14-18
NOW

14-18

Contemporary arts
commissions for the First
World War Centenary

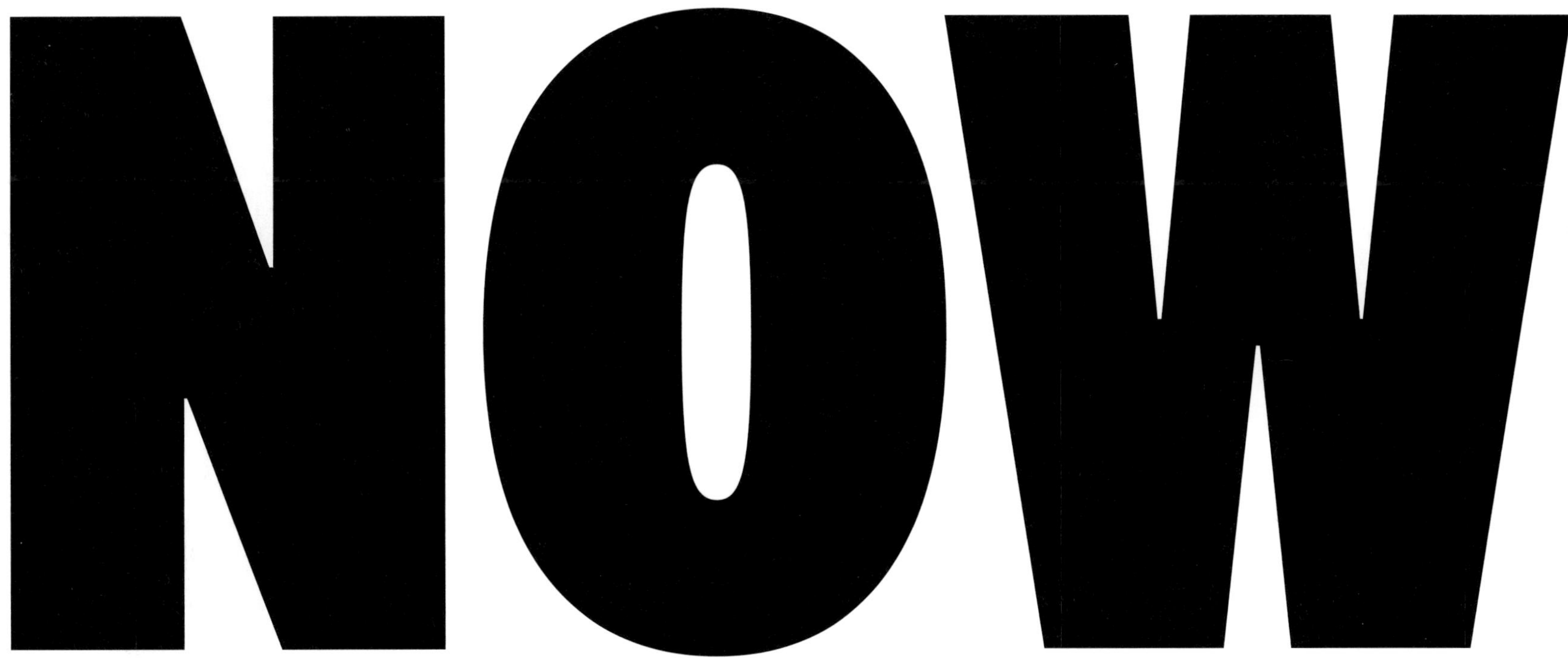

NOW

Profile Editions

First published in Great
Britain in 2019 by Profile
Editions, an imprint of
PROFILE BOOKS LTD
3 Holford Yard
Bevin Way
London WC1X 9HD
United Kingdom
www.profileeditions.com

A CIP catalogue record for
this book is available from
the British Library.

ISBN: 9781788161466

Editor: Angela Koo
Editorial team: Claire Eva,
Majeeda Goodall, Chloë Morley
and Nadia Vistisen
Design: John Dowling

Reprographics by Studio
Fasoli, Italy. Printed and
bound in Italy by Printer
Trento srl.

14·18-NOW
WW1 CENTENARY ART COMMISSIONS

14-18 NOW Principal Funders

Supported using public funding by

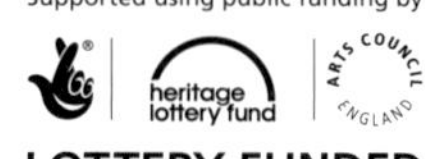
LOTTERY FUNDED

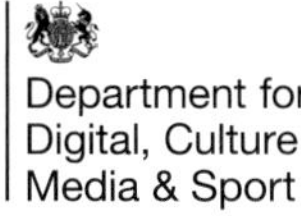
Department for
Digital, Culture
Media & Sport

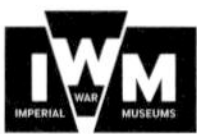

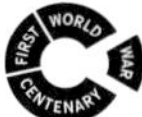

CONTENTS

*— Engaging over 35 million people
with the centenary of the First World
War, including 8 million young people*

*— 420 artists from 40 countries,
in 220 locations across the UK*

*— Produced with 600 arts, heritage
and community organisations*

*— Outstanding artists from all art
forms, including visual arts, theatre,
literature, dance, music, film, digital
and outdoor arts*

FOREWORD

Jenny Waldman CBE
Director, 14-18 NOW

From the poetry of Siegfried Sassoon to the paintings of Paul Nash, art has provided a prism through which we have come to understand the First World War. Inspired by the impact that such works have had on our perceptions of history, 14-18 NOW aimed to invite contemporary artists to forge fresh connections with the First World War and the period 1914–18, opening new perspectives on its resonance today.

14-18 NOW was established as an independent organisation with a brief to create a cultural programme as a complement to the more formal First World War centenary commemorations. Launched in 2013, we had less than a year to commission our first season of new works. Our programme focused on three main seasons: 2014, 2016 and 2018, with the Poppies tour and occasional commissions in the years between.

Our initial aim was for our five-year programme of new commissions to reach 10 million people, but that was soon to prove an underestimate. By the end of 2018, a total of 35 million people in the UK had engaged with our programme.

The name we chose, 14-18 NOW, was designed to emphasise how the impact of this conflict, 100 years distant, continues to be felt in the 21st century. We commissioned over 100 artworks that were inspired by events of both minor and major significance, from intimate personal stories to epic battles, and from the effects of social changes such as votes for women in the UK to the impact of the war around the world. We encouraged artists and partners to come up with large-scale, ambitious ideas that would engage hearts as well as minds. Great art packs an emotional punch, and has proved to be a powerful tool to connect us with our shared history and heritage.

We offered artists access to Imperial War Museums' astonishing archives and peerless historians, access that in many cases opened new avenues of enquiry and gave greater depth to their research. But we also gave them complete freedom to express whatever they wanted, however they wanted to express it — and our task was to help them realise their vision to the highest quality.

From the start we wanted 14-18 NOW to reach as wide an audience as possible — particularly young people, who may feel distant from formal centenary commemorations and from the war itself. From our opening season in 2014, when over 15,000 schoolchildren wrote a *Letter to an Unknown Soldier*, to our closing Armistice commemorations in 2018, when every UK secondary school received a copy of Peter Jackson's *They Shall Not Grow Old* and a special accompanying learning pack, we tried to draw young people closer to this pivotal moment in global history. Some 8 million young people engaged with our programme, a tribute to the power of the arts to bring our heritage alive for a new generation.

With arts and heritage partners, we presented the artworks across the whole of the UK, from Shetland to Cornwall and Derry/Londonderry to Ipswich. Many of the works were free, large-scale, outdoors, participative — or a combination of all these. Indeed, 67 per cent of our programme was free to the public. Some of the works are permanent and remain in museums and in the public realm. Others will have further presentations on stages, in concert halls and cinemas. Many were transient, such as Jeremy Deller's *We're here because we're here*, Artichoke's *PROCESSIONS* and Danny Boyle's *Pages of the Sea*, and will remain in people's minds and memories. Together, these artworks have had immense impact on the millions of people around the UK and abroad who engaged with our programme. 14-18 NOW has pioneered a new way of marking national moments through the arts, inviting artists to help us understand the past, look afresh at the present and shape the future.

Creating a programme of this scale and ambition depends on partnership and collaboration, and it was our privilege to work with a wide array of remarkable individuals and organisations from the UK and around the world. Our thanks go to the Department for Digital, Culture, Media & Sport, who conceived the idea of a cultural programme for the First World War centenary; the National Lottery through the Heritage Lottery Fund and Arts Council England, our main funders; 14-18 NOW's many supporters, from individuals and businesses to trusts and foundations; our invaluable colleagues at Imperial War Museums, who hosted and supported us from the very start; the historians who advised and inspired our artists; the volunteers and public who participated; the BBC and other media partners who ensured the widest reach for our projects; our 600 partner arts and heritage organisations, without whom our projects could not have happened; the deeply committed 14-18 NOW board and team; and, most of all, the 420 artists from 40 countries who created the inspiring artworks featured in the pages of this book.

14-18 NOW did an extraordinary job and a great service in reminding us of the complexity of the First World War's impact. It did not impose a single narrative. Rather, its many and varied projects opened up the possibility of many stories and many ways of reacting to the past. It was left to each of us to decide how we wanted to think and feel about the war.

INTRODUCTION

Professor Margaret MacMillan

Anniversaries of great events are never easy to commemorate. We in the present look back and ask ourselves what did it mean: the birth of Mozart or Mohammad? Luther nailing his theses to the church door or Einstein discovering the theory of relativity? The fall of Constantinople to the Ottomans or the German surrender at Stalingrad? The greater the consequences or the horror, the more difficult it becomes. How do we think now about the Holocaust without trivialising it? How can we — or should we — avoid bringing our own concerns and preoccupations as we try to grasp the meaning of past events? And, after all, who are 'we'? Governments often want to tidy up the past and impose a single unified version of what happened back then — at Waterloo, say, or the Battle of the Somme. But there can be no one view. Women, men, diverse ethnic groups, religions or social classes, start from different viewpoints, and what they see in the past may be guided by that.

So marking the 100th anniversary of the First World War, that vast and destructive struggle from 1914 to 1918, was never going to be easy. We can agree that it was a catastrophe that destroyed the old confident Europe and left a strangely and irrevocably altered world. Beyond that there are, and always have been, profound differences over how we remember and commemorate that war. We still cannot agree on how it started or why it went on for so long, and we still debate its meaning and its legacy a century later.

For most of the 1920s, the British — and many in the Empire — thought of the war as a necessary and just one. The war memorials talked of 'our glorious dead', while veterans met, as they continued to do until they passed from the scene by the 1960s, to reminisce and sing the songs they had learned in their war service. It was only in the 1930s, with the publication of some of the great critical memoirs and novels, that doubts started to take hold. After the Second World War, which seemed to be more of a clear-cut victory of good over evil, the First World War became much more problematic in the public memory. The loss of lives, the waste of resources, the exhausting of British power in that earlier war now seemed pointless rather than a noble sacrifice. The overwhelming image of the 1914–18 war has come to be the mud, the shattered landscapes and the corpses of the Western Front, with the single most important event in all four years for the British being the first day of the Battle of the Somme.

Yet that later picture leaves out so much. It does not take into account the other battlefields, in the Middle East or Africa, and it only notices in passing that there were soldiers from all over the British Empire fighting, too, from Canada, the Caribbean, Africa, the Antipodes — and a million Indians. And in our remembering, we have not always paid much attention to the home front, to the involvement of women in what had been considered men's work, or the lasting effects of the losses of loved ones on their families and friends.

14-18 NOW did an extraordinary job and a great service in reminding us of the complexity of the First World War's impact. It did not impose a single narrative. Rather, its many and varied projects opened up the possibility of many stories and many ways of reacting to the past. It was left to each of us to decide how we wanted to think and feel about the war. And contemporary concerns and issues, far from being kept at arm's length, were very much part of the enterprise. The editors of *1914: Goodbye to All That* invited their authors to consider both Robert Graves' famous memoir and current questions of artistic freedom and expression. *Fashion & Freedom* asked contemporary British designers to design clothes inspired by the big changes and simplification of women's fashions made necessary by the war. *PROCESSIONS* encouraged women all over the country to make banners and then come together in marches on 10 June 2018 in Belfast, Cardiff, Edinburgh and London to celebrate the first grant of women's suffrage. (This was also a wonderful example of the mix of grassroots and national activities that marked so many 14-18 NOW events.)

The clever use of contemporary artists and idioms to explore the past and its connections to the present made what might seem like a remote part of history accessible to younger generations. One of the final projects was *They Shall Not Grow Old*, a Peter Jackson film that employed modern technology to rework footage from the Great War, removing all the jerky movements and graininess that so distances us from the people depicted there. Jackson wanted to 'bring the First World War alive for 15 year olds'.

This is important, for the Great War was a watershed in history that still affects us. The great achievements of Europe in industry, science and technology, and in organisation and ideas, turned into deadly weapons, making possible a prolonged and debilitating struggle that consumed lives and resources on a massive scale. Indeed, a new term was coined to describe it: total war. And we live in a world that has been shaped by it.

*One key to the success
of 14-18 NOW was in that
word 'Now'. It reminded us
of the past without trying
to recreate it or impose
a false nostalgia.*

British artists were deeply involved in the First World War, as combatants often, and supporters and critics as well. Their skills were also enlisted for the war effort, to write propaganda or patriotic literature, design recruiting posters or paint heroic battle scenes. And when the war ended it was Britain's artists who helped to give voice to the loss and the mourning. So for 14-18 NOW to call on contemporary British artists to help us understand the First World War today was both inspired and right. Cartoonists, novelists, poets, painters, actors, musicians, dancers, composers, playwrights, photographers, sculptors, film-makers. Almost no one refused the invitation. 14-18 NOW did not tell them what to do — there is no 'official' art here — but it made possible an encounter between creative talents in the present and the past. Sometimes it was by making connections and creating partnerships; sometimes by commissioning works.

In the summer of 2018, to take just one example of many, New Yorkers saw an old fireboat that had been transformed into a thing of beauty by Tauba Auerbach, who had covered it from stem to stern with red-and-white patterns. 14-18 NOW made it happen and promoted it. And there were four other ships painted by other artists docked around Britain during the commemorations. These *Dazzle Ships* paid tribute to those of the First World War, which had come out of the desperate need to save Allied and friendly shipping from German U-boat attacks. Many of Britain's leading painters then had drawn on styles such as Cubism and Vorticism to camouflage hundreds of ships in patterns designed to bewilder hostile observers and disguise the size, direction and speed of the ships.

One key to the success of 14-18 NOW was in that word 'Now'. It reminded us of the past without trying to recreate it or impose a false nostalgia. On 4 August 2014, 100 years after Britain found itself at war, 16 million British people followed the invitation of *LIGHTS OUT* to turn off their lights for an hour. In windows across the country — in houses, flats, churches and government buildings — single candles or lights burned as people reflected on that anniversary either alone or together. It was a moment to wonder what we would do if our world was as suddenly turned upside down.

Two years later on 1 July 2006, the 100th anniversary of the first day of the Battle of the Somme, another haunting event took place across Britain. Commuters — I was one — rushing into railway stations on their way to work started noticing groups of young men dressed in military uniform, with their packs and their weapons. The men marched along the platforms in unison, or stood about or sat in groups waiting for their orders. Sometimes they sang, but only songs from the First World War. And something, we started to realise, was not quite right about the uniforms, for soldiers today do not usually wear puttees or dish-shaped metal helmets. The young men were among us but not of our world. If we tried to speak to them they remained mute but held out a small card with their name and time of death. The one I addressed represented a soldier who had died two weeks after 1 July in 1916, aged 20. *We're here because we're here*, the name from the famous wartime song, was both moving and jolted all of us who saw it out of our daily preoccupations.

The participants in that project were all amateurs who had been training in secret for months under the direction of the artist Jeremy Deller and Rufus Norris, director of the National Theatre, a fact that points to another strength of 14-18 NOW — it encouraged each of us to participate however we could. I was fortunate to become involved when I answered a simple invitation to write a letter to the soldier whose bronze statue, letter in hand, stands in Paddington Station in London. I tried to imagine what it would be like to write to someone on his way to the battlefront or perhaps already there, with both of us knowing that he might never come back. Some 20,000 of us — from schoolchildren to the elderly, and from all over Britain — wrote our letters, and it was decided to make a selection of those into a book.

14-18 NOW brought contemporary art into daily experience; it connected individuals to group projects; and it linked local and national commemorations. It created projects in schools and community centres, in parks and streets, across the British Isles. It showed repeatedly that it could follow as well as take the lead, making it possible for individual projects to evolve and grow. The remarkably successful *LIGHTS OUT*, for example, commissioned four international artists to consider a single beam of light shining in the darkness; their works were subsequently shown in Bangor, Belfast, Edinburgh and London.

Another 2014 project — *Blood Swept Lands and Seas of Red* — by artist Paul Cummins and designer Tom Piper, originally staged at the Tower of London in 2014, marked the beginning of the Centenary of the First World War. In total, 888,246 ceramic poppies filled the Tower's famous moat, attracting over 5 million visitors, each poppy representing a British or colonial life lost at the front during the war. When I saw it, the huge crowds moved slowly and quietly, while people talked in hushed tones. Along the fences were letters and photographs of long-dead forebears from the time of the First World War, placed there by individuals acknowledging a part of their family history. Public interest was so great that the artwork had to have a longer life. 14-18 NOW stepped in and took two sculptural elements of the original installation on tour to 19 places across the United Kingdom, from Orkney to Caernarfon to Southend-on-Sea. Individual poppies were also 'planted' online around the world.

That was also as it should have been, for the First World War was a truly global one and 14-18 NOW did much to remind the British of that. The Indian garden in Bradford painted by Imran Qureshi, the performances by the Orchestra of Syrian Musicians, and the installation *Dr Blighty*, about Indian soldiers convalescing in Brighton, showed the extent to which the war was an imperial project, drawing in men from all quarters of the world. *SS Mendi: Dancing the Death Drill*, a play by Fred Khumalo and the Isango Ensemble from South Africa, told the story of their compatriots who died at sea before they reached the battlefields, while William Kentridge's multimedia *The Head & the Load* was a tribute to the millions of African men and women who carried supplies for the fighting between Britain, France and Germany in Africa.

Other countries have had their commemorations of the First World War but none have had such a broad sweep or done anything remotely like this bold marrying of contemporary arts with the past. 'Fun' would be the wrong word for such a momentous endeavour, but while a profound appreciation of the tragedy of the war ran throughout it, there was also a lightness of touch in what 14-18 NOW made possible. It reminded us that life goes on, and that there is beauty created even out of horror. Its projects informed us all, engaged us, and made us reflect upon the present as much as the past. I like to think that those who died in the First World War would have approved.

ART AS LENS: RE-GLOBALISING THE FIRST WORLD WAR

David Olusoga

There is no other conflict in history — arguably no other major historical event — that is known more through the poetry and the art that it generated than through the writing of historians. In Britain, the First World War has become what David Reynolds calls the 'literary war', with the words of the war poets far better remembered than those of any general or statesman. When we recall, for example, the use of chemical weapons on the Western Front, what comes to us most vividly are not the words of the commanders who ordered the use of that new terror weapon, or the names of the scientists who learnt how to weaponise chlorine and phosgene, but lines from Wilfred Owen's poem 'Dulce et Decorum est'. If we picture such attacks or their aftermath, John Singer Sargent's panoramic painting *Gassed* comes to mind far more readily than any of the aerial photographs that show deadly clouds of gas creeping across No Man's Land towards lines of trenches and the lungs of doomed men.

We owe the poets of the trenches a great debt. Their imagery, especially since the 1960s, has become seared into our national imagination. The suffering they endured and the violence they witnessed and participated in have been transmitted to subsequent generations with unique force and poignancy. But another effect of the 'literary war' has been to obscure other aspects of the conflict — those upon which the poets were silent, and to which the war artists were not drawn.

Seventy million men were mobilised during the First World War; of them, around 4 million were non-white non-Europeans. Most were subjects of European empires. They fought, laboured and died in Europe and in various theatres of war across the globe. While some fought in their own homelands, others travelled vast distances and encountered lands and peoples that they would otherwise have never known. A few left fragmented accounts of their experiences.

The battles fought in Africa and the Middle East, like the arrival onto the European theatre of war of hundreds of thousands of men (and some women) from across the globe, fascinated contemporaries and was the subject of endless reportage and debate. Yet more books and plays have been written, and more movies and documentaries produced, about the few dozen war poets than the campaigns fought in the colonies and the colonial troops who fought on the Western Front.

Around 1.4 million Indians took up arms for the British Empire during the First World War. The decision to deploy them outside the subcontinent was taken within 48 hours of Britain's declaration of war, despite initial talk of a 'white man's war'. France threw her pre-war West and North African regiments into battle at the first opportunity. As the death toll climbed, France recruited thousands more men from her African colonies to fill the ranks. The French authorities justified the voluntary — and at times enforced — recruitment of Africans by regarding it as *l'impôt du sang*, 'blood tax'. French Africa was to pay for the supposed benefits of France's *mission civilisatrice* in the lives of her young men. Another great army of the war, the army of labourers who built and maintained the trenches and who fed the great war machine on the Western Front, was even more diverse and international. Men from every continent served in the labour battalions. Around 140,000 Chinese labourers served the British and French. Alongside them were Indians and black South Africans who, unlike white men from the same dominion, were not permitted to serve in combat, lest they should demand civil rights and equality at the conclusion of hostilities. The war in the Middle East against the forces of Ottoman Turkey was fought by British armies that included both Indians and West Indians; and the long and miserable struggle that played out in East and Central Africa led to the recruitment and impressment of hundreds of thousands of Africans. An unknowable number died serving as 'carriers', and an equally incalculable number of men, women and children died when the warring armies passed through their villages, commandeering scarce food and taking men away from their fields and harvests to swell the ranks of the carriers.

During the century since the end of the First World War, however, our vision of the conflict has narrowed and most of these men and their stories have been forgotten. We have come to remember the war as a purely European conflict and, influenced by the poets, to regard it as a uniquely European tragedy. But the realities of the war — the fact that sections of the British front line in 1914 and 1915 were held by men from the hills of the Punjab; that one of the most dynamic of the American battalions consisted of black men; and that the tanks that eventually helped break the German lines were repaired and maintained by Chinese labourers — did not simply fade from memory; they were erased. That process of erasure began soon after the guns fell silent and the vistas of the new, post-war world became visible to the victors.

On 19 July 1919, at the end of the month of celebrations that marked the signing of the Treaty of Versailles, a victory parade was held in London. Nearly 15,000 servicemen took part. Troops from Britain marched through the streets of the imperial capital alongside their comrades from the Australia, Canada, New Zealand and South Africa. Units of the Indian Army were also permitted to march, although arriving late they took to the streets in August. Yet veterans of the war from the West Indies and Africa were prevented from taking part in the victory parade. The West Africans were not given permission even to travel to London. This act of exclusion was part of a deeper and longer process of erasure. In the weeks leading up to the victory parade there were attempts to erase black people not just from the memory of the war but from post-war Britain itself. Men from Africa and the West Indies, many of them demobilised sailors and soldiers, were attacked by mobs in Liverpool, London, Cardiff, Newport and Barry. Now peace had come, these former allies had come to be regarded as unwanted aliens and unwelcome competitors for jobs.

The end of the war coincided with new efforts to codify and propagate virulent strains of scientific racism. In 1919, American racial theorists Madison Grant and Lothrop Stoddard were promoting their theory of 'Nordicism' and predicting a coming racial war. Stoddard believed that the First World War had been a 'white civil war' that had led to an 'unprecedented weakening of white solidarity'. Energies that would have been better used securing white dominance over the non-white peoples of the world had been squandered. The victors, Stoddard alleged, had won the war, but by using non-white soldiers to do so had jeopardised both their own empires and global white supremacy. Even before the war was over in 1917, the South African general Jan Smuts warned that although armies raised in Africa had proved themselves to be of 'great military value' in the post-war world, they could 'prove a danger to civilisation itself'. After 1918, therefore, the service of non-white men in the various theatres of war was a story that many wanted repressed, not memorialised or celebrated. Great efforts were made by the victorious nations to demonstrate to their non-white veterans that their service in the war had not earned them any new rights and that the lowering of racial barriers had been a temporary wartime necessity. In the southern states of the US this message was stamped onto the bodies of returning black soldiers, 19 of whom were lynched — some for wearing their army uniforms in public, something that all returning soldiers were officially permitted to do.

Recent efforts at historical recovery, the struggle to salvage lost experiences and find missing voices found greater energy and urgency during the centenary. Much of this work has been led by historians and professionals in the heritage sectors across the world. This desire to paint a fuller, more inclusive and more honest picture of the conflict has been felt everywhere, from Thailand to Tanzania. It has motivated the writing of new books, the production of new exhibitions, feature films and documentaries, all focused on forgotten battles and missing contributions. But critically, artists too have played a key role in the reframing of the war and the recovery of lost voices and experiences.

It was not until the 1960s that the war poets became the dominant voices in how the war was remembered in Britain. More than half a century later, other artists working in different mediums and new artistic forms have begun to fill in the gaps in the cultural memory of the conflict, re-globalising our understanding of the first global war. New pieces, like William Kentridge's *The Head & the Load*, John Akomfrah's *Mimesis: African Soldier* and the Isango Ensemble's *SS Mendi: Dancing the Death Drill*, have placed the experiences of the South Africans who died on the *SS Mendi*, the East Africans whose bones lie in unmarked graves across forgotten supply lines, and the Senegalese riflemen who fought at Verdun into the artistic and cultural landscape of war remembrance. They stand there alongside the words by war poets and images of the war artists.

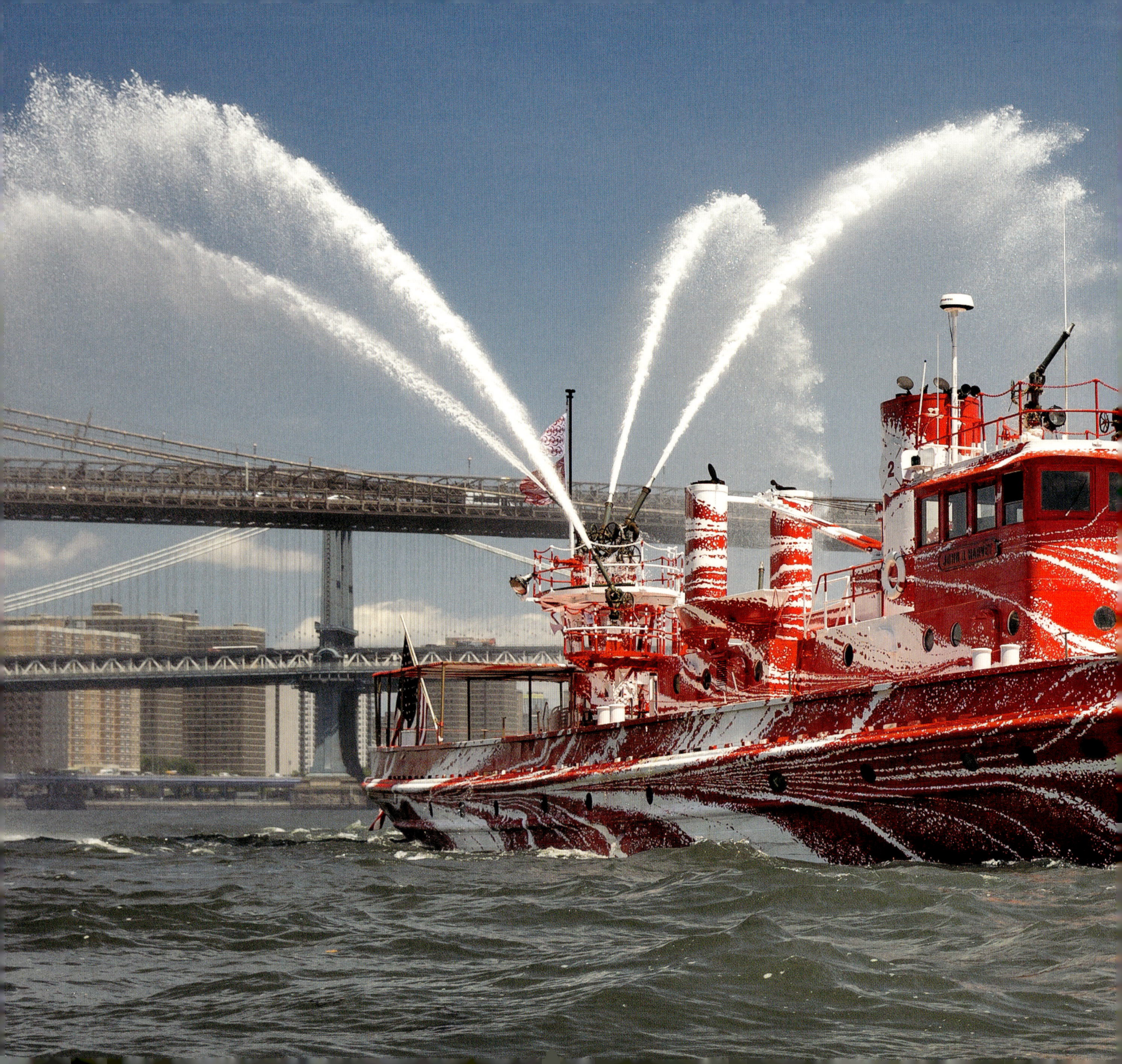

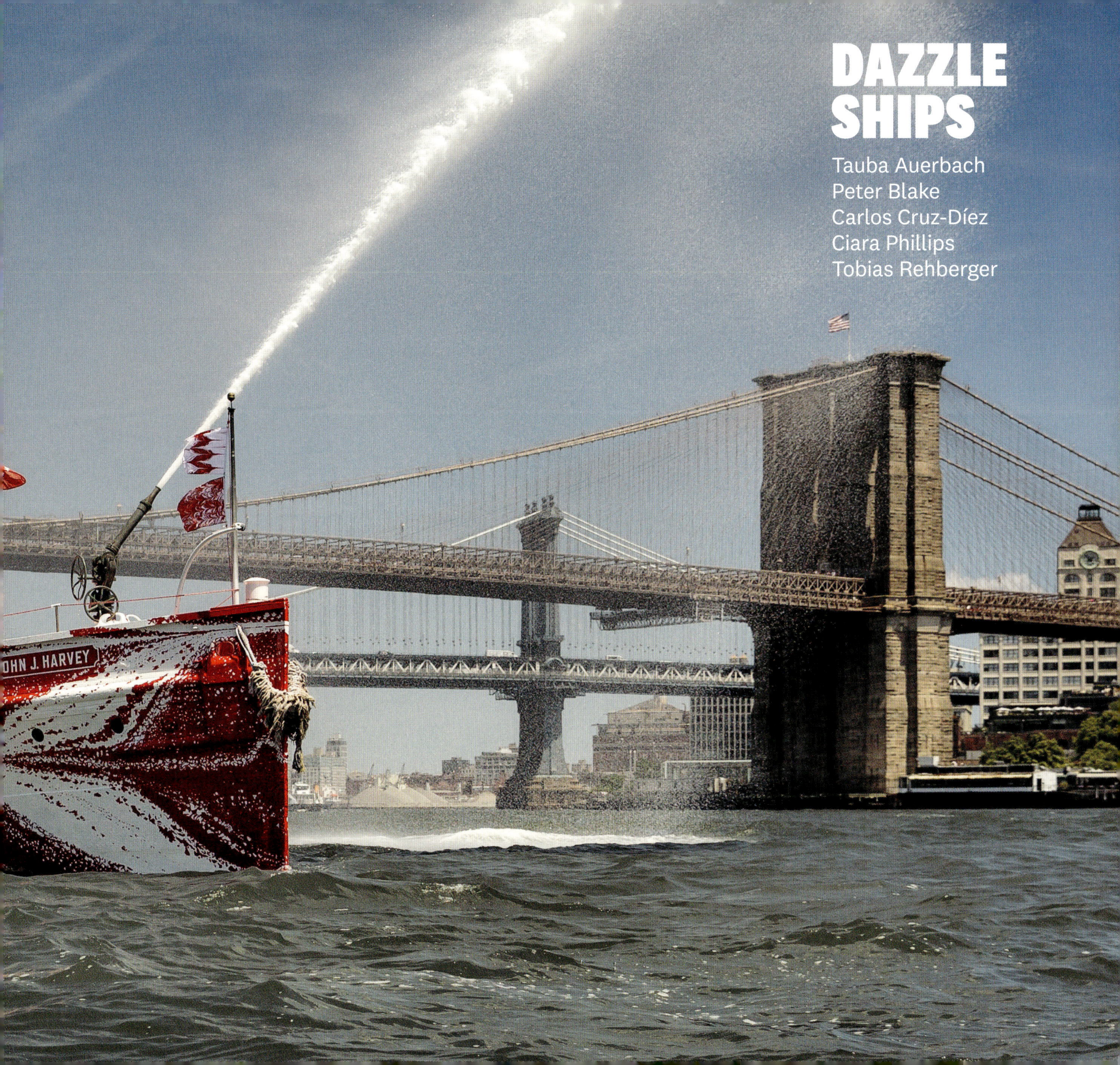
DAZZLE
SHIPS
Tauba Auerbach
Peter Blake
Carlos Cruz-Díez
Ciara Phillips
Tobias Rehberger

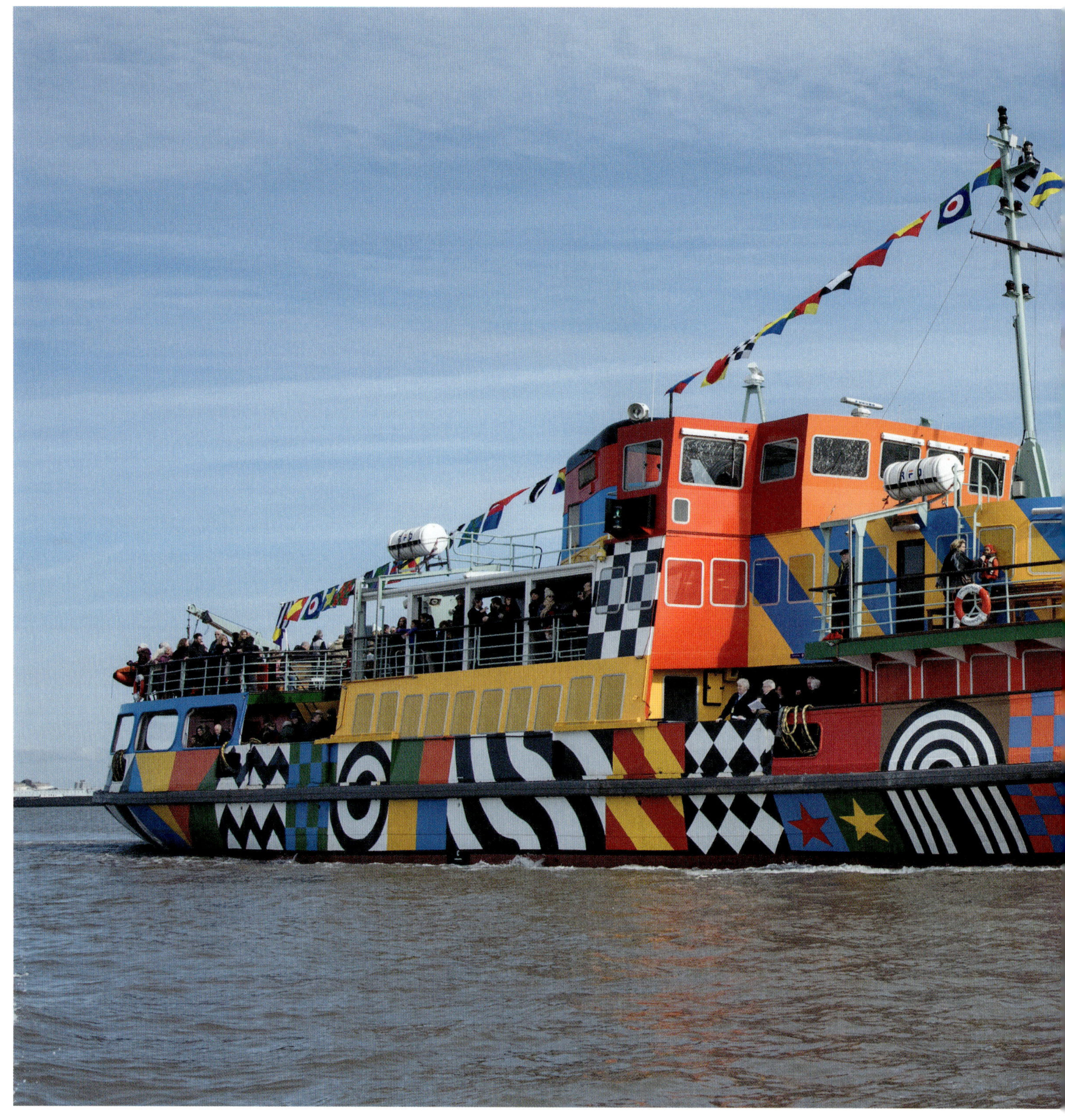

Previous page. Tauba Auerbach's *Flow Separation*, co-presented with Public Art Fund, 'dazzled' a 1930s US fireboat, transformed with red and white paint. Retired in 1994, the *John J. Harvey* was fleetingly recommissioned on 11 September 2001 to help evacuate people from New York's Lower Manhattan area.

Right. Peter Blake's *Everybody Razzle Dazzle*, his transformation of the Mersey ferry the MV *Snowdrop*. Mersey ferries like this one were requisitioned during the First World War as troop carriers.

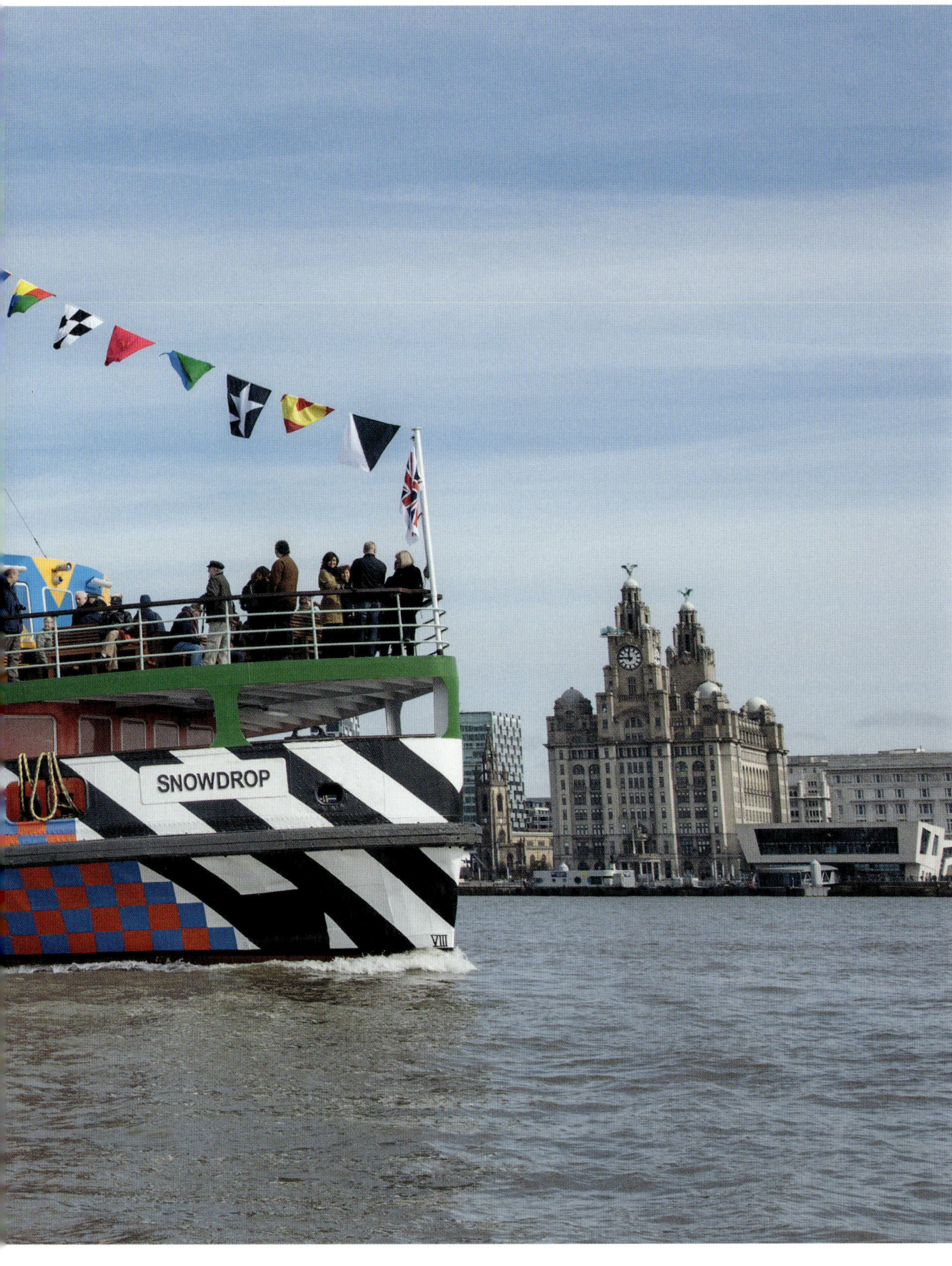

'Dazzle' was a style of naval camouflage characterised by brilliant, glaring geometric patterns. Widely used in the First World War and into the Second, 'dazzle' was not used to make a ship invisible to its enemies, but simply to confuse their attempts to sink it by making it difficult to gauge its distance, direction and speed.

Inspired in part by animal camouflage, the technique was developed by marine artist Norman Wilkinson, drawing on avant-garde movements such as Cubism and Vorticism that emerged at the start of the 20th century. The painter Edward Wadsworth then supervised the application of the designs to over 2,000 ships. The bewildering shapes and angles of these patterns continue to inspire artists today.

Throughout the five-year centenary, Liverpool Biennial and 14-18 NOW co-commissioned a series of five Dazzle Ships from artists — two in Liverpool, one in London, Edinburgh and New York. By responding to this little-known episode of design history, the five artists created large-scale, eye-catching public artworks that drew people's attention to the important role played by artists in the Allies' wartime survival.

In New York City, in a commission undertaken in partnership with Public Art Fund, Tauba Auerbach's contribution was entitled *Flow Separation*. This was the transformation of a decommissioned fireboat — the historic *John J. Harvey* — into a floating artwork to commemorate the centenary of the Armistice in 2018.

Right. The dazzle-camouflaged
HMS *Saxifrage*.

Below. Two dazzle camouflage
painted merchant ships moored
at a dockside in Leith, Scotland.

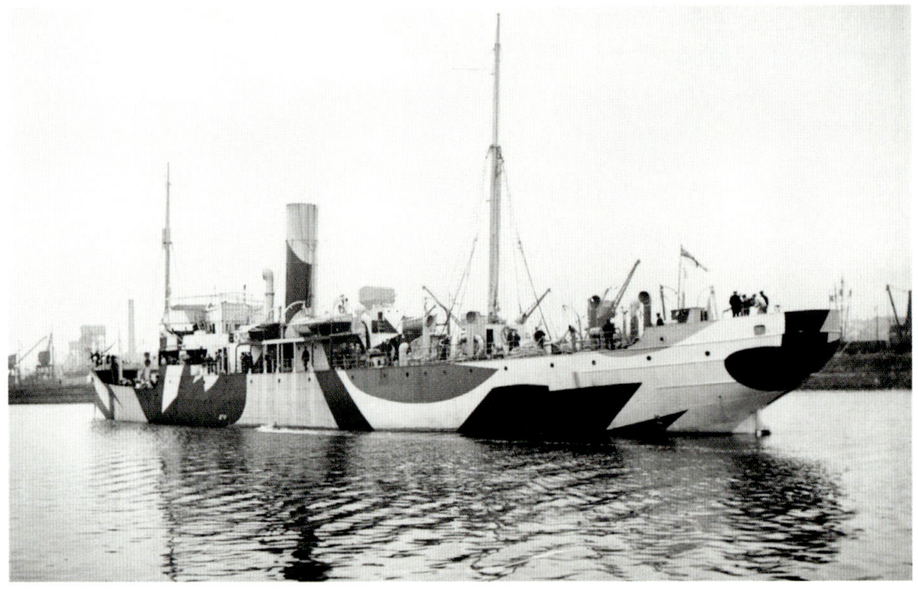

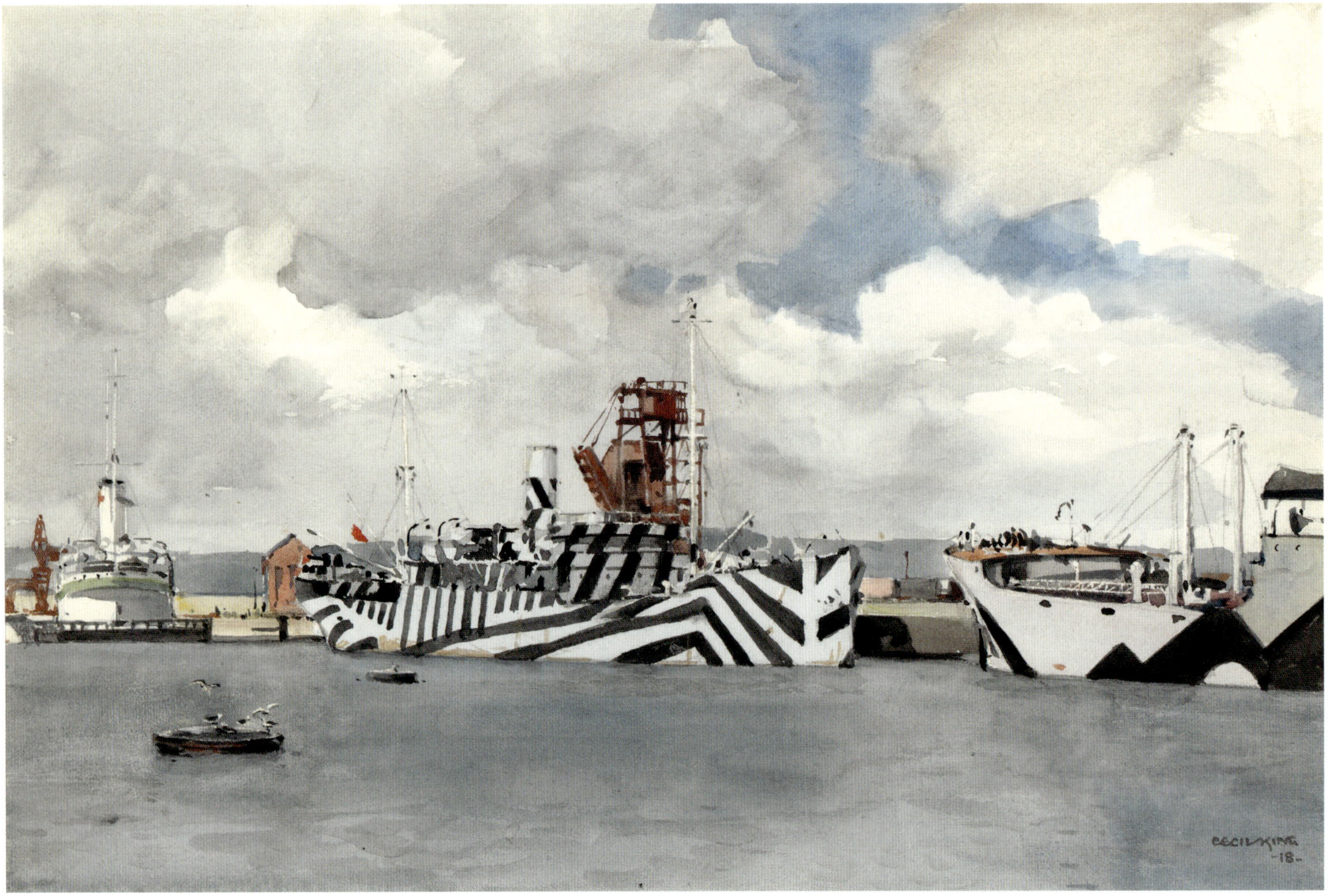

From top to bottom, dazzle designs for the HMS *Vindex* (port); the HMS *Vindex* (starboard) and HMS *King Alfred* (port); the HMS *Cumberland* and HMS *Berwick* (starboard and port); the HMS *Cornwall* and HMS *Donegal* (port) and HMS *Caledon* (port).

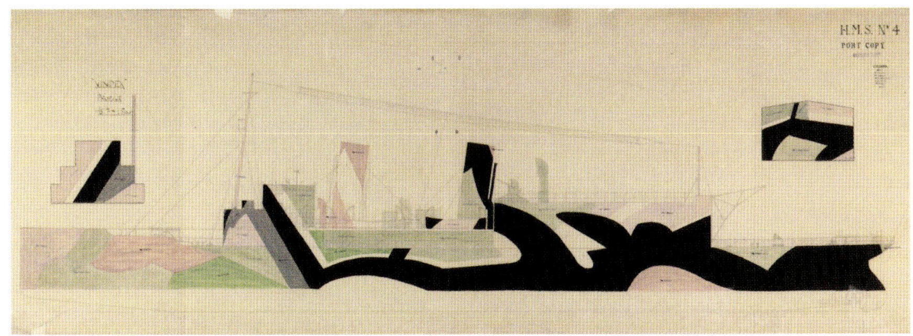

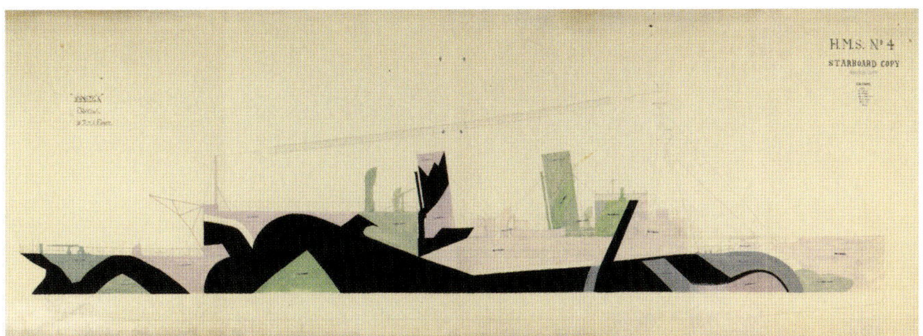

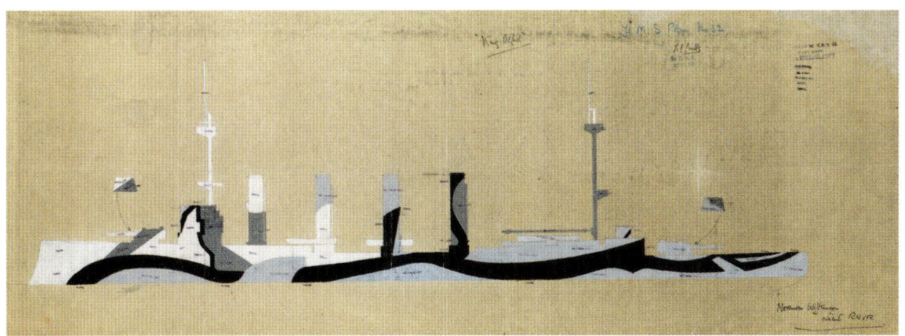

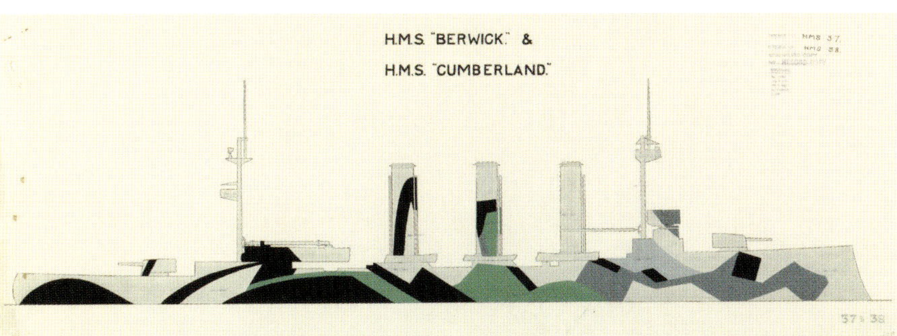

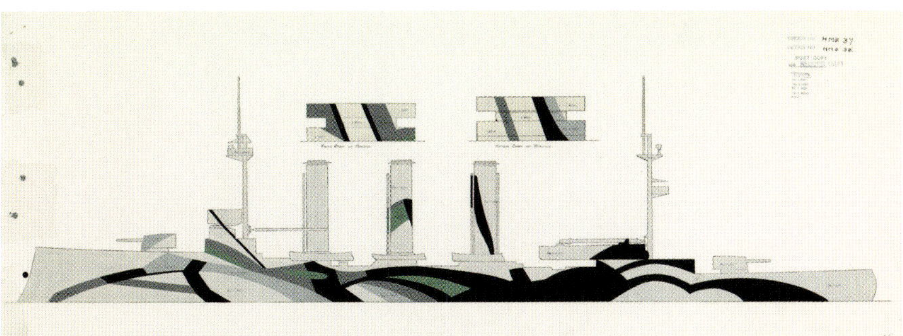

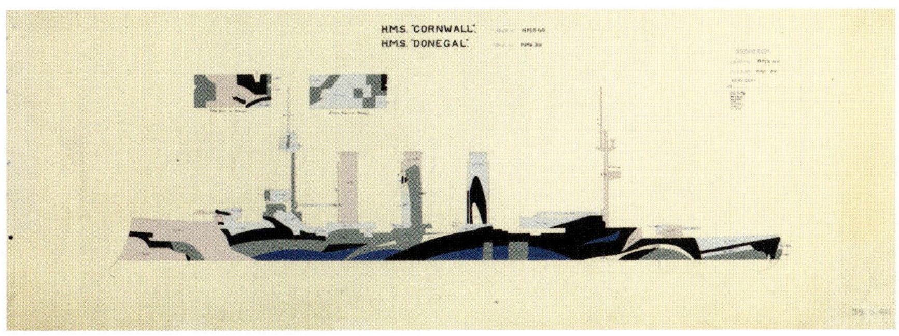

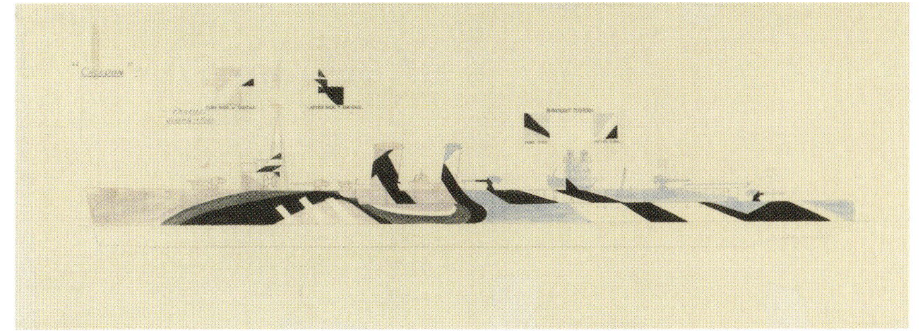

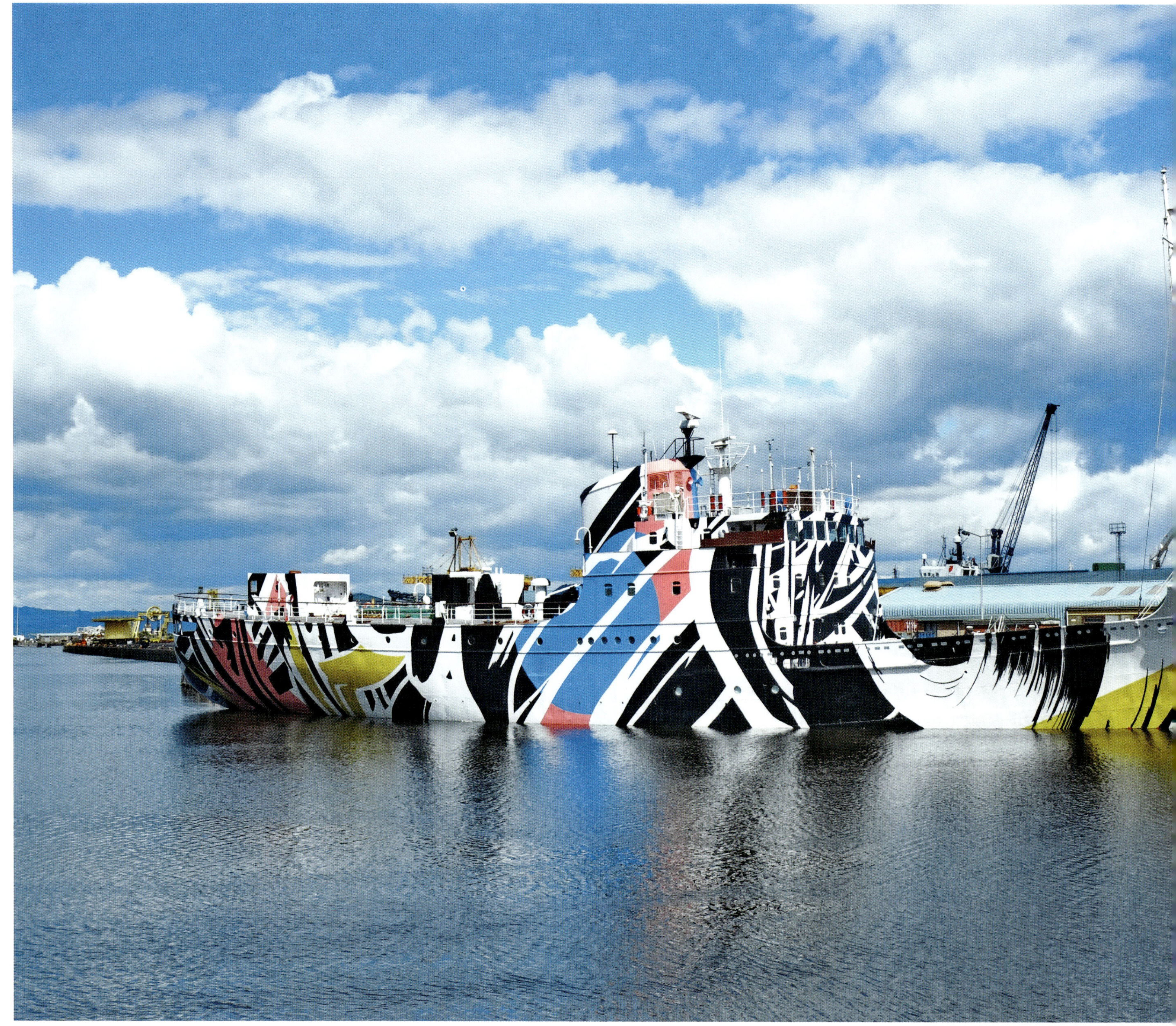

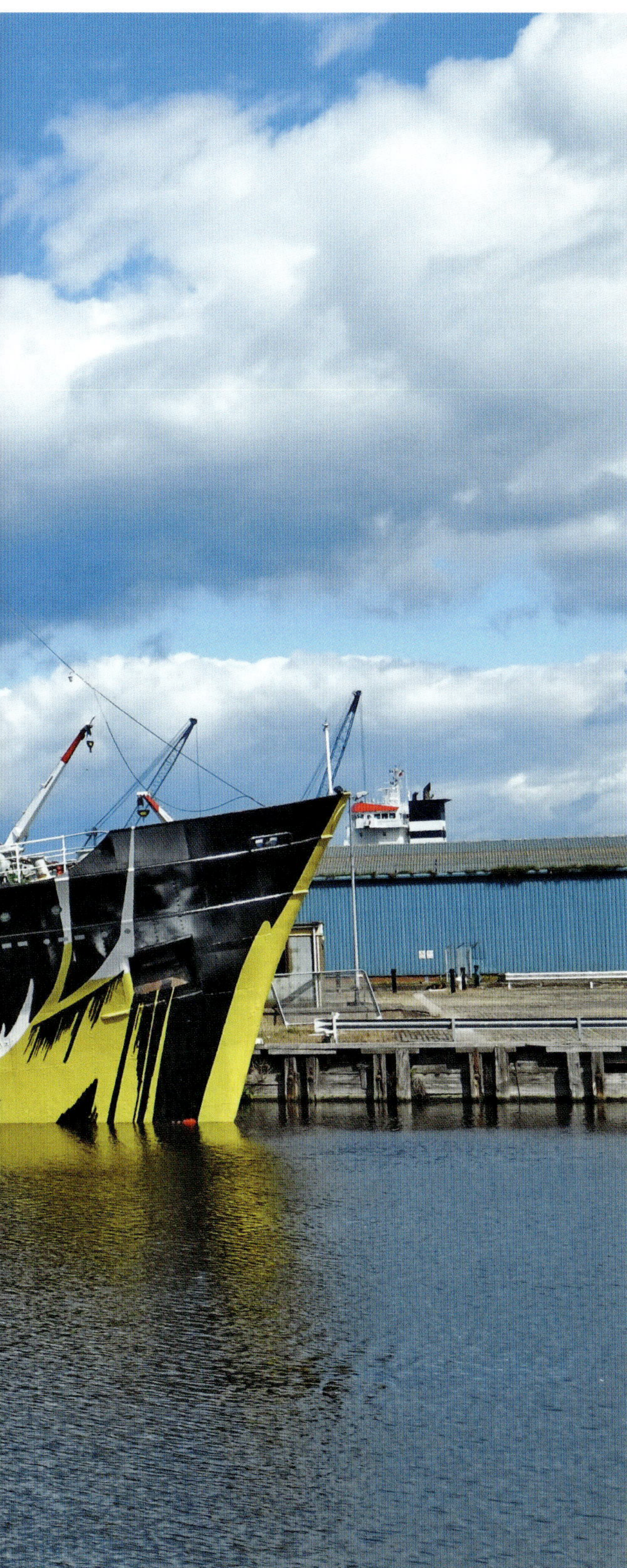

Ciara Phillips wrapped a Morse code message around the ship which read 'Every woman a signal tower', acknowledging the contributions made by women during war.

In Scotland, Ciara Phillips was given the task of creating a new livery for the former lighthouse boat the MV *Fingal*, berthed at the Prince of Wales Dock in Edinburgh. Commissioned by 14-18 NOW in partnership with the Edinburgh Art Festival, the launch of this Dazzle Ship was timed to mark the centenary of the Battle of Jutland on 29 May and 1 June 2016. Phillips' work paid homage not only to the work of artists during the First World War, but also to the contributions made by the women — particularly those who worked in the Royal Corps of Signals as telegraph operators.

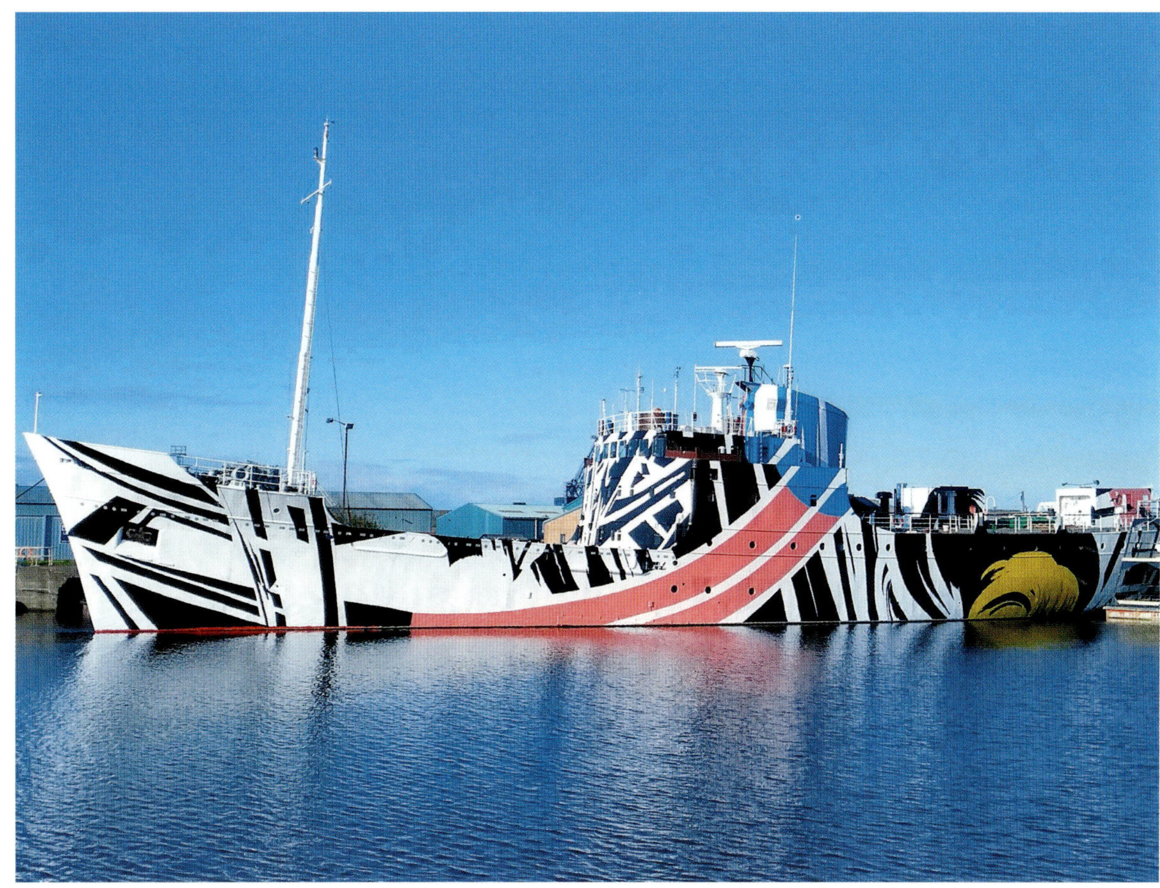

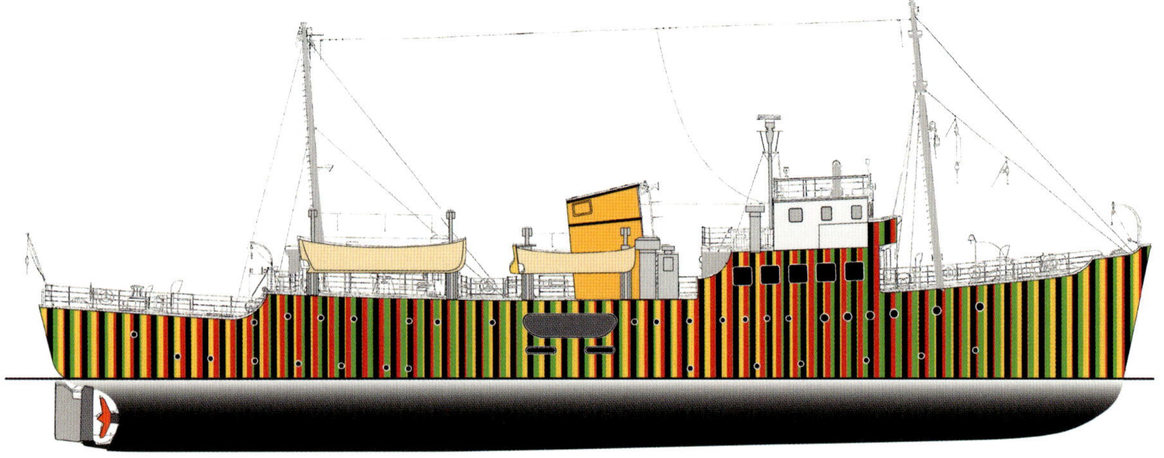

In London, the HMS *President* (1918) was 'dazzled' by the German sculptor Tobias Rehberger. This ship had, in fact, served as a Dazzle Ship during the First World War, under the name of HMS *Saxifrage*.

And in Liverpool, two commissions took place. The first was by Venezuelan artist Carlos Cruz-Díez, who decorated the *Edmund Gardner*, a historic pilot ship, owned and conserved by Merseyside Maritime Museum. Situated in a dry dock adjacent to the city's busy Albert Dock, it became a much-loved new public monument. The second commission was a new design for a Mersey ferry by renowned British pop artist Sir Peter Blake. Blake covered the *Snowdrop* with a pattern entitled *Everybody Razzle Dazzle*. As a working vessel, this ship continued to carry out its commuter service (River Explorer and Manchester Ship Canal Cruises) with its vivid new exterior.

Finally, as a postscript to the project, design agency Pentagram dazzled Room 131A at the Victoria and Albert Museum for the nine days of the London Design Festival 2018.

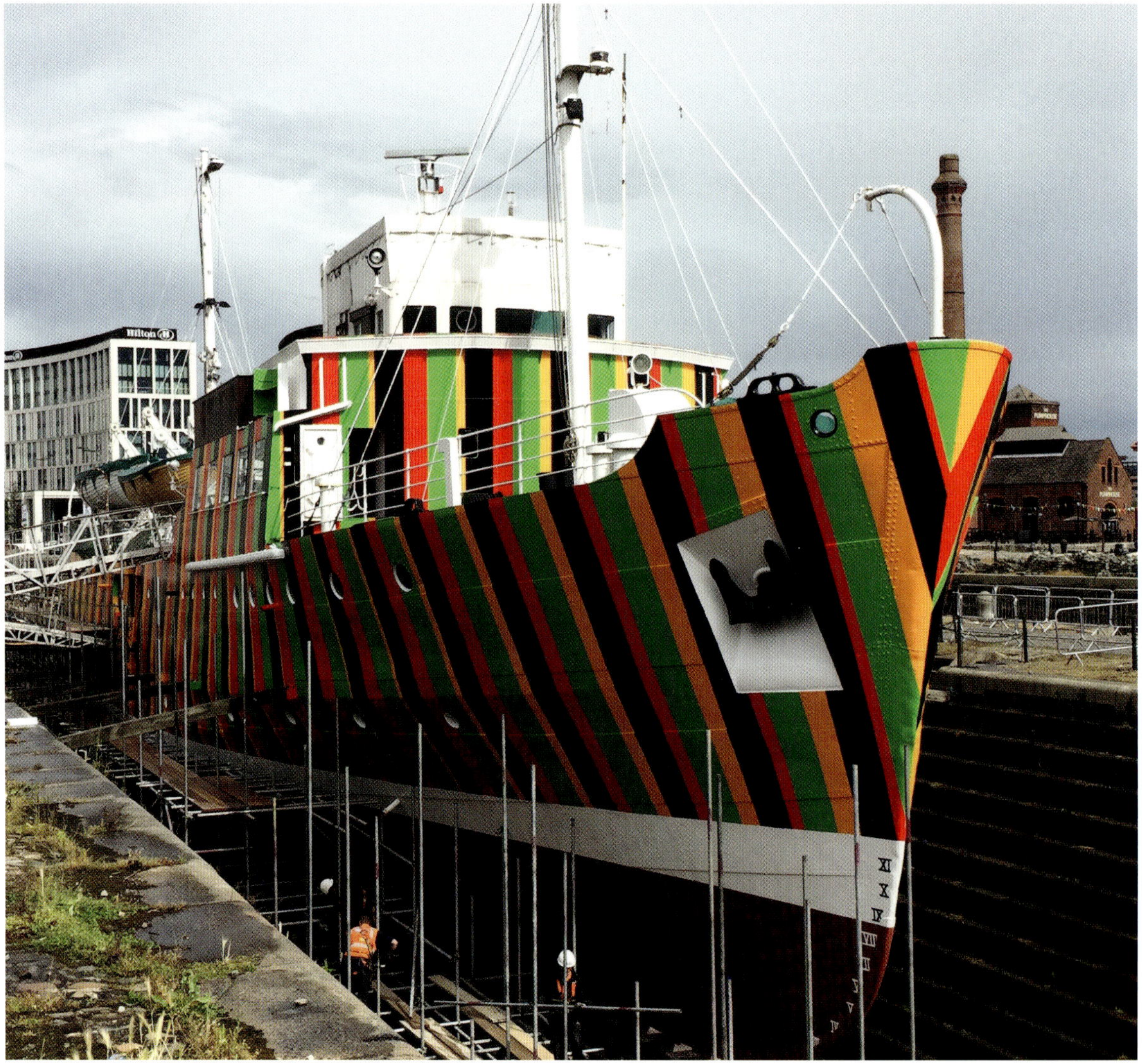

Edmund Gardner, *Liverpool, June 2014 — 2019*
HMS President *(1918), London, July 2014 — Dec 2015*
Snowdrop, *Liverpool, 2015 — 2021*
MV Fingal, *Edinburgh, May 2016 — Jan 2017*
John J. Harvey, *New York, July 2018 — May 2019*

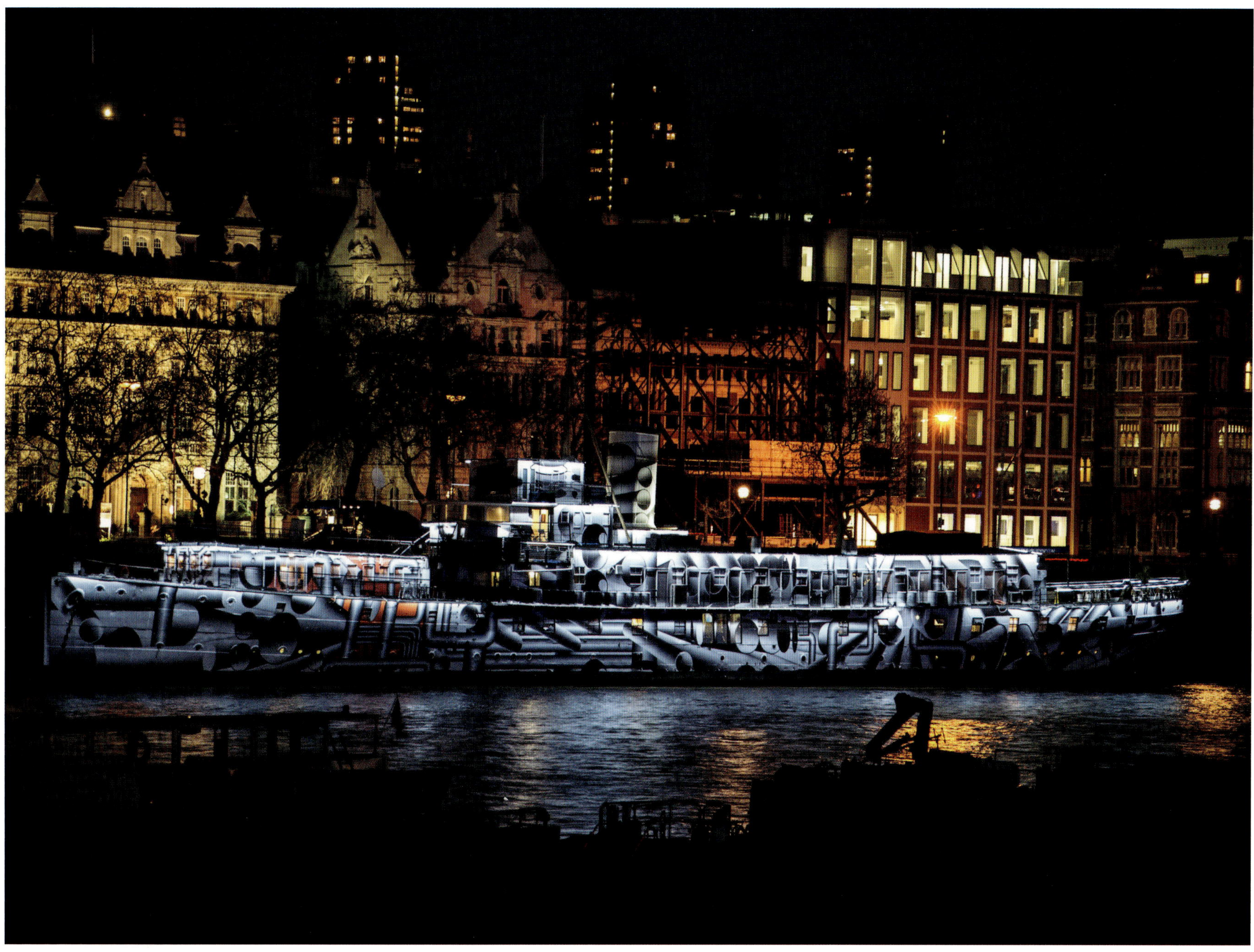

The HMS *President* (1918), moored on the Thames, bearing black-and-white 'camouflage' by Tobias Rehberger. This ship was one of only three remaining warships from the First World War.

MIMESIS: AFRICAN SOLDIER

John Akomfrah

John Akomfrah's multimedia installation *Mimesis: African Soldier*, unveiled at the Imperial War Museum in London, remembered the millions of Africans and people of colour from across the globe who fought and took part in the First World War.

Projected onto three screens, archive footage of the war was combined with newly filmed material shot in locations around the world, a powerful sound score, and tableaux reconstructions using live actors. This work by one of the UK's most celebrated installation film-makers highlighted the role of Africa and its inhabitants in the Great War.

At the start of the First World War, Britain, France, Belgium, Portugal and Germany controlled vast territories in Africa, and possessed empires that stretched across the world. Men from these colonies were enlisted to fight alongside Europeans on both sides, supported by legions of porters responsible for transporting food and equipment (see also page 82).

Colonial soldiers took part in key battles and campaigns throughout the war, in Africa, Europe and the Middle East. *Mimesis: African Soldier* recounted a story of vast scope, courage and human cost. In doing so it commemorated and celebrated the African and other colonial soldiers whose contributions have been marginalised and neglected for too long.

Imperial War Museum, London, 21 September 2018 — 31 March 2019 / New Art Exchange, Nottingham, September — December 2019

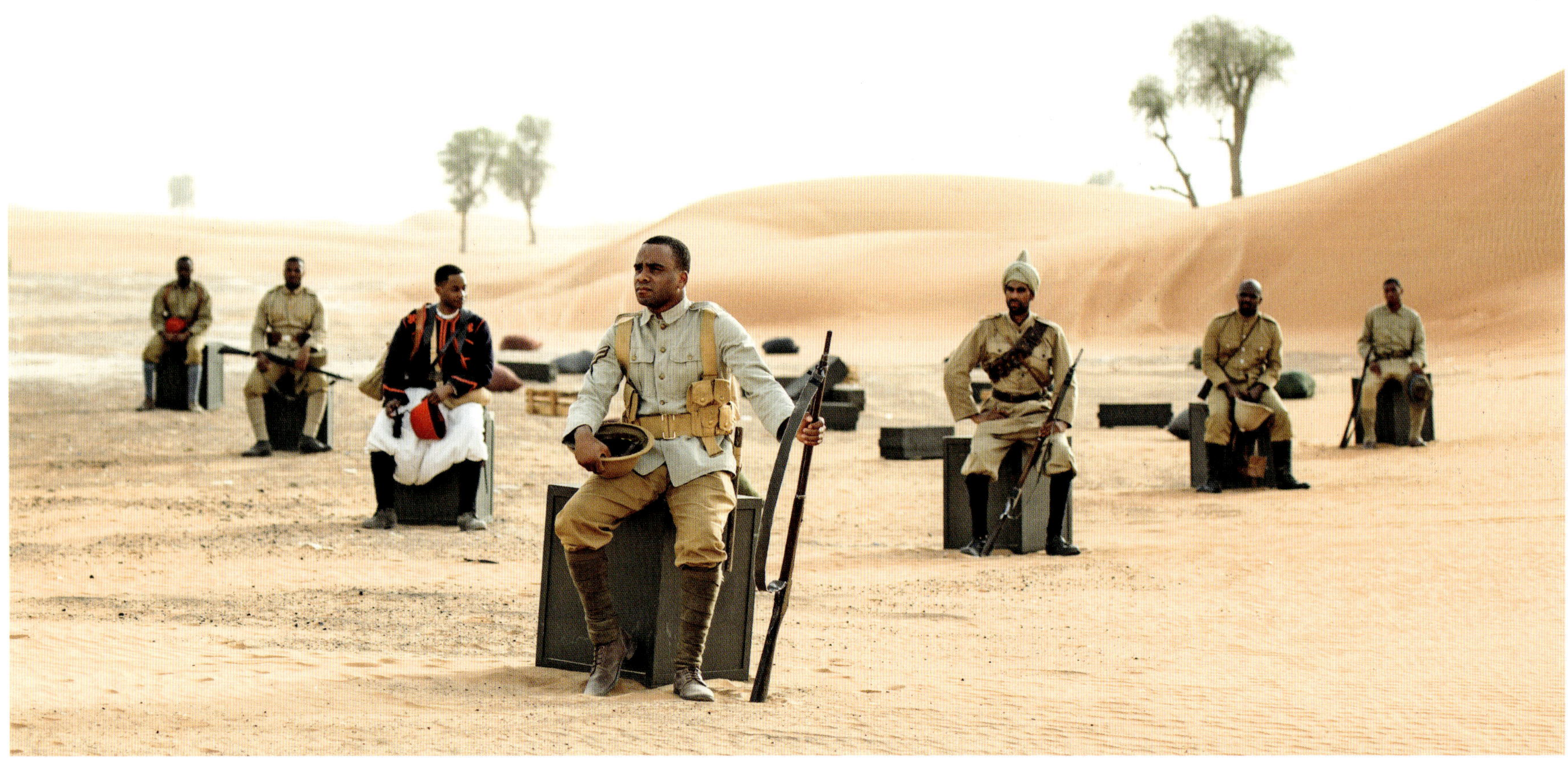

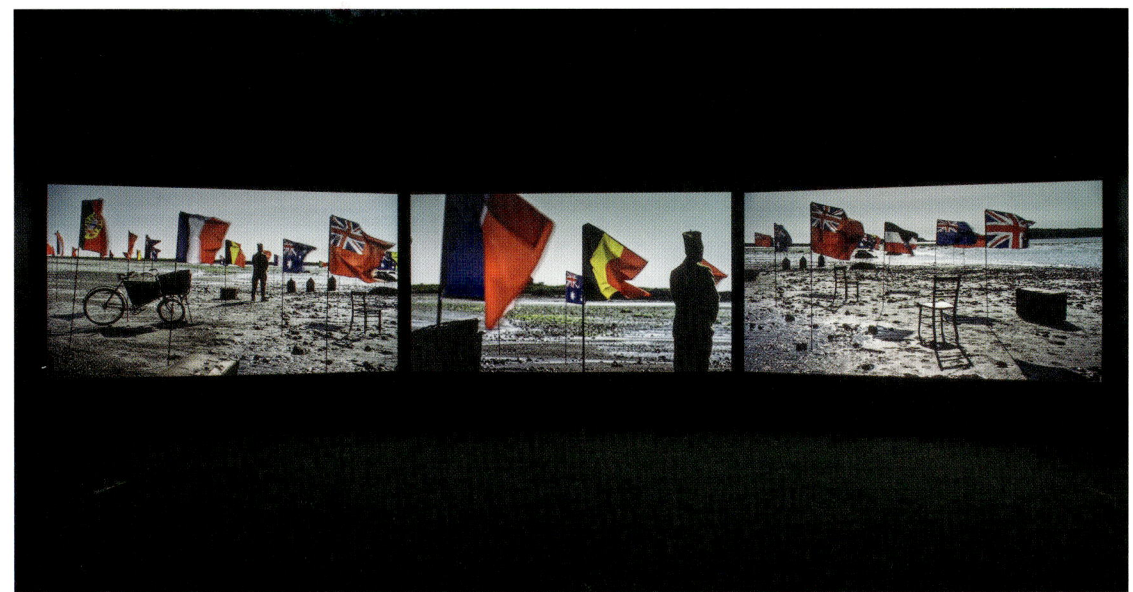

The film combined original back-and-white footage with modern reconstructions using actors, all set to a soundtrack of African music from the 1920s and '30s. The final work was then projected onto three screens.

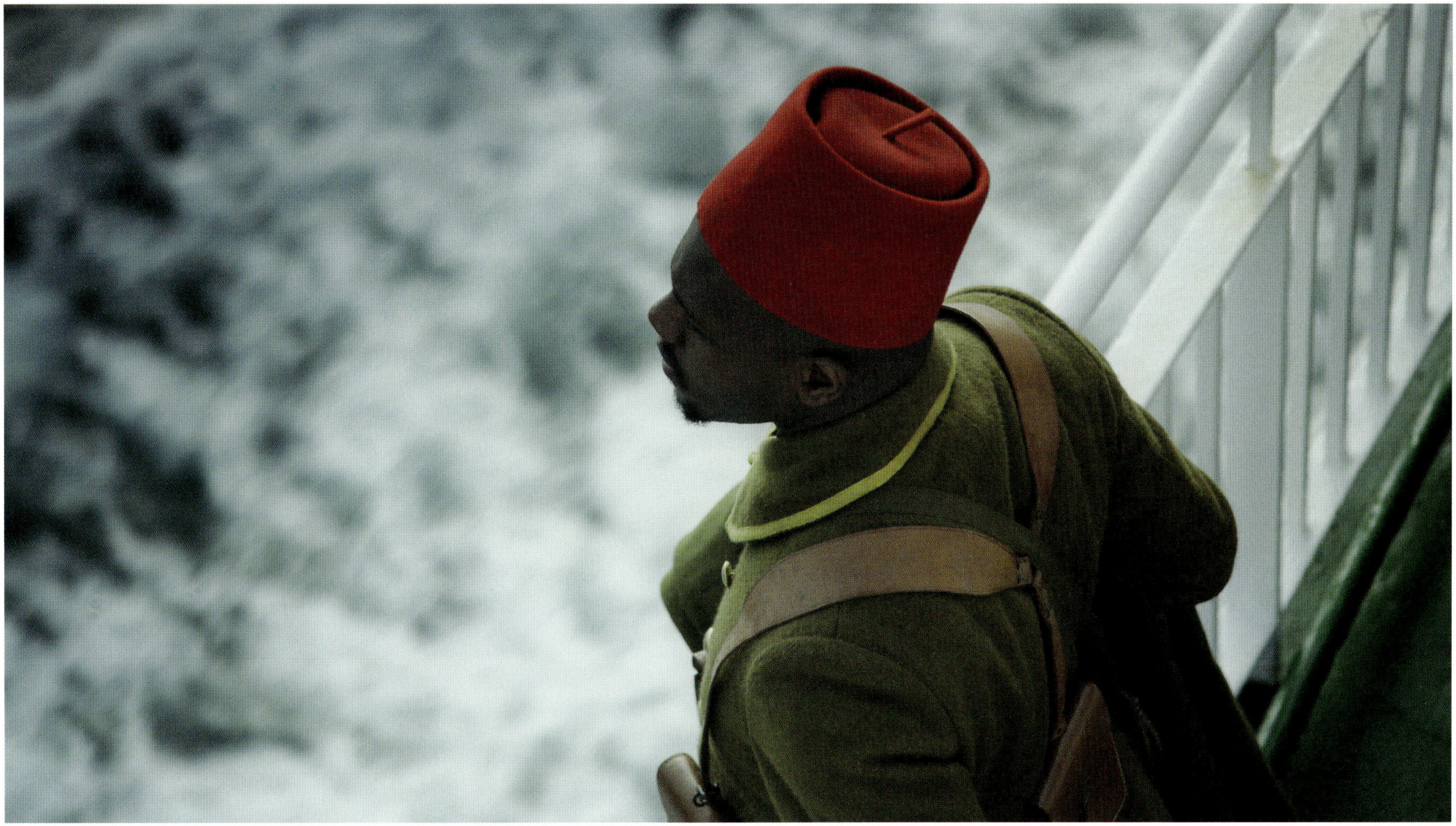

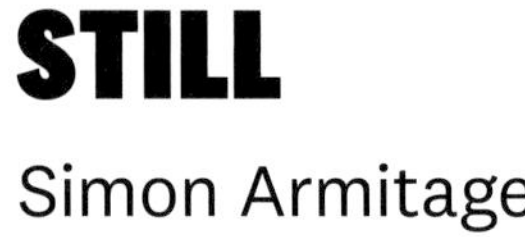

STILL

Simon Armitage

Still is a collection of poems by Simon Armitage — reworkings of Virgil's *Georgics* ('Agriculture'), an epic poem about the land, and man's place within it. Armitage wrote these poems in response to a series of panoramic and aerial photographs associated with the Battle of the Somme. These photographs show the scenes of battle from a rarely seen perspective, transforming the devastation on the ground into ghostly, abstract landscapes. Planes used to take such photographs on reconnaissance missions were one of the many technological developments that made the First World War unlike any that the world had seen before.

Armitage's poems were premiered, alongside prints of the images that inspired them, at the Norfolk & Norwich Festival in 2016, and the title poem of the set was read by Armitage at the *Fierce Light* exhibition held during the festival (see page 192). Fittingly, the poems were published by Enitharmon Press on the centenary of the battle.

*Norwich Playhouse and East Gallery, Norwich,
10 — 28 May 2016*

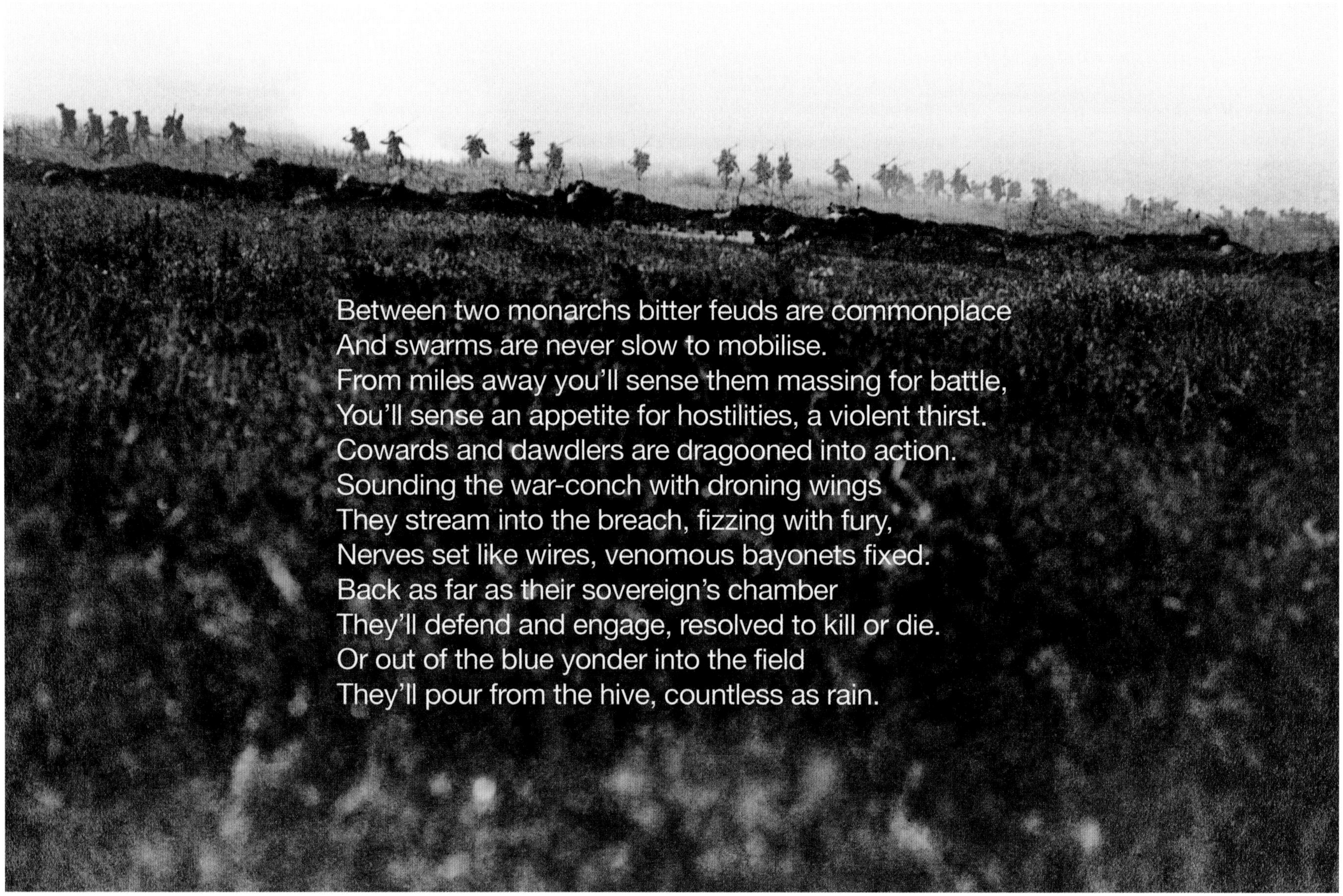

Between two monarchs bitter feuds are commonplace
And swarms are never slow to mobilise.
From miles away you'll sense them massing for battle,
You'll sense an appetite for hostilities, a violent thirst.
Cowards and dawdlers are dragooned into action.
Sounding the war-conch with droning wings
They stream into the breach, fizzing with fury,
Nerves set like wires, venomous bayonets fixed.
Back as far as their sovereign's chamber
They'll defend and engage, resolved to kill or die.
Or out of the blue yonder into the field
They'll pour from the hive, countless as rain.

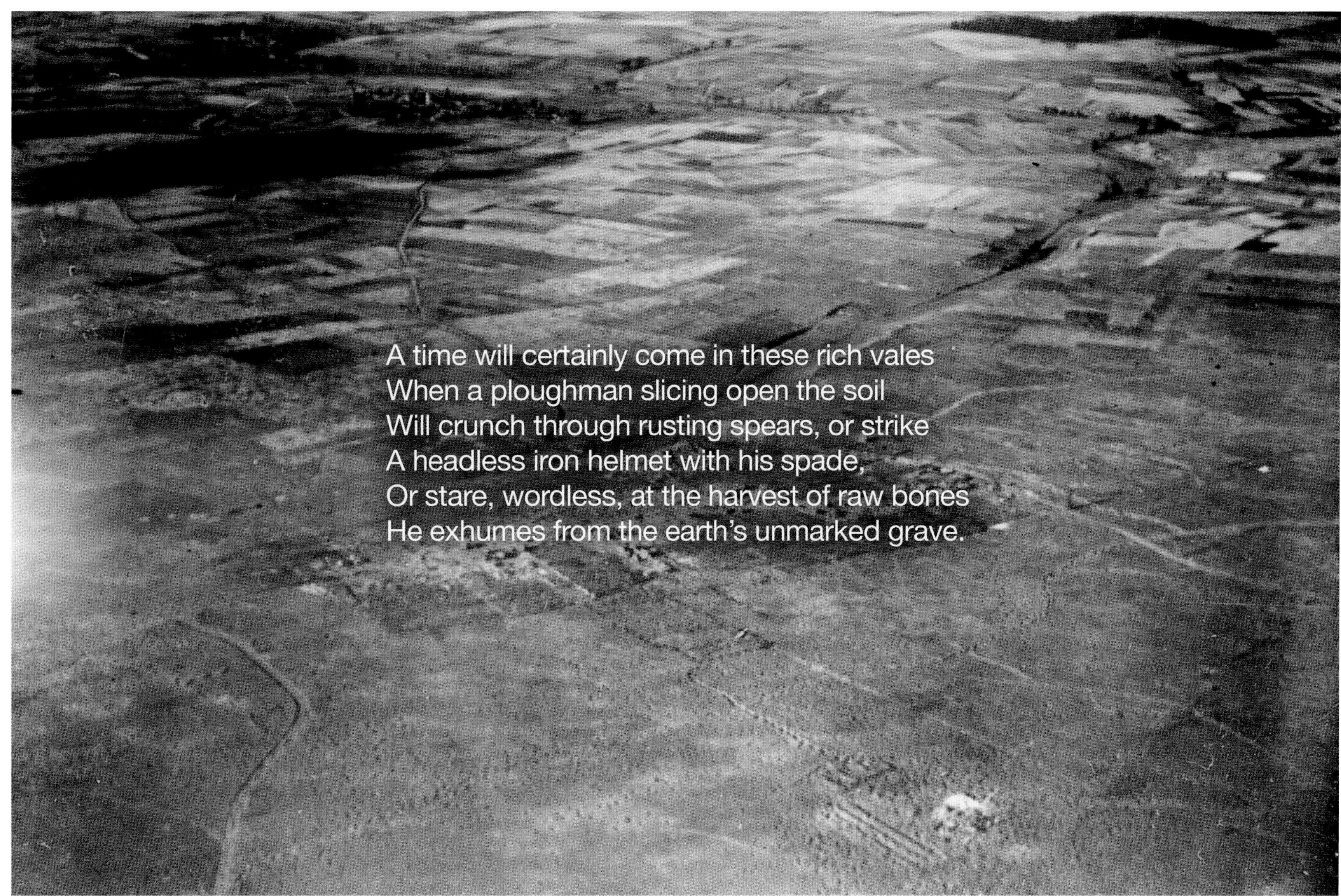

Armitage's poetry was inspired by, and offset against, haunting, grainy images of the First World War battlefields.

FASHION
& FREEDOM

Designers
Holly Fulton
J JS Lee
Roksanda
Vivienne Westwood
Emilia Wickstead
Sadie Williams

Film-makers
SHOWstudio
Luke Snellin

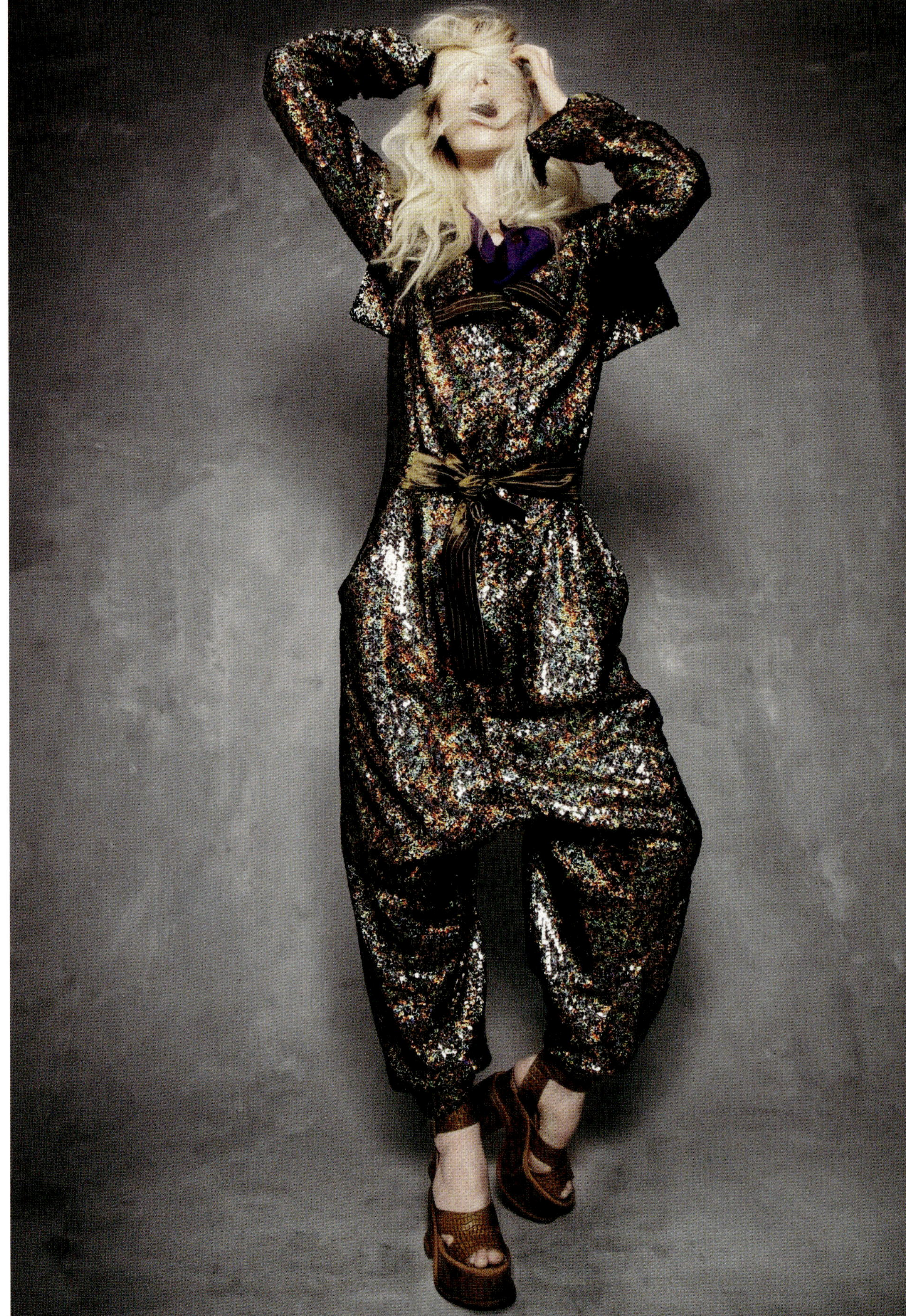

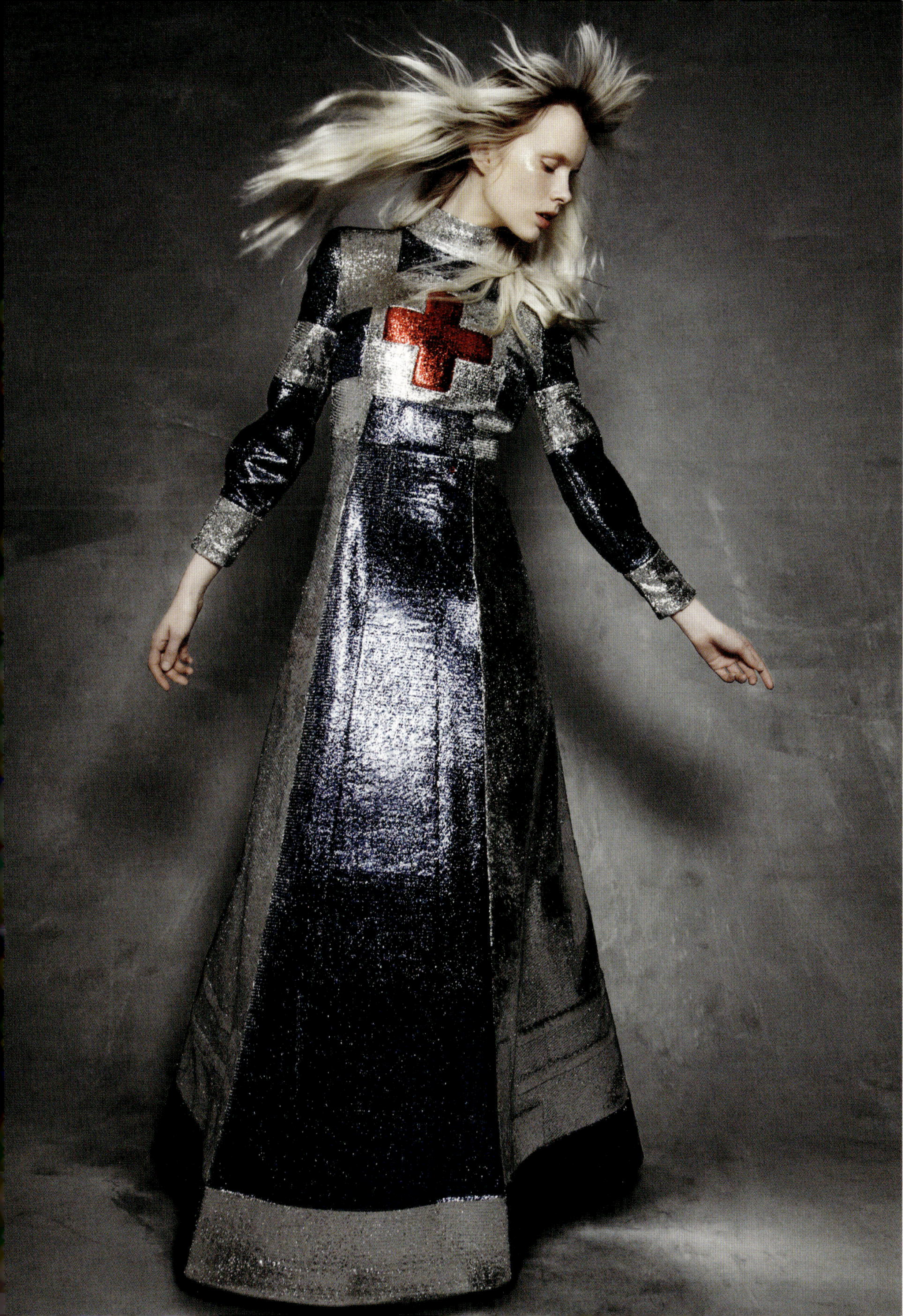

The First World War changed the role of women forever — not least because, with men away fighting, more than a million women were required to go out to work for the very first time: in munitions factories and on the buses, driving ambulances, and even 'manning' the London Underground. These new responsibilities gave women new freedoms — and new looks, as tight corsets and heavy skirts were replaced, out of necessity, by a more natural silhouette and shorter hemlines.

A century later, creative director Darrell Vydelingum launched *Fashion & Freedom*, a multifaceted touring exhibition that celebrated the fashion legacy of the war through contemporary pieces by Vivienne Westwood, Roksanda Ilinčić, J JS Lee, Emilia Wickstead, Holly Fulton and Sadie Williams. Some of the designers took their inspiration from the shift towards more utilitarian, masculine garments, while others focused on specific details of wartime work: Roksanda, for example, chose a colour palette that recalled the 'canary girls', female munitions workers whose skin turned yellow as a result of the toxic chemicals they came in contact with.

These exclusive designs were then presented in the exhibition alongside historic wartime selections drawn from Manchester Art Gallery's renowned costume collection. Also on display were contributions from students at five British fashion colleges, who had been invited to work to the themes of 'Restriction and Release', reflecting changing women's clothing during the First World War.

Vivienne Westwood celebrated the introduction of the jumpsuit for women (left), while the red cross and clean lines of Sadie Williams' gown (right) paid tribute to the nurses of the First World War.

A series of short films was also commissioned
to complement the garments. Three of these were
directed by members of Nick Knight's fashion website,
SHOWstudio: Rei Nadal explored the corset in a film
featuring designs by Phoebe English; Marie Schuller
worked with menswear designer Craig Green to explore
workwear; and George Harvey collaborated with Gareth
Pugh for a film that focused on military wear. A fourth
film was made by Luke Snellin, who wrote and directed
First, reimagining a young woman's first day at work as
a bus conductor, in uniforms designed by Manchester
fashion label Private White V.C.

*Manchester Art Gallery, 13 May — 27 November 2016
/ The Civic, Barnsley, 11 February — 8 April 2017 /
Freedom Festival, Hull, 1 August — 3 September 2017
/ Belfast International Arts Festival, 10 — 28 October
2017 / National Memorial Arboretum, Burton-on-Trent,
9 March — 30 November 2018*

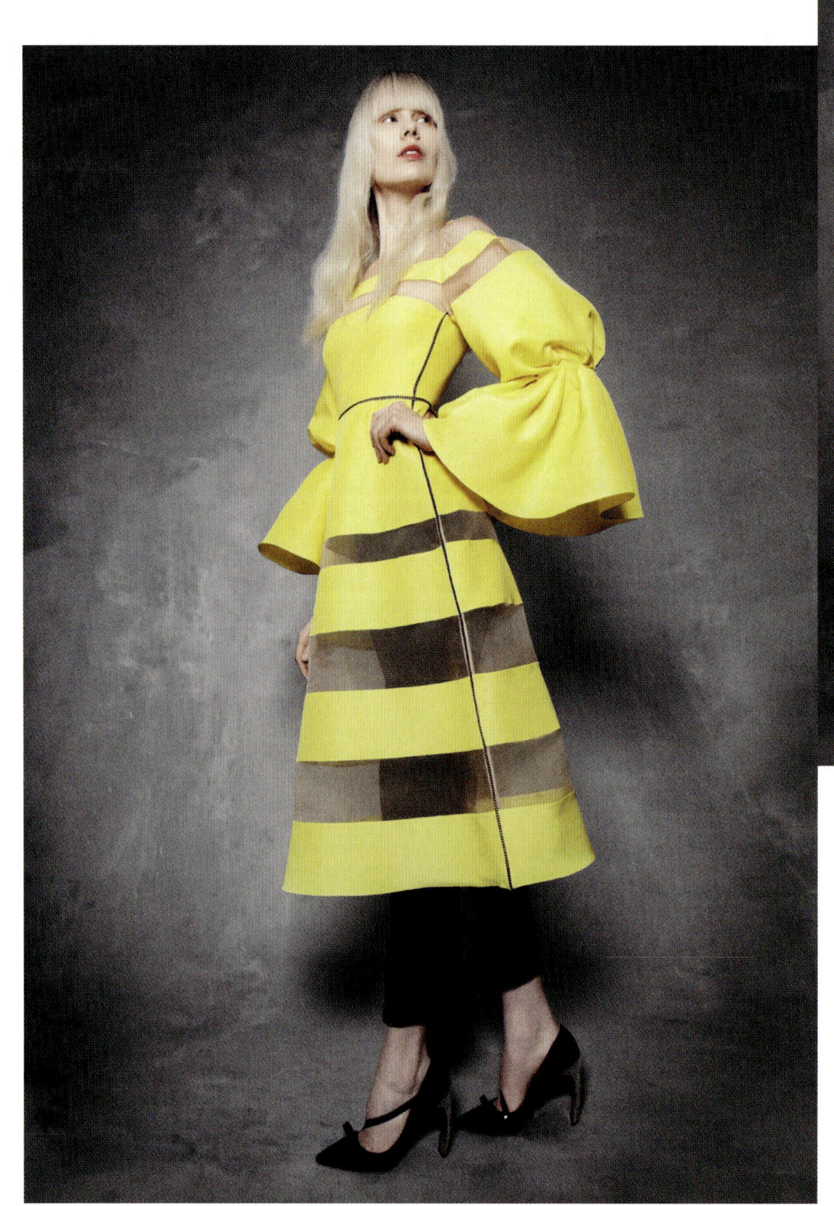

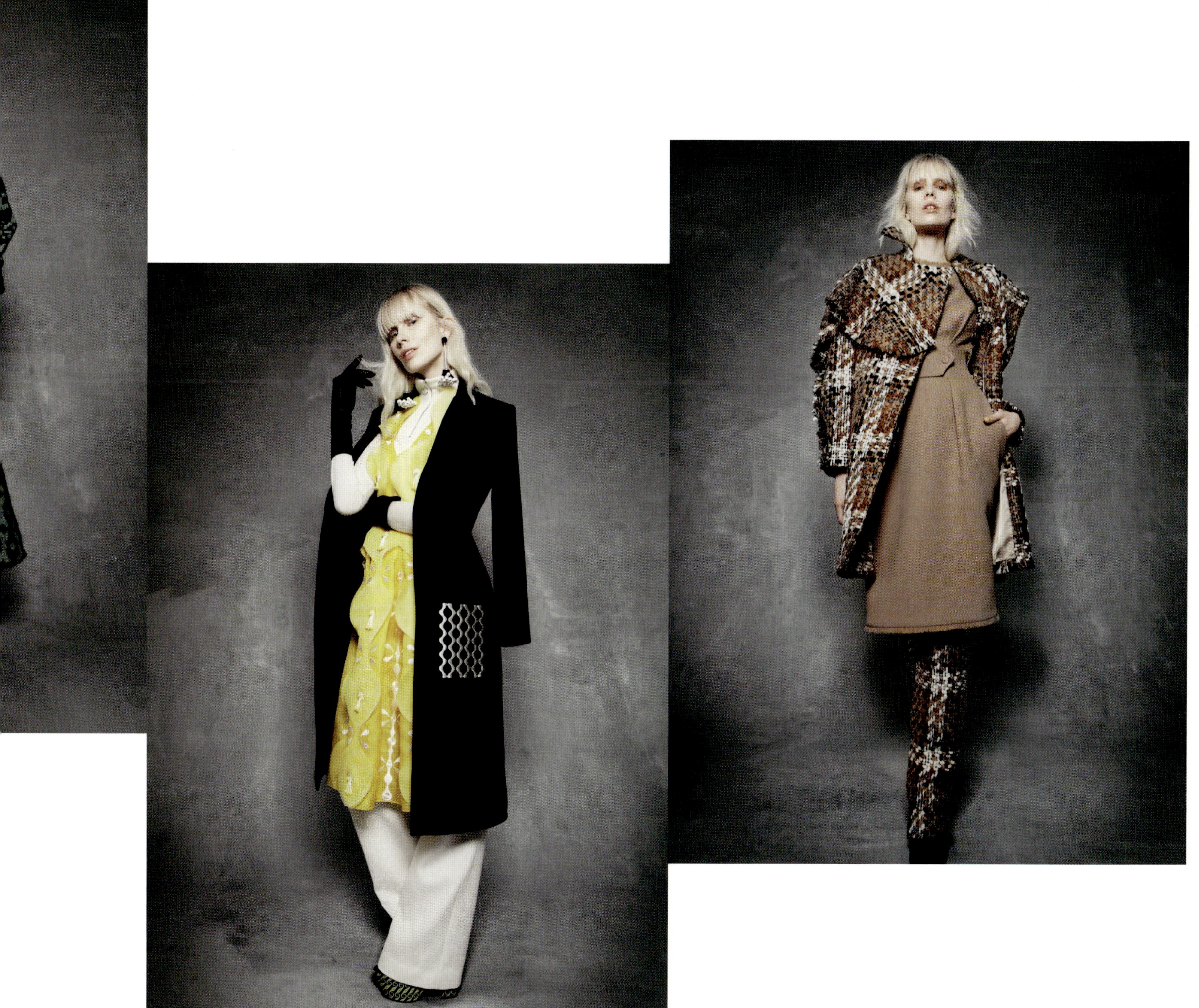

THE COFFIN JUMP

Katrina Palmer

Between June 2018 and 2019, visitors to Yorkshire Sculpture Park were able to see an intervention in the landscape, comprising a hand-painted fence above a trench. 'Activated' at certain times by a horse and rider leaping over it, Katrina Palmer's *The Coffin Jump* combined sculpture, soundtrack and performance, and was intended to symbolise the new challenges and freedoms afforded to women during the First World War.

The work was inspired by the role of women in the war, and specifically the First Aid Nursing Yeomanry (FANY). Founded in 1907, the all-female FANY was a courageous corps of women on horseback who treated wounded men on the battlefields before they were evacuated to a field hospital. However, when the First World War broke out, the British Army initially refused to be associated with the FANY, so the nurses gave medical support to the Belgian and French armies instead. Later, they helped to run medical convoys and drove ambulances in support of British forces.

For the fence inscriptions, Palmer drew on such sources as the diaries of FANY member Muriel Thompson, with phrases including 'woman saves man' and 'nothing special happened' paying simple tribute to the everyday heroism of the women of the war.

Yorkshire Sculpture Park, 16 June 2018 — June 2019

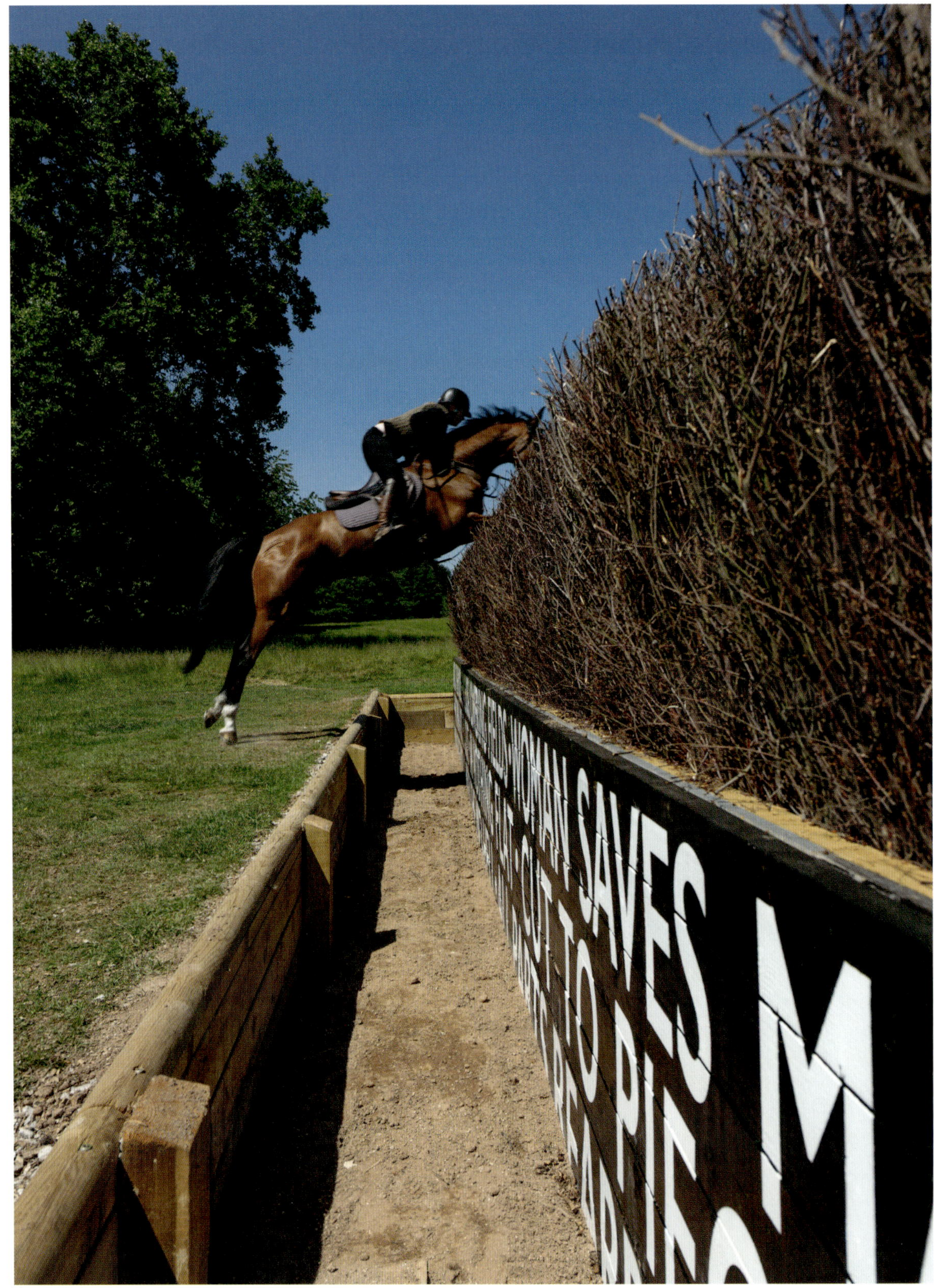

Katrina Palmer

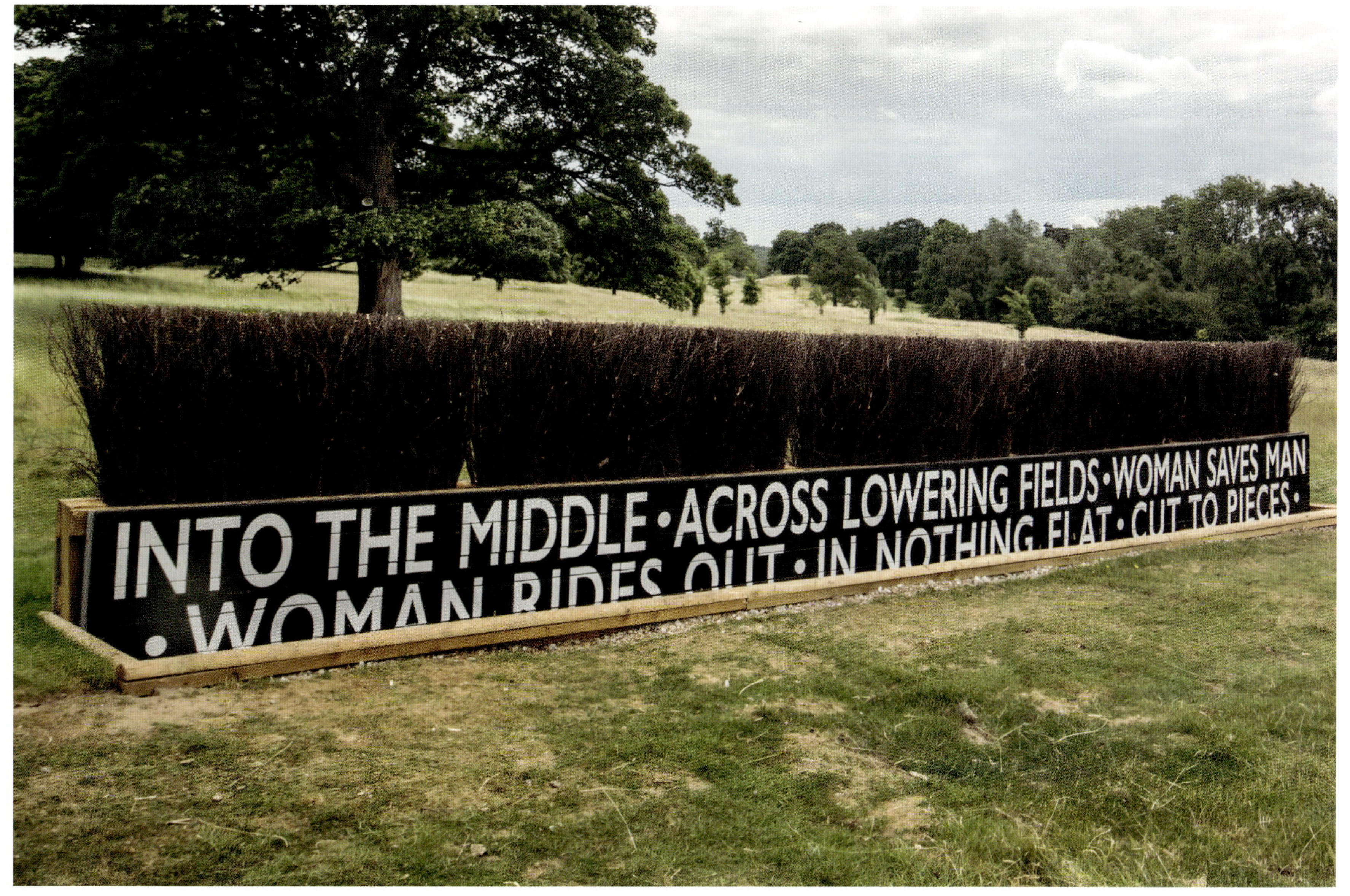

LONDON SINFONIETTA

George Benjamin

This special BBC Proms concert marked both 100 years since the Armistice and 50 years since the London Sinfonietta was founded to perform the best in contemporary music. Conducted by George Benjamin, the programme centred on four specially commissioned compositions inspired by the First World War and written by a quartet of leading European composers from countries that had once fought on opposite sides of that conflict: Luca Francesconi from Italy, Georg Friedrich Haas from Austria, Hannah Kendall from Britain and Isabel Mundry from Germany.

The prom also featured two pieces written either side of the war — Charles Ives' searching *The Unanswered Question*, and Igor Stravinsky's elegant *Symphonies of Wind Instruments* — along with a monumental work by one of the most important figures in 20th-century music: Olivier Messiaen's *Et exspecto resurrectionem mortuorum*, a memorial to the dead of the two world wars.

The Roundhouse, London, and BBC Radio 3, 21 July 2018

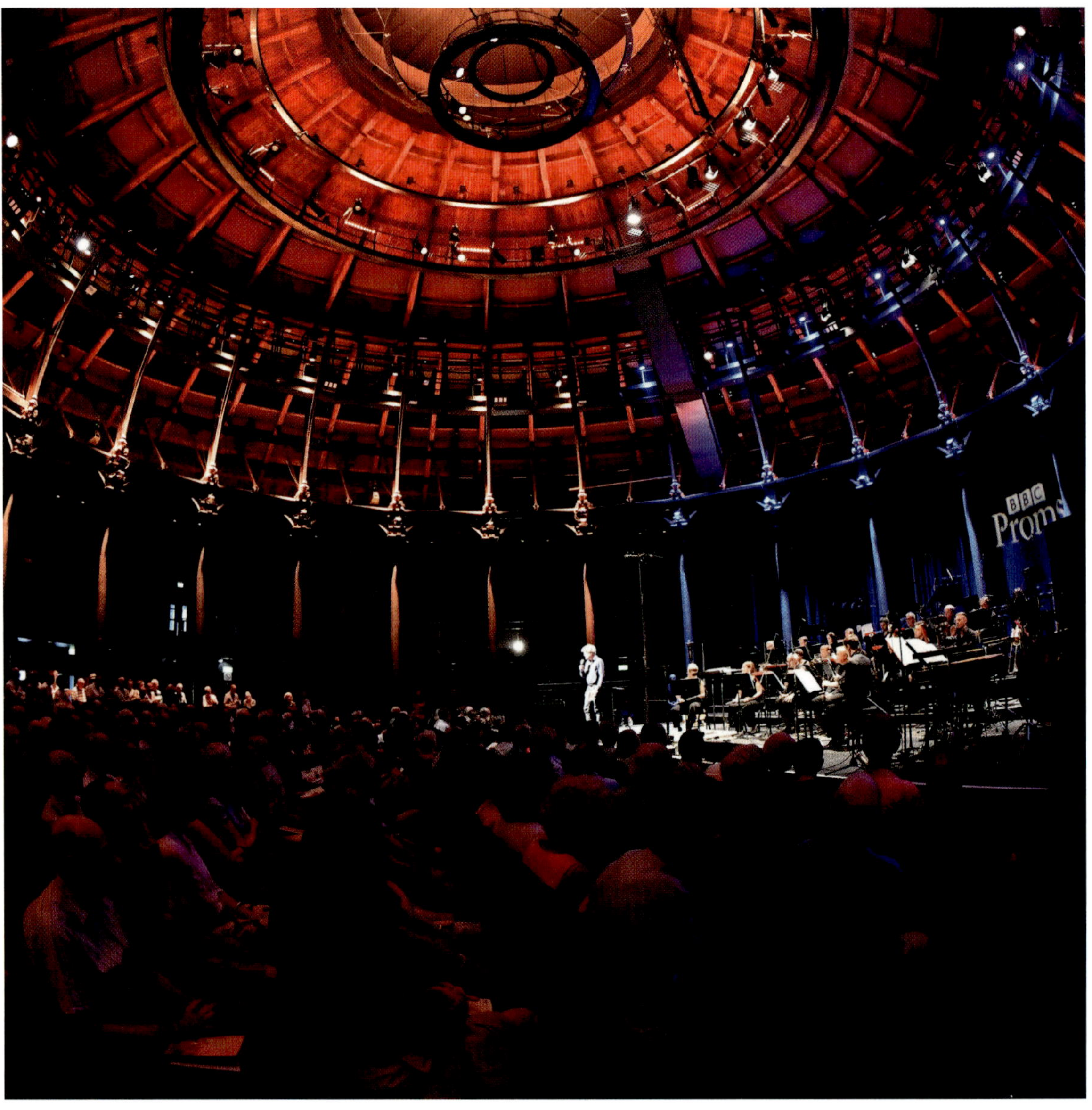

THE CASEMENT PROJECT

Fearghus Ó Conchúir

In 1916, the year of the Easter Rising, Irish rebel and international humanitarian Roger Casement, once knighted by the British crown, was hanged for treason in Pentonville Prison. Recognised for exposing human rights abuses in the Congo and the Amazon, his support for Irish nationalism and cooperation with Germany caused a scandal. His homosexuality was just as controversial.

The Casement Project, by choreographer Fearghus Ó Conchúir, used dance to explore themes of identity, belonging and becoming through the dichotomies of Casement's life — his acceptance into the upper echelons of the establishment, his rejection of it through his politics, and its rejection of him for his sexuality. The project encompassed a stage performance (*Butterflies and Bones*), a day of dance on the beach where Casement landed in Ireland shortly before the Easter Rising (*Féile Fáilte*), a dance film (*I'm Roger Casement*), two academic symposia and a variety of engagement activities.

The British Library, 3 June 2016 / The Place, London, 11 — 12 June / Banna Strand, Kerry, 23 July 2016 / The Mac, Belfast, 13 October / Project Arts Centre, Dublin, 20 — 22 October / RTÉ broadcast, 17 January 2017

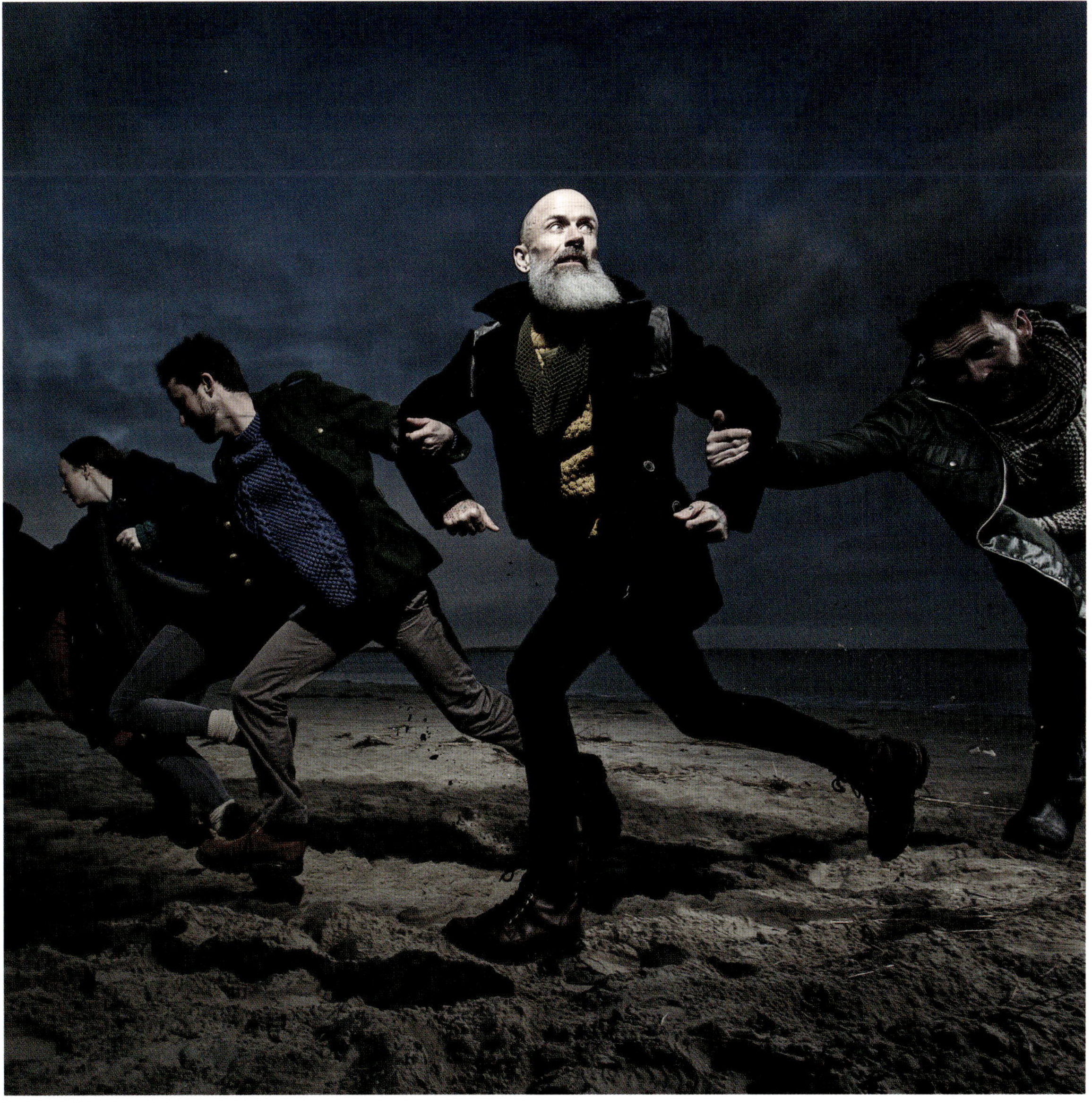

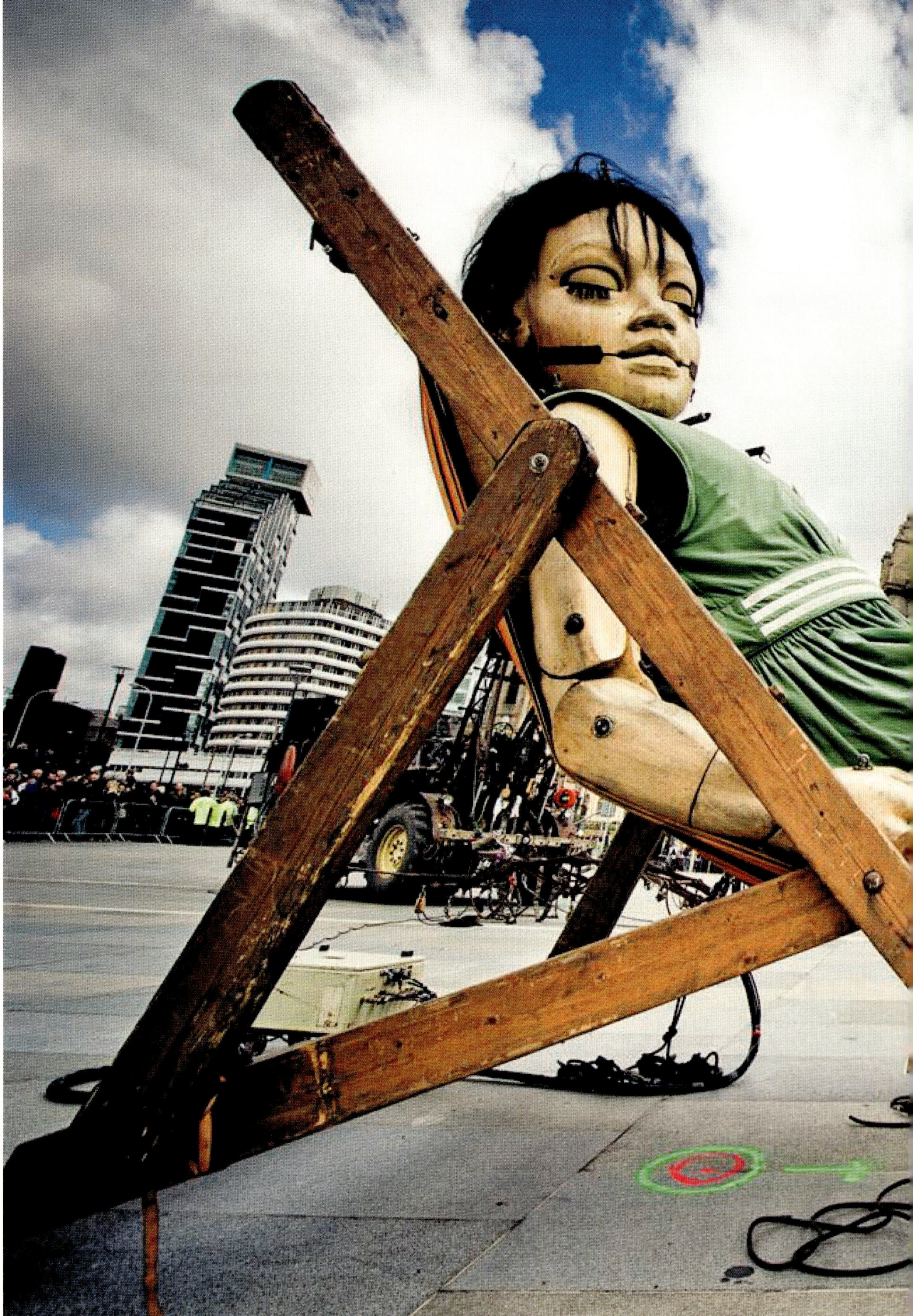

Liverpool hosted one of the most astonishing events of the 2014 centenary when it welcomed Royal de Luxe's iconic giants onto its streets for a city-wide five-day spectacular.

Jean-Luc Courcoult's world-renowned French street-theatre company retold the story of the famous Liverpool Pals battalions — the young men who volunteered alongside their next-door neighbours, family members and friends to fight for Britain on the battlefields of Europe. One battalion was called for, yet four were raised, such was the depth of patriotic fellow-feeling in this city renowned for its deep community ties.

One hundred years later, the *Little Girl* and her pet dog *Xolo* told their story, roaming the city to live music written by the company's regular collaborator Michel Augier, drawing captivated crowds into their ranks as they went, entranced by this extraordinary and emotive spectacle. Battalions of young men re-enacting their forebears' cheerful march towards the recruitment centre at St George's Hall were followed by legions of mourners in funeral dress, poignantly just a short distance behind.

MEMORIES OF AUGUST 1914

Royal de Luxe

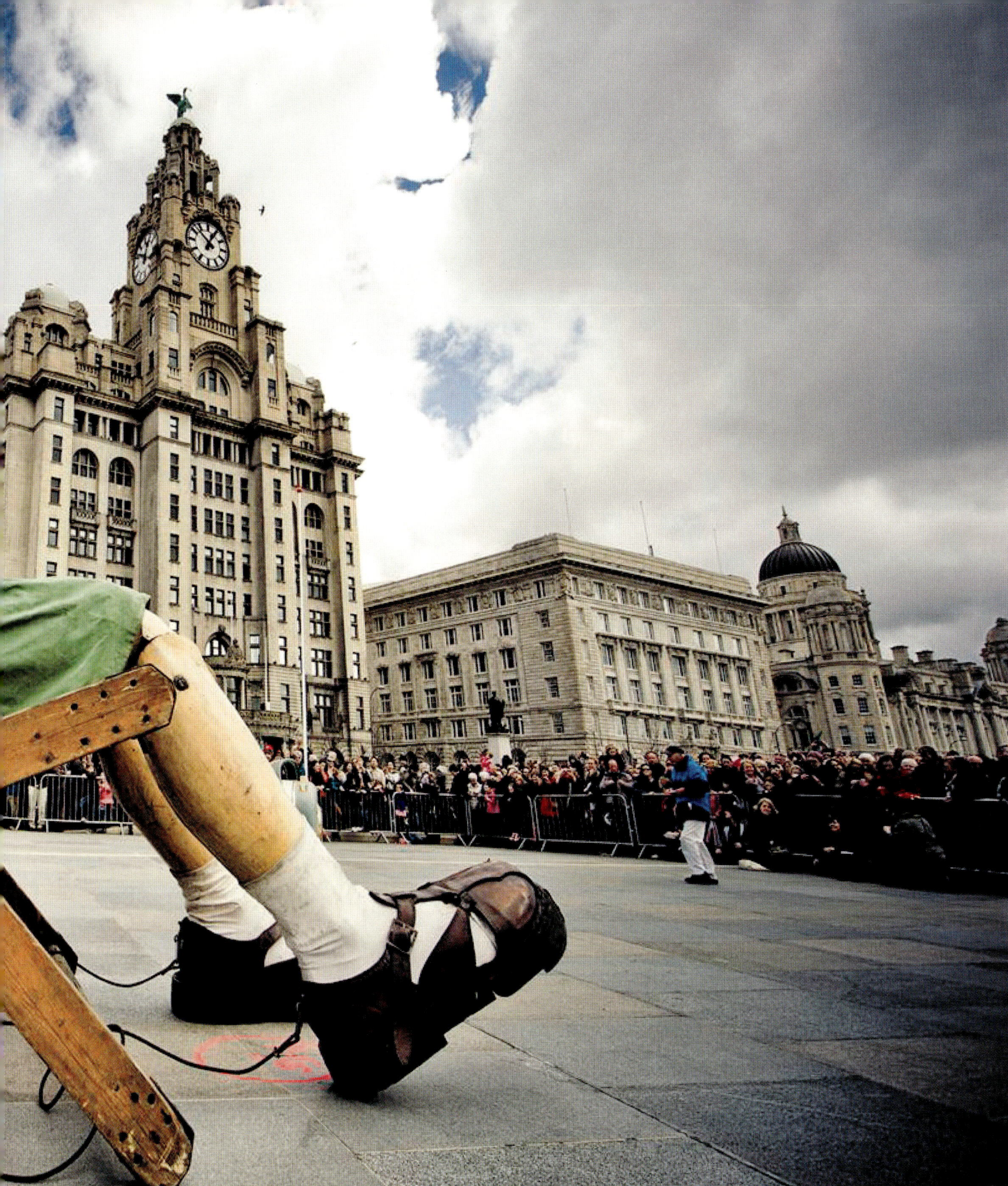

The *Little Girl*, seen here resting in front of the city's iconic Royal Liver Building.

Right and opposite. Royal de Luxe's giants were hoisted into action and controlled by a team of puppeteers; 22 operators alone were needed to escort the *Little Girl* through the city streets.

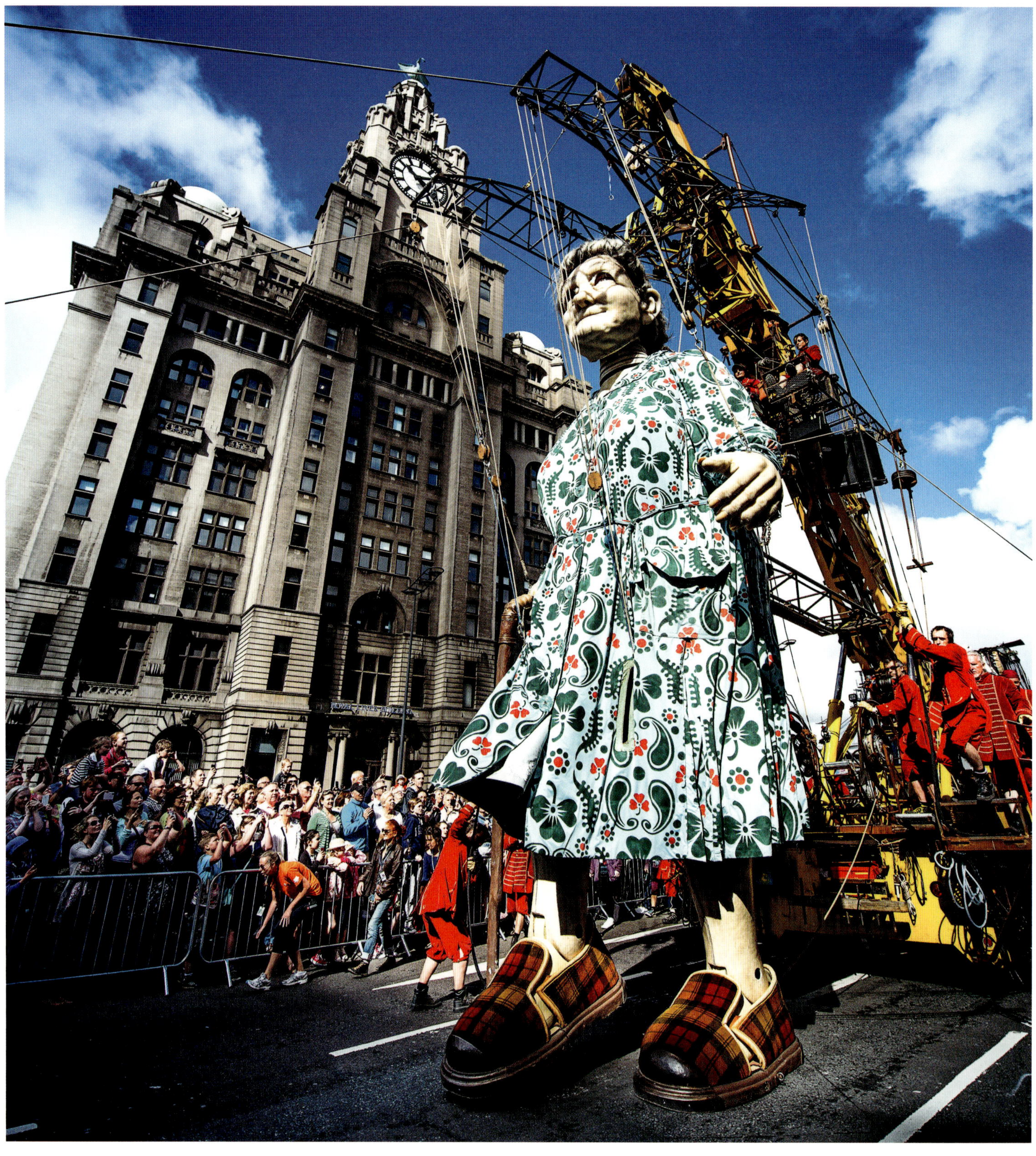

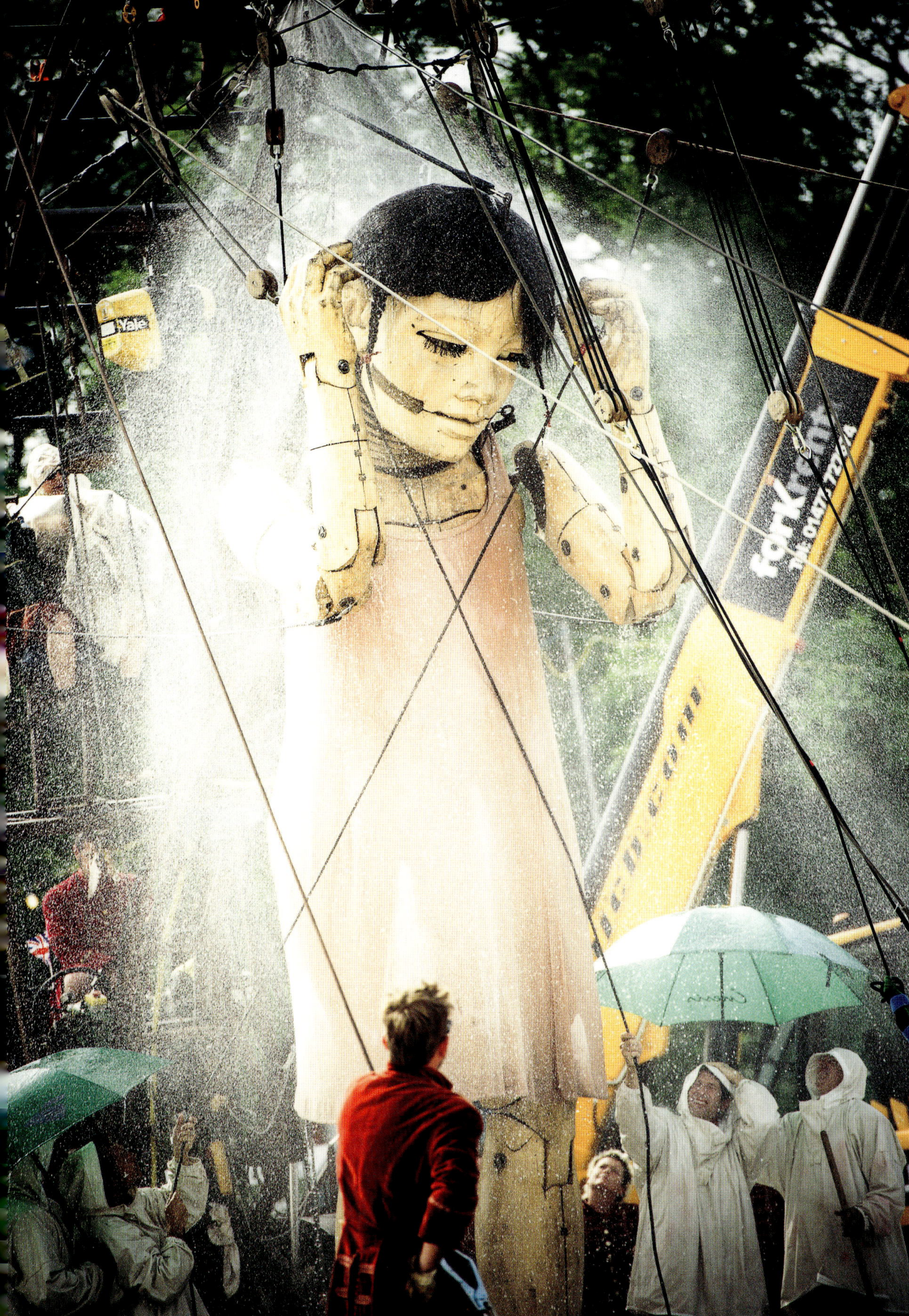

After an extended nap in St George's Hall — an exhibition that itself drew tens of thousands of visitors — the figure of another giant was hoisted back to life. The *Grandmother*'s vanilla-scented flatulence and furtive sips of whisky charmed all who came in contact with her.

The beauty of Royal de Luxe's giants comes not only from their size and their incredibly lifelike movements, but from the fact that their armies of puppeteers must travel with them, operating them by hand with ropes and pulleys like manic bell-ringers, revealing the fascinating workings that conjure these ingenious artworks into life.

In total, more than 1.5 million people — a mix of visitors and locals — came to see the spectacle and to honour a courageous generation of Liverpudlians whose memory lives on in sadness and in joy.

Liverpool, 23 — 27 July 2014

'42,000 people queued to see the latest show from French street-theatre specialists Royal de Luxe before it had even started.'

The Guardian

ACROSS AND IN-BETWEEN

Suzanne Lacy

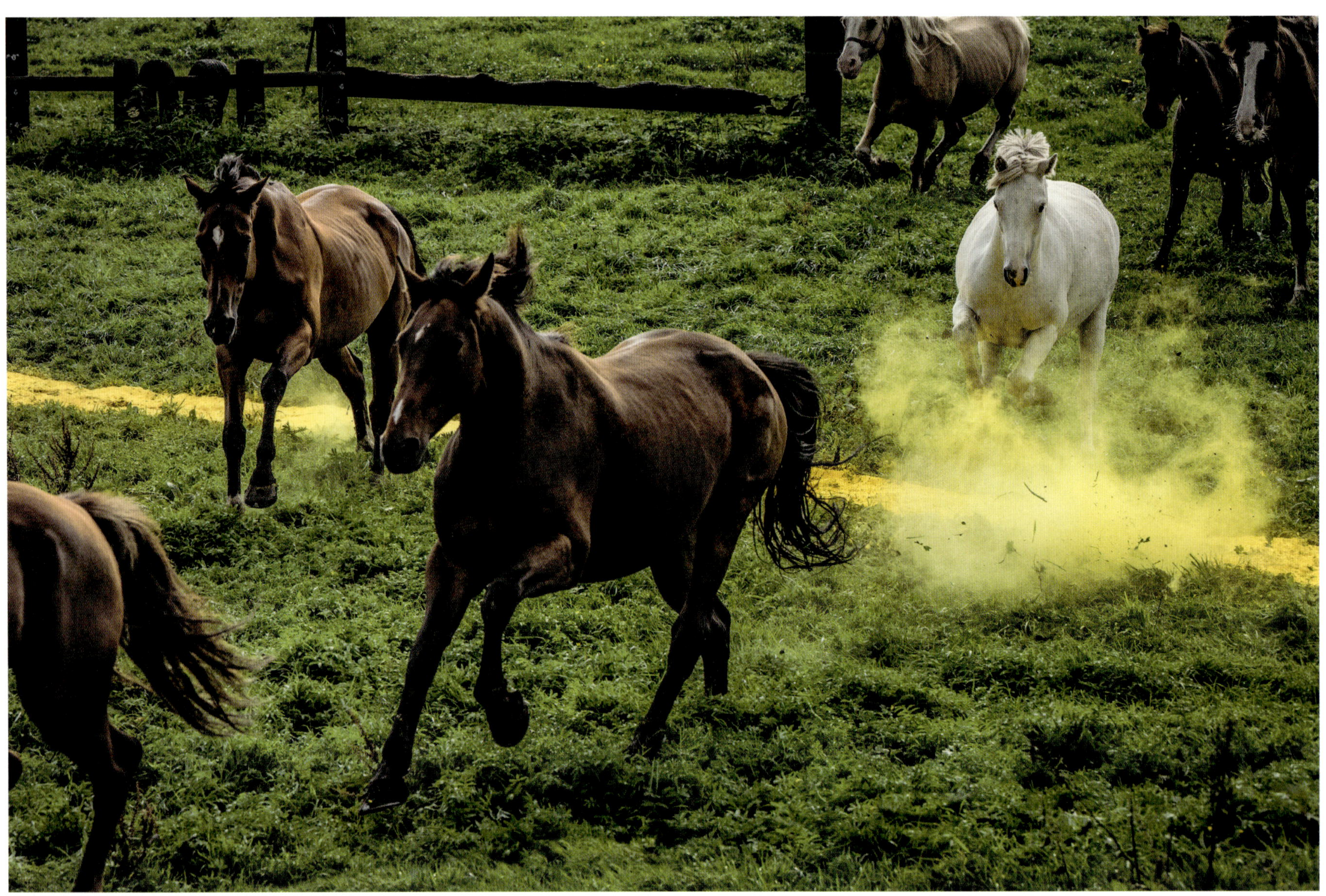

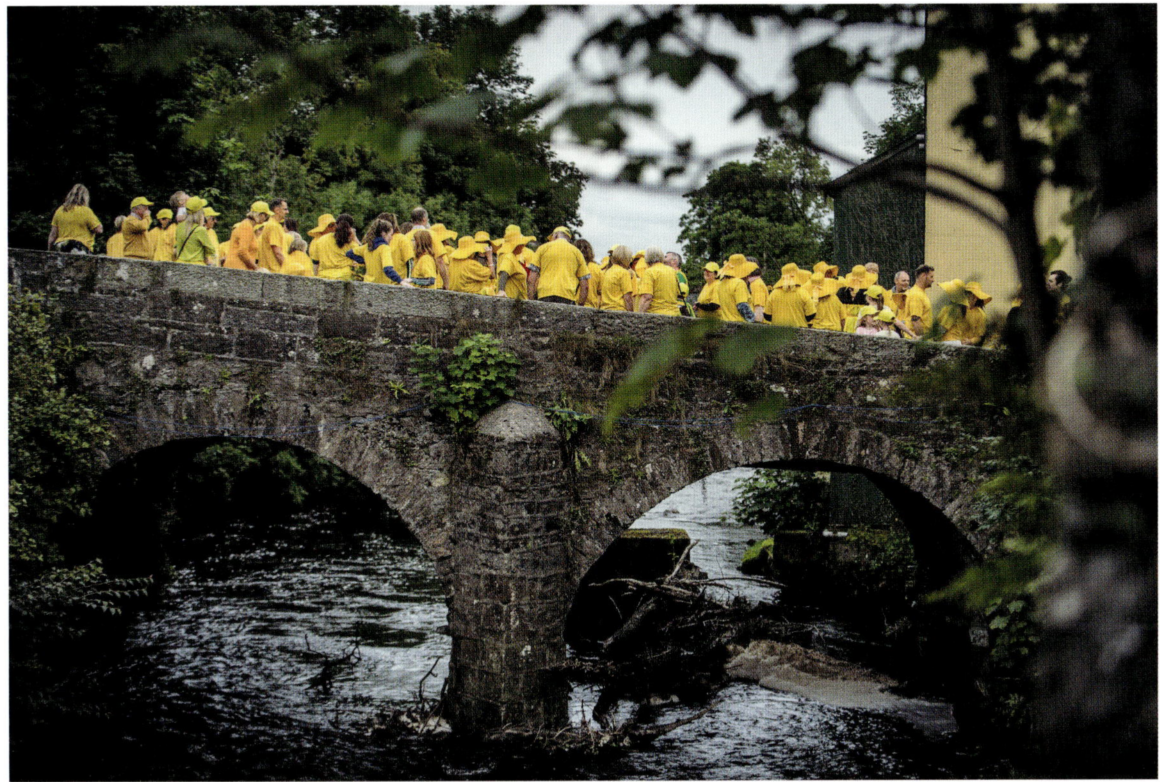

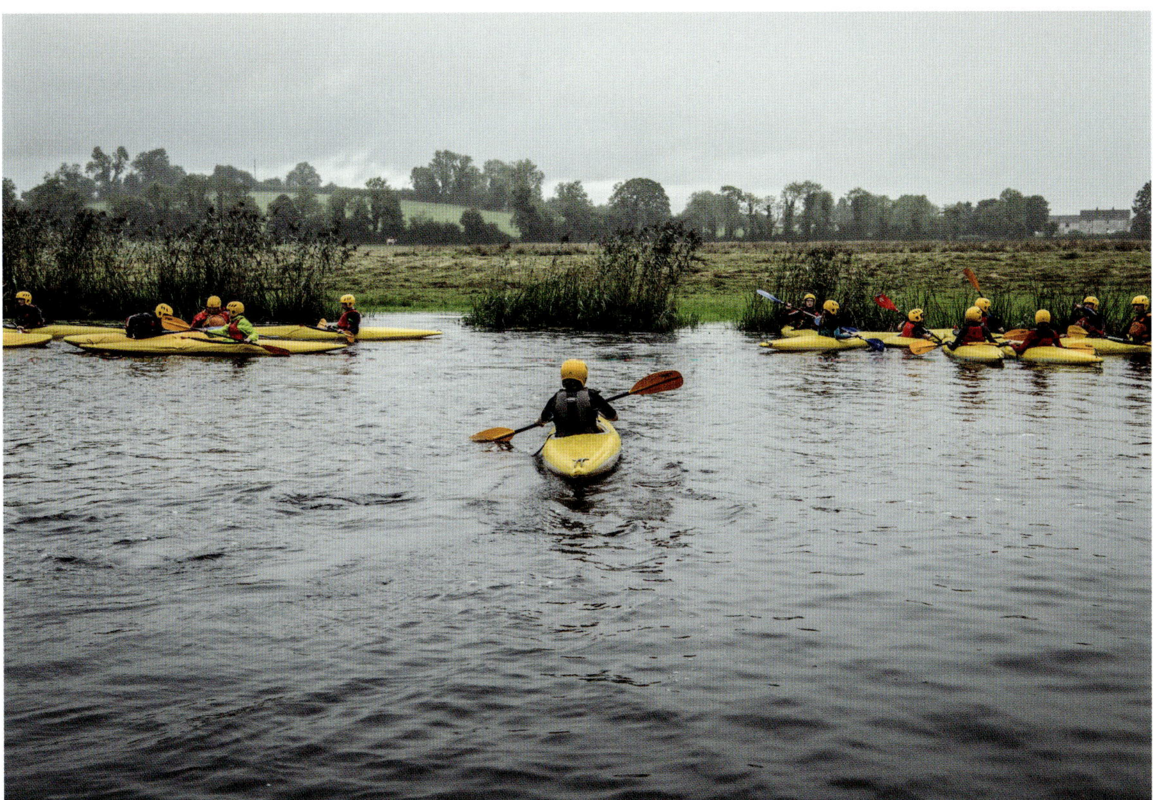

Borders have profound impacts on the lives of people who live on or near them. Some borders, such as the one dividing Northern Ireland from the Republic of Ireland, run through lakes, roads and farmland.

The journey towards the partition of Ireland dates from the end of the First World War. After the Easter Rising of 1916 and the assertion of independence by Sinn Féin in 1918, a devastating civil war broke out following the division of the country into north and south in 1921. The consequences of this division are still felt today. For this commission, Suzanne Lacy collaborated with artists and activists in Ireland while working with residents to create a series of localised gatherings and individual musings on visible and invisible borders, in order to investigate how the border frames identity and intervenes in the routine of everyday life.

The first part of the project was *The Yellow Line*, a large-scale three-channel film projected onto the Ulster Museum during the Belfast International Arts Festival. The second part was the *Border People's Parliament*, a performance event at Stormont, the home of the Northern Ireland Parliament. This brought together 120 people who live along the border across social, political and geographic divides, giving them an opportunity to eat and talk together, and to record their views about the border. The participants considered matters of global political significance that were also, to them, intensely local, and the outcome was a document entitled the 'Yellow Manifesto', which was then presented to MPs at the Houses of Parliament in London.

Ulster Museum and Stormont's Parliament Buildings, Belfast, 18 — 23 October 2018

THIS IS NOT FOR YOU

Graeae Theatre

Taking place on a mock parade ground, first in front of Woolwich's Royal Arsenal and then in Stockton-on-Tees, *This Is Not for You* was an epic outdoor performance paying moving tribute to Britain's wounded war veterans. The story of their fight for respect and remembrance was told with heft, beauty and wry humour, both on the ground and off it, with audio description and sign language as integral parts of the production.

The piece was directed by Jenny Sealey, written by Mike Kenny, with music composed by Oliver Vibrans, and performed by representatives of the charity Blesma, The Limbless Veterans, alongside professional performers and local community choirs. Graeae, together with the National Centre for Circus Arts, trained 25 disabled veterans in performance and aerial choreography especially for the piece.

Alongside its performances in Greenwich and Stockton, the work inspired an extensive education and digital engagement programme, encouraging both veterans and members of the public to share their stories, thereby honouring those men and women whose contributions to history often go unnoticed.

Greenwich + Docklands International Festival, London, 30 June — 1 July 2018 / Stockton International Riverside Festival, Stockton-on-Tees, 2 — 3 August 2018

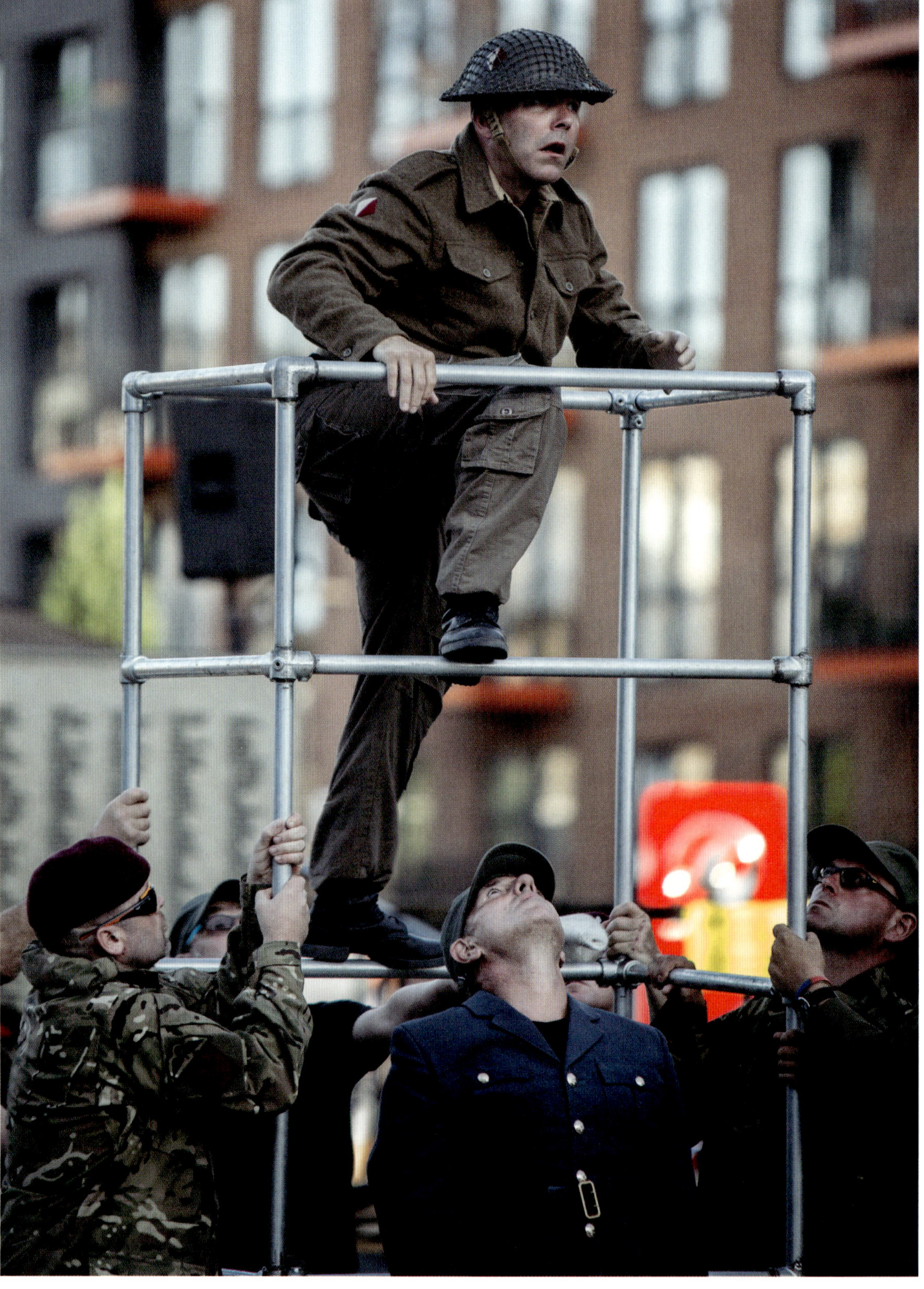

'You go past the Cenotaph and the crowd clap you. It's quite moving. We were waving to the crowd, and this little boy said: "This is not for you survivors. This is for the dead." It made me feel guilty.'

A veteran describing his experiences on Remembrance Sunday

Opposite. The company in performance at Woolwich.

Below. Performers rehearsed for two weeks, and were trained in how to work interactively with the cuboids that formed a key part of the show's design.

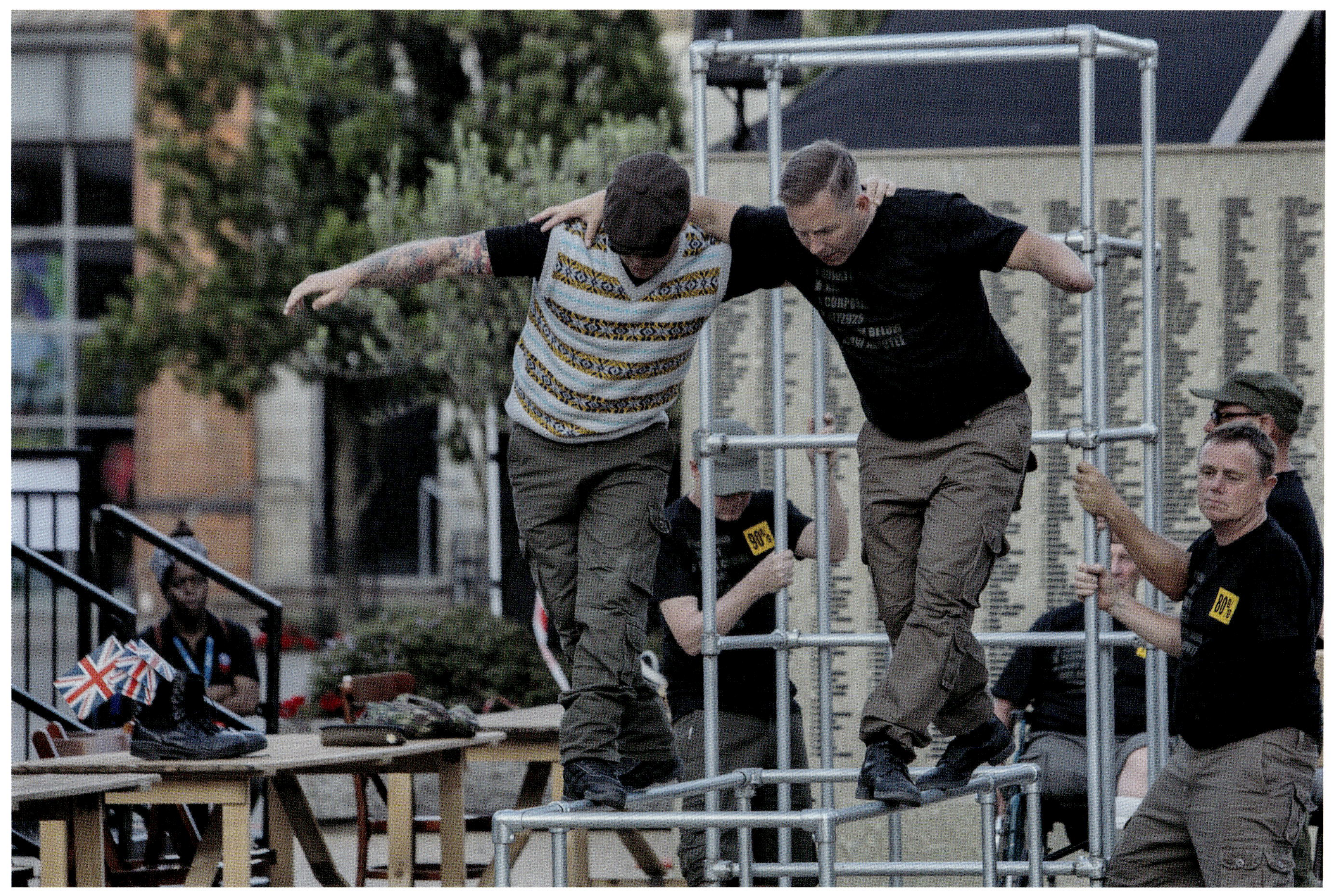

SHELTER

Anne Tallentire

The mass mobilisation of troops across the Continent a century ago left an architectural legacy: the Nissen hut (see also page 150). The simple curved structure that we associate now with barracks, refugee camps and internment blocks was invented by a British Army officer, Major Peter Norman Nissen, in 1916 to house soldiers and supplies.

Today, that mass movement of soldiers finds an echo in the millions of refugees who are seeking refuge across Europe, and emergency architecture is once more having to respond to a humanitarian crisis. This was the subject that Irish artist Anne Tallentire was keen to explore in a work commissioned by 14-18 NOW and Northern Irish art organisation the Nerve Centre.

Tallentire sought the advice of architect Gráinne Hassett — founder of the Calais Builds Project, which contributed to the infrastucture of the refugee camp that sprang up near Calais in 2015, housing thousands of migrants hoping to seek asylum in the UK. Hassett advised on what materials would be required for an equivalent building today. Using one of two galleries at Eighty81, Tallentire created an initial iteration in the form of a store of these materials. Then each morning she carried, for example, corrugated iron, steel poles, nails and wood to the adjacent Ebrington Square (the site of a former army parade ground), where she choreographed and recorded on video the construction of a 'material diagram'. At the end of the day this work was dismantled, brought to the second gallery and transformed into a new sculptural entity. On the following day another set of materials from gallery 1 was selected to make another diagram on the parade ground, which became another sculpture in the second space, and so on, until gallery 1 (the store) was emptied and gallery 2 full of work. The entire process, with its emphasis on ephemerality and process-based making, reflected Tallentire's long-standing interest in cultural displacement and the lived environment. The work was exhibited at Eighty81 before travelling to Belfast and Limerick.

Nerve Centre at Eighty81, Ebrington Square, Derry/Londonderry; Ulster Museum, Belfast; FabLab, Limerick / 16 June — 29 September 2016

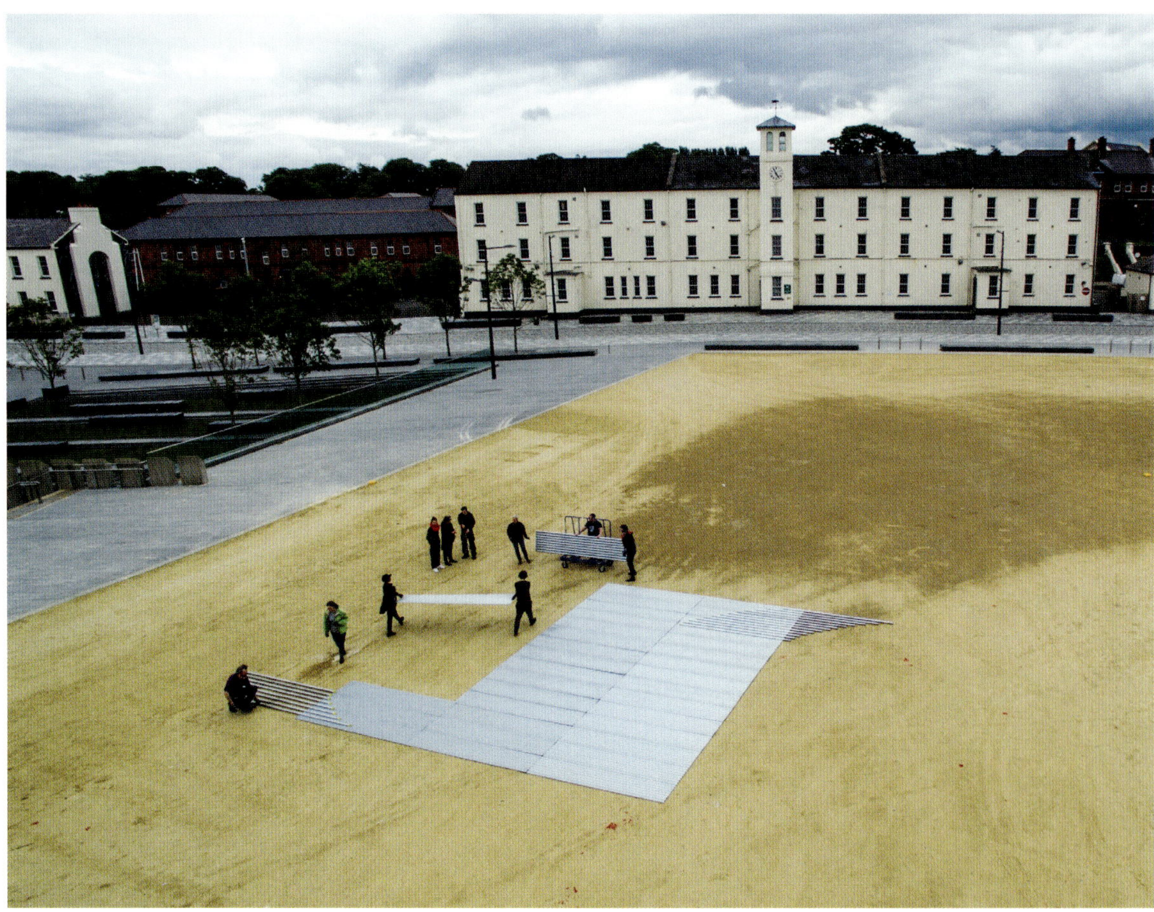

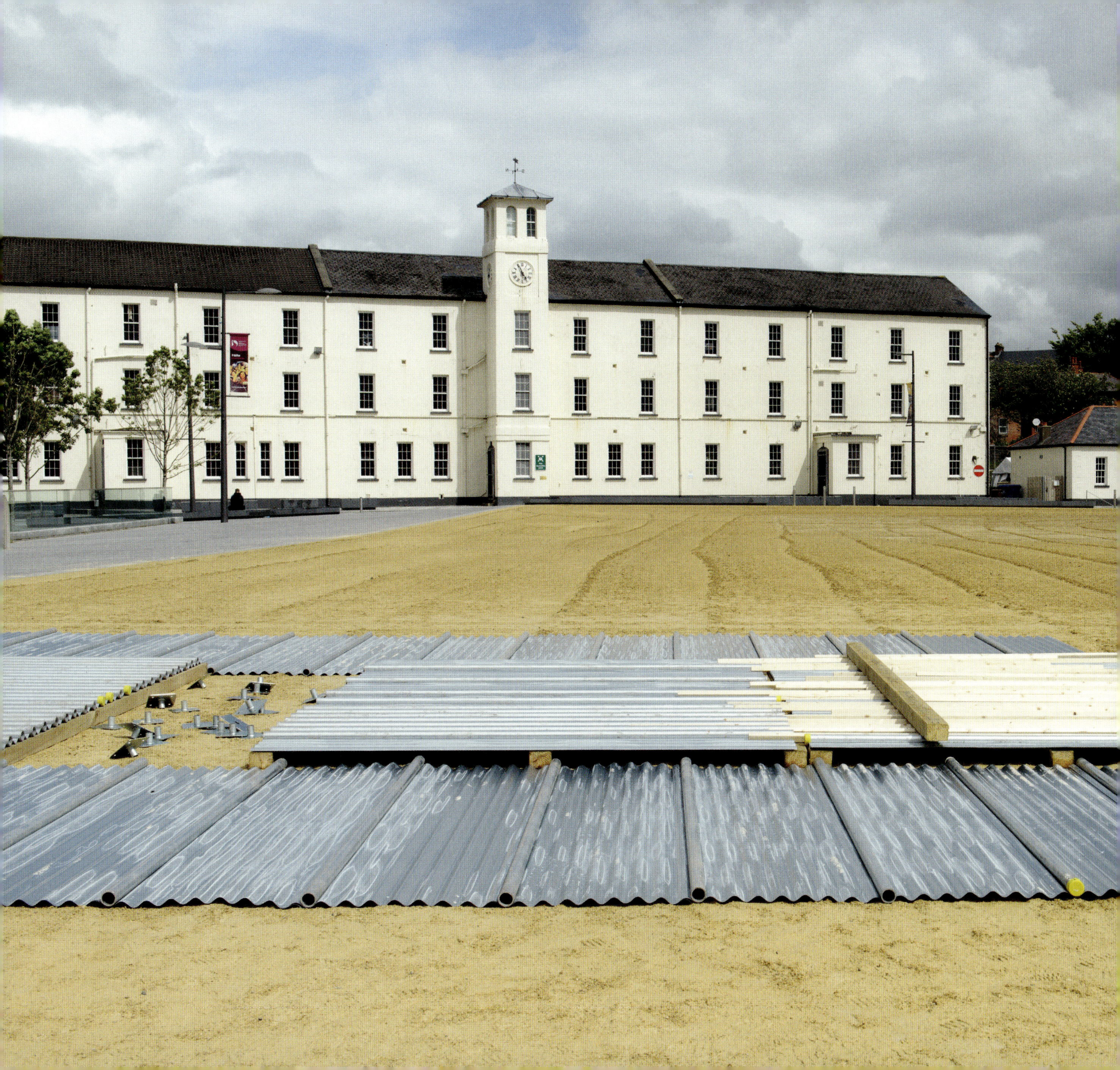

TRIUMPH TO EXIST

Magnus Lindberg

Magnus Lindberg, the London Philharmonic Orchestra's Composer in Residence from 2014, marked the eve of the Armistice with a major new setting of wartime poems by Finnish poet Edith Södergran. Although written in 1916, during the tumult of the First World War, Södergran's 'Triumph to Exist' is a vital exultation on the wonders of life — or, as Lindberg put it, the cry of someone who 'refuses to submit to the hopelessness all around her'.

The London Philharmonic Orchestra and Choir premiered Lindberg's piece alongside three other works with wartime resonance: Debussy's sombre *Berceuse Héroïque*, written as his fellow Frenchmen went into battle at the start of the conflict; *Requiem Canticles*, Stravinsky's adaptation of the Catholic requiem mass; and *The Eternal Gospel*, Janáček's ecstatic 1914 oratorio.

Royal Festival Hall, London, 10 November 2018

'*For me, the poem says something deeply essential about the tragedy of millions of young men who gave their lives in that useless slaughter. They were deprived of the simple human triumph to merely exist. Every syllable cries out to be set to music.*'

Magnus Lindberg

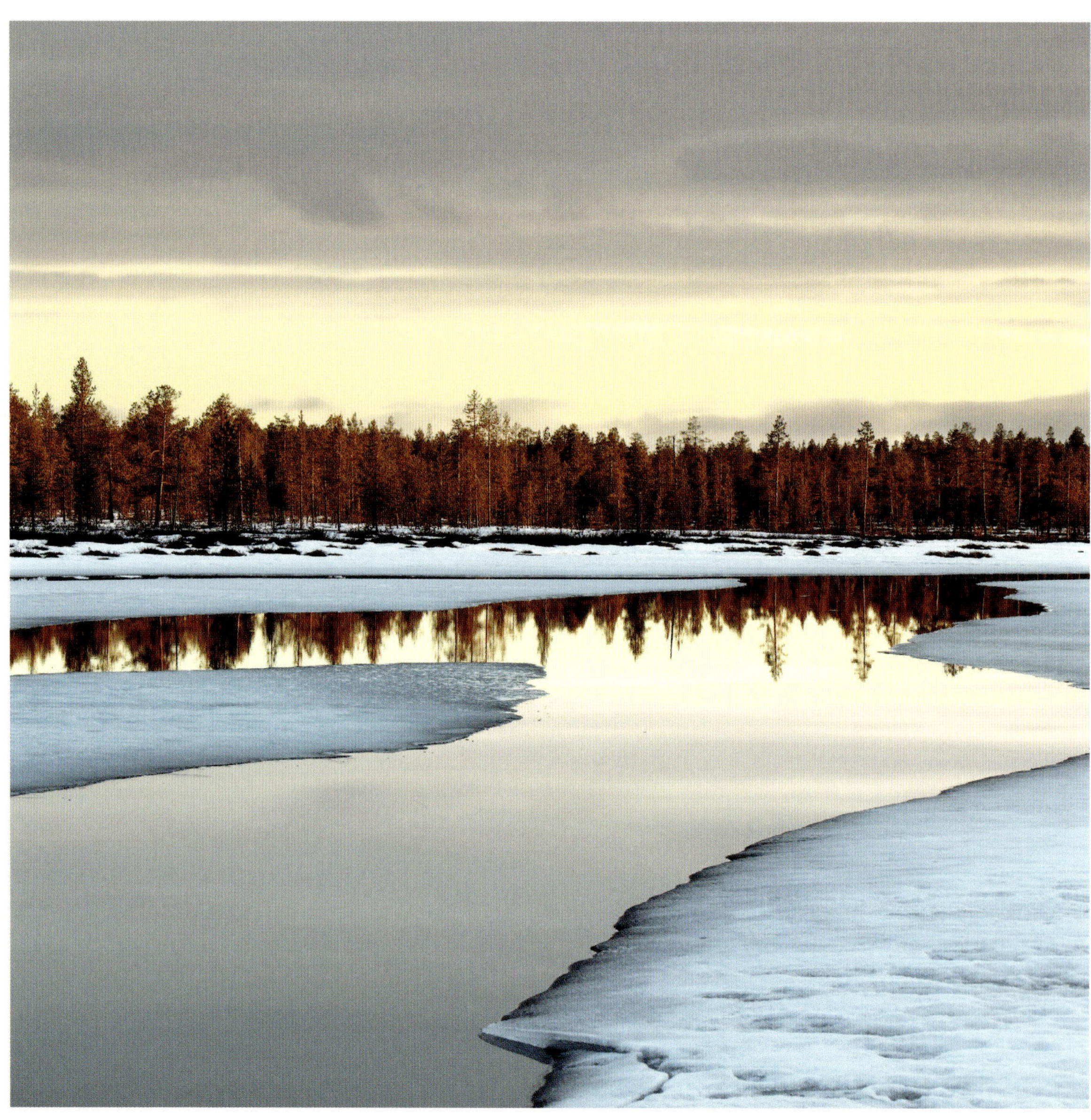

ALDEBURGH FESTIVAL

Charlotte Bray
Gary Carpenter
Vassos Nicolaou
Steingrímur Rohloff

This series of four concerts, curated by Oliver Knussen and Pierre-Laurent Aimard, featured Knussen conducting the BBC Symphony Orchestra, alongside soloists including the German baritone Benjamin Appl, and pianists Aimard, Tamara Stefanovich and Håkon Austbø. The programme used a blend of new and historical works to explore the music of the First World War period — an era of frenetic change and diversity almost unparalleled in musical history.

Four contemporary composers took inspiration from the music and events of 100 years before: orchestral pieces were provided by Charlotte Bray (*Stone Dancer*) and Gary Carpenter (*Willie Stock*) alongside piano studies by Vassos Nicolaou (*Études*) and Steingrímur Rohloff (*Three Études*). These were set amongst works by wartime composers such as Alban Berg, George Butterworth, Claude Debussy, Alexander Scriabin and Karol Szymanowski, all of whom experienced a time of energy and experimentation, as musical styles fragmented, creative imagination flourished and radical new directions were forged.

Snape Maltings Concert Hall, Suffolk,
17 — 24 June 2016 / BBC Radio 3

The BBC Symphony Orchestra, with conductor Oliver Knussen, performing at the 2016 Aldeburgh Festival.

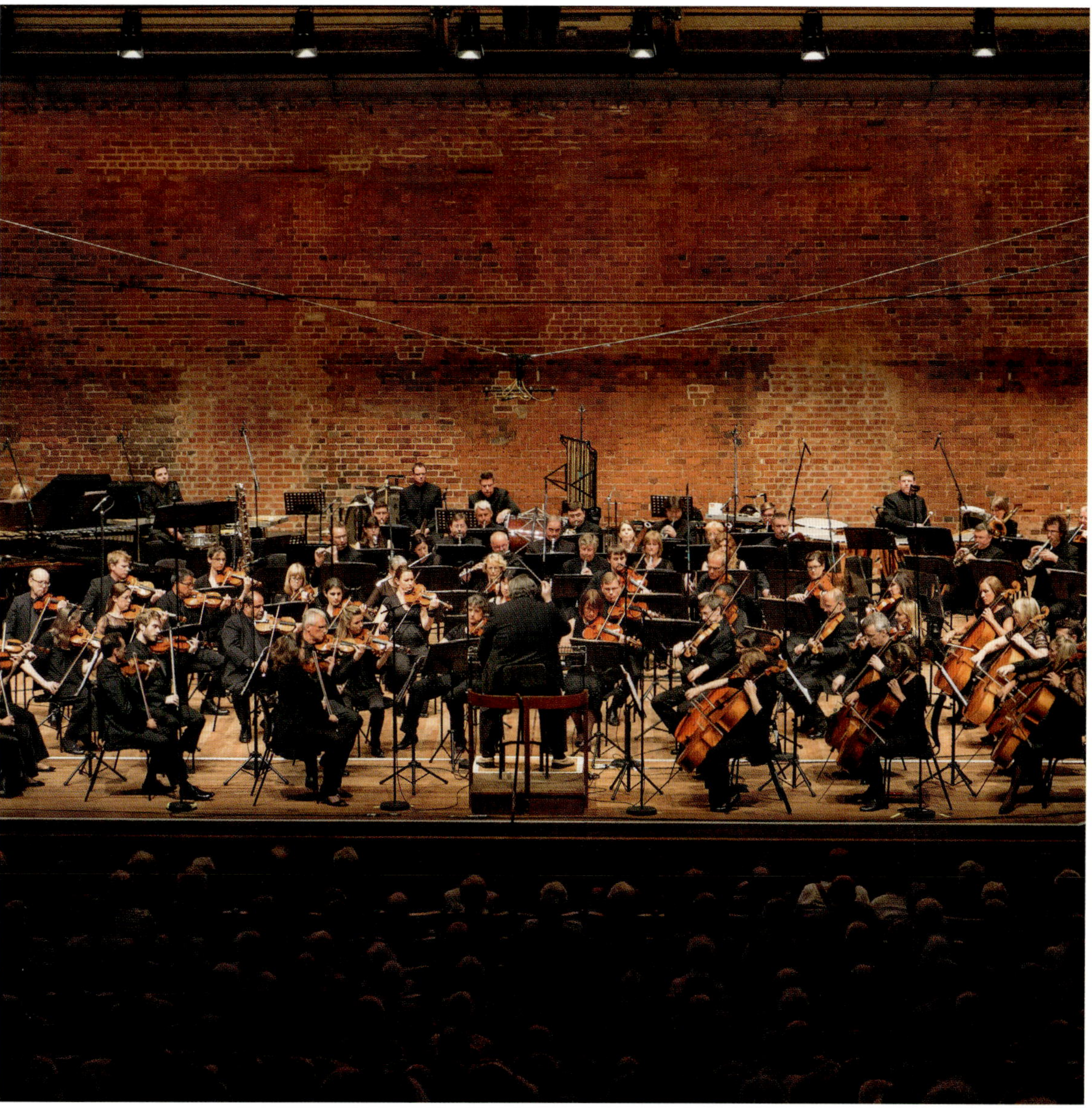

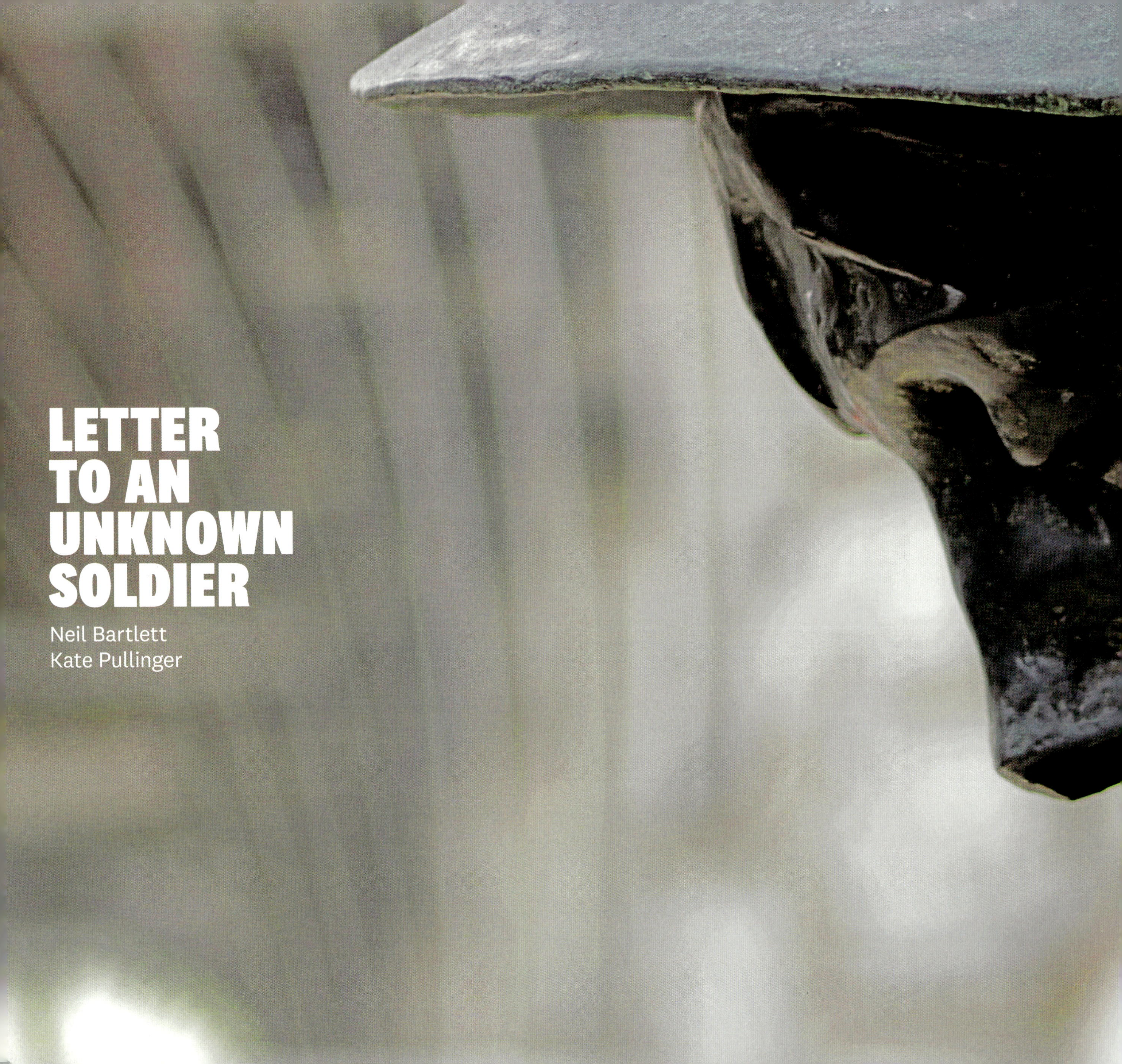

LETTER
TO AN
UNKNOWN
SOLDIER

Neil Bartlett
Kate Pullinger

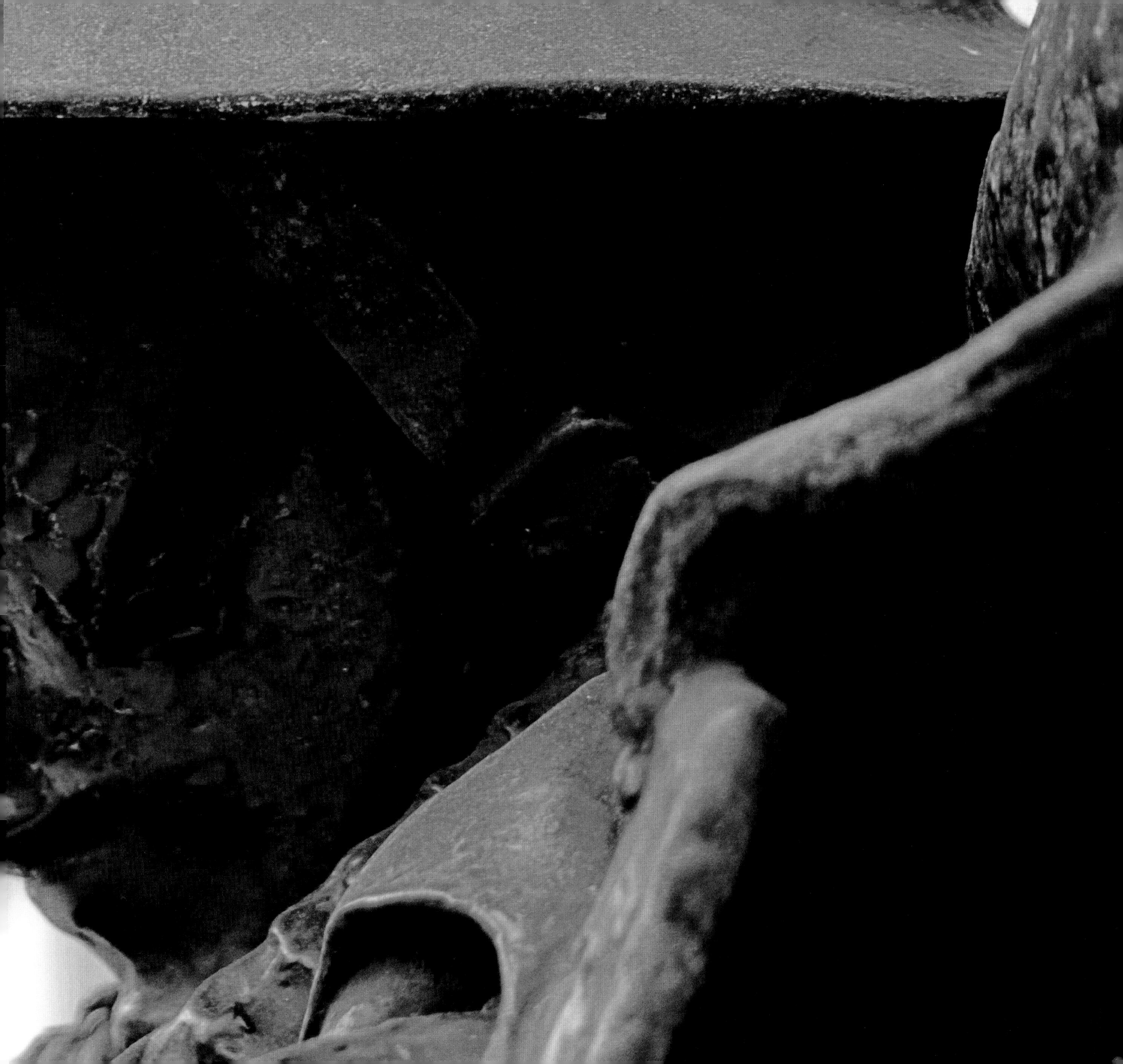

On Platform 1 of Paddington Station in London, there is a bronze statue of an Unknown Soldier by Charles Jagger; he's reading a letter. Letters from home were considered crucial to morale in the First World War, and at the height of the conflict an average of 12.5 million letters were sent each week by family, friends and lovers to soldiers fighting on the Western Front, as well as in the Middle East, Africa and India. They were processed by a mostly female staff of thousands, and then distributed swiftly and accurately by a fleet of ships, lorries and trains to their many destinations across the Channel, where they were handed out with the evening meal.

On the 100th anniversary of the declaration of war, in a year jammed full of remembrance and commemoration, Neil Bartlett and Kate Pullinger prompted people to step back from the public ceremonies. Reconsidering the familiar imagery associated with war memorials — cenotaphs, poppies and silence — they invited everyone in the UK to take a few private moments to think, and to write that letter in the hands of the Unknown Soldier: 'If you could say what you want to say about that war, with all we've learned since 1914, with all your own experience of life and death to hand, what would you say?'

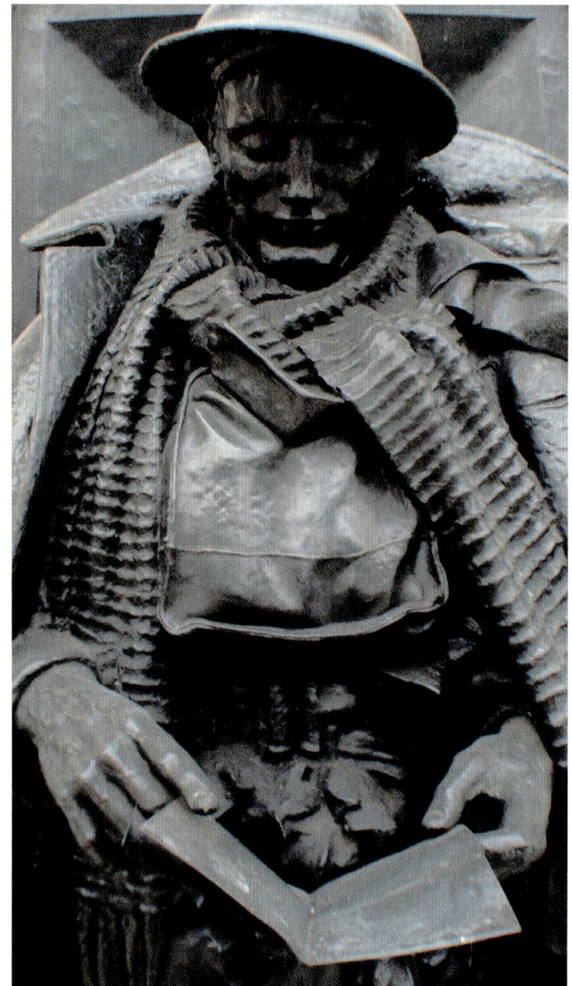

'A letter is not a text message nor a "like" on Facebook — in order to write one you have to stop, and think, and feel, and compose not just your letter but yourself ... A letter is private. A letter is everyday. A letter is familiar. A letter is, above all, personal.'

Neil Bartlett and Kate Pullinger, introduction to *Letter to an Unknown Soldier: A New Kind of War Memorial*

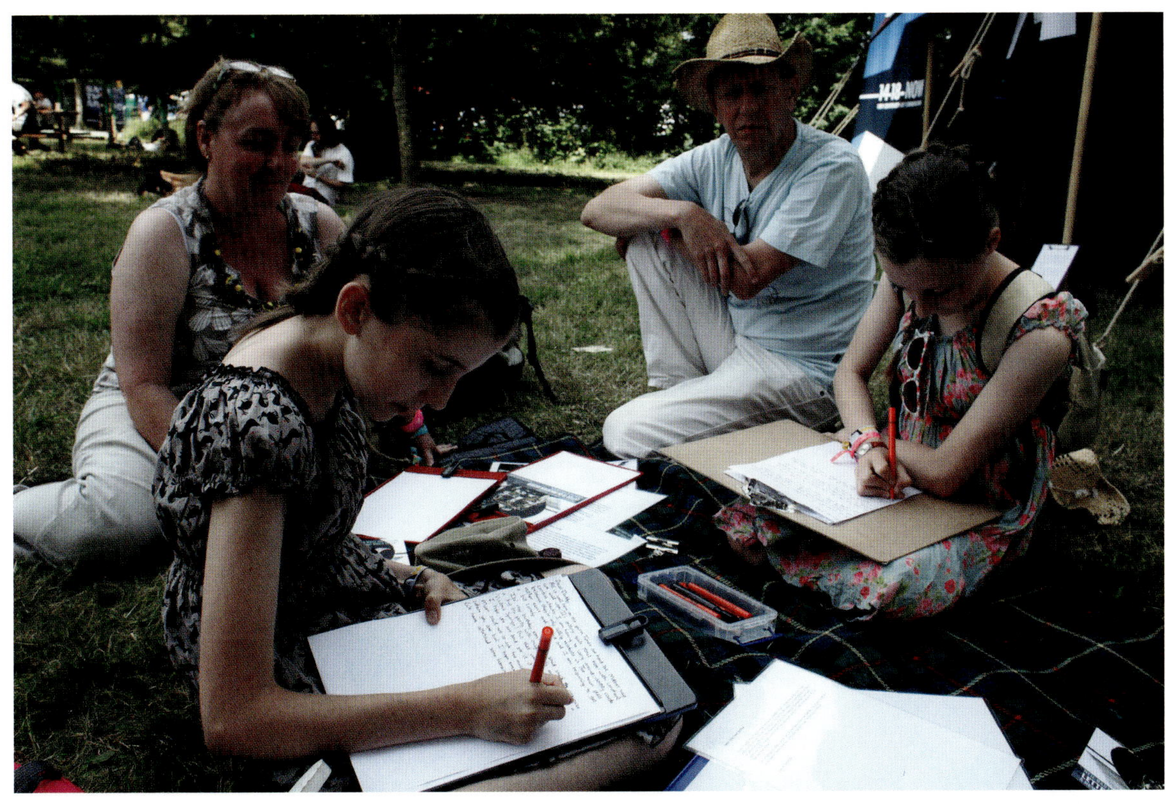

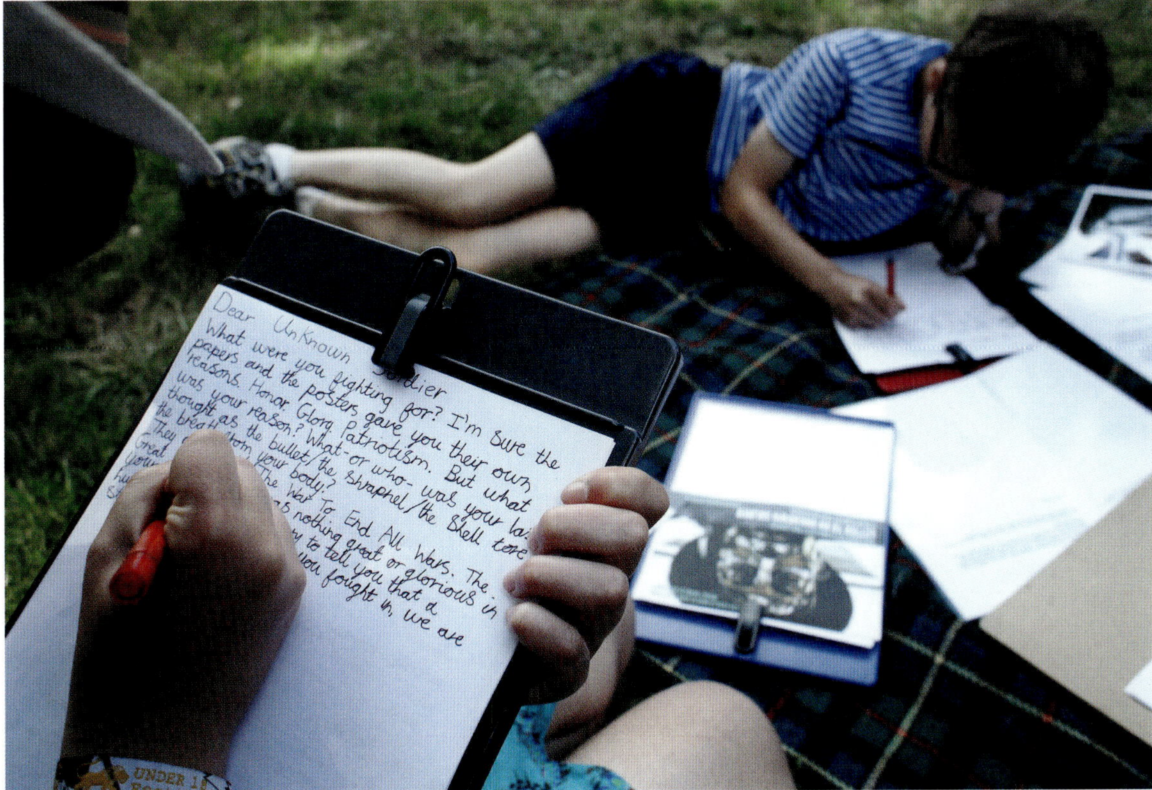
Dear Unknown Soldier
What were you fighting for? I'm sure the
papers and the posters gave you their own
reasons. Honor. Glory. Patriotism. But what
was your reason? What- or who- was your la...
thought as the bullet/the shrapnel/the shell tore
they...tom your body?
Great...The War To End All Wars. The...
you...as nothing great or glorious in...
hu...y to tell you that d...
S...you fought in, we are

The response to the project was extraordinary, with letters coming from schoolchildren, pensioners, students, nurses, serving members of the forces, and even the Prime Minister. By the end of its second week nearly 10,000 people had written to the soldier; by its close, a staggering 21,439 letters had been received, creating a new kind of war memorial — one made of words.

As the letters arrived, they were published on the website set up for the project and made available for everyone to read. The website opened on 28 June 2014, the centenary of the Sarajevo assassinations, and closed at 11pm on the night of 4 August 2014, the centenary of the moment when Prime Minister Asquith announced to the House of Commons that Britain had joined the First World War.

A selection of letters were published as a book by HarperCollins entitled *Letter to an Unknown Soldier: A New Kind of War Memorial*. Around 50 of the letters had been written in Gaelic, and these were published as a smaller book, launched at the Aye Write! book festival in Glasgow in 2016. At the end of 2014 the letters were transferred to an archive at the British Library, where they remain permanently accessible online, providing a snapshot of people's thoughts and feelings in that centenary year.

UK-wide, 28 June — 4 August 2014

Dear Alfred

This is the grandson you've never met – Andrew. I am now 66 years old, and I too was a soldier, serving in some conflicts, but none as terrible as yours. You fell in 1915 in Gallipoli, with thousands of your friends and mates in the Regiment.

I would dearly love to have known you and chatted to you about your life. My dad was a soldier too serving in all the major battles of the war after your one including D-Day, Alamein and Dunkirk. You would have been proud of him, but he was only 4 when you died.

My son is a soldier now and has served in Iraq, and Afghanistan… I am so proud of him and all his soldiers in how they face the dangers of today.

Next year I am coming to visit you in Gallipoli at the Cape Helles memorial, so stay there! and wait for me and my group – there will be about 30 of us including some children and serving soldiers from the Regiment… we can't wait to tell you all about ourselves, and you will see how much we admire, you, and what you did. I'm bringing a piper and bugler and you will love their playing.

With much love Grandad Alfred.

Yrs with huge admiration
Andrew

———————

Anonymous
66, Kinross, Retired regular army, Soldier

Dedicated to all the Scottish soldiers who fell in the Great War.

Dear Dad,

I hope you come back alive instead of dead because I would have no chance surviving in the frontline but I know you would because of your bravery and strength. If you do happen to die I will remember you with all my heart and I will tell everyone how brave you were. Please can you try not to die so the fun can go on. So just remember I am Supporting you, even when you're in a tough situation.

When you come home (if you survive) there will be a huge suprise! And I promise it will be fun. Even though you're in the front line I know you Can do it. The only three things I ask are: number one: send me a letter every week number two: try not to die and number 3: win the war!! I knew I know I have been putting you ass but heres the fun part. If you come back mum is going to take you to a famous night Club and wants to kiss you! all right?

Love your son Ryan
P.S don't tell mum about the night Club

SJ breaks into an army base to bury the ashes of her great-grandfather, a conscientious objector during the First World War. Inside, surrounded by soldiers and the ghosts of past wars, she finds a place where her certainty begins to falter.

For one night only on 14 October 2018, the UK's first-ever interactive feature film, *Bloodyminded*, was screened. Created by pioneering art group Blast Theory, the film had been inspired by research into First World War conscientious objectors carried out at the Imperial War Museum, alongside interviews with living British Army veterans who generously shared their experiences of training, frontline combat, banter, bullying and post-traumatic stress disorder.

Bloodyminded was shot in a single take and broadcast live to cinemas and online. Guided by the narrator, viewers were asked to consider their own relationship with violence — as individuals and as members of a society that continues to wage wars on their behalf. And as the story unfolded, they were invited to interact by expressing their opinions via a specially designed mobile app. The result was a moving and disturbing journey that asked audiences to make their own decisions about the morality of war.

ACCA, Brighton; Barbican, London; HOME, Manchester, Watershed, Bristol; Queen's Film Theatre, Belfast; Tyneside Cinema, Newcastle; plus cinemas in Munich, Basel, Berlin and online, 14 October 2018

BLOODYMINDED

Blast Theory

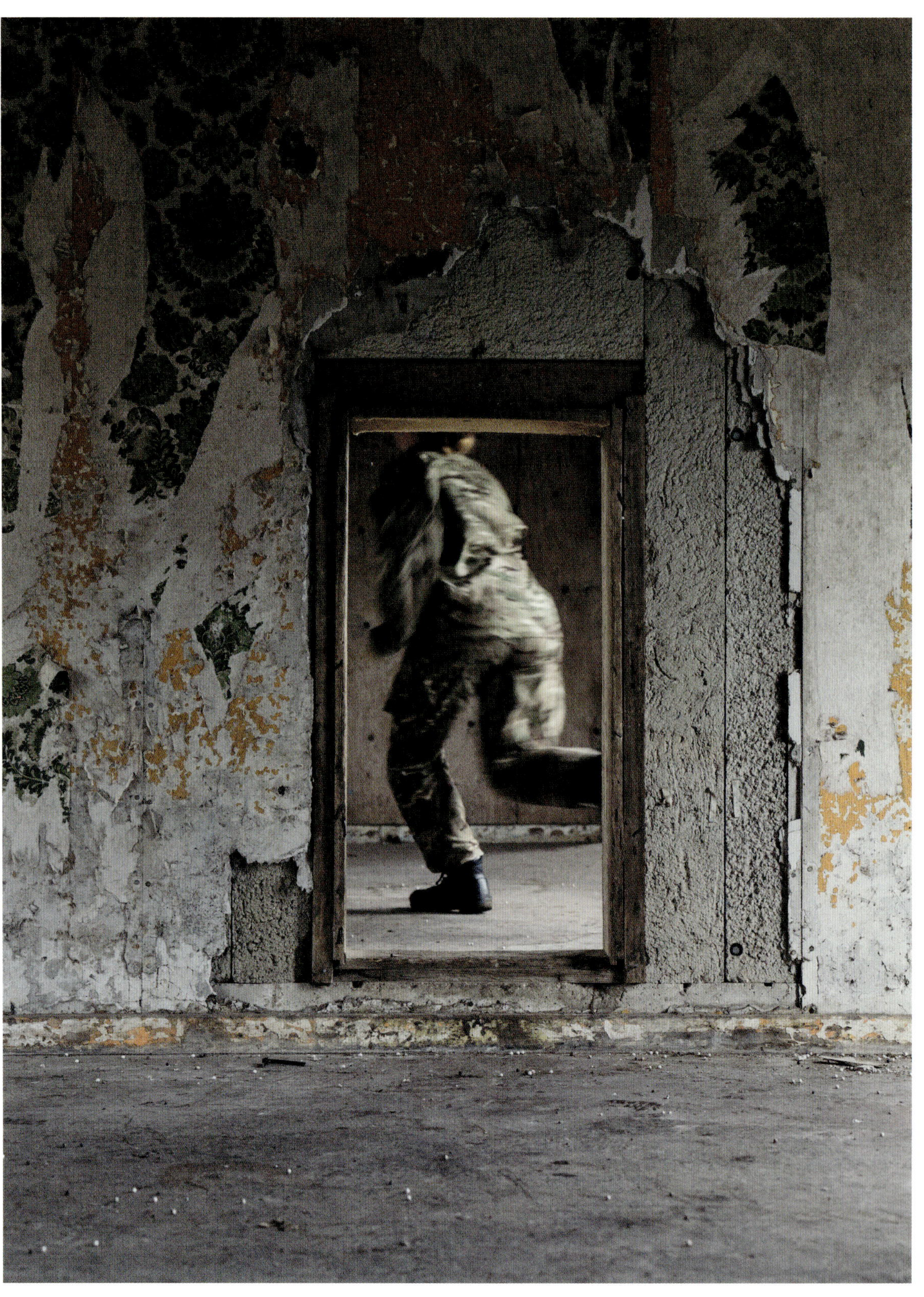

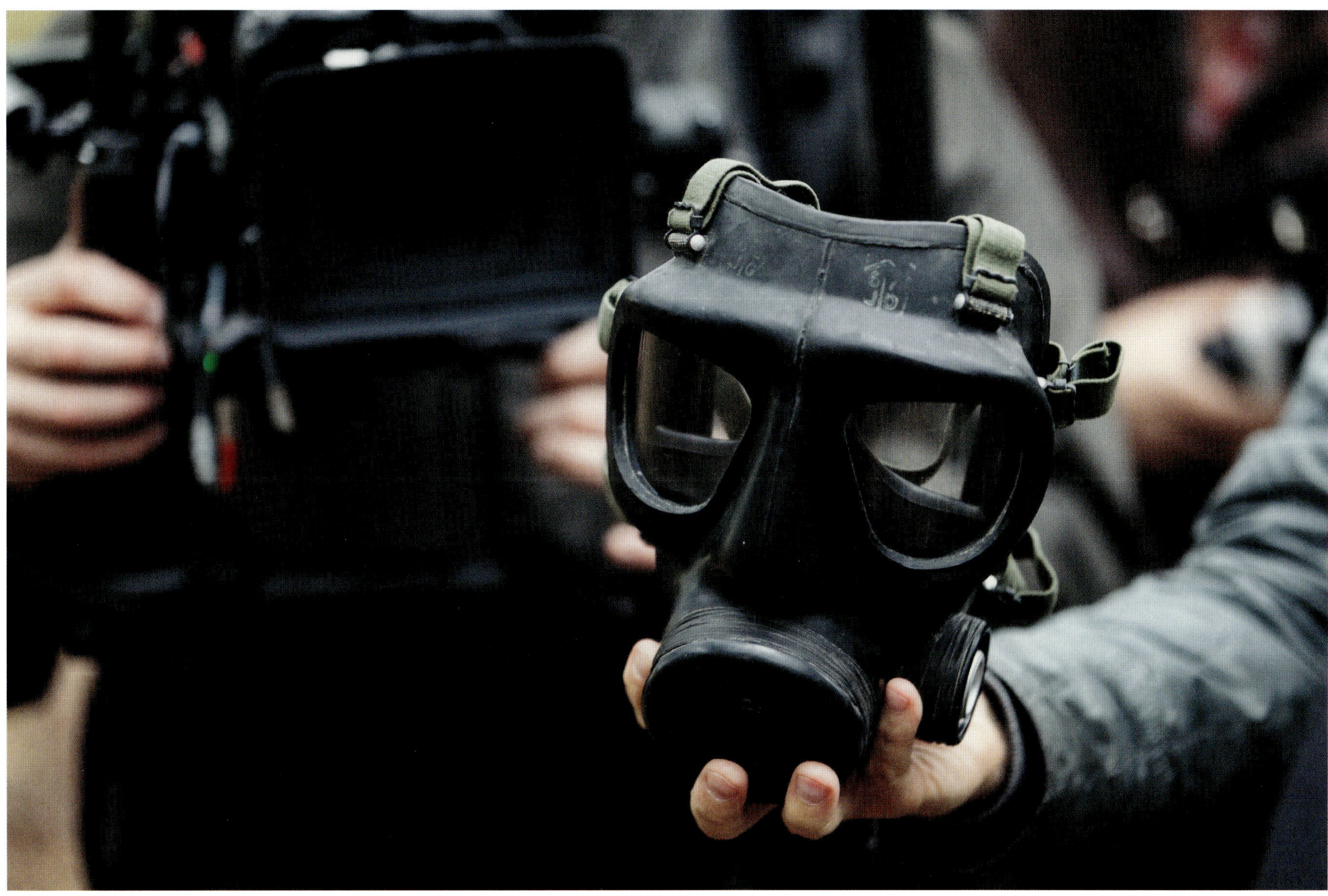

Bloodyminded was the UK's first-ever interactive feature film. It was shot on an army base, in a single take, and streamed live online and to cinemas across the UK and Europe.

END OF EMPIRE

Yinka Shonibare CBE

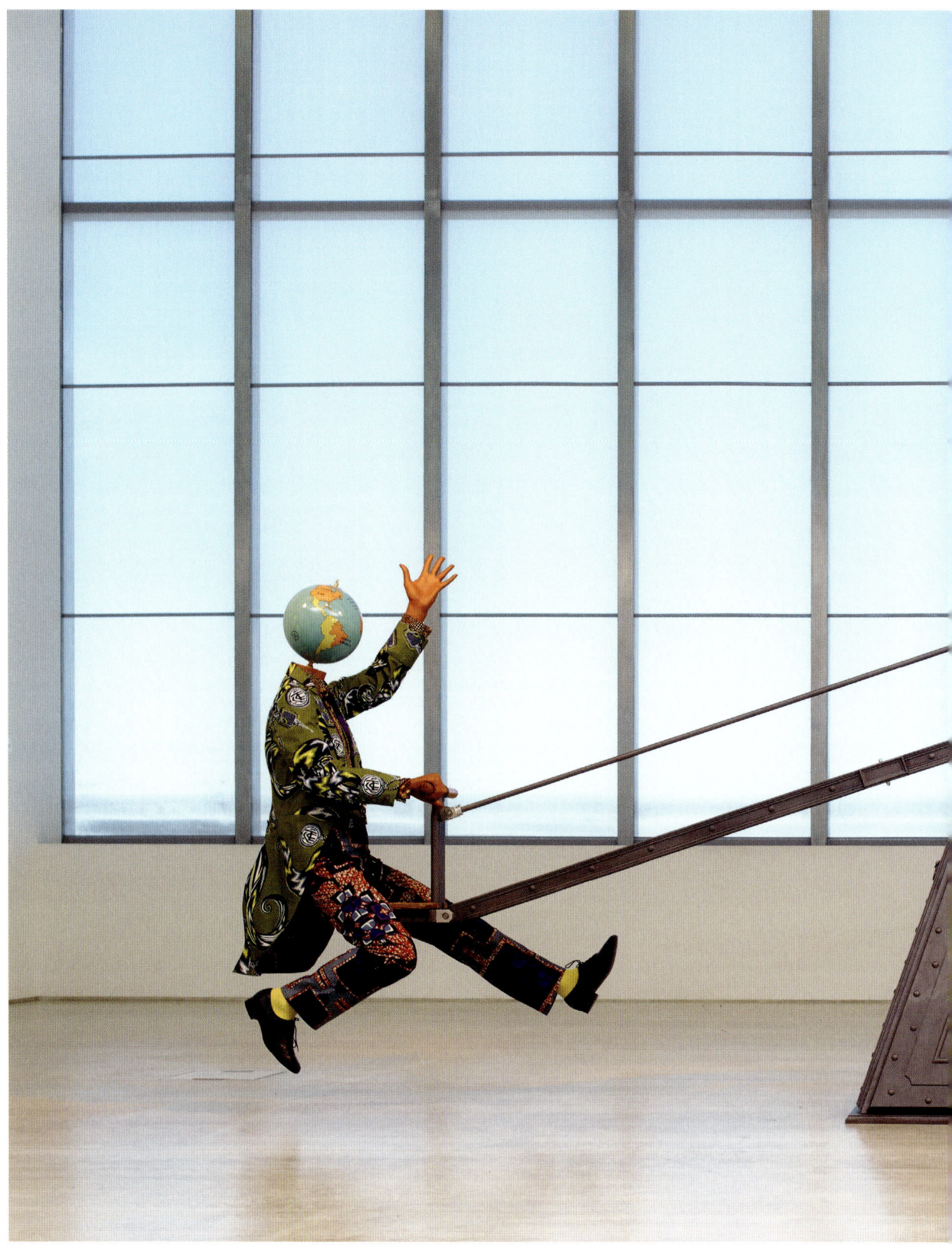

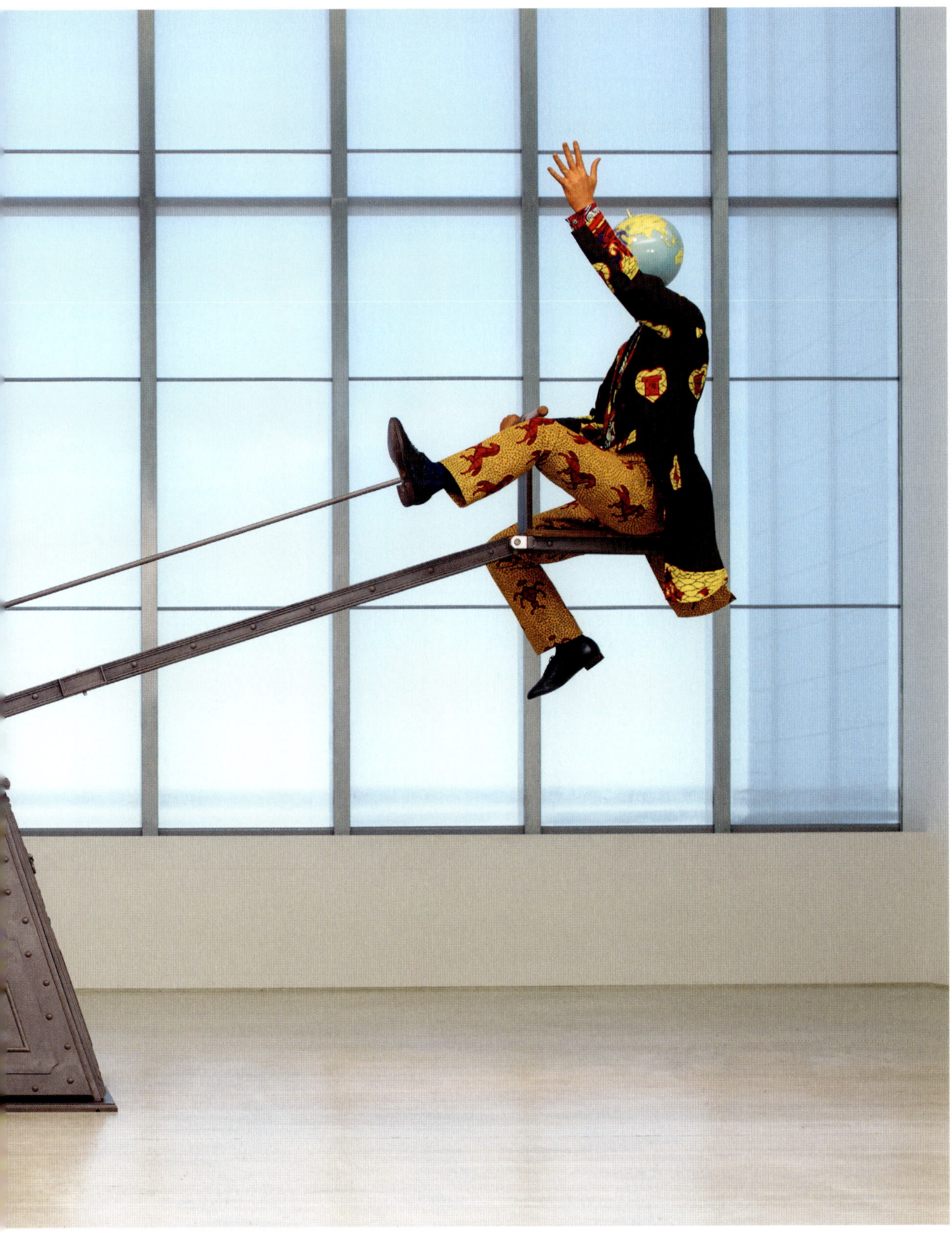

How has immigration contributed to our culture? How have immigrants shaped what it means to be British? How did the First World War affect the way Britain related to the members of its empire? Questions of immigration and cultural identity have always dominated the work of British-Nigerian artist Yinka Shonibare CBE, and for this 14-18 NOW/Turner Contemporary commission, he eschewed the carnage of the battlefield, choosing instead to explore how the new alliances forged in the war changed British society at the time, and continue to affect us today.

End of Empire addressed these questions through an arresting visual metaphor — two figures poised on opposite ends of a seesaw. The figures were attired in the 'African' fabrics that often characterise Shonibare's work, superimposed onto the tailcoats of Edwardian statesmen, underlining the fact that such fabrics were, ironically, designed and produced in Europe for export to Africa. The globe heads of these figures highlighted the countries involved in the war, while their perpetual motion symbolised the dialogue, balance and conflict that ensued between these nations. Pivoting within the gallery space, the seesaw also represented the possibility of compromise and resolution between two opposing forces.

End of Empire pointed out that while the war was nominally fought between two opposing European alliances, it was also a tangled mess of proxy wars fought between their constituents' respective colonies — including Nigeria, Shonibare's birthplace, from where soldiers were deployed by the British to fight in Cameroon and the East Africa Campaign. The work was a timely reminder that the global displacement of communities that results from war has far-reaching and lasting consequences on our cultures and attitudes.

Turner Contemporary, Margate, 22 March — 30 October 2016

IOLAIRE

Iain Morrison
Dalziel + Scullion
Julie Fowlis
Duncan Chisholm

Late on New Year's Eve 1919, HMY *Iolaire* set sail from Kyle of Lochalsh in northwest Scotland, carrying nearly 300 seamen home to the Isle of Lewis after the war. But in the early hours of New Year's Day, the ship sank at the entrance to Stornoway Harbour; at least 205 servicemen perished in one of the most devastating maritime disasters in modern British history.

To mark the centenary of the tragedy, 14-18 NOW and An Lanntair commissioned two new suites of Gaelic music. *Sàl* ('Saltwater') — composed by Lewis-born musician Iain Morrison, whose great-grandfather was among those who drowned — was presented with imagery by pioneering Scottish artists Dalziel + Scullion. *Sàl* has its roots in *ceòl mòr*, the 'great music' of the Highland bagpipes. *An Treas Suaile* ('The Third Wave'), by BBC Radio 2 Folk Award winner Julie Fowlis and violinist-composer Duncan Chisholm, mixed new and traditional music, archive recordings and visuals. Its title was inspired by the actions of John Finlay MacLeod, who swam ashore with a rope from the *Iolaire* and helped save dozens of lives.

An Lanntair Arts Centre, Stornoway, October — December 2018

Below. *An Treas Suaile* in performance at An Lanntair.

Opposite. Dalziel + Scullion's film emphasised the repercussions of the tragedy for those left behind, with scenes that captured the precious stability of domestic life, such as the act of salting and preserving mackerel.

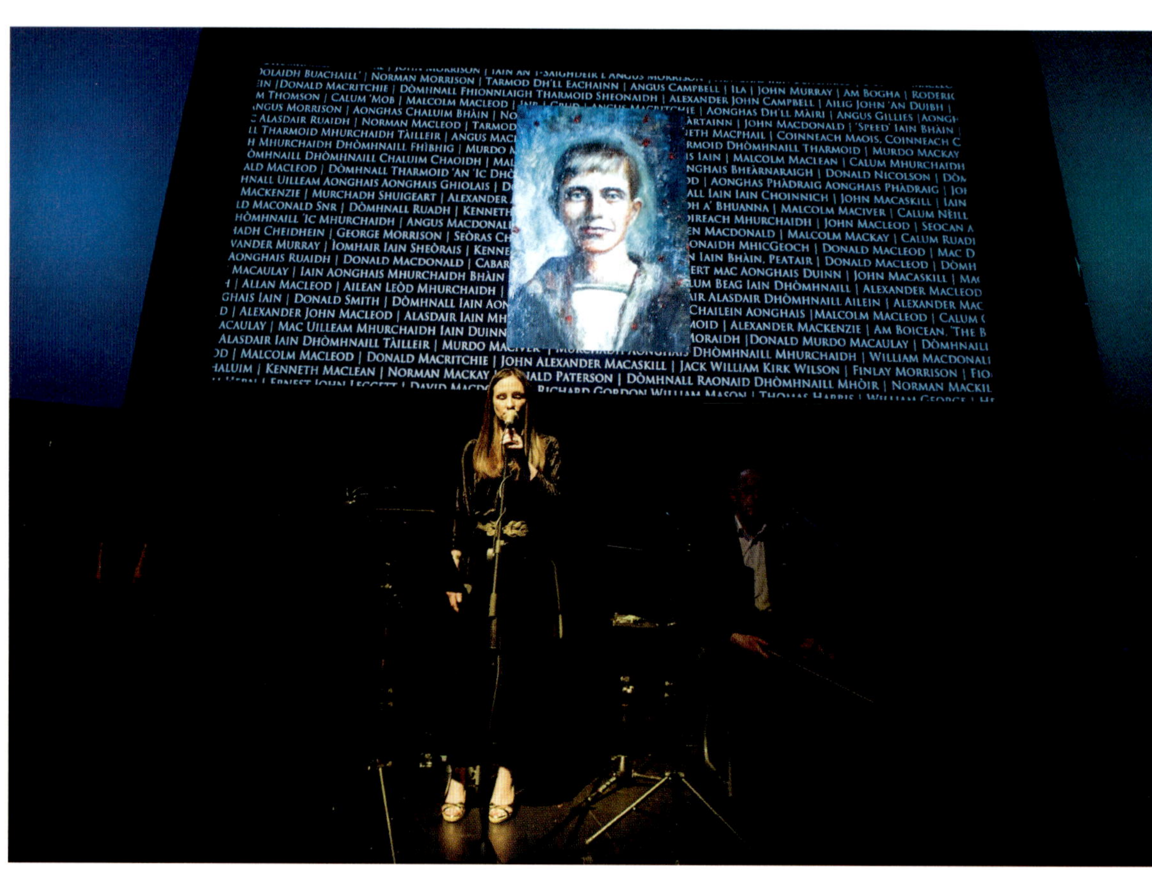

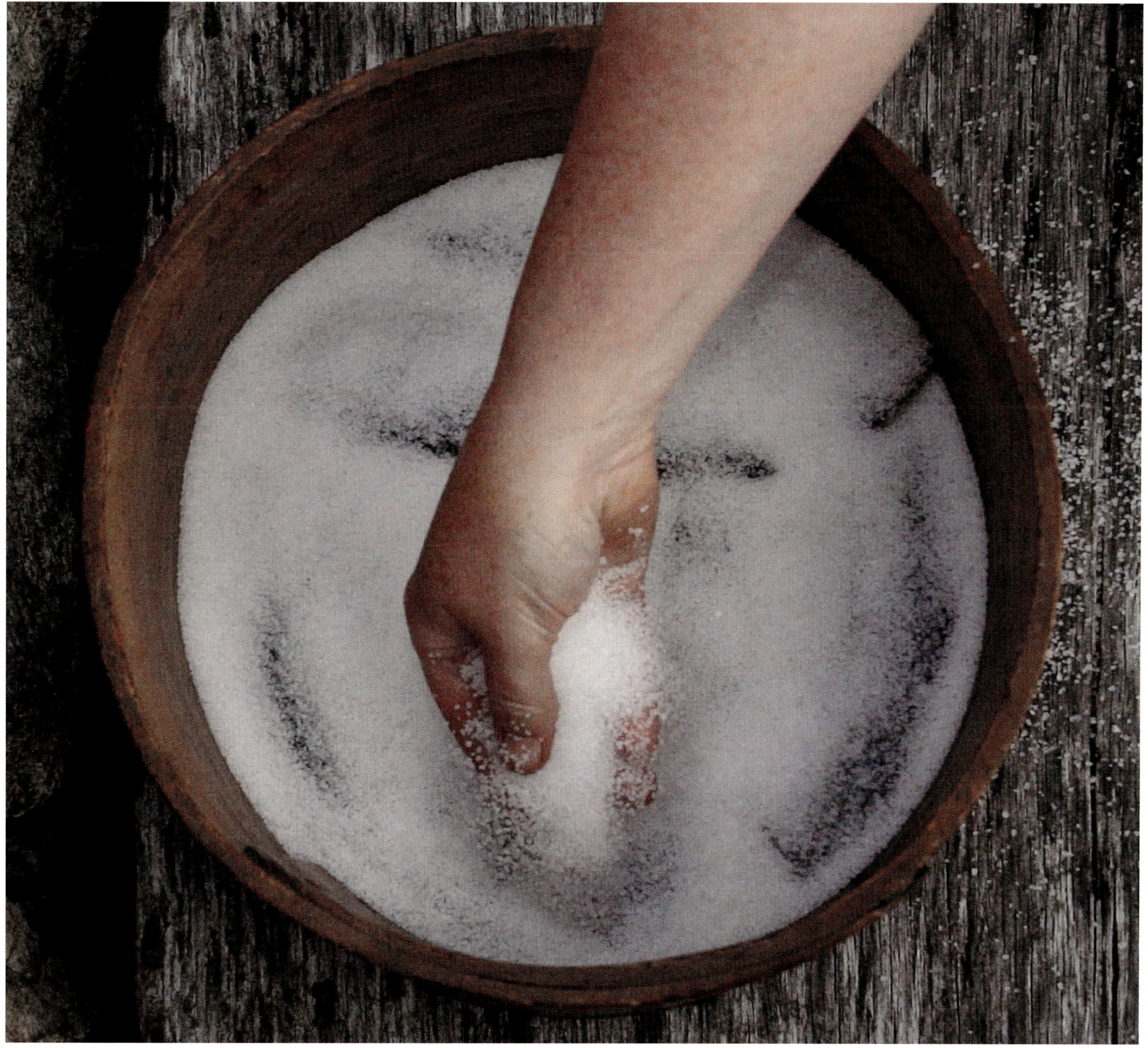

100: The Day Our World Changed was a collaboration between Cornish theatre-makers WildWorks and The Lost Gardens of Heligan in Cornwall — a one-day theatrical event that took place on the anniversary of Britain declaring war on Germany, reliving and retelling the stories of the local men and their families whose lives were changed forever on that day.

For this epic project, WildWorks worked with several community choirs, local children, sewing and crafting groups, gardening experts, banner and bunting makers, brass players, motorbike enthusiasts, comedians, fishermen and their boats, pyrotechnicians and hundreds of volunteers.

At dawn the names of soldiers from the parishes of Mevagissey, Gorran and St Ewe were called out one by one. Crowds gathered around Mevagissey harbour as a lugger — a traditional fishing boat — arrived fresh from a night at sea. The cast (both amateur and professional) then moved throughout the course of the day from the harbour to the sweeping fields of Heligan, creating impact via the tiniest of theatrical details and vast, extraordinary landscapes.

Tying it together was the story of the local squire, Jack Tremayne, his gardener and Mary, his true love. After following Jack, the marching naval reservists and the St Austell Town Band up into the grounds of Heligan, the audience were invited for a harvest picnic in Valentine's Field below Heligan House, where a stage of traditional rural activities was set.

An audience of over 5,000 found themselves in the thick of the action: seeing, hearing, learning and feeling something of the actual events and experiences that would have occurred among the residents of the three parishes on that fateful day 100 years before.

By channelling community spirit through theatrical spectacle, this event relived the outbreak of war in 1914 and prolonged the memory of it in the minds of a new generation.

Cornwall, 3 August 2014

100: THE DAY OUR WORLD CHANGED

WildWorks

Professional actors merged with local volunteers to recreate the scenes that would have taken place in Cornwall 100 years before.

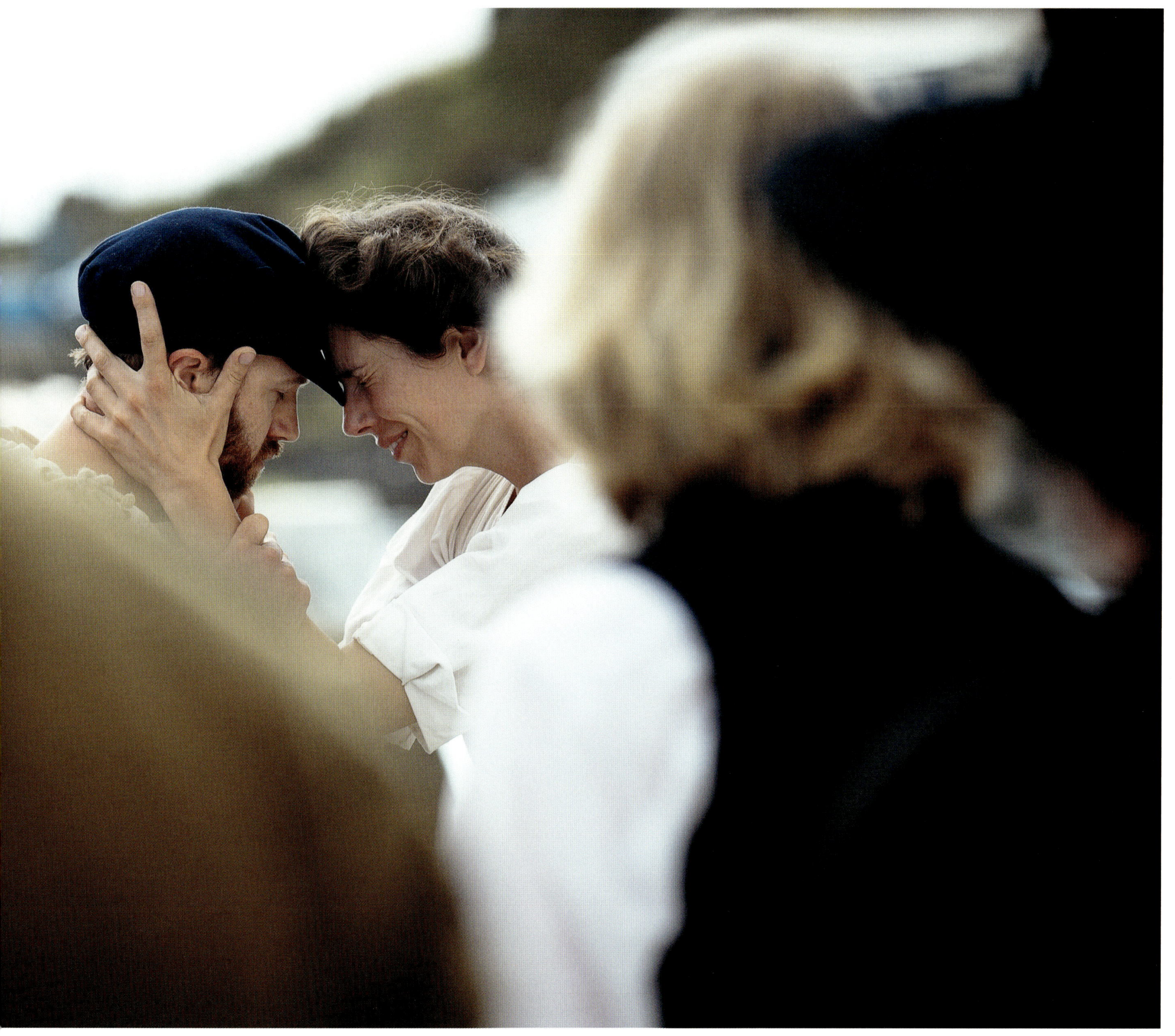

'They say we all die twice.
The first time when our body
dies and the second time when
people stop saying our names
and stop telling the stories of
the things we did in our lives.'
Bill Mitchell, artistic director of WildWorks

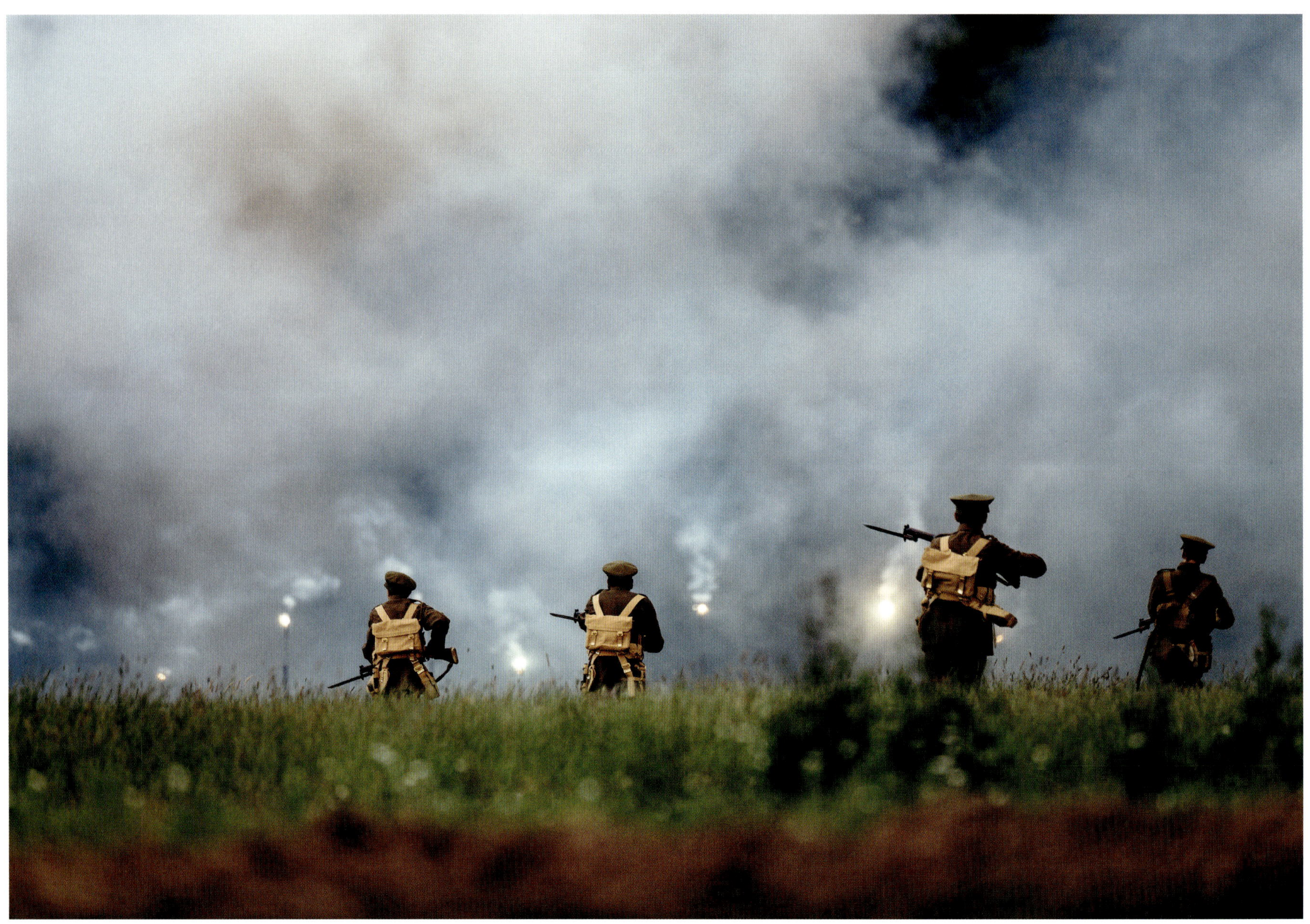

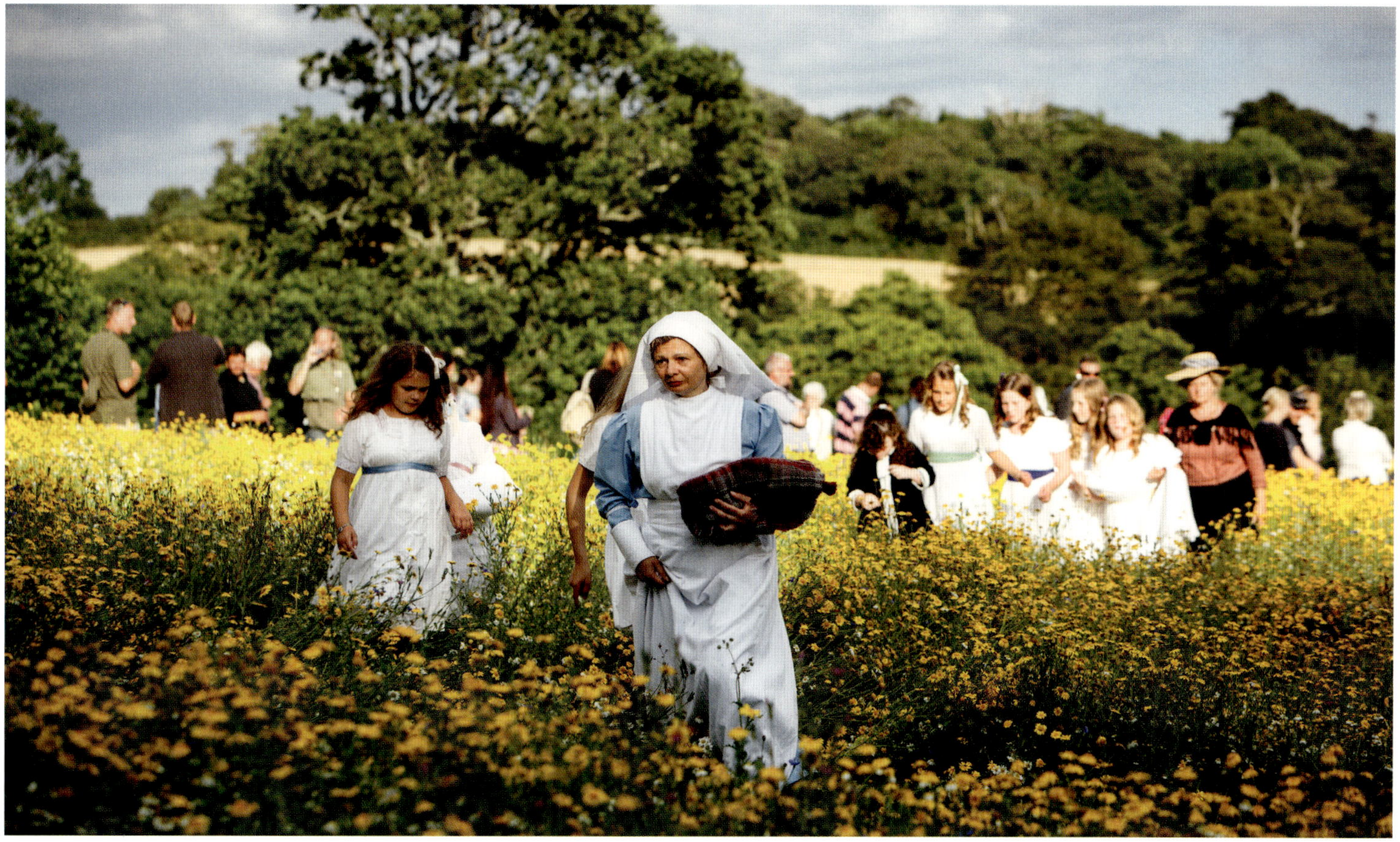

Having followed the performance from its starting point in Mevagissey harbour (below), the audience travelled from the village and on to Heligan House, following scenes that recreated the lost world of 1914.

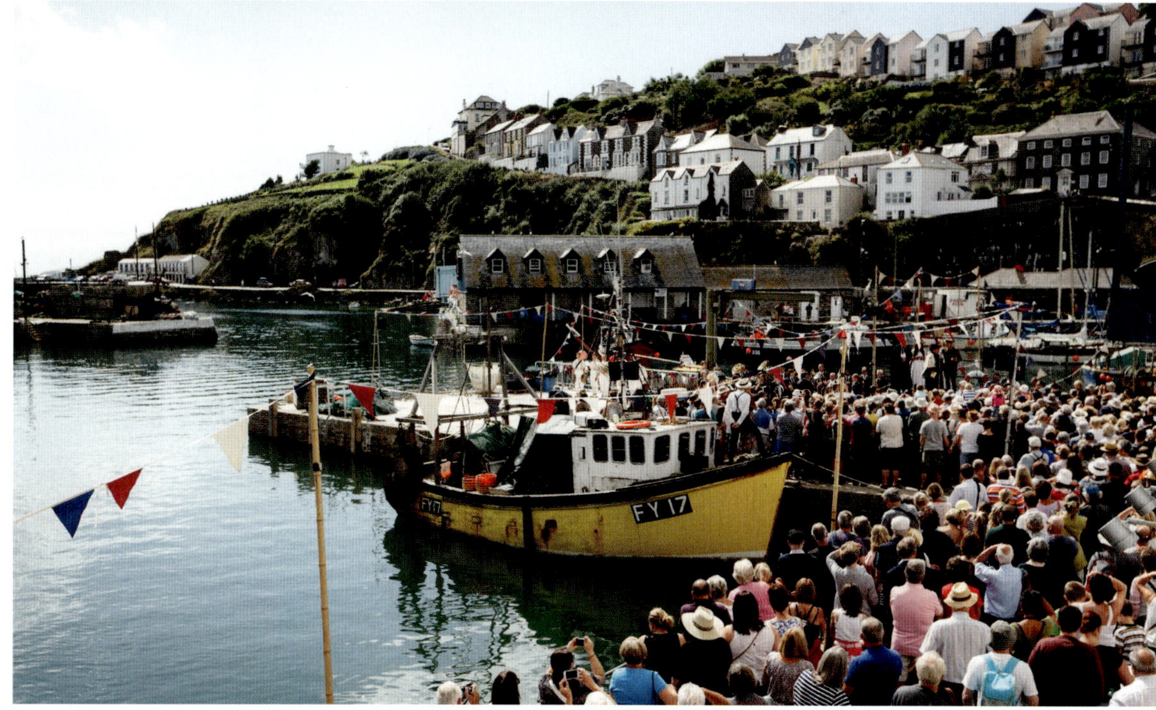

100: UNEARTH

WildWorks

In 2014, WildWorks presented *100: The Day Our World Changed* (see page 60), a dawn-to-dusk piece that focused on a generation walking into battle in 1914. In 2018 they returned to The Lost Gardens of Heligan with a companion piece that recreated the homecoming of those soldiers in a series of evening performances. This follow-up show — *100: UnEarth* — explored the devastating aftermath of that war and others since — for returning soldiers who must readjust to normal life, for those who must rebuild a life with them after years spent apart, and for those forced to live on alone.

As with the previous work, WildWorks employed a cast of hundreds — artists, musicians, veterans and members of the local community — to create a narrative that was brought to life in locations around the grounds of Heligan, thereby rooting the story in the Cornish landscape where it was both set and performed. Based on the Greek myth of Orpheus and Eurydice, audiences of *100: UnEarth* were invited to accompany Orpheus as he ventured into the Underworld to retrieve his lost love. The story also drew on soldiers' first-hand accounts of the war, sourced from the archives of the Imperial War Museums and elsewhere.

Conceived and created by Bill Mitchell, WildWorks' founder and artistic director, before his untimely death in 2017, *100: UnEarth* explored the grief and tragedy of war, and the struggle to leave the past behind — alongside the enduring power of hope, love and courage.

The Lost Gardens of Heligan, Cornwall,
3 — 22 July 2018

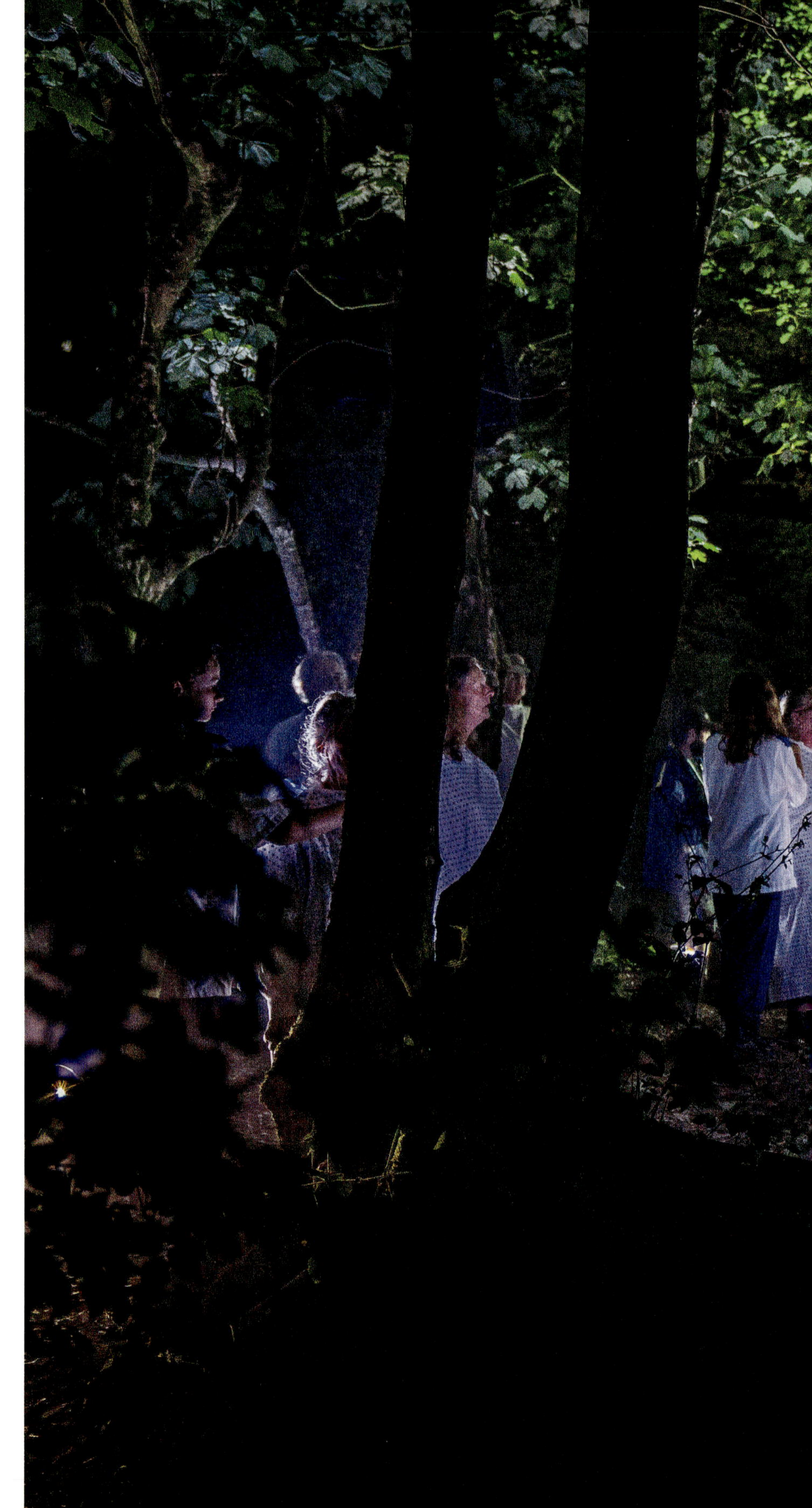

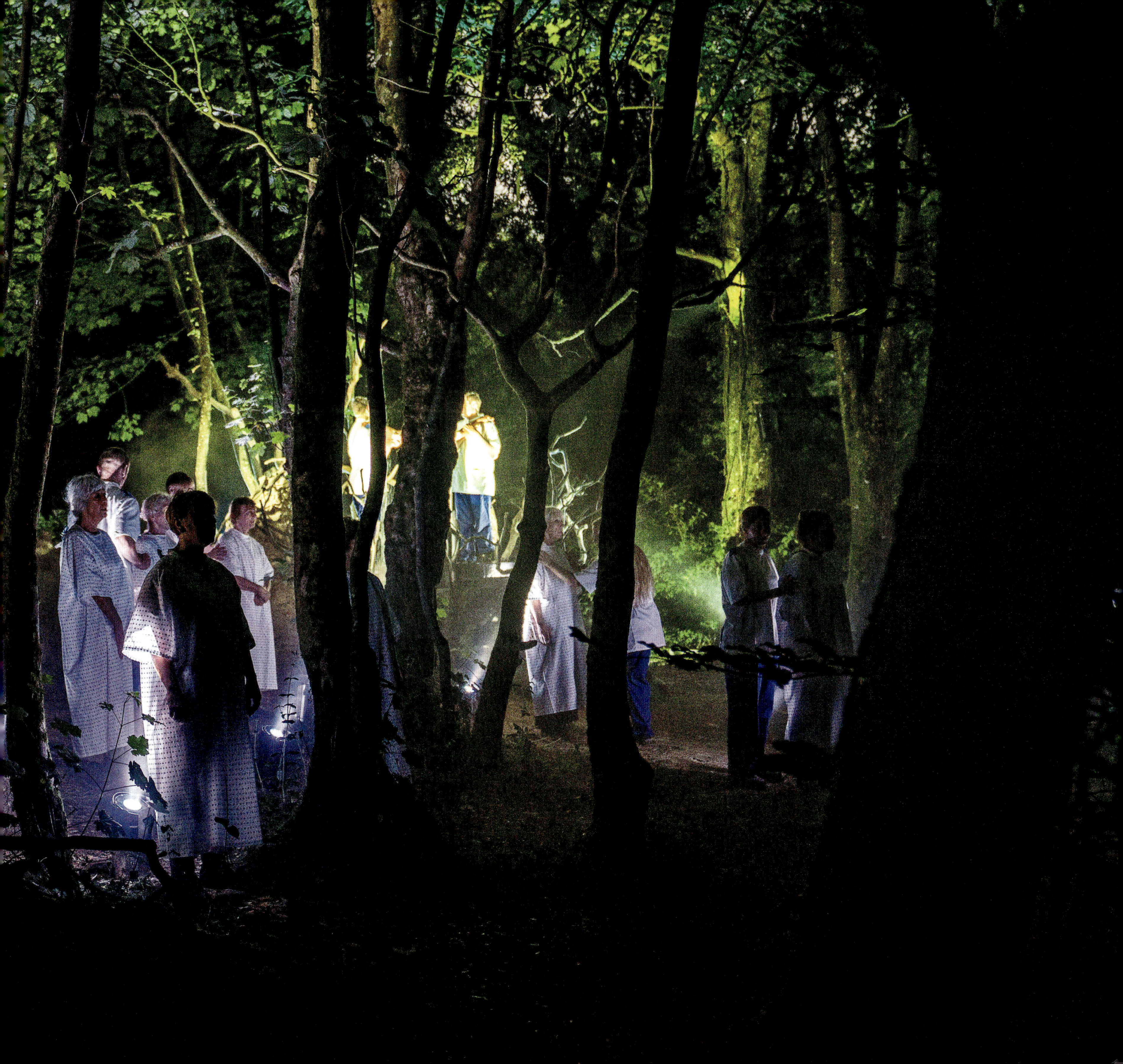

WildWorks' return to Heligan
for this piece of 'landscape
theatre' combined the efforts
of professionals and volunteers
in a number of striking set
pieces in Heligan's woods,
lawns and walled gardens.

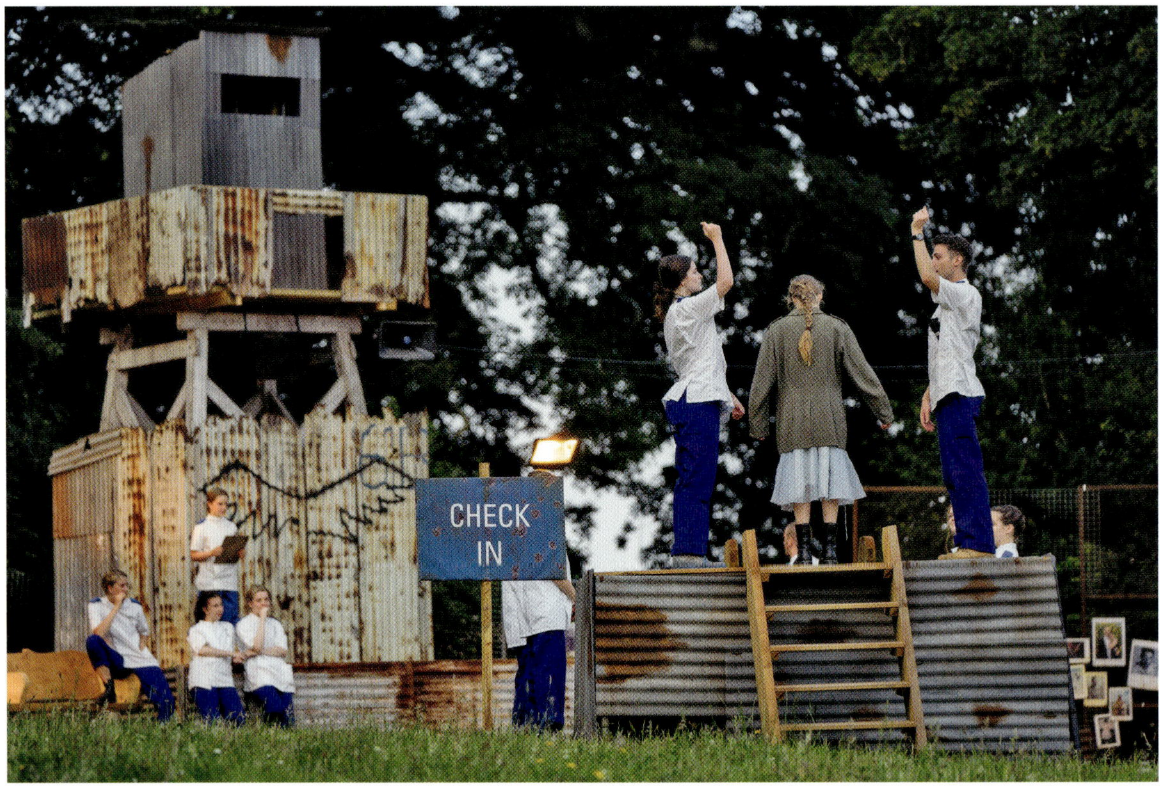

CHECK
IN

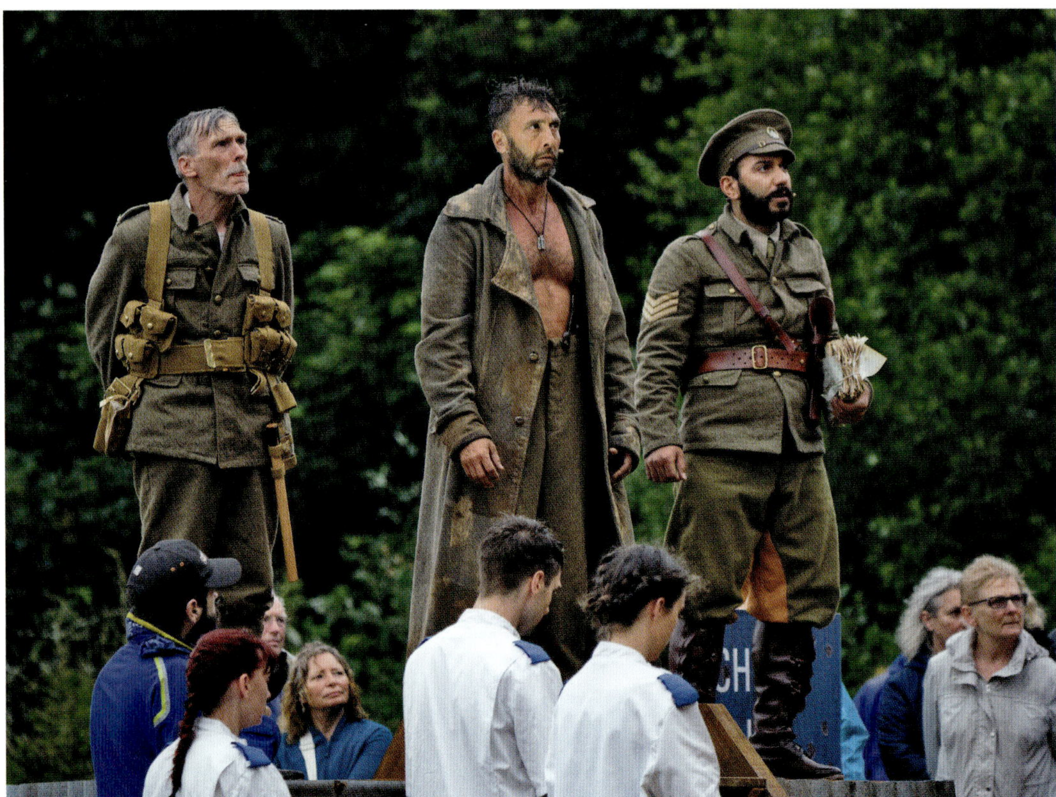

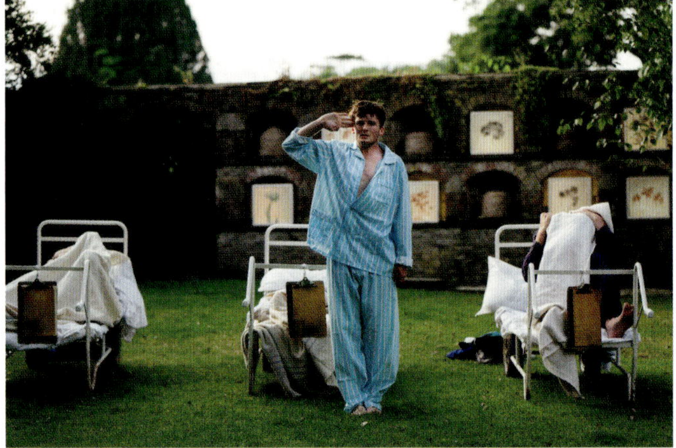

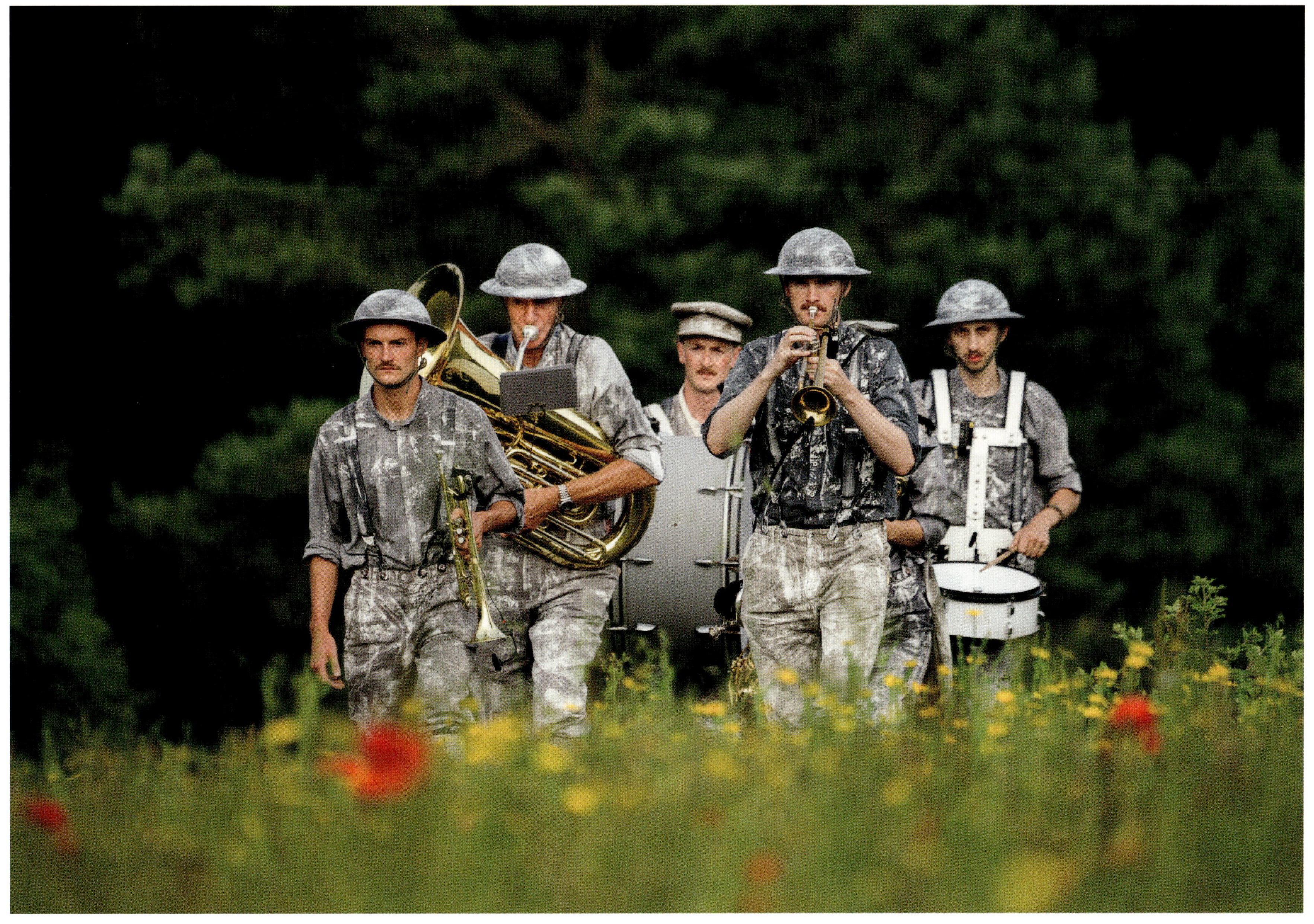

BBC LATE PROMS

John Tavener

On 4 August 2014, as the nation remembered Britain's entry into the war 100 years before, the music of one of its most loved composers carried an audience through an evening of reflection at the BBC Proms. This was part of a countrywide programme of events marking the hours leading up to 11pm, the exact time at which Britain's ultimatum to Germany expired (see *LIGHTS OUT*, page 90).

Combining silence and sound, simplicity and radiance, John Tavener captured the public imagination like few other 20th-century composers. For this performance the Tallis Scholars and conductor Peter Phillips were joined by the Heath Quartet for Tavener's *Ikon of Light*, celebrating light as a symbol of hope in dark times. This was followed by the world premiere of *Requiem Fragments*, a meditation on loss composed by Tavener just before his death in 2013 at the age of 69. As 11pm approached, the audience held tea lights while Samuel West read Wilfred Owen's 'Anthem for Doomed Youth', before the performance concluded with a beautiful rendition of Tavener's *The Lamb* by the choir as lights were extinguished.

Royal Albert Hall, London, 4 August 2014 /
BBC Radio 3 & BBC One

Peter Phillips conducted the Tallis Scholars and the Heath Quartet for the posthumous premiere of Tavener's new work at the 2014 Proms.

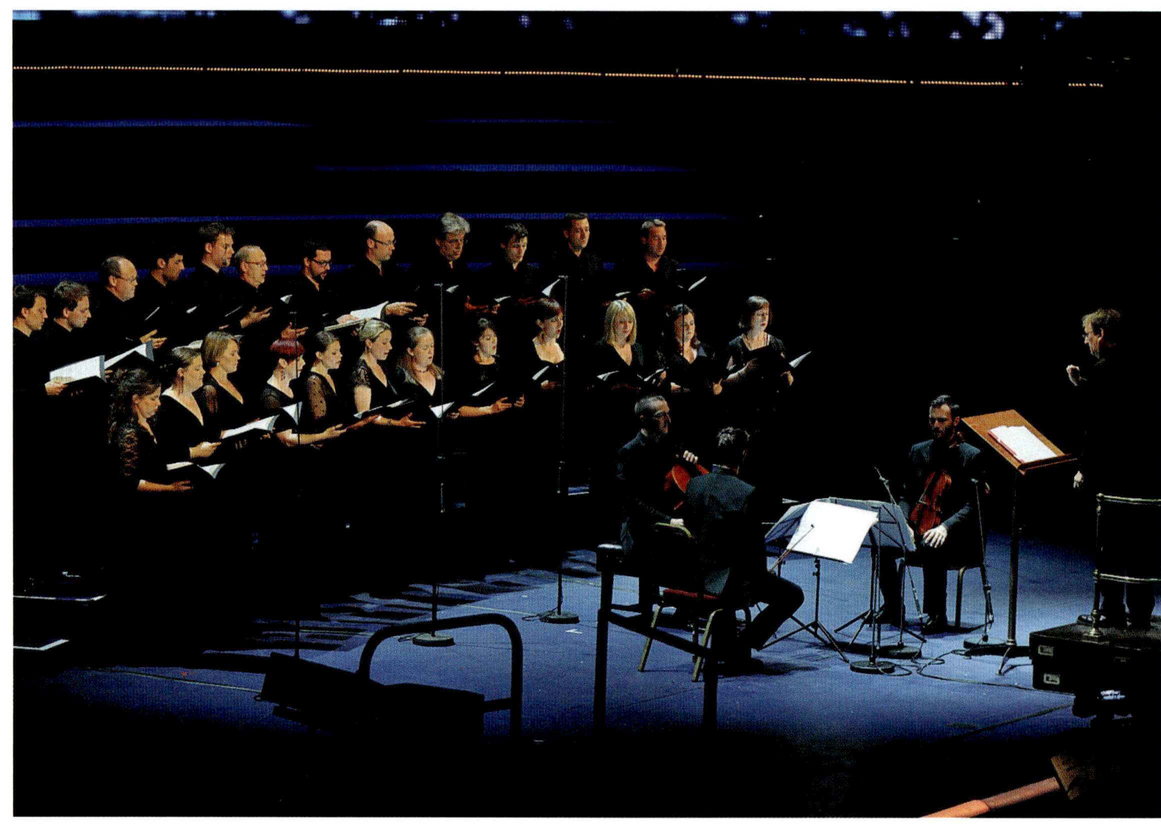

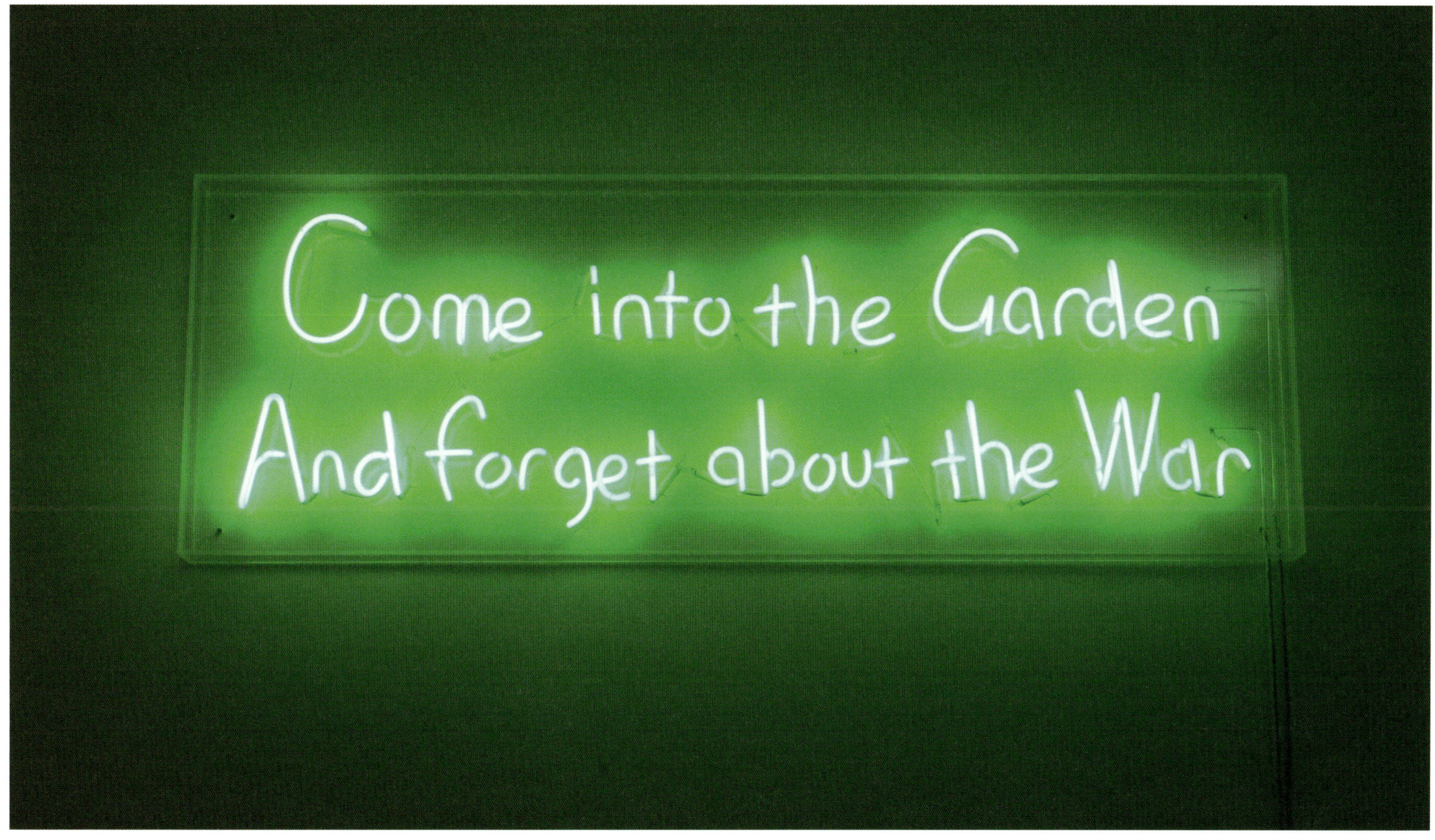

RADIO RELAY

Paddy Bloomer
Colm Clarke
Graham Fagen
Philip Hession
Gareth Moore
Sara Morrison
Mhairi Sutherland

The invention of radio changed our world, and continues to empower us today. *Radio Relay* was a co-commission with Belfast's Golden Thread Gallery designed to acknowledge both that power and the milestones in the early development of radio with Irish connections (including Marconi's transmission of his first signals in 1898, and the world's first pirate-radio broadcast during the 1916 Easter Rising).

A team of artists headed by Graham Fagen created works for a nationwide programme with participation at its core, including lessons on building a lo-fi radio transmitter. Then, over a midsummer weekend connecting sites such as Grey Point Fort, the Black Mountain and Belfast's ancient Giant's Ring, participants helped to make silver kites in a recreation of early experiments in radio antennae.

Golden Thread Gallery, Belfast, 17 — 20 June 2016

The phrase seen here in neon is a work by the artist Graham Fagen; it formed a focal point for an audio installation by Fagen entitled *The Garden*. The artist borrowed a slogan he found on the wall of the Talbot House Museum in Belgium, which was once a clubhouse — and oasis — for soldiers stationed in the area in the First World War.

EVERYTHING THAT HAPPENED AND WOULD HAPPEN

Heiner Goebbels

Everything that happened and would happen was a major new work that spanned 100 years of European history: its giddy contradictions, false promises and consuming crises. Taking the First World War as a starting point, rather than attempting to distil the last century into a linear narrative, this co-commission with Artangel proposed a landscape of fragmented incident without differentiating between the trivial and the supposedly meaningful. Together with 20 musicians, dancers and performers, the German artist and composer Heiner Goebbels led audiences to a Manchester storage depot filled with the props of the past, the burden of the present and the key to possible futures.

The work consisted of live music, performance, sound, movement, image and moving image, and was inspired by contrasting source materials: Patrik Ouředník's 2001 book *Europeana*; elements from Goebbels' 2012 staging of John Cage's *Europeras*; and a live feed from TV channel Euronews' *No Comment* — original, unedited footage of the news, without commentary or mediation. Part-performance, part-construction site, *Everything that happened and would happen* was an invitation to imagine an alternative history of the 20th century through the poetry of collaboration and chance. This world premiere was presented with Manchester International Festival as a pre-Factory event.

Mayfield, Manchester, 10 — 21 October 2018

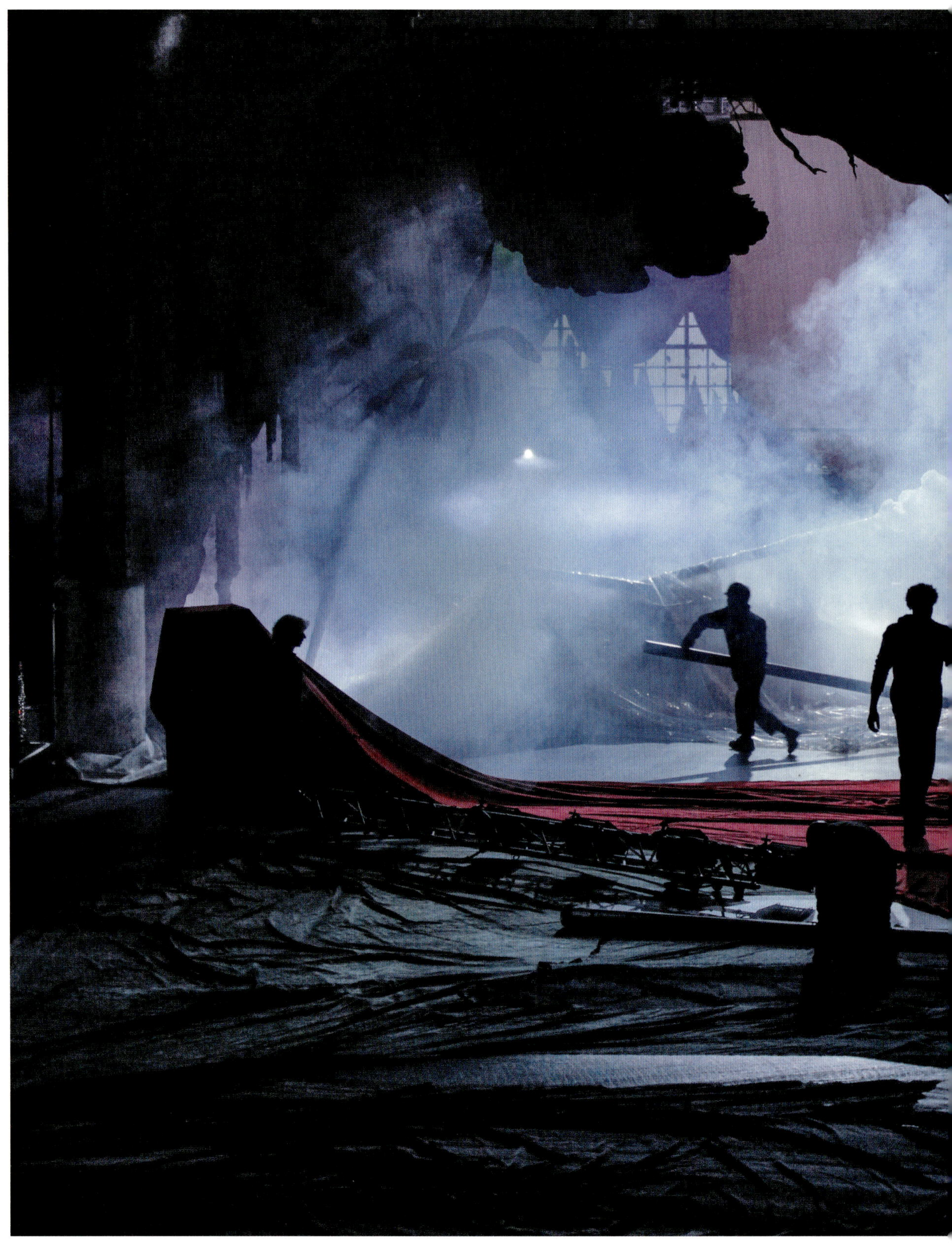

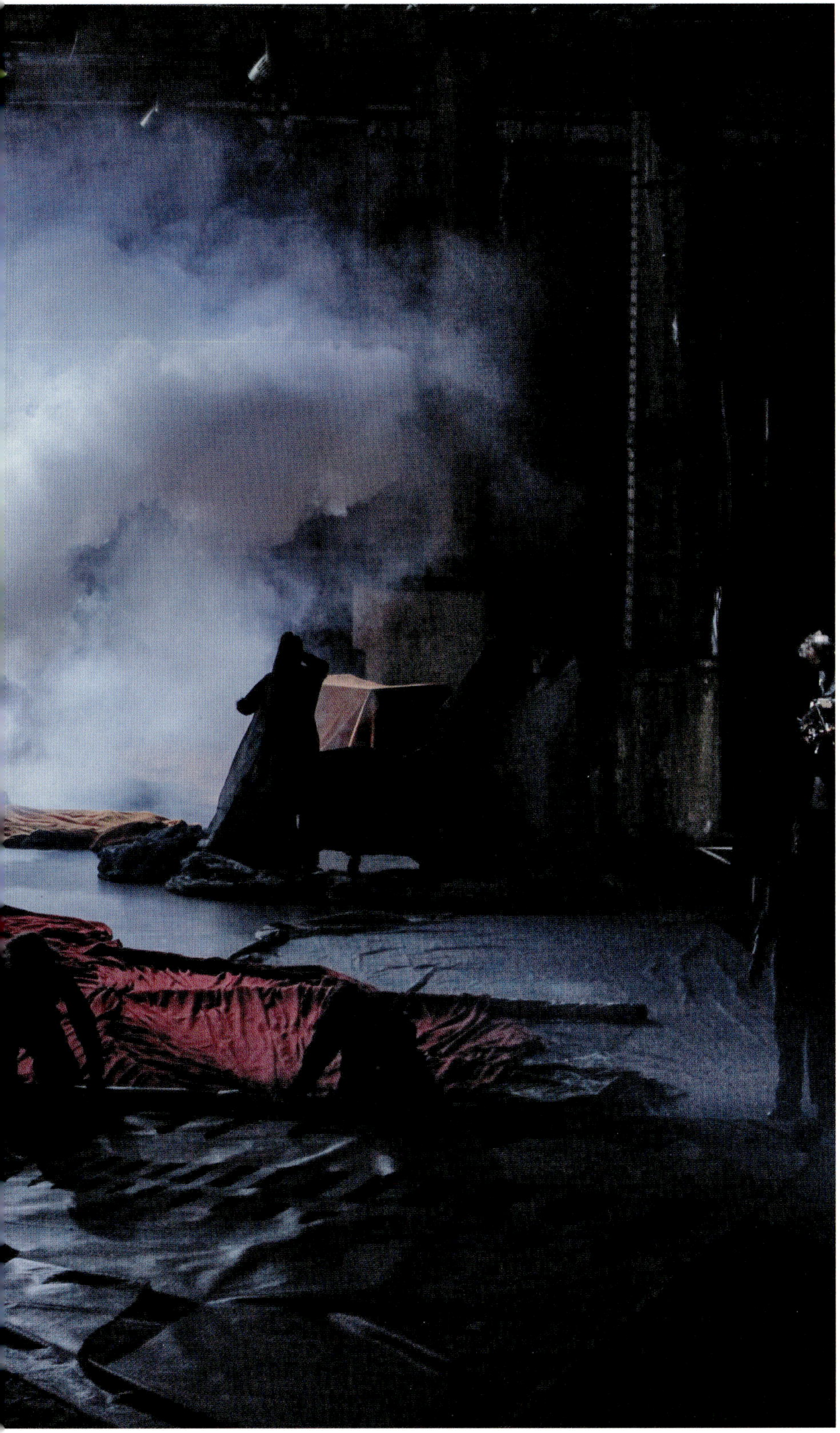

Inside this cavernous venue,
the team of performers acted
as stage hands, assembling
and disassembling elements
of the set in order to create
a series of dramatic vistas.
These were complemented
by striking light effects,
projected still and moving
images, and a multilayered
soundtrack of dialogue,
industrial sounds and music.

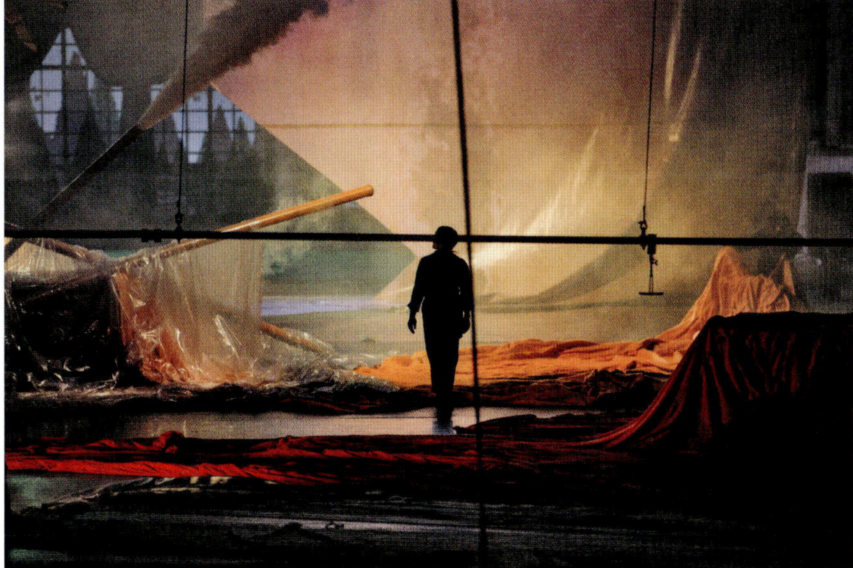

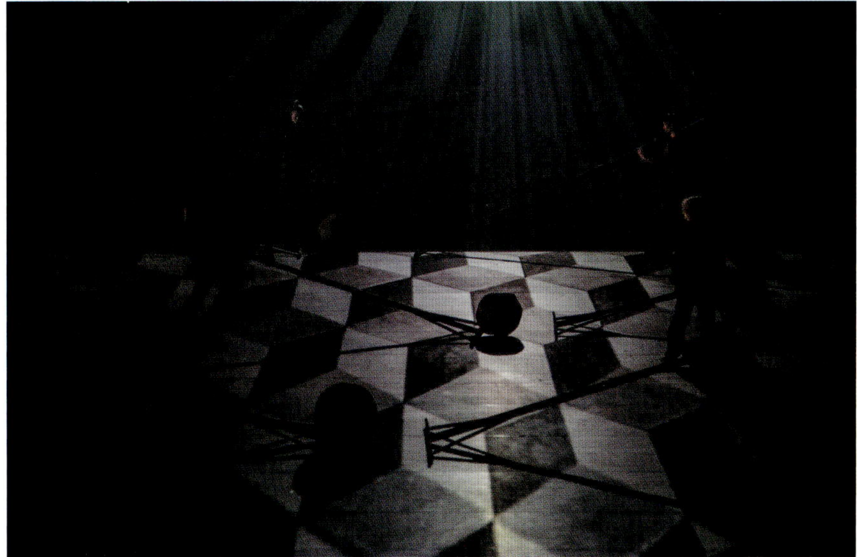

SHOT AT DAWN

Chloe Dewe Mathews

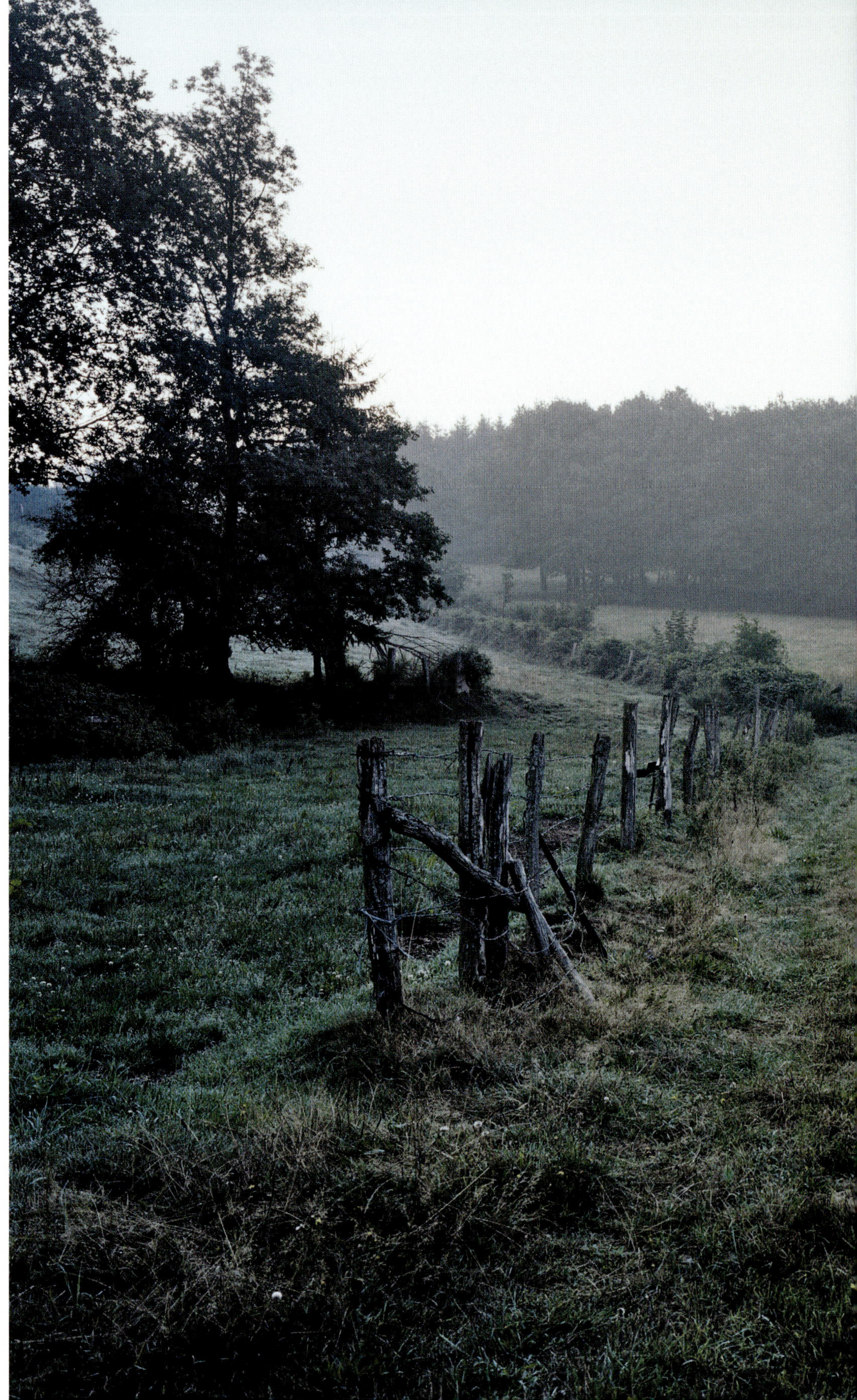

Not all deaths during the First World War were at the hands of the enemy. Hundreds of soldiers — some of them only in their teens — found guilty of cowardice, desertion or breaching military discipline were executed by firing squads made up of soldiers from their own regiment. Seen as necessary for order and morale at the time, many of these victims were undoubtedly suffering from psychiatric conditions that today would result in treatment rather than in execution.

Some 1,000 soldiers on both sides of the conflict were killed in this way during the war, and it was the deaths of 74 of these that photographer Chloe Dewe Mathews chose to commemorate in a series of images recording the places where they were executed.

Dewe Mathews spent two years meticulously researching the project, identifying the exact sites where the executions had taken place. She then took her photographs as close as possible to the precise time at which the executions themselves had taken place — usually at daybreak, hence the title of the series. Each photograph was titled simply with the name of the soldier and the time, date and location of execution.

The photographs were published in book form by Ivorypress on 14 July 2014, while the prints embarked on a two-year international tour.

Touring (Paris, Edinburgh, London, Essen, Antwerp, Dresden, Dublin, Madrid), January 2014 — July 2016

Below left. *Second Lieutenant Eric Skeffington Poole, 07:25 / 10.12.1916. Town Hall (prison cell), Poperinge, West-Vlaanderen.*

Below right. *Soldat Casimir Canel, Soldat Jean-Louis Lasplacette, Soldat Alphonse Didier, 05:00 / 12.6.1917. Cellar (holding cell), Maizy, Picardie.*

Right. *Soldat Lucien Baleux, Soldat Émile Lherminier, Soldat Félix Louis Milhau, Soldat Paul Regoult, Time unkown / 23.5.1916. Roucy, Picardie.*

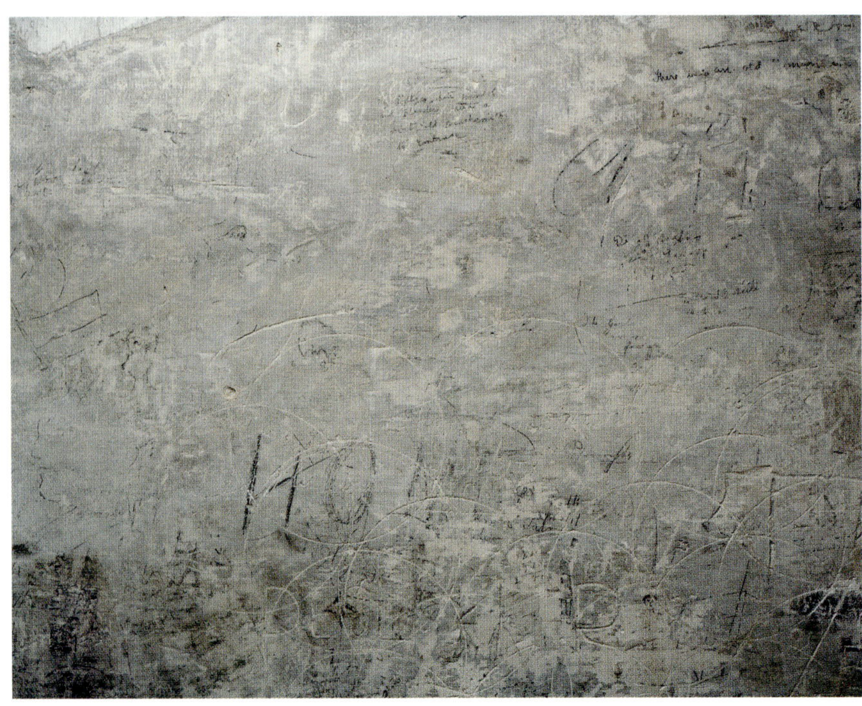

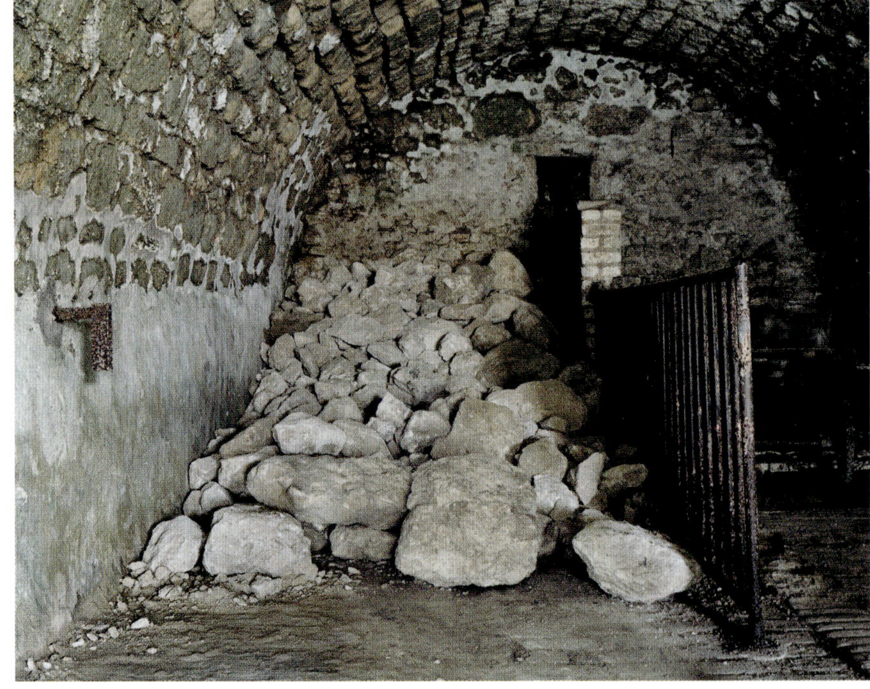

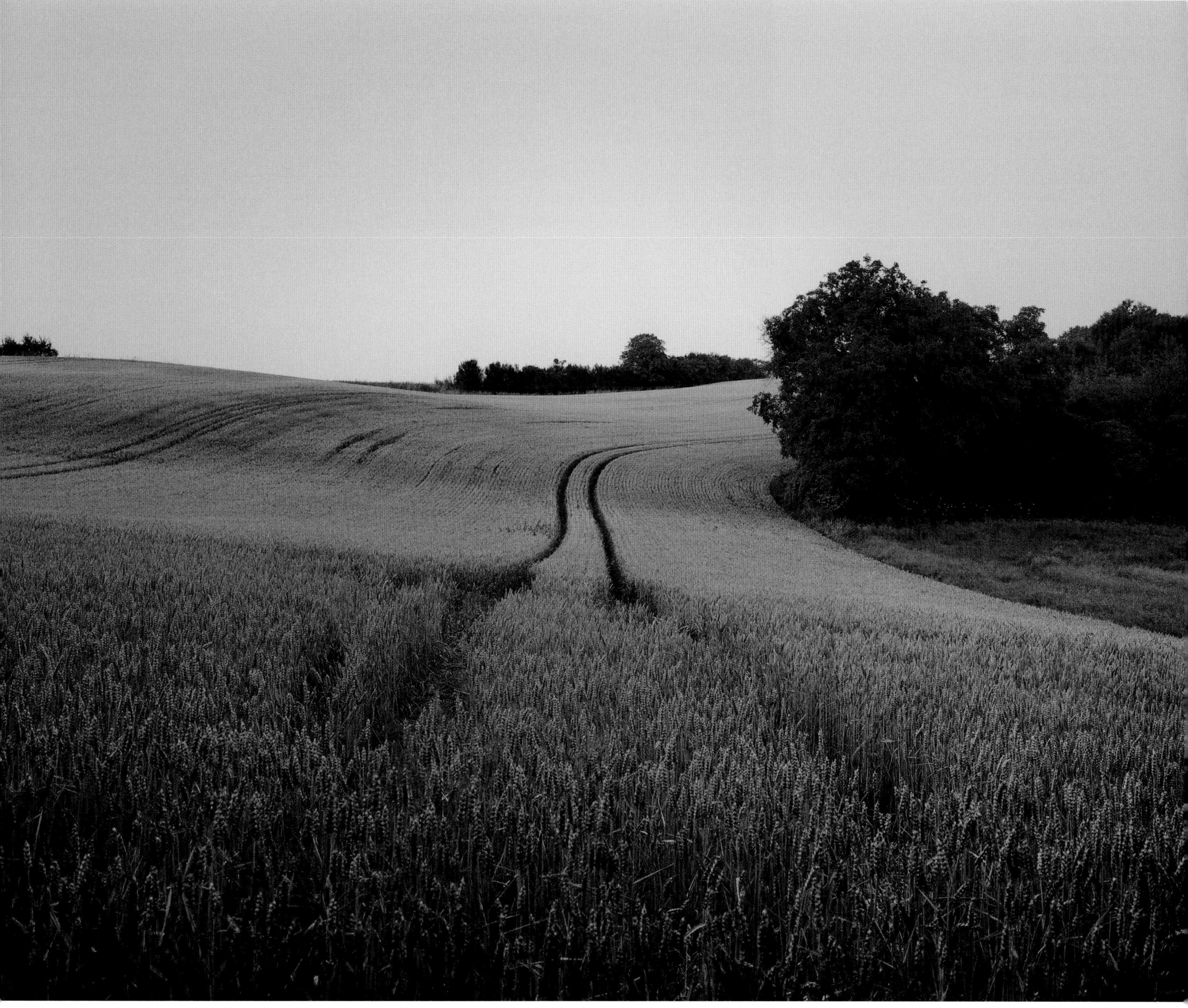

NOW THE HERO \ NAWR YR ARWR

Marc Rees

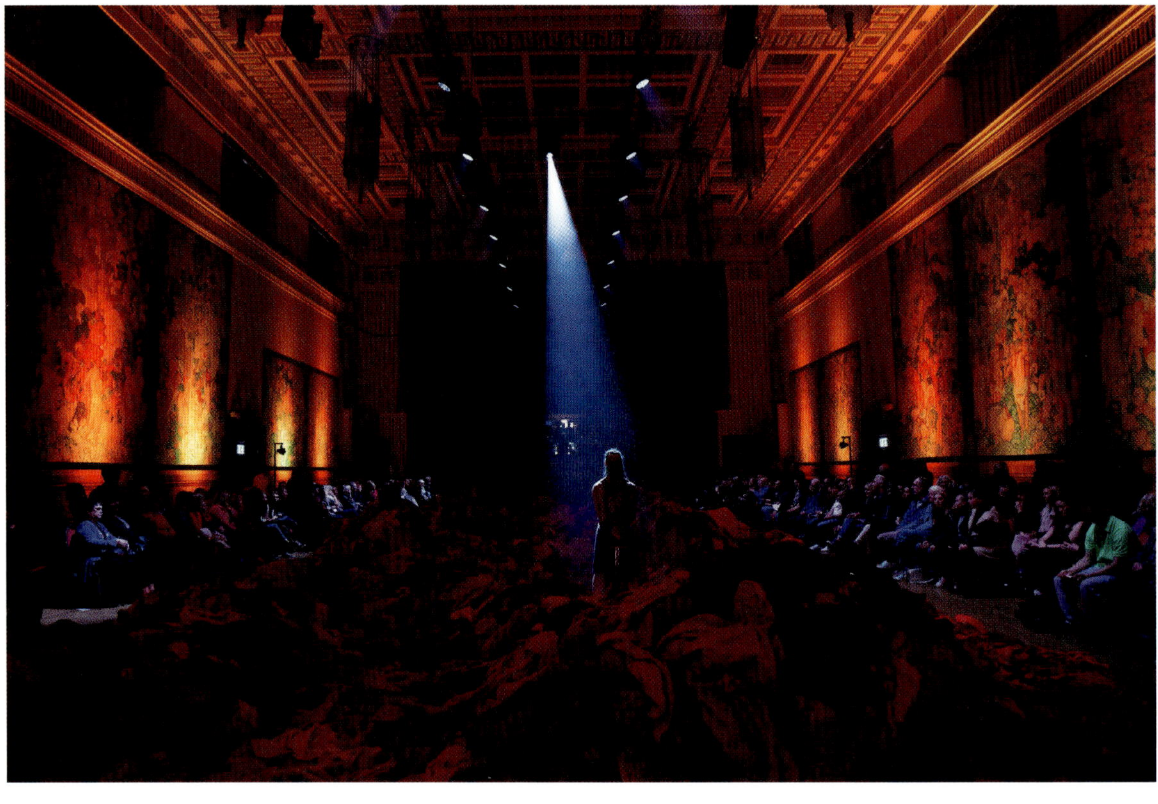

Now the Hero \ Nawr yr Arwr was a site-specific, immersive theatrical experience created by Marc Rees, one of Wales' most inspired artists. The event took the audience from Swansea Bay through the surrounding streets to the Brangwyn Hall, experiencing an imaginative journey through three distinct periods of war — from Celtic history, the First World War and contemporary conflict — with a counterpoint of peace and hope. Rees took his inspiration from an epic medieval poem, an intimate portrait of a serving Swansea soldier, an original Greenham Common protestor and a set of paintings by Frank Brangwyn, to subvert the role of the hero and to question the act of remembrance.

Brangwyn's little-known British Empire Panels, a set of idyllic, fantastical landscapes, provided the starting point for the First World War component of the work. Originally commissioned by the House of Lords to commemorate the war, these paintings were rejected by Parliament as 'too colourful and lively'; instead, they found a home in Swansea, where they have been displayed since 1934. The panels offer an uncompromising vision of the colourful and optimistic possibilities of post-war empire, and Rees used them as a springboard for exploring the narratives of war and hope proposed by the paintings.

At the heart of *Now the Hero \ Nawr yr Arwr* was a requiem composed by Owen Morgan Roberts (realised from an original collaboration by the late Jóhann Jóhannsson and Roberts). It featured a libretto by Owen Sheers, sung by Stephen Layton's world-famous choir, Polyphony.

The performance moved through scenes that reflected on war and peace via a battle, a wedding party, a Tibetan sand mandala, a protest dance and a traditional wake. The work culminated with an outdoor harvest supper created and curated by the artist Owen Griffiths and framed around the symbolism of Brangwyn's work through Griffiths' GRAFT — a soil-based syllabus; a new permanent edible garden and teaching space located at the National Waterfront Museum.

To coincide with *Now the Hero \ Nawr yr Arwr*, Swansea played host to an extended 'art weekender' entitled *Now For More*, where all of the city's cultural institutions and organisations presented work connected to the British Empire Panels, the legacy of the First World War, and the impact of war and conflict on human relationships.

Swansea Bay and Brangwyn Hall, Swansea, 25 — 29 September 2018

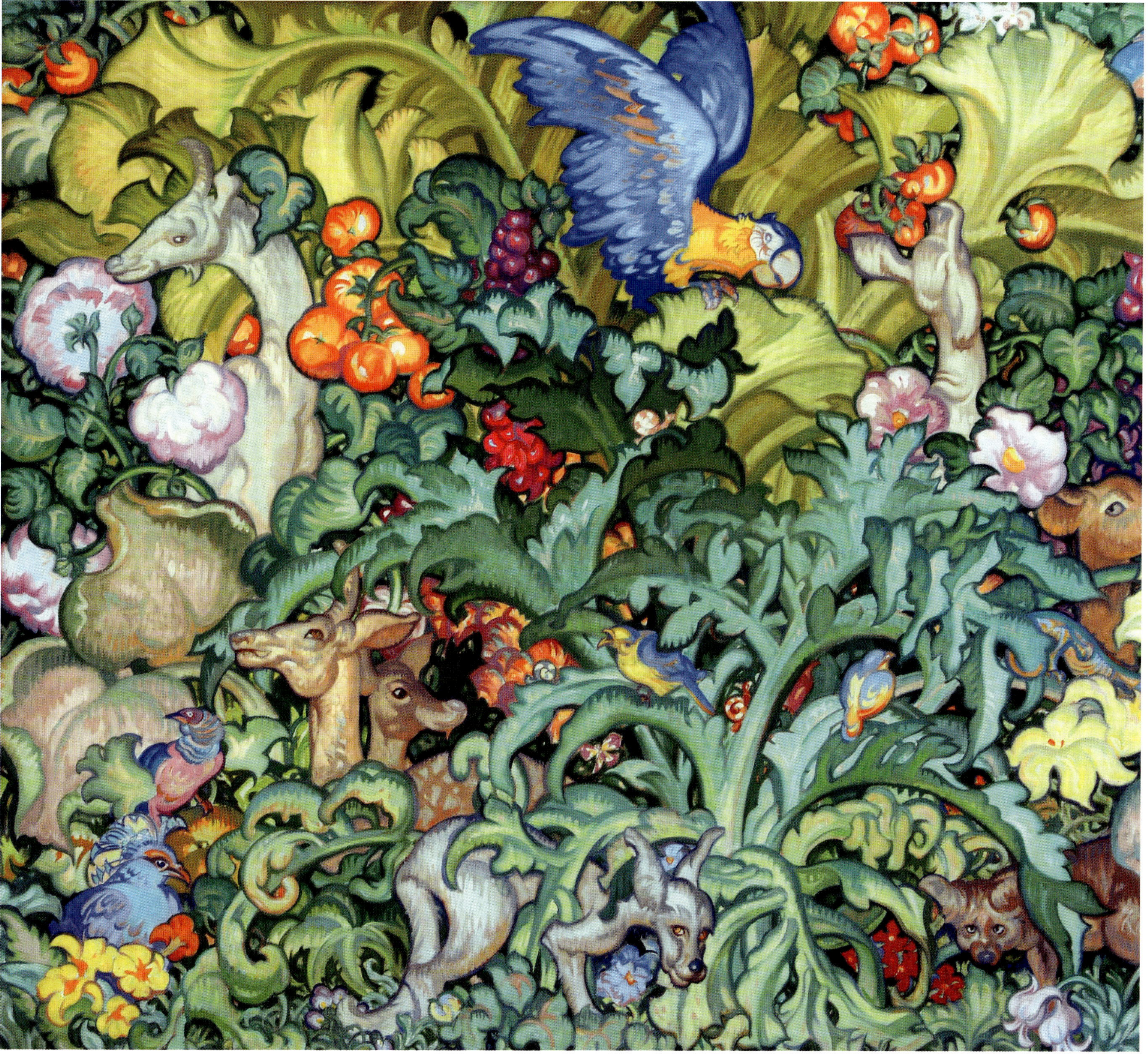

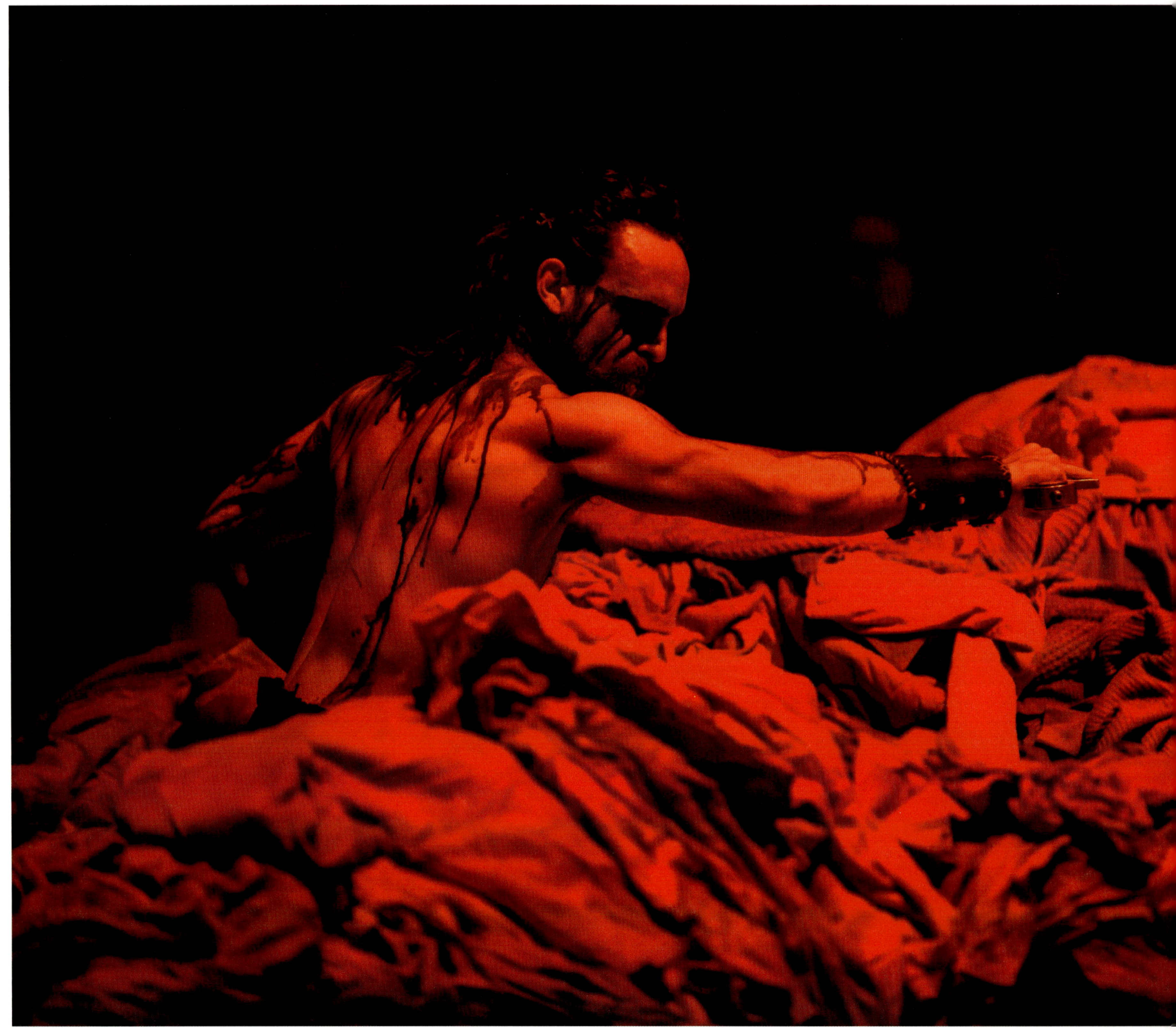

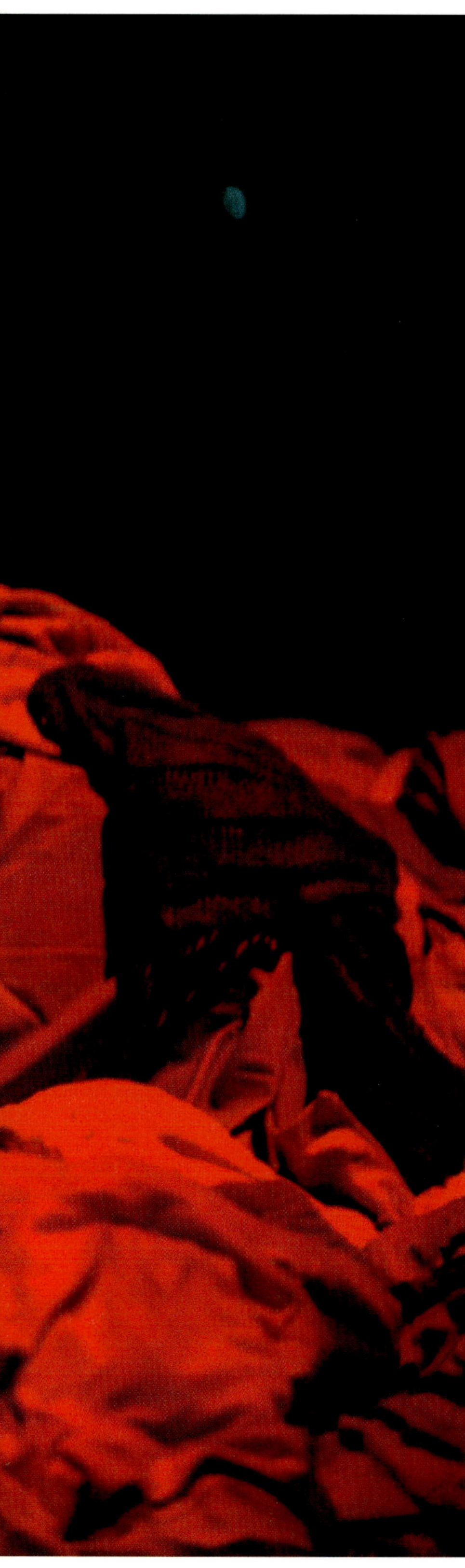

Left. The Celtic warrior, engulfed in a stylised sea of blood.

Right. Each performance began with the three men emerging from the waves at Swansea beach.

Below. A new garden project provided the ingredients for a special harvest supper.

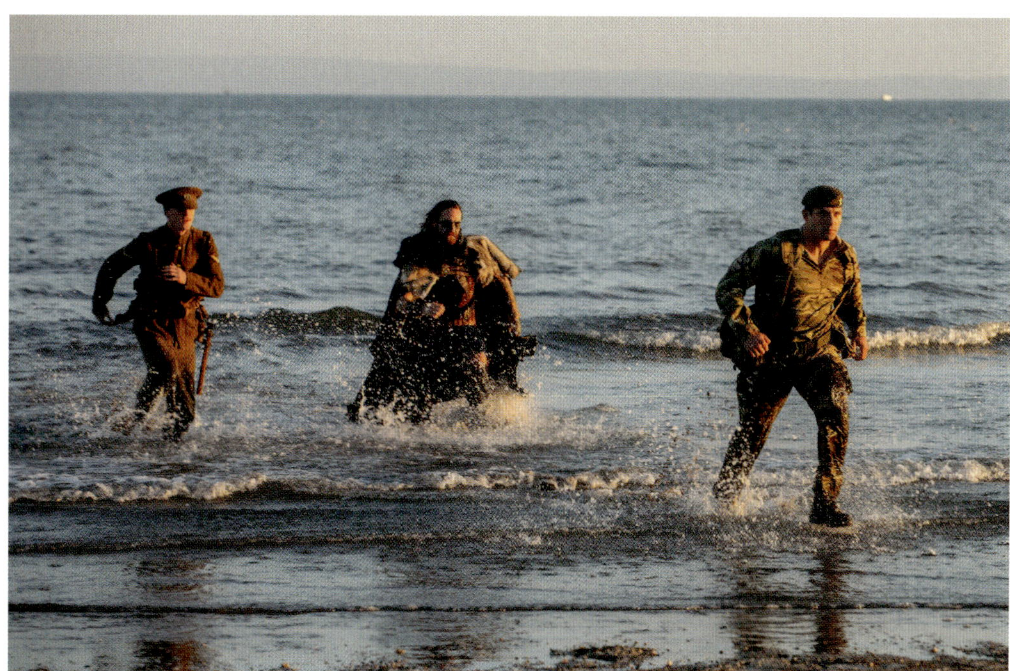

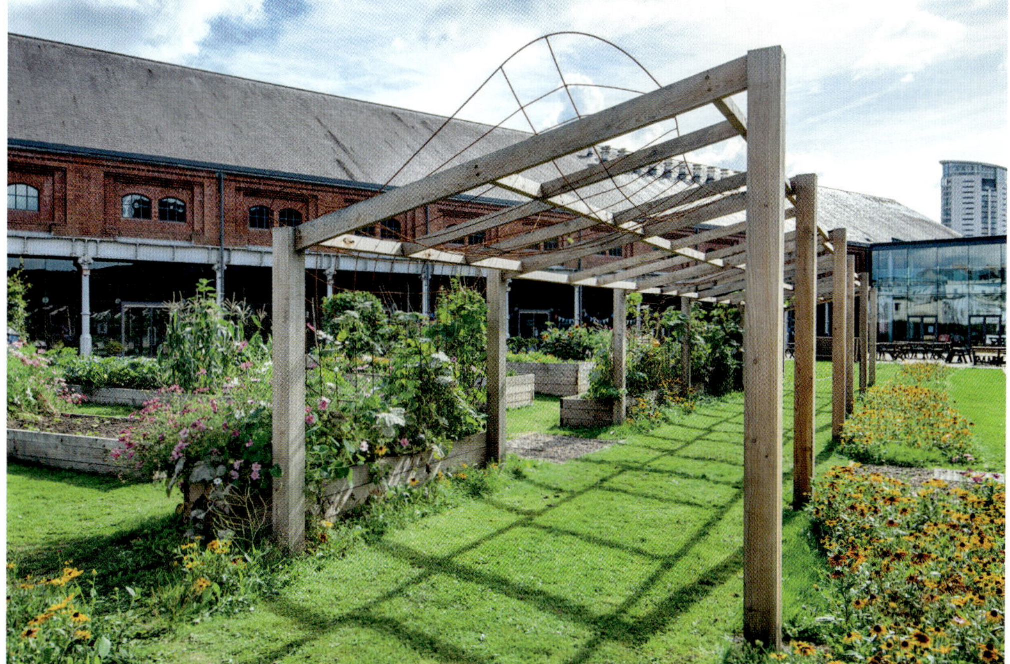

SOME THOUGHTS ON *THE HEAD & THE LOAD*

William Kentridge

Every Remembrance Sunday the headmaster would read out the names of ex-pupils and masters who had died in the war. Our conversation was with these English boys, not with the hundreds of thousands of African carriers. All Quiet on the Western Front, stereoscopic photographs of the Flanders trenches, the great English war poets, took all my air.

The following is an edited extract from a series of notes on the thoughts and processes behind *The Head & the Load*.

When I was an undergraduate student in the 1970s, studying colonial history, I came across the obscure history of a Baptist minister, John Chilembwe, who wrote a letter to the *Nyasaland Times* in 1914 entitled 'The voice of the African native in the present war', in which he stated:

> *In times of peace, everything for Europeans only, and instead of honour, we suffer humiliation with names contemptible. But in time of war, it is found that we are needed to share the hardships, and shed our blood in equality ... the poor Africans who have nothing to own in this world ... are invited to die for a cause which is not theirs.*

Chilembwe's letter was never published, and he and his followers were executed. A copy of this letter has sat in a box in my studio for the last 45 years, waiting its moment to be used.

When the letter was taken out of the box and presented to the group, it was clear that it would be central to the production. But there was the question of how one changes this letter into a performance on stage. We needed to be led not only by books and texts. There was traditional research at the Imperial War Museum: photos, letters, copies of military instructions. In different archives there was a search for African oral histories of the War (there were remarkably few of them that we could track down).

We were looking both for the broad strokes, the broad shapes of what happened, but also for surprising thoughts, for particular turns of phrase; for the idiosyncratic.

I invited Philip Miller and Thuthuka Sibisi to join the team to find the musical language of the piece. Collaborations never start from an emptiness, they start from the work that we have done before. There was a familiarity of a way of working, which involves using a mixture of found and altered musical material — a collage.

When the large-scale workshop of 60 participants began in my studio, there was a wealth of materials waiting to be used: different musical fragments and pieces of animation, waiting to be tested and to see what happened when we put movement and image together. The days were spent in a mixture of rehearsing and watching. The chorus and the musicians having to master the provisional pieces of music. The performers having to learn how to carry the shadow cutouts that had been made in the studio prior to the workshop and those that were made during the course of the ten-day workshop. (These shadows included a boat in three parts; loads that were literal, cutouts that looked like loads; loads that were metaphoric, like an entire mineshaft and headgear carried on someone's shoulders; loads that were historic, figures from past and future African independence movements, nationalist leaders who would be carried like saints in a religious procession.)

Our starting point was the width of the stage. We started with the idea of different musical forces at each end. Europe at one end of the stage, Africa at

the other, and a space of negotiation in between. This became musically Africa's choral and percussive tradition at one end; European high modernism at the other. This gave us a horizontal extent. Then through the middle, vertically, we dropped the Dadaists. Not so much an extra voice to add to the music, but as a strategy for working, to work with what they showed us, the cut-up, the illogical ... performers reading in between and over each other; a series of different thoughts on top and next to each other, often with no obvious connection.

The colonial incomprehension — Europe not understanding Africa, Africa's uncomprehending of Europe's intentions — also found expression in the range of languages used, a kind of broken telephone along the length of the stage: English into isiZulu to French back to English, translations and mistranslations projected on to the screen; Morse code made of Hungarian phrases, German phrases, English phrases, messages sent from Africa to Europe, hovering at the edge of comprehensibility, a series of words unmoored from their context.

When the project began, one of its energies was a frustration, a frustration at my own ignorance about the material, about the war in Africa (an ignorance I shared not only with my audience, but also with the other participants in the project). I think there are three kinds of ignorance here. Firstly, a deliberately constructed ignorance, a conscious effort by the colonial powers to silence voices, to hide history ... the absence of memorials to Africans, the absence of medals, the fact that they were not allowed to participate in the 1919 victory parades, were

deliberate acts of erasure. 'Lest their behaviour merit recognition, their deeds must not be recorded', wrote one colonial officer.

The second ignorance I am complicit in. Every Remembrance Sunday the headmaster would read out the names of ex-pupils and masters who had died in the war. Our conversation was with these English boys, not with the hundreds of thousands of African carriers. *All Quiet on the Western Front*, stereoscopic photographs of the Flanders trenches, the great English war poets, took all my air.

The third ignorance is a slowness in making connection. Allowing fragments to remain as fragments. It needs a heating up, a galvanising of energy for these connections to spark. This heating up is the richest part of the collaborative process. Ideas and images tumbling over each other, an over-determination of the project. These connections happen during improvisations, taking a section of material designed for one part of the project and placing it in a completely different context. The most obvious connections are usually the least interesting, and the ones that arrive through all these other processes are what give new insight, not just into the material we are working with, but sometimes illuminate the corners of the larger questions behind the project itself.

William Kentridge is an internationally acclaimed artist whose evocative vision combines the political with the poetic. Dealing with subjects as sobering as colonialism and totalitarianism, his highly personal work is often imbued with lyrical undertones and references to his native South Africa. *The Head & the Load*, created with his long-time collaborator, composer Philip Miller, co-composer and music director Thuthuka Sibisi and choreographer Gregory Maqoma, was his most ambitious project to date. This was a live multimedia event — an imaginative and absurdist landscape on an epic scale that told the story of the millions of Africans who worked as porters and carriers during the First World War. Taking its title from the Tswana proverb 'The head and the load are the troubles of the neck', its world premiere took place against the dramatic backdrop of Tate Modern's Turbine Hall.

THE HEAD
& THE LOAD

William Kentridge
Philip Miller
Thuthuka Sibisi
Gregory Maqoma

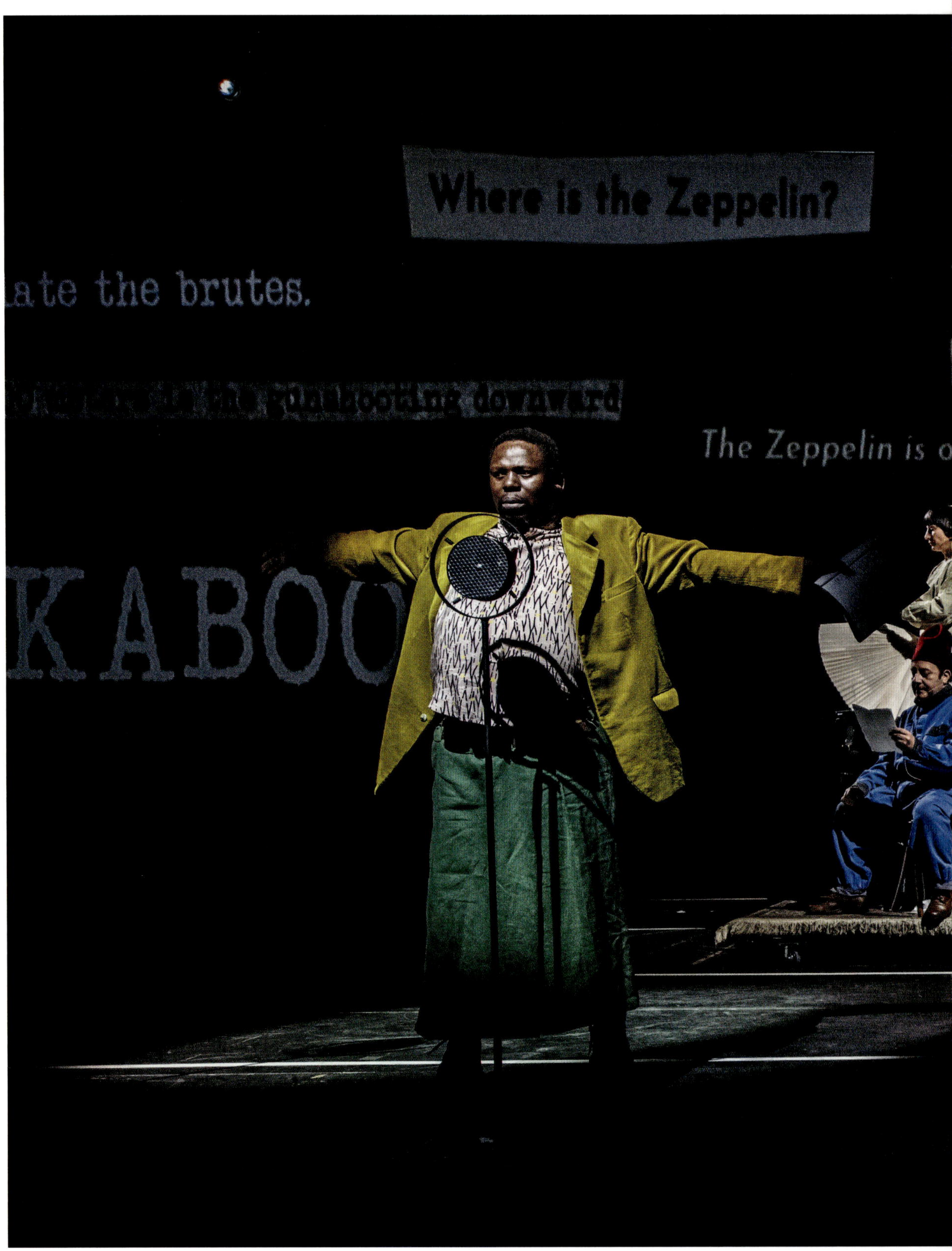

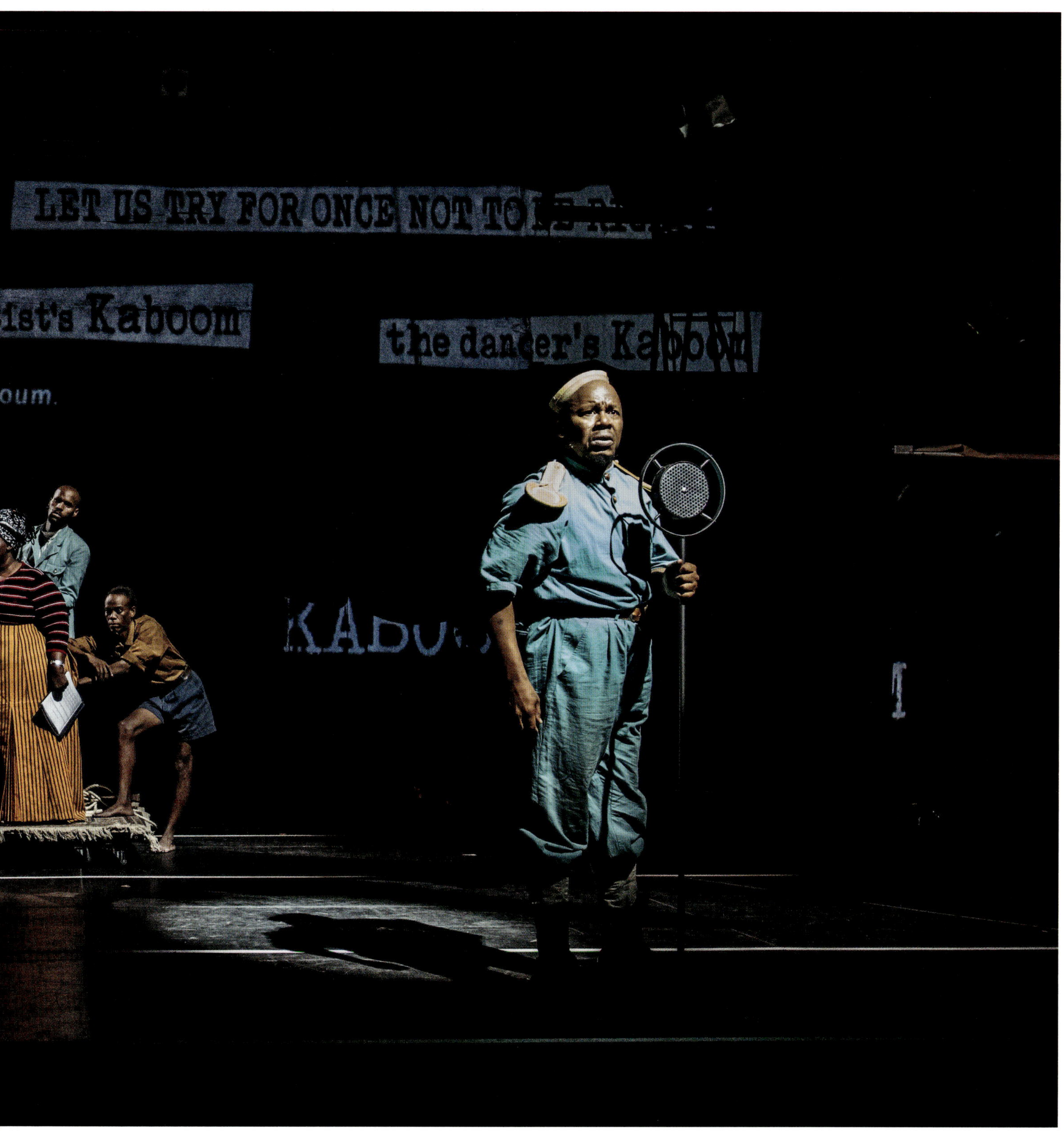

The cast who brought the story of the wartime African porters to life included some whose own grandfathers had served in this way, and who had preserved their shamefully modest reward of a coat and a bicycle as treasured possessions.

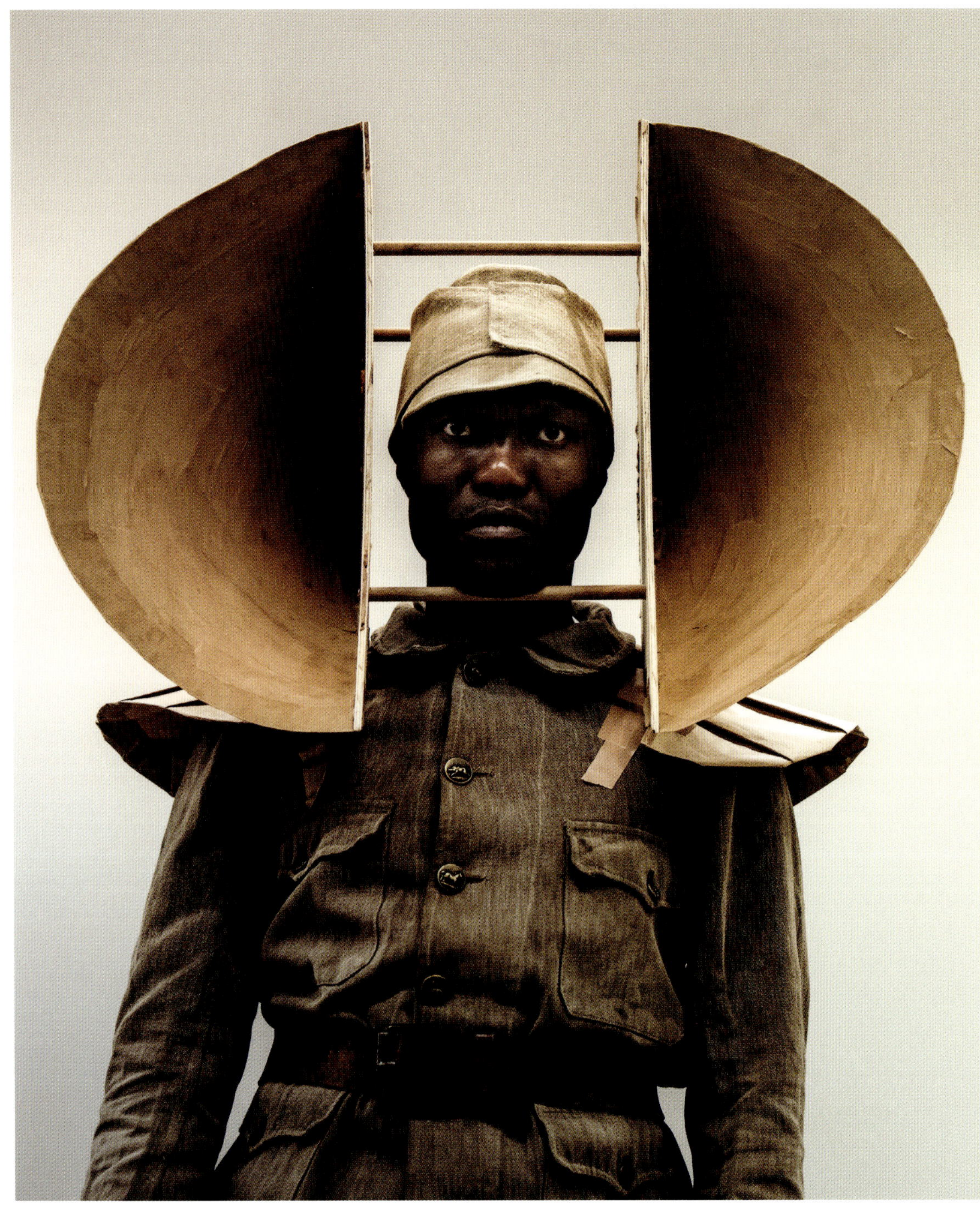

The Head & the Load drew on every aspect of Kentridge's practice — drawing, printmaking, painting, sculpting, performance and film-making — to produce a work that combined music, movement, art and animation. It was brought to life by a cast of singers and dancers, many of whom were based in South Africa. Performers carried props across the stage in a recreation of the great distances and heavy loads borne by the wartime porters, the shadows they cast melding with film projections of further shadows to create processions across the stage; layered voices delivered fragments of text in an often cacophanous blend of European and African languages; dance choreographed by Gregory Maqoma dramatised the action, and the musical journey, created by Philip Miller and Thuthuka Sibisi, drew on both African and European traditions and combined performances by the orchestra collective The Knights and an international cast of other musicians and singers.

The Head & the Load was a hugely impressive audiovisual monument to those who died for a cause that was not their own. As Kentridge himself explained, in summarising his intentions for the work: 'The colonial logic towards the black participants could be summed up: "Lest their actions merit recognition, their deeds must not be recorded." *The Head & the Load* aims to recognise and record.'

Tate Modern, London, 11 — 15 July 2018 / Ruhrtriennale, Germany, 9 —12 August 2018 / Park Avenue, Armory, New York, 4 — 12 December 2018

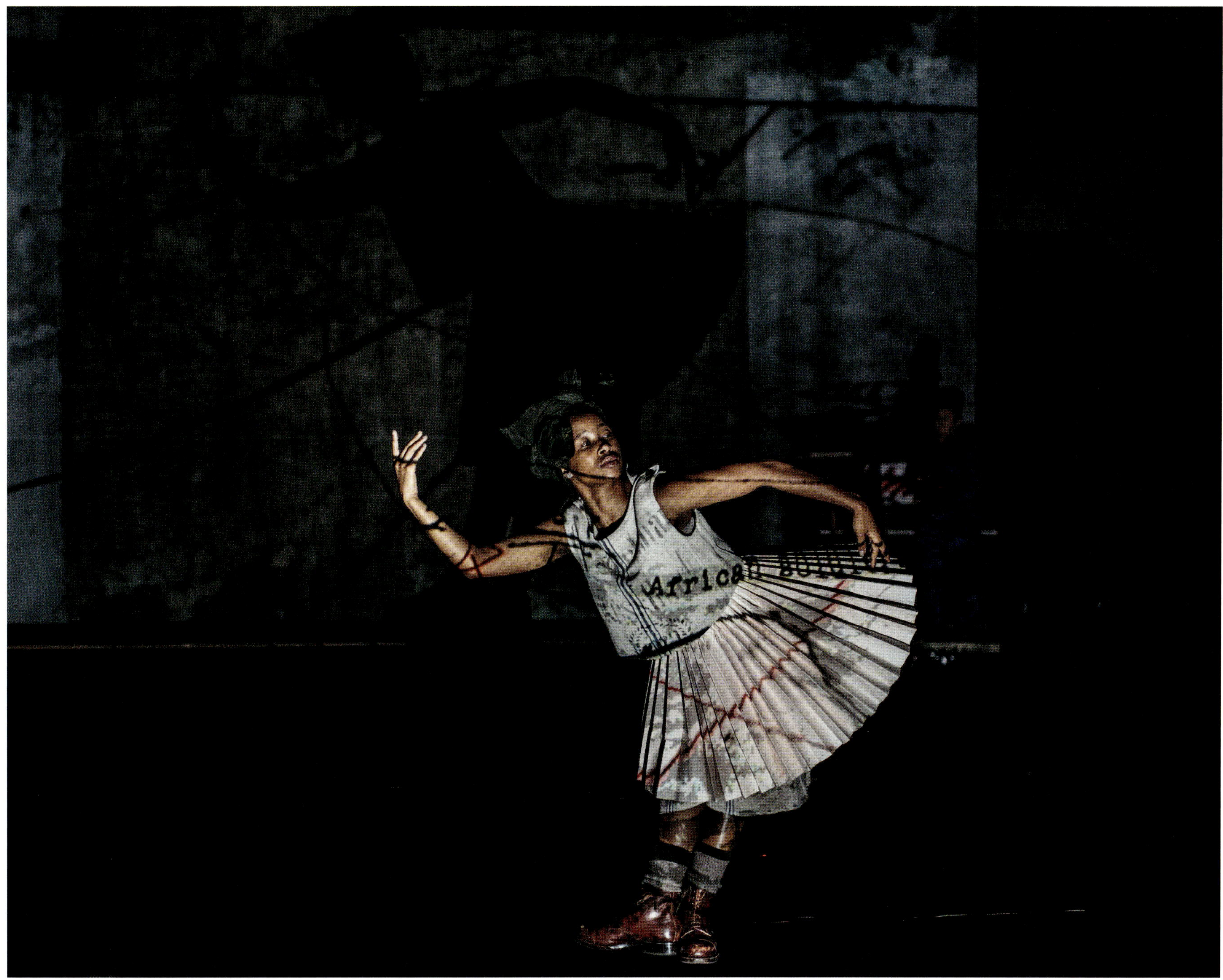

Above. The work included a blend of shadow play, projections and movement.

Opposite. A First World War listening device — one of many props used to recall the hardships of the porters' role.

FIVE TELEGRAMS

Anna Meredith
59 Productions

Five Telegrams was an exuberant, multi-layered 'light and sound' show that captured the complex and messy reality of the war. It fused a new piece by contemporary composer Anna Meredith with projected visuals by the design company 59 Productions. The first performance was led by Sakari Oramo conducting the BBC Proms Youth Ensemble, the National Youth Choir and the BBC Symphony Orchestra, against the spectacular backdrop of the Royal Albert Hall on the First Night of the Proms, illuminated as never before.

The starting point for the creators had been the discovery of field service postcards written home by soldiers at the front and preserved at the Imperial War Museum. These multiple-choice cards restricted communication to a few brief and impersonal options ('I have been sick / wounded / admitted into hospital'; 'I have received no letter from you lately / for a long time'). Soldiers were allowed to score out any irrelevant information, then to sign and date their card — nothing more.

The work then evolved to take the form of five movements, each based on a different example of wartime communication: Spin (newspaper articles of 1918, featuring propaganda eerily akin to today's 'fake news'); Field Postcards; Redaction (freely written postcards that were sent back from the front but then censored by the authorities); Codes (the use of codes during the war); and the announcement of the Armistice.

Before the premiere, *Five Telegrams: Sender* was presented as the Proms' free curtain-raiser. An outdoor audience watched visuals projected onto the exterior of the hall, while the score was transmitted live from inside the building. On the following evening, *Five Telegrams: Receiver* opened the Proms, with projections that lit up the hall's interior. A repeat performance of *Five Telegrams* then took place at the start of the 2018 Edinburgh International Festival. A further iteration of the work — *Nothing to Be Written* — became the very first 'Virtual Reality Prom' that year, combining music from *Five Telegrams* with visuals that took audiences on the journey made by soldiers 100 years before.

Royal Albert Hall, London, 12 — 13 July 2018 / Usher Hall, Edinburgh, 3 August 2018 / BBC TV & BBC Radio 3

> ## 'We were clear that we didn't want to create a sepia-toned, lone-bugled kind of piece.'

Anna Meredith, *The Guardian*

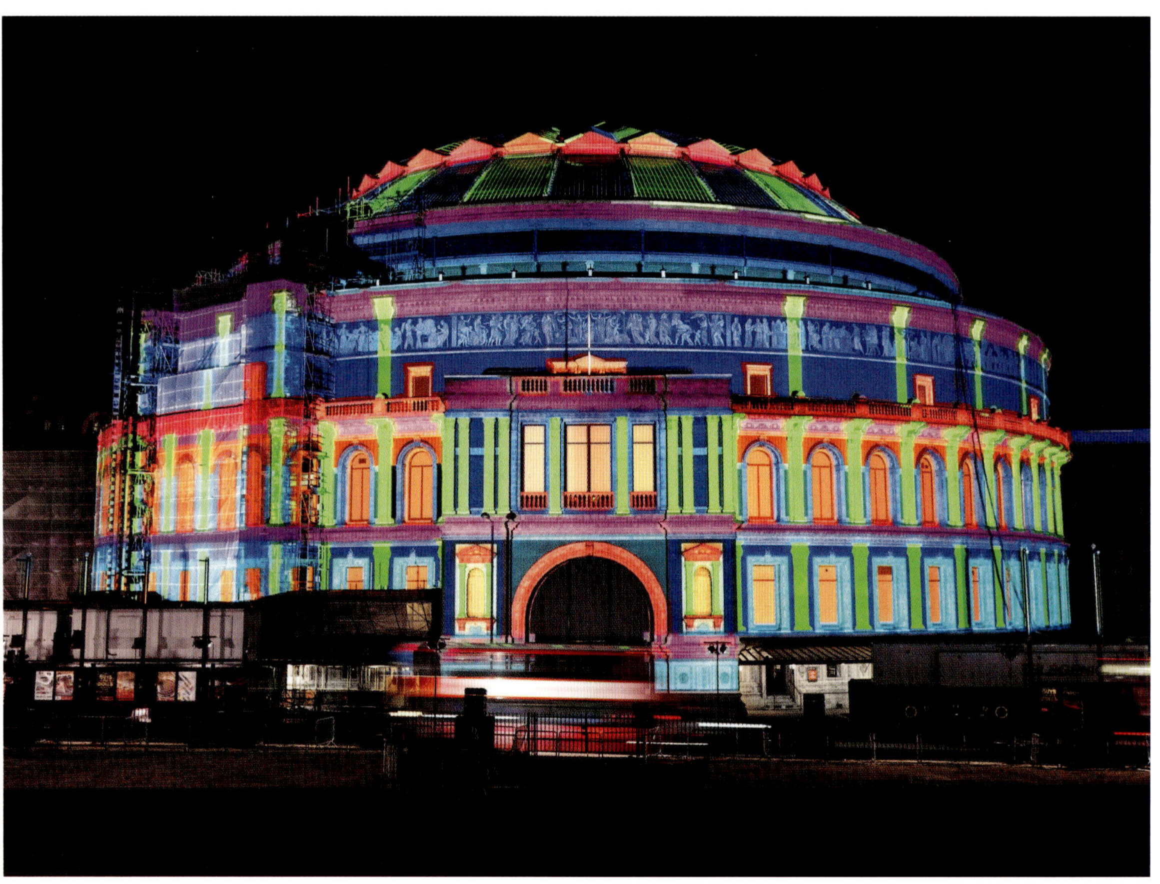

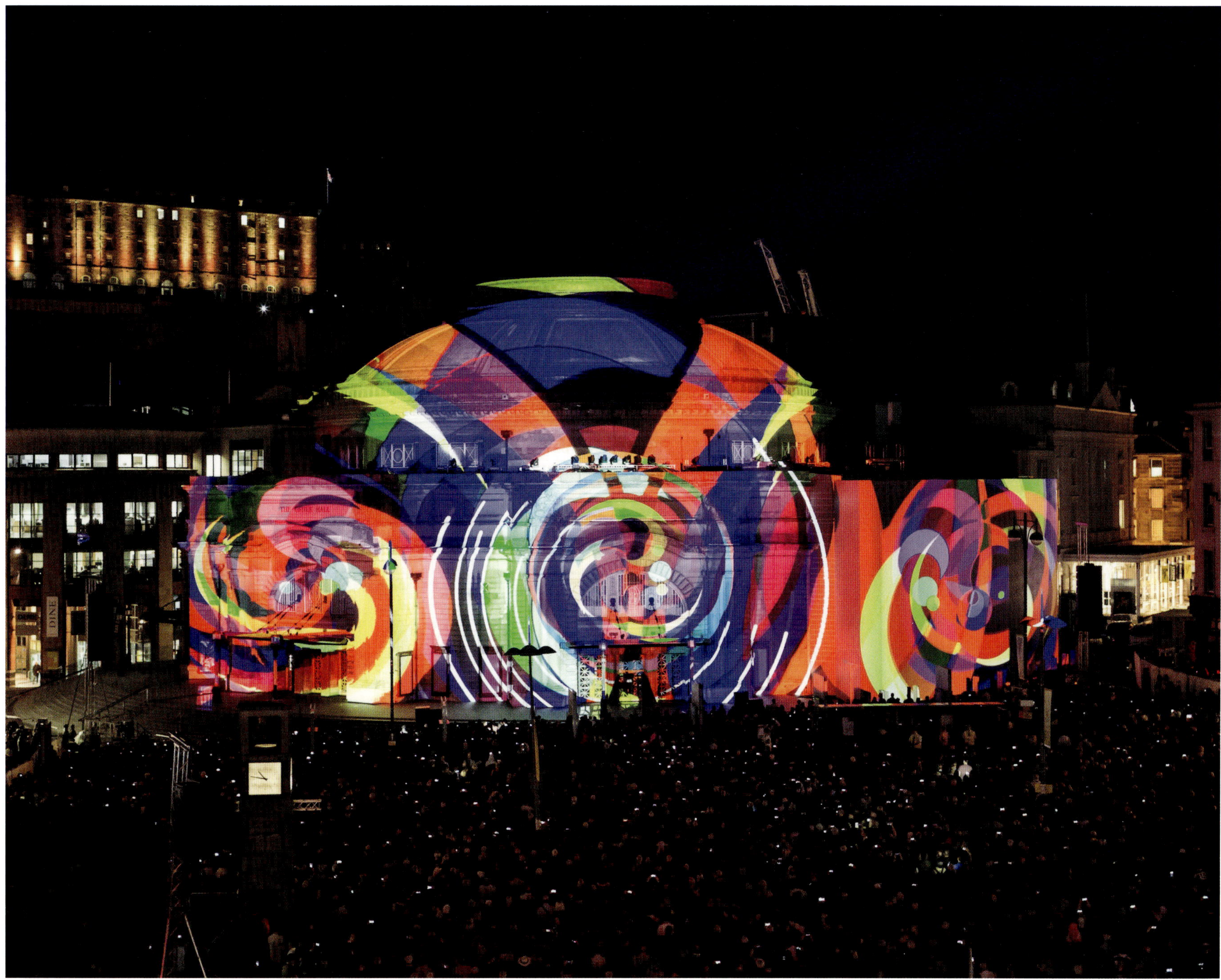

Above. The performance that subsequently opened the 2018 Edinburgh International Festival.

Opposite. The Royal Albert Hall, lit up for the work's premiere in London.

GOODBYE TO ALL THAT

Lavinia Greenlaw (editor)
NoViolet Bulawayo
Xiaolu Guo
Daniel Kehlmann
Erwin Mortier
Elif Shafak
Kamila Shamsie
Ali Smith
Aleš Šteger
Colm Tóibín
Jeanette Winterson

Lavinia Greenlaw, one of Britain's most eminent poets and respected literary figures, invited ten writers from countries involved in the First World War to respond to the title of Robert Graves' famous autobiography *Goodbye to All That*. Each took the poignant phrase of the title as a starting point for a personal reflection on the aftermath of war, as well as the continuing struggle for artistic freedom in the face of conflict in all its forms.

A poet, novelist and classicist, Graves fought at the Battle of the Somme alongside his close friend and fellow soldier-poet Siegfried Sassoon. He was among the most celebrated writers to emerge from the conflict. His autobiography, which he described as a 'bitter leave-taking of England', depicts the horror of war and documents the momentous social changes it brought about.

The ten authors' written responses to Graves' famous title were published as an anthology by Pushkin Press, broadcast on BBC Radio 3, and discussed at live events in London and Edinburgh. These stories, investigations and essays paid tribute to the spirit of Graves, an artist who remained true to himself in the face of personal trauma and public hostility.

The essays include: *Good Voice* by Ali Smith; *Goodbye To Some of That* by Kamila Shamsie; *A Visit to the Magician* by Daniel Kehlmann; *Tea at the Museum* by Aleš Šteger; *In Search of Untold Stories* by Elif Shafak; *Clarity* by NoViolet Bulawayo; *The Community of Sealed Lips: Silence and Writing* by Erwin Mortier; *Coolies* by Xiaolu Guo; *Fearing the Night* by Colm Tóibín; and *Writing on the Wall* by Jeanette Winterson.

London and Edinburgh, July 2014 / BBC Radio 3

'The First World War changed the course of life. It also changed the course of lives to come. A hundred years on, it is still in sight but has slipped out of reach … I didn't want writers simply to return to the past but to formulate and reinvigorate questions we should never stop exploring.'

Foreword to *Goodbye to All That*
Lavinia Greenlaw

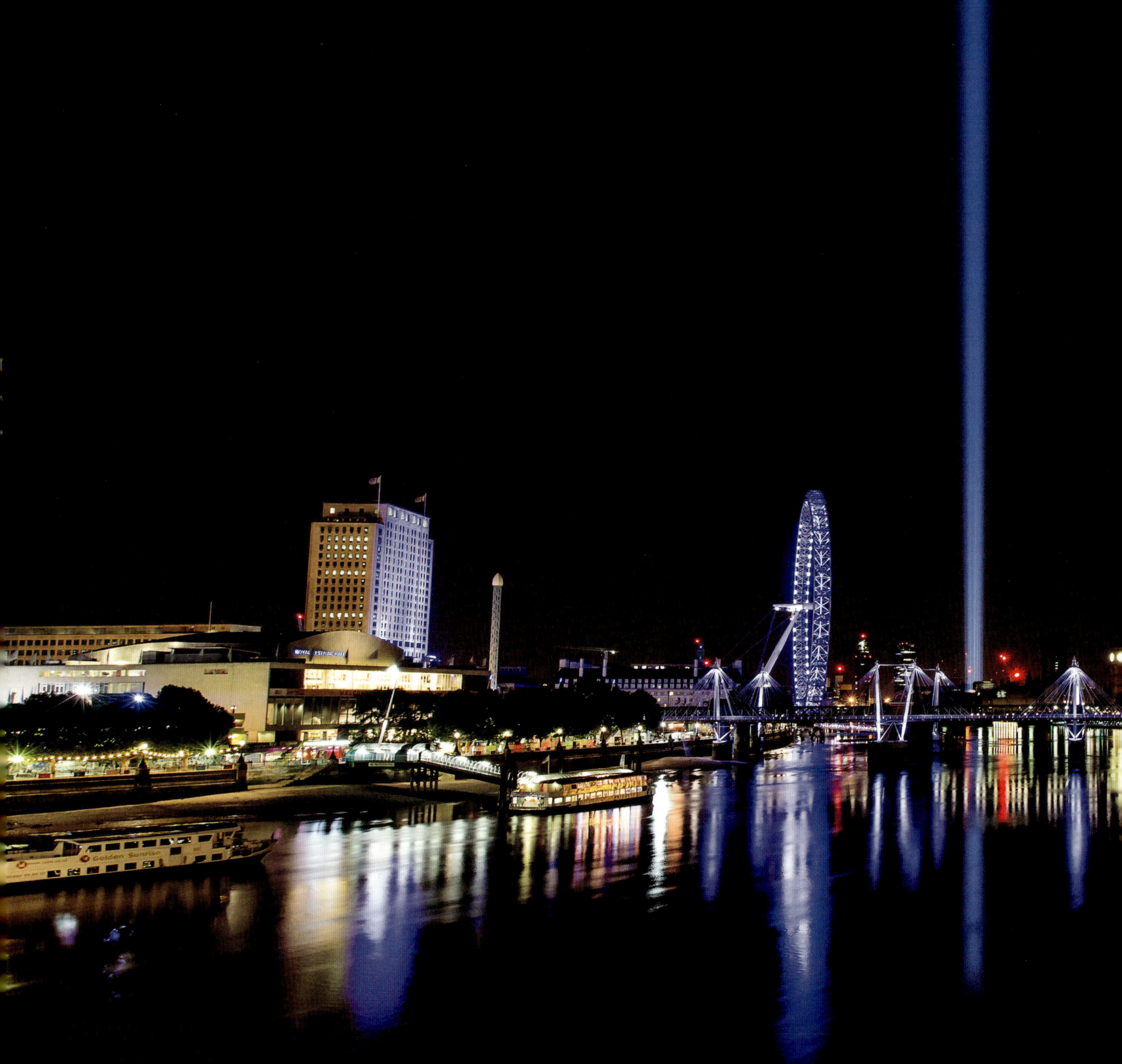

LIGHTS OUT

Jeremy Deller
Ryoji Ikeda
Nalini Malani
Bob and Roberta Smith
Bedwyr Williams

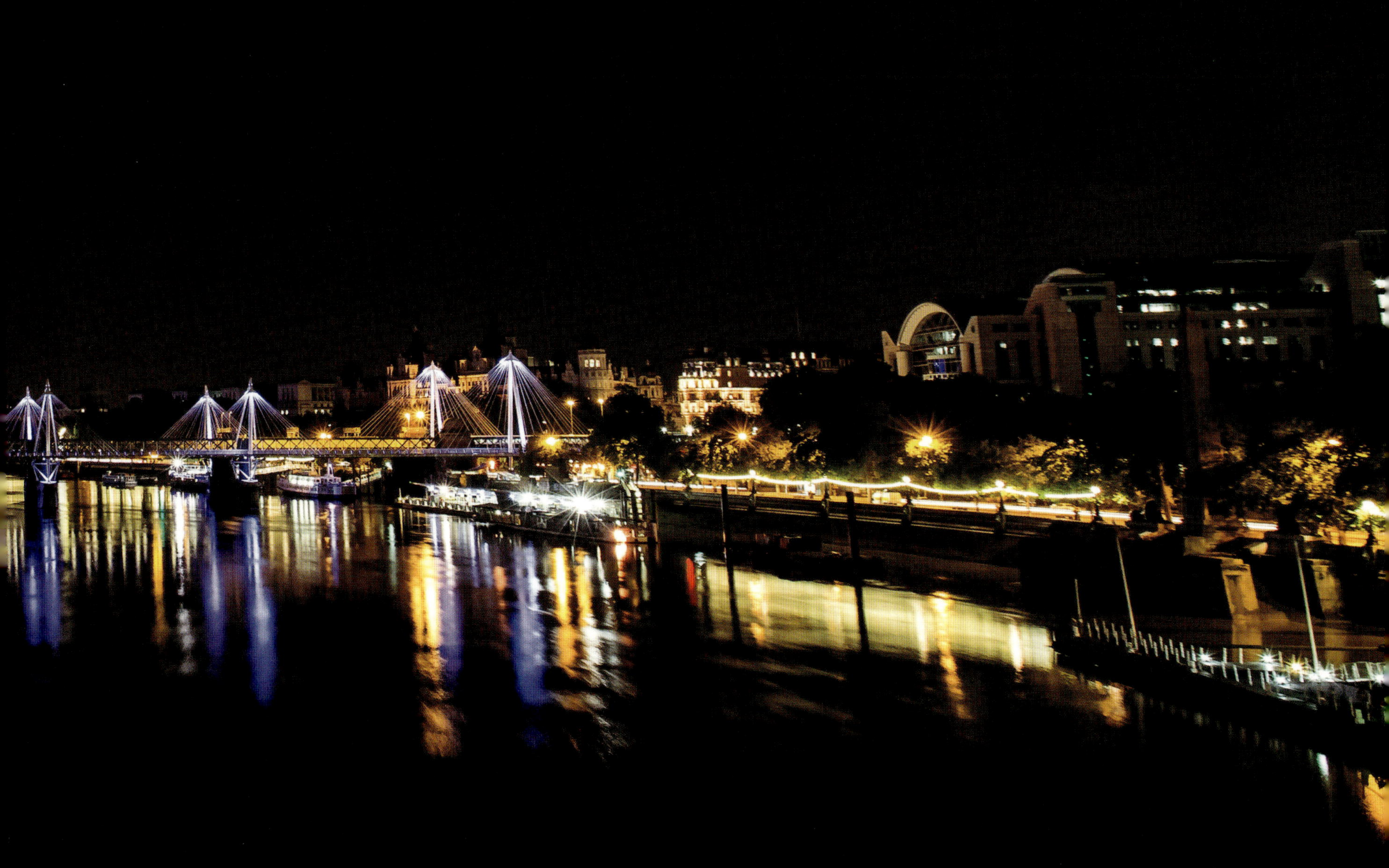

Previous page and this
page. Ryoji Ikeda's
Spectra directed a cluster
of 49 blue searchlights up
into the London night sky,
where, from a distance,
they appeared as a single
column of light.

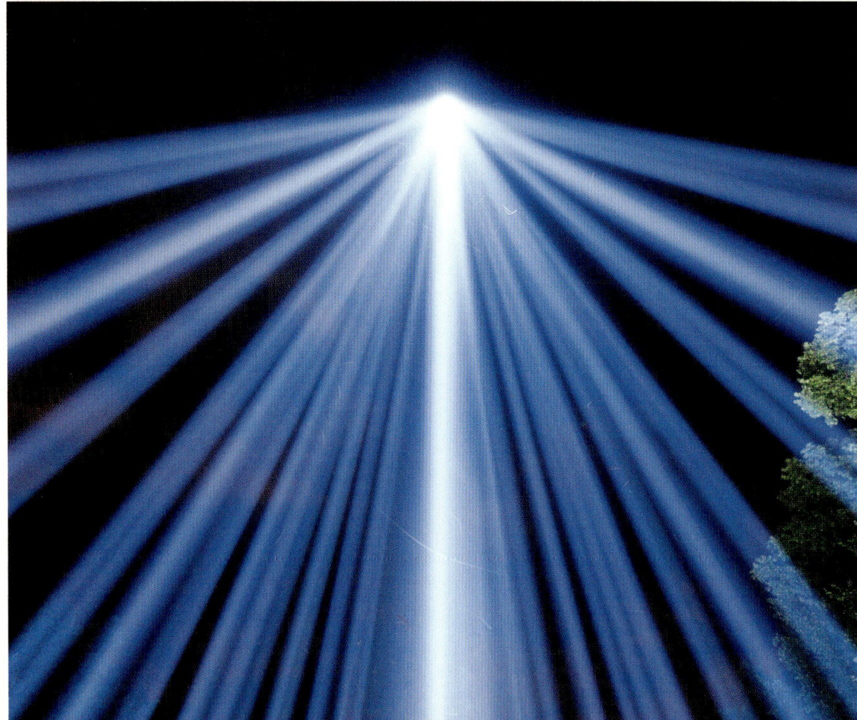

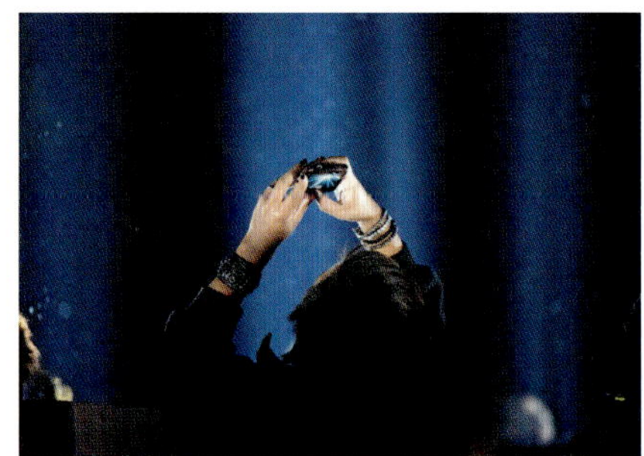

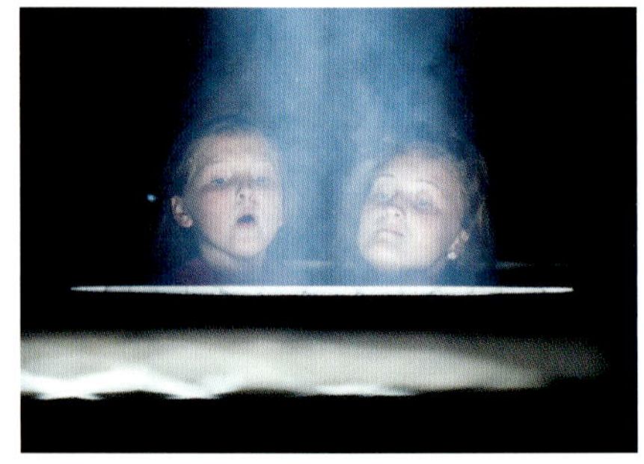

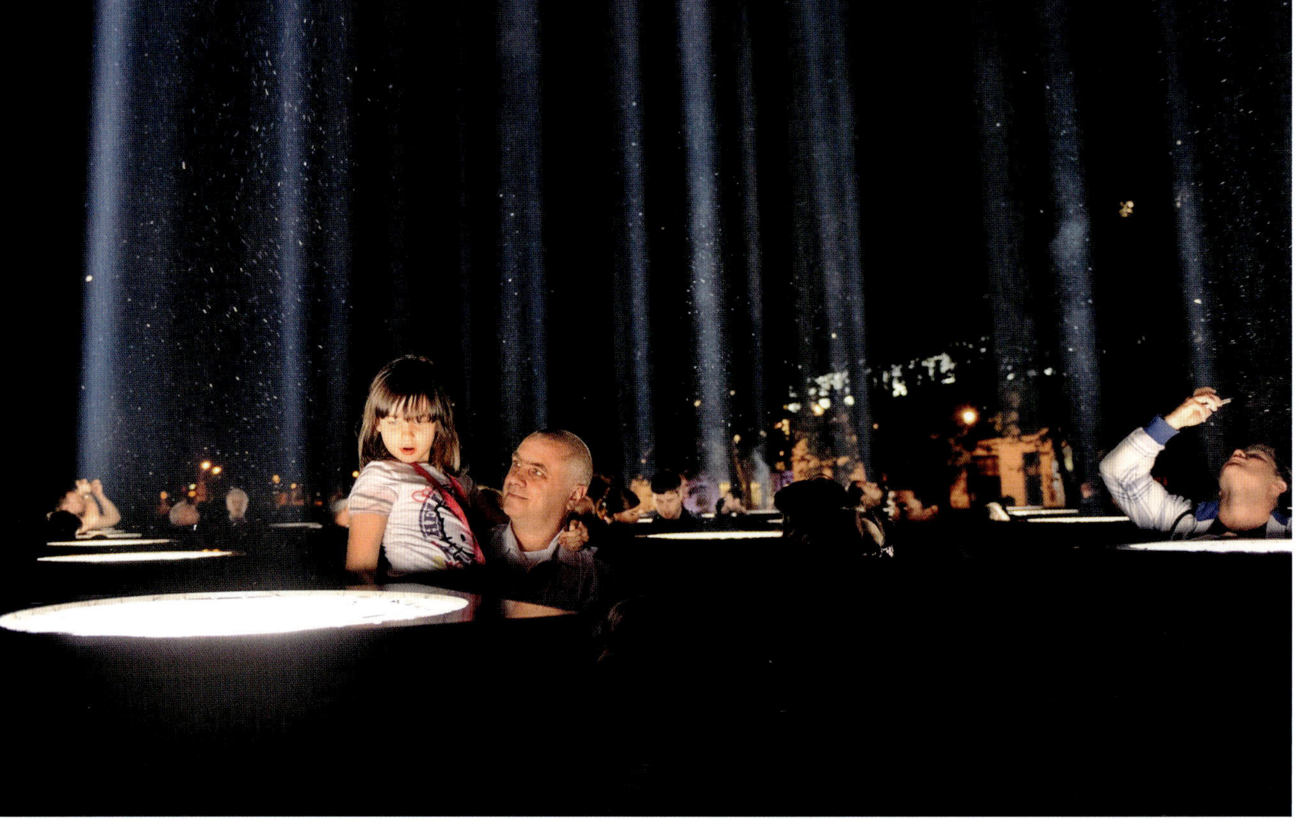

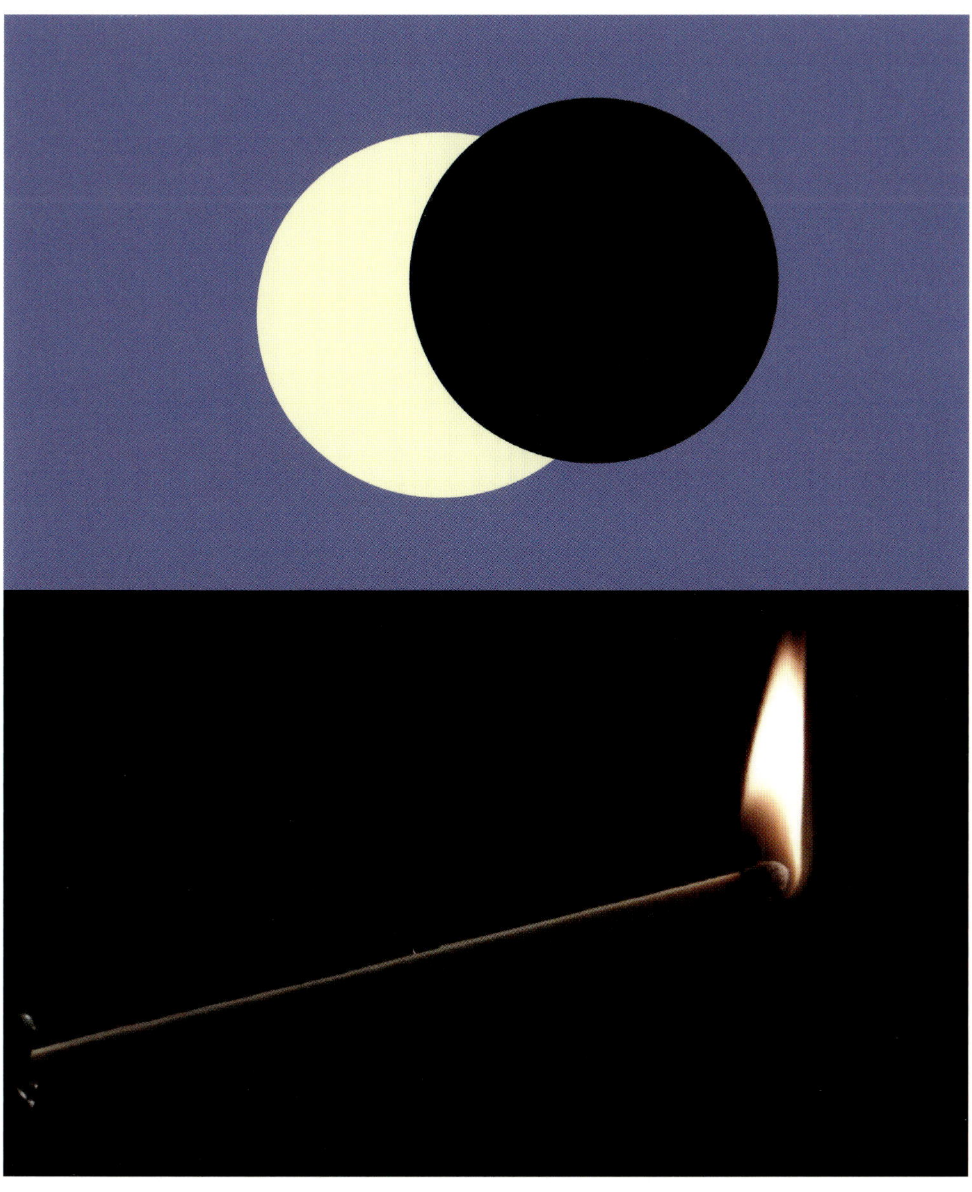

On 4 August 2014, the people of the United Kingdom were invited to participate in *LIGHTS OUT* by turning off their lights from 10pm to 11pm, leaving on a single light or candle for a shared moment of reflection. The event was called *LIGHTS OUT*, in reference to Sir Edward Grey's famous observation that 'the lights of Europe are going out and we shall not see them lit again in our lifetime'.

More than 16 million people around the country participated in marking the centenary of the outbreak of the First World War in this way, whether in the privacy of their own homes, or at one of the many communal events that took place across the nation. Over 1,000 local authorities, iconic buildings, national organisations — including the BBC and the Royal British Legion — parish councils and places of worship extinguished all but one of their lights to mark the occasion.

As part of this remarkable event, 14-18 NOW commissioned four international artists — Ryoji Ikeda, Nalini Malani, Bedwyr Williams, and Bob and Roberta Smith — to create public artworks in London, Edinburgh, Bangor and Belfast that responded to the idea of a single light continuing to shine through darkness. To tie them together, the artist Jeremy Deller designed a free-to-download app for the occasion; its four short films were viewable only on the four days leading up to the event.

Japanese artist Ryoji Ikeda's *Spectra* was a column of intense white light that punctuated the London sky from sunset until dawn for seven nights, emanating from 49 static high-powered searchlights based adjacent to the Palace of Westminster. The work was visible across London, and audiences could also walk within the installation and experience an accompanying sound composition of pure sine waves.

Working with the Edinburgh Art Festival, visual artist Nalini Malani developed a major new outdoor presentation of her highly acclaimed work *In Search of Vanished Blood*, illuminating the western and southern facades of the Scottish National Gallery with large-scale projections and shadow play. A choreographed succession of images of war, including actual film footage of the Cameron Highlanders marching to war, was combined with a powerful soundtrack to create a mesmerising reflection on war and its impacts.

Nalini Malani transformed
the Scottish National
Gallery in Edinburgh with
choreographed projections
set to a dramatic soundtrack.

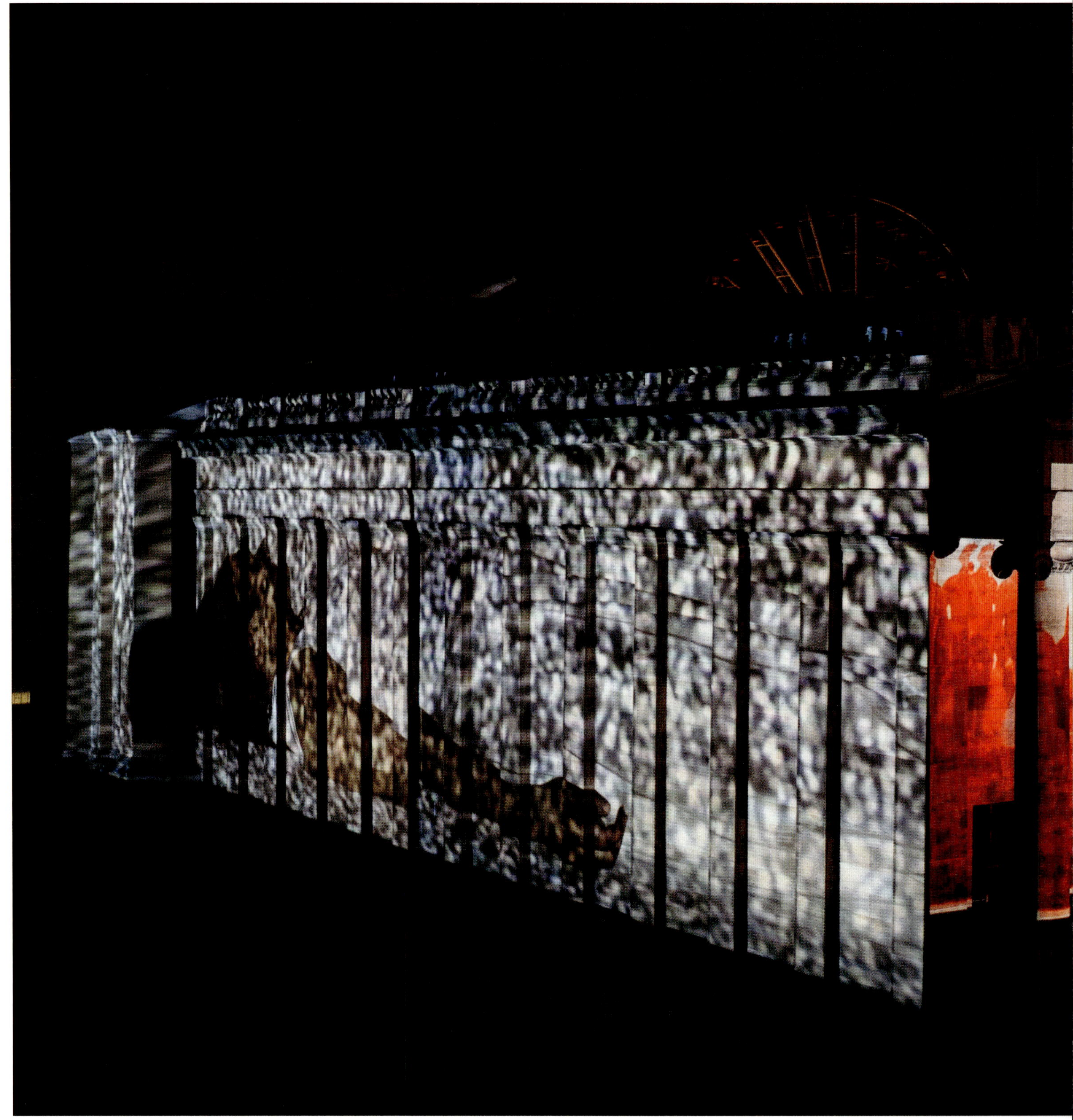

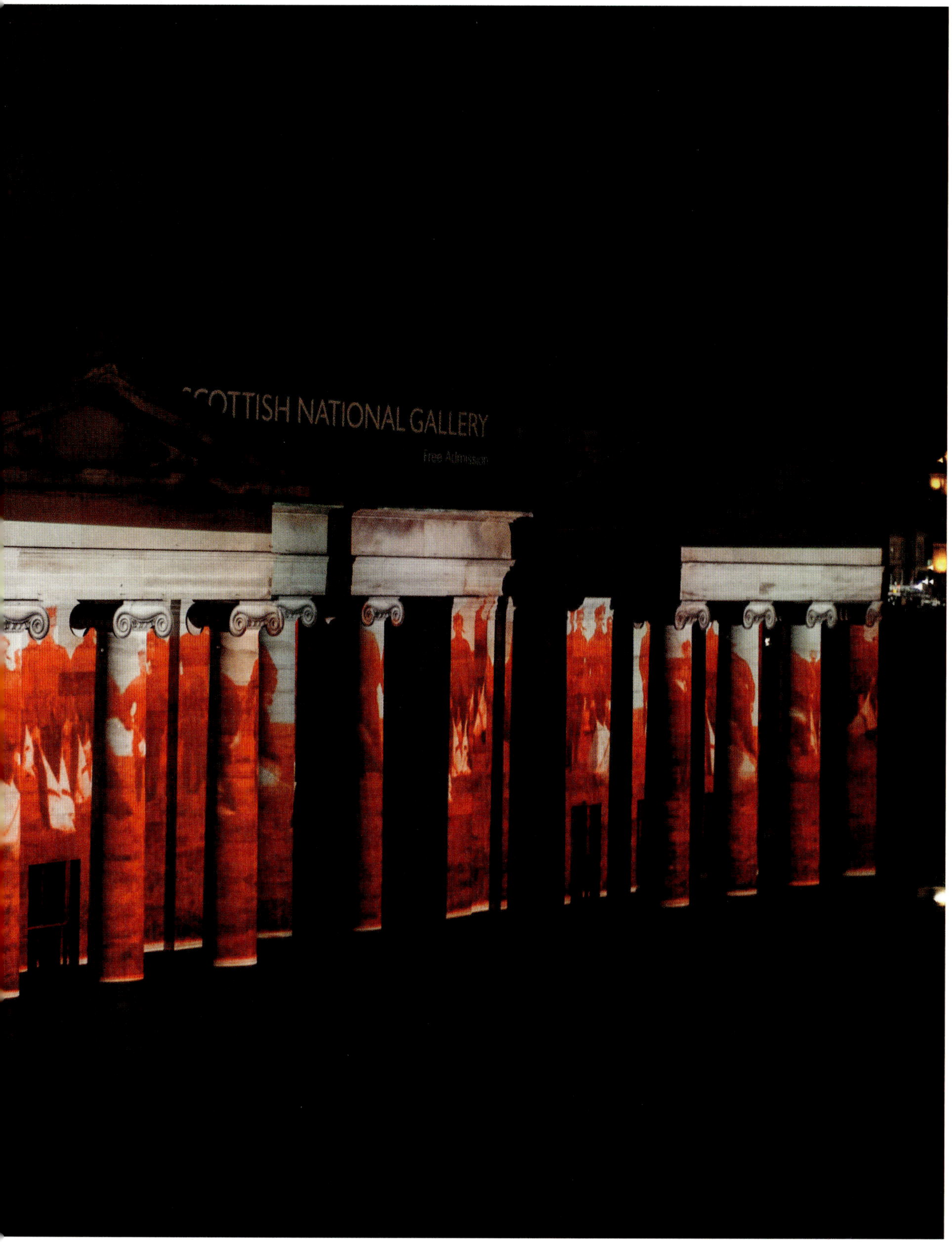

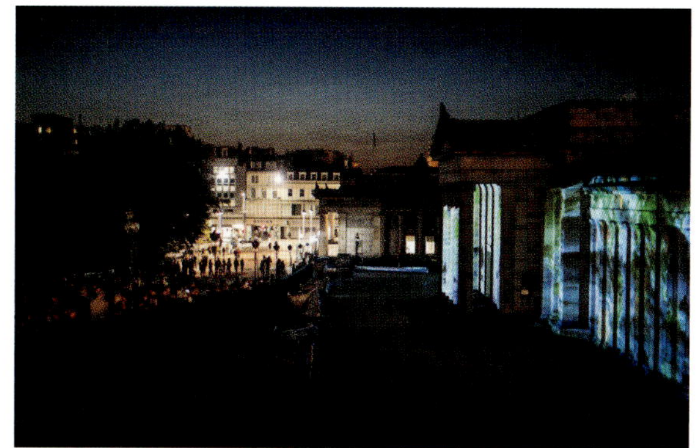

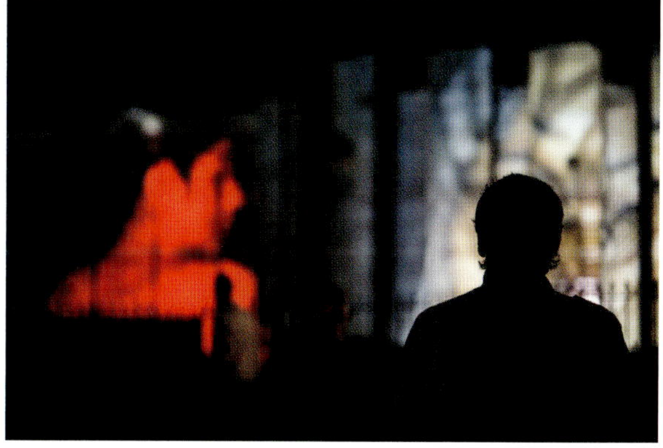

Bob and Roberta Smith's work, in partnership with Factotum, was called *What Unites Human Beings, Ears, Eyes, Loves, Hopes and Toes is Huge and Wonderful. What Divides Human Beings is Small and Mean*. The title was taken from the artist's *Letter to an Unknown Soldier* (see pages 48–53) and embodied his belief that the common goals humanity aims for — love, peace and wellbeing — outweigh the things that divide us. The artist took over the East Lawn of the City Hall in Belfast to create an illuminating installation of the statement, using letters designed and constructed together with local artists and community groups, each containing candles that were then lit by city residents in a moment of shared reflection.

Bedwyr Williams' work *Traw*, co-commissioned with Artes Mundi, took the form of a large-scale video and sound installation at the site of the North Wales Memorial Arch in Bangor. Combining photographs found in the Cymru 1914 archive with the slowed-down sound of a ticking clock (*traw* means 'to strike'), Williams created a montage of local personnel affected by the war. Excising all uniforms and references to rank, close-up faces instead drew focus to individual personalities and personal sacrifice in a war where death was measured in the millions.

UK-wide, 4 August 2014

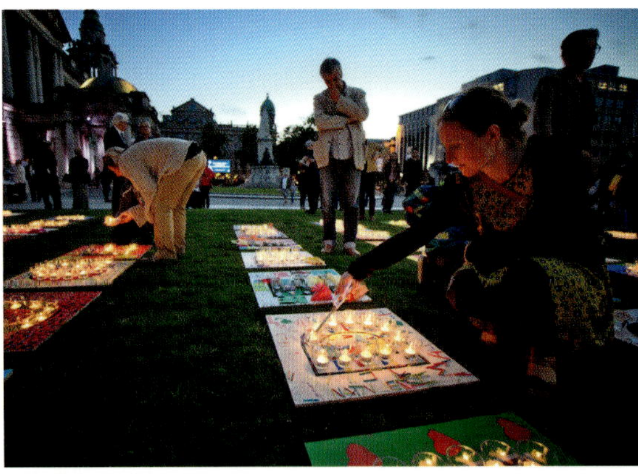

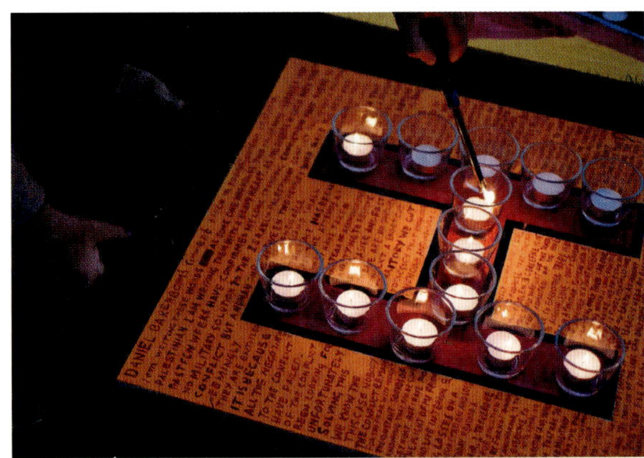

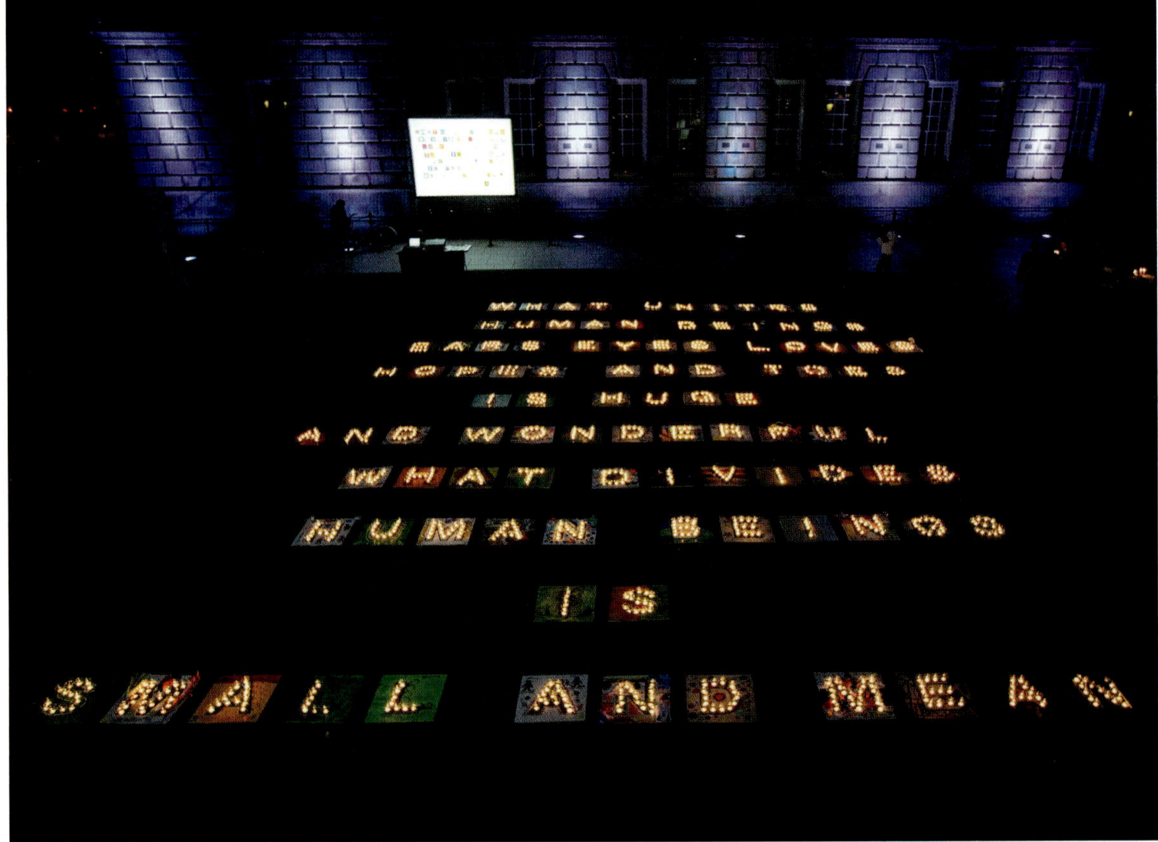

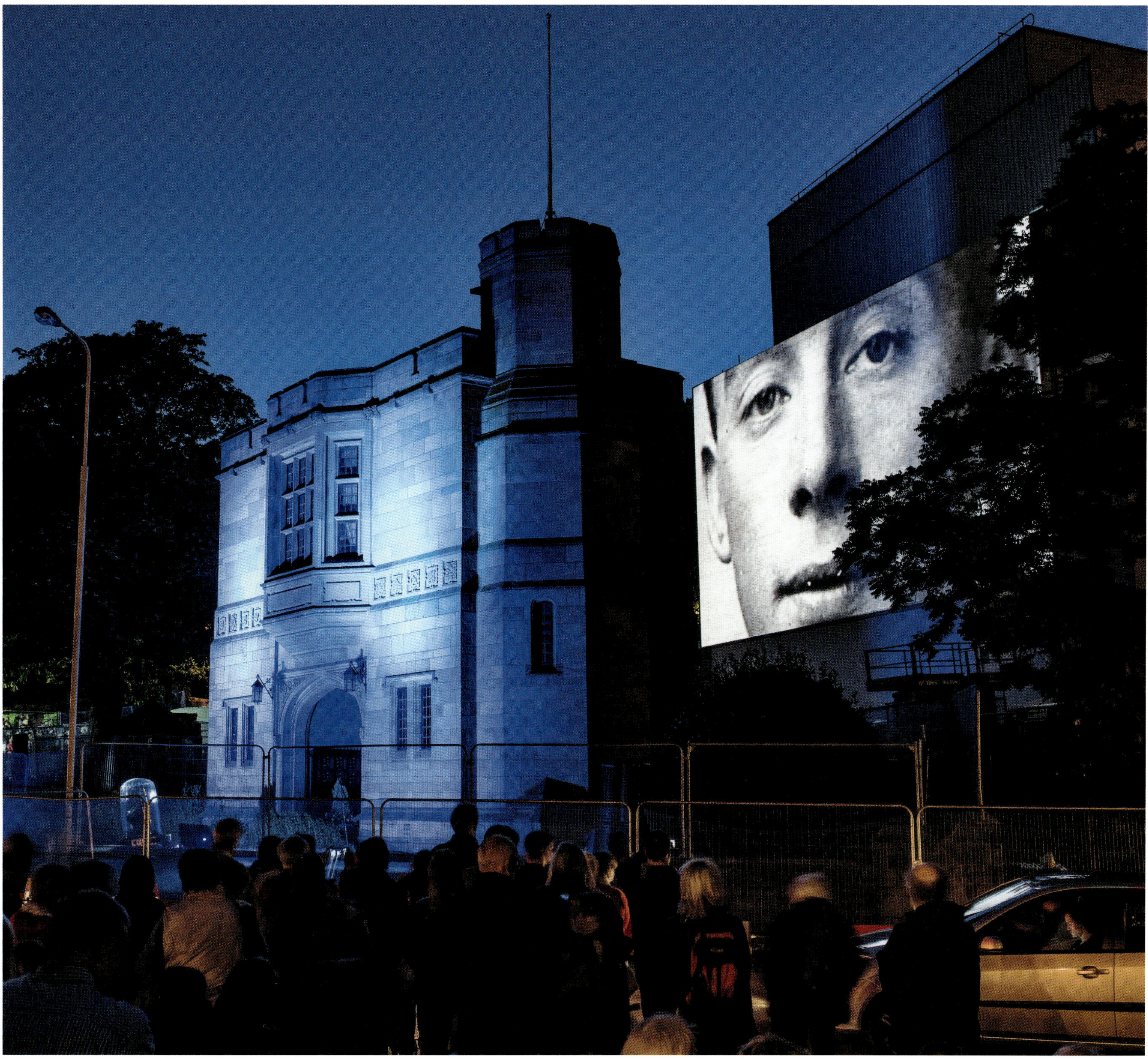

BLACK DOG:
THE DREAMS
OF PAUL NASH

Dave McKean

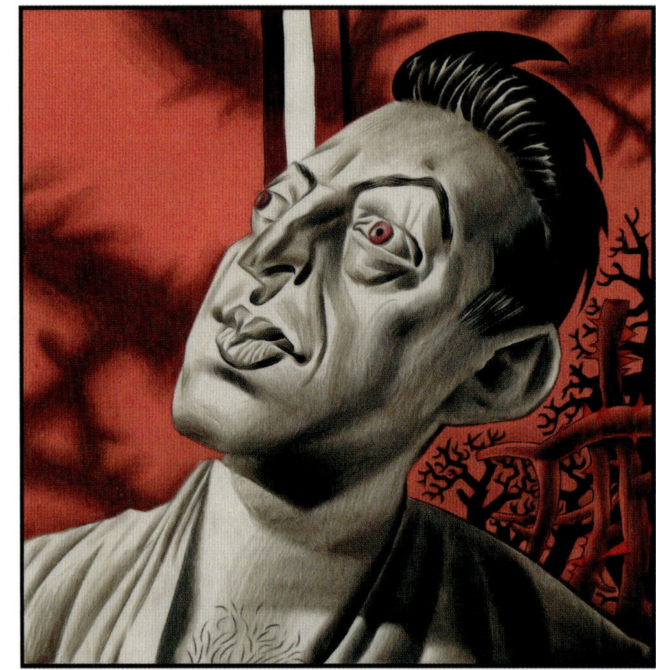

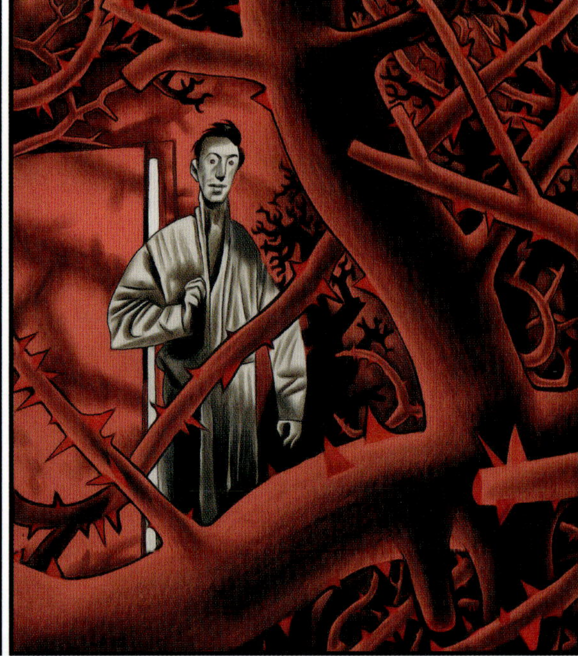

'I am no longer an artist.
I am a messenger who will
bring back word … to those
who want the war to go on
forever … it will have a bitter
truth, and may it burn their
lousy souls.'

Paul Nash, writing home from the
Western Front

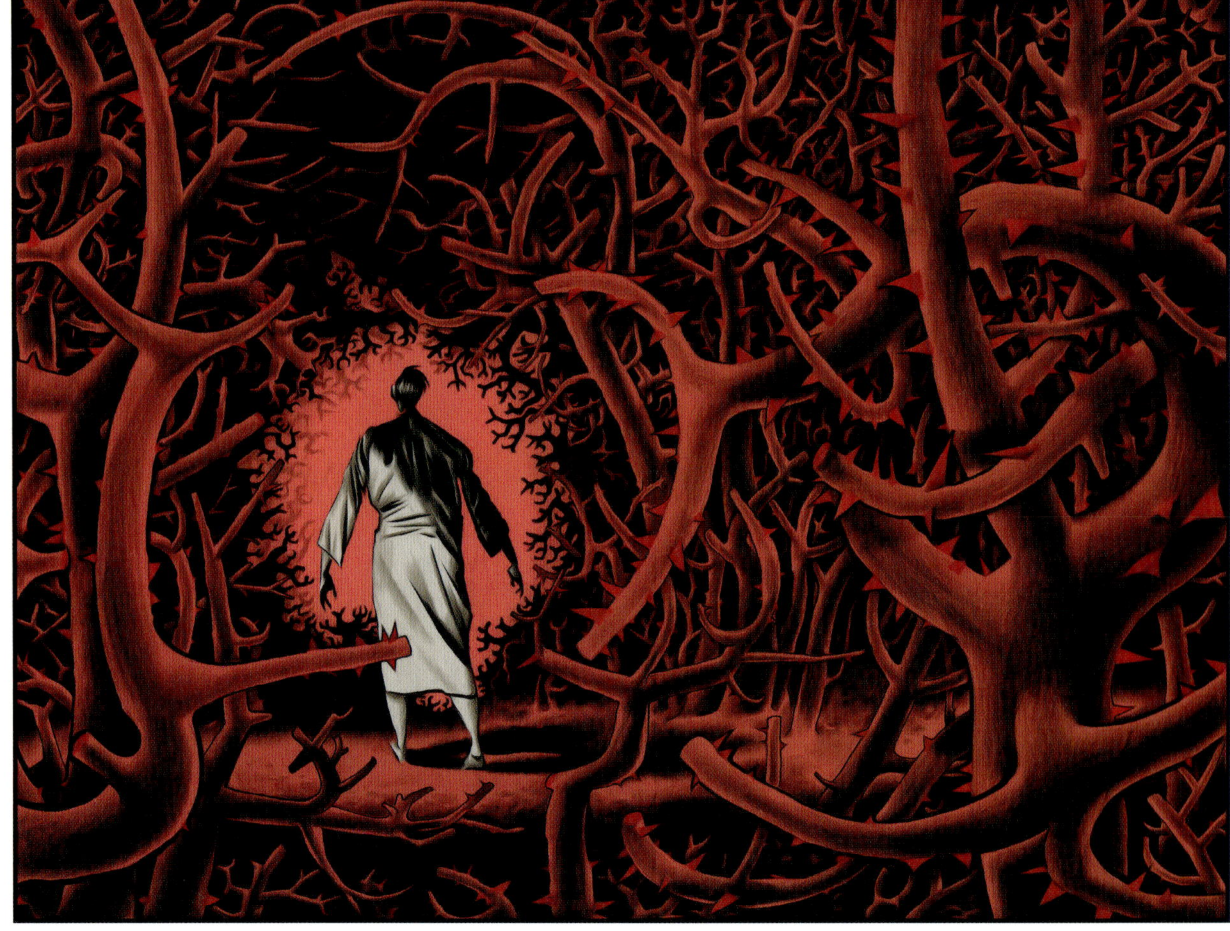

The painter Paul Nash joined the British Army when he was 25 years old, six weeks after the start of the First World War. After serving as an officer in the Ypres Salient, on the Western Front, a broken rib forced him to return to London for medical treatment in the summer of 1917. During his convalescence, Nash exhibited a group of artworks depicting the Western Front and, as a result, he was commissioned to return to Belgium as an official war artist.

In Nash's absence, Ypres had been the scene of one of the war's most brutal battles, and the painter was appalled and outraged by what he returned to – both the destruction of the landscape, and the plight of the troops stationed there. Compelled to respond, he wrote, 'I realise no one in England knows what the scene of the war is like … If I can, I will show them.'

During his second spell at the front, Nash made dozens of sketches. Then, back in England he translated these sketches into paintings that were shocking, dark and bleak: muddy landscapes, tiny figures that move miserably across obliterated landscapes. With their jagged edges and harsh contrasts, they captured the hopelessness of life at the front, and made clear that the natural landscape had been tortured by war into something weird, frightening and inhumane. The paintings made a huge impression when they were first exhibited, helping to change public perceptions about the war.

Opposite. An image belonging to a sequence in McKean's graphic novel in which Nash finds a rare and precious kingfisher's egg — symbolic of the fragility of nature amid the destruction of war.

Right. Nash's troubled state of mind is set against the background of a looming war.

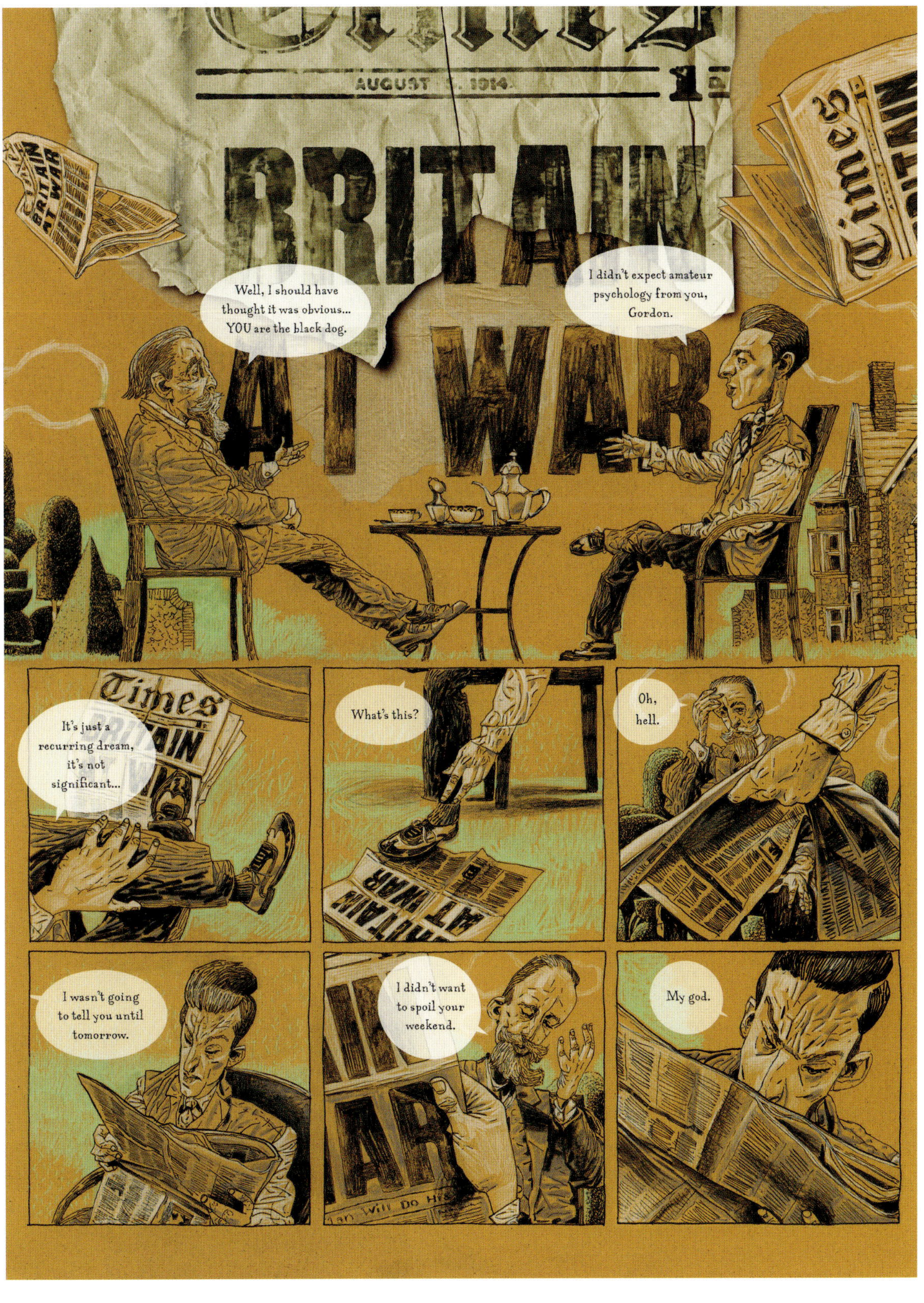

In 2016, the acclaimed illustrator, film-maker and musician Dave McKean was inspired by the work of Nash to create a graphic-novel based on the artist's work, thoughts and dreams, entitled *Black Dog: The Dreams of Paul Nash*. McKean wanted to explore Nash's 'dream-/nightmare-like battlefields of the war' and their place within the Modernist and Surrealist movements of the early 20th century. He took the title of the novel from Nash, too, who often referred to a black dog that haunted his dreams — a sign of foreboding, a warning.

In May, McKean's work was issued as a limited-edition book before being published by Dark Horse as a graphic novel in October. *Black Dog: The Dreams of Paul Nash* launched with a series of multimedia performances, with text, images and music performed by McKean and musicians including Matthew Sharp. The book was nominated for an Eisner Award in 2017.

As well as a tribute to one of the most powerful artists of the 20th century, *Black Dog: The Dreams of Paul Nash* is a meditation on conflict, loyalty and creativity in war.

Kendal Town Hall, 28 May 2016 / House of Illustration, London, 13 July 2016 / Rye Arts Festival, 18 September 2016 / Revelation St Mary's, Ashford, 11 November 2016 / Tate Britain, 13 November 2016 / The Lakes International Comic Art Festival, Brewery Arts Centre, 16 October 2016 / QUAD, Derby, 17 June 2017 / St Mary's Church, Rye, 18 September 2018

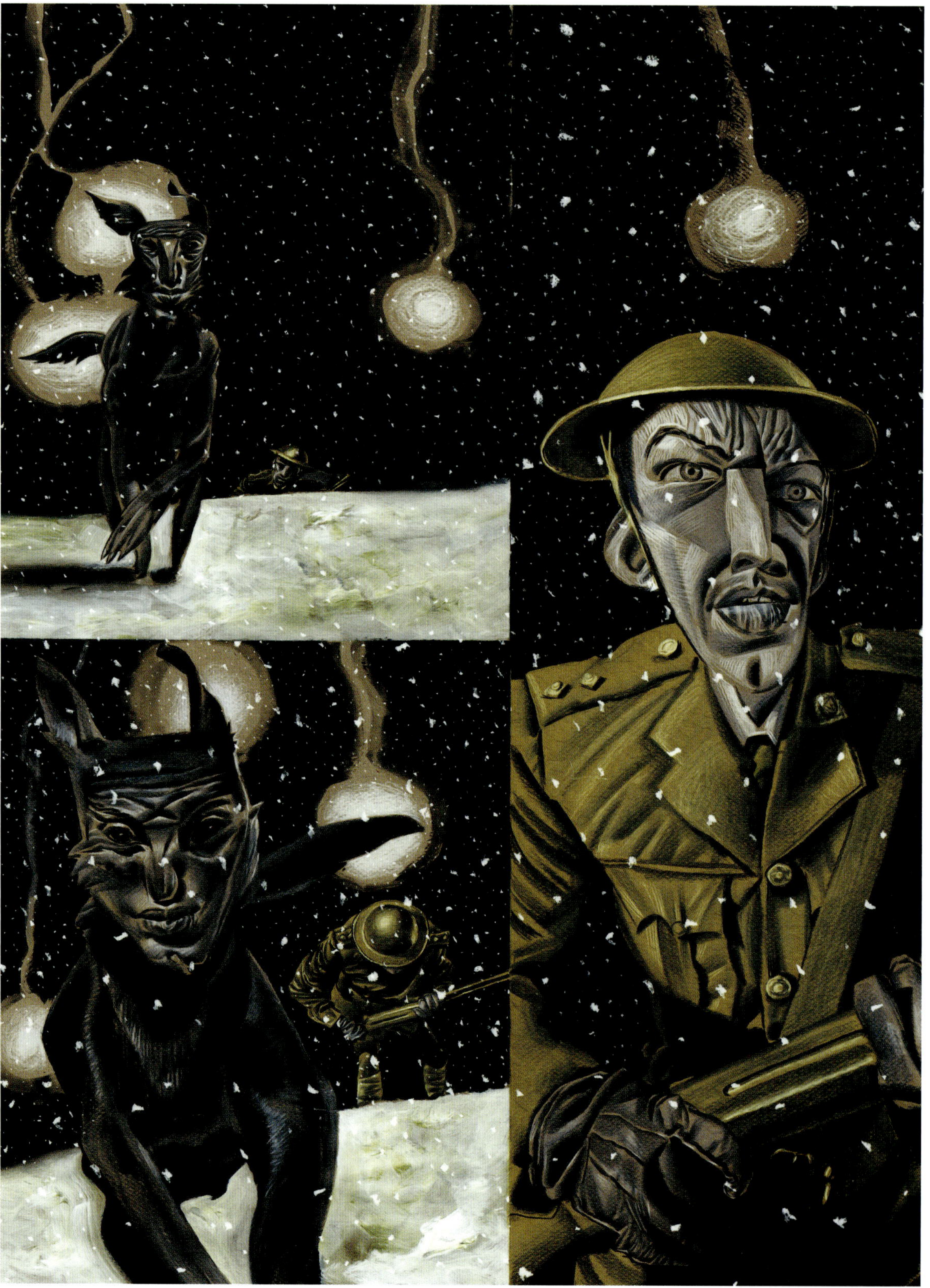

The black dog of Nash's imagination is a recurring presence as the world descends into war, giving McKean's storytelling a dreamlike, foreboding quality.

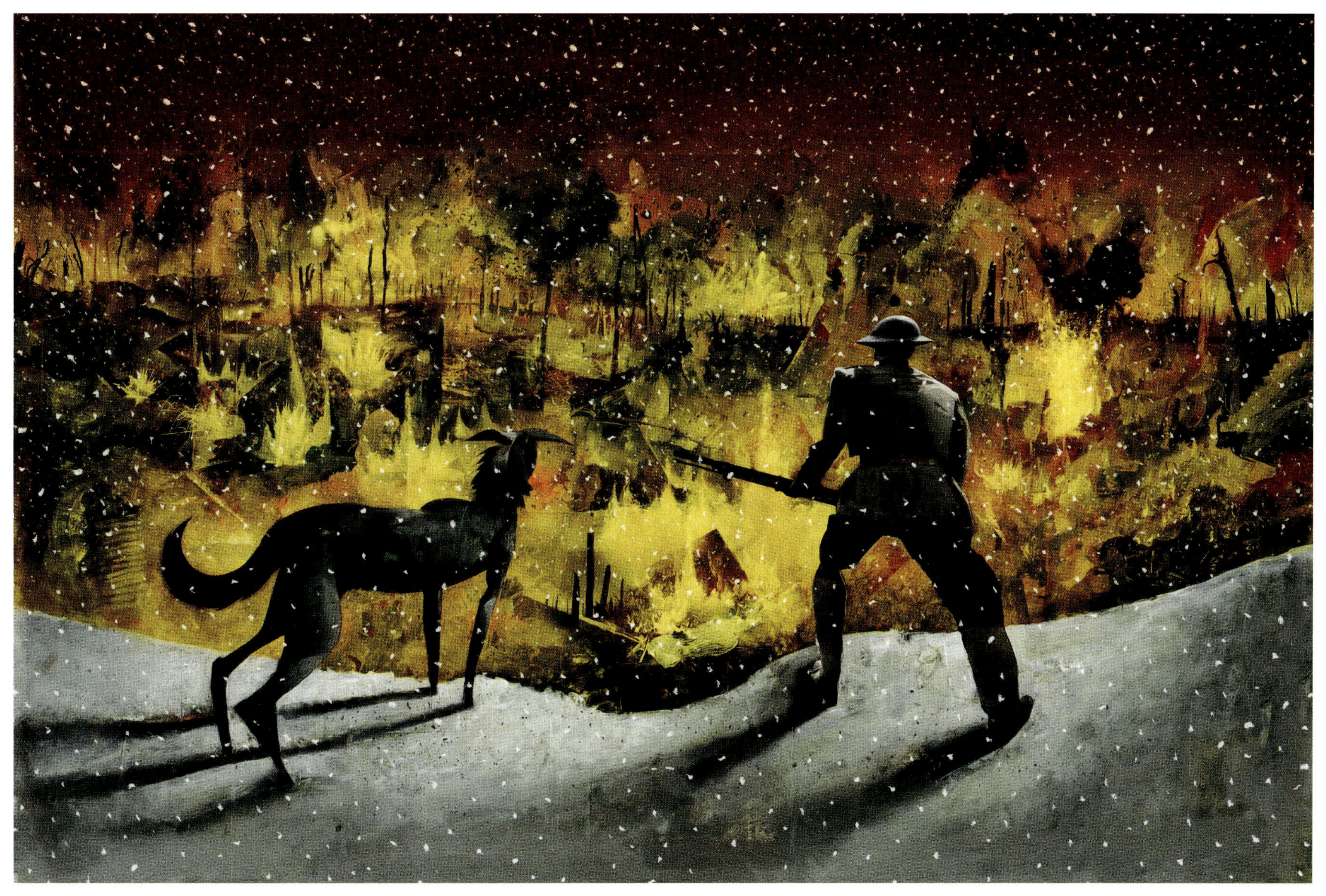

Mark Anderson took the
Dadaists' use of the chaotic,
disorienting and occasionally
grotesque to create a work
that questioned the First
World War.

FURIOUS FOLLY

Mark Anderson

In Zurich, 100 years ago, a group of radical young artists faced with the horror and the folly of the First World War began to question the role of art in a broken society. While millions were losing their lives at the front, art that was restricted to the few and merely concerned with ideas of beauty had begun to feel false. The madness of the battlefield and the futility of the war led these artists to a new artistic language that deliberately eschewed structure and meaning, rejecting everything that had gone before in an attempt to reflect the times they were living in. The movement that they founded — and named Dada — embraced the chaos, aggression and senselessness of the war, and their approach soon inspired others in Berlin, Paris and New York.

For *Furious Folly*, Mark Anderson revisited the Dadaists' anti-war sentiment, and employed the same ethos to create an immersive, large-scale, open-air event that questioned the war afresh. It took place as night fell, staged in the empty space between the two lines of battle — No Man's Land. Performing to around 2,000 people a night, it immersed its audience in a war-torn landscape, made evocative, disorienting and moving with the use of sound, devices set in motion, pyrotechnics and performance.

Railing against the inconceivable madness of the First World War, just as the Dadaists had a century before, *Furious Folly* challenged the inhumanity and senselessness of conflicts past and present.

Magdalen College School, Oxford, 17 — 18 June 2016 / Sutton Park, Birmingham, 8 — 9 July 2016 / Preston Park, Stockton-on-Tees, 4 — 5 August 2016 / Mount Pleasant Park and Ride site, Weymouth, 20 — 21 September 2018

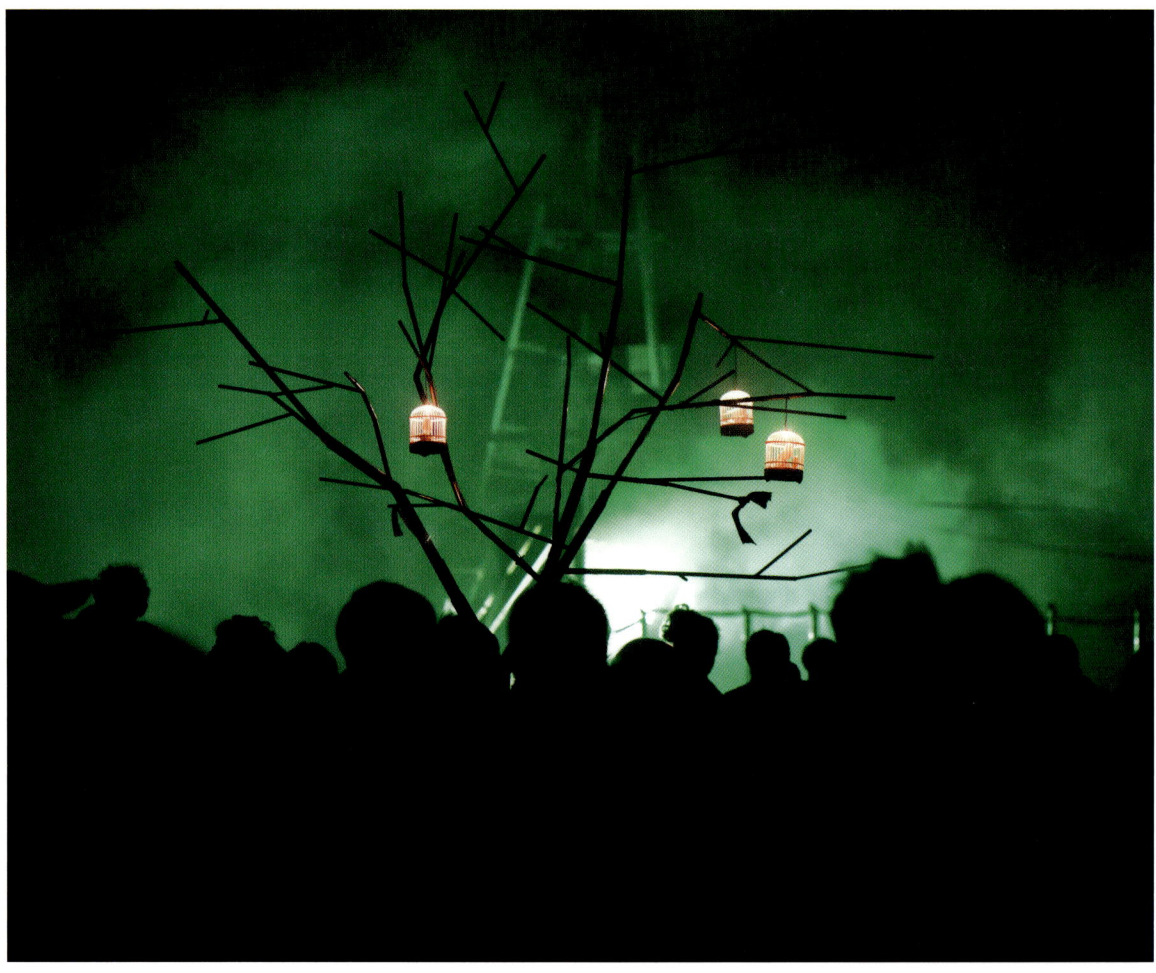

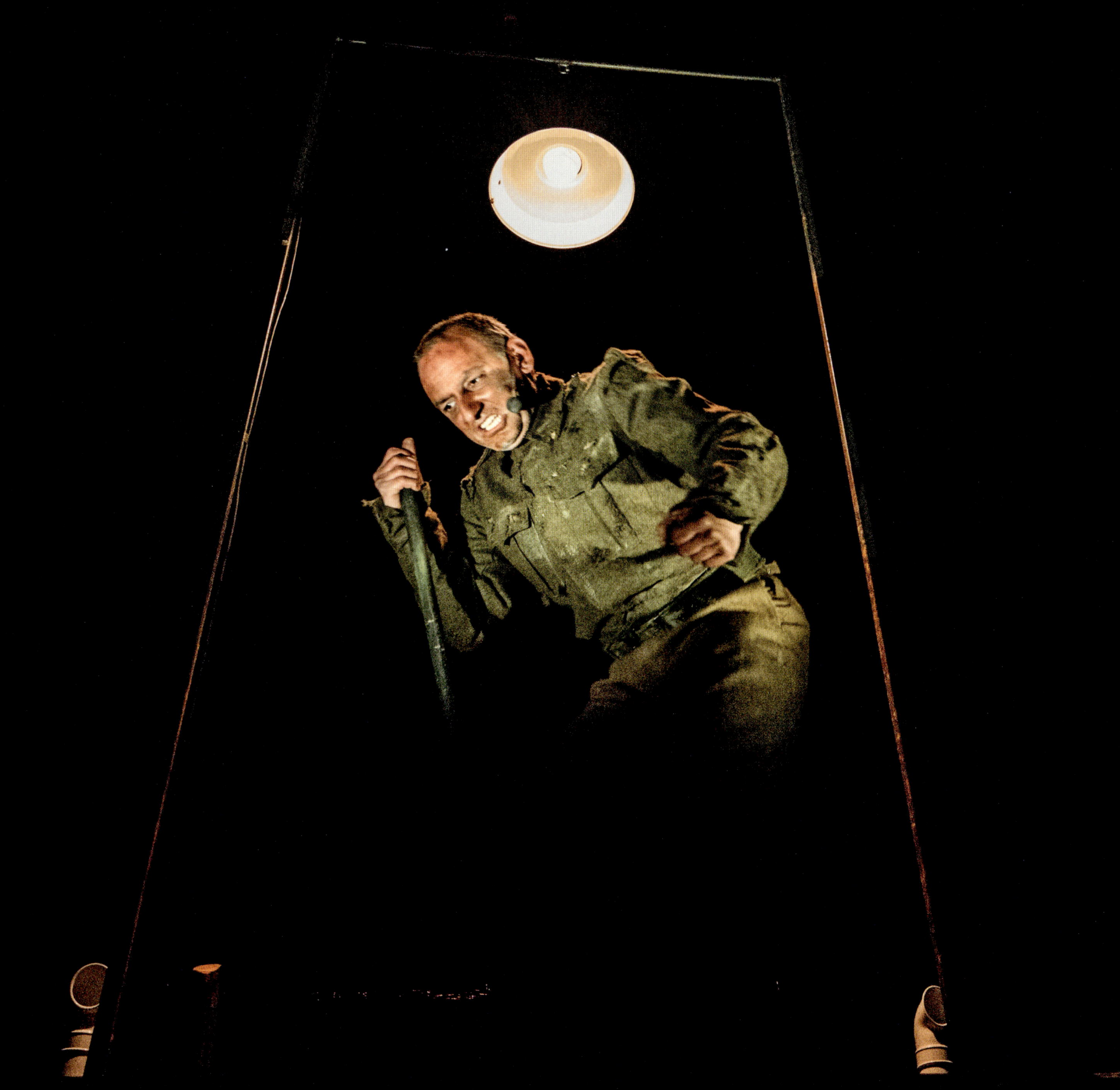

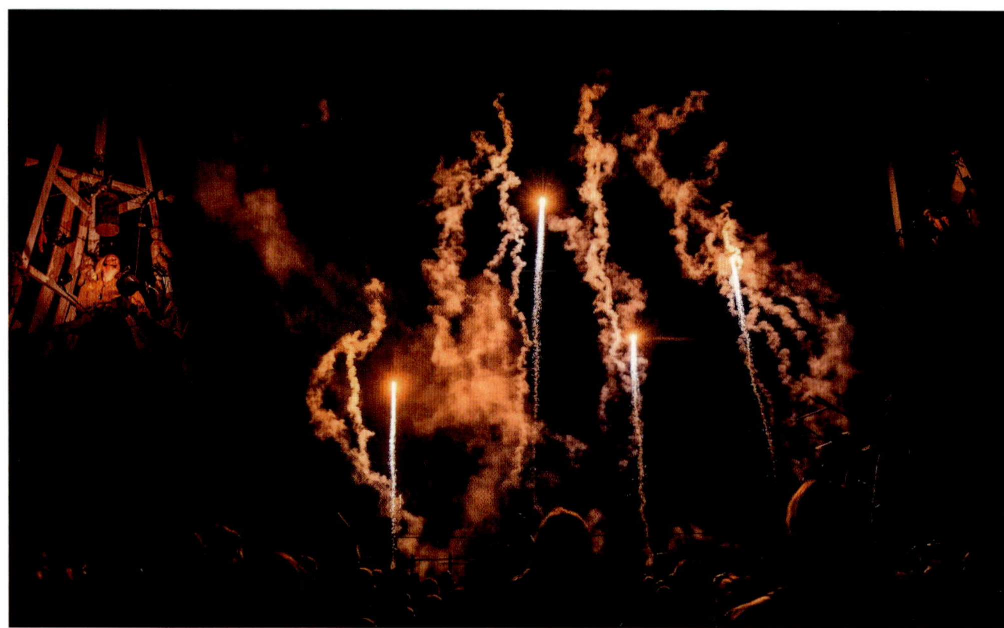

'In Zurich in 1915, losing interest in
the slaughterhouse of the world war,
we turned to the fine arts. While the
thunder of the batteries rumbled in the
distance, we pasted, we recited, we
versified, we sang with all our soul.
We searched for an elementary art
that would, we thought, save mankind
from the furious folly of these times.'

Hans Arp, founding member of the Dada movement

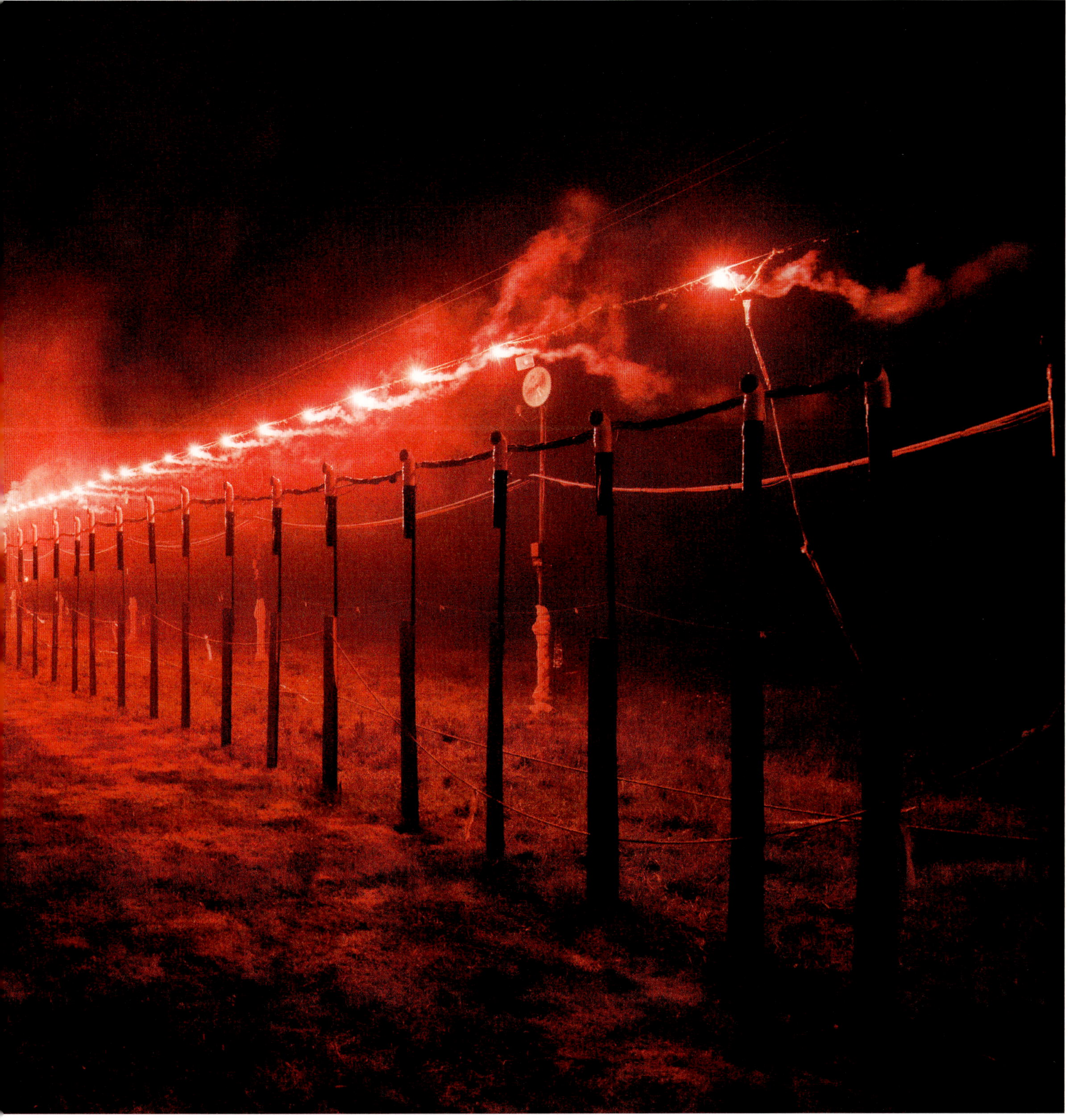

For each performance, the location was transformed into No Man's Land circa 1915, a disorienting nightmare of sound, light and movement.

ALL THE HILLS AND VALES ALONG

James MacMillan

This five-movement choral work received its chamber premiere in the intimate setting of Cumnock Old Church, under the conductorship of both Eamonn Dougan (shown here) and James MacMillan.

Charles Hamilton Sorley, one of the great British war poets, was promoted to the rank of captain in August 1915 aged just 20, having postponed his education to volunteer for service in the British Army. Two months later, he was shot and killed at the Battle of Loos.

James MacMillan, one of Britain's leading composers, chose five of Sorley's poems for the text to *All the Hills and Vales Along*, a major new oratorio written to commemorate the Armistice. MacMillan composed this powerful work especially for internationally acclaimed British tenor Ian Bostridge, who performed it in two distinct arrangements.

MacMillan conducted the world premiere of the chamber version alongside Eamonn Dougan at MacMillan's Cumnock Tryst festival, before Gianandrea Noseda directed the world premiere of the orchestral version by the London Symphony Orchestra.

Cumnock Old Church, Cumnock, 6 October 2018 / Barbican, London, 4 November 2018 / BBC Radio 3

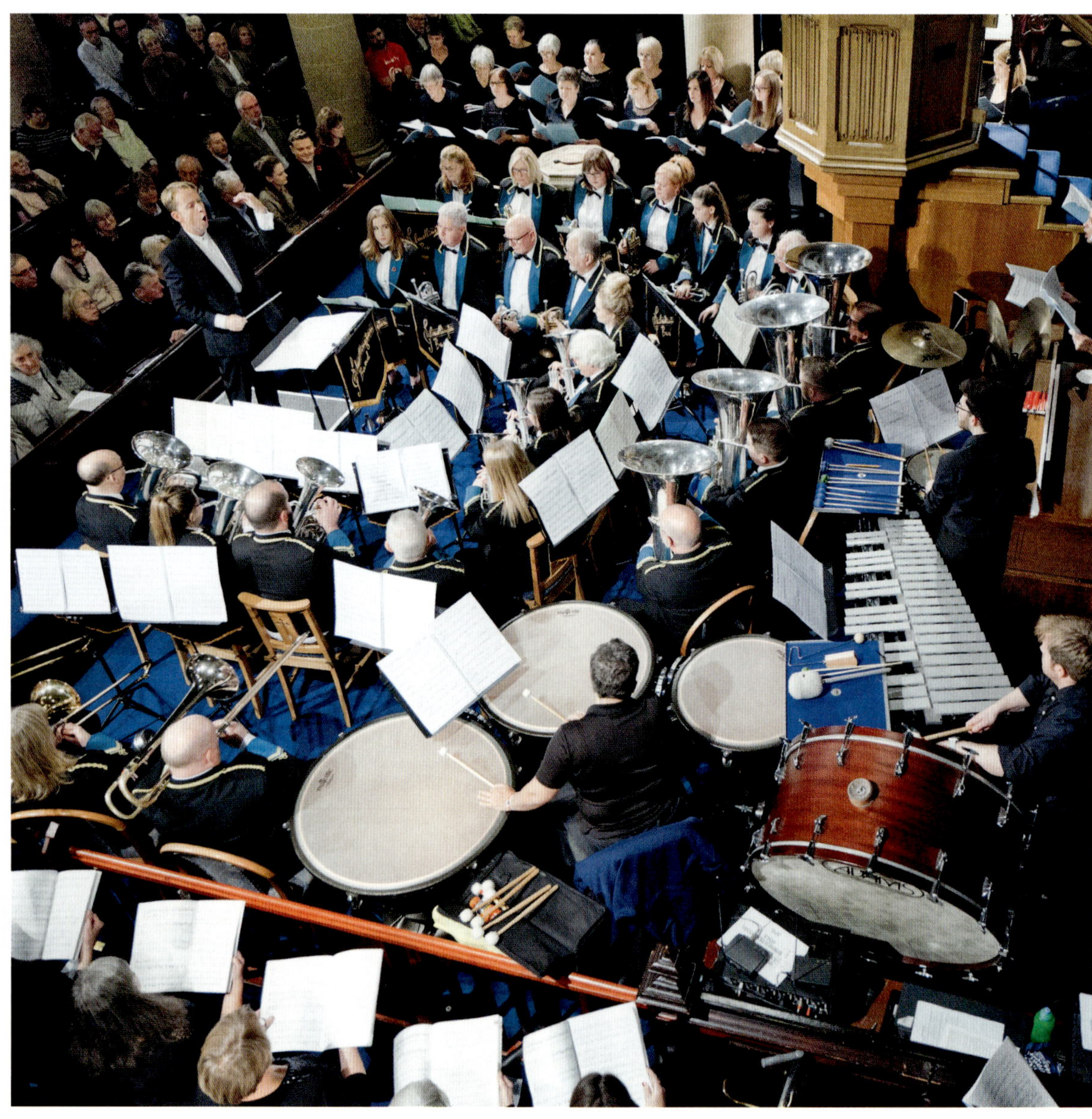

14-18 NOW AT WOMAD

Siyaya

An exuberant performance by Siyaya told the story of Zimbabwe's involvement in the First World War and that country's struggle for liberation.

During the first season of centenary commemorations, 14-18 NOW worked with the WOMAD Festival to commission a new work by Zimbabwean music, dance and theatre collective Siyaya. Since 1982, WOMAD has showcased the role of music and performance in world culture and, like 14-18 NOW, WOMAD recognises the vital part played by the arts in the maintenance and enrichment of a society's shared heritage.

Originally from Bulawayo in Zimbabwe, a country that experienced great internal conflict throughout the 20th century, Siyaya's performance showed how a healthy musical culture can help to sustain communities through bloodshed and political upheaval.

The Shona name *Siyaya* means 'we are on the move', a fitting name for this high-energy group of musicians, percussionists, vocalists and dancers. Their outreach work with schools and community programmes has been a living demonstration of the persistence of culture in the face of tumultuous social change. This new work, created specifically for the 2014 concert, was performed at the festival alongside their traditional repertoire of songs and dances.

Charlton Park, Wiltshire, 24 — 27 July 2014

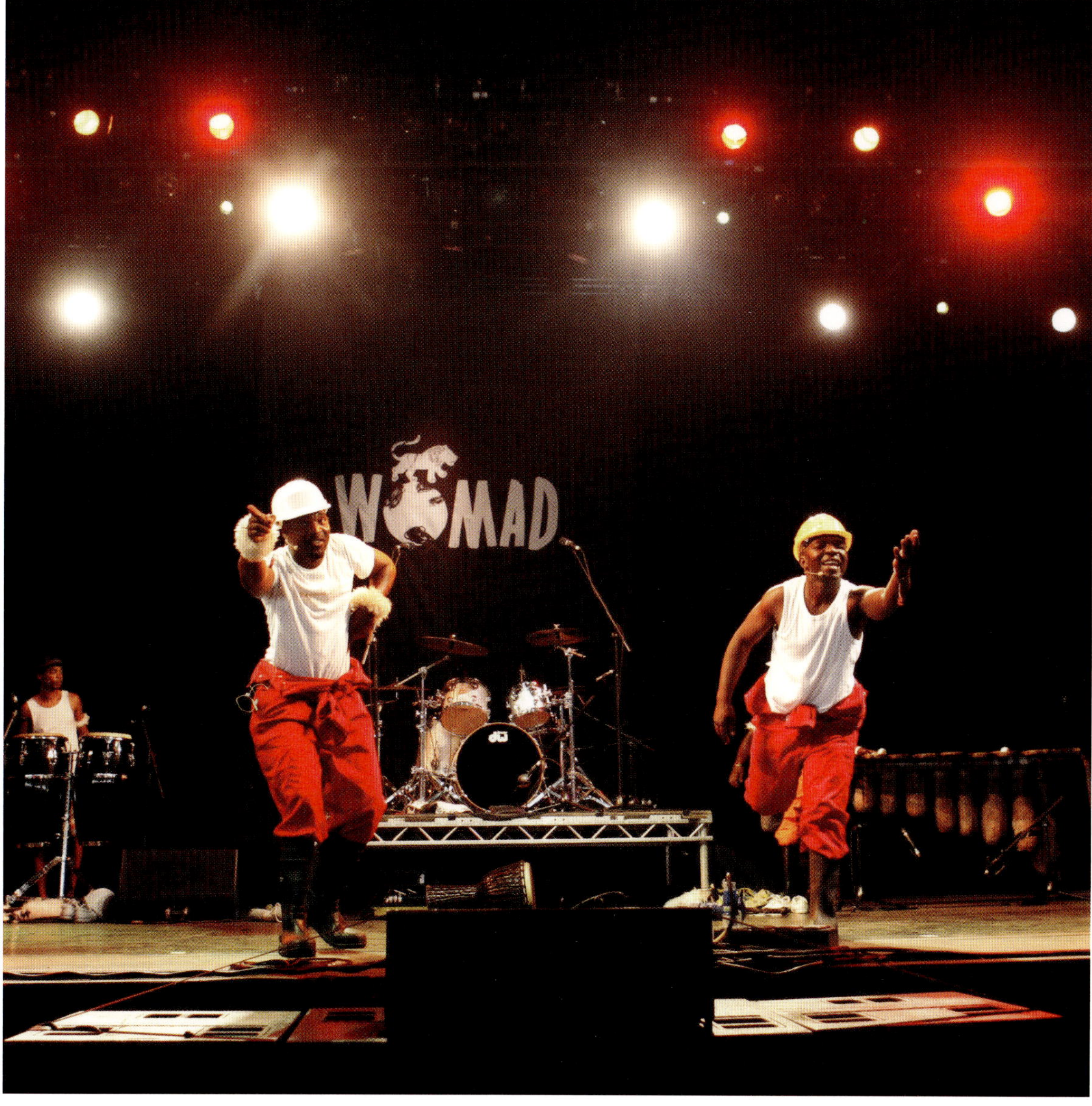

GARDEN WITHIN A GARDEN

Imran Qureshi

The garden is usually a place of peace and safety. But in 2016, in a co-commission with Cartwright Hall Art Gallery, and in partnership with Yorkshire Festival, two parks in Bradford hosted new gardens that provided neither refuge from conflict, nor a haven from the outside world. Instead, inspired by the history of the million-strong Indian Army that fought alongside the British in the First World War, Pakistani artist Imran Qureshi transformed these spaces into zones in which light and dark mixed, and horror and hope collided.

Qureshi lives and works in Lahore, a region that as part of the British Raj sent many Sikh, Muslim and Hindu soldiers to fight in the war. It was their experiences of being at war in a distant land and a hostile climate that informed the Bradford gardens. Qureshi is known for his large-scale installations and for exploring the delicate style and intricate techniques of the 16th-century Mughal art of miniature painting. He uses both approaches to reflect upon contemporary conflicts, and the complex interplay between Islamic and European history and culture.

Rather than being constructed from plants, the Bradford gardens were painted directly onto the paving using acrylics. The first, in City Park, was a vibrant circular work in blue. The second, in the Mughal Water Gardens in Lister Park, used a more sombre palette of black and grey, with subtle splashes of red. An accompanying display of photographs and videos of Qureshi's work was held in adjacent Cartwright Hall. Alongside, a broad engagement programme ensured schools and community groups benefited from the project, with the creation of other commissions in photography, calligraphy, sculpture, song and video by seven Bradford artists.

Garden within a Garden highlighted the experiences of those from around the world who made such a profound contribution to the war effort, and acted as a reminder that although war creates division, it can also bring people together.

City Park and the Mughal Water Gardens, Bradford, 22 June — 30 October 2016

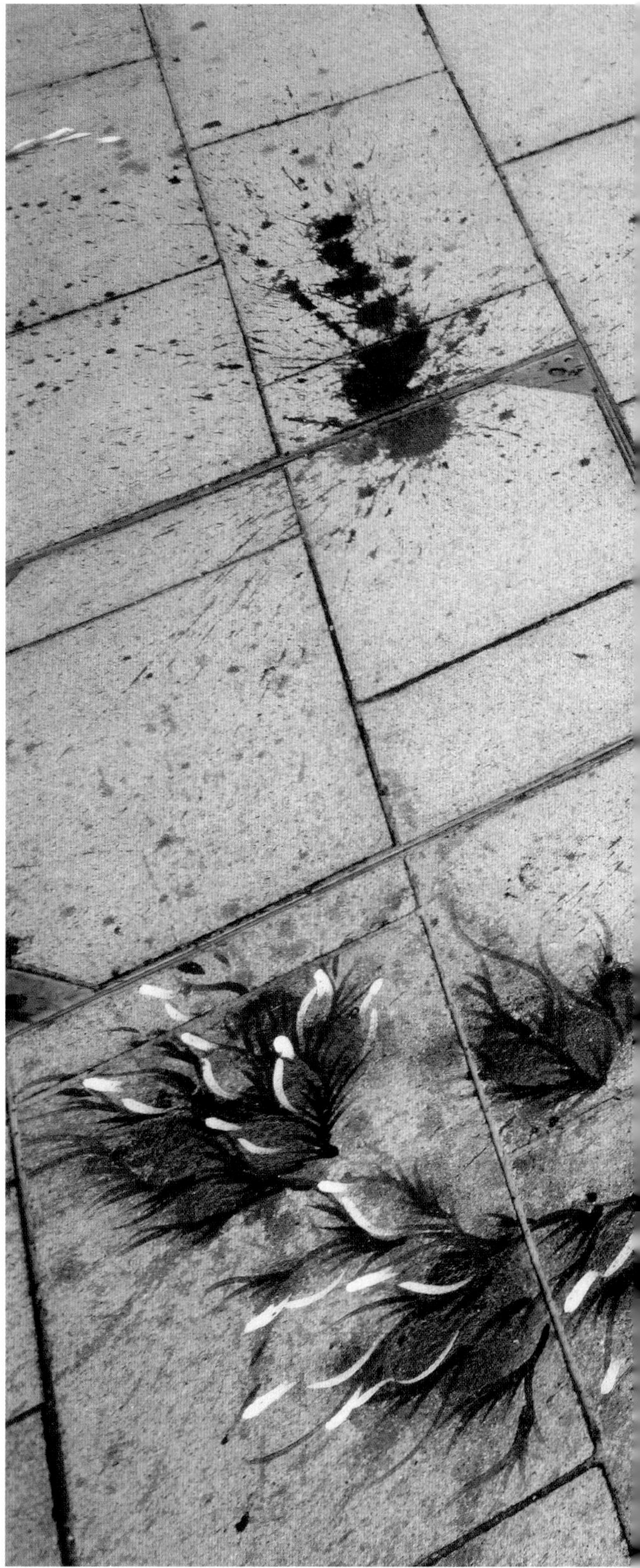

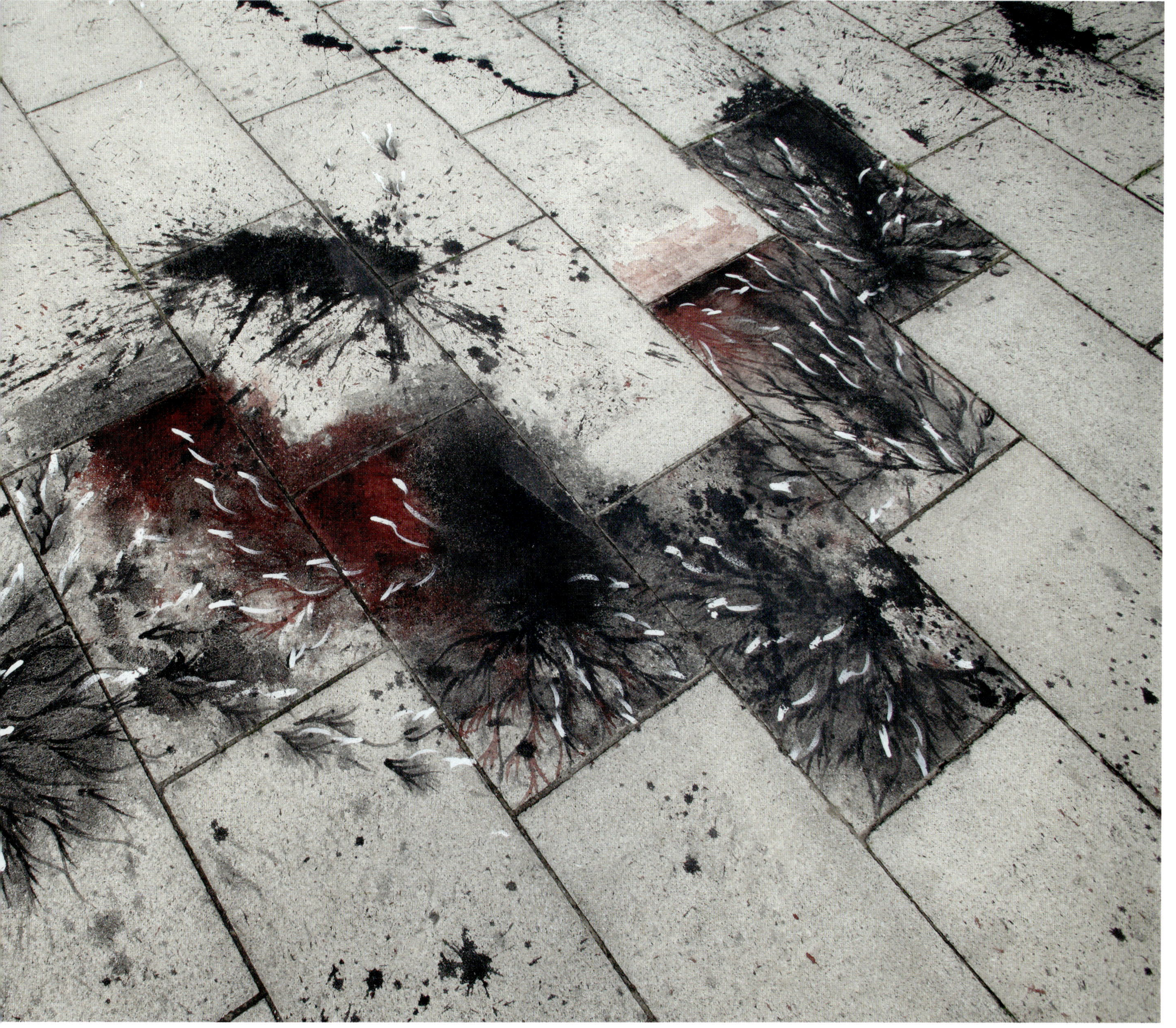

Below. Qureshi's piece for City Park in Bradford city centre was created in vivid hues of blue with white.

Opposite. The work in the Lister Park Mughal Water Gardens was completed in black, grey and white, enlivened with occasional splashes of red, reflecting the monochrome images that remain our only photographic record of the First World War.

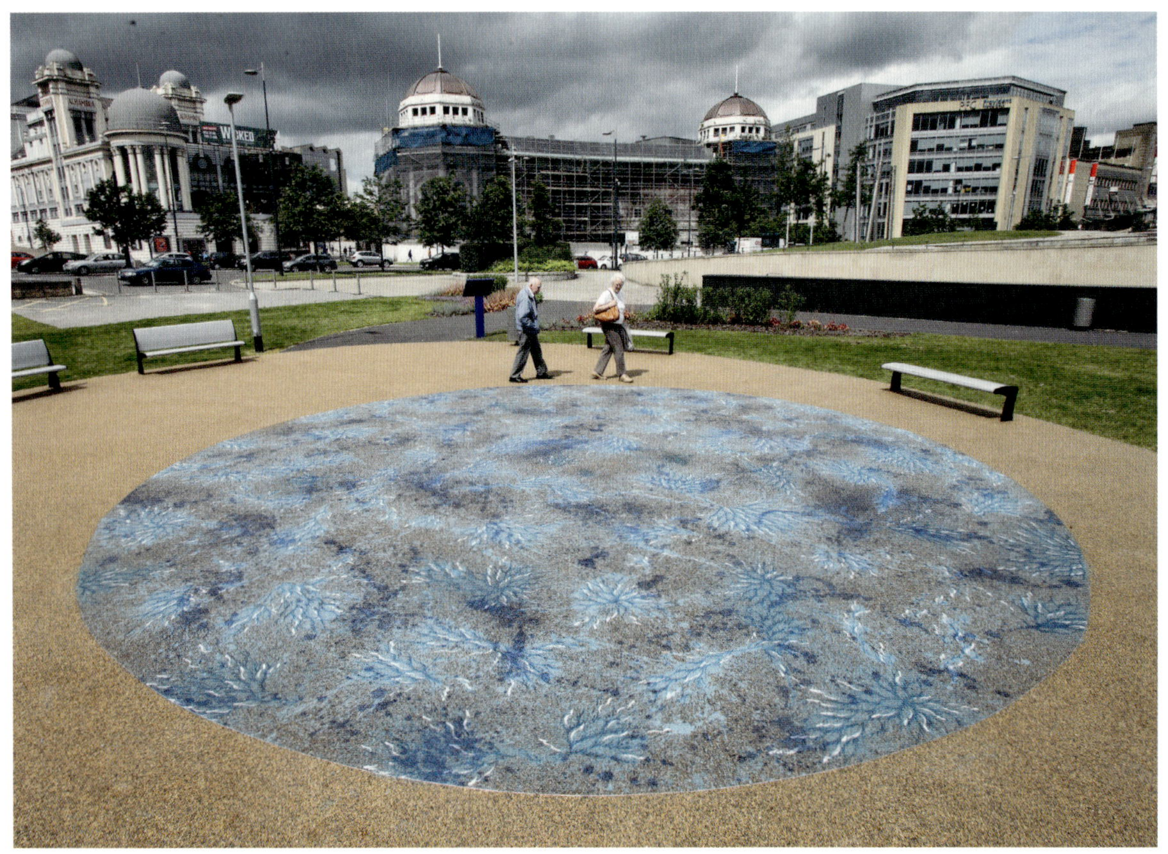

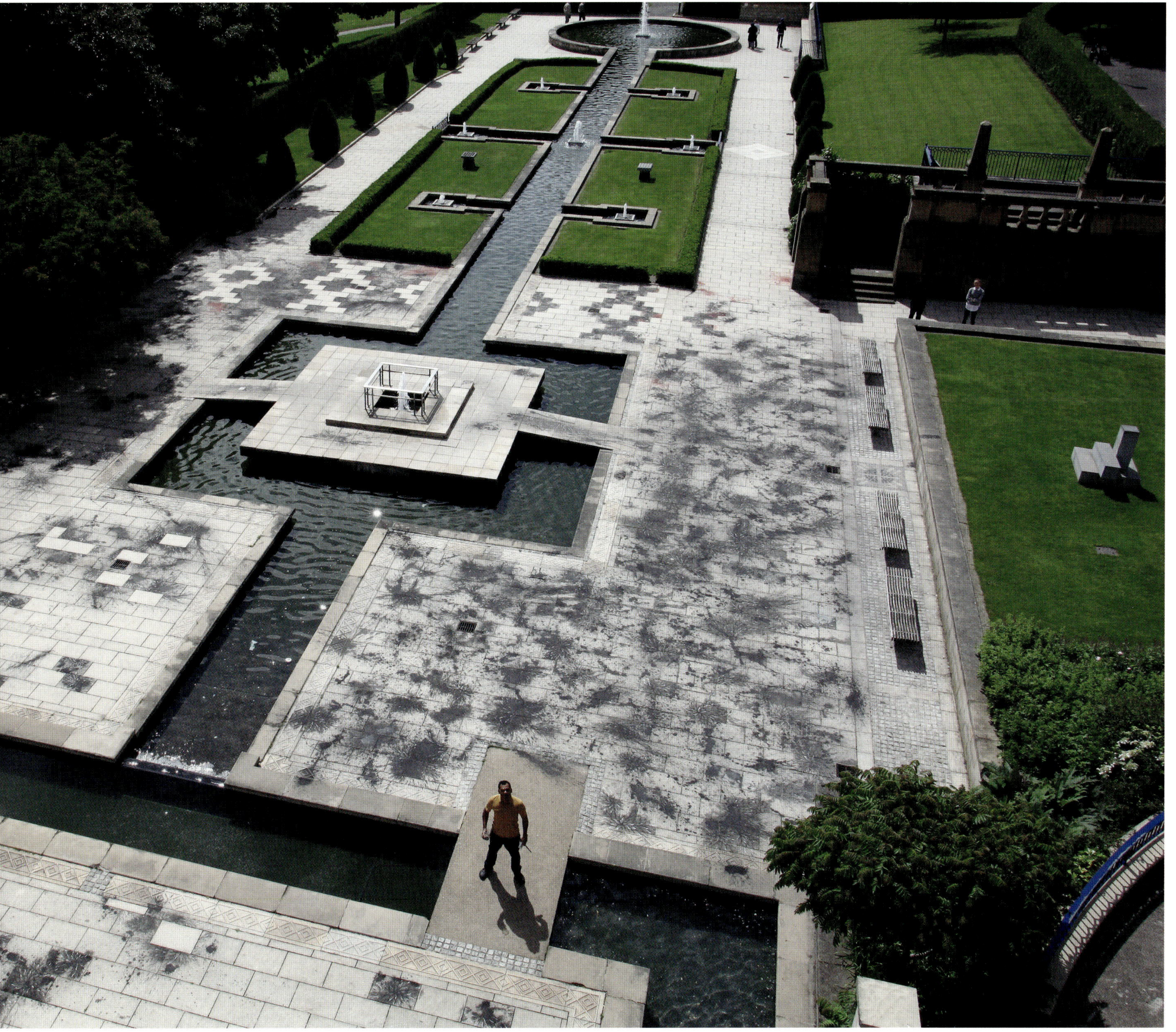

ORCHESTRA OF SYRIAN MUSICIANS

With Damon Albarn and guests

Instabilities in the Middle East today can trace their roots back to the Sykes–Picot Agreement of 1916, which divided the Arab provinces of the Ottoman Empire into spheres of British and French influence. Its ongoing effects can be seen clearly today in the civil war that continues to rage in Syria. In the world of music, this has had a lasting impact on the once-prestigious Orchestra of Syrian Musicians, as most of its members have been forced to flee their homeland and find work elsewhere around the world.

Damon Albarn first worked with the orchestra, led by principal conductor Issam Rafea, at the Damascus Opera House back in 2008. The orchestra then went on to collaborate with Albarn and the Gorillaz on their track 'White Flag', and joined them on their 2010 'Escape to Plastic Beach' world tour, which included shows at the 11th-century Citadel of Damascus.

In 2016, Damon Albarn and Africa Express reunited the Orchestra of Syrian Musicians for the first time since the conflict began, in a series of rare performances designed to highlight and celebrate the remarkable music and culture of Syria. The first of the UK shows took place at Glastonbury Festival, where the British rappers Kano and Bashy joined the orchestra on the Pyramid Stage.

This was followed by an evening at the Royal Festival Hall on 25 June (live-streamed to audiences in Syria and a refugee camp in Jordan), when the orchestra and Albarn were joined by a number of guest performers including Malian ngoni player Bassekou Kouyaté, Egyptian singer Bu Kolthoum, Lebanese-Syrian rapper Eslam Jawaad, Syrian singer Faia Younan, US singer and songwriter Julia Holter, Tunisian tenor Lotfi Bouchnak, French hip-hop performer Malikah, Tunisian jazz and Sufi singer Mounir Troudi, Mauritanian instrumentalist Noura Mint Seymali, British singer Paul Weller, Algerian singer Rachid Taha, and London-based musician TALA.

Other artists, including Senegalese superstar Baaba Maal, then joined the line-up on four more dates in Europe throughout June.

Holland Festival, Amsterdam, 22 June 2016 / Glastonbury Festival, 24 June 2016 / Royal Festival Hall, London, 25 June 2016 / Cemil Topuzlu Open-Air Theatre, Istanbul, 27 June 2016 / Roskilde Festival, Denmark, 29 June 2016

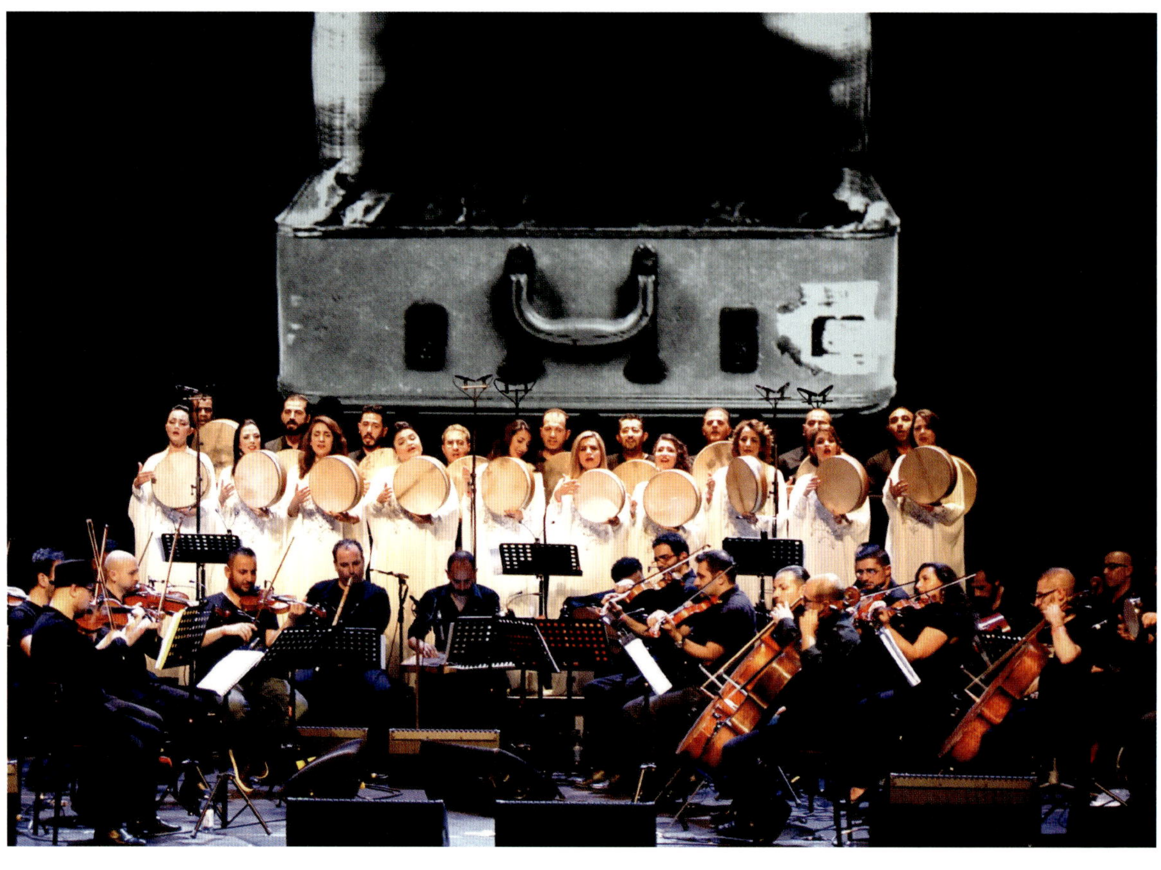

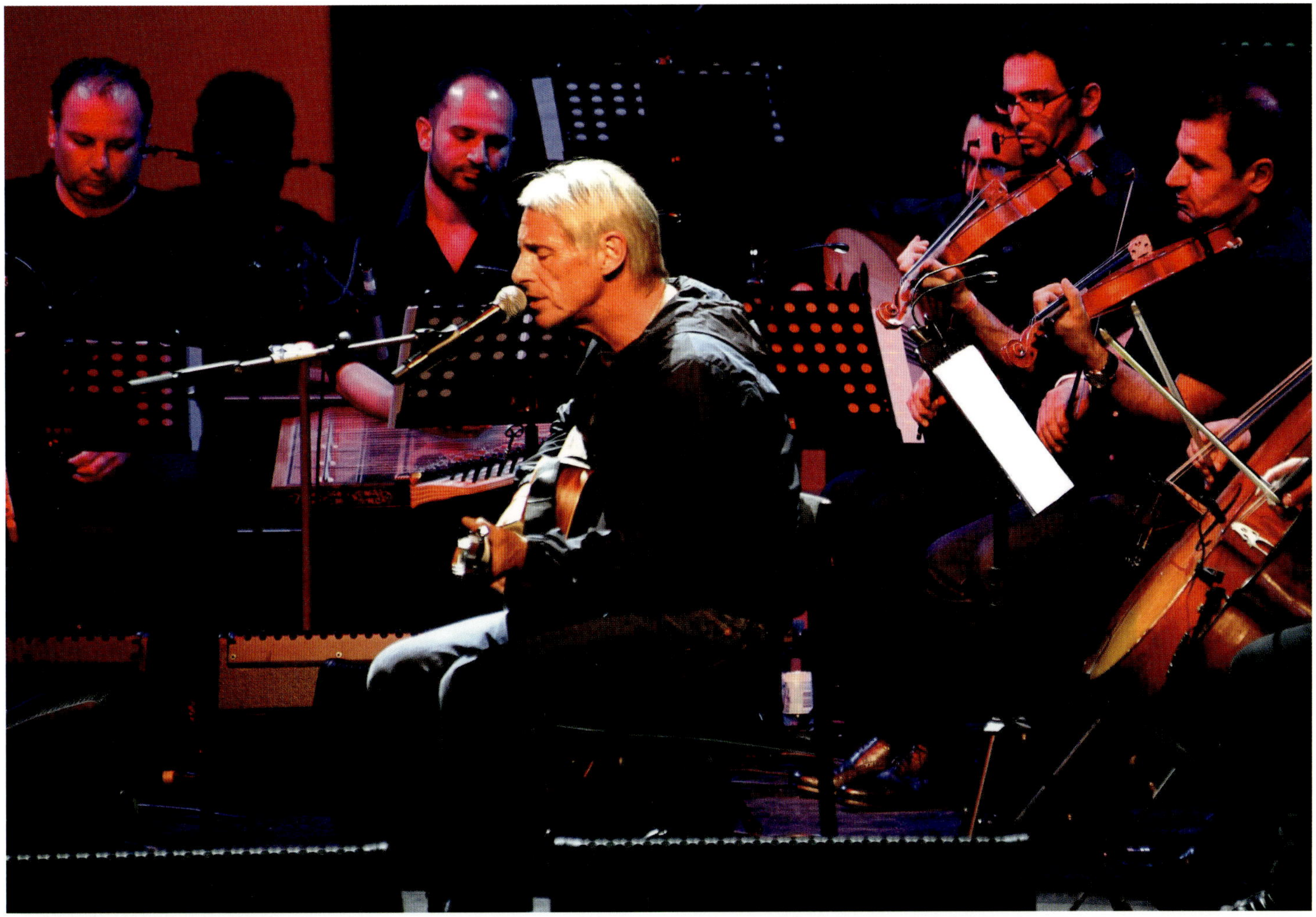

Opposite. The Orchestra of
Syrian Musicians came together
for the first time in many years
to perform an initial concert
in Amsterdam.

This page. The Syrian
musicians were joined in
performance by Paul Weller
(top), Noura Mint Seymali
(below left) and Bassekou
Kouyaté (below right).

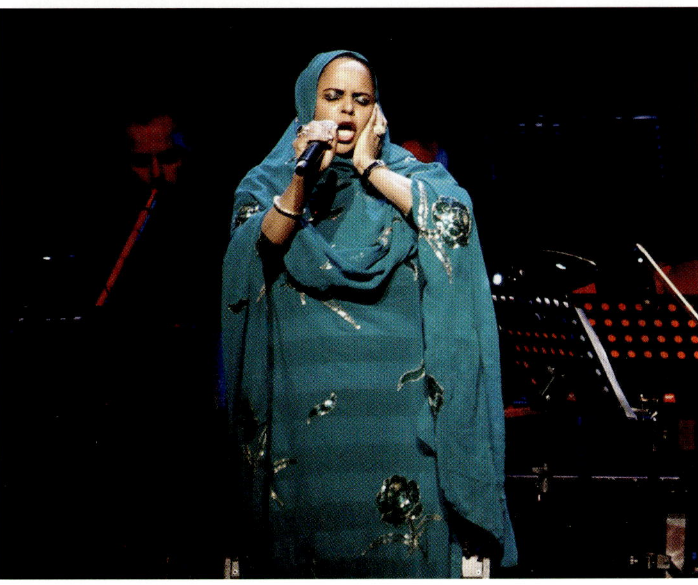

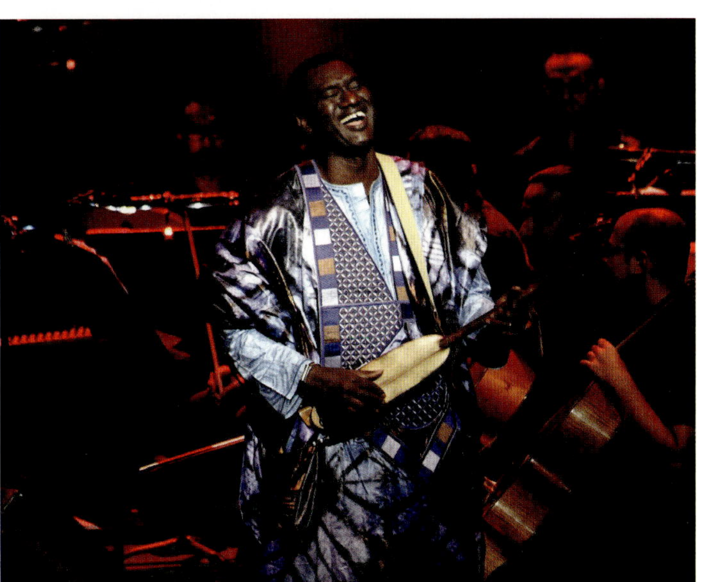

'The result is an exploration of organic matter, its structure, the forces of decay and destruction, and the intriguing beauty that a location with so much to say has both on and off the page.'

Glass magazine

ANYA GALLACCIO

Scottish-born artist Anya Gallaccio creates site-specific installations that draw on the heritage of a particular site, employing organic materials to underline the shifting forces of decay and destruction. For her contribution to 14-18 NOW she created a work that was inspired by the striking landscape and hidden history of Orford Ness, a remote shingle spit off the Suffolk coast.

The Royal Flying Corps (RFC) was formed in 1912, just nine years after the Wright brothers achieved man's first powered flight. A year later, the RFC established a base on Orford Ness — better known today as a nature conservation site. Here, secret trials were conducted in the aerial photography and bombing that would prove so crucial to the war effort.

Gallaccio took photographs of sample material from the site, then applied extreme magnification to these in order to create a set of alternative 'landscapes', both reflecting the geology of the site, and the abstract quality of contemporary aerial photographs housed in the Imperial War Museum's archive. These were printed onto metal structures that were then distributed throughout the site at Orford Ness and at nearby Snape Maltings, each tilted at an angle for viewing.

Orford Ness and Snape Maltings, Aldeburgh Festival, Suffolk, 14 — 29 June 2014

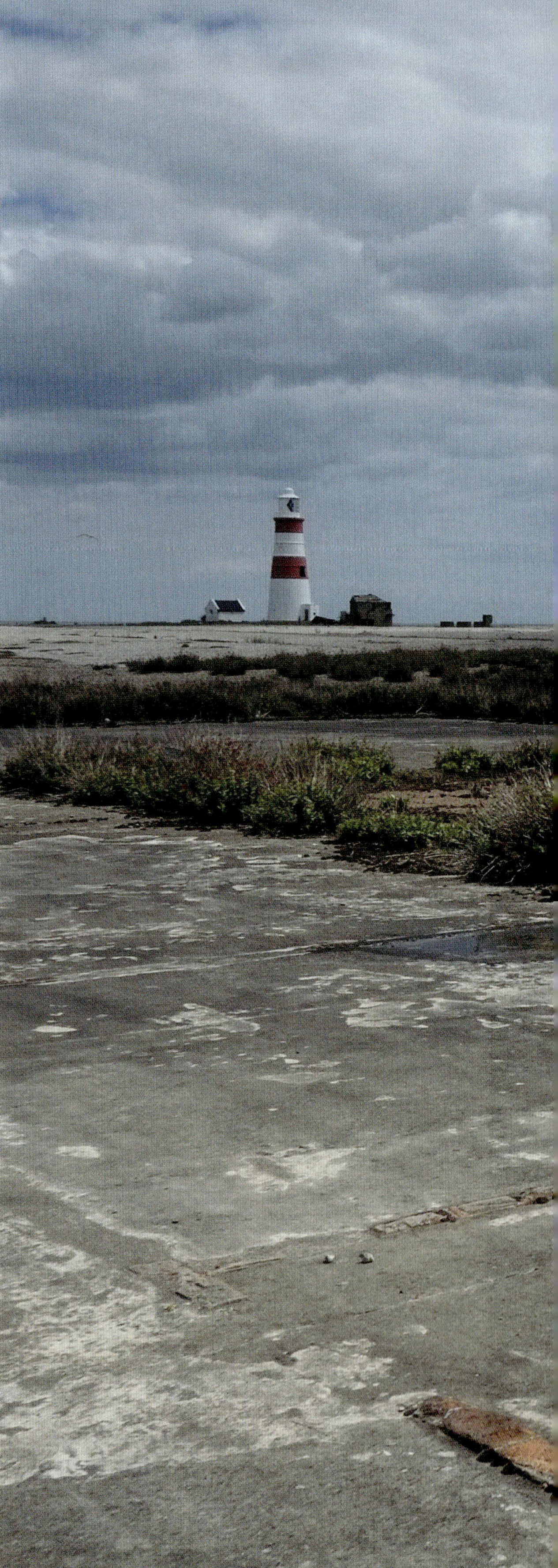

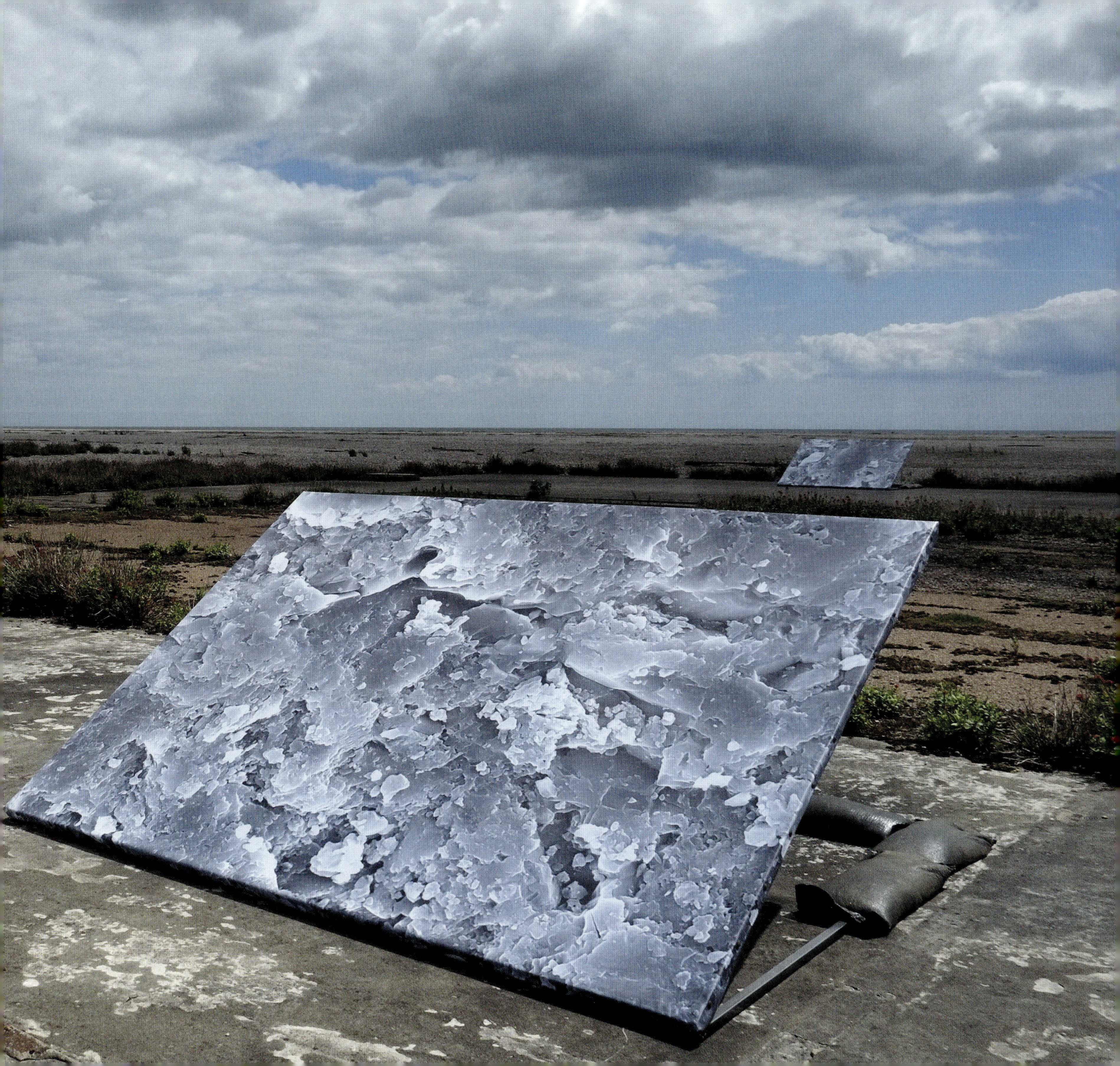

Performed first as a short excerpt at London's Roundhouse in the summer of 2014, then as a full-length stage performance at Sadler's Wells in January and October 2015, this moving dance piece went on to be filmed in a lavish production that was broadcast on BBC Two and on iPlayer. An evocative score by folk rock musician, poet and visual artist Keaton Henson was combined with the choreography of Iván Pérez to tell the story of a group of young soldiers sent to fight in a brutal war that ultimately consumed them.

Drawing inspiration from images of the First World War, *Young Men* was an exploration of warfare through the bonds that form between men who train and fight together. The live show also featured film and projection by BalletBoyz, a common feature of the work of this award-winning dance company, who have revolutionised the way dance is presented on stage and are in the vanguard of digital dance creation.

YOUNG MEN

BalletBoyz

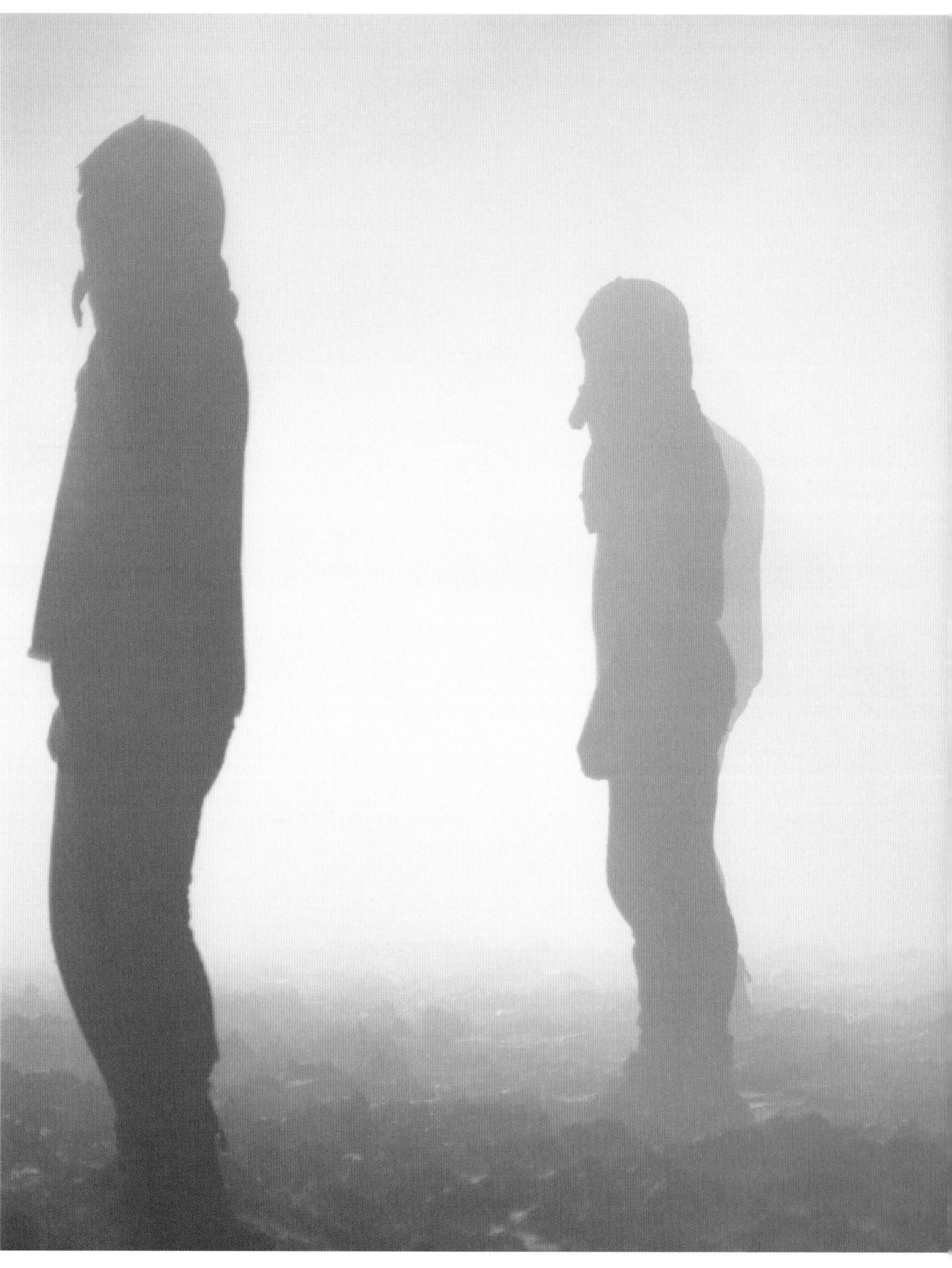

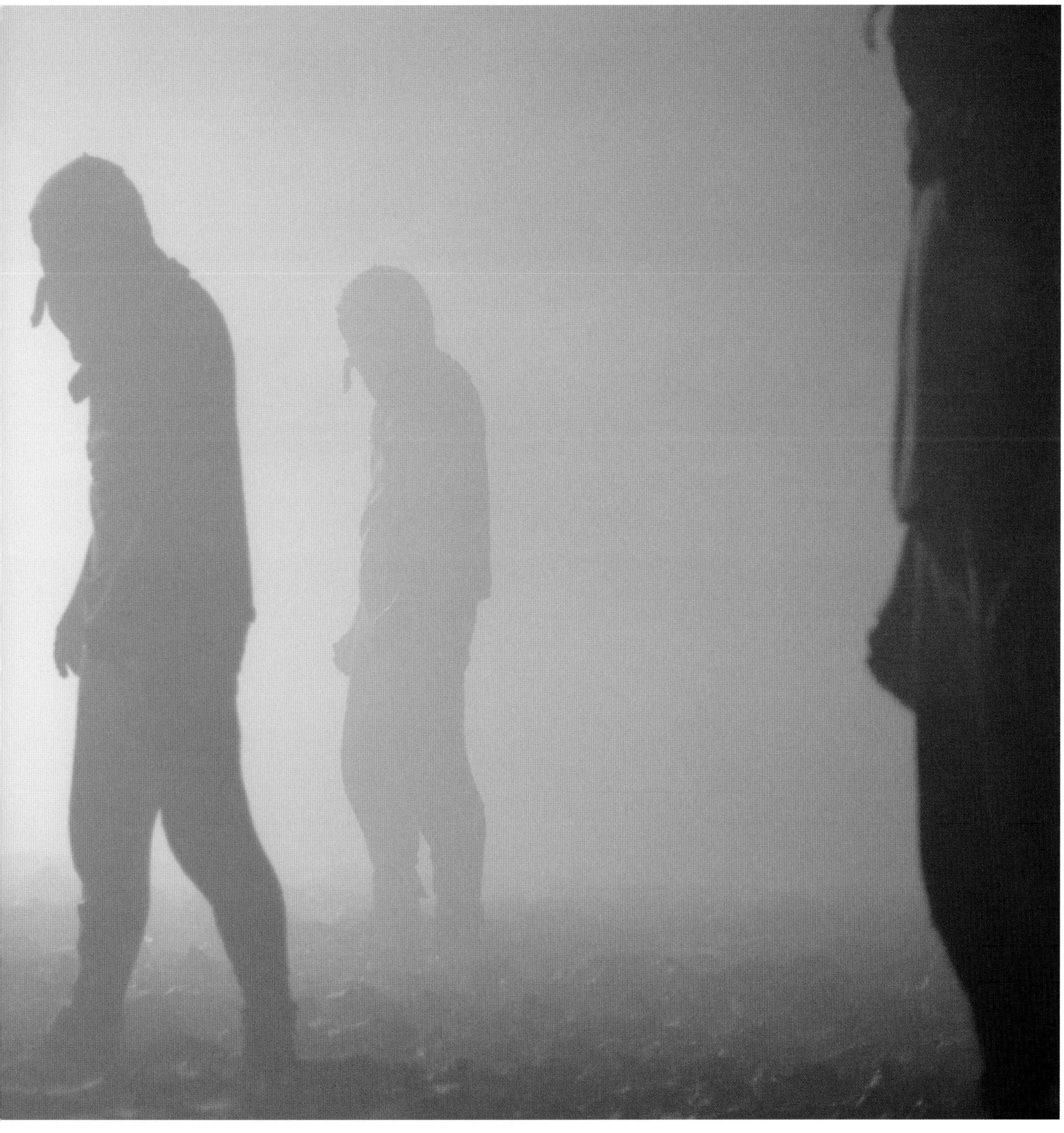

Young Men was made into a feature-length film, with no dialogue, and a haunting soundtrack by Keaton Henson. It was shot on location in France, featuring dancers from the company.

'As we watched the show for the stage being created in the studio, we became aware that here were characters and choreography that demanded both the scale and intimacy that only film can bring. We were determined to bring this particular story to the big screen.'

Michael Nunn and William Trevitt

Following the success of the stage production, BalletBoyz artistic directors Michael Nunn and William Trevitt adapted the work for the screen with the support of BBC Music. Shot entirely on location in France with a reworked score and production design, the film version of *Young Men* is a bold and powerful drama, and one of just a few great silent movies to have been made since the advent of synchronised sound in the late 1920s. It was the company's debut feature film and provided an impactful new outlet for its trademark synthesis of classical dance and intense physical performance. The film went on to win a Eurovision Rose d'Or award in 2017, which recognises originality, quality and creativity, and a highly coveted Golden Prague at the International Television Festival.

The Roundhouse, London, 31 July — 1 August 2014 / Sadler's Wells, London, 14 — 18 January and 5 — 10 October 2015 / BBC Two premiere broadcast, 12 November 2016

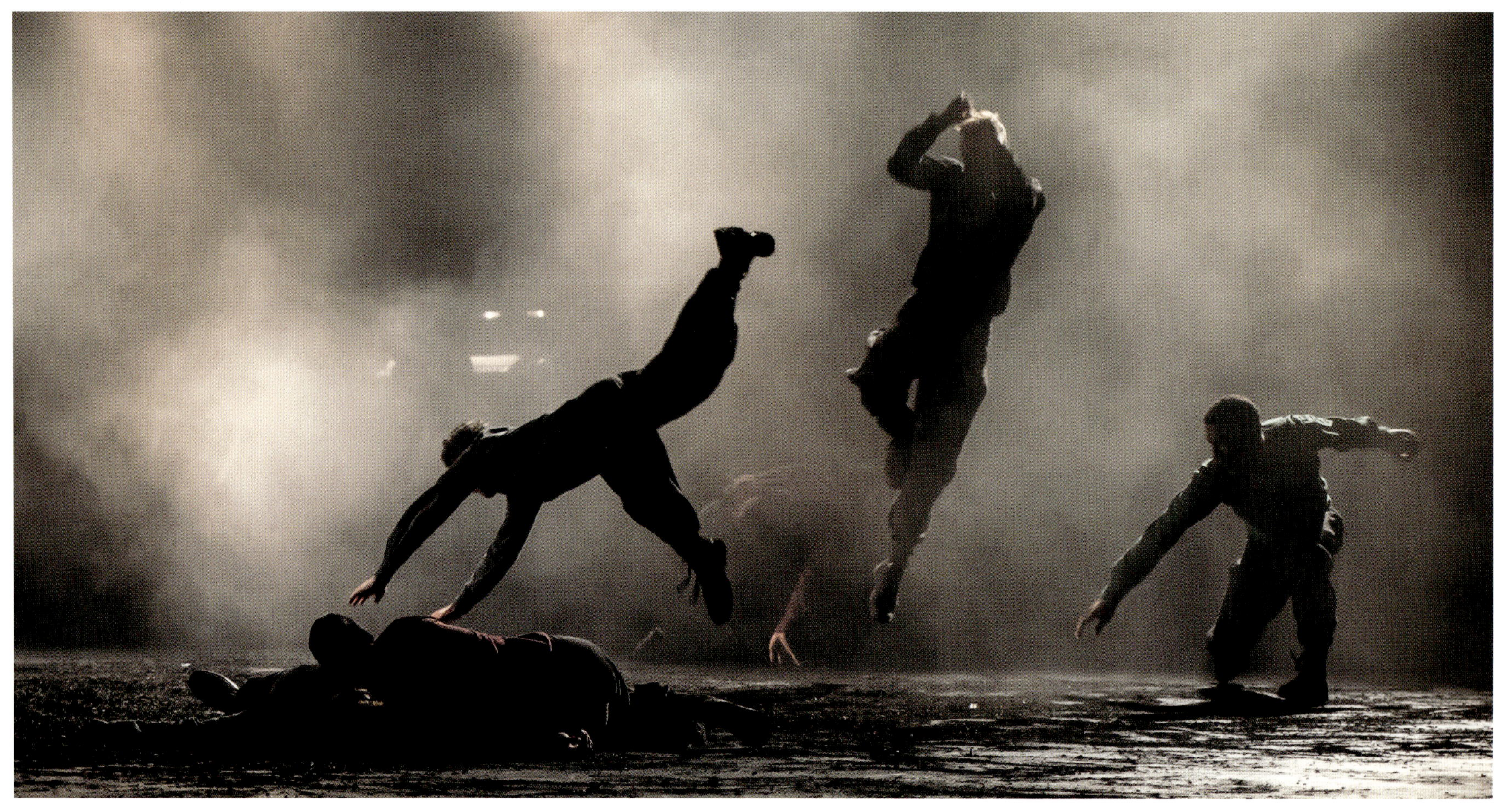

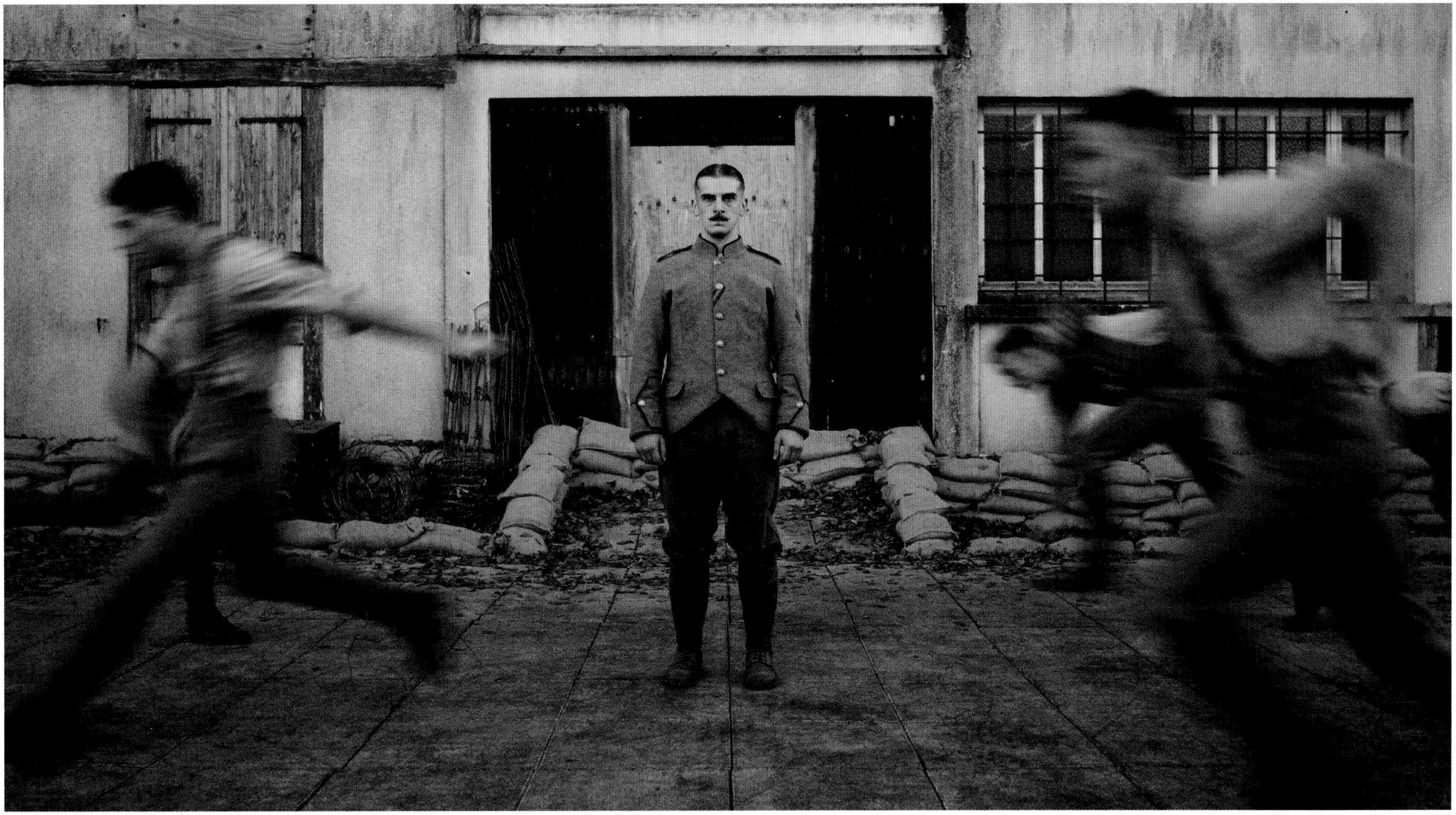

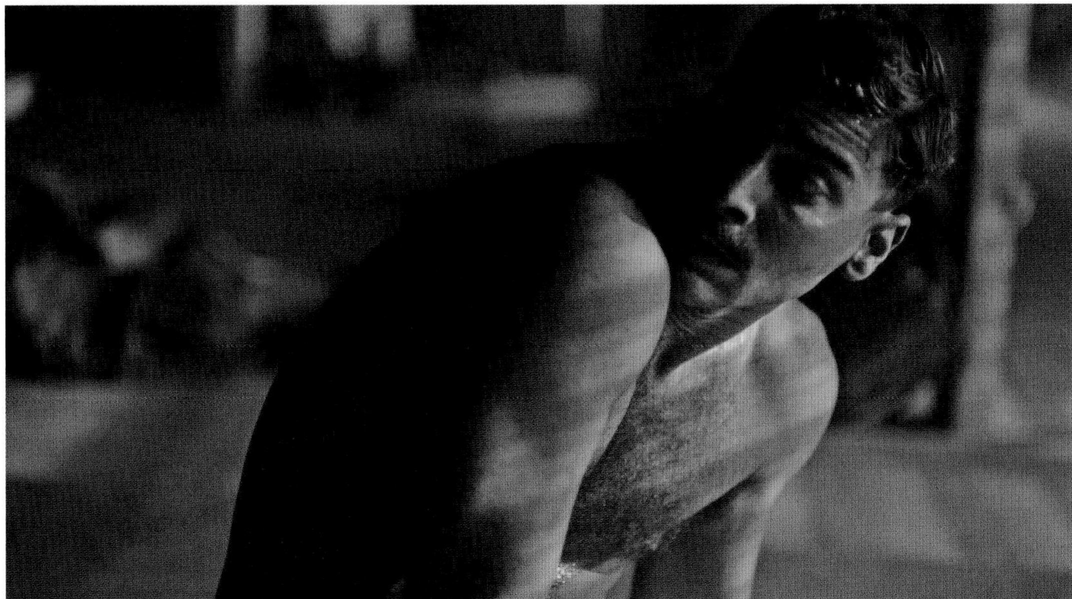

Left and above. Iván Pérez's choreography for both the stage show and the film explored the conflict, companionship, love and loss experienced by young men plunged into war.

Opposite. The intensely physical and highly charged live show captured the horrors of war in a series of set pieces featuring 11 male dancers and 2 female guest artists.

WHEN YOU LOOK YOU MAY NOT SEE; IF HISTORY COULD BE FOLDED, WHERE WOULD YOU PUT THE CREASE?

Richard Wentworth

The First World War was the first to be fought by an almost entirely literate generation. On a personal level, this made it possible for soldiers abroad to keep in touch with their wives, sweethearts and children via an extraordinarily swift postal service. Official agencies, meanwhile, took advantage of the potential of mass communication via such innovations as the public information poster. A century later, these two very different modes of communication provided British artist Richard Wentworth with the starting point for a three-part commission.

When You Look You May Not See was a poster based on a postcard written by soldier Herbert Ernest Wilson to his wife Martha Emily Wilson on 4 September 1918, sourced from the First World War Poetry Digital Archive, at the University of Oxford. Written just months before the Armistice was signed, its poignancy is heightened by the halting style in which it is written: Herbert enquires after his wife's health, hoping that she might write to him soon, and complaining only of the weather. The poster also made use of Johnston, the typeface designed in 1916 by Edward Johnston for use across the Underground system and still in use today. By reversing the text, Wentworth emphasised the distance that separates us from the experiences, attitudes and expressions of the Wilsons' day, and by presenting it via the format and typography of an official notice, he asked viewers to consider the relationship between public and private notions of duty.

Two further, large-scale works expanded upon these themes and techniques, under the shared title of *If history could be folded, where would you put the crease?* The first, covering the hoardings at Southwark station, featured reversed and mirrored text. The second was a text and mirror installation in the subways of Piccadilly Circus station. The difficulty of reading the text in each case forced the reader to dwell upon the notion of 'foldable' time and hidden pasts. What would it mean to blot out a part of our history?

Reminding us that the Tube has always served as a space for the transmission of official ideas, all three works of art asked us to reconsider our perspective on the past.

London Underground stations / 25 July 2014 — 12 December 2016

The mirrored text that was displayed on the hoardings outside London's Southwark Underground station.

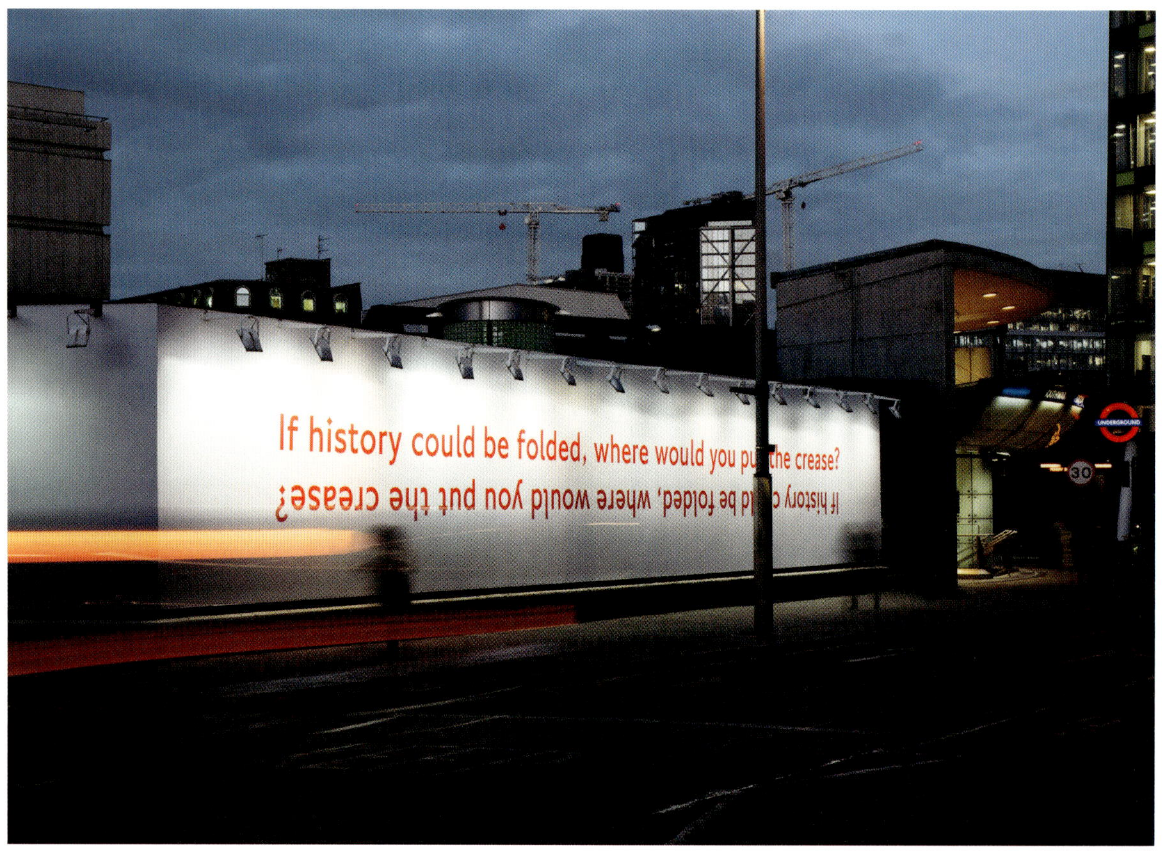

art.tfl.gov.uk

When You Look You May Not See, Richard Wentworth, 2014
From a postcard by Herbert Ernest Wilson, to his wife Martha Emily Wilson
The Great War Archive, University of Oxford © Marilyn White

France
4 September 1918

Dear Wife,
Just a line hoping you are in the best
of health as it leaves me quite well.
I have not had a letter off you today
so shall be expecting one tomorrow.
We are having some awful weather just
now. I shall be pleased when this month
is out we might get a bit better then.
Well remember me to all.
I hope they have heard from George
by now. I hope Dot is keeping well.
Remember me to all, will write when
I get a letter from you.
Well I think this will be all this time,
so will close.
With best love from loving husband,

Herbert

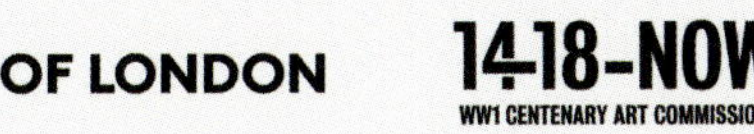
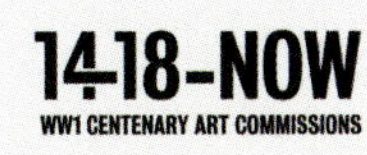
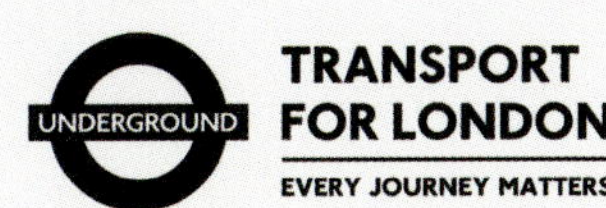

MAYOR OF LONDON

14-18-NOW
WW1 CENTENARY ART COMMISSIONS

UNDERGROUND
TRANSPORT FOR LONDON
EVERY JOURNEY MATTERS

The short yet poignant message written by serving soldier Herbert Wilson to his wife back home — in the classic type designed by Edward Johnston for the London Underground.

24-DECADE HISTORY OF POPULAR MUSIC: THE WW1 YEARS AND MORE

Taylor Mac

The year 1916 was a particularly important and turbulent one in Ireland's history. This was the year of the Easter Rising at home, and the Battle of the Somme on the Continent — a battle in which thousands of soldiers from the 36th (Ulster) Division lost their lives.

One hundred years on, in his first Northern Ireland appearance, the fabulous and fearless American playwright, actor, singer-songwriter and performance artist Taylor Mac brought three special participative concerts to the Belfast International Arts Festival, reflecting on Ireland's experiences during the first decades of the 20th century.

In the first two concerts, Mac presented his own colourful take on the music and culture that spanned the years before, during and after the First World War, from 1896 through to 1926. His third concert featured songs from the century spanning 1916 to 2016. Accompanied by a live band and dressed in a dazzling array of theatrical outfits designed by his costume designer Machine Dazzle, Mac inspired both laughter and reflection as he investigated notions of authority, class, empire, gender, patriotism and war, and the different ways in which history itself is both made and viewed.

The MAC, Belfast International Arts Festival, 25, 26 & 29 October 2016

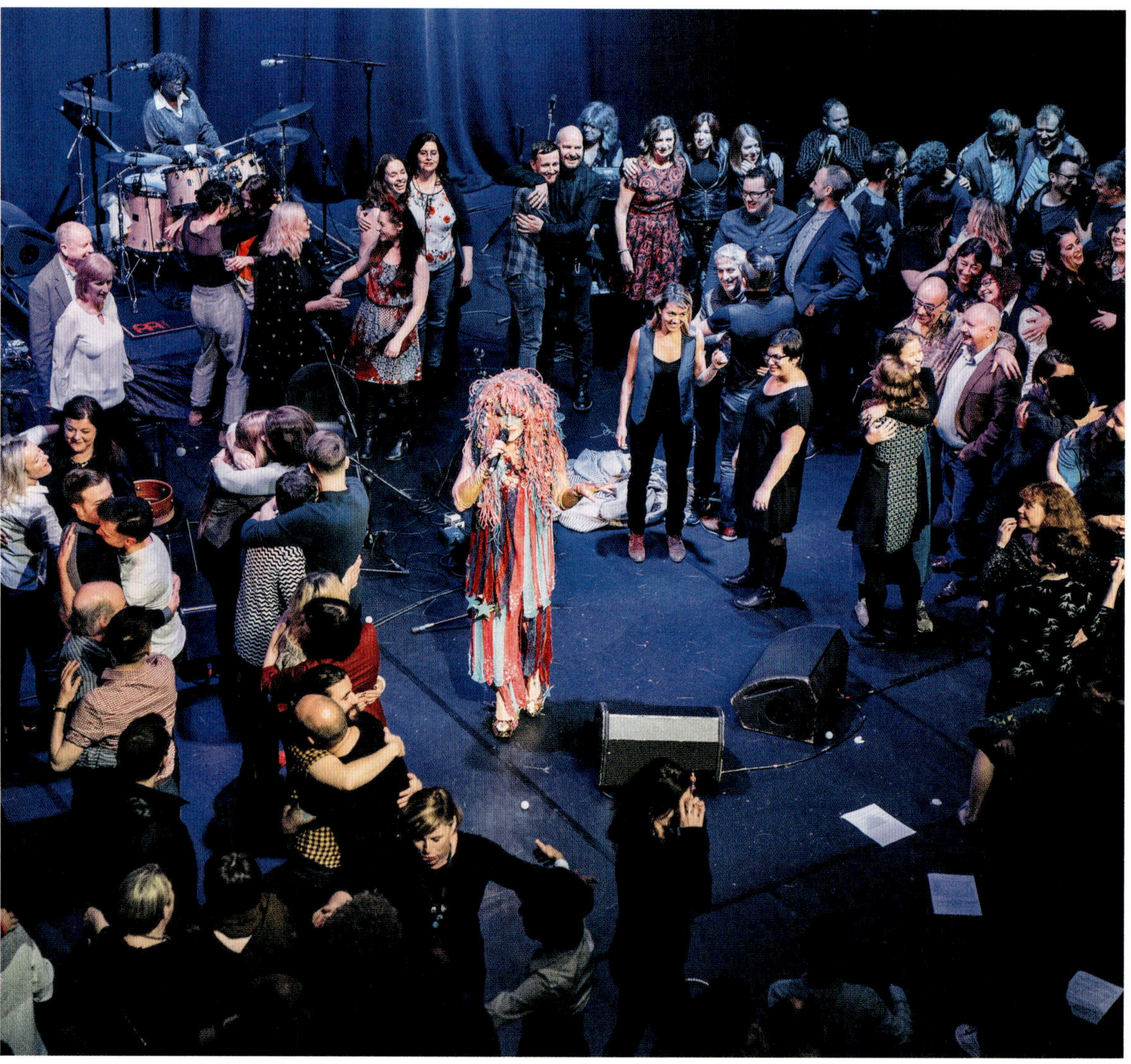

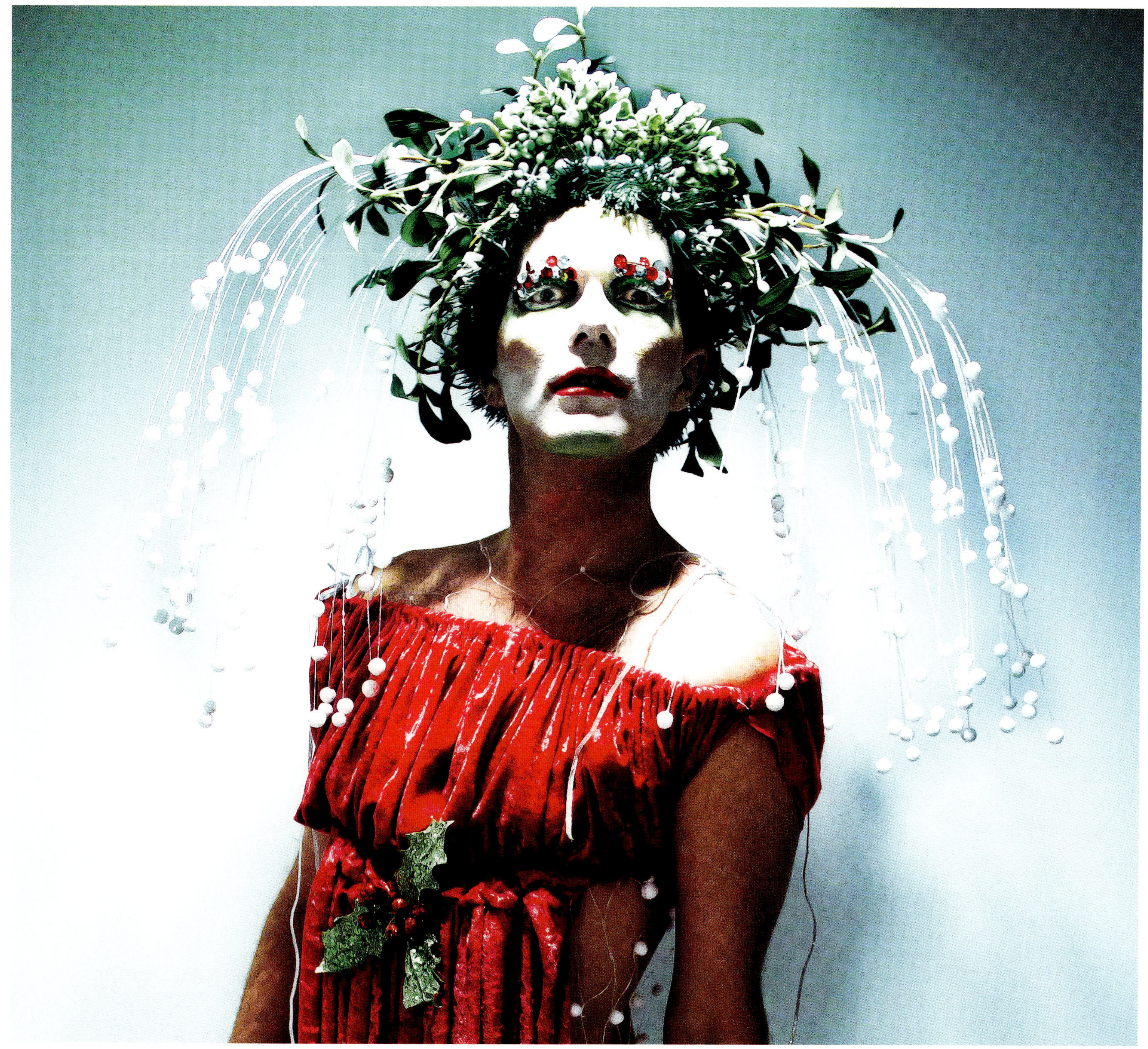

THESE ROOMS

ANU
CoisCéim Dance Theatre

The performance propelled audiences through the domestic spaces and rooms of the civilians, each one recreated from the testimonies and archive material, depicting the lived experience of the victims and the rupture caused by this tragic event on both their homes and lives.

On 28 April 1916, five days into the Easter Rising, 15 civilian men were killed in house-to-house raids by British soldiers on a single Dublin street. *These Rooms*, an intense, immersive blend of theatre, dance and visual art created by David Bolger, Owen Boss and Louise Lowe, told two sets of stories: those of the civilians who were victims of the North King Street Massacre, and those of the men of the South Staffordshire Regiment who committed this act — their identities largely anonymous, their actions controversially exonerated at a military inquiry. The piece took as its starting point the testimonies of the 38 women who witnessed the massacre first-hand.

Created by two of Ireland's most original companies, *These Rooms* received unanimous critical acclaim when it was first presented in a dilapidated Dublin building in 2016 as part of the centenary commemorations of the Easter Rising. It was then wholly reimagined for a London run in 2018, in a co-commission between 14-18 NOW, LIFT and the Shoreditch Town Hall; a riveting work shedding new light on a pivotal moment in British–Irish relations. It was accompanied by *Beyond These Rooms*, an installation and symposium at Tate Liverpool as part of Tate Exchange.

Shoreditch Town Hall, London, 4 — 22 June 2018 / Tate Liverpool, 17 January — 9 February 2019

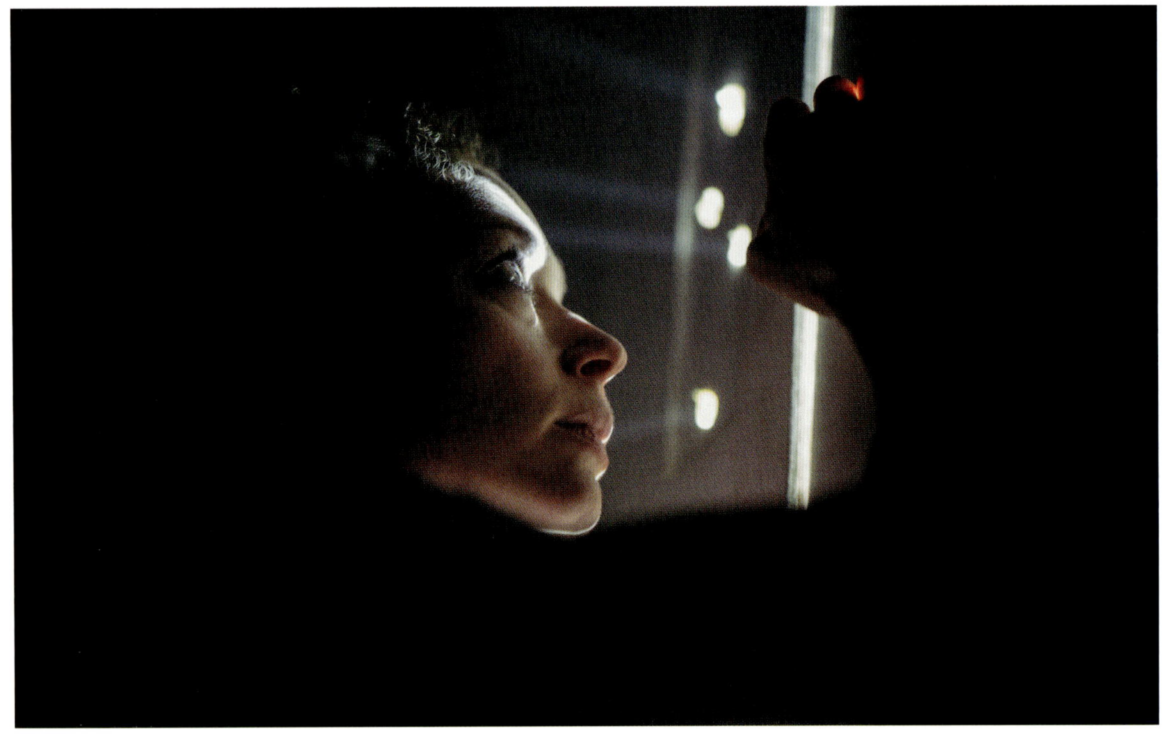

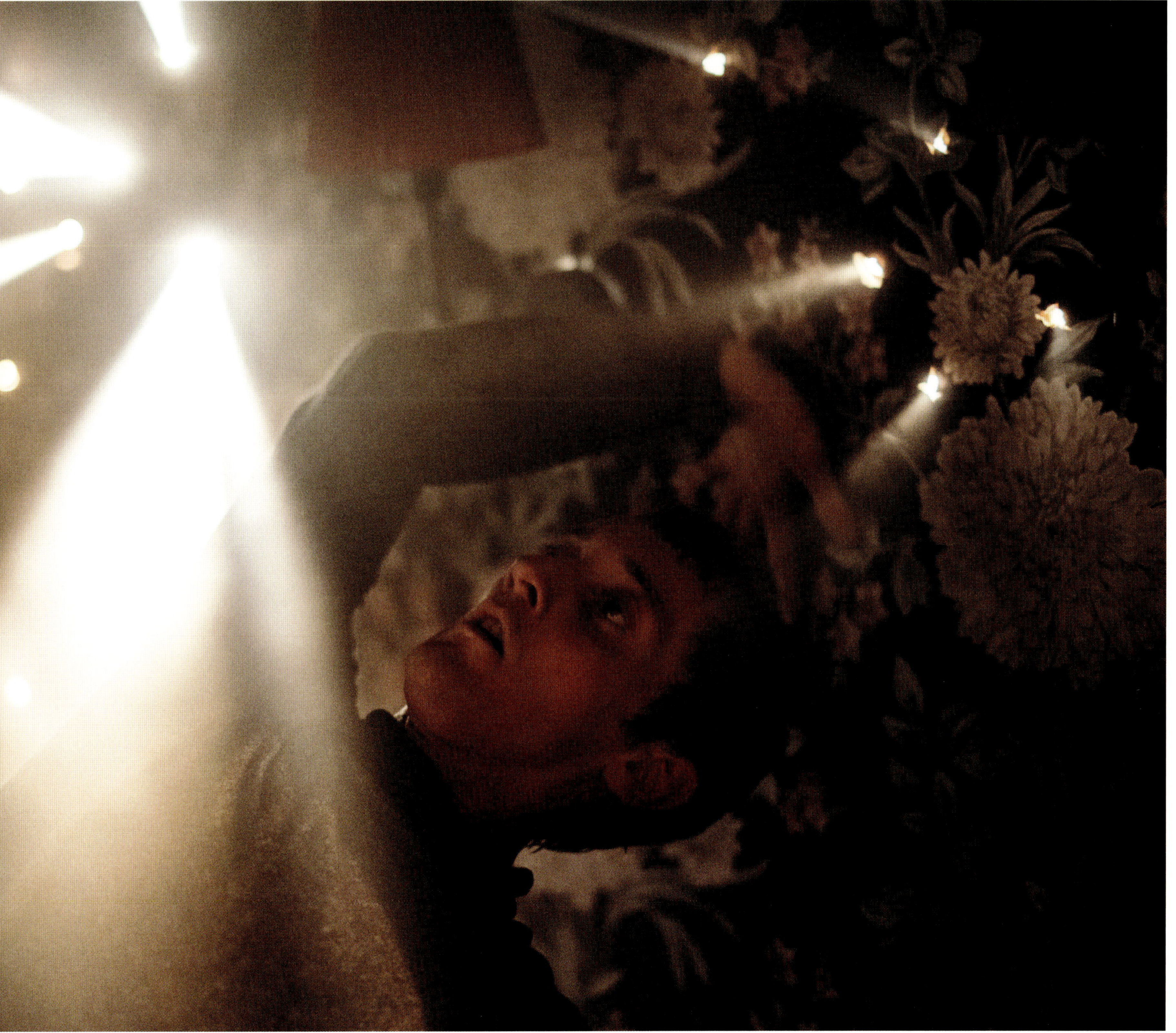

Set in 1916 and 1966, the
50th anniversary of the
Easter Rising, *These Rooms*
also explored the concepts
of truth and time in
attempting to narrate
conflicted histories.

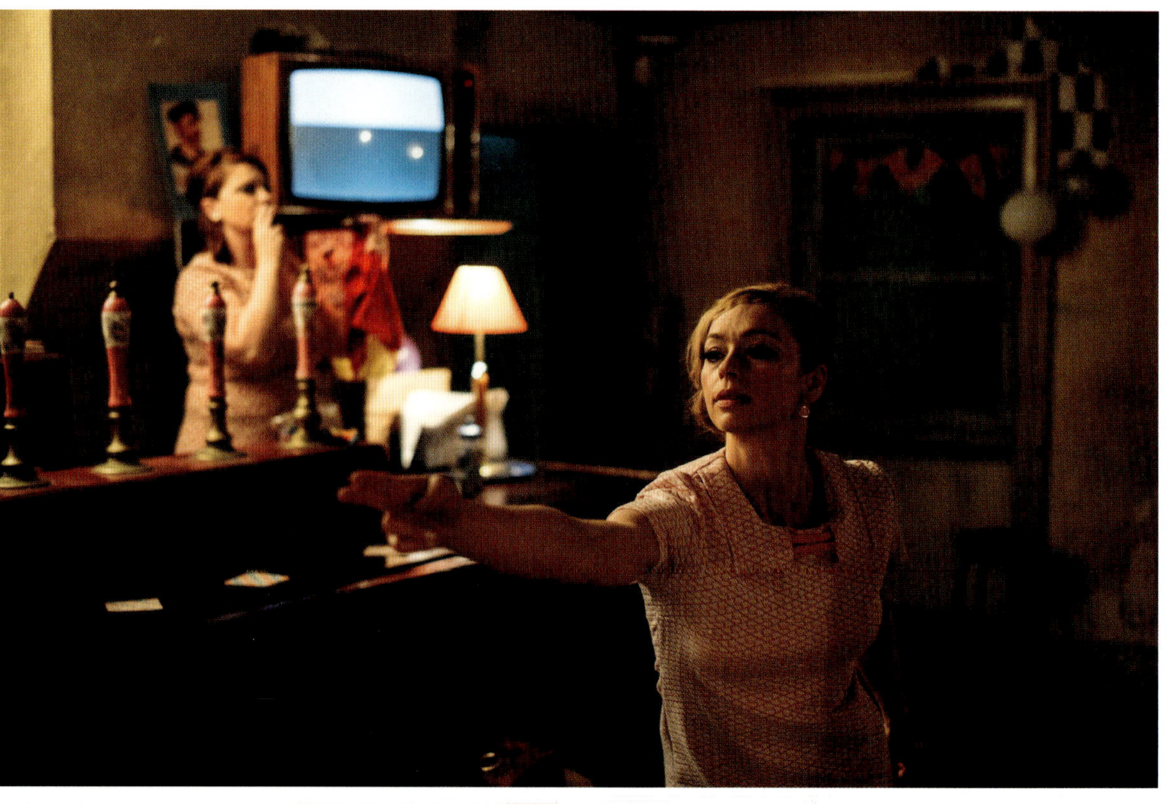

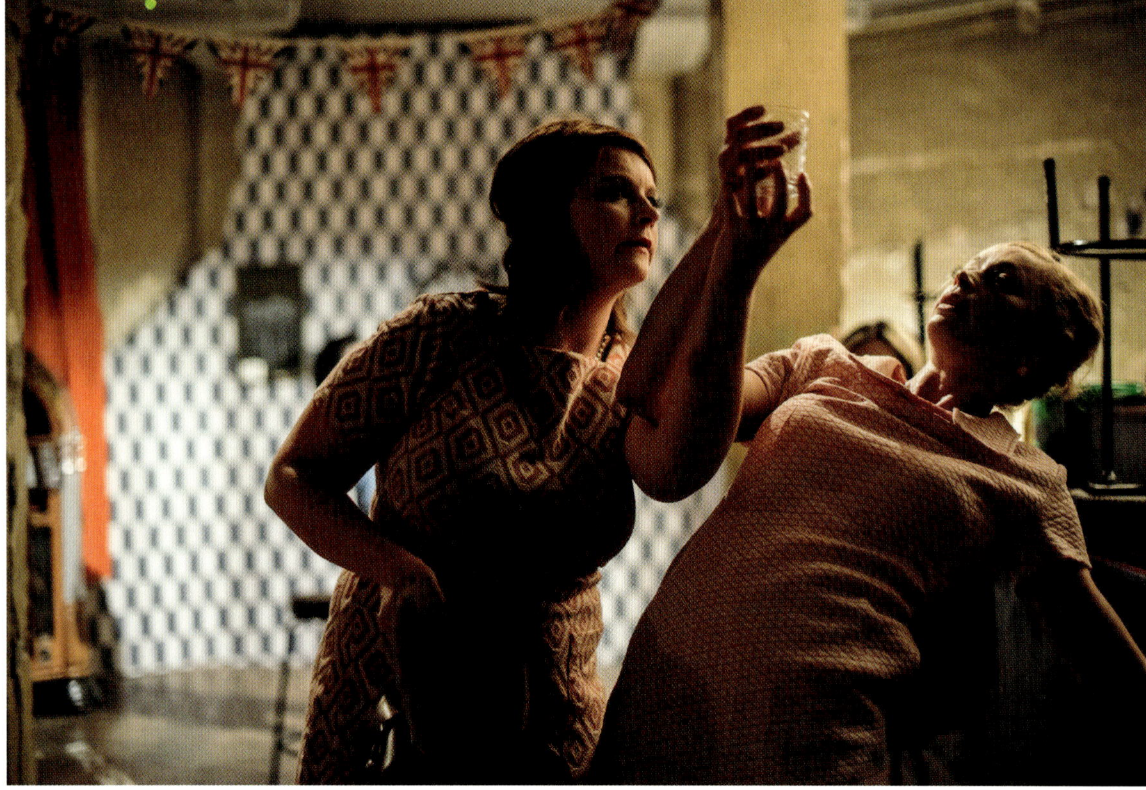

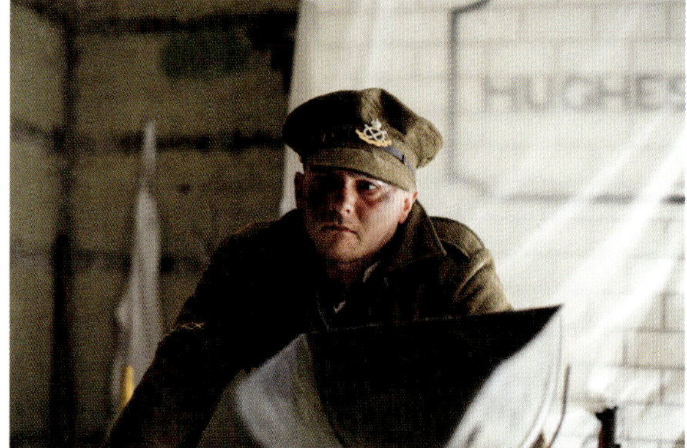

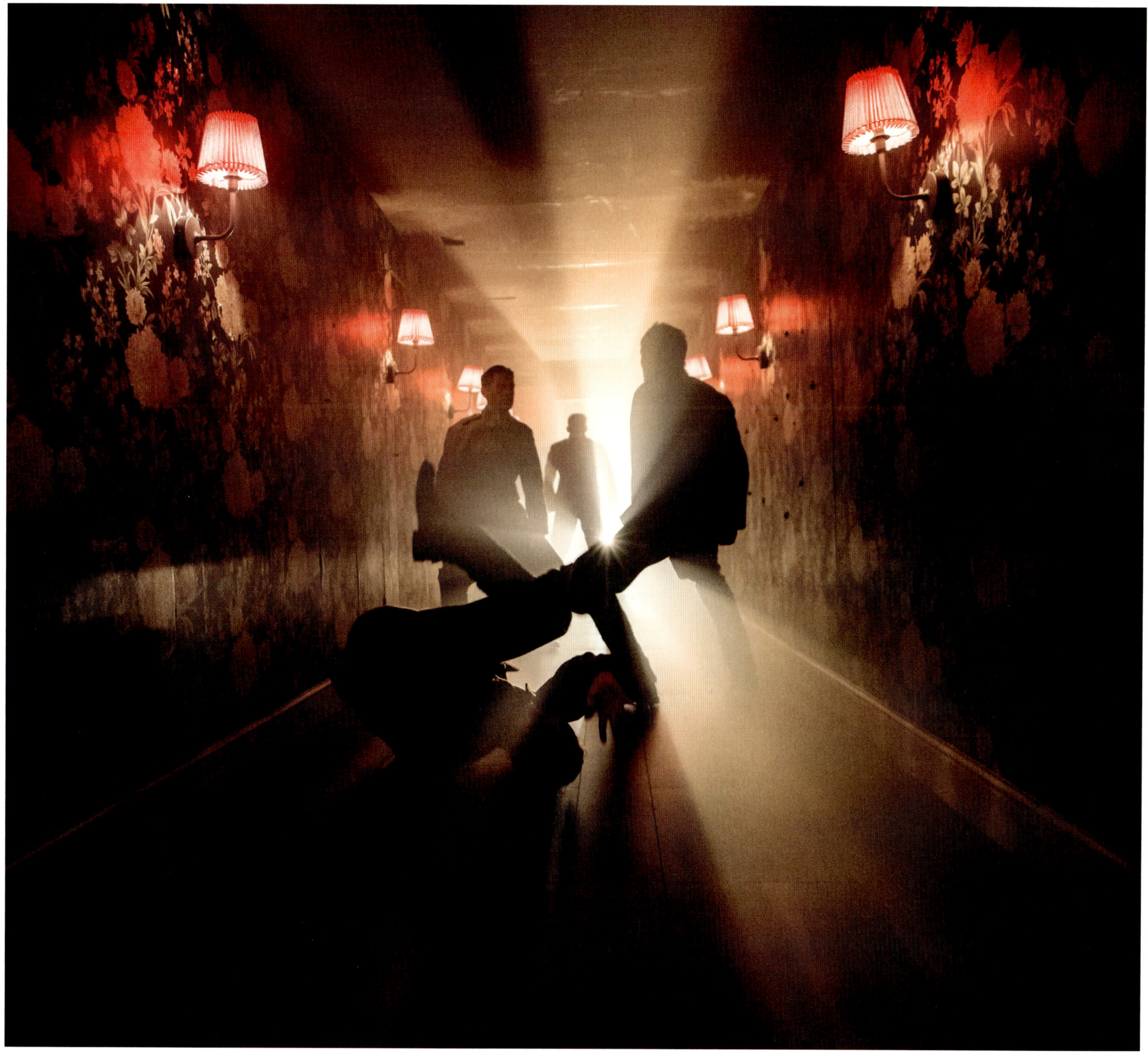

*It was not to be a static memorial
in bronze or stone — there are
already too many of those,
their significance often quickly
forgotten. The work was about
an encounter — with an idea of
the past, and, perhaps crucially,
an encounter with another,
unknown person.*

YOU HAD TO BE THERE

Charlotte Higgins

A week after the Brexit referendum, on the morning of 1 July 2016, something strange and compelling began to unfold quietly, discreetly, completely unheralded. Young men, dressed in the uniforms of First World War soldiers, began to gather at railway stations around the UK. They spoke to no one — not to each other, not to members of the public. They sat and waited, stood around in clumps, smoked. They were ghostly. It was as if they had slipped through time.

Later, they would board trains, then walk out into the streets of other cities and towns. People began to see them in markets, in shopping malls. If one of the soldiers had his eye caught by a passerby, he would silently pass them a card. On it was the name, rank, regiment and age of a man who had been killed on the first day of the Battle of the Somme, exactly 100 years earlier, when at 7.30am British soldiers began to walk across No Man's Land to be met with machine gun fire, and 19,240 perished. At some preordained time, the men began to sing, to the tune of 'Auld Lang Syne', 'We're here because we're here because we're here because we're here' — a weary, resigned chorus that was sung in the trenches. The song gave its name to the work itself, which had been devised by the artist Jeremy Deller with the collaboration of Rufus Norris, artistic director of the National Theatre. But its authorship was announced only at the end of the day. Until then it remained completely unexplained, a mystery.

Thousands of volunteers had trained and rehearsed for the day, keeping the secret of the memorial they were to embody. I was in the know: I had been invited to watch Norris rehearse a large group of men in a drill hall in London's Bethnal Green. Similar rehearsals were going on throughout the country. There was a seriousness to these gatherings, as well as fun; a sense that some responsible task had been undertaken. Norris wanted the men, he said then, to be 'alive. You don't have to "act". The most compelling thing you can do is be alert, be present.'

The work was, by its very nature, fleeting. You either saw it or you didn't, though it wasn't long before pictures and stories began to amass on social media. Deller had been clear that he wanted to avoid 'heritage places — churches, war memorials. I wanted to take it to the public'. It was not to be a static memorial in bronze or stone — there are already too many of those, their significance often quickly forgotten. The work was about an encounter — with an idea of the past, and, perhaps crucially, an encounter with another, unknown person.

I wrote about the work in the *Guardian*. Contemporary art can receive an impatient reaction in the paper's online comments section, but *We're here because we're here* was an exception. 'I'm still thinking about it this morning,' wrote one reader, on 2 July. 'It had far more effect than a cannon salute, or a two-minute silence for me.' Another described going up to one of the men and asking him where he was going. 'He just stared at me and reached into his pocket. Gave me a card saying "Private Arthur Blackburn, 1st Battalion, London Regiment, Royal Fusiliers, Died at the Somme on 1st of July 1916 aged 23 years". He then took off his helmet, looked at the ground and walked slowly off without saying a word. I was nearly in tears.' A third, from Manchester, wrote of going to buy lunch from a supermarket, 'when I saw a man in a captain's uniform cross a walkway. They looked like they were just sitting and standing around waiting for something — or just displaced, like they shouldn't be there. It was very eerie and I've had it in my head all day.'

I wonder if those readers still ever think of *We're here because we're here*. I do — as if the material of the work were memory itself, evanescent but powerful. The other day I opened a paperback and a card fell out of it. 'Lance Corporal John Arthur Green,' it read. '1st/9th Battalion, London Regiment (Queen Victoria's Rifles). Died at the Somme on 1 July 1916. Aged 24 years.' I stopped for a moment. Then I tucked it back inside another book, ready for memory to ambush me some other day.

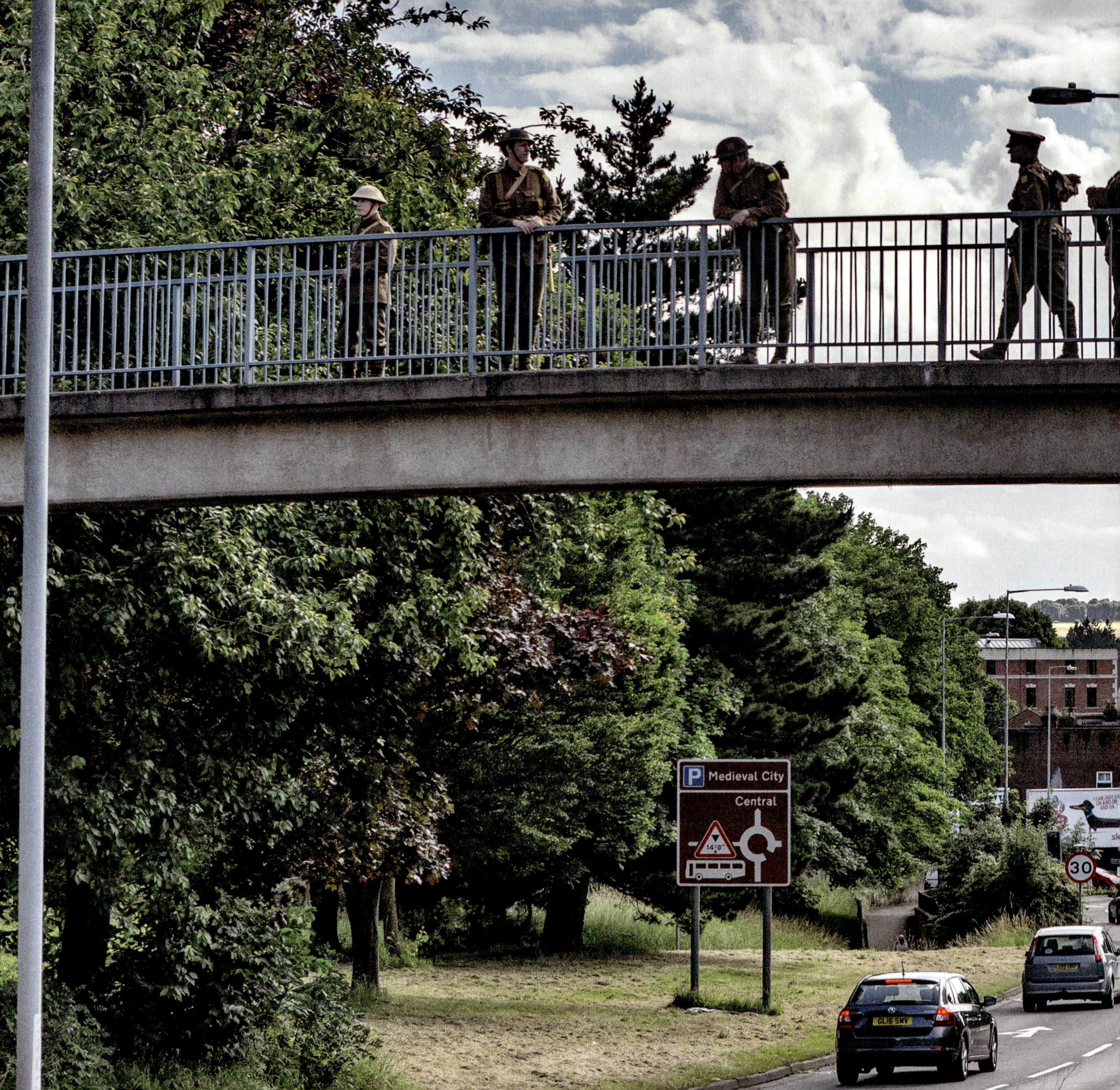

Medieval City
Central
14'9"
30

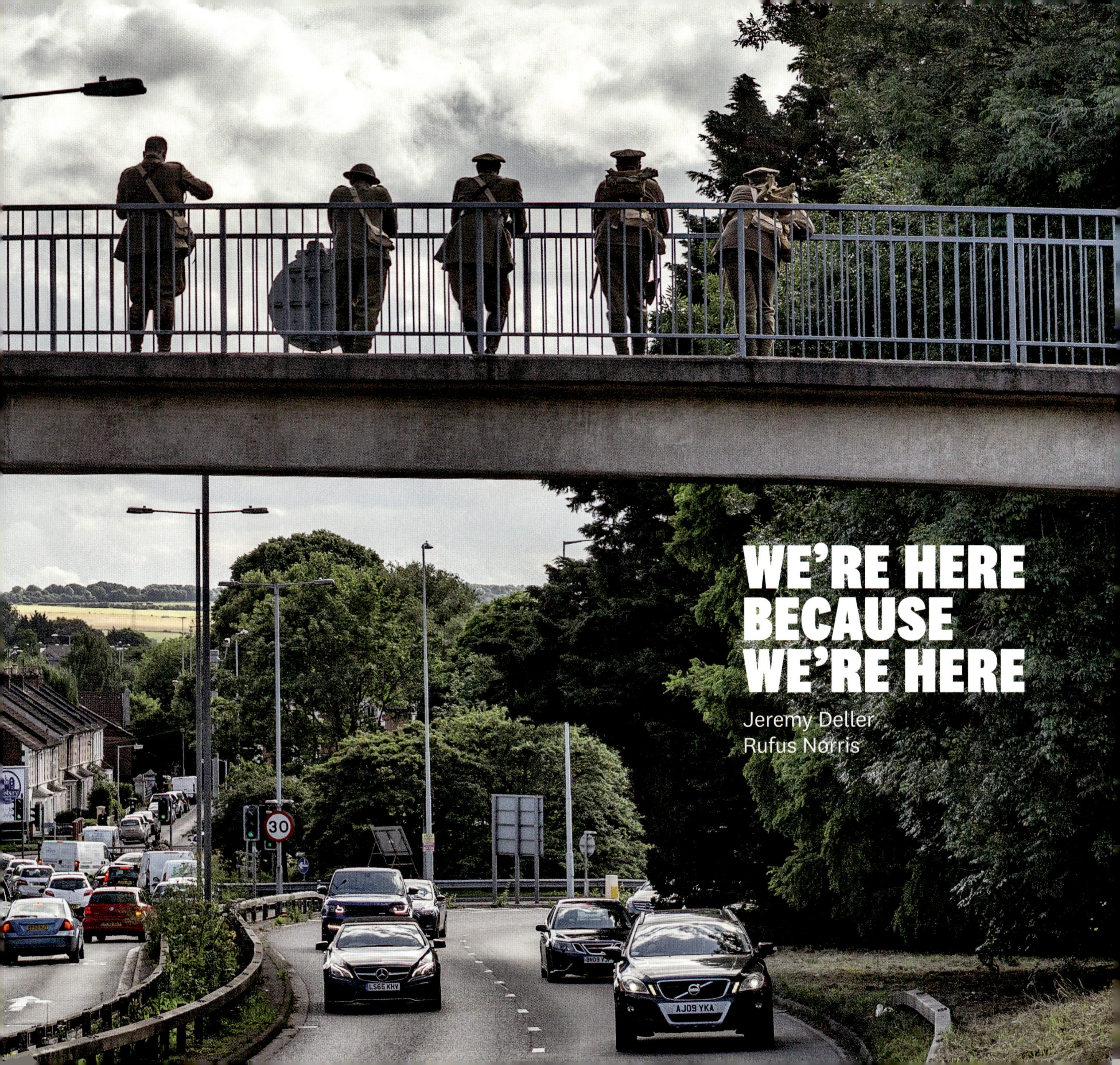
WE'RE HERE
BECAUSE
WE'RE HERE
Jeremy Deller
Rufus Norris

On 1 July 2016, wholly unannounced, some 1,400 men dressed in First World War uniforms emerged silently in small groups across the UK, standing in train stations, streets, on public transport and in shopping centres. When approached, they did not speak, but simply handed out a card, each bearing the name of a soldier who had died on that same day 100 years earlier. It was the anniversary of the first day of the Battle of the Somme and the men were participating in a living artwork created by artist Jeremy Deller in collaboration with Rufus Norris, director of the National Theatre.

From 7am to 7pm, thousands of volunteers, each representing a fallen soldier, took this unique and living memorial out onto the streets of contemporary Britain.

Private Robert Wallace

9th Battalion
Royal Inniskilling Fusiliers

Died at the Somme on 1st July 1916
Aged 17 years

#wearehere

Lance Corporal
George Frederick Tarrant

1st/9th Battalion
London Regiment (Queen Victoria's Rifles)

Died at the Somme on 1st July 1916
Aged 22 years

#wearehere

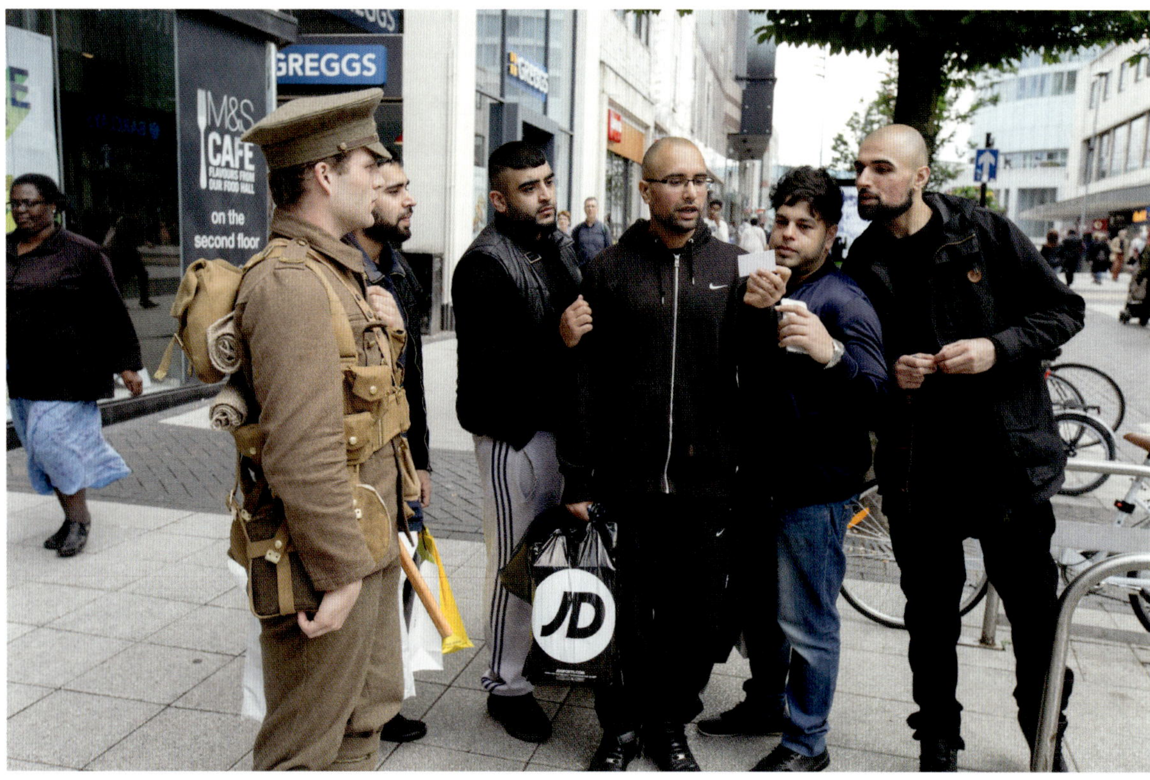

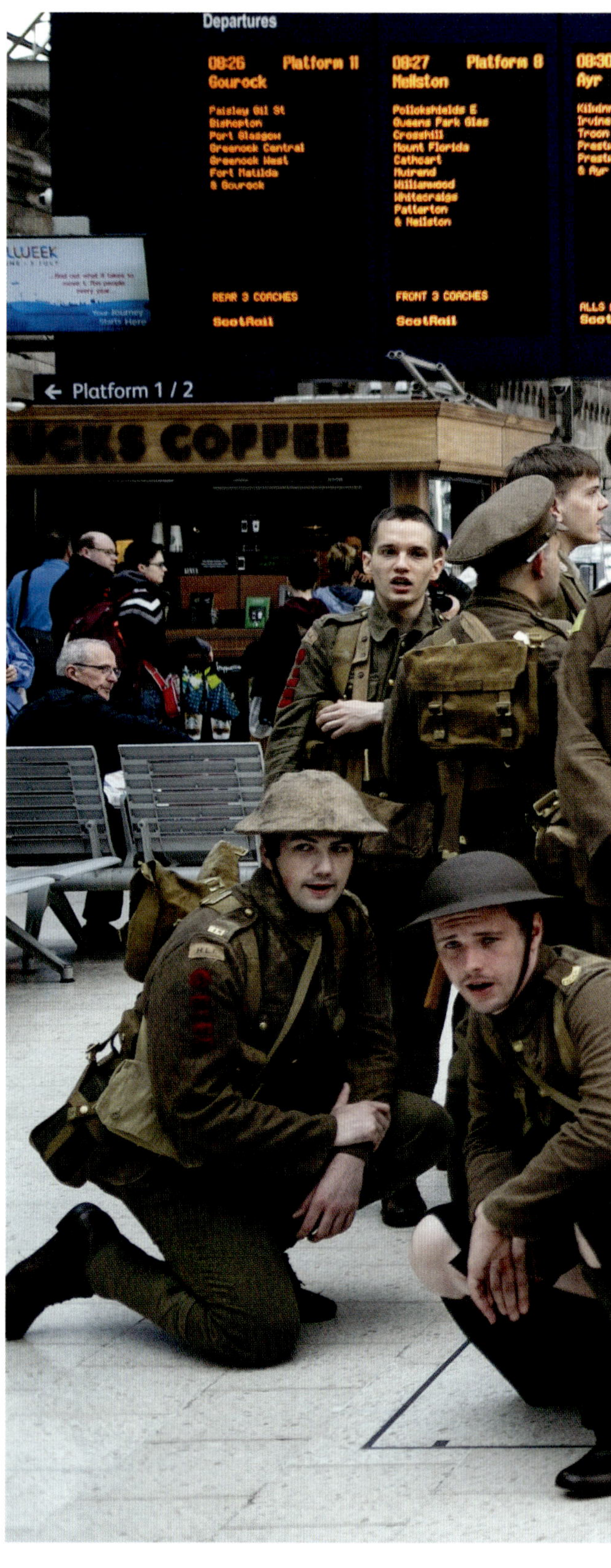

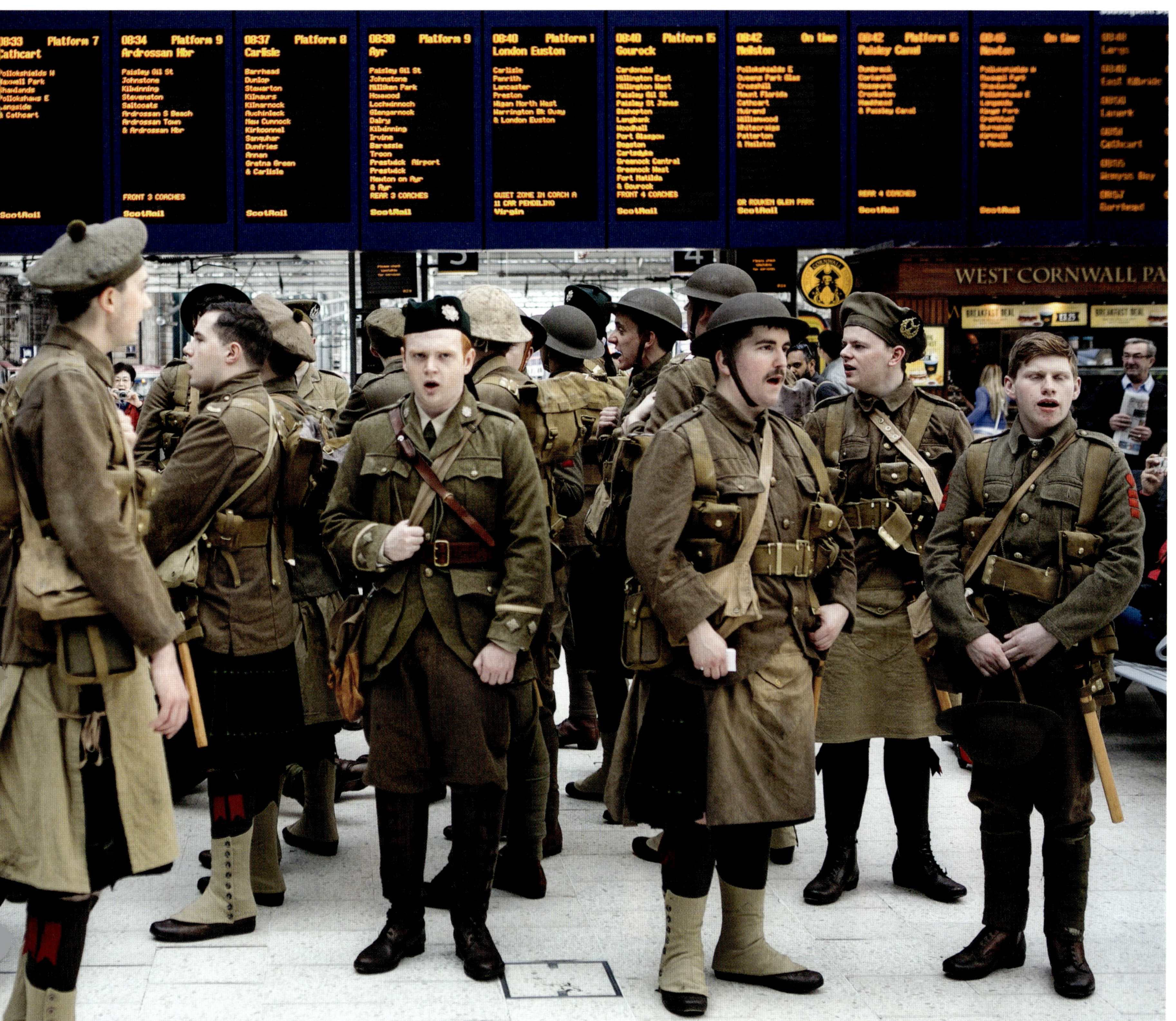

WEST CORNWALL PA

Deller was clear from the outset that the event needed a powerful human element. In order to have the fullest impact on its audience, it also needed to be mobile, unpredictable – even intrusive. This was to be a memorial that came to the people, rather than the other way round.

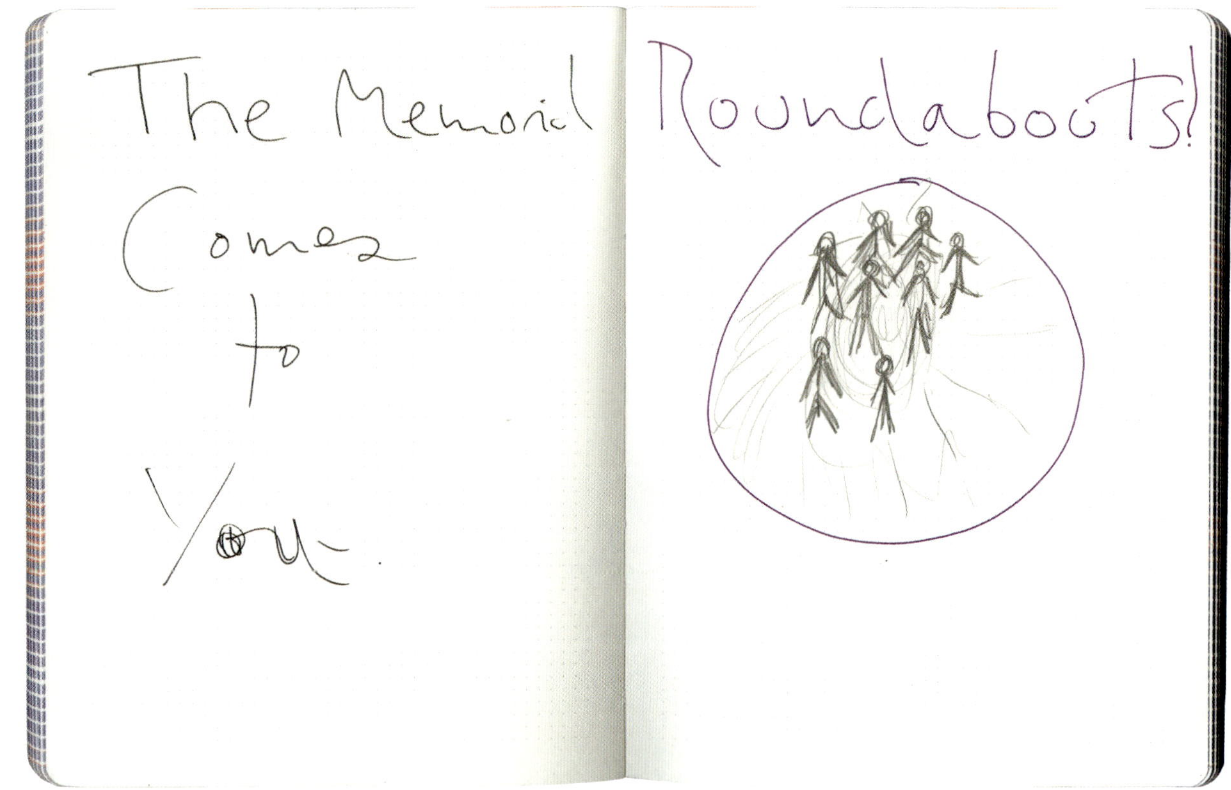

NOT. [Manchester] Open
Miserable Kind.
Statues——— Friendly.
Sculptures-
Posi
Intimidating. receptive.
Smiling x. (—
⟶ Handshake Be Interested
Nod [Photo] Comfortable

How is it possible National Event
Nat to create a Dynamic figurative
an. Public High Vis Seep by]
Intervention. if not Random. millions
not expecting Life of its own.
or necessarily wanting. Living Sculpture.
Memorial
Avoid Sentimentality
unsettling
obstructive
Intervention in Daily Life.
Corner of Eye.
or Stepping Over

1916

'We're here because we're here' was a refrain often heard in the First World War trenches, sung over and over to the tune of 'Auld Lang Syne' as a reaction to the tedium and apparent pointlessness of trench life. It was also the title of Deller's performance piece and was sung at intervals, hauntingly, by the groups of uniformed men. On that first day of fighting in 1916 in the fields of France, 19,240 men were killed. (The battle itself would last another four and a half months, with an eventual death toll of 420,000 British, 200,000 French and 500,000 German soldiers.) Each of the volunteer participants in the work represented one of those soldiers.

Recruitment and rehearsal of the volunteers (all sworn to absolute secrecy) had begun many months earlier, through an unprecedented collaboration between 28 theatres, led by the Birmingham Repertory Theatre. There was no advance publicity of the event. Deller's aim was to create an unsentimental living memorial that would come to the people, and he had wanted people to encounter the soldiers in everyday settings — 'shopping centres and carparks and outside schools' — rather than in traditional 'heritage places' like churches and war memorials, where people arrive prepared and full of preconceptions.

We're here because we're here had a profound effect on its audience, stopping people in their tracks and moving many to tears. The cards that the soldiers handed out included the hashtag #wearehere, and photographs and accounts of the men flooded social media throughout the day. According to a YouGov poll, an astonishing 30 million people (63 per cent of the UK adult population) were aware of the soldiers that day, 2 million of whom saw the soldiers first hand.

After the event, 14-18 NOW and the National Theatre presented a touring exhibition at theatres and venues across the UK, telling the story of the one-day memorial through images of the volunteers. A BBC documentary was also made, charting the making of the project. And a year later, on the battle's 101st anniversary, Deller and 14-18 NOW published a book containing 100 photographs of the event.

UK-wide, 1 July 2016

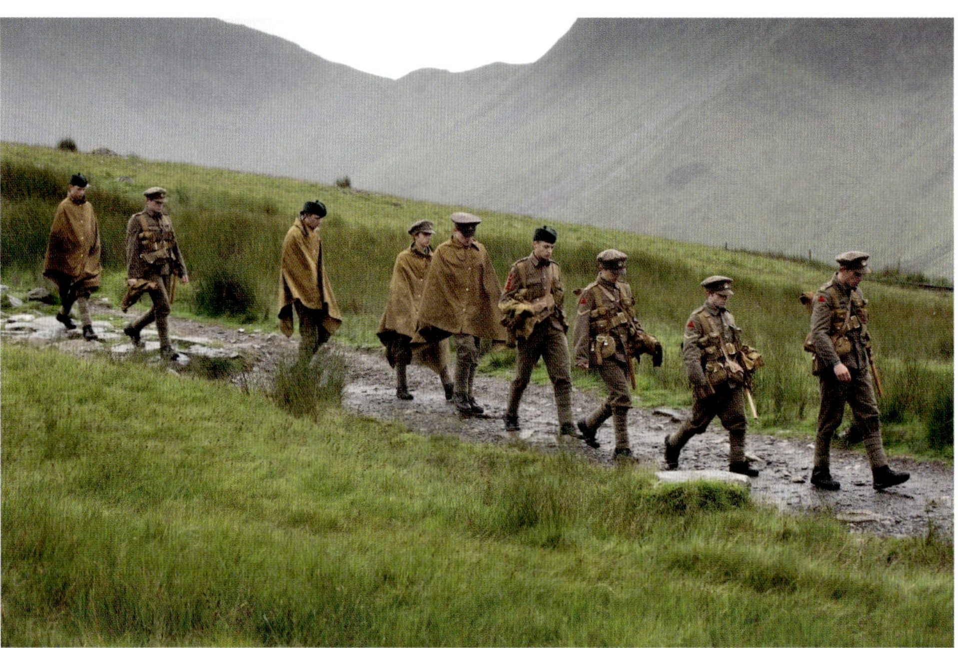

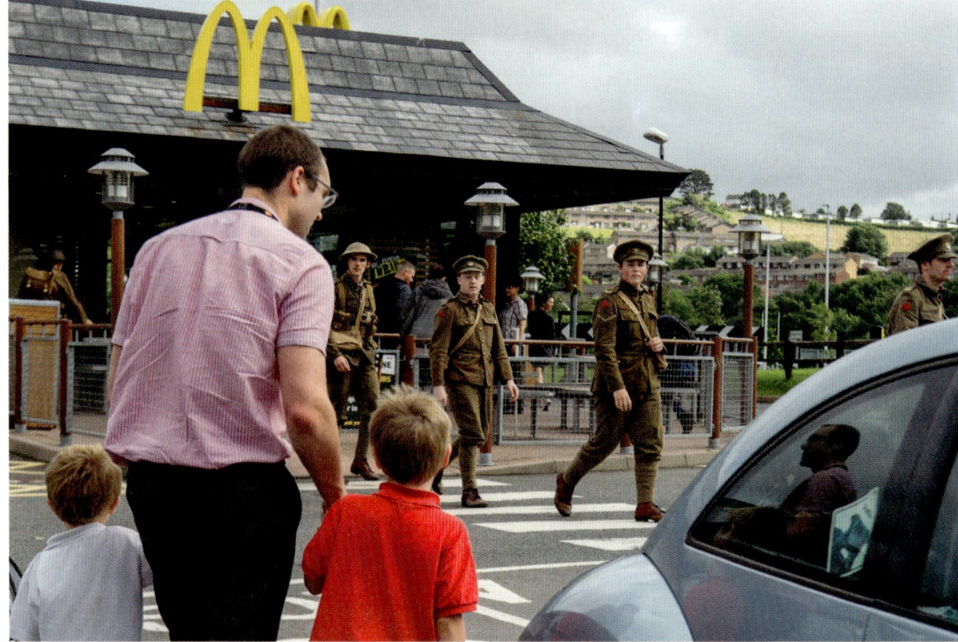

Participants aged between 16 and 52 dressed in historically accurate uniforms to reflect the men who had died in battle a century earlier. All were volunteers who had undergone rehearsals to achieve the right balance of impact and restraint.

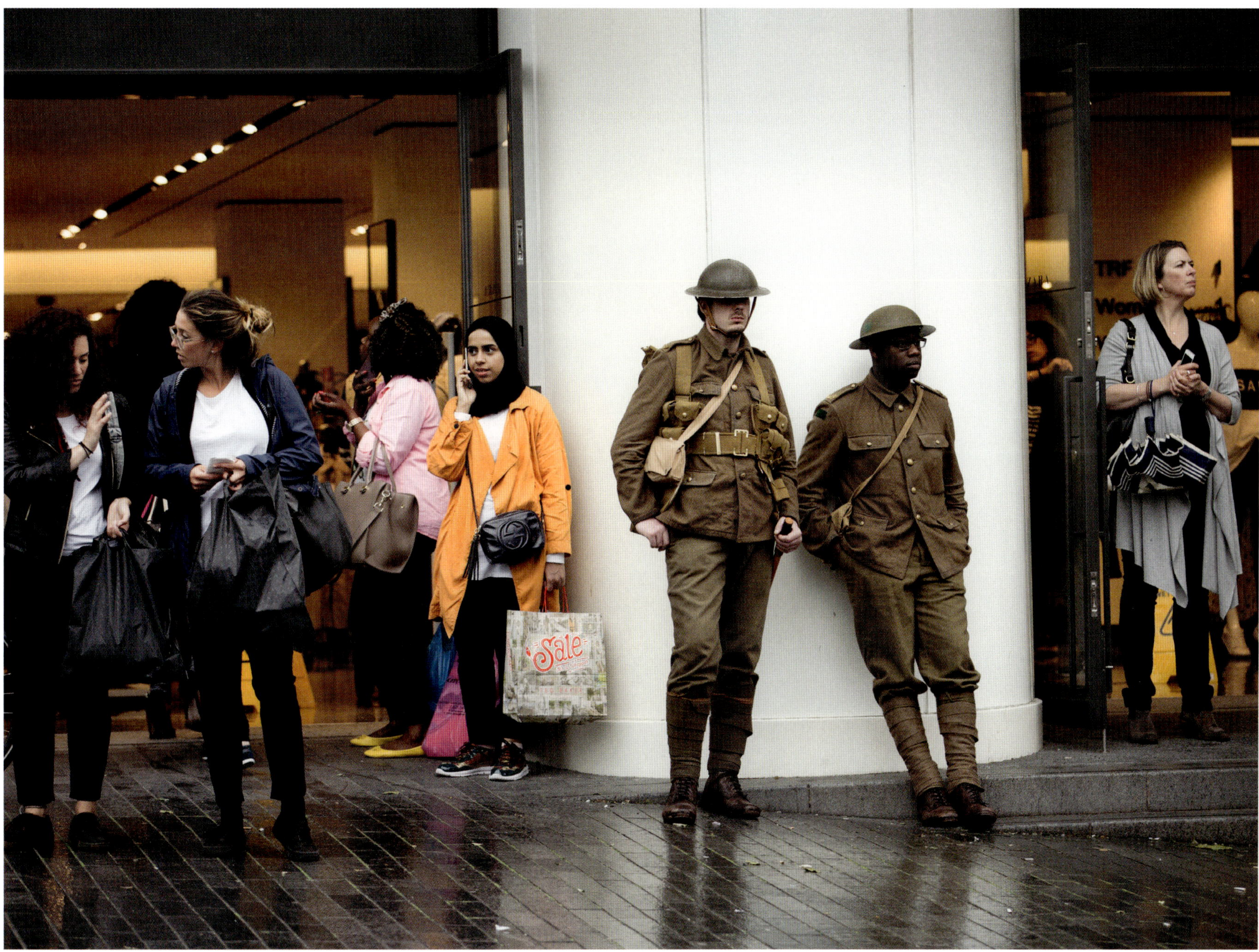

Up and down the country, groups of soldiers gathered then dispersed, blending into their everyday surroundings in a silent — and often static — tribute to the men whose names they carried.

TRACES OF THE GREAT WAR

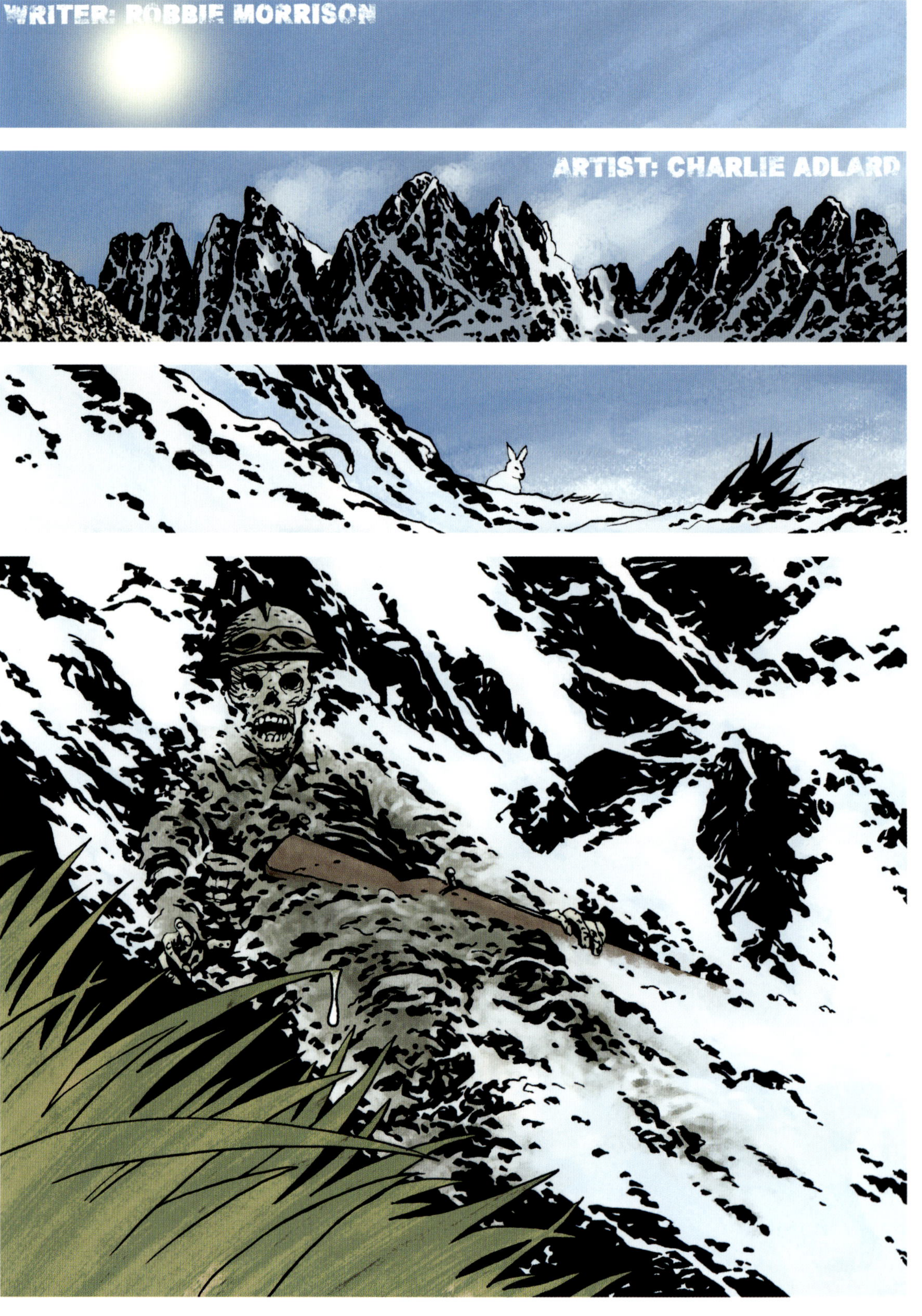

Traces of the Great War was an ambitious anthology of new illustrated short stories by internationally acclaimed comic book artists, graphic novelists and writers, all of whom explored the continued relevance and resonance of the First World War and its aftermath in our lives today.

An international collaboration between the Lakes International Comic Art Festival (LICAF) and On a Marché sur la Bulle in Amiens, France, commissioned by 14-18 NOW and La Mission du Centenaire de la Première Guerre mondiale, *Traces of the Great War* featured contributions from both the UK and around the world. The anthology included a number of collaborations between graphic artists and writers (Dave McKean with poet Simon Armitage, Sean Phillips with novelist Ian Rankin), and between artists and illustrators who had never worked together before (Juan Díaz Canales and Kris, Régis Hautière and Thomas von Kummant).

The Lakes International Comic Art Festival, Cumbria, 12 — 14 October 2018 / Salon du Livre d'Albert, France, October 2018

Opposite. The pairing of British comics writer Robbie Morrison and cartoonist Charlie Adlard produced *Without a Trace*…

Right. *Really?*, by the French illustrator and writer Edmond Baudoin.

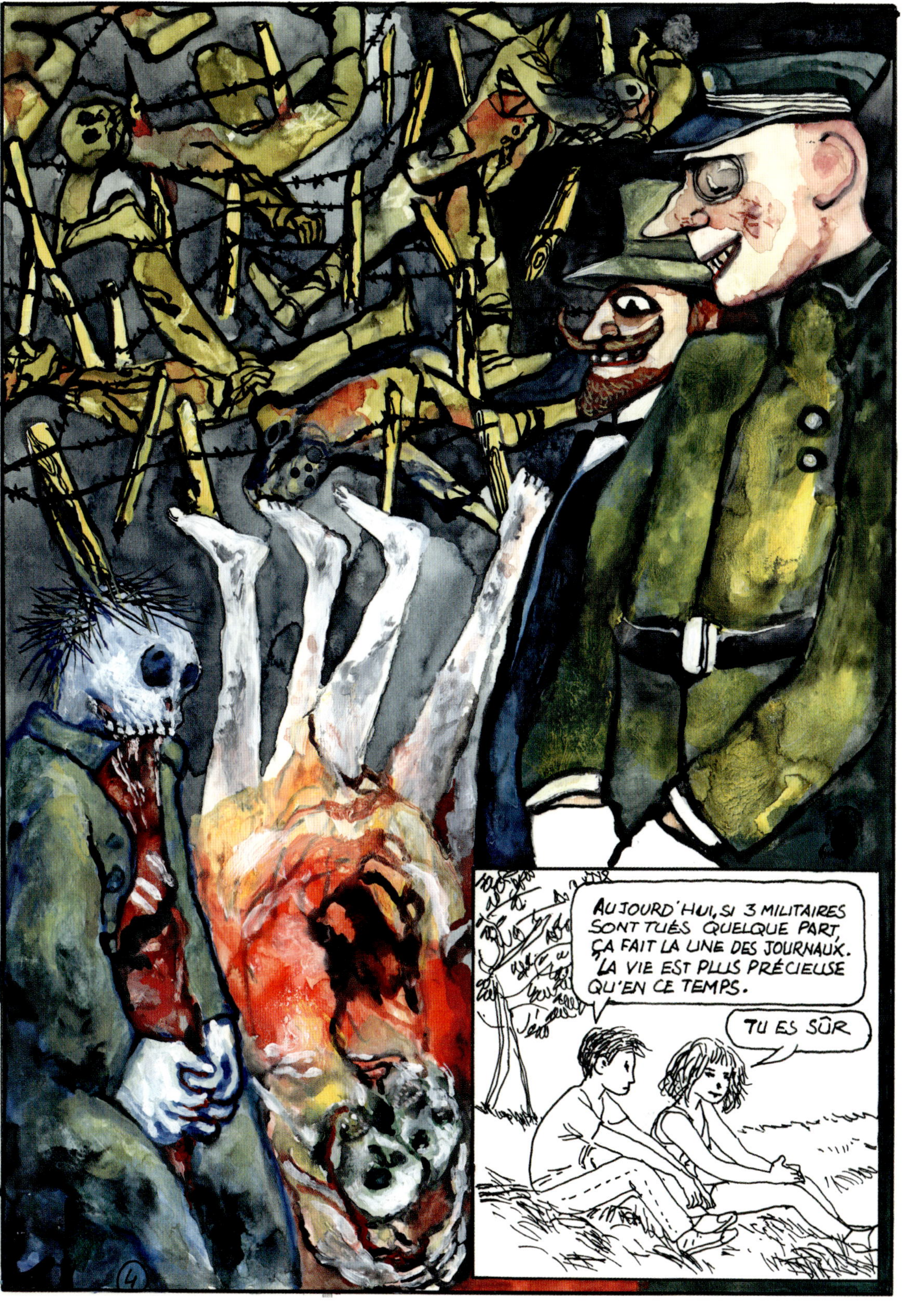

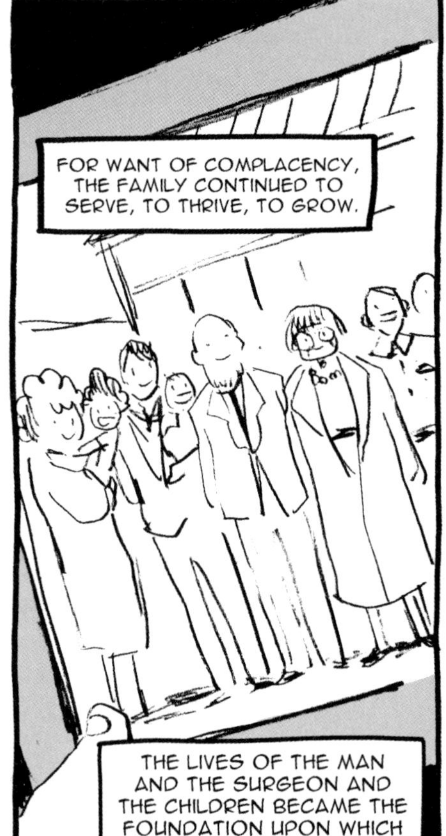
FOR WANT OF COMPLACENCY, THE FAMILY CONTINUED TO SERVE, TO THRIVE, TO GROW.
THE LIVES OF THE MAN AND THE SURGEON AND THE CHILDREN BECAME THE FOUNDATION UPON WHICH THE NEXT GENERATION WOULD BUILD.

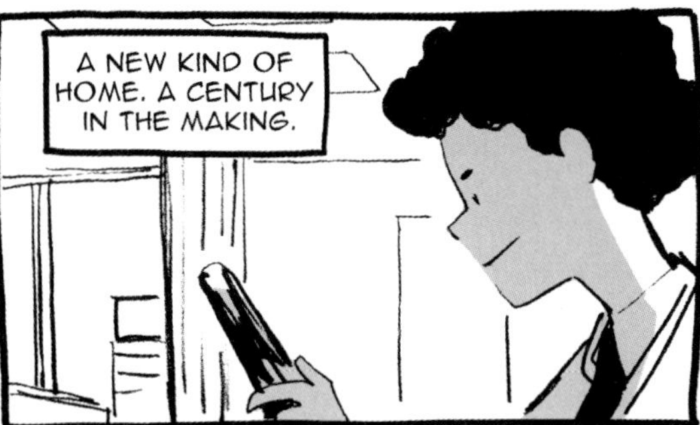
A NEW KIND OF HOME. A CENTURY IN THE MAKING.

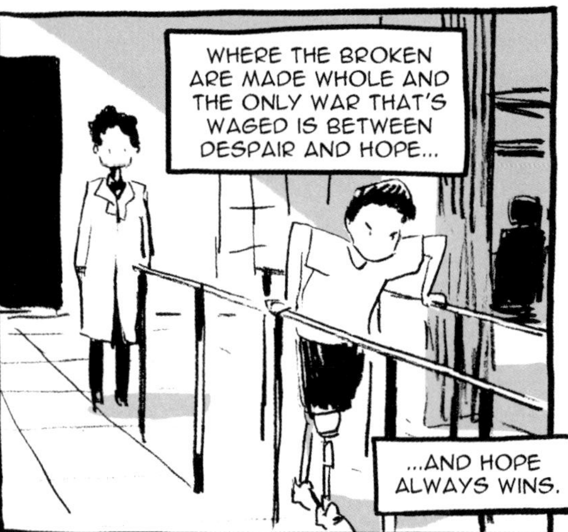
WHERE THE BROKEN ARE MADE WHOLE AND THE ONLY WAR THAT'S WAGED IS BETWEEN DESPAIR AND HOPE...
...AND HOPE ALWAYS WINS.

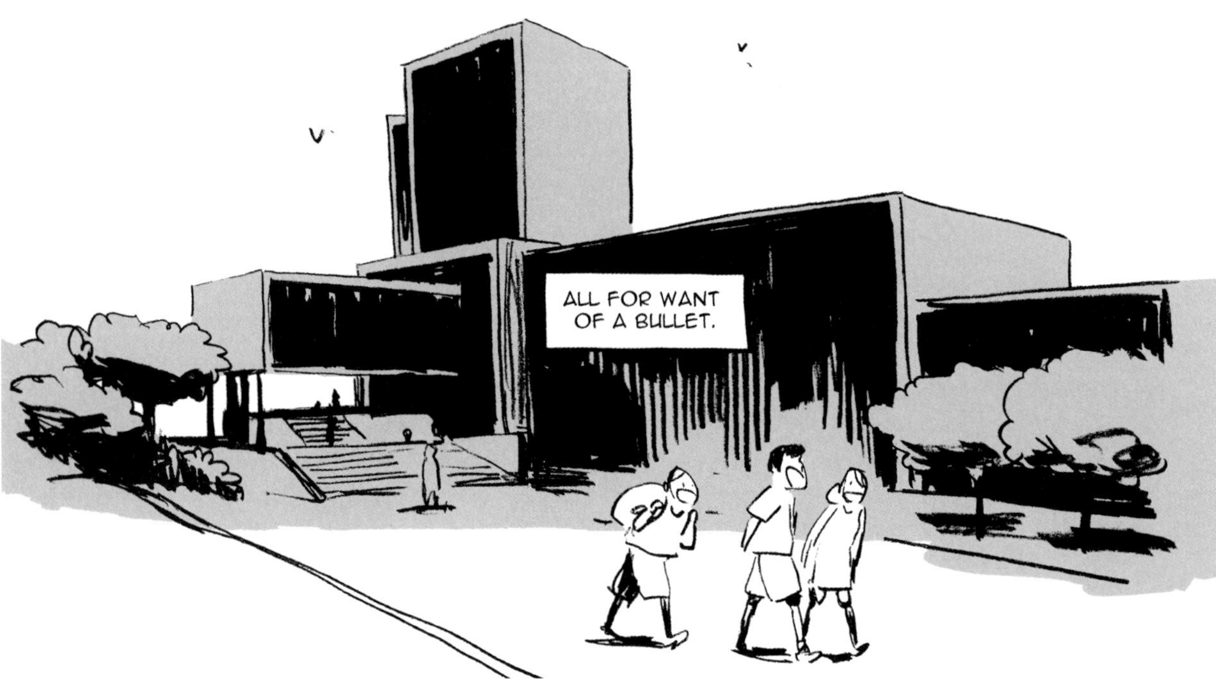
ALL FOR WANT OF A BULLET.

MAKE GERMANY PAY!

Script: Mary M Talbot Art and lettering: Bryan Talbot

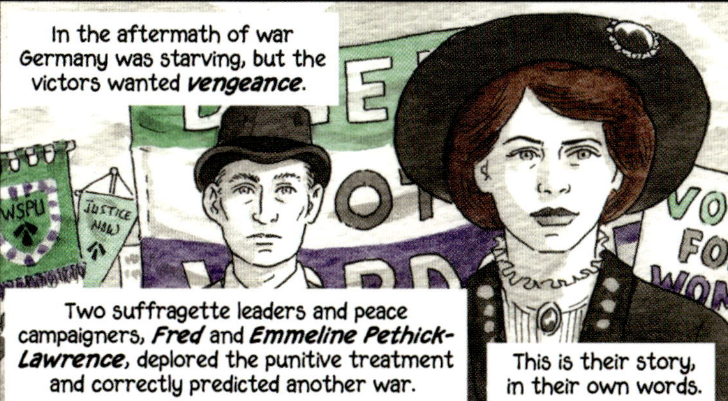

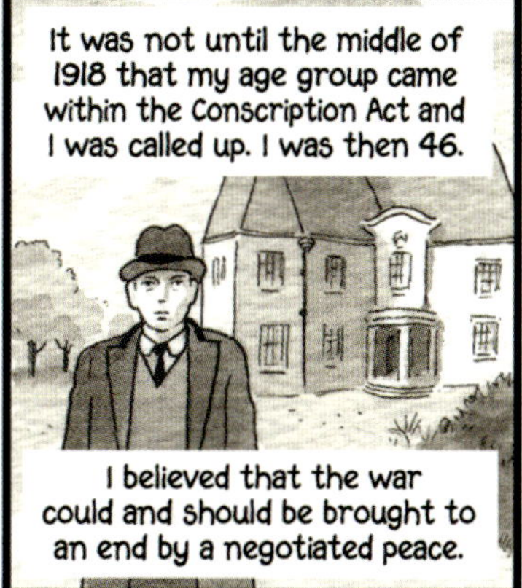

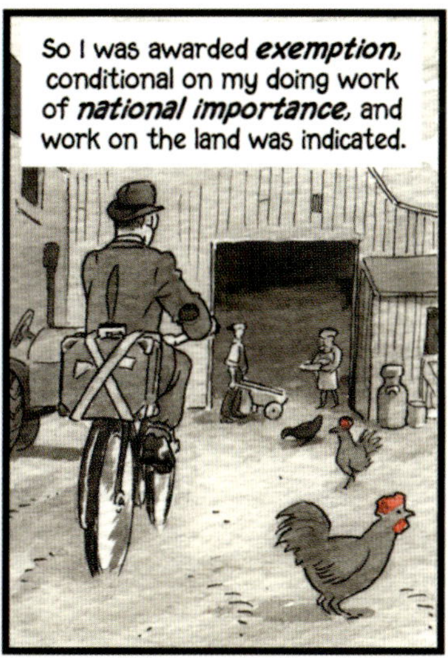

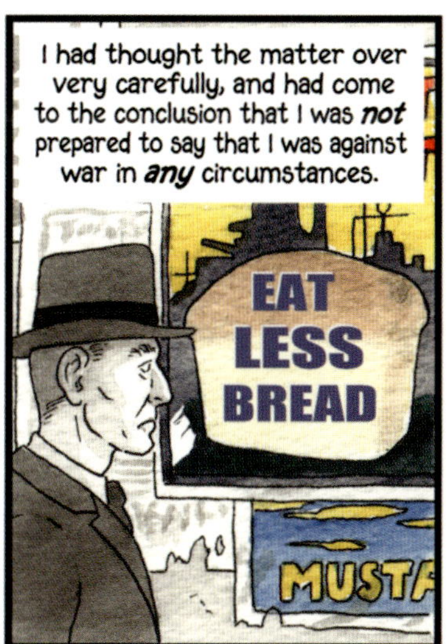

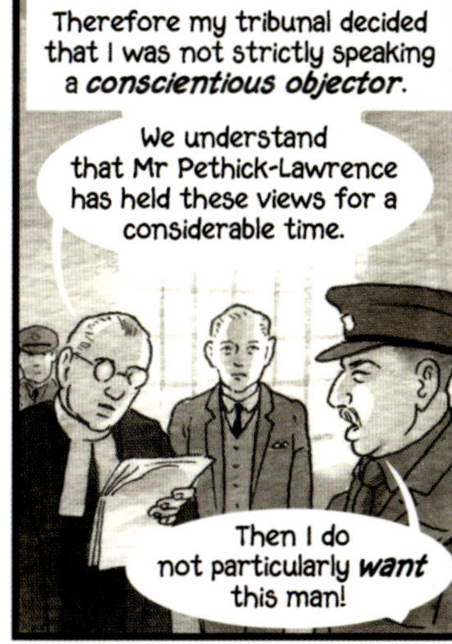

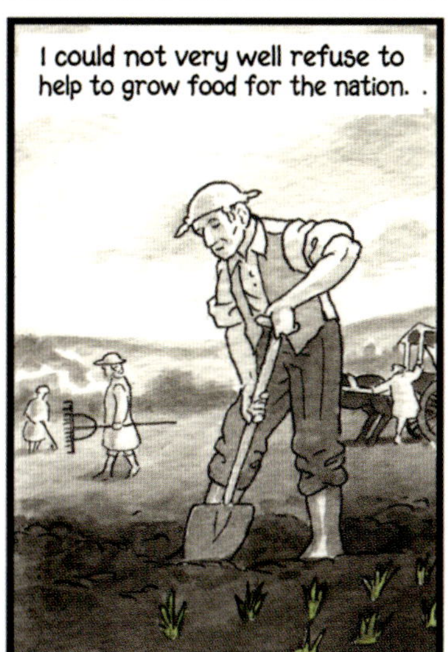

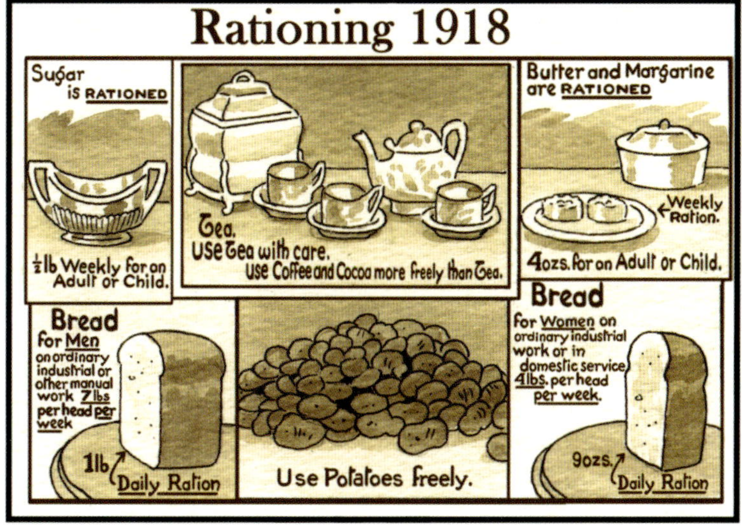

Rationing 1918

Sugar is RATIONED
¼ lb Weekly for an Adult or Child.

Tea. Use Tea with care. Use Coffee and Cocoa more freely than Tea.

Butter and Margarine are RATIONED
Weekly Ration
4 ozs. for an Adult or Child.

Bread for Men on ordinary industrial or other manual work 7 lbs per head per week
1 lb Daily Ration

Use Potatoes freely.

Bread for Women on ordinary industrial work or in domestic service 4 lbs. per head per week.
9 ozs. Daily Ration

BEWARE OF PITY

Complicité
Schaubühne Berlin

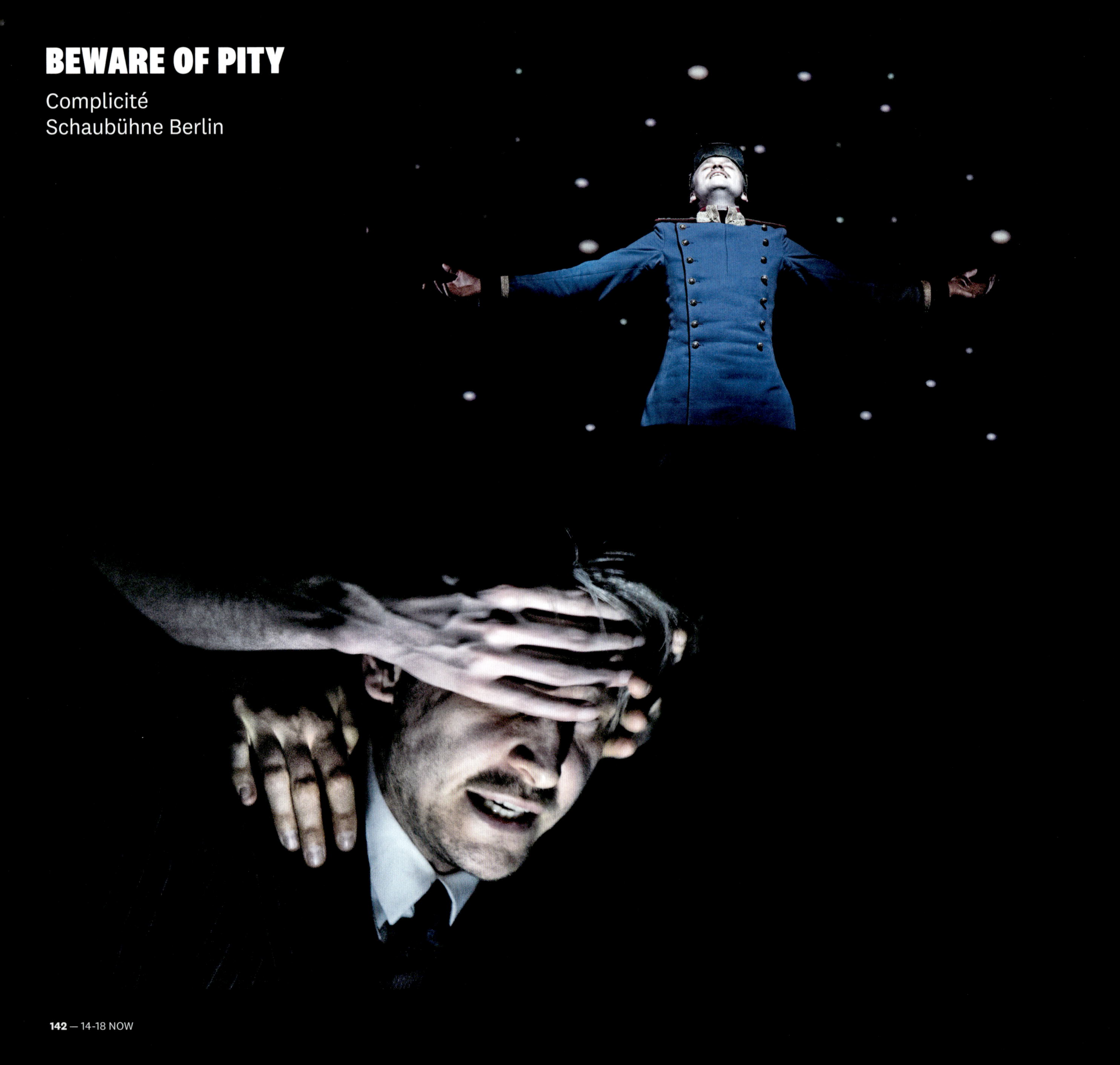

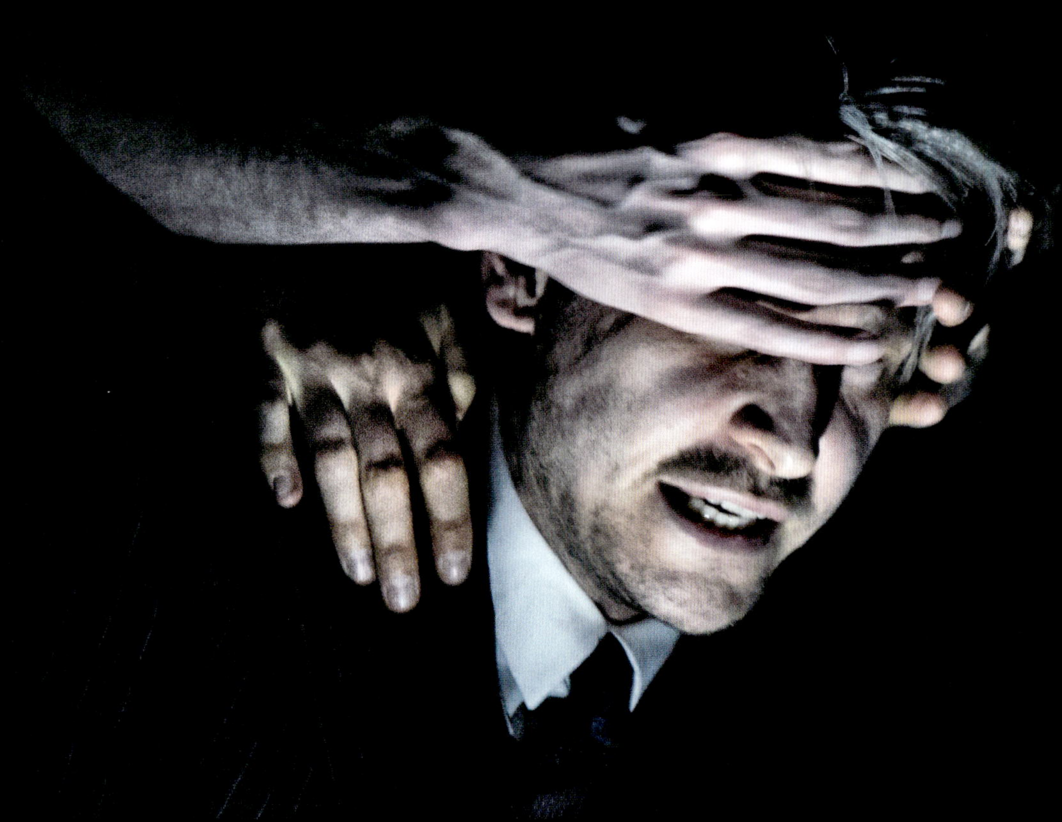

Beware of Pity is a novel by Stefan Zweig, written in 1939, on the eve of the Second World War, but set on the eve of the First. It tells the story of a young officer, Hofmiller, who commits a faux pas at a soirée held by a local landowner, unwittingly asking his paralysed daughter to dance. The mistake pulls Hofmiller into a relentless train of events in this devastating depiction of honour, love and betrayal, set against the disintegration of the Austro-Hungarian Empire — a catalyst for the outbreak of the First World War.

Director Simon McBurney presented this story in dramatic new form in 2017, in a co-production that brought two of Europe's most imaginative, boundary-pushing theatre companies together for the first time — McBurney's own Complicité and the German Schaubühne. Seven German-speaking actors (with the aid of English surtitles) tested the limits of physical theatre on an equally innovative set, enhanced by video projections and a compelling soundscape, to create a tense and emotionally charged telling of Hofmiller's slide into disaster.

Following on from the Schaubühne's success at the Barbican with *The Forbidden Zone* (see pages 154–157), *Beware of Pity* was an eloquent work of theatre that depicted an individual and a society on the verge of collapse, raising questions of consciousness and compassion.

Barbican, London, 9 — 12 February 2017

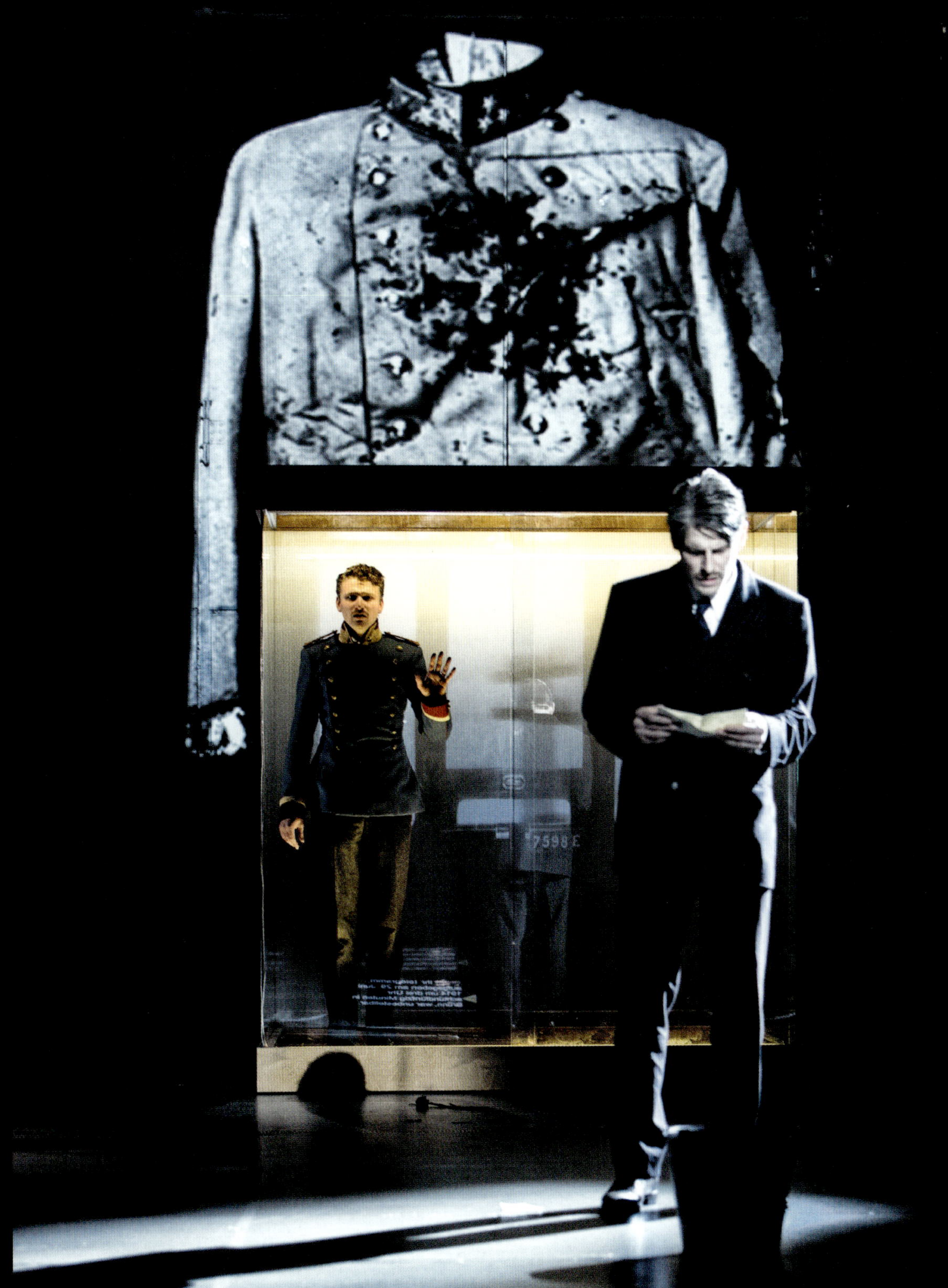

A sound score, video projections and a stylised set design created the tension and claustrophobia of a world on the brink of collapse.

DOES IT MATTER?

Katherine Araniello
Jez Colborne
Claire Cunningham
Tony Heaton
Simon Mckeown

More than 2 million British servicemen were wounded in the First World War, and many returned home with a permanent disability. They were one of the most visible legacies of the war, and their sheer numbers meant that society's attitudes towards disability were forced to change. On a practical level, major advances in prosthetics, research into physical and psychological trauma, and the provision of workplaces and accommodation for disabled veterans were all developments that would benefit future generations.

In 2014, a series of short films titled *Does It Matter?* co-commissioned by 14-18 NOW and Channel 4, and produced by Artsadmin and Xenoki, explored this subject. Five disabled artists were commissioned to create unorthodox, irreverent and unexpected takes on the legacies of war and disability in Britain today.

Oh! What a Lovely Lovely Ward by Katherine Araniello turned sentimentality on its head in a playful and absurd reimagining of a wartime hospital, in which the wounded waited their turn to have their morale lifted by Matron, while a jolly war song was bashed out on an old piano, and a frenzied special-effects team tended to the injured.

For *Soldiering On*, Jez Colborne collaborated with Mind the Gap to explore his fascination with the pomp and ceremony surrounding war, in contrast to its brutal reality. Set in an old cinema, with Colborne performing an original song at a piano, it explored the belief that 'learning-disabled people don't go to war'.

Claire Cunningham's *Resemblance* was a solo performance created around the act of assembling (and disassembling) a crutch in the manner of a soldier assembling his gun, thereby comparing a weapon of destruction with an object of support.

In *Breathe Nothing of Slaughter*, Tony Heaton examined the potent symbol of the memorial against the realities of those disabled by the devastating effects of war. Heroic, enduring, Adonis-like bodies waving flags or in prayerful repose were set in stark contrast to archive images of blackened faces, rotting feet and malnourished bodies.

Simon Mckeown's *Ghosts* used motion capture and animation to follow a cast of disabled veterans from the various countries of the conflict as they talked, cooked and tended to pigeons in a landscape filled with the artefacts of war.

These five short films were screened at the Southbank Centre's Unlimited Festival on 2 September 2014, and on the Channel 4 website.

Southbank Centre, London, 2 September 2014 / Channel 4 online

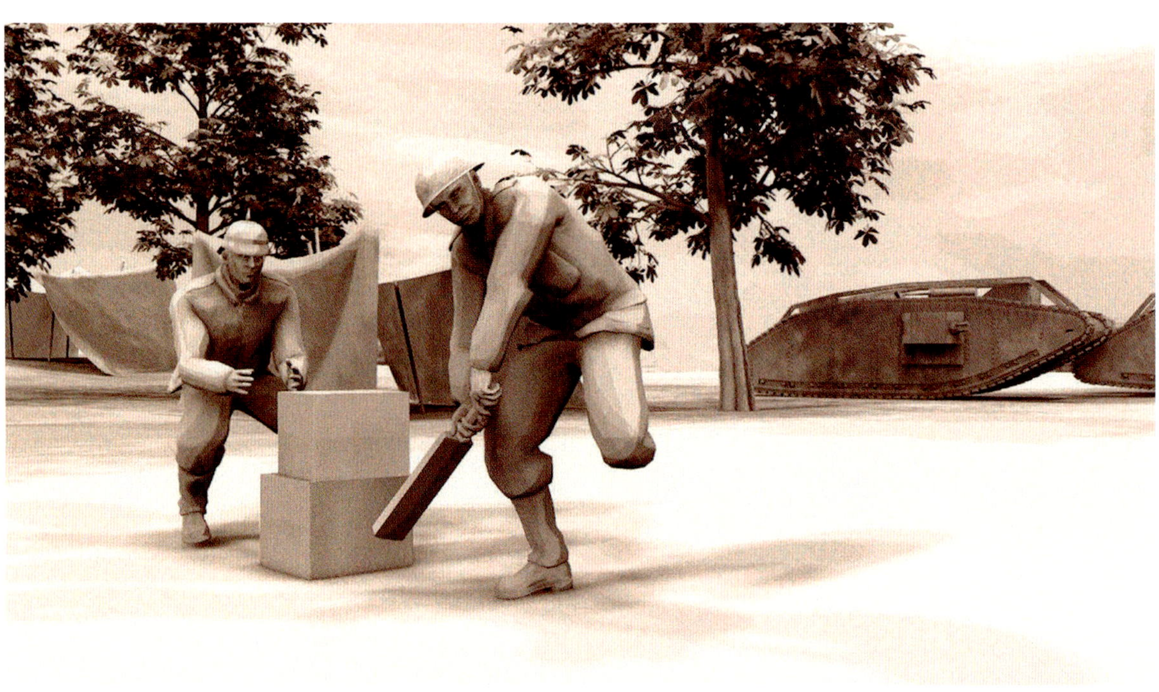

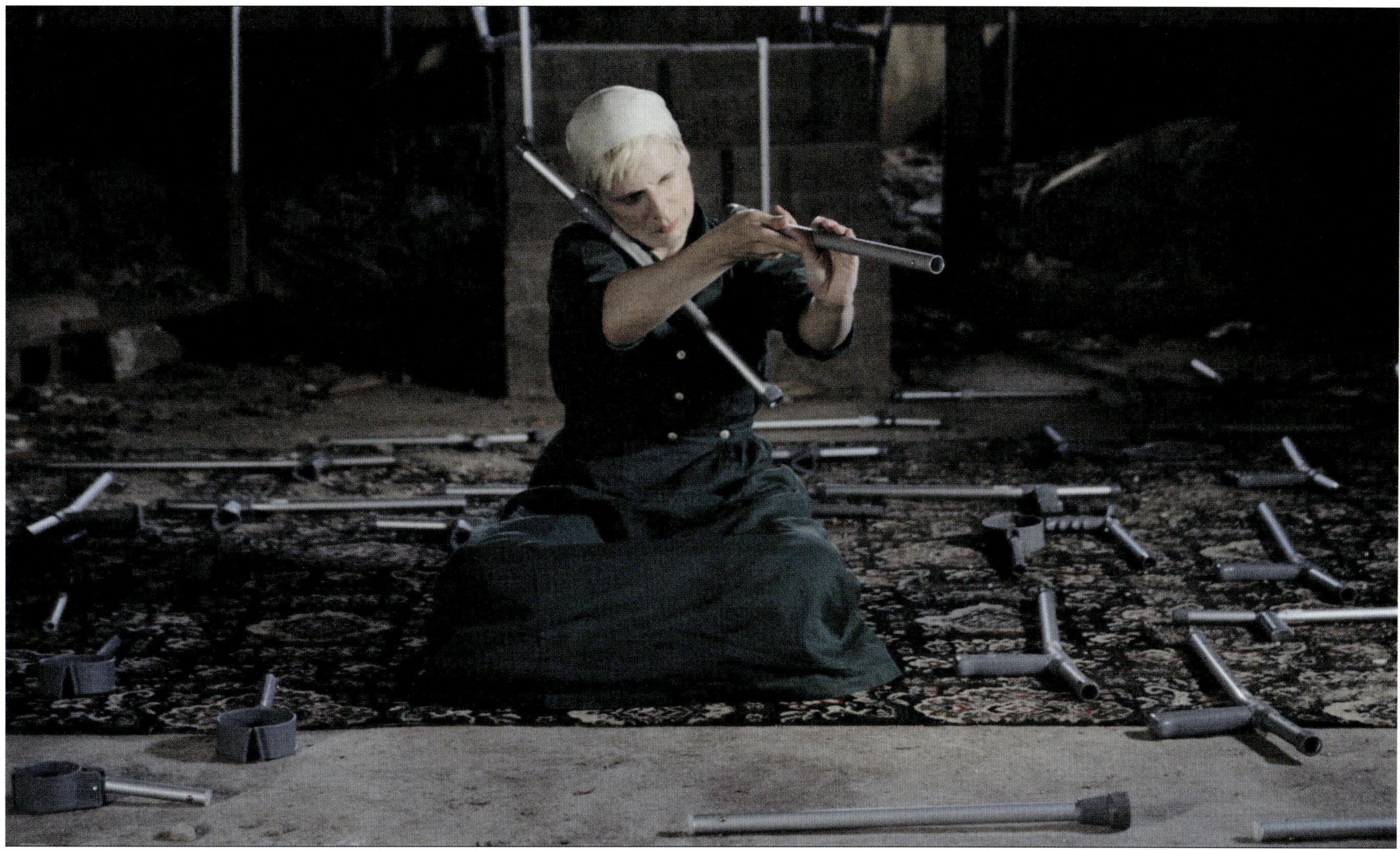

Above. In *Resemblance*,
Claire Cunningham enacted
the 'ritual' of dismantling
a crutch as if she was
handling a weapon.

Opposite. Simon Mckeown's
Ghosts featured a virtual
cast of disabled veterans.

> '*Memorial honours the dead in the simplest, most honest way … through collective compassion and the classic inspiration of art — in eloquent music, the words of great poets and the performance of a great actor.*'
>
> *Stage Noise*

MEMORIAL

Alice Oswald
Jocelyn Pook

Alice Oswald's powerful book-length poem 'Memorial' was inspired by *The Iliad*. But rather than attempting to retell Homer's monumental tale, Oswald's poem instead focuses on the fates of the soldiers named within it, turning a heroic epic into a human lament for the lost and forgotten. It was published to widespread critical praise in 2011, but according to Oswald herself, 'it was written to be spoken out loud' — a claim that was fulfilled when director Chris Drummond of Australia's acclaimed Brink Productions took *Memorial* from page to stage at the Barbican in 2018. This poignant and atmospheric theatre work captured the essence of Oswald's poem while drawing fresh connections between its Homeric narrative and the First World War.

Australian actress Helen Morse performed the text, joined by a chorus of 215 local men and women — one for every soldier in Oswald's poem. The chorus was drawn from local community choirs, with music composed by Jocelyn Pook, and movements directed by Yaron Lifschitz, artistic director of the Australian contemporary circus company Circa.

Barbican, London, 27 — 30 September 2018

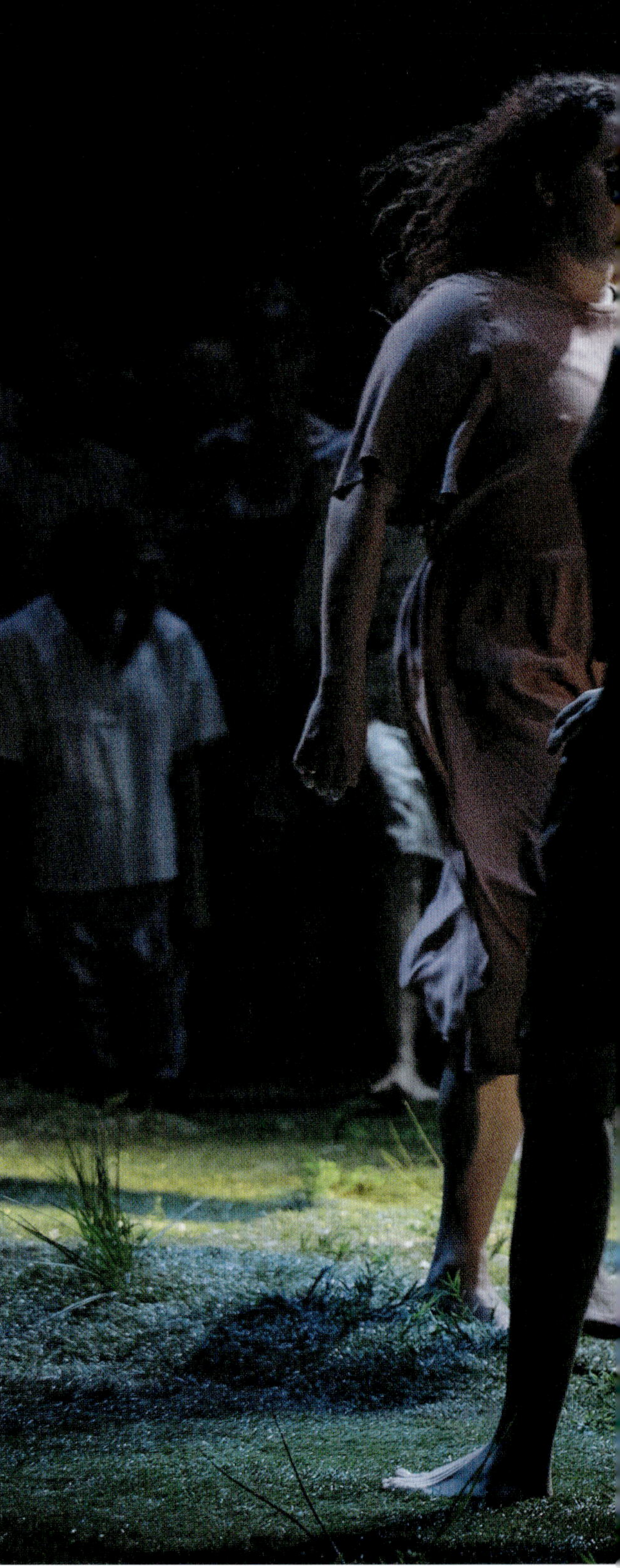

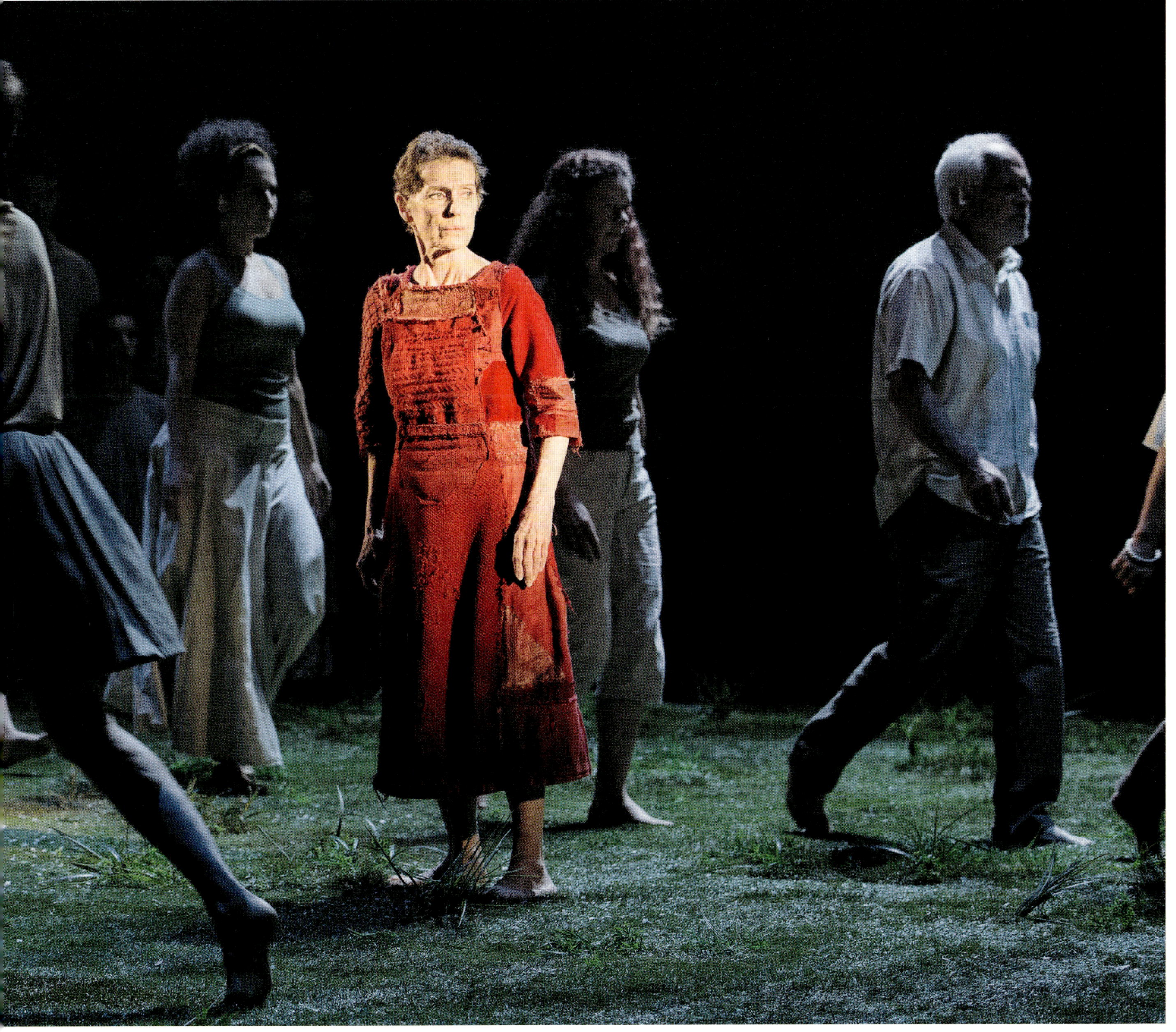

*Mostly these sculptures are cast in situ
and replaced back into the landscape.
The journey to visit the piece is considered
part of the experience, and the pieces
are often placed in remote places — on
islands, in woodlands, by lakes or in the
desert. The location chosen for this work
was a remote part of Dalby Forest in North
Yorkshire, so the viewer would have to
travel on foot to see the piece, or would
come across it unexpectedly amongst
the trees and bracken.*

A WALK IN THE FOREST: ANOTHER SHY SCULPURE

Rachel Whiteread

In 2016 I was approached by 14-18 NOW to see if I would propose a work for its programme — a project that I was delighted to accept.

It seemed appropriate to continue with the theme of my 'Shy Sculptures', which I have been working on for the past decade. These are a series of works that encapsulate the essence of certain archetypal buildings and structures set in the landscape worldwide. The works are cast in concrete from the interior of the buildings. All of the elements — the fireplaces, doors, windows and so on — are cast blind, so the building has no means of entry.

Mostly these sculptures are cast in situ and replaced back into the landscape. The journey to visit the piece is considered part of the experience, and the pieces are often placed in remote places — on islands, in woodlands, by lakes or in the desert. The location chosen for this work was a remote part of Dalby Forest in North Yorkshire, so the viewer would have to travel on foot to see the piece, or would come across it unexpectedly amongst the trees and bracken.

I eventually chose to work with a Nissen hut — a peripatetic structure developed during the First World War and used as workshops, dormitories, hospitals, housing and even churches. These huts have become an indigenous part of our post-war architectural story and can be seen dotted all over the country, where their usage — as barns and farm buildings, village halls and warehouses, amongst many other functions — remains as diverse as it was in the war years.

These huts were originally developed in 1916 by Peter Nissen, a Canadian-American-British mining engineer, inventor and army officer in Ypres, northern France. While serving there Nissen realised that cheap mass-produced huts needed to be developed that could be easily installed by unskilled labour, to house the thousands of troops that were mobilised during the First World War.

Nissen developed these structures so that a team of six people could erect them in no more than four hours. They were exemplary structures — cheap, versatile — and they became a model for prefabricated buildings that used simple and versatile materials at their core: bolts, wood and corrugated iron.

The particular hut used for this project measured 5 metres by 11 metres by 3 metres. It had been moved a number of times during its lifetime and had had several incarnations.

The location in Dalby Forest was also of significance as the forest was originally planted to replenish dwindling timber supplies, beginning after the war in 1921. Nissen huts were used to house labour-camp workers and prisoners of war who began the planting of the forest, and were used in other forests across the country as prisoner-of-war camps. The foundations of the buildings of the camp can still be seen in the location that we selected as the site of the sculpture.

I chose to use a material that is as old as the history of architecture; concrete is a material that has been used in all its guises for millennia. I also used a casting and laminating technique that will last for decades. The work in its structured presence will sit quietly in the evergreen forest in its new ghostly, concrete embodiment for many years to come.

Nissen Hut was created to mark the centenary of the Forestry Commission as well as the centenary of the First World War. Its presence in this remote location serves as a reminder that the Forestry Commission was set up in 1919 to expand Britain's forests and woodland after depletion during the war.

Deep in the heart of Yorkshire's Dalby Forest stands
a ghostly white cabin. *Nissen Hut* is a concrete cast
of the interior space of a Nissen hut, the distinctive
military structure invented by Major Peter Nissen
during the First World War to provide easily erected
shelters for a variety of different uses.

The Forestry Commission, which manages
Dalby Forest, came into being in 1919 to replenish the
nation's strategic timber reserve, which was entirely
depleted after the First World War, and Nissen huts
were used to house the labourers who supported the
planting of the forest, just as they had sheltered so
many others across Europe during the war.

By focusing on empty space and transforming it
into sculpture, this permanent public work created
a haunting testament to the war's impact on every
part of the British landscape. It also brought visitors
into the heart of the forest — a living, breathing space in
which to view art.

Dalby Forest, Yorkshire, from 10 October 2018

NISSEN HUT

Rachel Whiteread

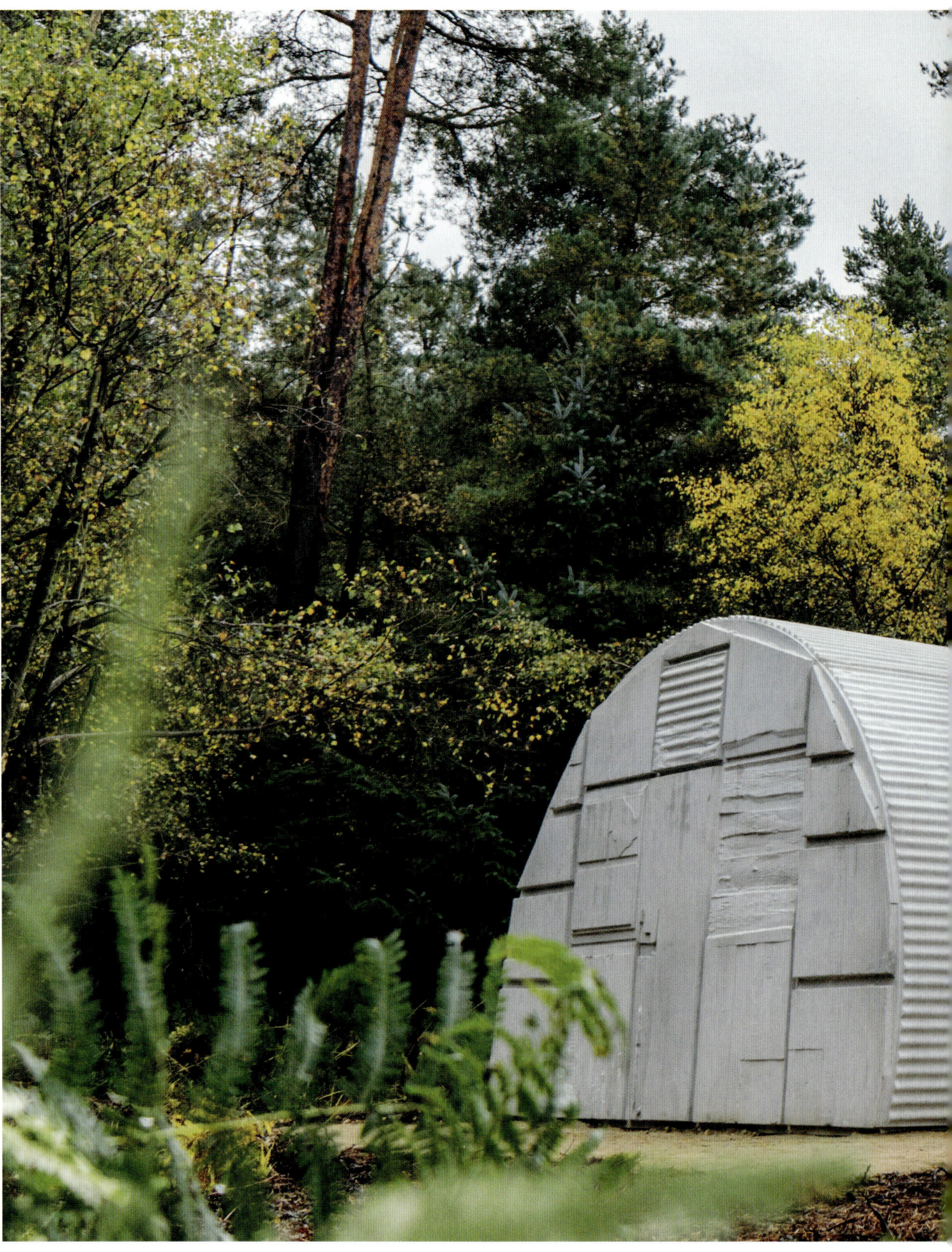

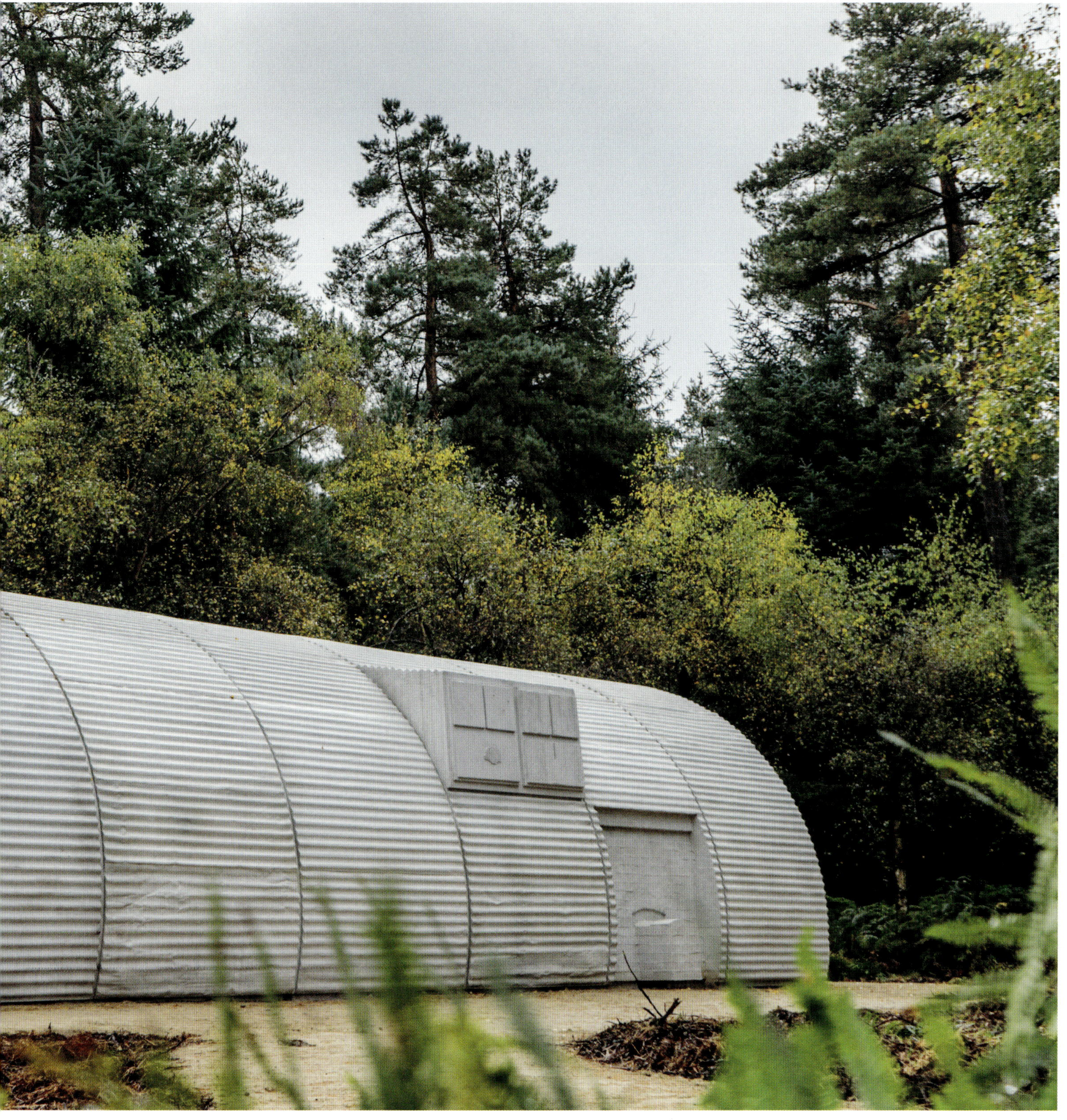

The simple half-cylinder created by making a solid from the empty space inside the original hut. The sculpture was hidden deeper in the forest than the hut had been, so that only those who sought it out would find it.

THE ART OF BORDER LIVING

Claire-Louise Bennett
Garrett Carr
Peter Curran
Paul McVeigh
Nuala O'Connor
Kamila Shamsie
David Thomas

There was no Irish border in 1918, yet in Yeats' words, Ireland was 'changed utterly' by the Easter Rising of 1916. Thousands of volunteers from the Unionist and Nationalist traditions were fighting in France, Belgium and Gallipoli, all wearing the British uniform, but fighting for different things. What they shared were homes and families along what would soon become the border between the United Kingdom and the Republic of Ireland.

In 2018, documentary maker Peter Curran and sound designer David Thomas collaborated with a number of leading writers and Verbal Arts in Northern Ireland to make *The Art of Border Living* for BBC Radio Ulster — a creative documentary inspired by the borderlands over the past 100 years. The project also featured live performances and a series of podcasts combining the written word with soundscapes, textures from Ulster's natural world, and voices from local communities.

BBC Radio Ulster, 11 November 2018 / Poetry Ireland, Dublin, 14 November 2018

The 7.5-km Legnabrocky trail, Cuilcagh Way, in County Fermanagh.

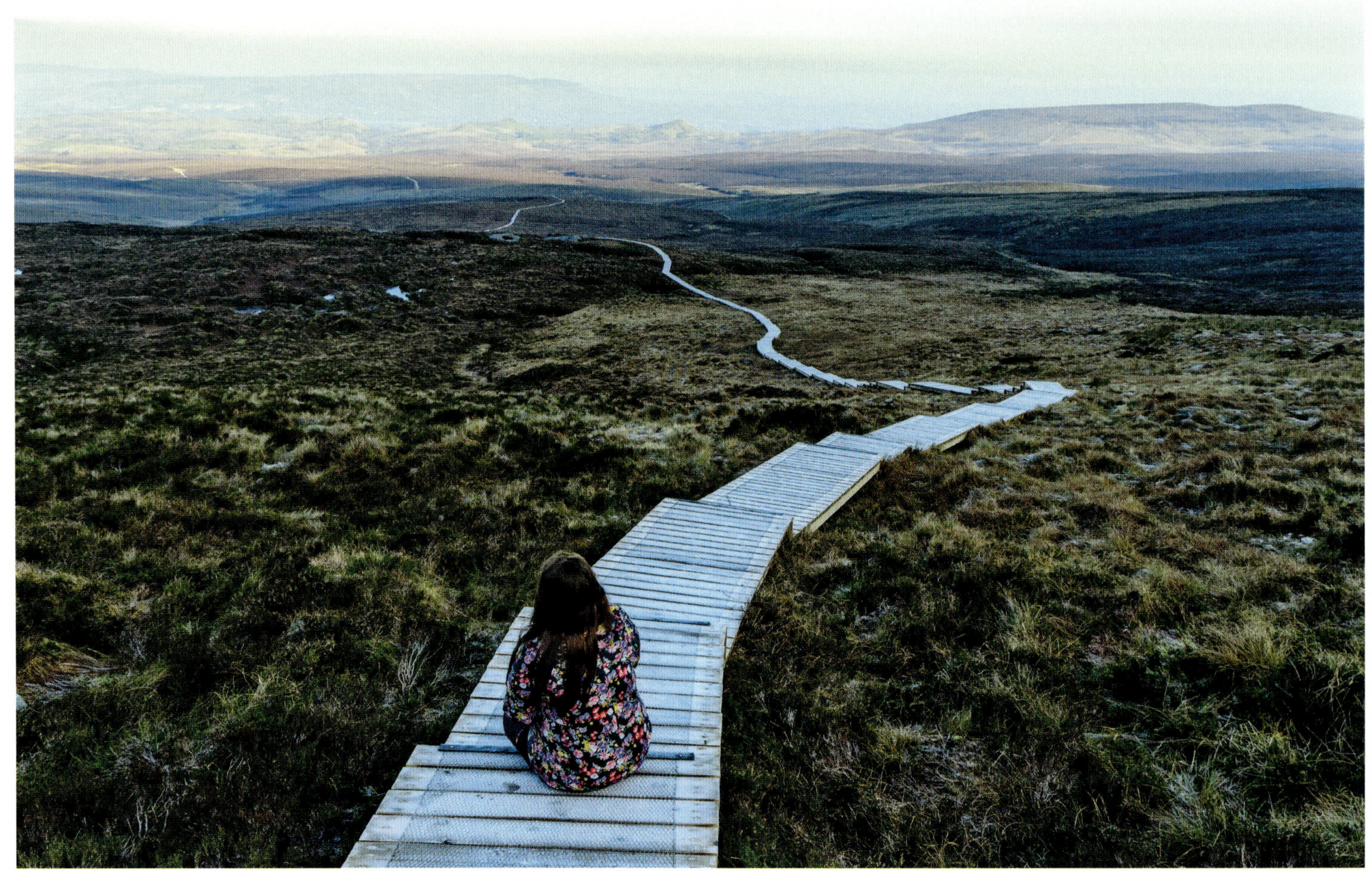

MEMORIAL GROUND

David Lang

This choral commemoration was premiered at the East Neuk Festival, a day after the centenary of the first day of the Battle of the Somme.

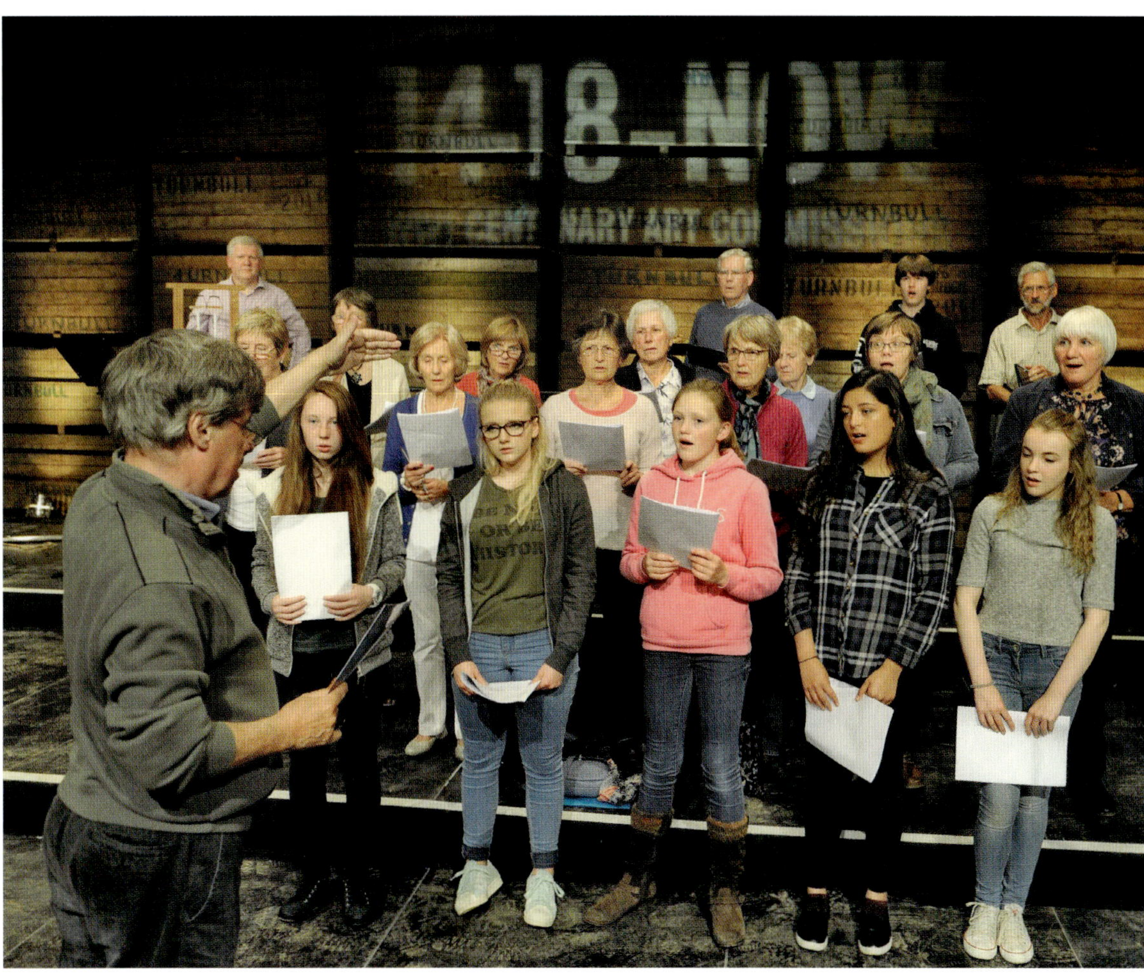

'An outstanding performance that caught the sadness, the spirituality and courage of all those men who fell not just at the Somme, but at all the great battles.'

Memorial Ground participant

Memorial Ground is a choral piece by Pulitzer Prize-winning composer David Lang, composed in 2016 to mark the centenary of the Battle of the Somme. More than 1.1 million people from all over the world were killed or wounded during that battle, and no single text or piece of music can respond to such a scale of loss, so Lang wanted to offer people a way to voice their own response.

The piece received its world premiere at the East Neuk Festival on 2 July, performed by Paul Hillier and his acclaimed Theatre of Voices, with singers from the Scottish Chamber Orchestra Chorus and amateur choirs from around Fife. Afterwards, choirs around the country, of all levels, sizes and abilities, were able to download the score in order to sing customised new versions of the work. (The music had been written to be as accessible as possible to a wide ability range of singers.) Some kept it simple and short; others added instruments, video projections, staging, poetry, prayers or whispered names of the fallen — but all were unique. Choirs were also able to add the names of those they wished to recognise, resulting in very personal acts of remembrance.

The project culminated in November 2016, with choirs performing their own versions of *Memorial Ground* at concerts, services and school assemblies on and around Remembrance Sunday, honouring the many who made sacrifices in order that we may live the lives we do. In 2017 the project won a Music Award for Audiences and Engagement from the Royal Philharmonic Society.

East Neuk Festival, Fife; UK-wide, July — November 2016

THE FORBIDDEN ZONE

Duncan Macmillan
Katie Mitchell
Schaubühne Berlin

Renowned for her innovative, immersive theatrical staging, Katie Mitchell is one of the most inventive directors in Britain. This production used five video cameras and four film sets — including a moving subway train — to create a dynamic live-cinema event telling the tragic multi-generational story of the Haber family.

The Habers included two women whose lives were at the heart of the brutal race to weaponise poison gas — the first ever weapon of mass destruction, and a defining feature of what became known as the 'Chemists' War' of 1914–18. Clara Immerwahr gave up a career in chemistry when she married the Nobel Prize-winning Fritz Haber. When Haber's research turned to the development of chlorine gas and its implementation on the battlefields at Ypres, Clara's protests at this 'perversion of science' went unheard. Her fate was then tragically echoed in 1949 in Chicago when their grandchild, Claire Haber, saw her poison-gas antidote research terminated as military funding was diverted to support atomic warfare.

Barbican, London, 2 August 2014 (streamed from Salzburg Festival) and 26 — 29 May 2016 (live performance by Schaubühne Berlin)

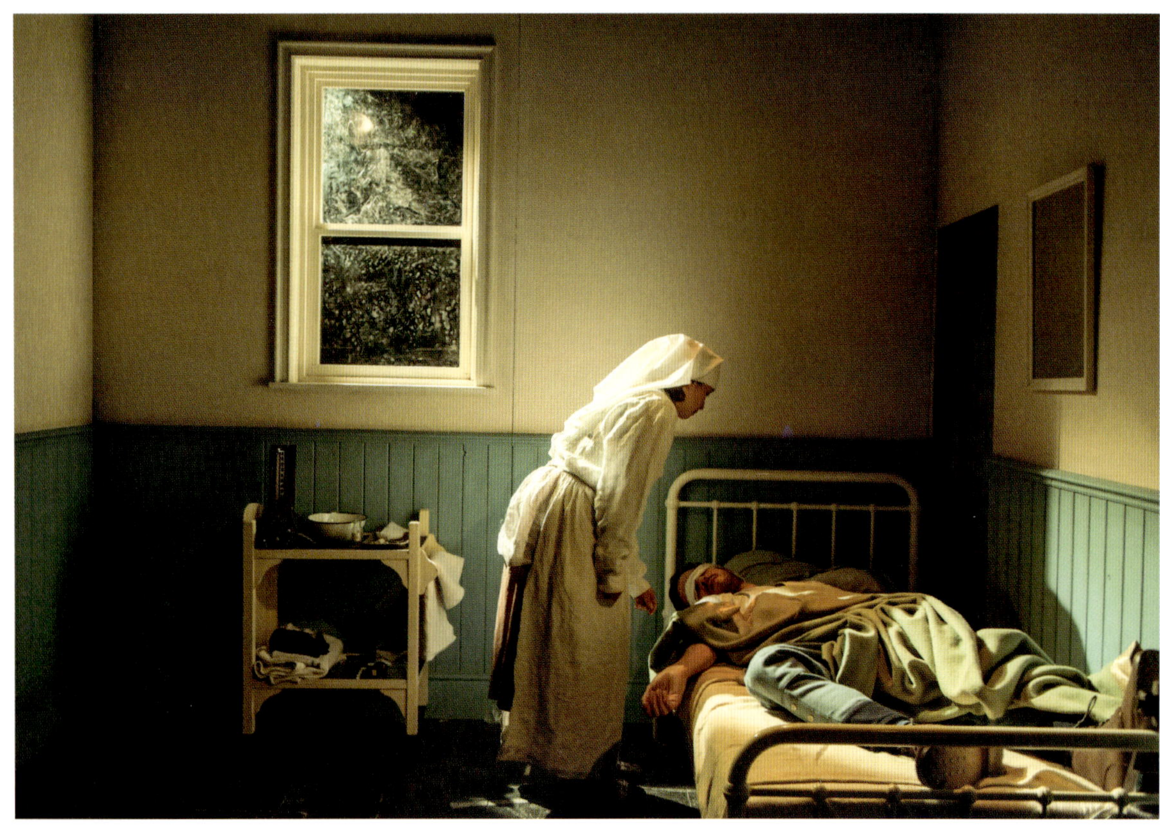

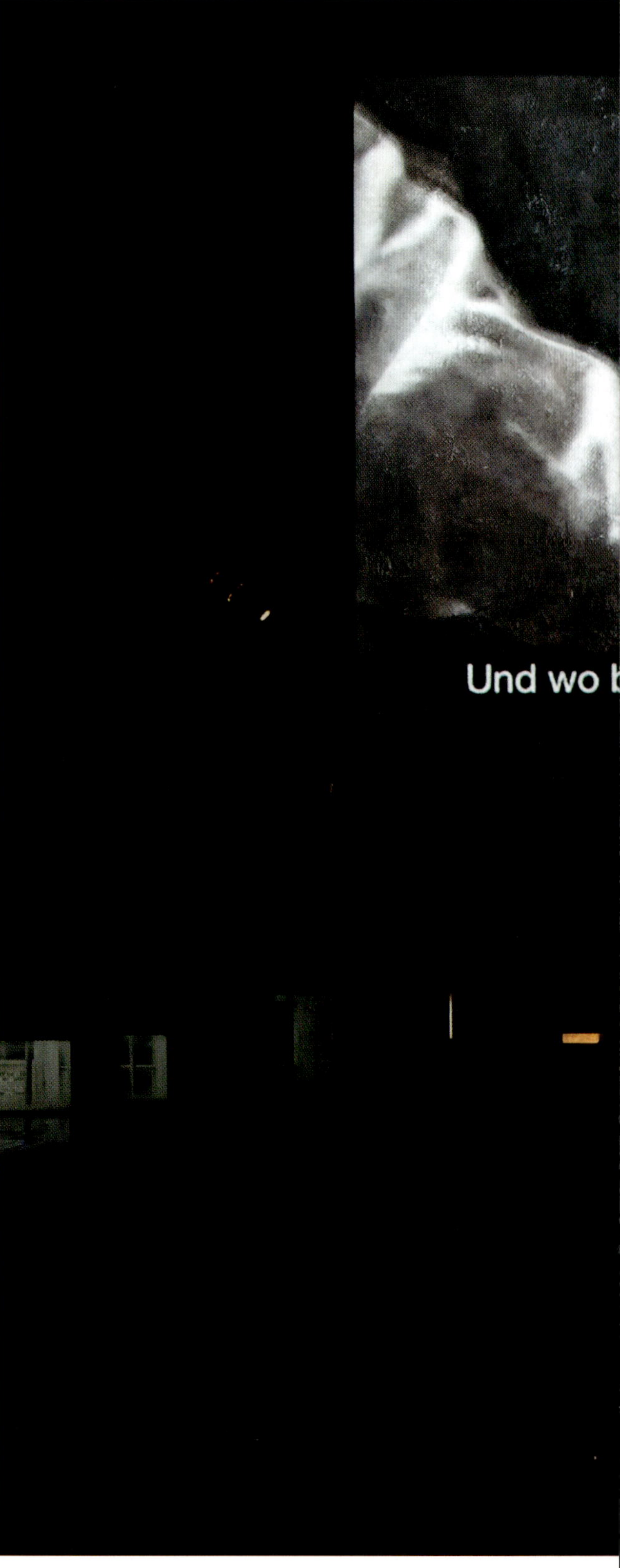

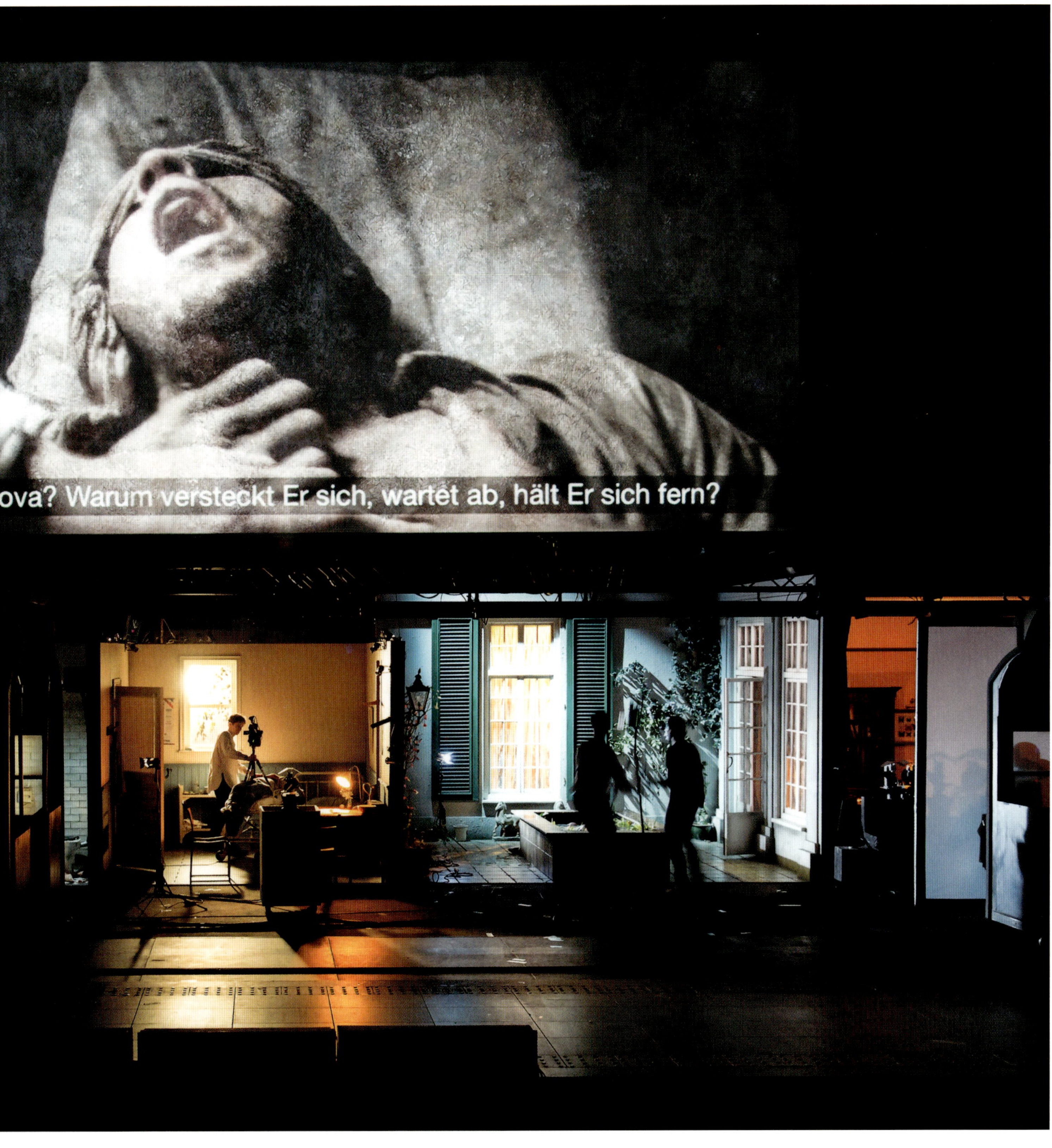

Written by Duncan Macmillan, and incorporating texts by Mary Borden, Virginia Woolf, Hannah Arendt and others, this production was performed in English, German and French with surtitles. Its 2014 premiere at the Salzburg Festival (seen here) was live-streamed at the Barbican, where it returned for a four-night run of live performances in May 2016.

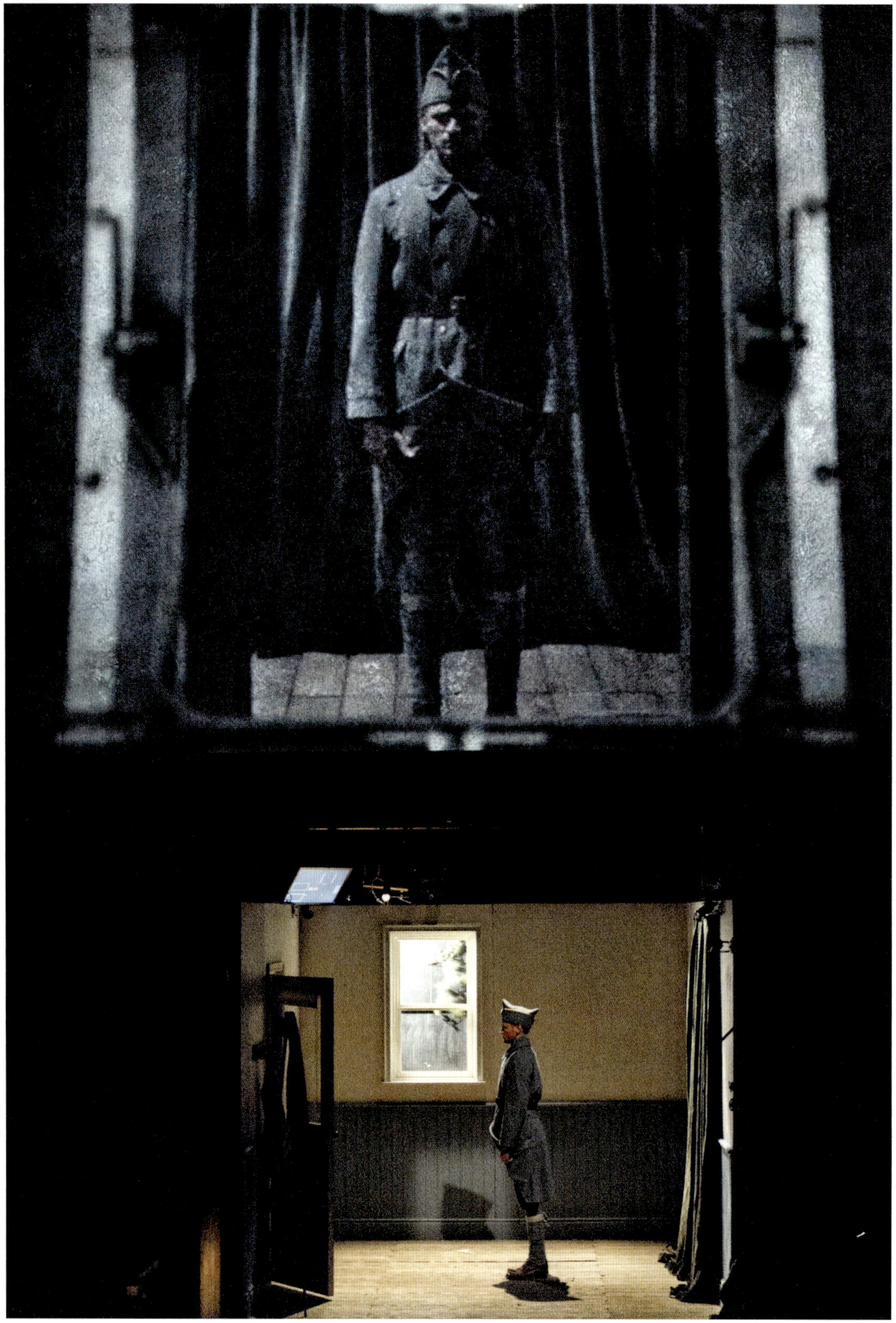

The Haber women's story
was relayed in a series
of flashbacks, and a
blend of live and digital
storytelling, captured
by camera operators who
moved nimbly among
the performers to record
close-up moments as they
happened in real time.

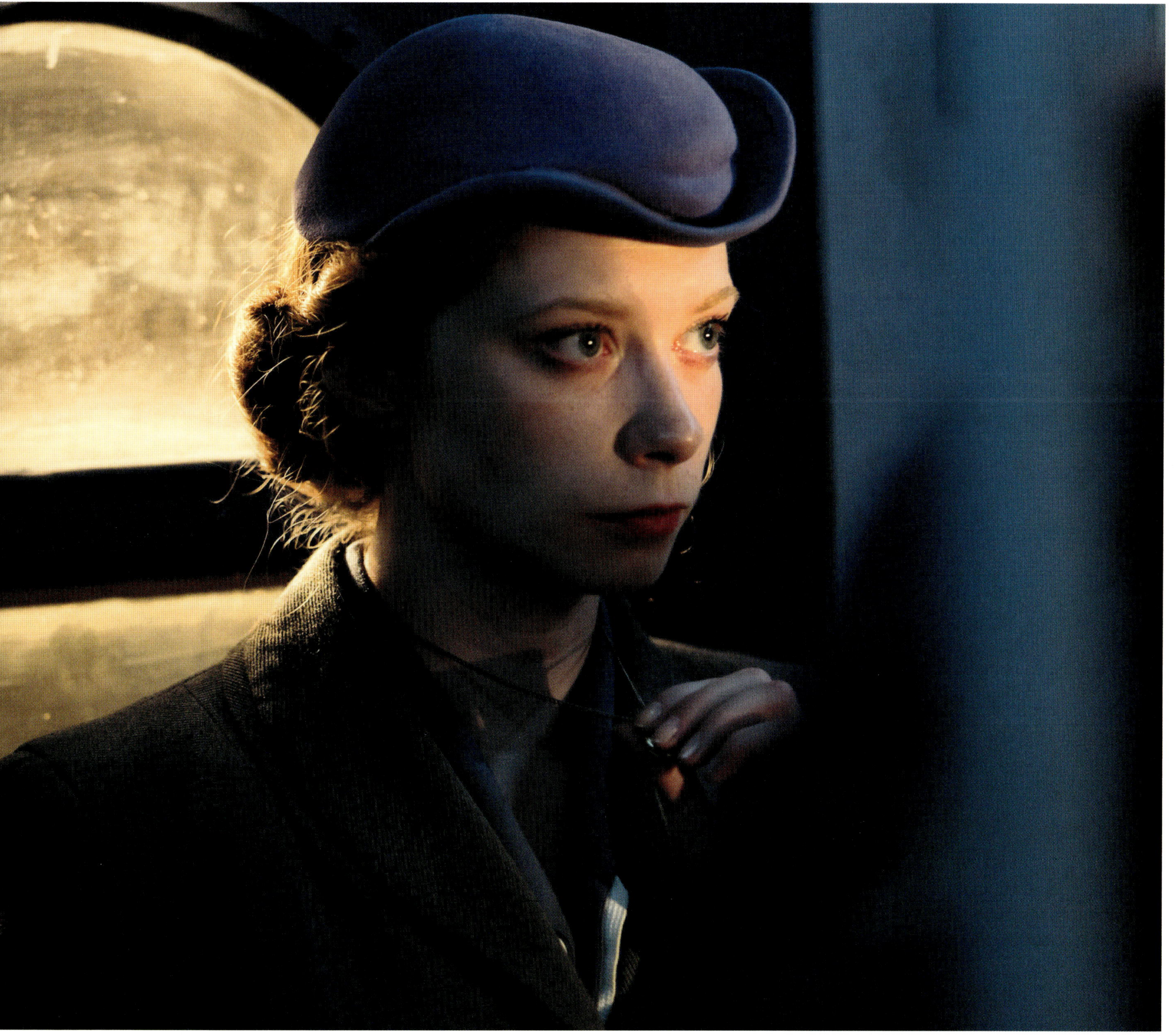

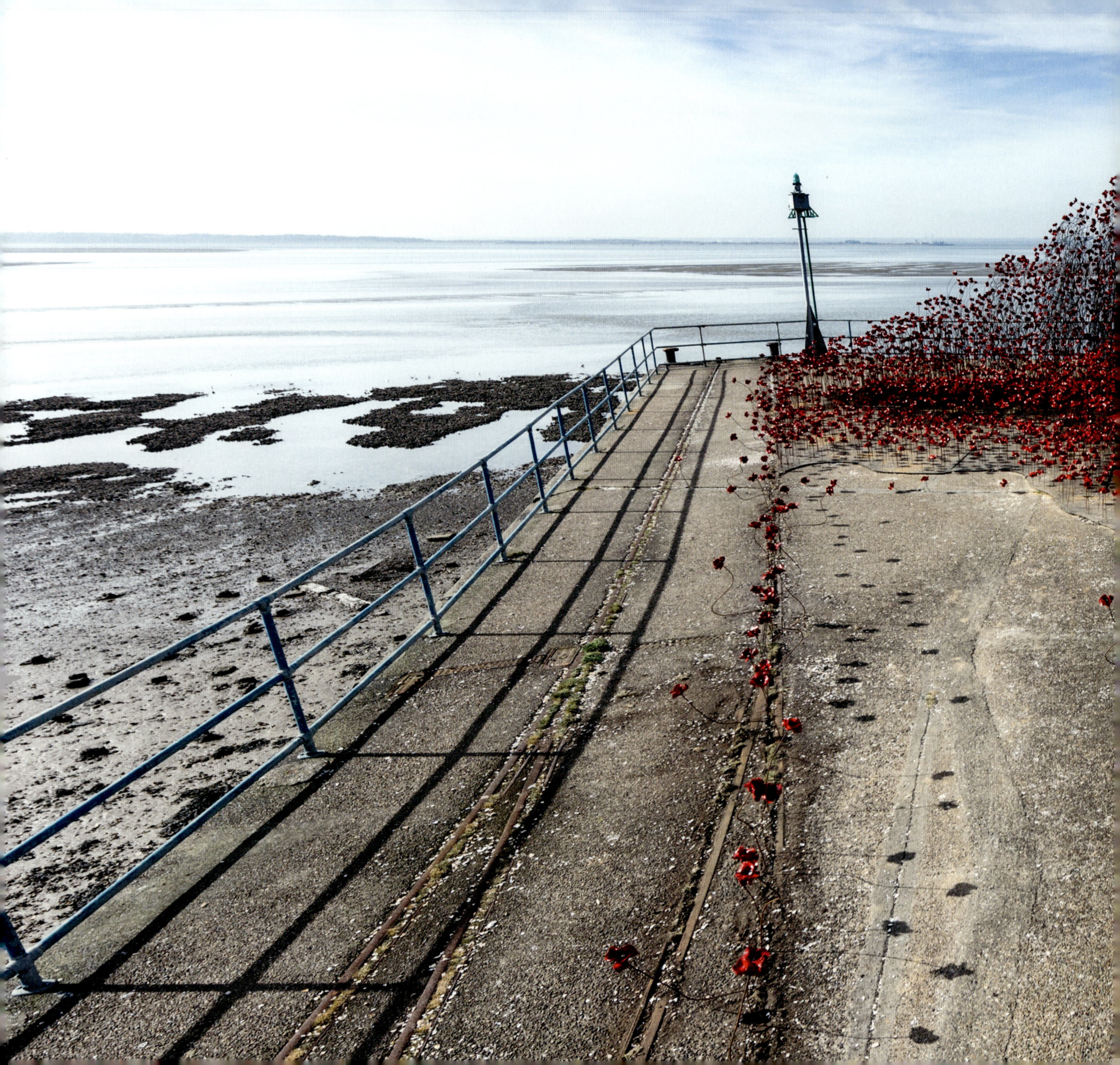

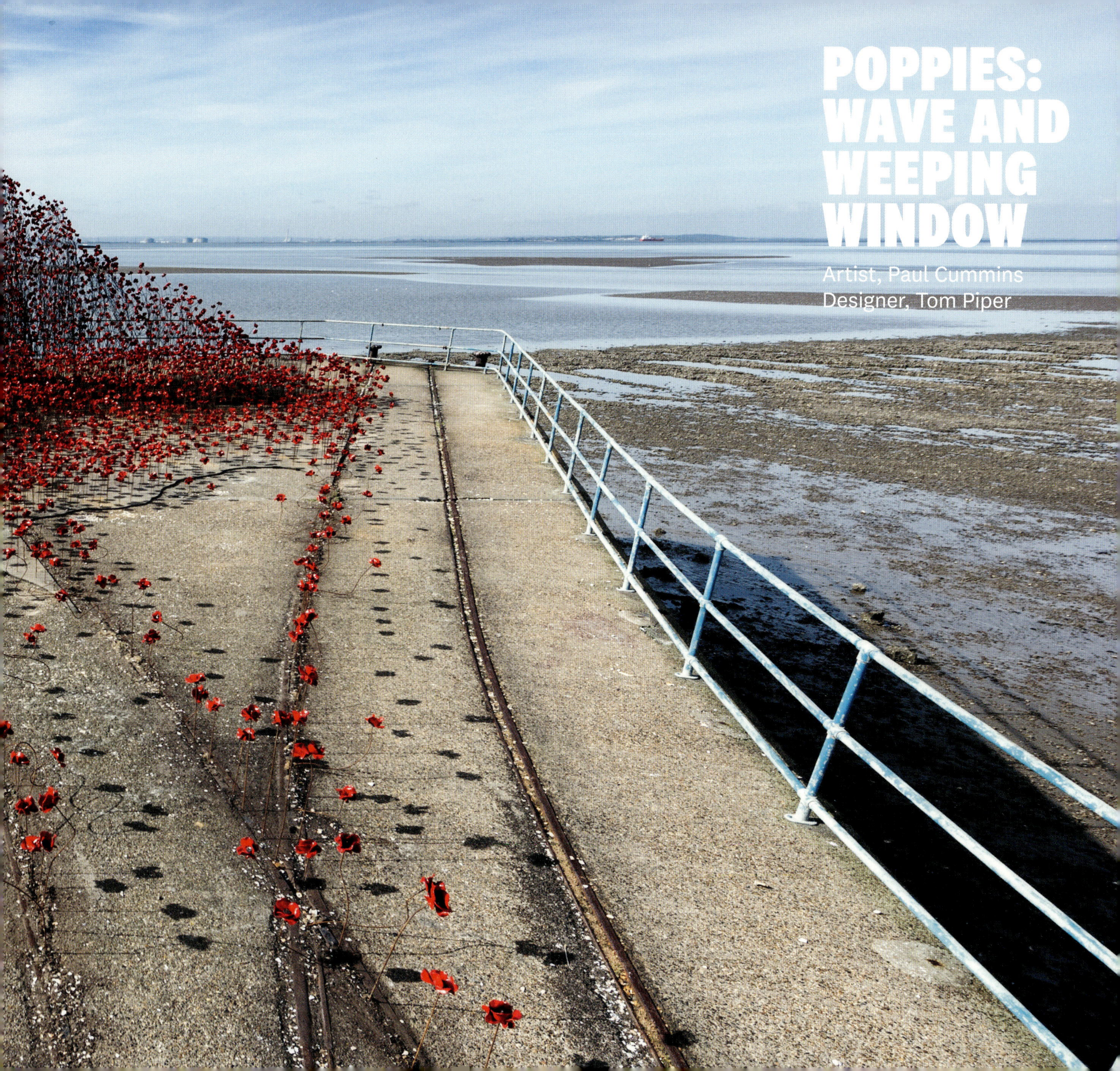

POPPIES:
WAVE AND
WEEPING
WINDOW
Artist, Paul Cummins
Designer, Tom Piper

Blood Swept Lands and Seas of Red was a large-scale outdoor installation of ceramic poppies displayed at the Tower of London in 2014. It comprised 888,246 handmade flowers, one for every British and colonial life lost at the front in the First World War. It was the work of artist Paul Cummins and designer Tom Piper, and was seen by an estimated 5 million people during its stay in the Tower's grounds, including politicians and royalty.

The installation was intended to be transitory, only lasting from August until November. So while there was great public demand for its run to be extended, the artist and designer remained true to their vision, and the work was dismantled carefully, beginning on 12 November, the day after the final flower was 'planted'.

Two striking sculptural sections of the installation (*Wave* and *Weeping Window*) were preserved for the nation through the generosity of two philanthropic trusts and foundations, and whose support secured the sculptures for posterity. The sculptures were taken on tour by 14-18 NOW between 2015 and 2018 so that the intricate beauty and emotional impact of the work could be experienced by audiences in public spaces of significance right across the United Kingdom.

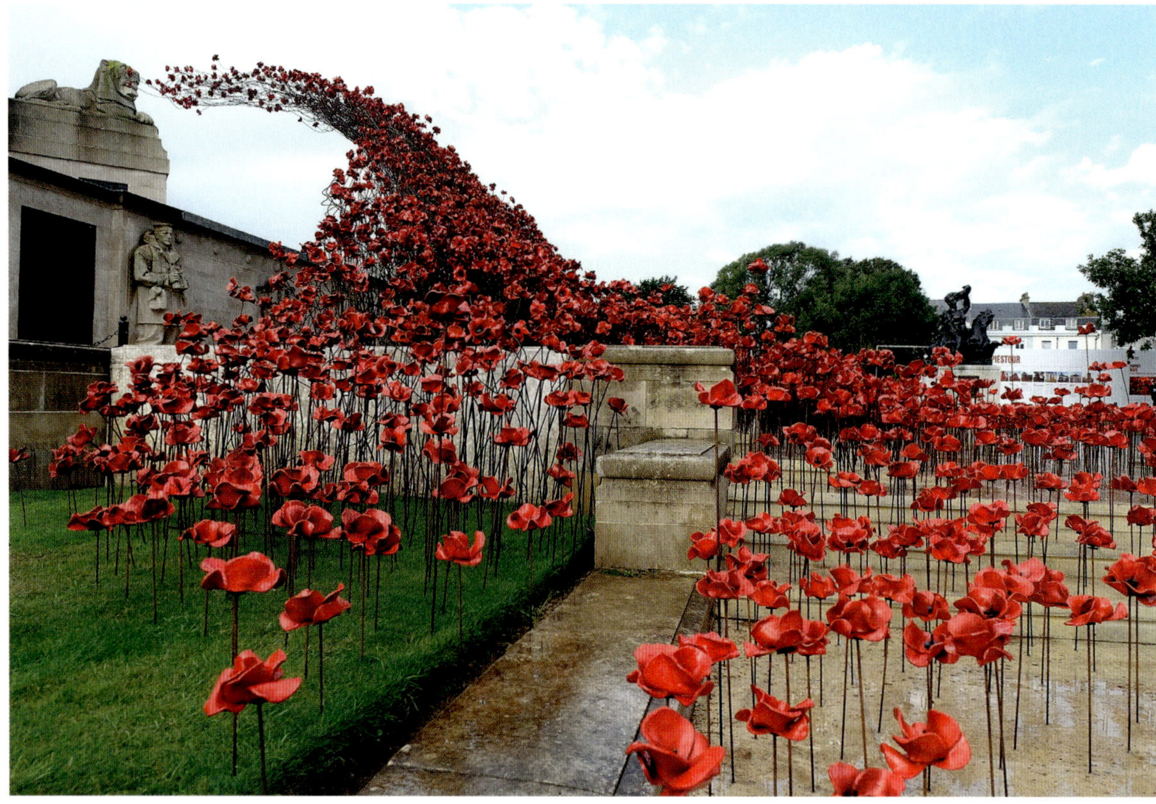

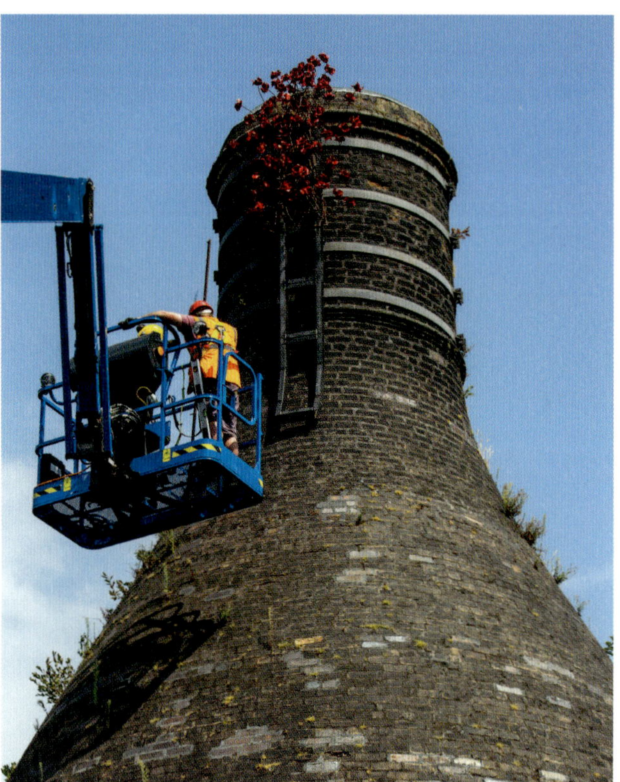

Previous page. *Wave* at The Barge Pier in Shoeburyness, Southend-on-Sea, where was the scene of one of the first air-raid attacks on the UK.

Above. *Wave* at CWGC Plymouth Naval Memorial, which commemorates the thousands of naval servicemen and women of the First World War with no known grave.

Left. *Weeping Window* at Middleport Pottery in Stoke-on-Trent, the ceramic-producing centre that saw a huge increase in output as a result of the war.

Opposite top. Designer Tom Piper (left) and artist Paul Cummins planting poppies at Lincoln Castle.

Opposite bottom. *Wave* at Lincoln Castle, which was used by the Lincolnshire Regiment for fundraisers and parades in the war.

Visitor to Caernarfon Castle

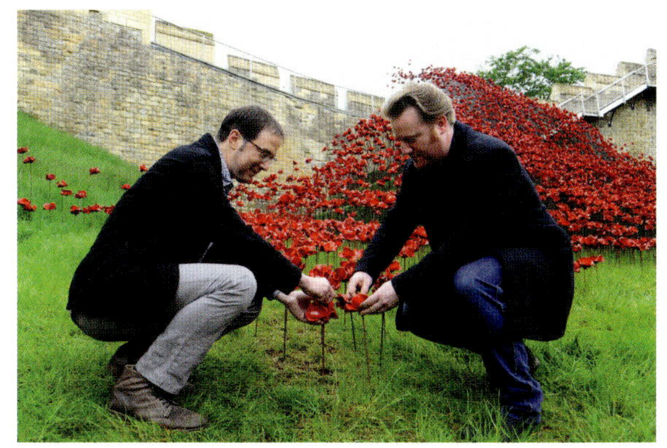

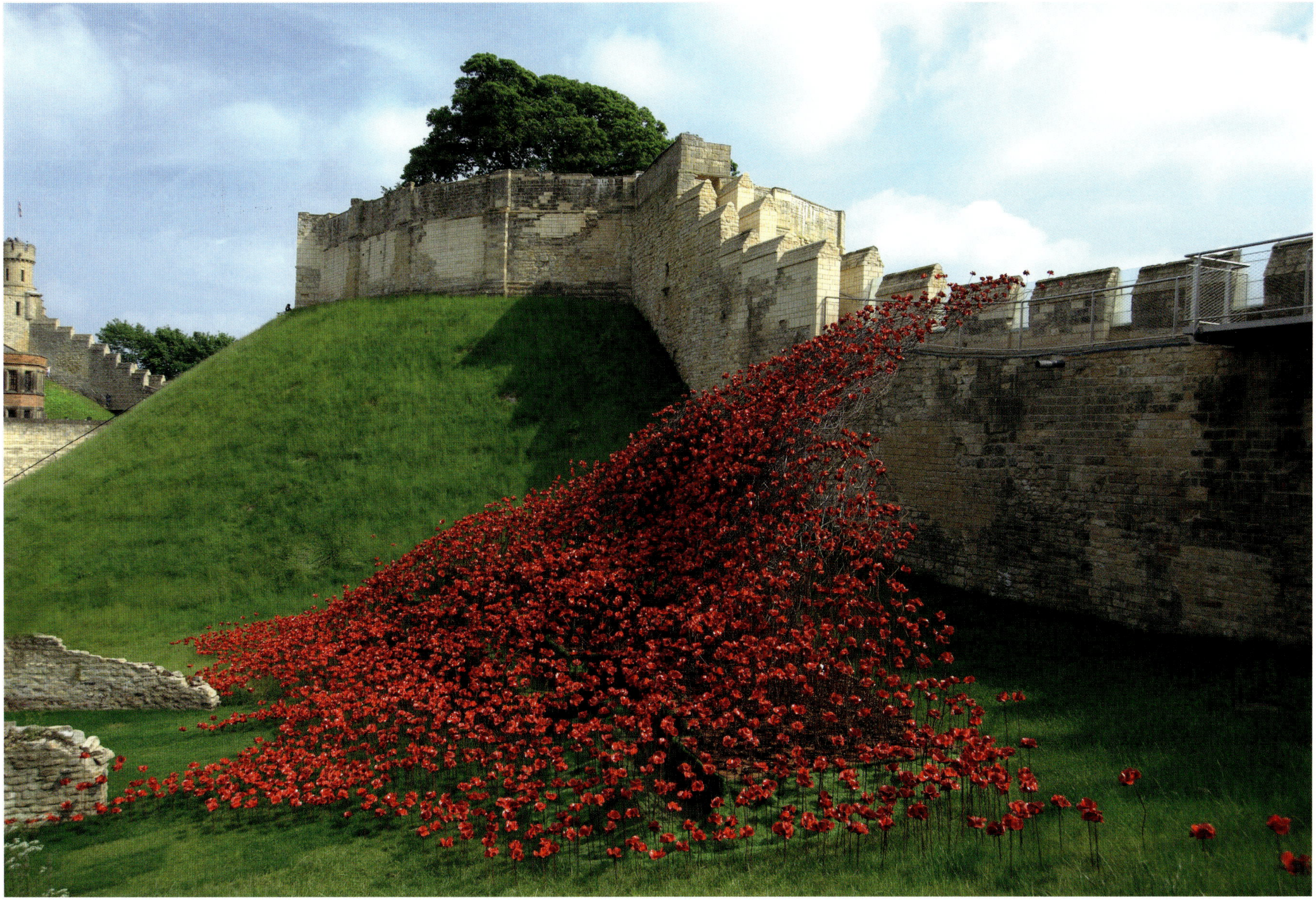

In all, 19 cities and towns in the UK were visited:
Wakefield, Ashington, Liverpool, Orkney, Lincoln,
Perth, Caernarfon, Hull, Southend-on-Sea, Derby,
Cardiff, Plymouth, Carlisle, Belfast, Hereford,
Fareham, Stoke-on-Trent, Manchester and London.
As a result, the sculptures were seen by over 4.5
million people who came to reflect and admire these
evocative artworks, while thousands of young people
took part in the accompanying learning programme.

The tour itself was a massive logistical operation,
with the works being completely dismantled,
transported on trucks and then meticulously
reassembled in their new locations. At the close
of the tour, the two sculptures became part of the
collection of the Imperial War Museums.

**Below. *Weeping Window*
flowing from a turret window
of the Black Watch Castle and
Museum in Perth, Scotland —
a focal point for remembrance
and learning about the First
World War.**

**Right. *Weeping Window*
was displayed on St Magnus
Cathedral, Orkney, to mark
the centenary of the Battle
of Jutland.**

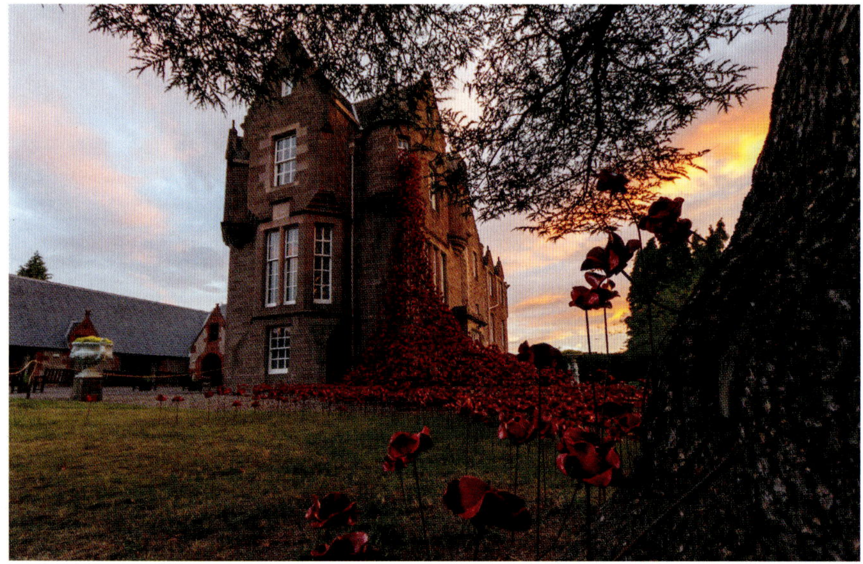

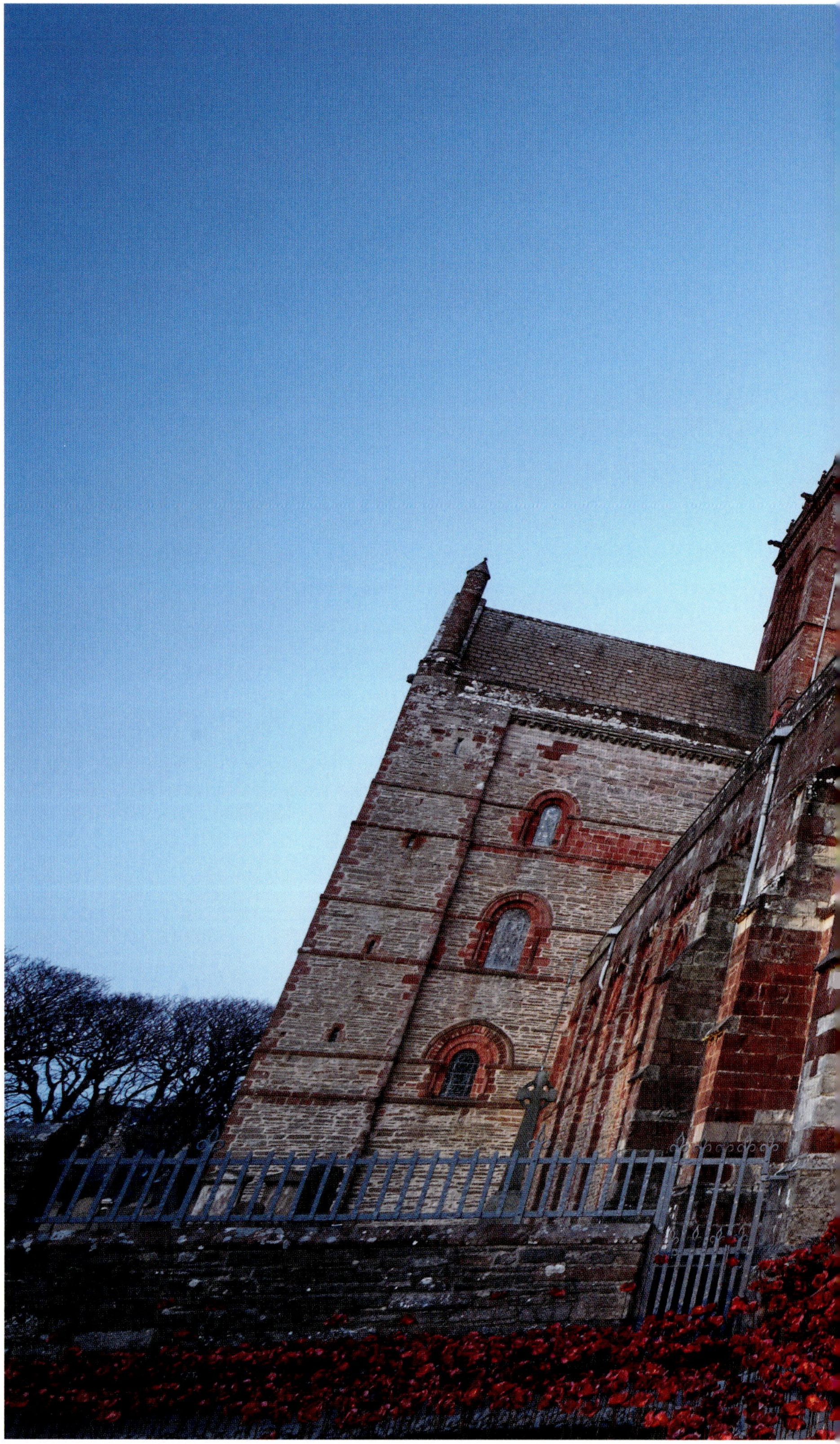

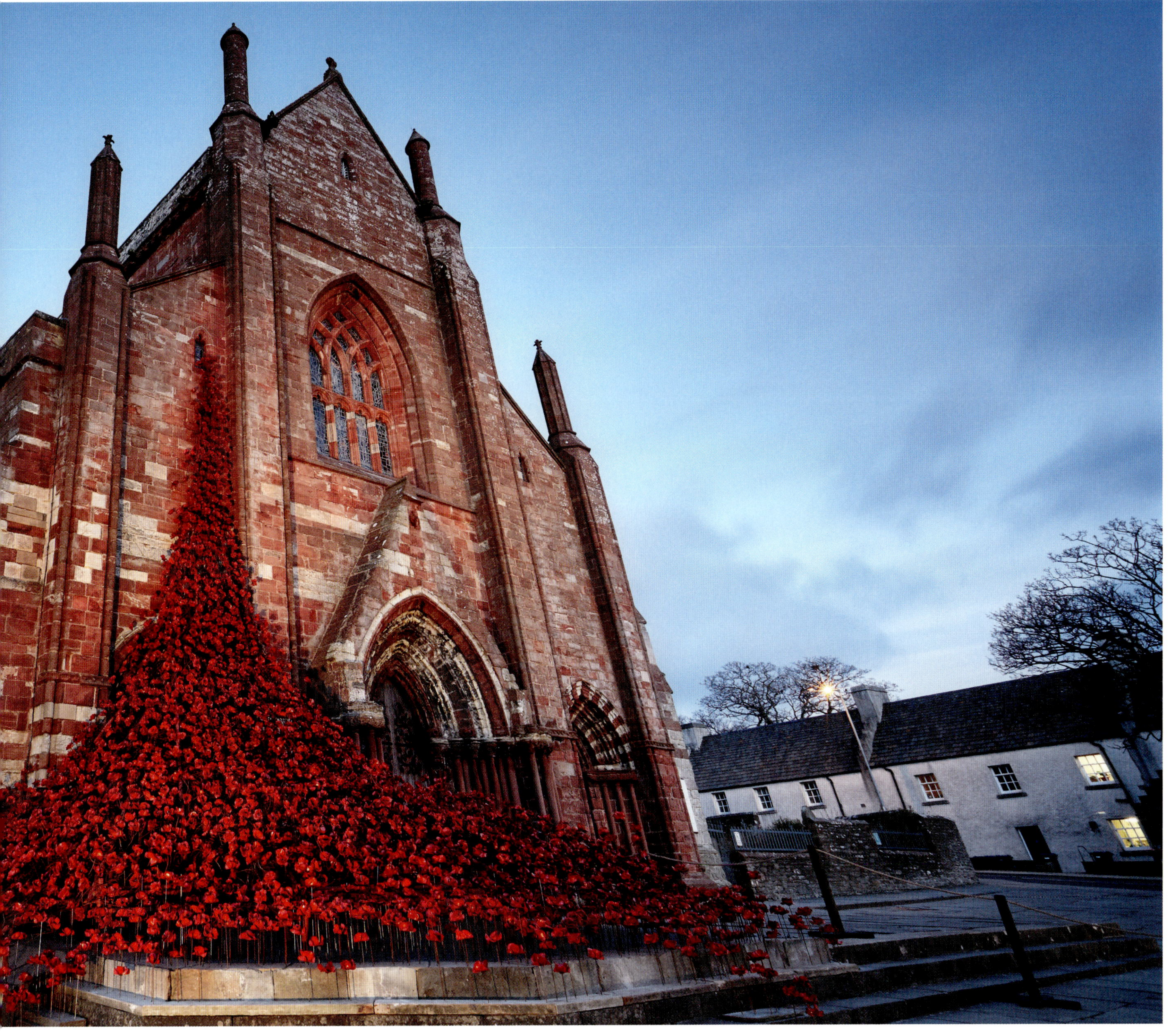

Visitor to Caernarfon Castle

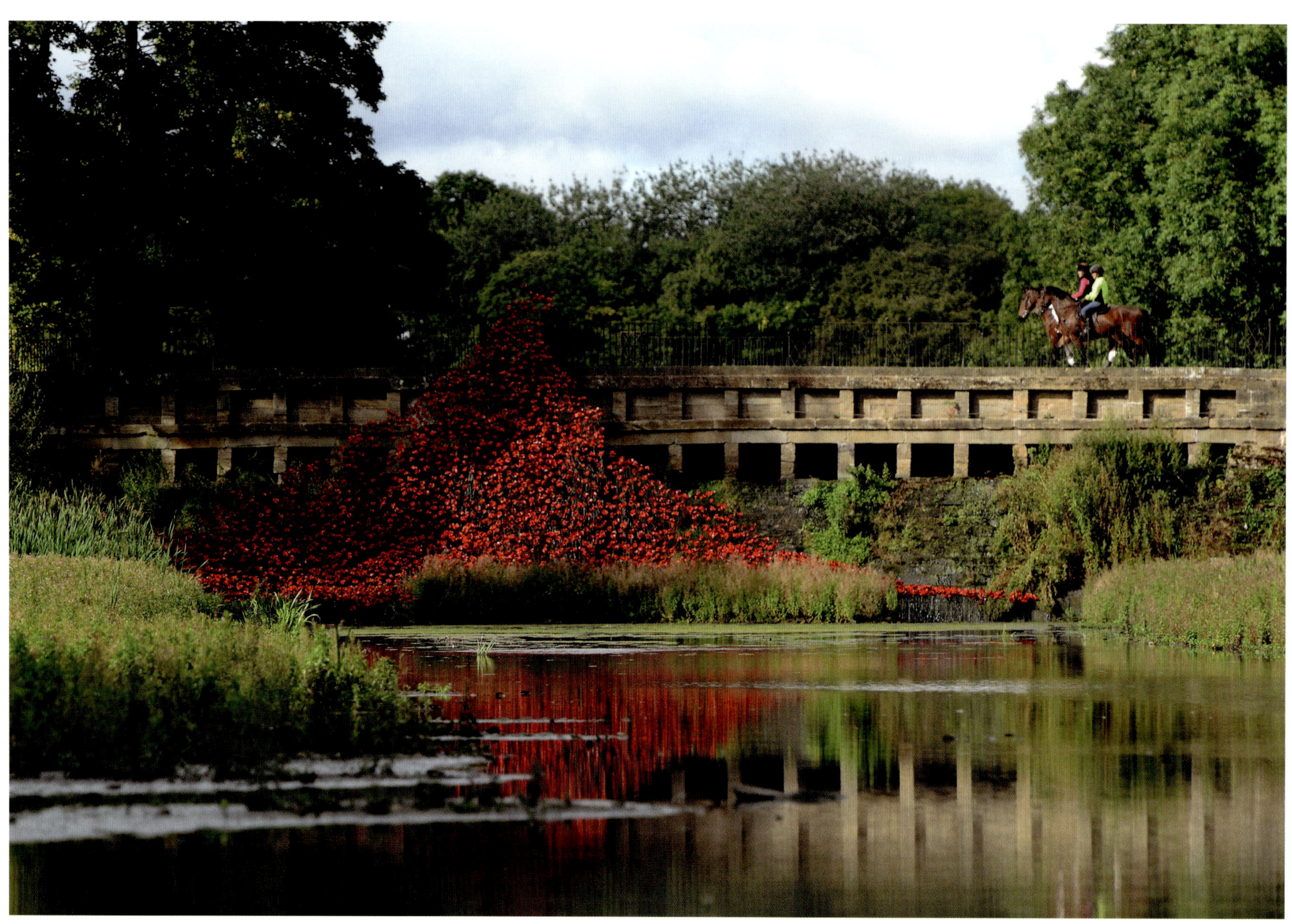

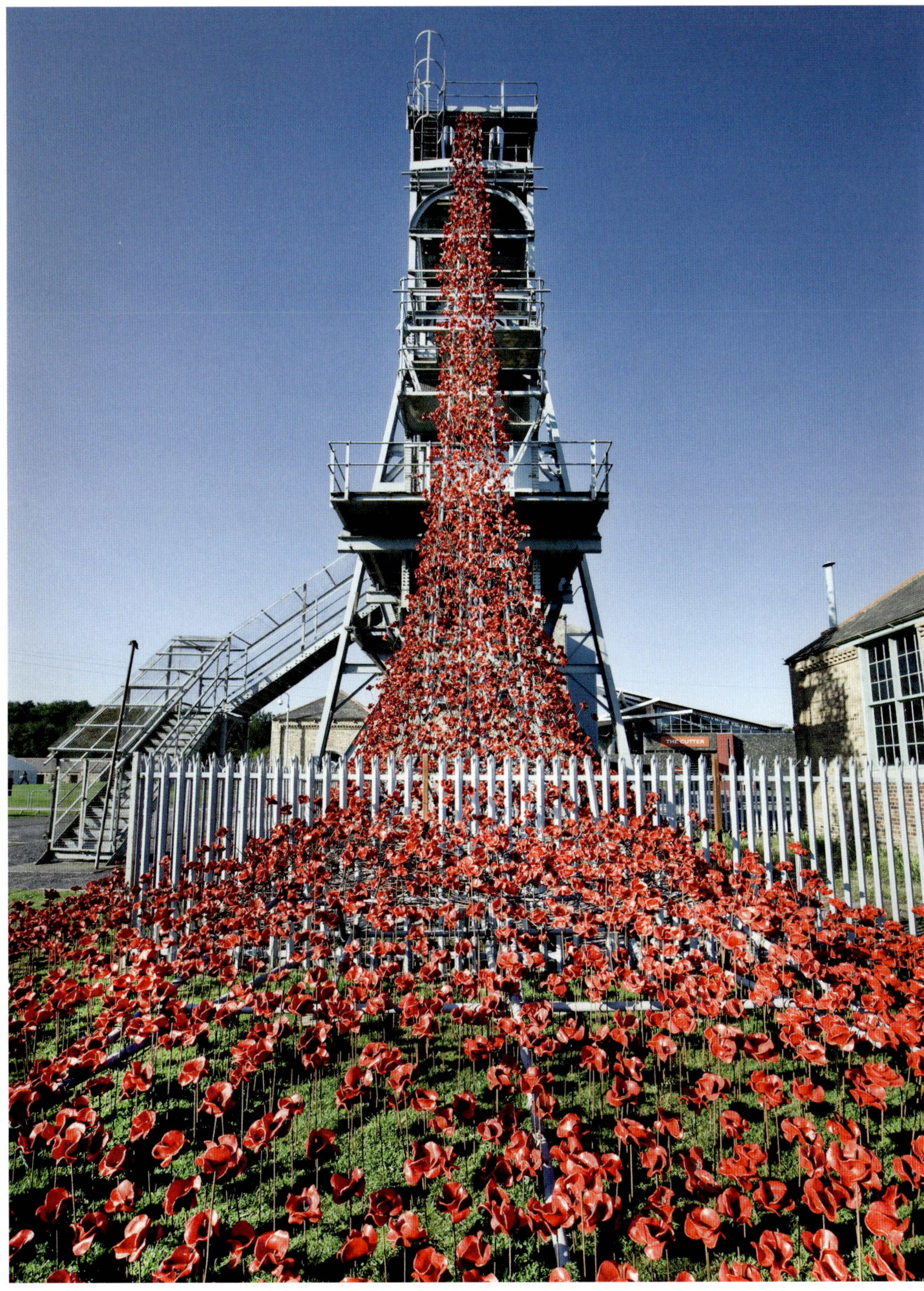

Wave and *Weeping Window* from the installation *Blood Swept Lands and Seas of Red* — poppies and original concept by artist Paul Cummins, and installation designed by Tom Piper — by Paul Cummins Ceramics Limited in conjunction with Historic Royal Palaces, originally at HM Tower of London 2014.

Opposite. *Wave* at Yorkshire Sculpture Park.

Left. *Weeping Window* at Woodhorn Museum, a colliery heritage site in Northumberland, source of both coal and skilled miners during the war.

All the poppies from the original installation were sold to the public, raising £9.5 million for six service charities. An online archive — *Where Are the Poppies Now?* — was created by 14-18 NOW to document where the ceramic poppies were in the world. This archive featured personal stories of those who purchased a flower and an interactive map of where the poppies are now. The flowers have been planted in homes and gardens in Australia, New Zealand, Canada, Dubai, Brazil and Malaysia, as well as at war graves in France and Belgium, to remember and reflect on those who lost their lives.

UK-wide, July 2015 — November 2018

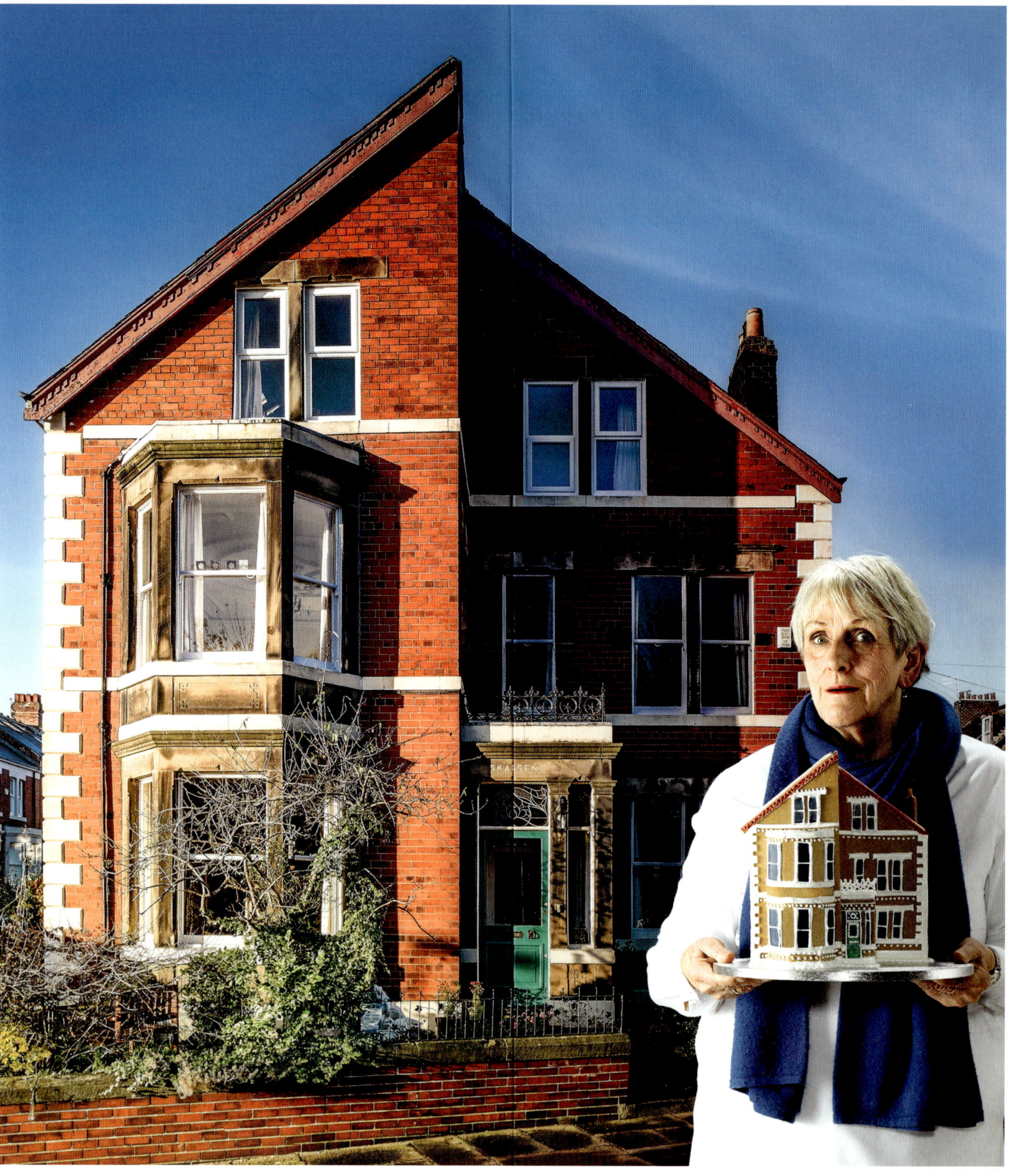

GREAT & TINY WAR

Bobby Baker

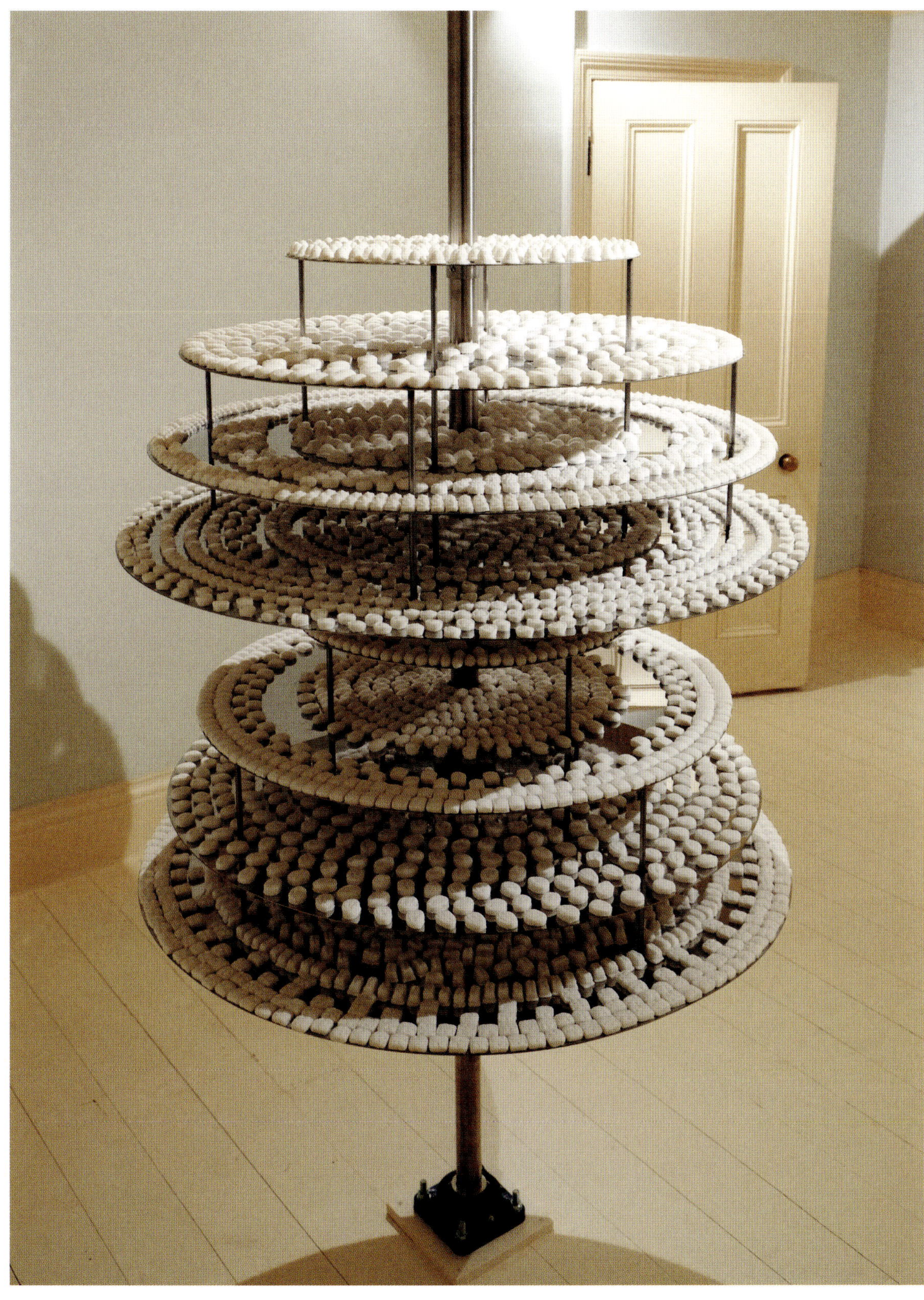

In 2014, 100 years after the start of the First World War, artist Bobby Baker began reimagining what day-to-day life was like in times of conflict. For three months in 2018, she invited audiences on a tour of a transformed house in Newcastle upon Tyne — an ingenious, immersive multimedia installation inspired by real stories, passed down through her family and shaped by the domestic and emotional labour of international conflicts.

In *Great & Tiny War*, guests were met with unexpected experiences as the house's contents juxtaposed the spectacular with the everyday: a ghostly heroine, an edible armoury and 4,701 reinvented dinners were among the incongruous phenomena to be found.

Baker's installation cast light on the role of women during wartime and the impact of conflicts, historical and contemporary, on the mental health of whole families through generations. In doing so, she celebrated the women today who carry on running houses, bringing up children, and keeping families together at the most harrowing of times.

Great & Tiny War was a monument to unacknowledged private struggles and personal strength, and resonated in particular with a great many visitors whose own families have been touched by war.

Newcastle upon Tyne, 7 September —
28 November 2018

ASUNDER

Bob Stanley

In July 1916, British, French and German forces began one of the most traumatic battles in military history. Over the course of just four months, more than a million soldiers were captured, wounded or killed at the Battle of the Somme. By delving into personal stories from the North East of England, and combining film with live music, *Asunder* took audiences on a journey through unexplored experiences of the First World War.

The film, by Esther Johnson, used local archive footage to convey the story of the city's involvement in the war, from the men who fought on the battlefields, to those who stayed behind to work in the region's shipyards and munitions factories, and the women and children for whom life continued on the home front. The film's soundtrack was created by two renowned bands from the North East, Sunderland's Field Music and Newcastle's Warm Digits, who performed live with the Royal Northern Sinfonia and the Cornshed Sisters.

Created by writer and musician Bob Stanley, *Asunder* received its world premiere in the old Sunderland Empire music hall on 10 July, close to the 100th anniversary of the first salvos of the Somme, before touring around the UK.

Sunderland Empire, 10 July 2016 / Barbican, London, 12 February 2017 / Sage Gateshead, 11 November 2018 / Cinema screenings across the UK, 2017 — 2018

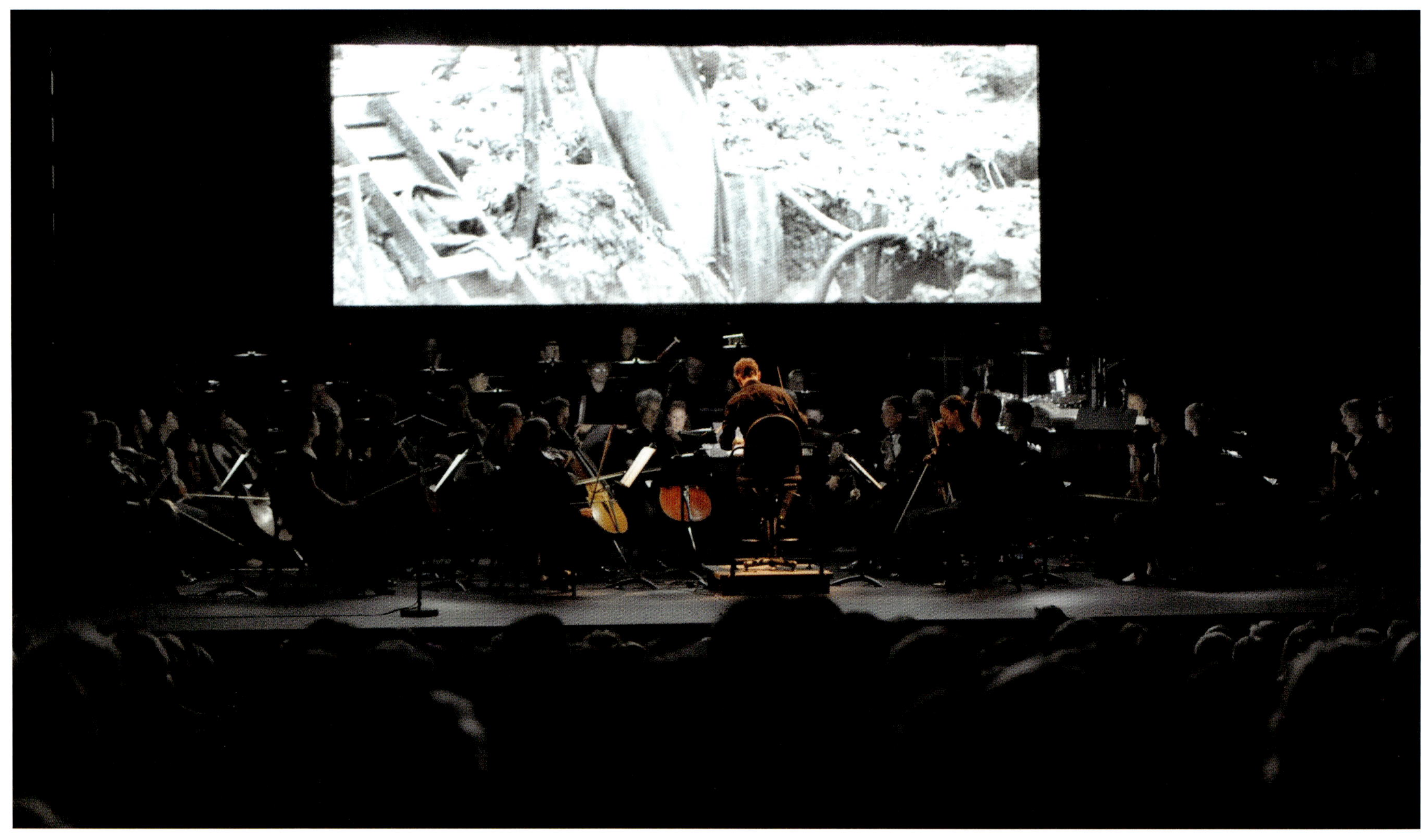

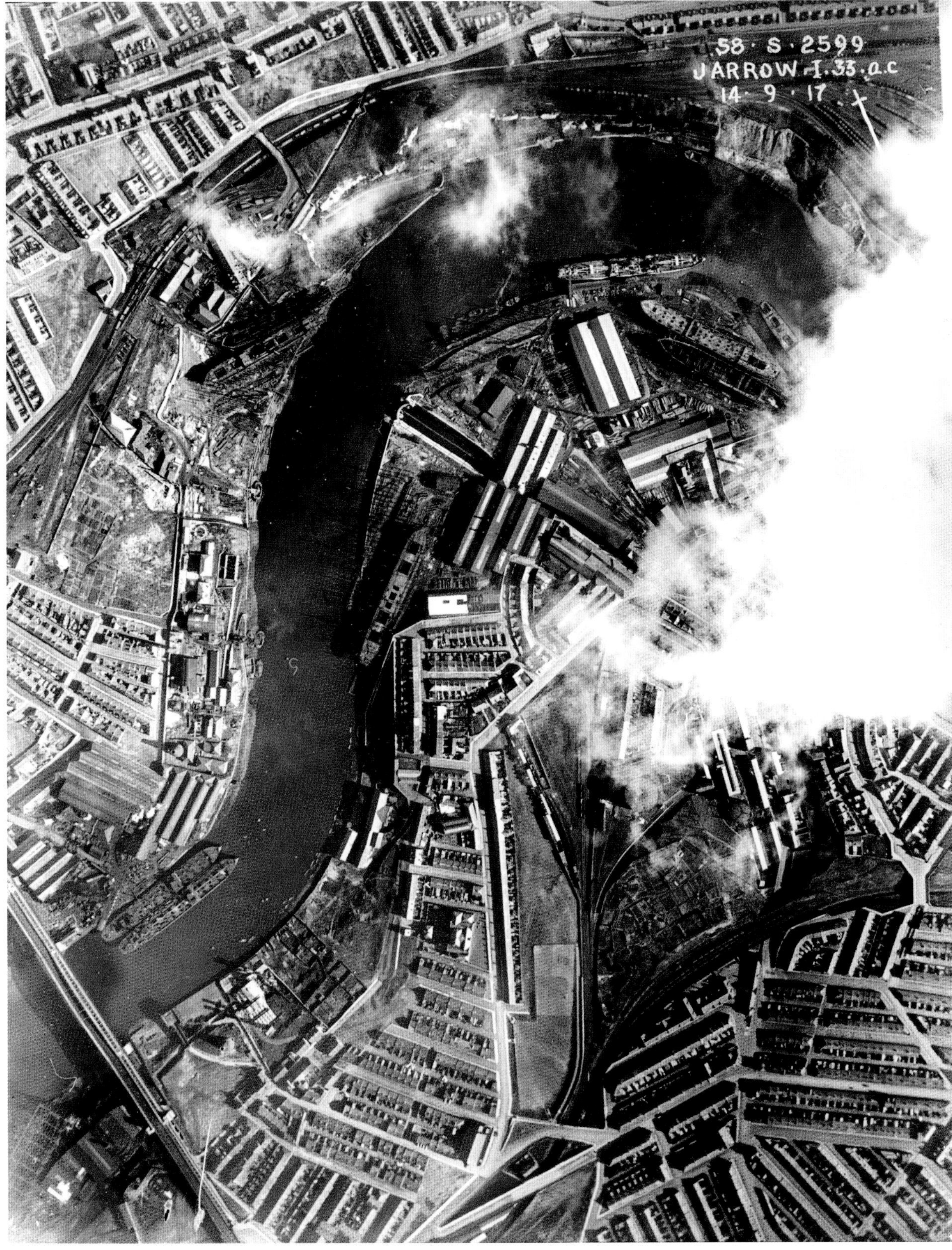

Asunder combined archive footage of wartime Sunderland and its inhabitants with contemporary views of Tyne and Wear to provide a fresh view of the past and its links to the present. Musicians from the North East provided a live-music backdrop to this very local story.

AFTER A WAR

Mark Ball and
Tim Etchells

Various artists, including:
Hotel Modern and
 Arthur Sauer
Forced Entertainment
Lola Arias
James Bridle
The Tiger Lillies

Over one week in June 2014, the biennial LIFT festival staged a programme of events related to the theme of conflict. Having opened at the Southbank Centre at the beginning of the week, the programme fittingly culminated in a weekend of new commissions at the Battersea Arts Centre, which from 1916 onwards housed the trials of many of London's conscientious objectors. *After a War* was curated by LIFT's artistic director Mark Ball and the artist Tim Etchells, who invited an eclectic line-up of international artists to reflect on the enduring legacies of the first truly global conflict.

The programme opened with *The Great War* by Dutch theatre company Hotel Modern and Arthur Sauer, which combined live animation and a miniature film set to recreate the experiences of the many millions of First World War soldiers. The Western Front was reconstructed on a tiny scale, from soil, parsley trees and rusty nails. Foley artist and composer Sauer provided the soundtrack, and original letters and spoken testimonies were woven throughout the performance.

Based on the 1986 novel *The Notebook* by Hungarian writer Ágota Kristóf, Forced Entertainment's performance of the same name told the story of twin brothers evacuated to their grandmother's farm during the Second World War, in a world still feeling the territorial divisions imposed at the end of the First World War. Directed by Tim Etchells, this production captured Kristóf's bold, crisp language and subversive humour to create a performance that questioned politics and personal ethics in wartime.

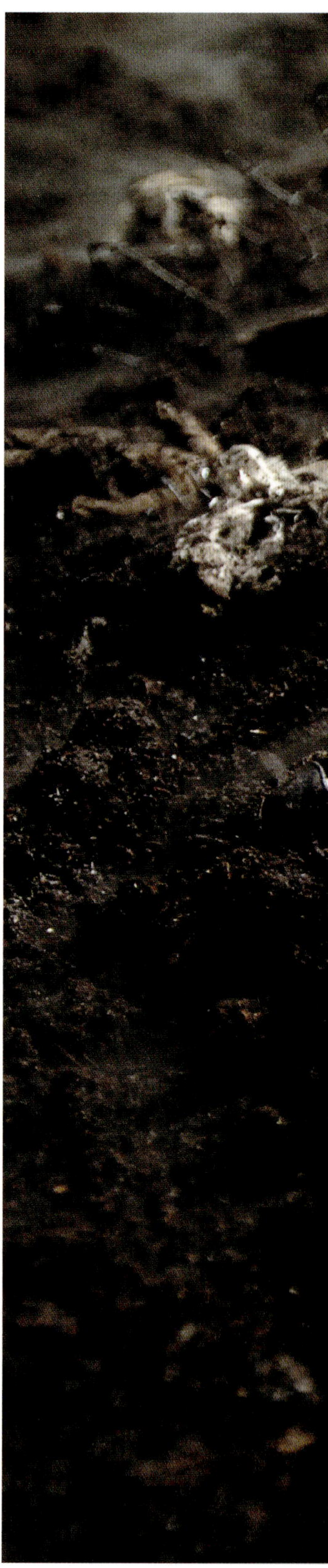

Right. The Western Front brought to life in miniature in *The Great War*.

Below. The poster for *The Notebook*, the unsettling story of twin brothers who take their own moral stance against a crumbling wartime society.

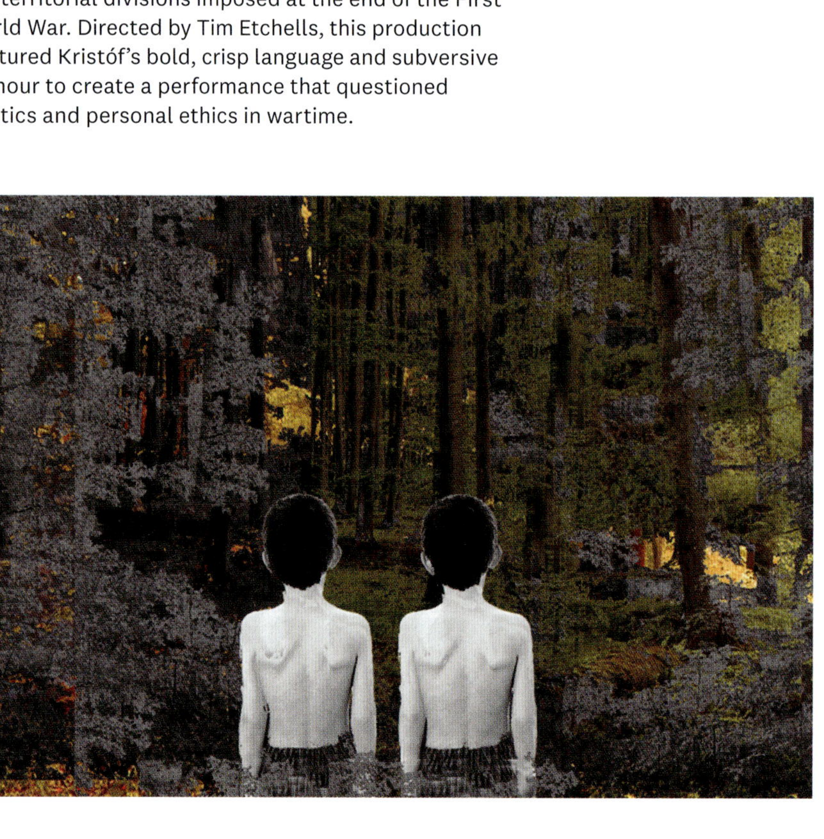

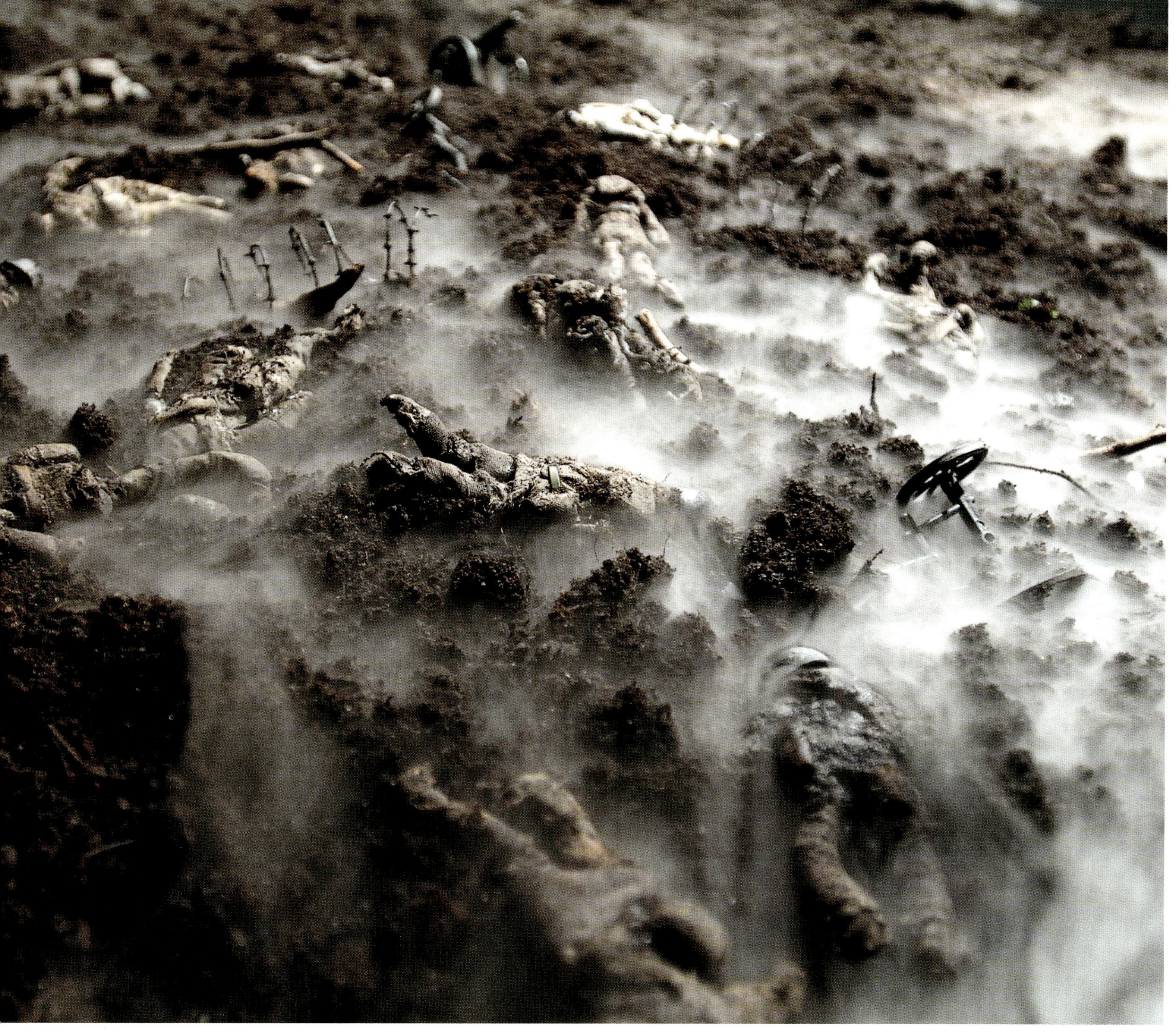

The Argentinean artist Lola Arias presented the UK premiere of *The Year I Was Born*, in which 11 performers born in Pinochet's Chile in the 1970s and early 1980s told the stories of their parents living in the grip of dictatorship, recalling this bloody moment in history with the use of photographs, letters, cassettes, clothing and anecdotes.

James Bridle's *Drone Shadows* have been installed in numerous places (including the atrium of London's Imperial War Museum), and featured on the streets of Battersea for *After a War*. Simple yet ominous outlines act as a reminder of the invisibility, threat and sheer size of these weapons of modern warfare.

The rousing finale to the programme was provided by the Tiger Lillies, with a new performance entitled *A Dream Turns Sour*. This was their excoriating take on poetry and songs from the First World War period — a startling mixture of opera, gypsy song, Left Bank Paris and black humour.

These artists were joined by Inua Ellams, Lucien Bourjeily and many others across the weekend, creating work in a range of disciplines, with widely varying perspectives on the First World War and subsequent conflicts, and taking audiences on a journey through the varied spaces of the centre into deep reflection on the lasting impact of war.

Southbank Centre and Battersea Art Centre, London, 24 — 29 June 2014

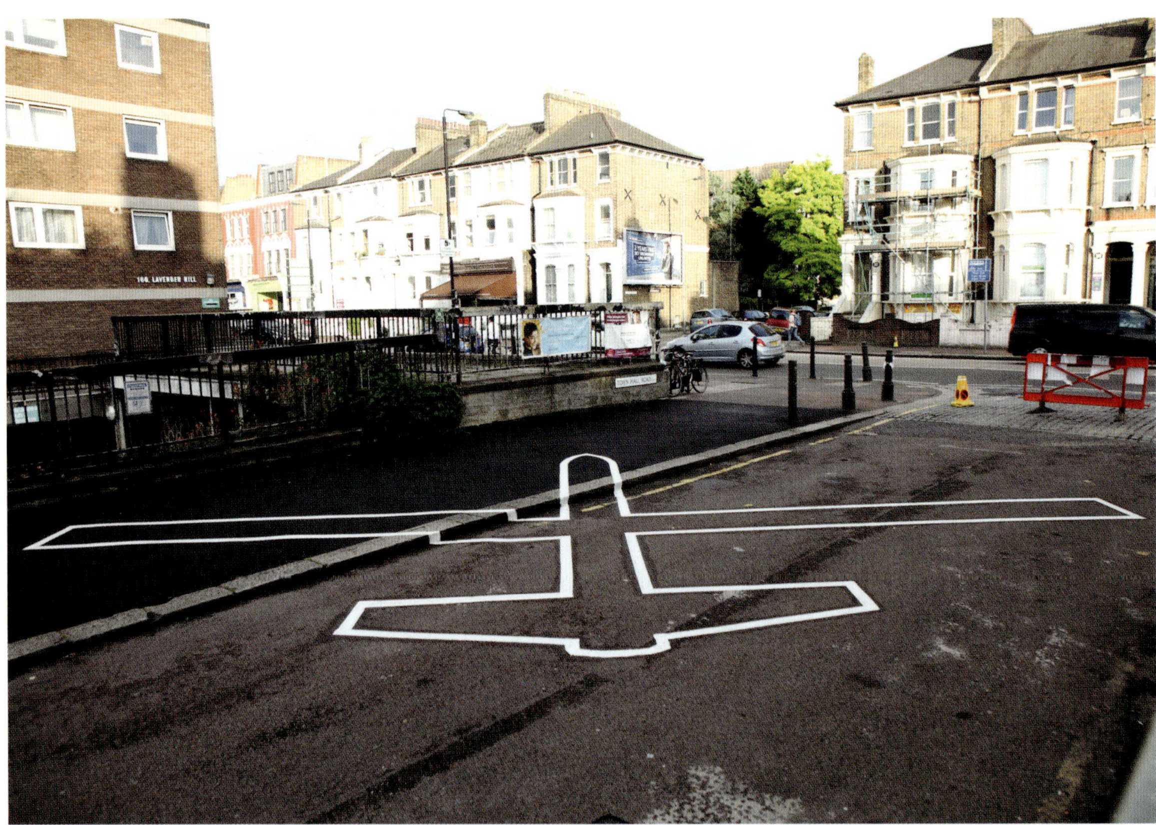

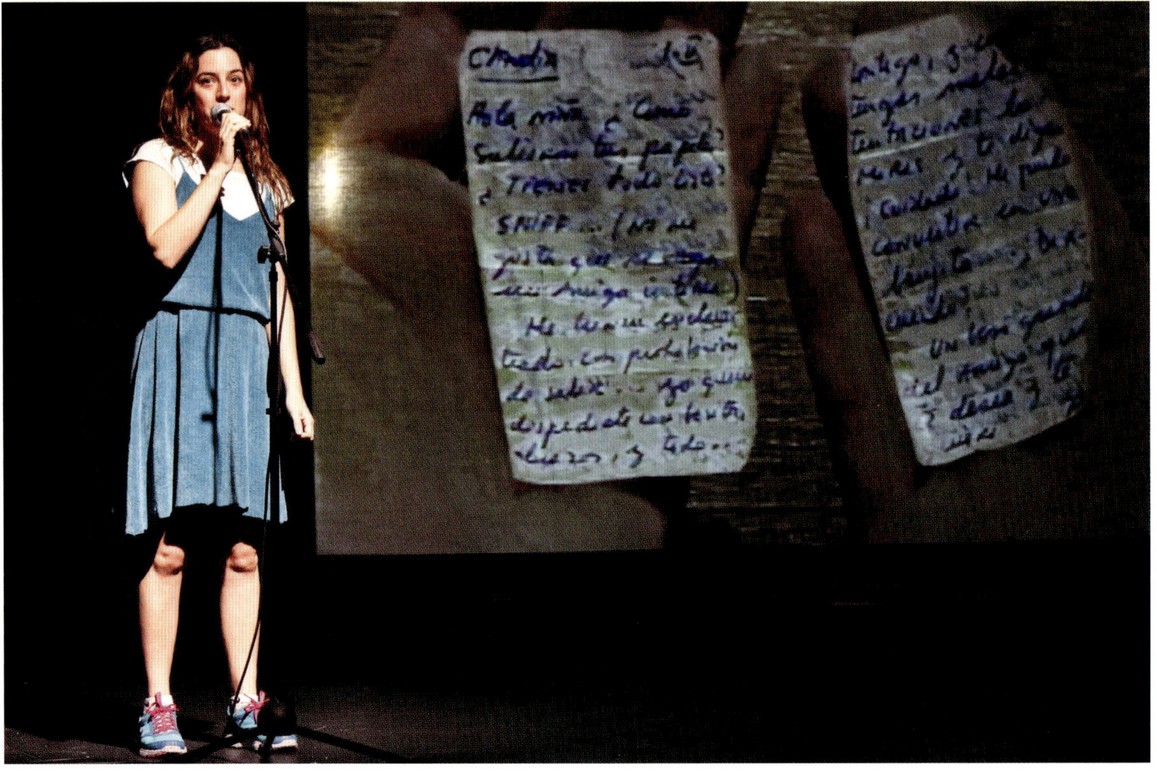

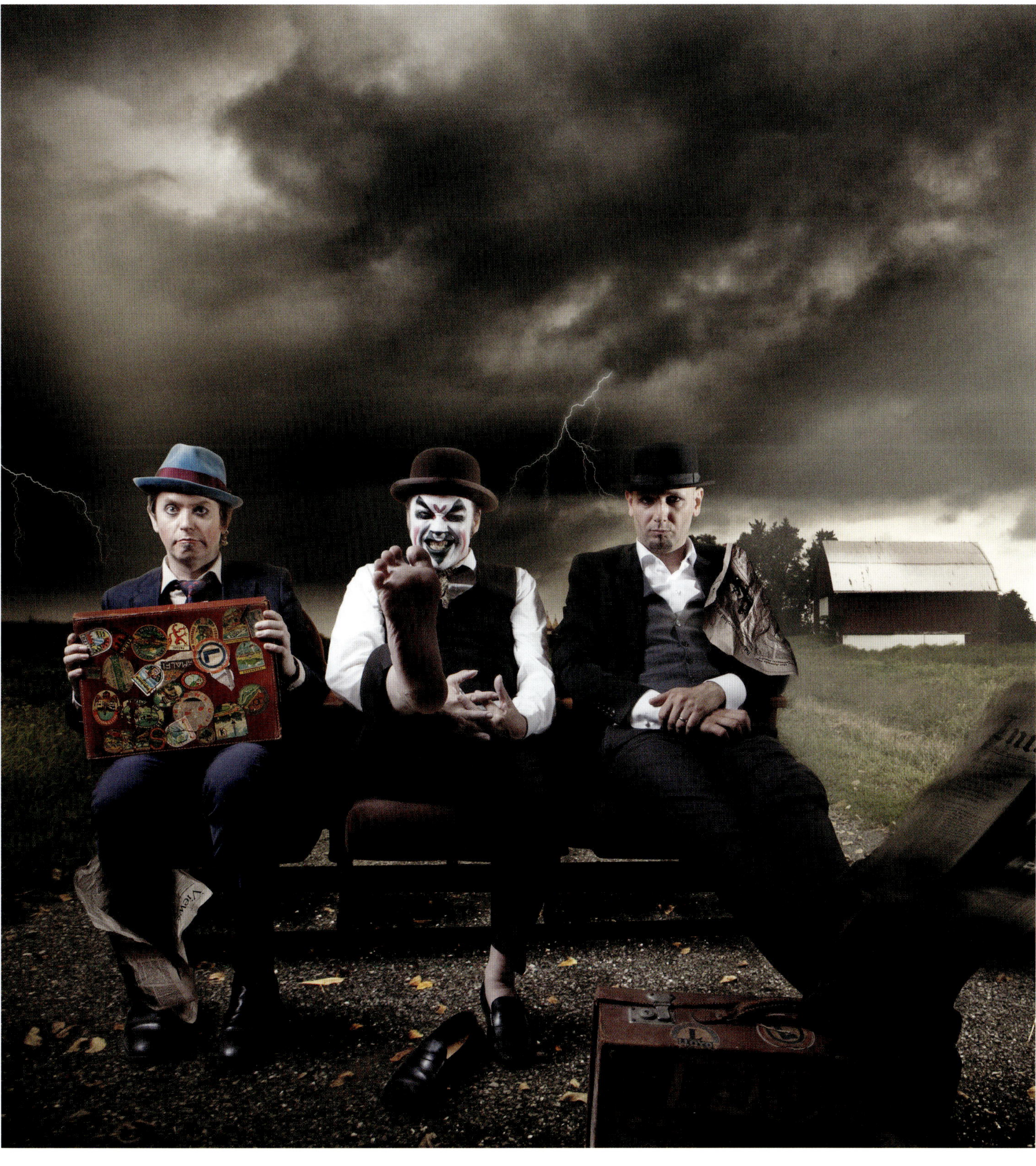

Opposite top. The shadow of a drone, created by artist James Bridle, passed over the streets of Battersea as part of *After a War*.

Opposite bottom. *The Year I Was Born* drew on real-life experiences of life under a harsh dictatorship.

Left. The Tiger Lillies were inspired to create what they described as a 'doom-laden tale of death' using English and German poetry from the First World War.

CHARLIE WARD

Sound&Fury

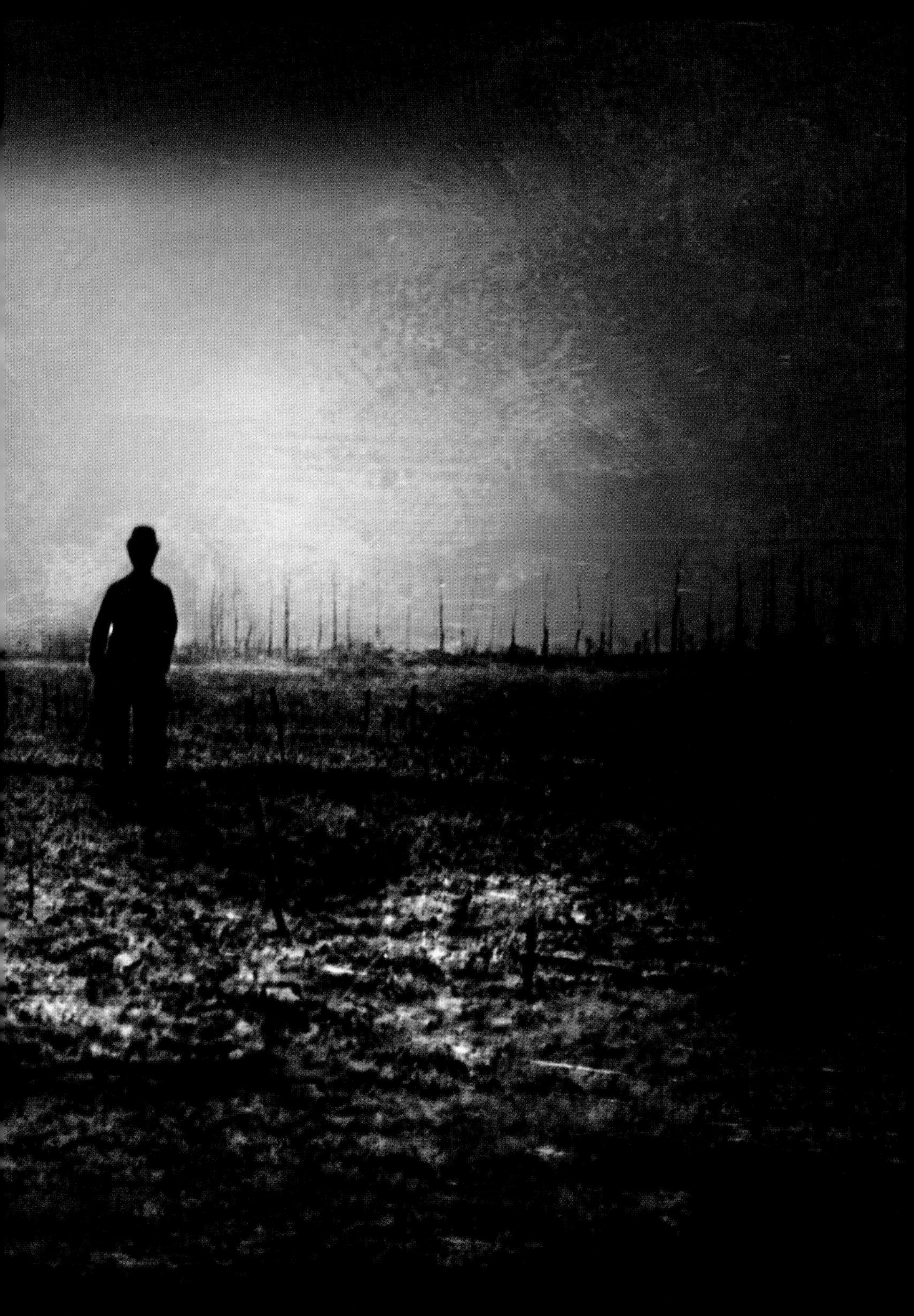

This intimate and powerful sound installation by Sound&Fury placed audiences in the heart of a makeshift wartime hospital, where an unlikely therapy brings solace to the injured.

It is rumoured that British soldiers in the trenches held up cardboard cutouts of Charlie Chaplin's tramp in the hope that the enemy would die laughing. But as the carnage of war set in, Chaplin's image was put to a different use. In the makeshift hospitals behind the front line, medical staff would show Chaplin films to the bedridden to boost their morale, with the ward's ceiling serving as the silver screen.

Using their distinctive style — total darkness, minimal lighting and immersive sound design — Sound&Fury conjured up the extraordinary experience of being a patient on Charlie Ward. For one soldier, the flickering images, whirring projector and Chaplin's perfect comic timing trigger complex emotions and memories. Cast from the trenches to childhood, and from trauma to dreams, the soldier is sent on a journey into a personal No Man's Land.

Appropriately, the first performances of *Charlie Ward* took place among the many artefacts of cinema history at the Cinema Museum, which itself is housed in the former Lambeth Workhouse, where Chaplin lived for a time as a child.

Cinema Museum, London, 23 July — 3 August 2014 / York Army Museum, 24 September — 6 October 2018 / Theatre Deli, Sheffield, 10 — 22 September 2018 / Perth Theatre, 15 — 20 October 2018 / Leeds Town Hall, 30 October — 11 November 2018

FLIGHT

Geraldine Pilgrim

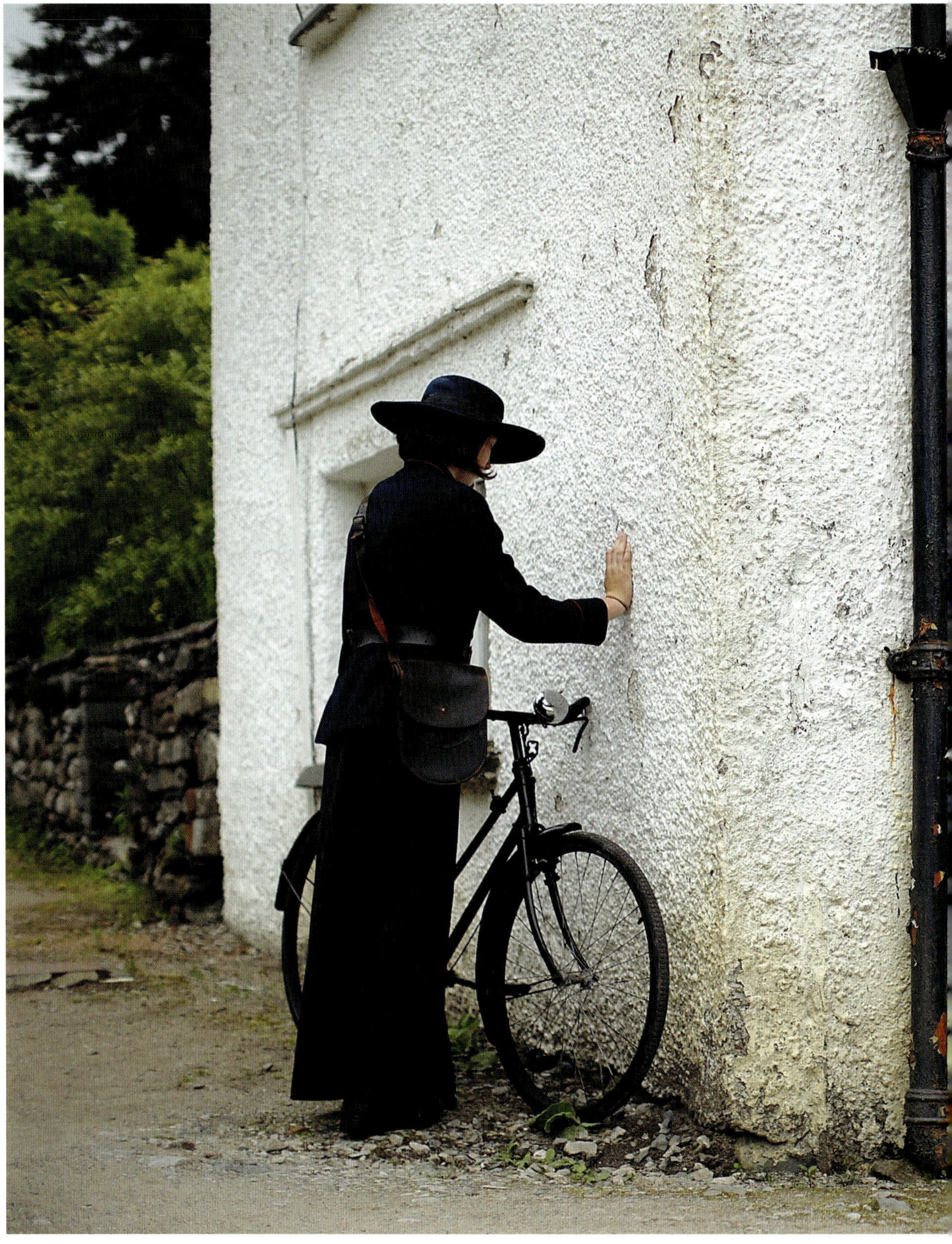

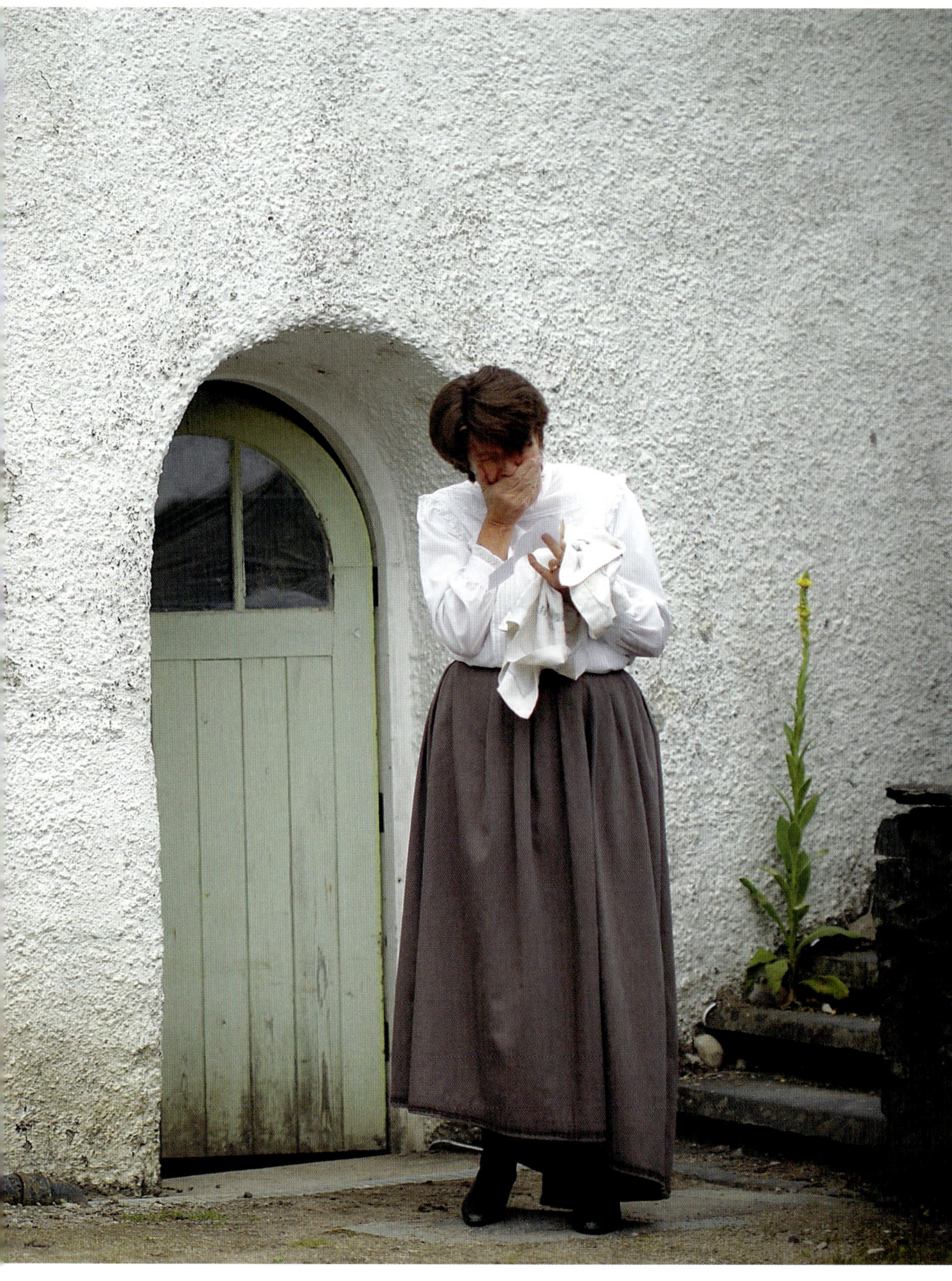

The Wright brothers made their first flight in 1903, and changed our world overnight. The ability to fly has transformed modern life, from the practicalities of industry and war to more intangible dreams. Capturing the beauty, power and drama of flight in all its forms, *Flight* was a multi-layered performance and installation created by the artist Geraldine Pilgrim, in conjunction with the Lake District National Park. The work paid particular tribute to its setting on the banks of Lake Windermere: Hill of Oaks was the birthplace of the first seaplane in 1911 and it became the site of a flying school for the Royal Naval Air Service in 1916. The vast majority of its young students, eager to learn to fly in the years leading up to the war, were tragically swept up in the conflict.

   Flight began with a number of site-specific performances over four days, featuring local volunteer performers, then continued in the form of an installation trail through the historic house and grounds of the Brockhole visitor centre. At the heart of the project were those young airmen, and the people they left behind — looking up at the sky and waiting for their loved ones to come home, like migrating birds, although so few ever would.

Brockhole on Windermere, Cumbria, 7 — 17 July 2016

*'When I read that the Royal
Flying Corps' new pilots, often
in their teens, lasted on average
just 11 days from arrival on the
front to death, I thought of the
Cumbrian landscape dreaming
of its missing airmen, realising
they would never return ...'*

Geraldine Pilgrim

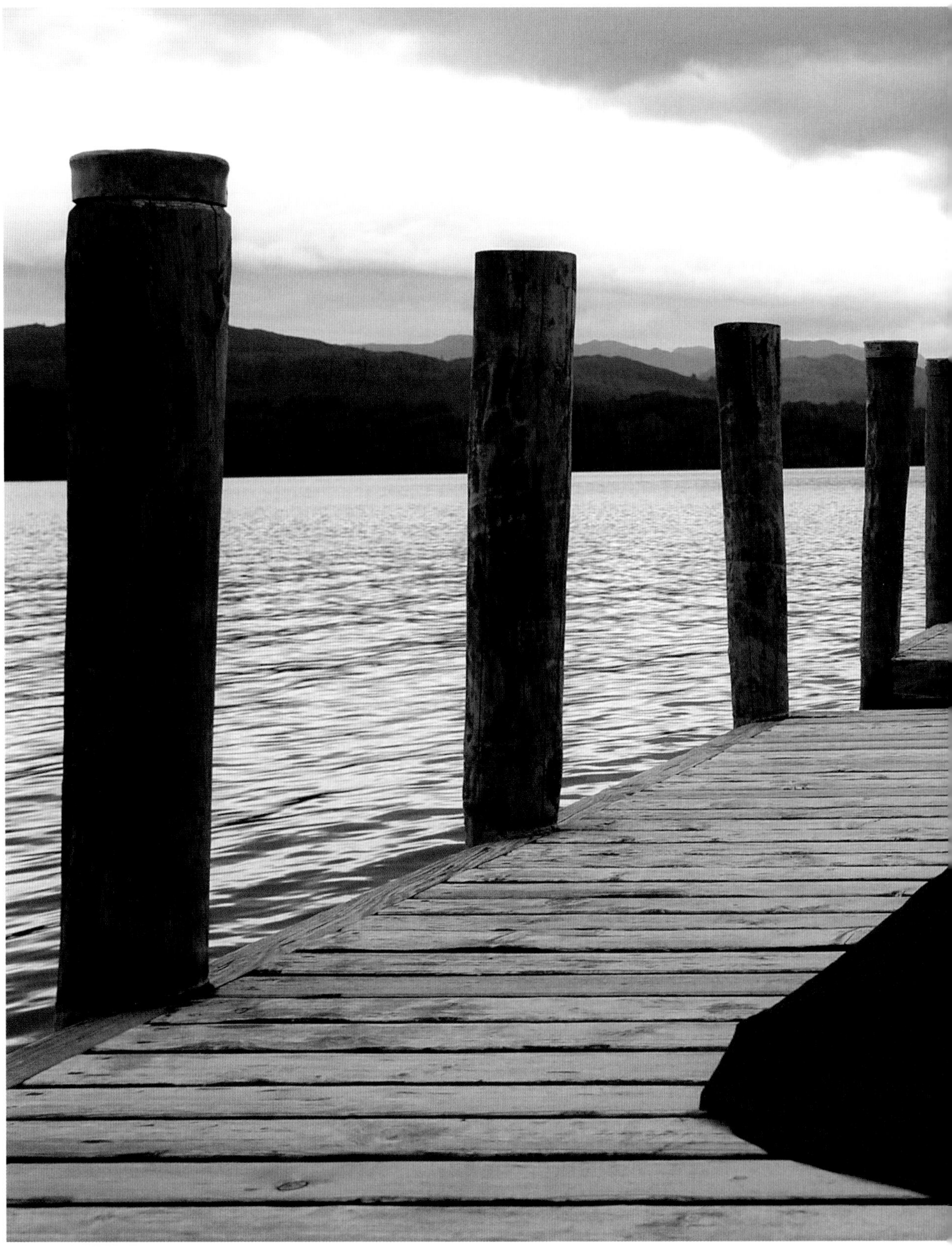

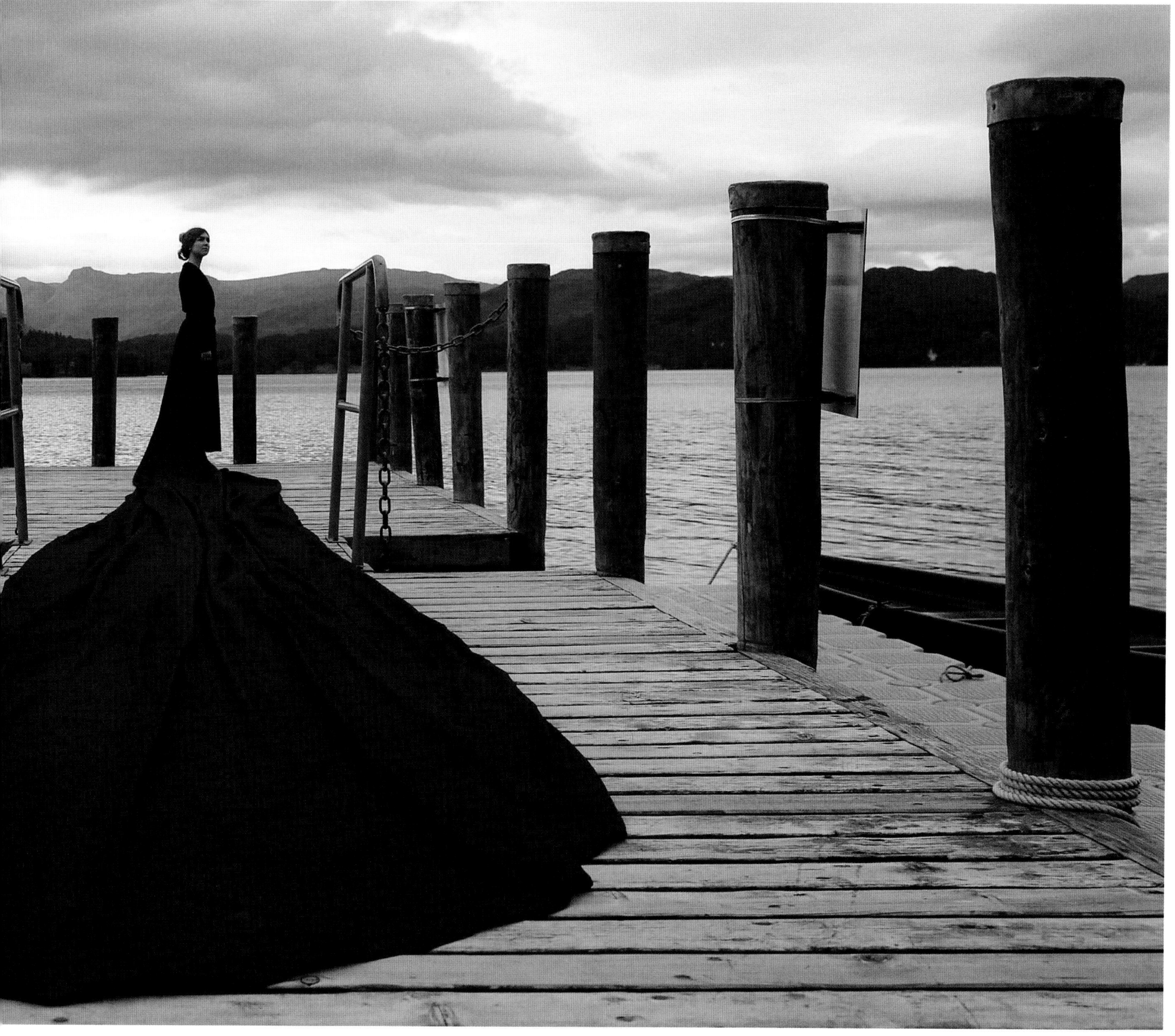

The 19th-century Briggait, in the heart of Glasgow's thriving Merchant City, was originally the city's fish market. It has now been transformed into a home for artists and cultural organisations. The Empire Café was a week-long event held here during the 2014 Commonwealth Games, exploring the context of Scotland and the North Atlantic slave trade. As part of the wider programme, 14-18 NOW commissioned a new film from the Scottish artist Graham Fagen.

War c/w I Murder Hate documents a contemporary recording session of two songs, pairing Bob Marley's 'War' (which started life as a speech given by Haile Selassie calling for world peace) with Robert Burns' 1790 anti-war song 'I Murder Hate'. The work considered the stories of Jamaican soldiers during the First World War, and the way in which Jamaican identity developed as status shifted from slave to citizen. In doing so, the film presents an even broader message of humanity, condemning inequality and championing love over hate.

The Briggait, Glasgow, 24 July — 1 August 2014

THE EMPIRE CAFÉ

Graham Fagen

Stills taken from Graham Fagen's film, which combined the disparate works of the Scottish Burns and Jamaican Marley to explore Jamaica's role in both the First World War and the British Empire.

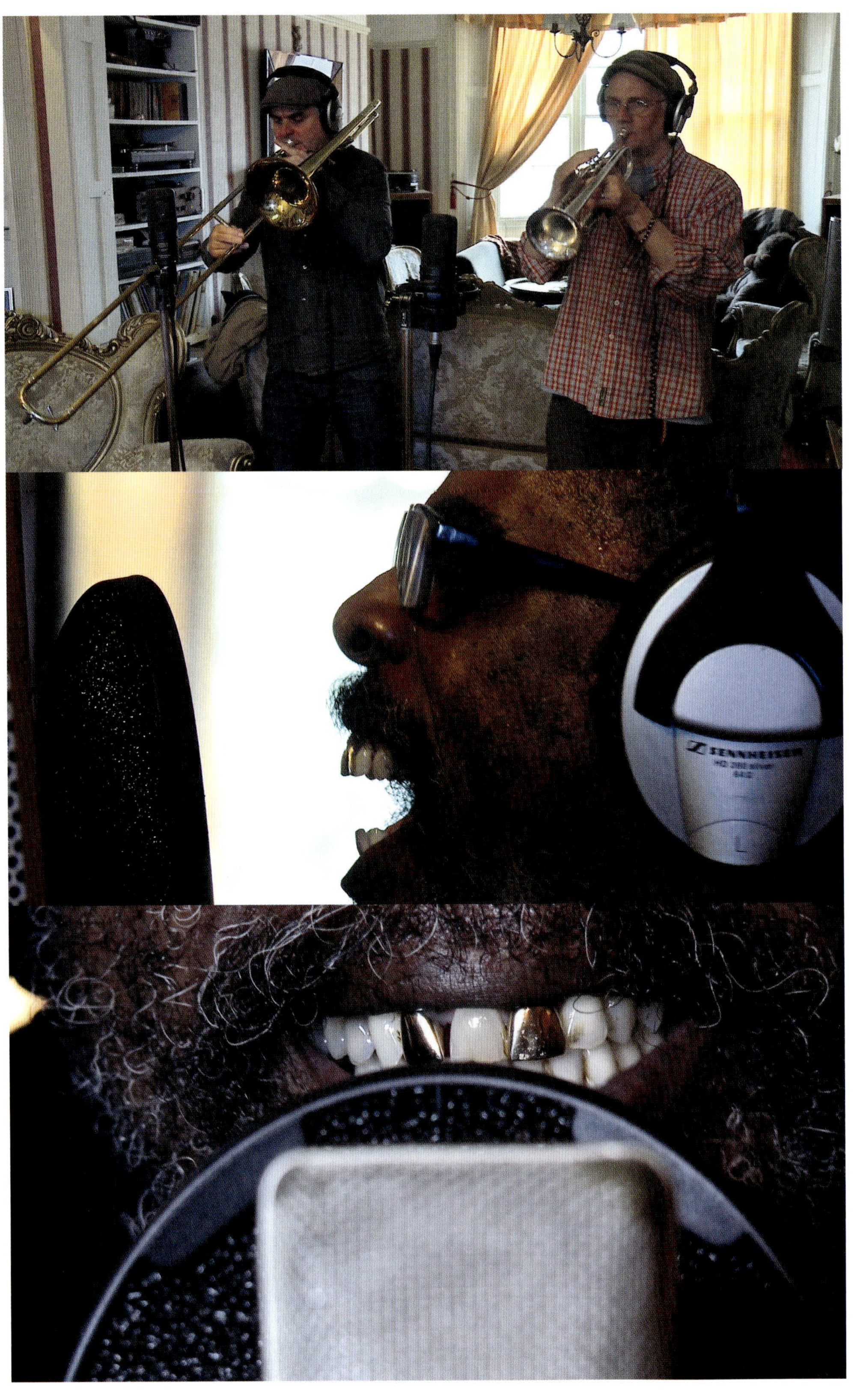

The assassination of Archduke Franz Ferdinand on the streets of Sarajevo on 28 June 1914 was among the defining events of the modern world. One hundred years later, musician and activist Billy Bragg hand-picked six artists to write and perform new songs at Glastonbury Festival inspired by that event.

Bragg performed Thomas Hardy's 'The Man He Killed' set to a folk tune; Sam Duckworth wrote 'Invisible Lines', inspired by the Archduke himself; Robb Johnson (whose two grandfathers both spent time on the Western Front) performed 'The Day My Grandfather Played Football'; folk duo O'Hooley & Tidow perfomed 'The Pixie', about Daisy Daking, who taught dance to rehabilitated soldiers in France; singer-songwriter Mat Skinner performed 'The Scarecrow', set to a First World War poem by James Lyons; and folk singer Lucy Ward sang 'Lion', about rifleman Robert Loveless Barker, who was shot at dawn for cowardice.

*Left Field stage, Glastonbury Festival,
25 — 29 June 2014*

'As Iraq struggles to throw off the borders drawn for it in 1919 by the victorious allies, you can see the events of the First World War still reverberating through our daily news bulletins.'

Billy Bragg

THE OPENING ACT

Billy Bragg
Sam Duckworth
Robb Johnson
O'Hooley & Tidow
Mat Skinner
Lucy Ward

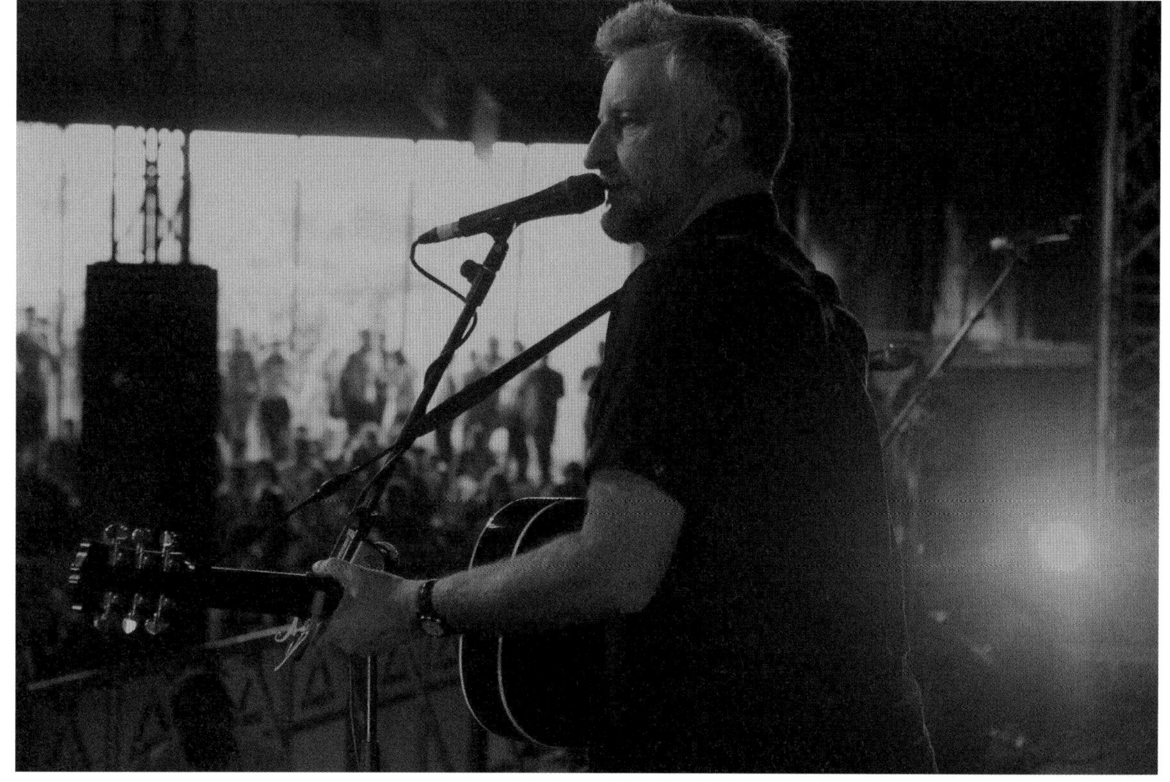

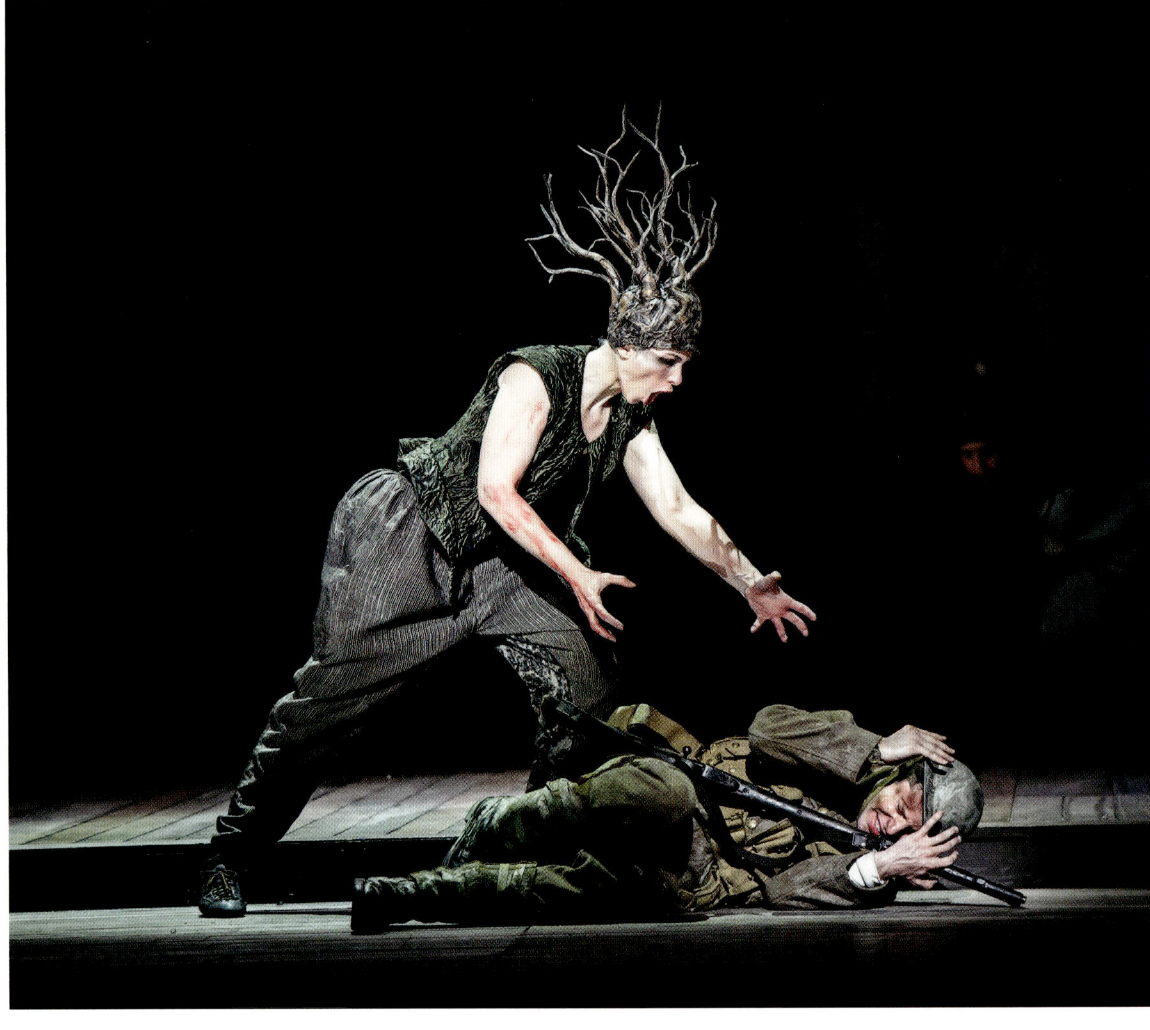

IN PARENTHESIS

Iain Bell
Welsh National Opera

Commissioned to mark the centenary of the Battle of the Somme and to celebrate the 70th year of Welsh National Opera, *In Parenthesis* was young British composer Iain Bell's adaptation of the 1937 epic poem of the same name by writer and artist David Jones, based on Jones' own wartime experiences. Bell's beautiful score combined traditional Welsh song with moments of otherworldliness, terror, humour and transcendence, while director David Pountney's production provided both a powerful evocation of the period and a commemoration of the devastating events that took place that fateful July.

The story opens in December 1915, with its protagonist, Private John Ball, and his comrades in the Royal Welch Fusiliers posted to fight in France. Upon landing in that country, the soldiers find themselves in an eerie, foreboding world, where they linger through Christmas and into the following year. However, by July 1916, they have reached the Somme battlefield, where the order is given to attack Mametz Wood (see also pages 264–267). Entering a strange, timeless realm, Ball's comrades are killed one by one, leaving Ball a wounded survivor. However, as the story concludes, the character of the Queen of the Wood appears to bestow garlands on the dead, creating a fragile sense of regeneration and rebirth amid a scene of horror and destruction.

Wales Millennium Centre, Cardiff, 13 May — 3 June 2016 / Birmingham Hippodrome, 10 June 2016 / Royal Opera House, London, 29 June — 1 July 2016

'Bell's richly multilayered score
supports the deft interweaving
of realism and mythic fantasy.
A powerful act of remembrance.'
The Independent

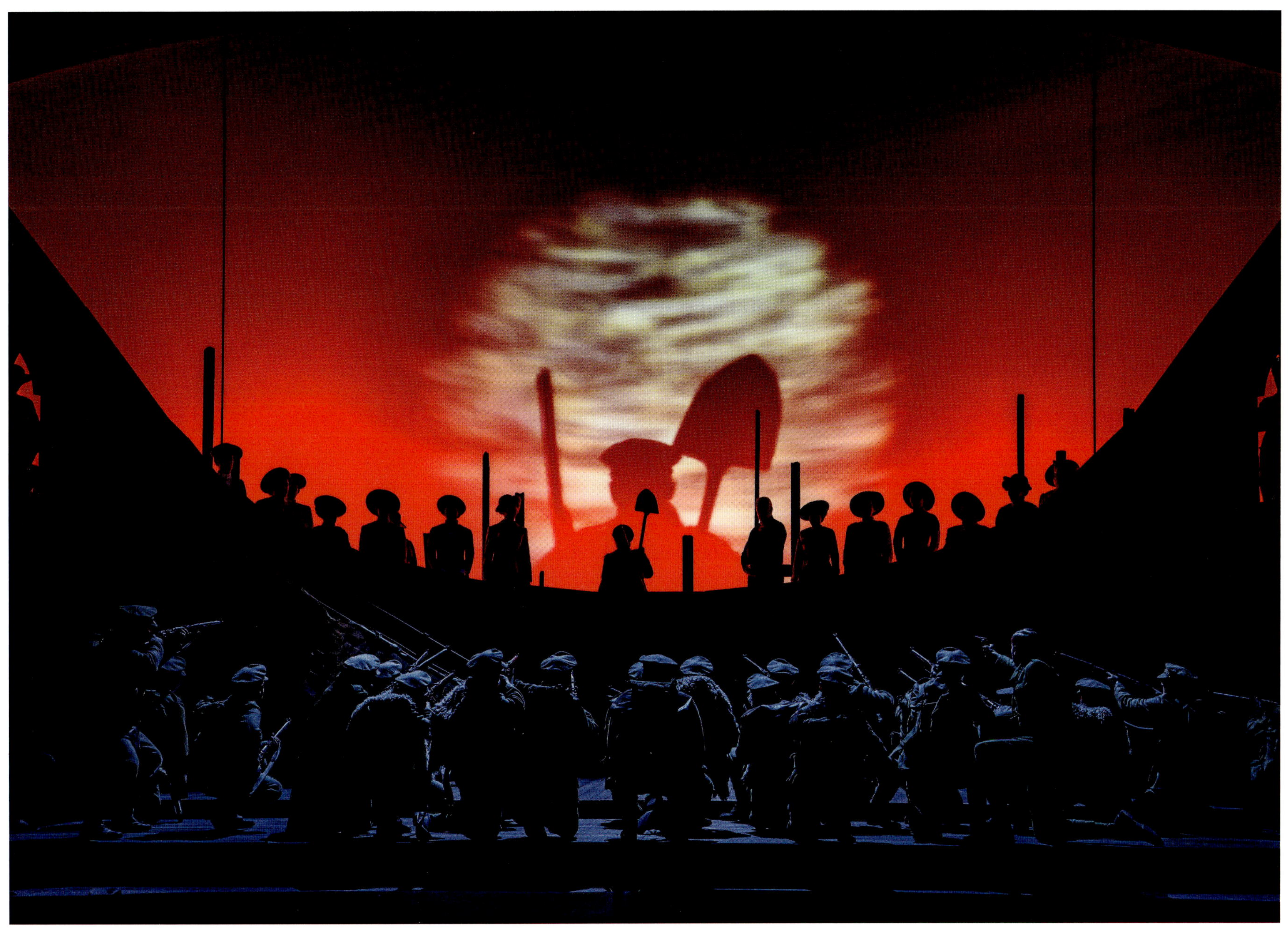

Although we had started this piece of work as an examination of the past, it became obvious that the themes we were exploring remained hugely relevant … Whether we're white, black or brown, we all know what it means to be a stranger because we're all, to a certain extent, powerless as citizens because of the actions of the government of the time.

WHOSE WAR?
WHOSE FIRE?

Akram Khan

When I first started to think about *XENOS* it was in the context of creating my final solo dance work, so it became very important to me, very quickly. I found myself thinking about my mother frequently because she was the one who taught me my first dance steps. Making *XENOS* became a very emotional and personal process, both in that it was my final solo piece, but also in that the subject matter began to feel extremely close to me and my heritage.

The process started from the position of examining the Prometheus story and the idea of men and gods making the same mistakes, trapped in eternal torment. When I started to talk to 14-18 NOW we looked at the similarities that are often drawn between the First World War and Greek mythology, and the work started to evolve of its own accord as I explored these themes with my creative team. I like to work collaboratively with artists I have an existing relationship with but also to bring in new voices — often this is when things begin to evolve.

Greek for 'stranger' or 'foreigner', *XENOS* was inspired by the legend of Prometheus and the untold story of the 1.3 million Indian soldiers who fought in the First World War. The more I delved into the history, the more surprised I was to learn about the soldiers' experiences because it wasn't something that was taught in school. But at the same time it was no surprise at all, because history is always written from one side, predominantly from the Anglo-Saxon perspective, and the winners will always tell the story. Those who survived the trenches returned home to discover that, post-colonisation, India had little interest in men who had fought on behalf of the British.

The idea of these men who were plucked from their homes in India to take part in a war on foreign soil for a country that they knew nothing about really struck us. How strange the experience, the countryside and the treatment of them must have been. But also the way that these men were viewed as strangers, too — treated differently to the other British men taking part in the conflict.

We came up with the idea that the solo dancer should be the depiction of one Indian soldier, one body who represented all of those who were plucked from their home and spat out into the conflict. We decided that this man would be someone who was a dancer at home and was coming to terms with the huge change in his circumstances and how he would struggle to confront it. This of course allowed me to incorporate some of the Kathak movements that represent where my dancing started, and have always been present in my work. It also meant that we could work with amazing musicians to root the piece firmly in India as the audience entered. The work throughout is really a dialogue between the classical Indian and the contemporary, which felt right for this presentation — both in terms of the subject matter, and also as my final solo piece of work. I felt a strong desire to meld the historical with the contemporary.

Although we had started this piece of work as an examination of the past, it became obvious that the themes we were exploring remained hugely relevant. The parallels across different periods of time in which xenophobia has been, and remains, a huge concern — the same set of symptoms that were there before the First and Second World Wars being still present today.

Whether we're white, black or brown, we all know what it means to be a stranger because we're all, to a certain extent, powerless as citizens because of the actions of the government of the time.

Creating *XENOS* was both a beautiful and exciting way to end my solo dancing career, as well as a homage to those who took part in the First World War — those who were the *XENOS*.

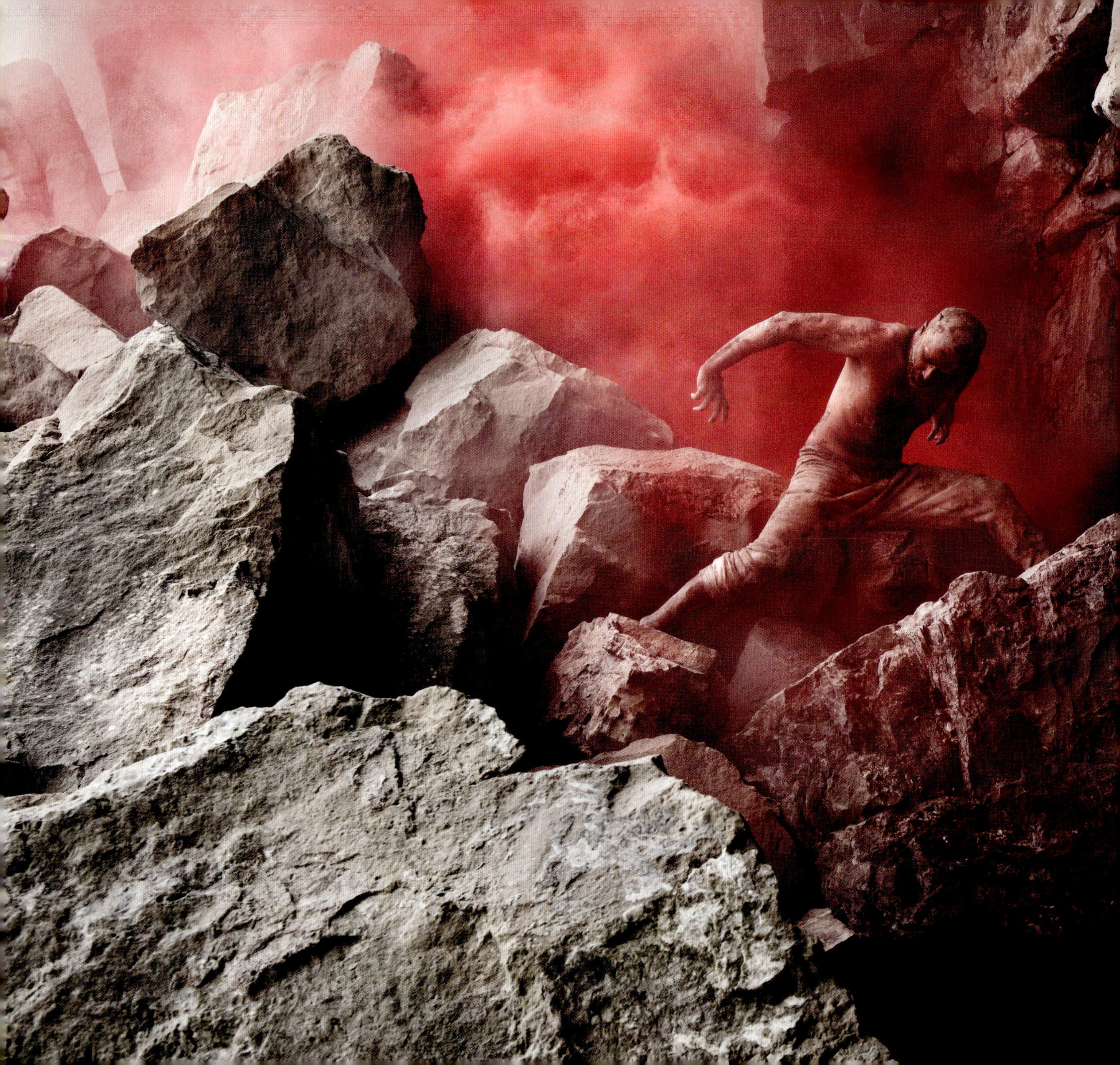

XENOS

Akram Khan

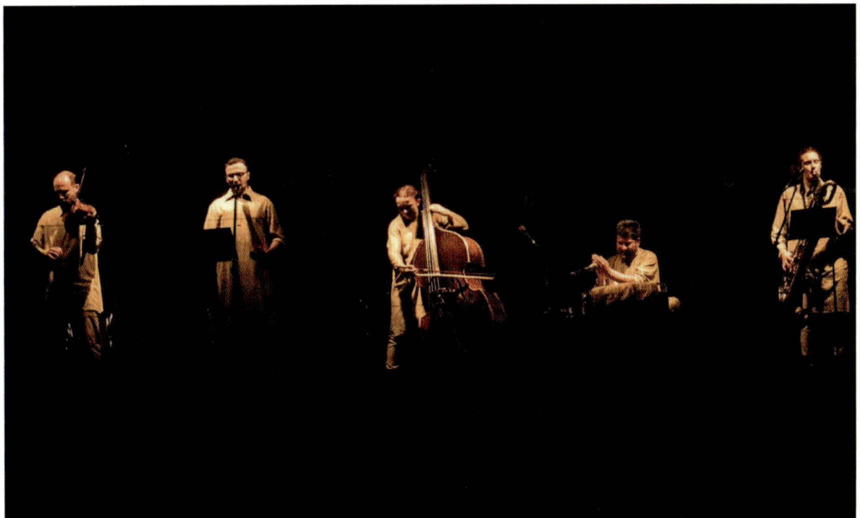

Above. The score was performed live by five musicians — violinist Andrew Maddick, vocalist Aditya Prakash, bass player Nina Harries, percussionist B. C. Manjunath and saxophonist Tamar Osborn.

Left. Akram Khan's lone dancer struggles in a smoke-filled trench — a stark landscape of rocks and clay that threatens to engulf him.

Internationally revered choreographer and dancer Akram Khan's swansong as a full-length solo performer in 2018 (aged 43) was a moving tribute to the sacrifices made by Indian colonial soldiers in the First World War. *XENOS* (Greek for 'foreigner') explored the experience of a single shell-shocked soldier who had once been a traditional Indian dancer, his skilled body having become an instrument of war. The work combined dance and movement with complex sound design, music and lighting to capture the beauty and horror of the human condition.

Working with his literary team (dramaturg Ruth Little and playwright Jordan Tannahill), Khan drew on archive accounts of soldiers' testimonies, which he juxtaposed with the Greek myth of Prometheus, who formed man from clay and was punished by the gods for stealing fire. The result was a dream-like journey into the mind of a man scarred by his experiences of combat, in which physical and psychological punishment is meted out on him as an individual for mankind's collective decision to create such a war.

Khan, whose family came to England from Bangladesh, employed a shifting hybrid of classical Kathak and contemporary dance in the piece, merging influences of East and West, past and present. Kathak influences in the choreography were used to represent the dancer's heritage and identity — his very humanity — which returned to him at moments throughout the piece, despite the dehumanising effects of battle.

The elaborate set viscerally recreated the trenches of the Western Front, using steep slopes, ropes, flows of real mud and a raised dais on which five musicians played Vincenzo Lamagna's score live, positioned above the action like Olympian gods. An oversized gramophone read out the names of real soldiers who lost their lives in the war, and sophisticated lighting effects were used to bring the nightmare to life, generating surreal shifts from high-society Indian house parties filled with classical music and dancing to the horrors of the Western Front.

XENOS was a haunting conclusion to an illustrious career, and a profound tribute to the 1.3 million Indian soldiers who fought in the conflict.

Sadler's Wells Theatre, London, 29 May — 9 June 2018 / Edinburgh International Festival, 16 — 18 August 2018

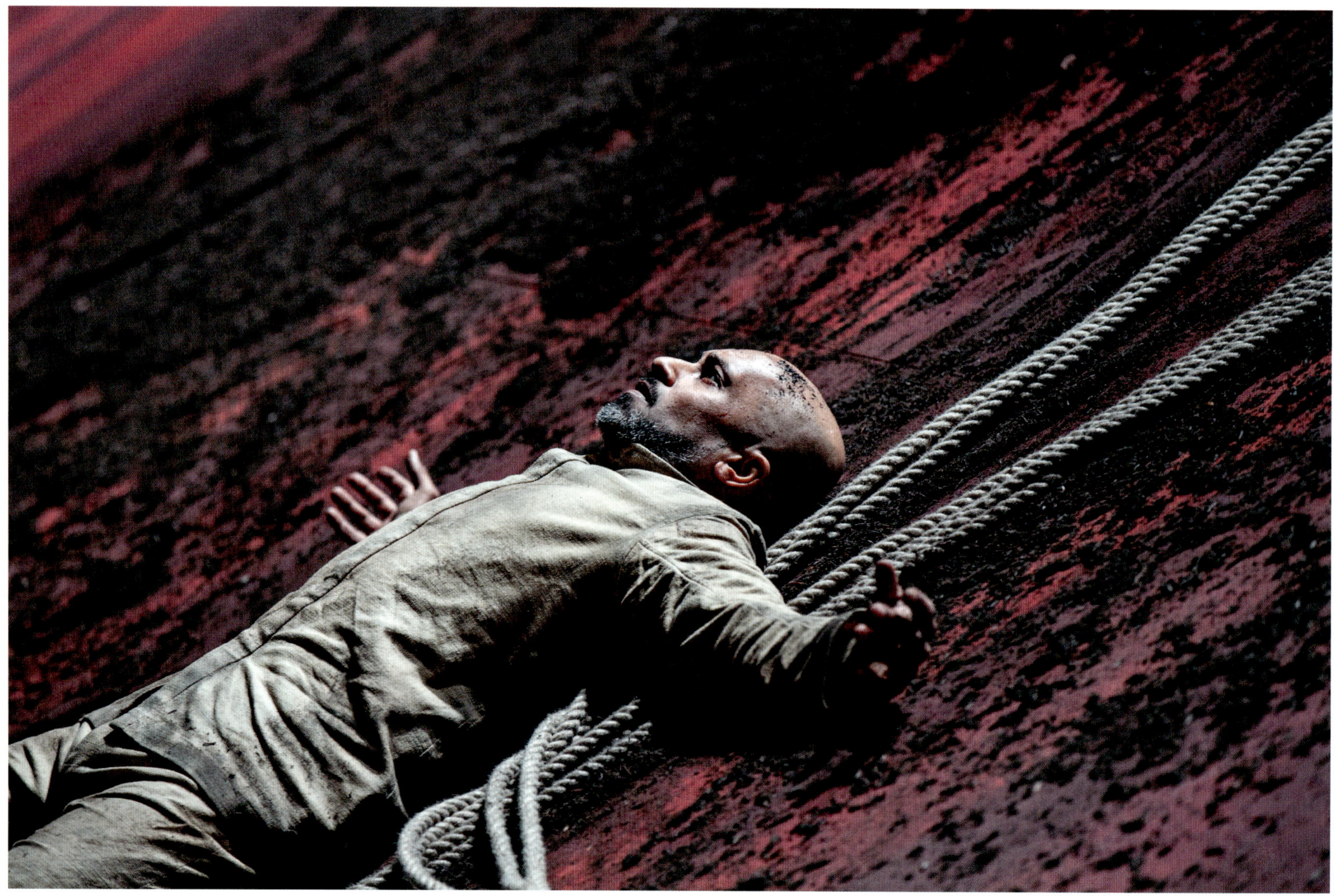

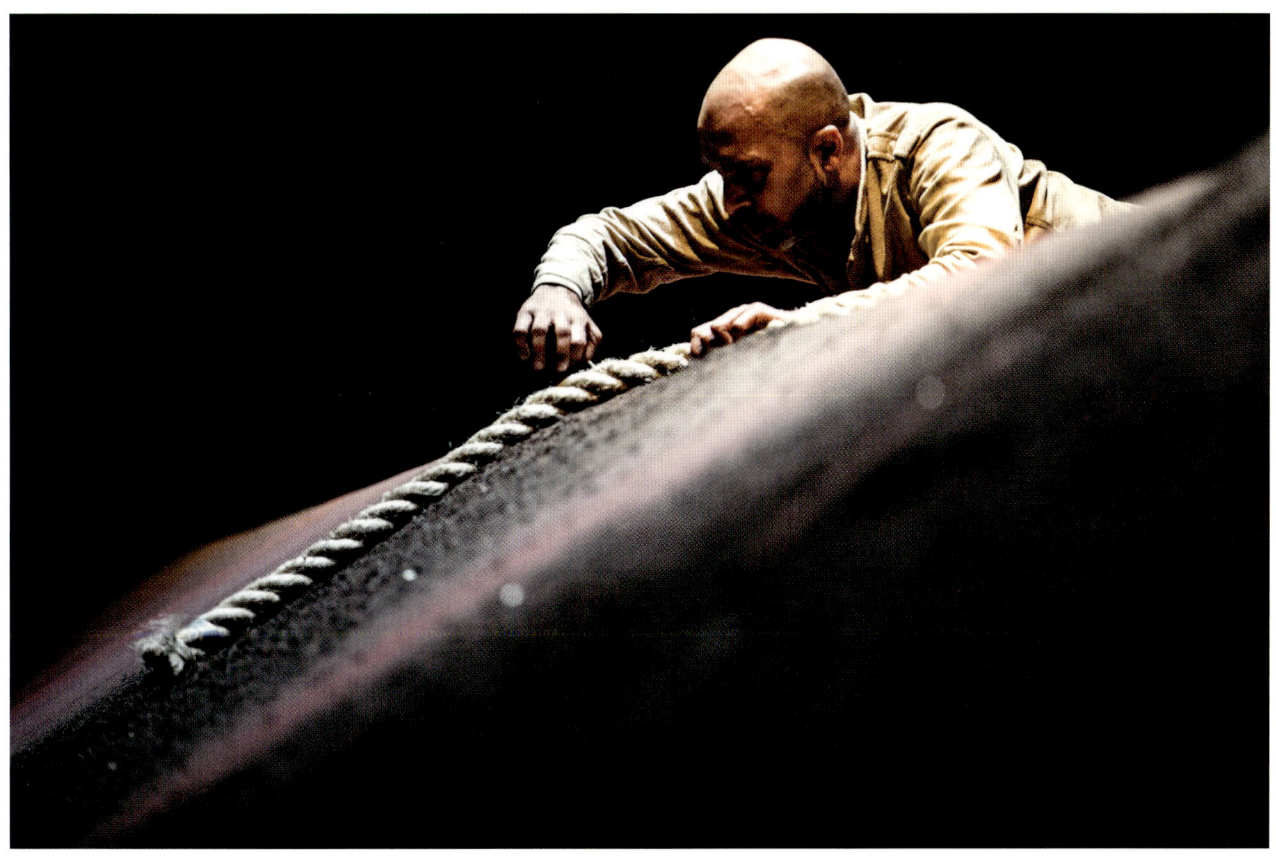

Left and opposite. Ropes that trailed down a steep slope appeared to offer the soldier an escape, but only ended up emphasising his entrapment.

Below. In an echo of the Promethean myth, Khan's dancer was ultimately defeated by a landslide, merging with the earth to become clay once more.

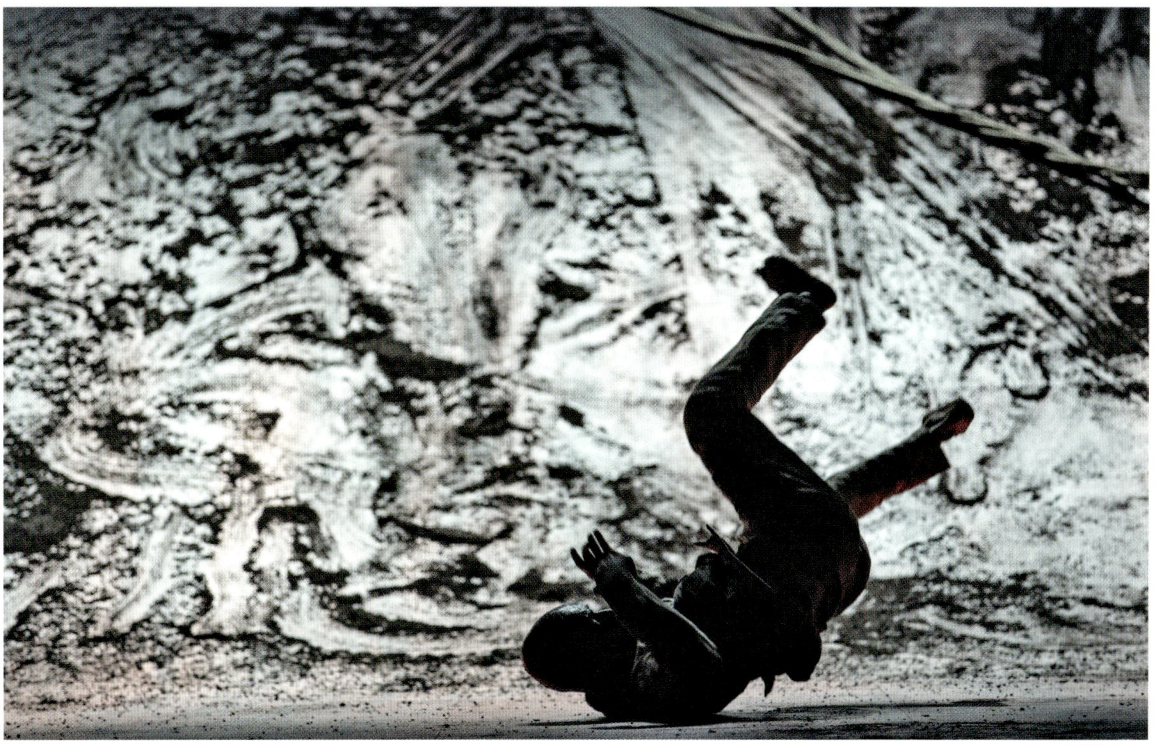

The First World War had a major impact on the way we think about the human body. The huge numbers and the nature of some of the physical injuries inflicted by mechanised warfare — machine guns, bombshells, chemical weaponry — were without precedent in human history, and demanded from both art and medical science new ways of thinking about prosthetics, disability and beauty.

The Body Extended: Sculpture and Prosthetics was an ambitious exhibition at the Henry Moore Institute in Leeds, telling the story of how we have extended and supplemented the body over the past century. Featuring objects and artworks from museums and medical collections from Europe and the United States, it demonstrated the ways in which the medical sciences and the arts have often looked to each other for new ideas of what it means to be human.

As a key element in the exhibition, the Henry Moore Institute and 14-18 NOW co-commissioned a major new outdoor sculpture from the artist Rebecca Warren. The massive bronze *Man and the dark* consists of a pair of legs, simplified in their anatomy, exaggeratedly muscled, the feet heavily shod, striding with a grimly heroic energy of thwarted purpose across the surface of a wheeled slab. This slab, reminiscent of an ancient cannon base, or the rudimentary vehicles used by amputee veterans, is in turn immobilised on a large, stepped plinth. Sited at the entrance to the building, on the busiest thoroughfare in Leeds, the work welcomed visitors to an exhibition that explored the impact of the war on how we understand and represent the human body today.

*Henry Moore Institute, Leeds, 21 July —
23 October 2016*

MAN AND THE DARK

Rebecca Warren

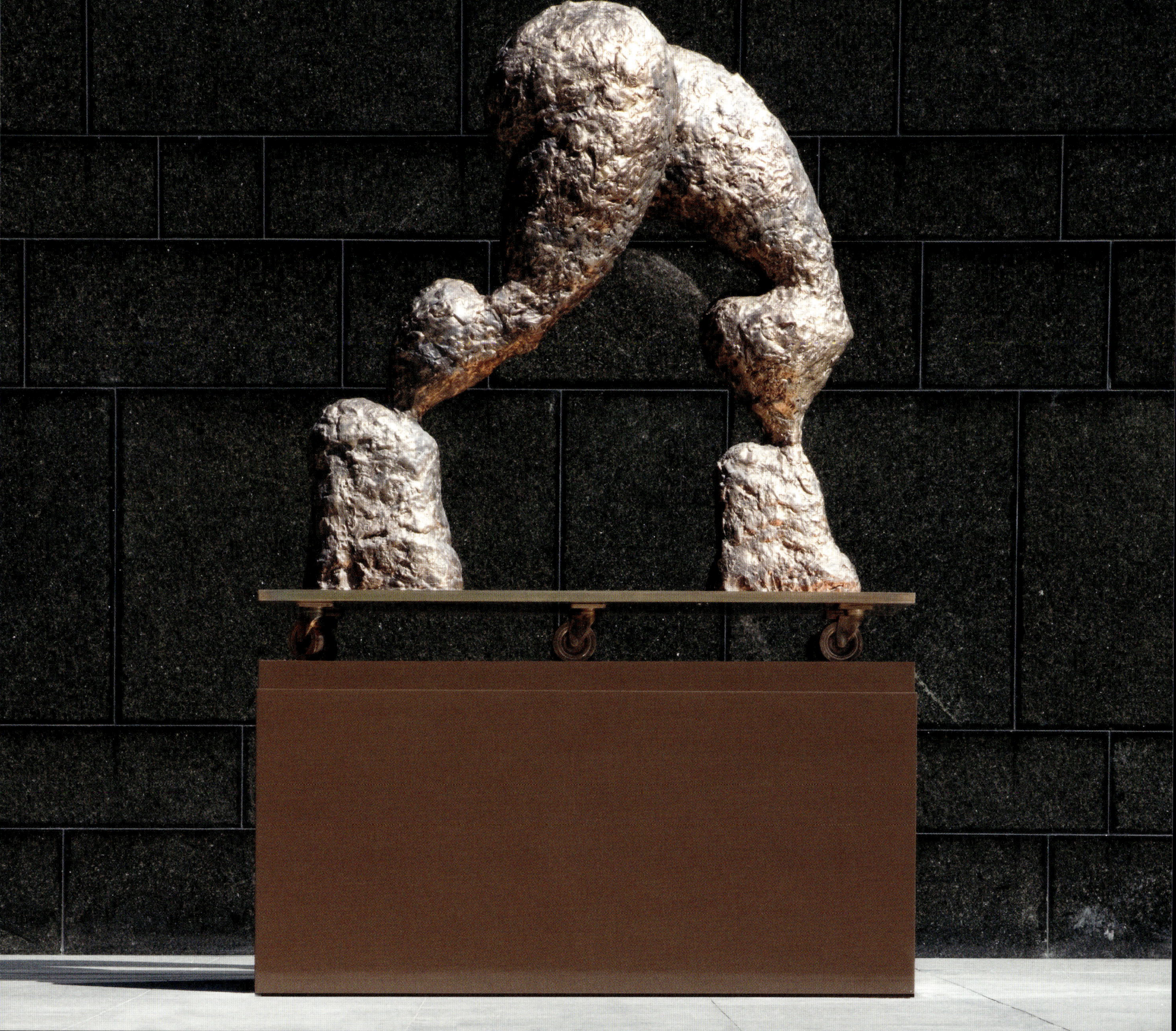

Song sheets flutter. Blood, bo
Ballads slide down the years,
My father, ninety, still singing
The past is lively, impossible
There's life in the old dog yet,
Private Joseph Kay takes a lo
Hits the sharp note, hands on

From 'Dedicated to Private Joseph Kay'
Jackie Kay

air,

roken lines.

s father

pin down.

ohn pipes

breath

blows out.

FIERCE LIGHT

Poets
Yrsa Daley-Ward
Jackie Kay
Bill Manhire
Paul Muldoon
Daljit Nagra

Film-makers
George Belfield
Tim Davies
Suzi Hanna
Matt Kay

Drawing on their experiences, the First World War poets used their art to reflect on the war's impact: from the horrors of the battlefield, to the ways in which the conflict rendered a familiar world unrecognisable to those left living in it.

As the centenary of the Battle of the Somme approached, *Fierce Light* brought together several leading contemporary poets to write new works that endeavoured to make sense of that deadly battle and its legacy in the 21st century. The project launched with a live event that opened the 2016 Norfolk & Norwich Festival, where the poems were read alongside new short films inspired by them and the themes they raised.

The film-maker Matt Kay created *Paid to Flight* in response to Yrsa Daley-Ward's poem 'When Your Mother Calls You, Come', and *Private Joseph Kay* in response to Jackie Kay's poem of the same name. 'Known Unto God' was the title of Bill Manhire's poem and Suzie Hanna's film response. Poet Paul Muldoon wrote 'July 1, 1916: With the Ulster Division', inspiring a short film with a matching title by George Belfield. And Tim Davies responded to Daljit Nagra's poem 'On Your "A 1940 Memory"' with a film entitled *Across Fields*.

The poems and films were then featured in an exhibition at the East Gallery, and presented on radio, at other literary festivals and online.

Also included at the live event was a reading of 'Still' by Simon Armitage (see pages 26–27).

Norwich Playhouse, 13 May 2016 / East Gallery, Norwich, 10 — 28 May 2016

CONTAGION
Shobana Jeyasingh Dance

The casualty count of the First World War was immense, but it came to be dwarfed by the deadly Spanish flu pandemic that swept through the world during the conflict's final year. The strain that emerged in 1918 infected up to 500 million people around the globe, its spread accelerated by wartime troop movements. By some estimates, as much as 5 per cent of the world's population died from the disease.

Contagion, a piece of dance from choreographer Shobana Jeyasingh that toured venues around England in late 2018, was inspired by the rapid spread of the flu virus — the unseen enemy attacking mankind indiscriminately while the business of war raged on, and women around the world risked their lives to care for the sick. The work of the Austrian painter Egon Schiele, one of many who fell victim to the disease, formed a visual footnote to the piece.

Set to an atmospheric soundscape and presented in promenade style with striking digital visuals, *Contagion* was presented in unconventional venues, many with connections to the First World War, including the Imperial War Museum North in Manchester. An innovative digital learning and engagement programme allowed the public to immerse themselves in the history of the epidemic alongside the emotion and visual drama of the performance.

Gymnasium Gallery, Berwick-upon-Tweed, 15 — 16 September 2018 / The Great Hall, Winchester, 22 — 23 September 2018 / Jerwood DanceHouse, Ipswich, 5 October 2018 / St Gabriel's Church, Sunderland, 18 — 19 October 2108 / Imperial War Museum North, Manchester, 21 October 2018 / British Library, London, 2 — 3 November 2018

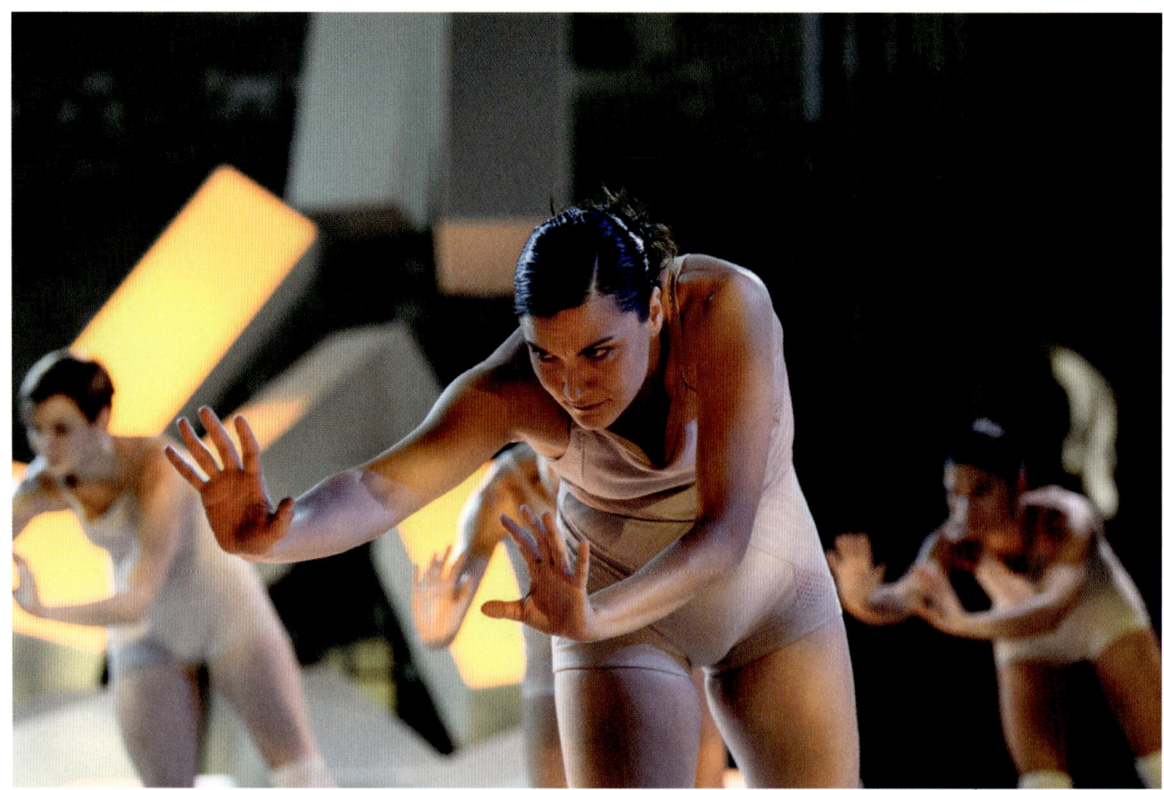

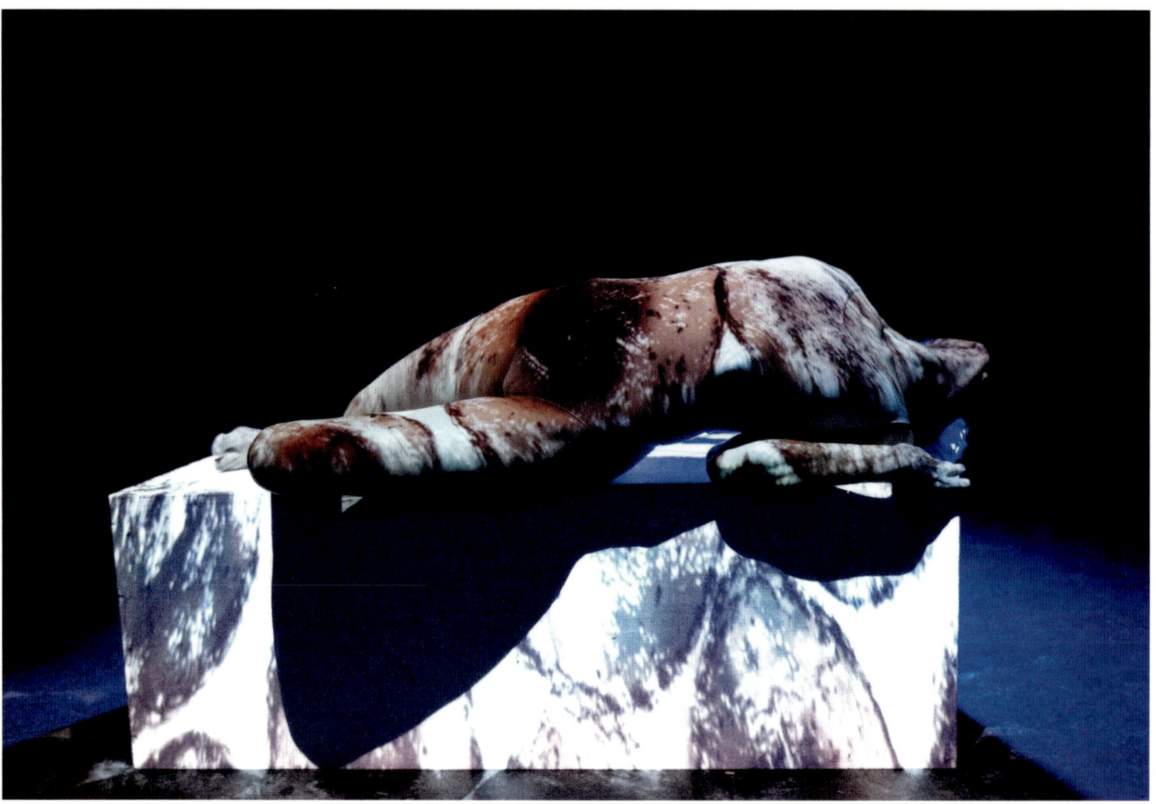

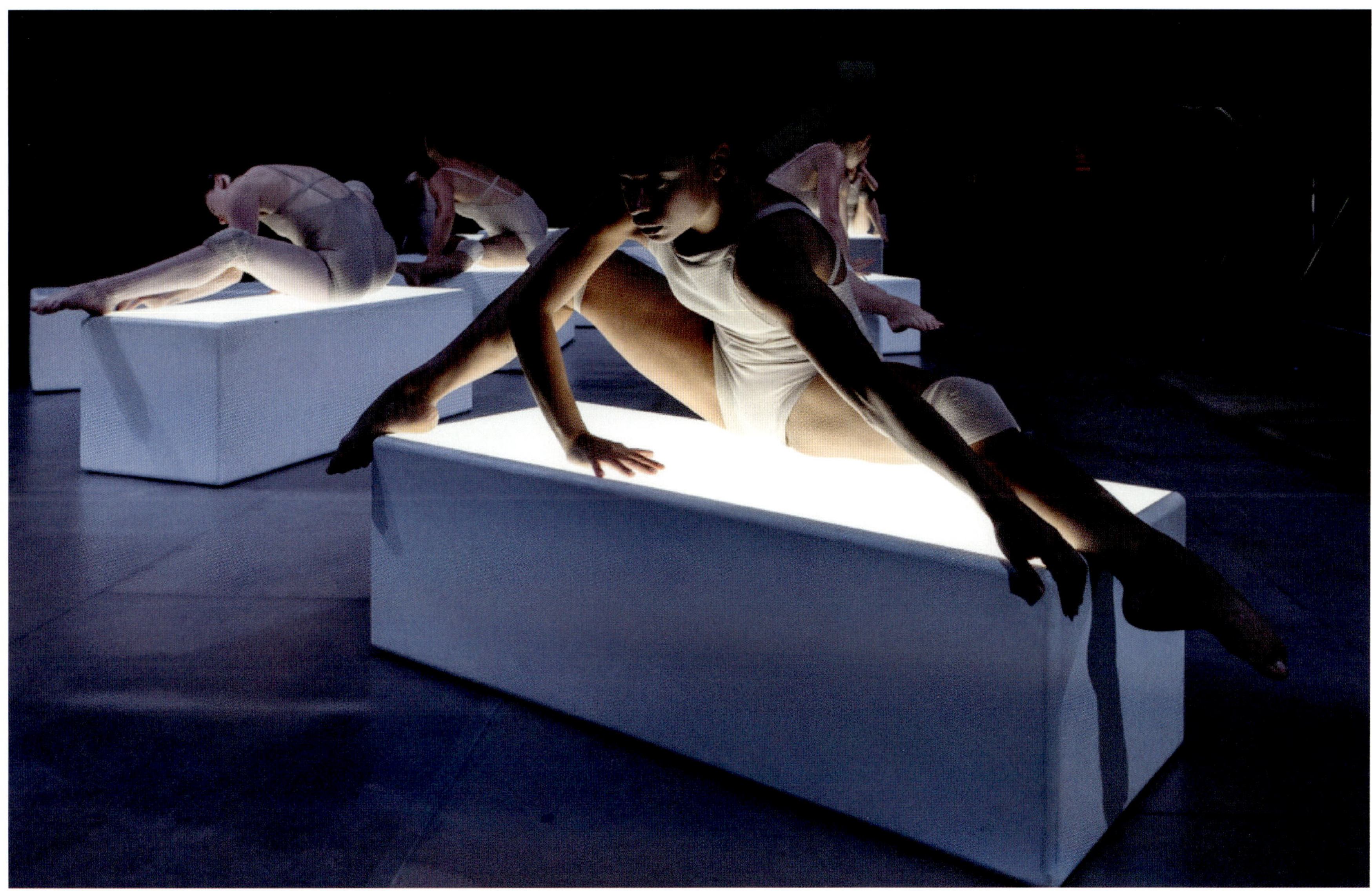

Eight female dancers explored the resilience and vulnerability of the human body in a 30-minute performance that was shown in numerous venues around the UK.

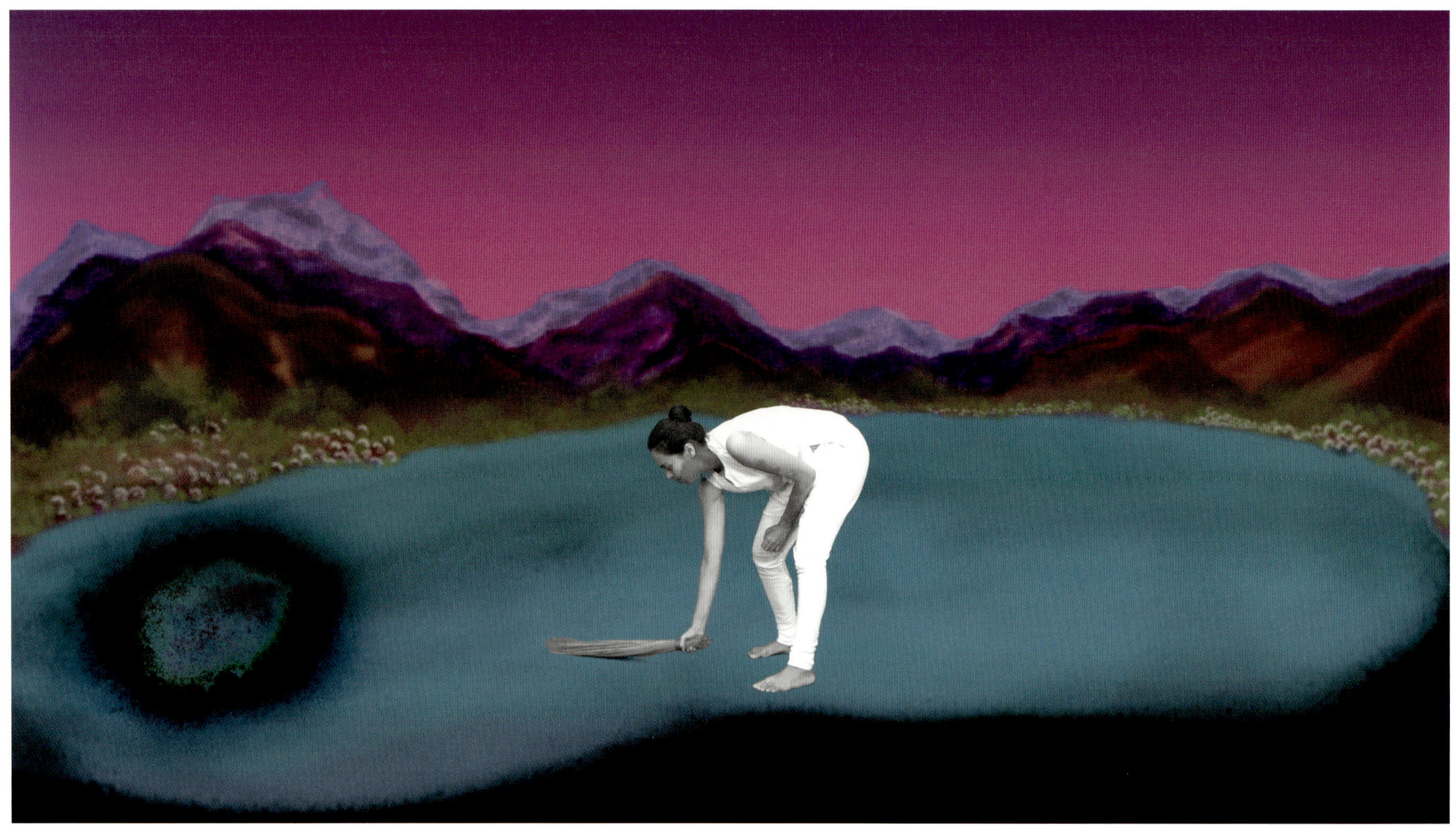

NOT YET AT EASE

Raqs Media Collective

Not Yet At Ease, by the Delhi-based artists Raqs Media Collective (Jeebesh Bagchi, Monica Narula and Shuddhabrata Sengupta), was inspired by the artists' investigations into materials and structures used in institutions that housed injured and distressed soldiers while they awaited remission, recovery and release during and immediately after the First World War.

Co-commissioned by 14-18 NOW and Firstsite, the artwork explored the history of psychological disorders resulting from conflict, and the stigmas attached to them. It was based on the understanding that symptoms of profound neural and psychic distress induced by violence during the war, now recognised as PTSD, were first observed by military censors reading the correspondence of Indian soldiers. The censors noticed what they called 'a tendency to break into poetry' — in the letters that the soldiers wrote from battlefields, barracks and hospitals — 'as an ominous sign of mental disquietude'.

Not Yet At Ease featured transcripts of letters and diaries, readings of medical records and official dispatches, extracts from novels and poetry, and accounts of dreams and nightmares — all interspersed with fragments of archival film and photography, reworked and animated, and spectral snatches of voices that were 100 years old, installed within a labyrinth-like construction in the gallery. Viewers approached via a giant mural featuring drawings depicting archival medical sketches of nerves used by doctors of the period, and phrases such as 'a bag of nerves', but with the word 'nerves' removed, creating a moving metaphor for what a person might have lost through conflict. An extensive accompanying events programme completed this study of the relationship between conflict and mental health, then and now.

Firstsite, Colchester, 28 September 2018 — 20 January 2019

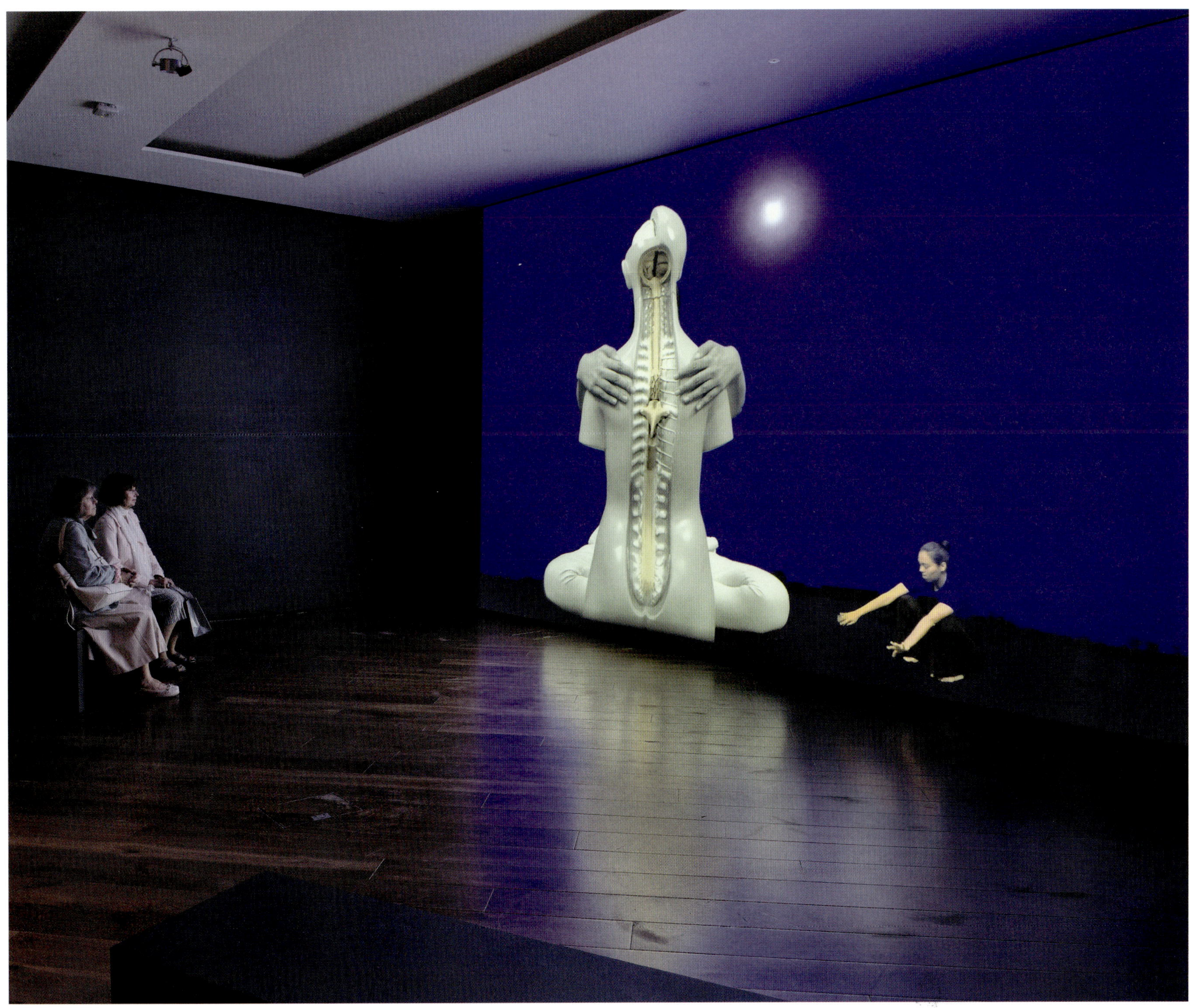

A series of video
projections combining
sound and animation
were shown throughout
the gallery.

Stepping through the looking glass, we find ourselves right there in the trenches, surrounded by young men whose faces are as close and clear as those of people we would pass in the street. I've often argued that cinema is a time machine, but rarely has that maxim seemed so true.

THROUGH THE LOOKING GLASS

Mark Kermode

When I asked Peter Jackson what drove him to make *They Shall Not Grow Old* — a remarkable revivification of the Imperial War Museum's archive of First World War footage — his answer was clear and simple. 'We set about trying to bring these guys to life,' he told me. 'The one thing that the film restoration does is to put the humanity back into the footage. And it really affected me when I saw it.'

It's ironic that computer technology has often been accused of taking the humanity out of cinema. In an age when it's possible to conjure spectacular action from digital effects, many modern movies have developed a sense of weightlessness — the inconsequentiality of artifice. Along with *Avatar* director James Cameron, Jackson has long been at the forefront of this digital revolution, with his twin Tolkien trilogies (*The Lord of the Rings* and *The Hobbit*) pushing the boundaries of computer-generated entertainment. Yet with *They Shall Not Grow Old* he has used that same technology to bring us face to face with the young men who fought in the Great War, bridging the vast divide of history through the miracle of digital film restoration.

The results are astonishing. As we watch a line of soldiers marching through mud towards the front, the film seems almost miraculously to change from silent black-and-white footage to colour film with sound, as though 100 years of film history had been suddenly telescoped into a single moment. Stepping through the looking glass, we find ourselves right there in the trenches, surrounded by young men whose faces are as close and clear as those of people we would pass in the street. I've often argued that cinema is a time machine, but rarely has that maxim seemed so true.

'I thought the best thing was to make this their story,' Jackson told me, remembering his profound reaction to seeing the results of some early test footage. 'Not a story about the First World War, but about what it was like to be a soldier.' Fittingly, his film uses no historians, narrators or political commentators. The voices we hear are those of veterans, many gathered by the BBC during the making of its 1964 documentary series *The Great War*.

The challenges involved in Jackson's restoration were extensive, not least correcting the pace of the original film, which was shot at anything from 10 to 18 frames per second. Computers were used to build interstitial frames that helped recapture the rhythms of real life, tuning in to the music of the soldiers' movements, breathing intimate life into their smallest gestures. A rich tapestry of background sound-effects also transports the viewer to training camps and battlefields, with actors providing regionally authentic dialogue based on forensic lip-reading of the silent footage. 'Hello mum!' chirrups one Private as he marches past the camera. Later, we see and hear an officer issuing instructions for the forthcoming attack.

Amid such artifice, the authentic archived voices of soldiers who were 'scared that the war would be over before we got out to it' strike a vibrant chord. While the unspeakable horrors of conflict are everywhere in evidence, Jackson's film still finds unexpected life and laughter in the company of those who walked in the shadow of death. 'I sort of understand these soldiers more than I ever did before,' Jackson reflected on the eve of the film's premiere in London. 'We always look at them as victims of the machine — which they were

— but they didn't see themselves as victims. They didn't see it in the negative way that we see it because they were proud of what they did. And the thing about it, too, that really touched me was that some of them came from quite hard lives, and went back to hard lives. The quote that almost made me cry was when someone says "There was a terrific lot of kindness". They may not have had it at home, but in the trenches people were kind to each other. Their lives depended on each other. If someone got a parcel from home, a cake from their mother, it would all be chopped up and given to their friends. People were kind to each other in a way that many hadn't experienced before, and probably didn't experience again. Complete strangers had to help each other survive, and I think they were all very affected by that.'

Jackson's words chime with the human thread that runs throughout *They Shall Not Grow Old*. For all its evocations of the grim realities of war, it is that tangible sense of empathy that lends the film such force. As the titular (mis)quotation from Laurence Binyon's poem 'For the Fallen' suggests, Jackson has attempted to take ageing footage and make it young again — to bring history, and those who lived it, into the present. It is an endeavour in which he has succeeded superbly.

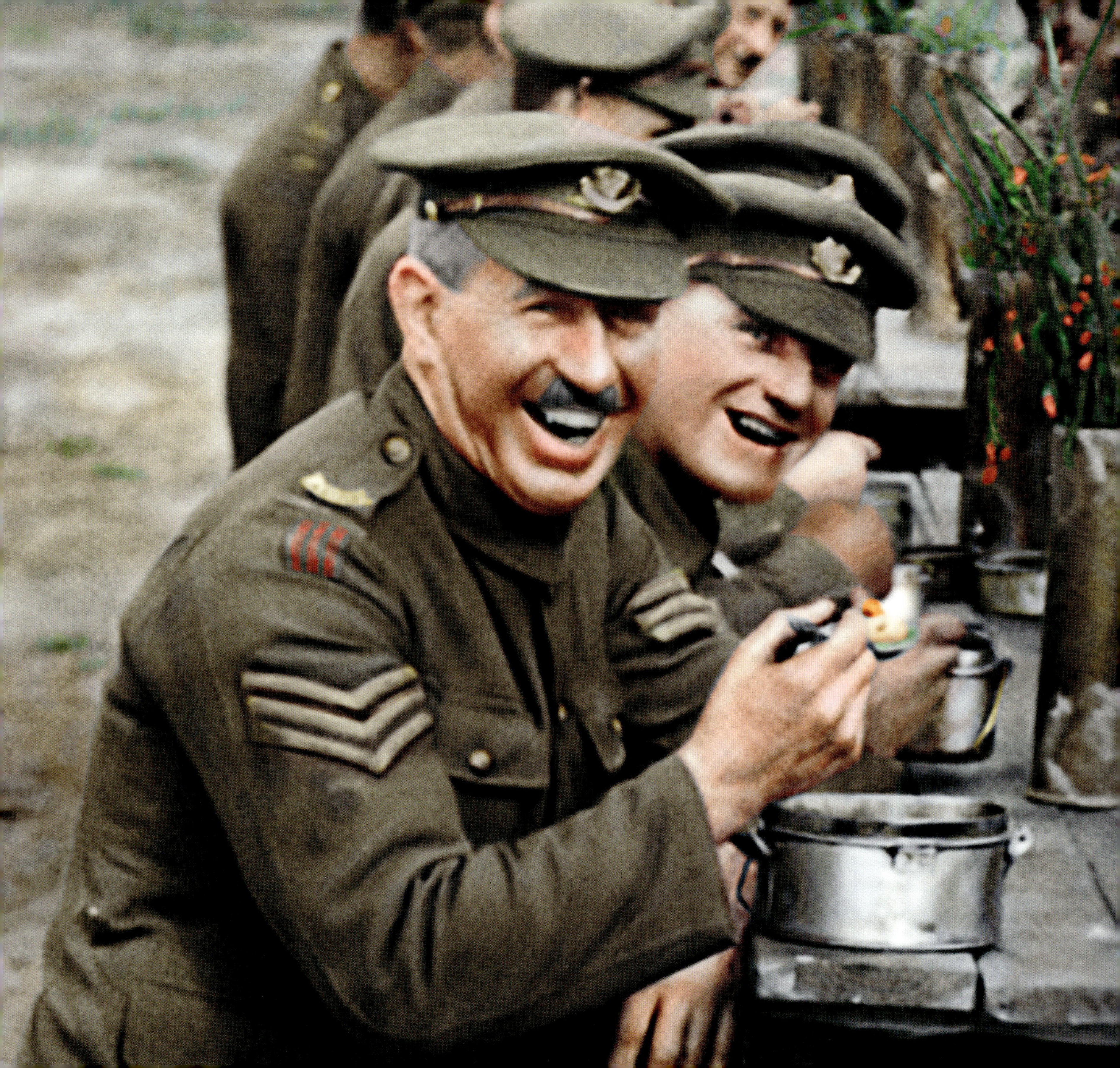

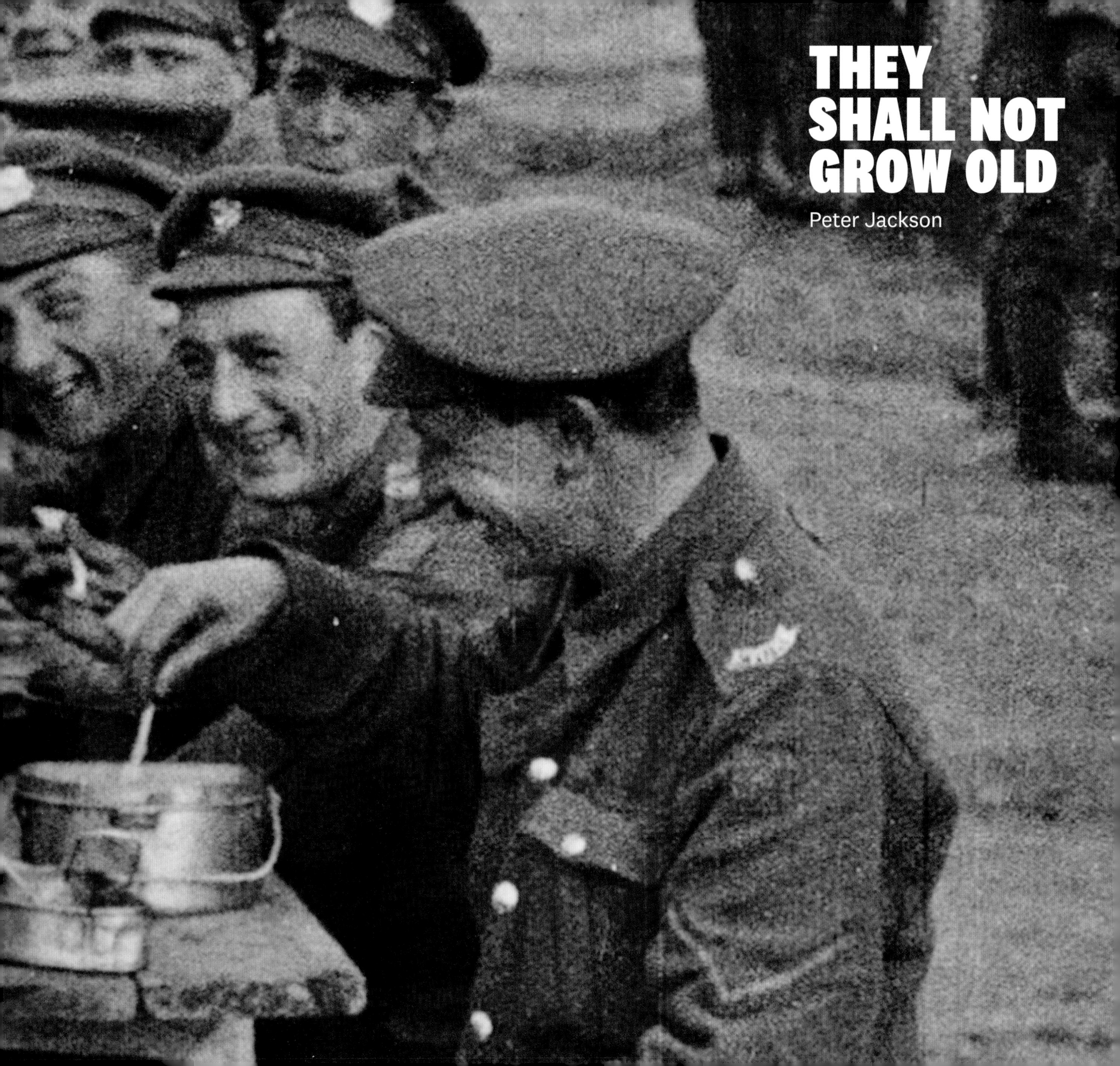

THEY
SHALL NOT
GROW OLD
Peter Jackson

Original footage from
Imperial War Museums'
archive was used to create
the film, much of it previously
unseen. The footage was
silent, so this was combined
with a modern soundscape
to recall the sounds of the
time, and overlaid with
recorded interviews of
servicemen who returned
home from the front.

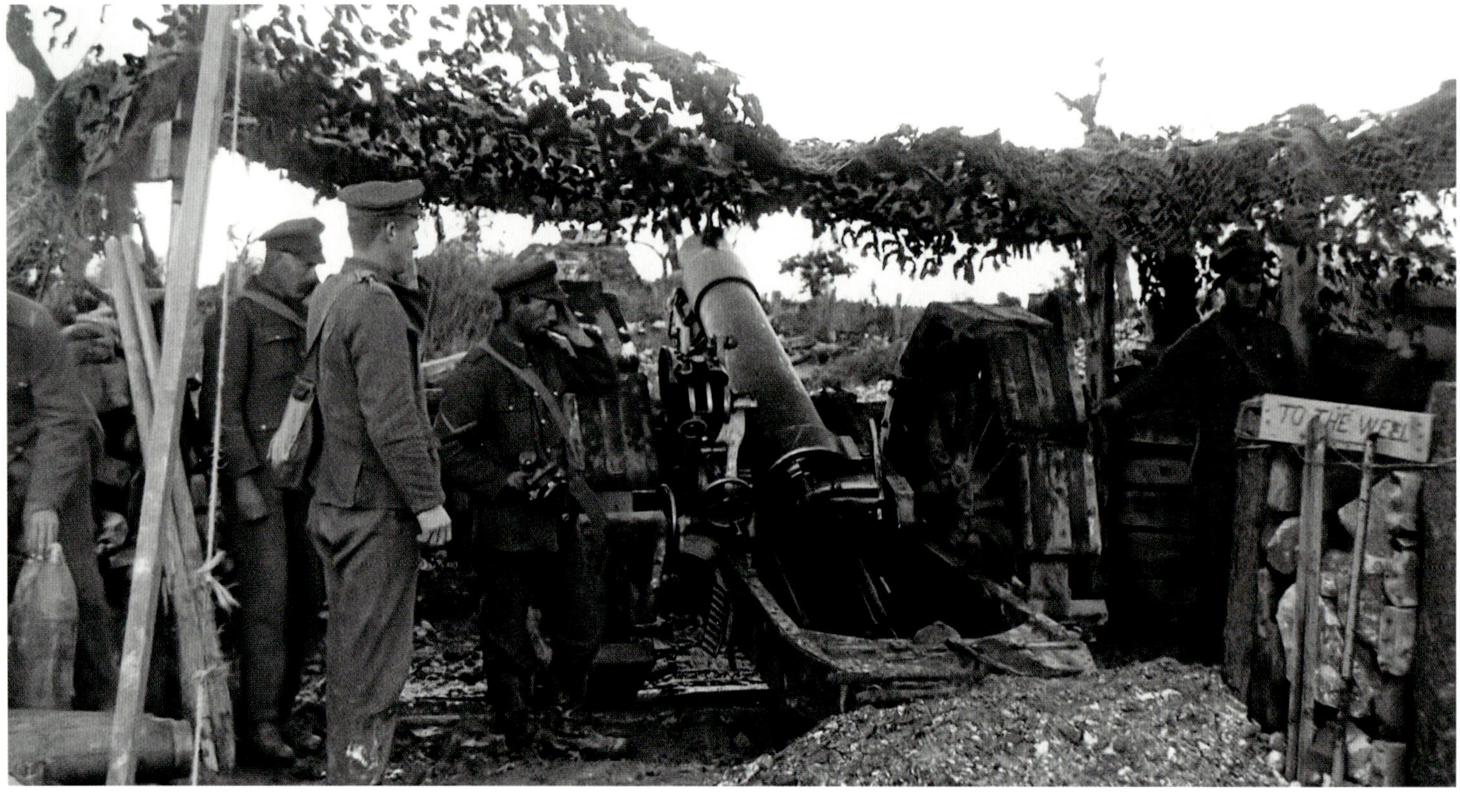
TO THE WELL

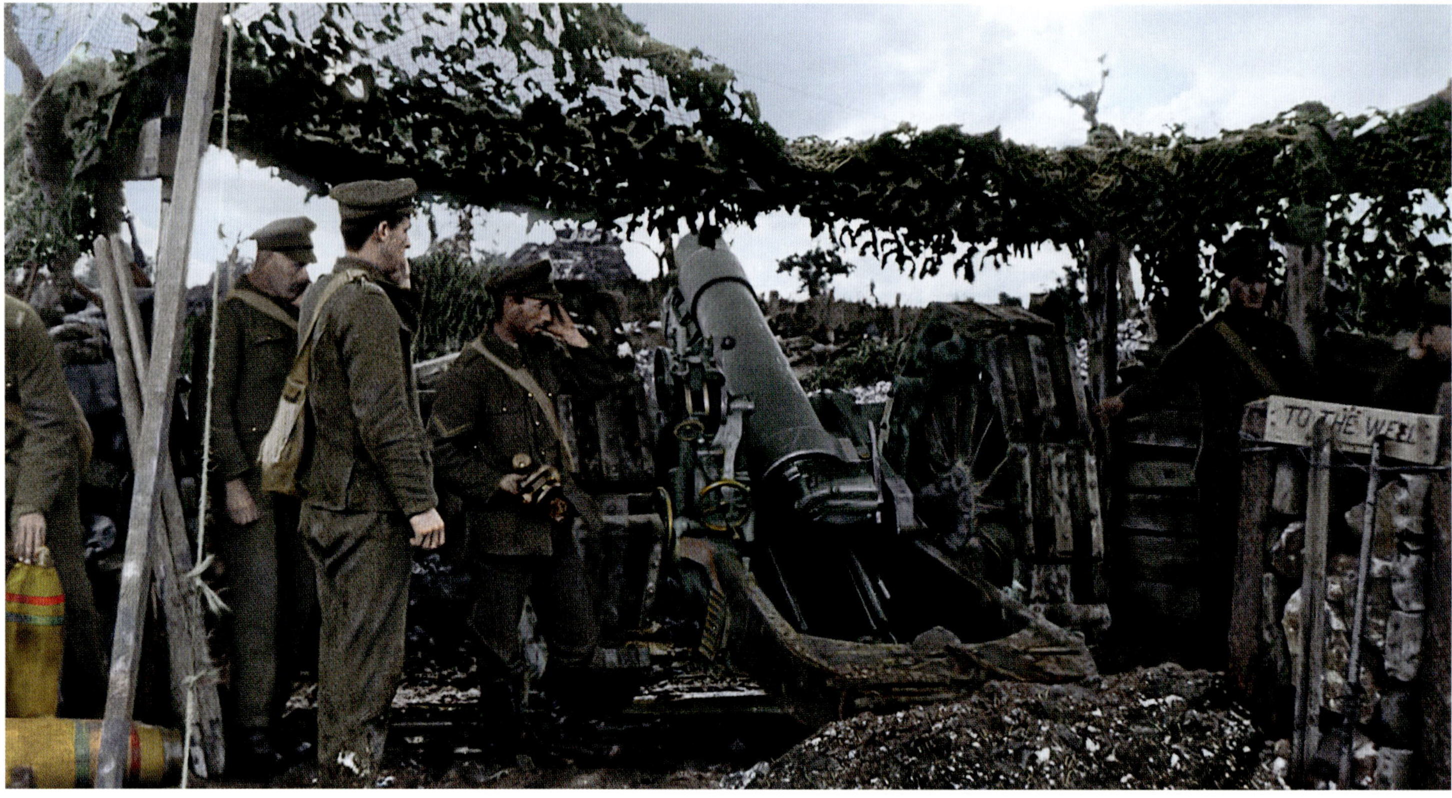
TO THE WELL

A hundred years after the end of the First World War, director Peter Jackson premiered his First World War documentary, *They Shall Not Grow Old*, at the London Film Festival.

The First World War was a landmark in cinematic history with warfare being caught on film for the first time. Cameramen captured the conflict in remarkable detail, from the recruitment halls in Britain to the front line trenches, and provided the public at home with an unprecedented view of war. With hundreds of hours of this film in its archive, 14-18 NOW and the Imperial War Museum approached Peter Jackson to make a unique documentary as part of the First World War Centenary commemorations.

For *They Shall Not Grow Old*, Jackson set out to bring to life the day-to-day experience of soldiers on the Western Front. Jackson and his team used cutting-edge techniques to make century-old images look as if they were shot yesterday. Black-and-white footage was transformed into colour and converted to 3D, to show the war as the soldiers themselves saw it.

Jackson also drew upon the Imperial War Museum's and the BBC's extensive collection of audio interviews. Using only the voices of the men involved, the film explores the realities of their lives as front line soldiers — from training, to the trenches, and then their return to civilian life.

By painstakingly selecting from over one 100 hours of footage and 600 hours of audio, Jackson reaches into the mists of time to reveal the hopes and fears of these veterans, the humility and humanity that represented a generation changed forever by a global war.

BFI London Film Festival, 16 October 2018 / UK-wide and global screenings from 16 October 2018 / BBC Two, 11 November 2018 and 2 February 2019 / DVD release, 10 December 2018

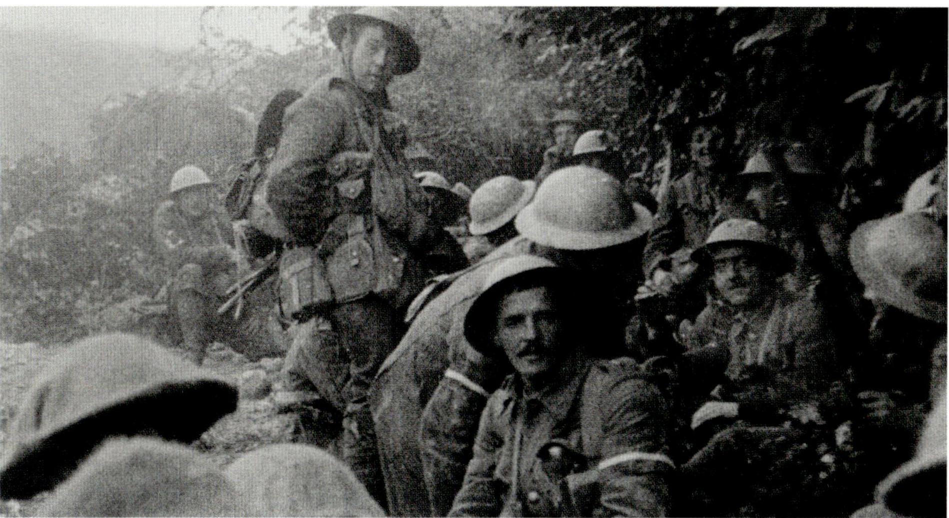

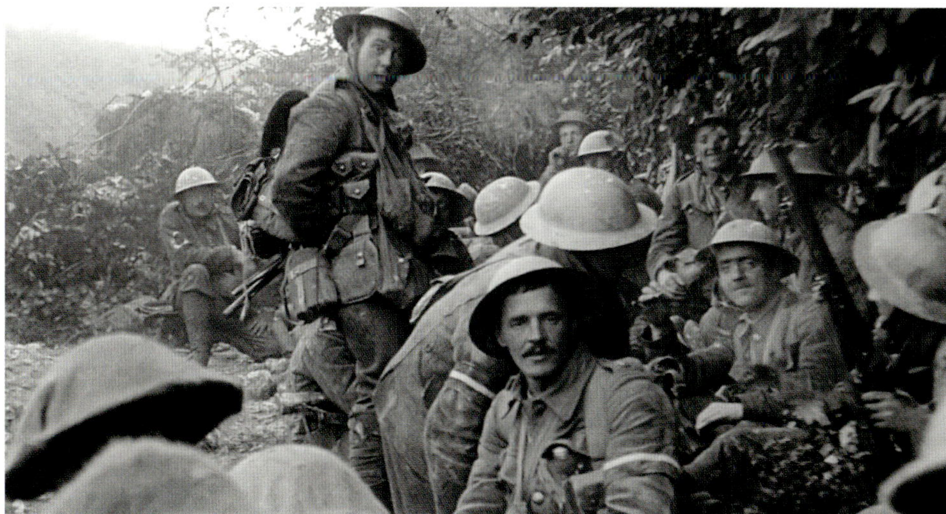

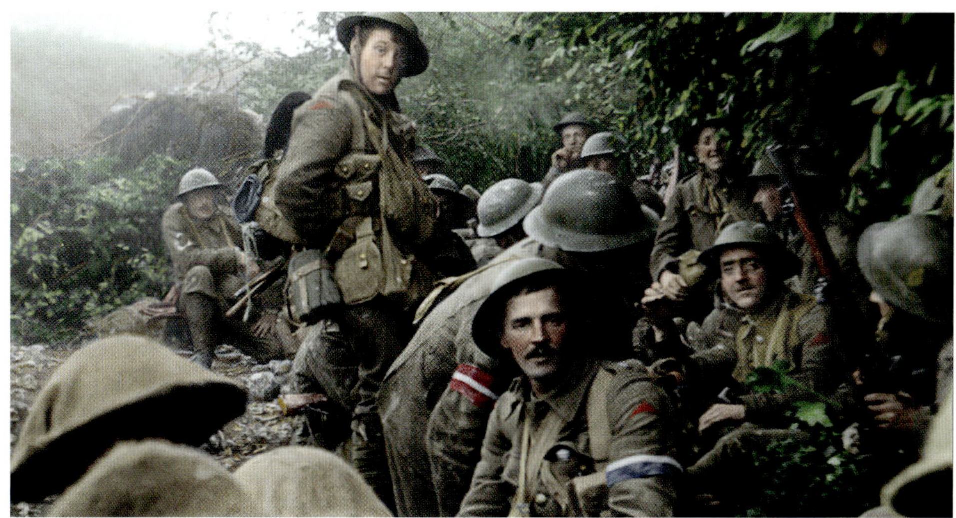

The 100-year-old footage was painstakingly colourised, slowed down and converted to 3D, bringing viewers closer to the reality of the First World War than ever before.

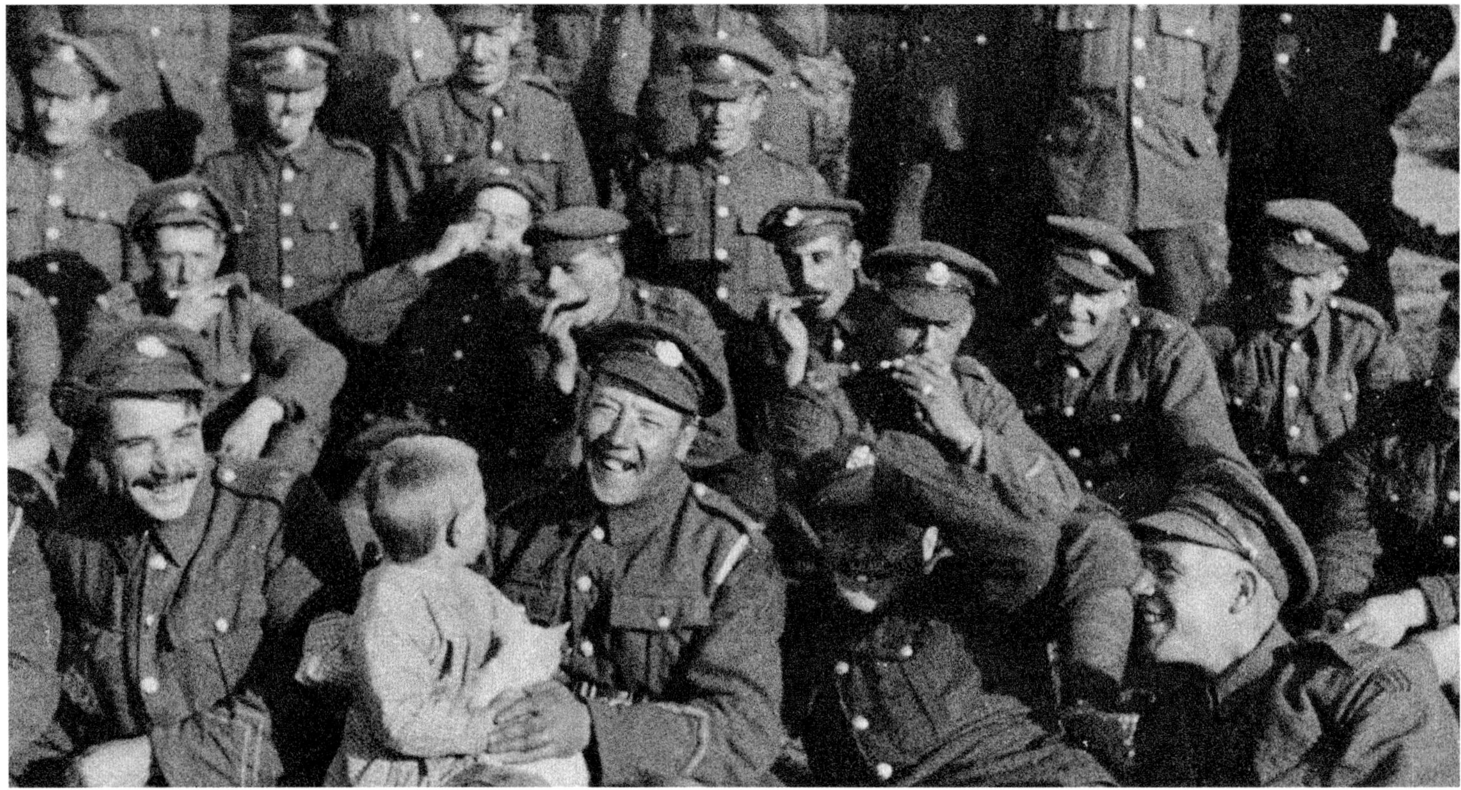

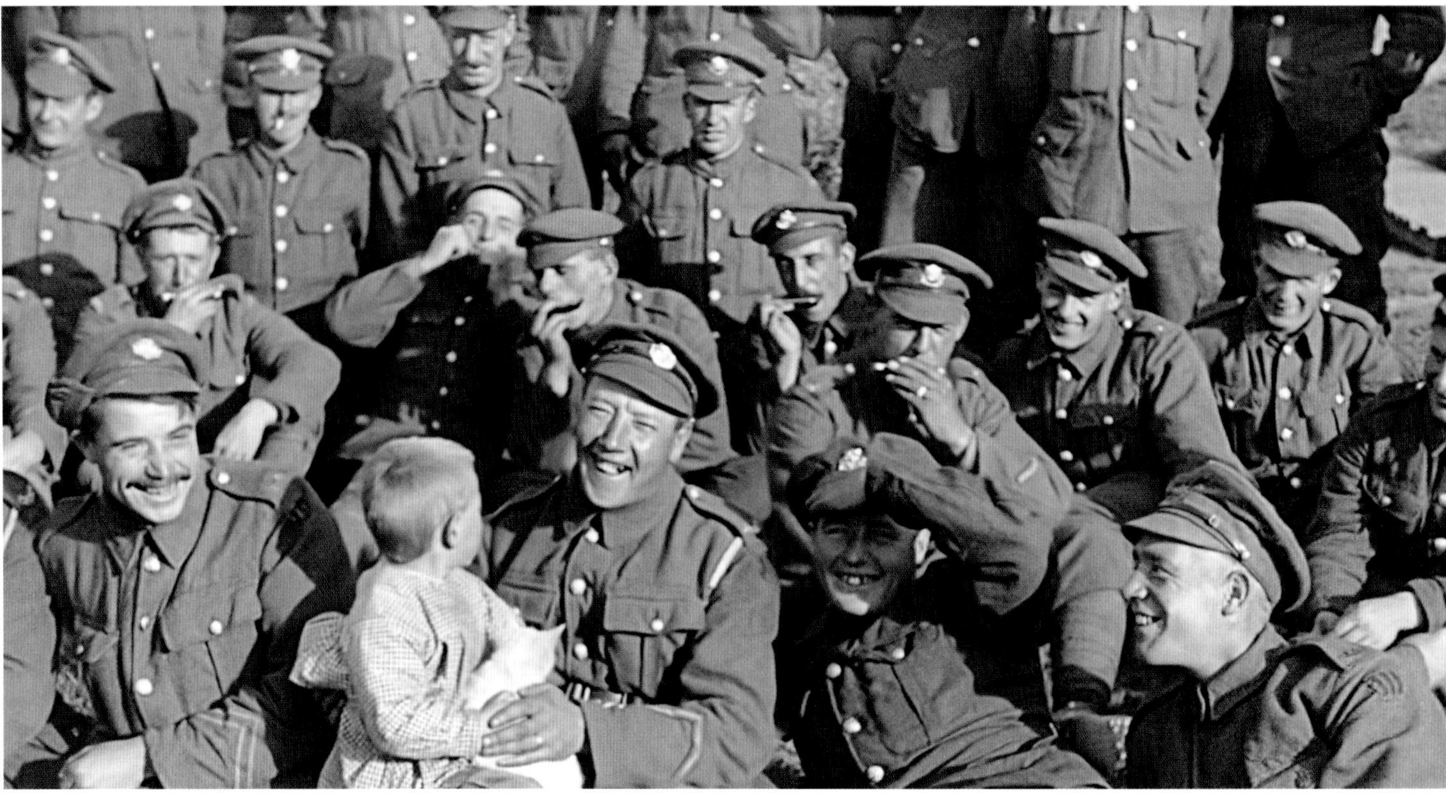

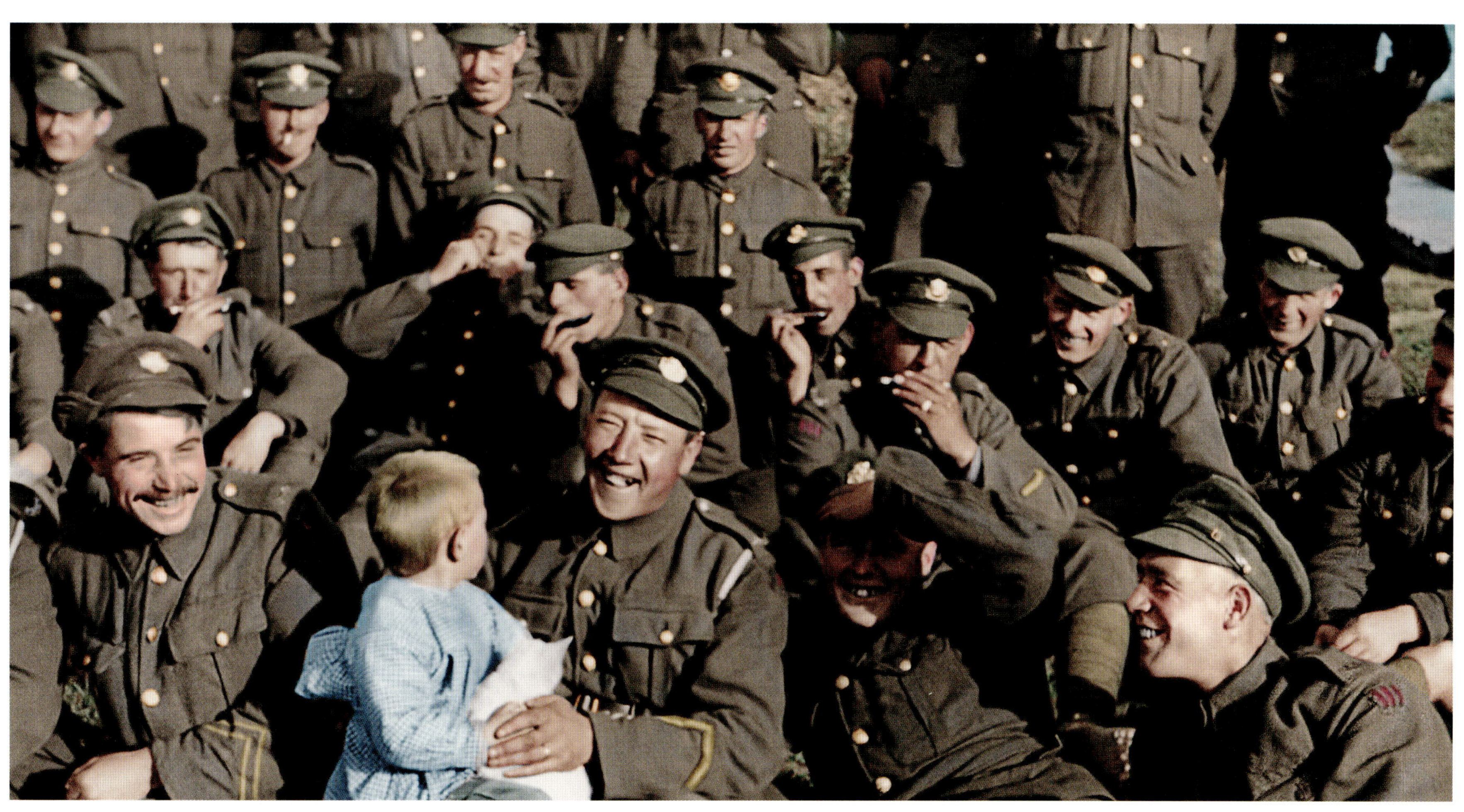

SYLVIA

ZooNation: The Kate
  Prince Company
The Old Vic
Sadler's Wells

SYLVIA was a hip-hop musical based on the life of suffragette Sylvia Pankhurst. This brand new musical had its first lease of life in 2018 at The Old Vic, and took place 100 years after the passing of the Representation of the People Act (1918), which granted the first British women the right to vote, although it would be a further ten years before women's suffrage was finally extended to be on the same terms as men's.

The middle daughter of Emmeline Pankhurst, Sylvia was a campaigner, independent thinker and a significant historical figure in her own right. Unlike her mother and sisters, Sylvia remained a lifelong socialist, and the political and personal rifts this created within her increasingly conservative family provided the subject matter for this show's text and lyrics, which director and choreographer Kate Prince co-wrote with author Priya Parmar and the musical team of Josh Cohen and DJ Walde. Cohen and Walde also provided the score, which fused dance music, hip-hop, soul and funk: a dynamic historical juxtaposition that underscored *SYLVIA*'s contemporary relevance, casting new light on a remarkable figure at the heart of one of the 20th century's defining political movements.

While still overshadowed in the history books by her mother, Sylvia Pankhurst was a progressive whose views on race, religion, class and gender would make her very much at home among liberal campaigners today. The radical stands she took against injustice in its many forms more than 100 years ago placed her in an elite vanguard, and her legacy was aptly celebrated in this provocative show.

The Old Vic, London, 3 — 22 September 2018

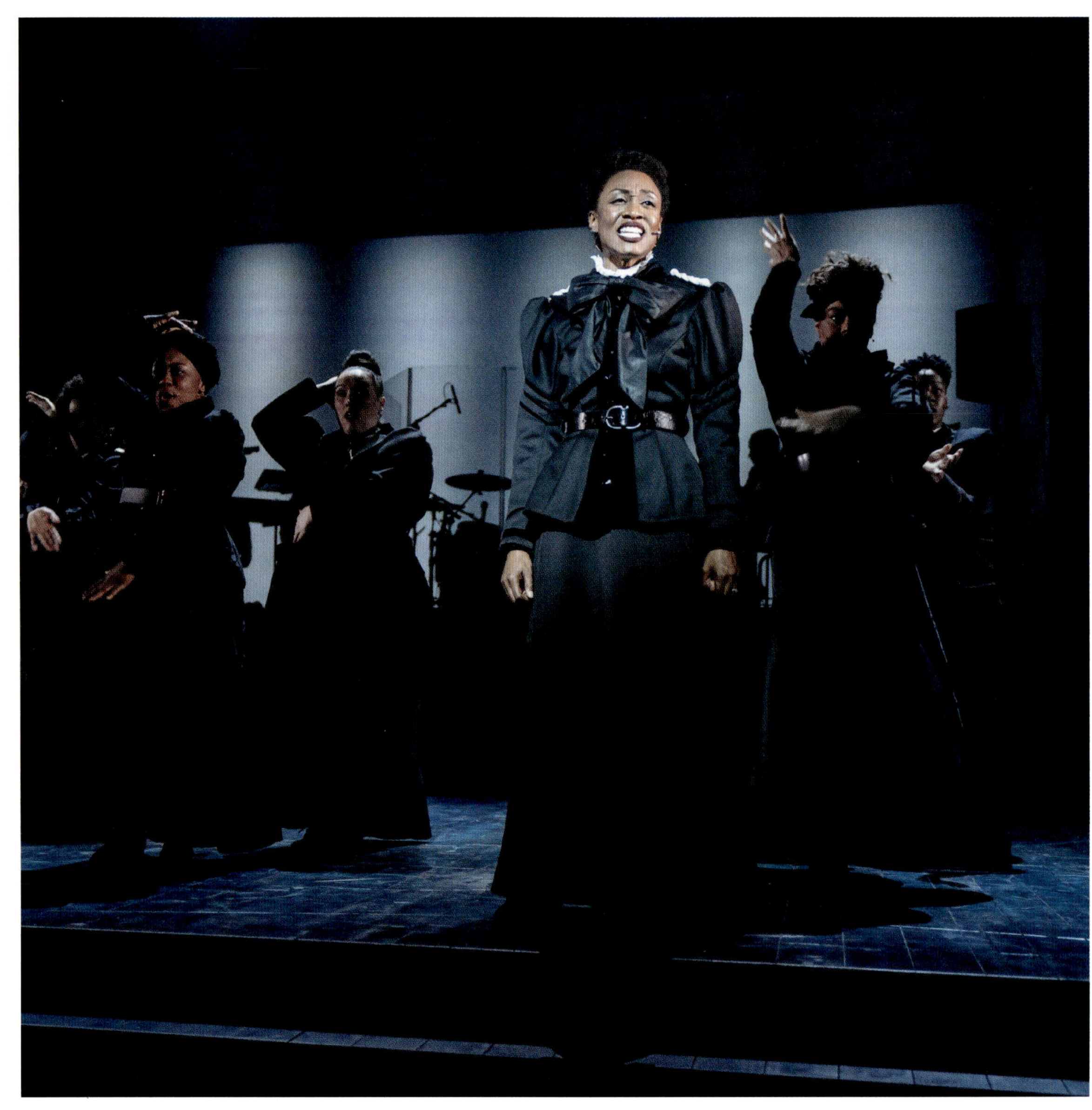

The cast of the funk, soul and hip-hop musical included Beverley Knight as Emmeline Pankhurst and Witney White as Christabel Pankhurst, both pictured.

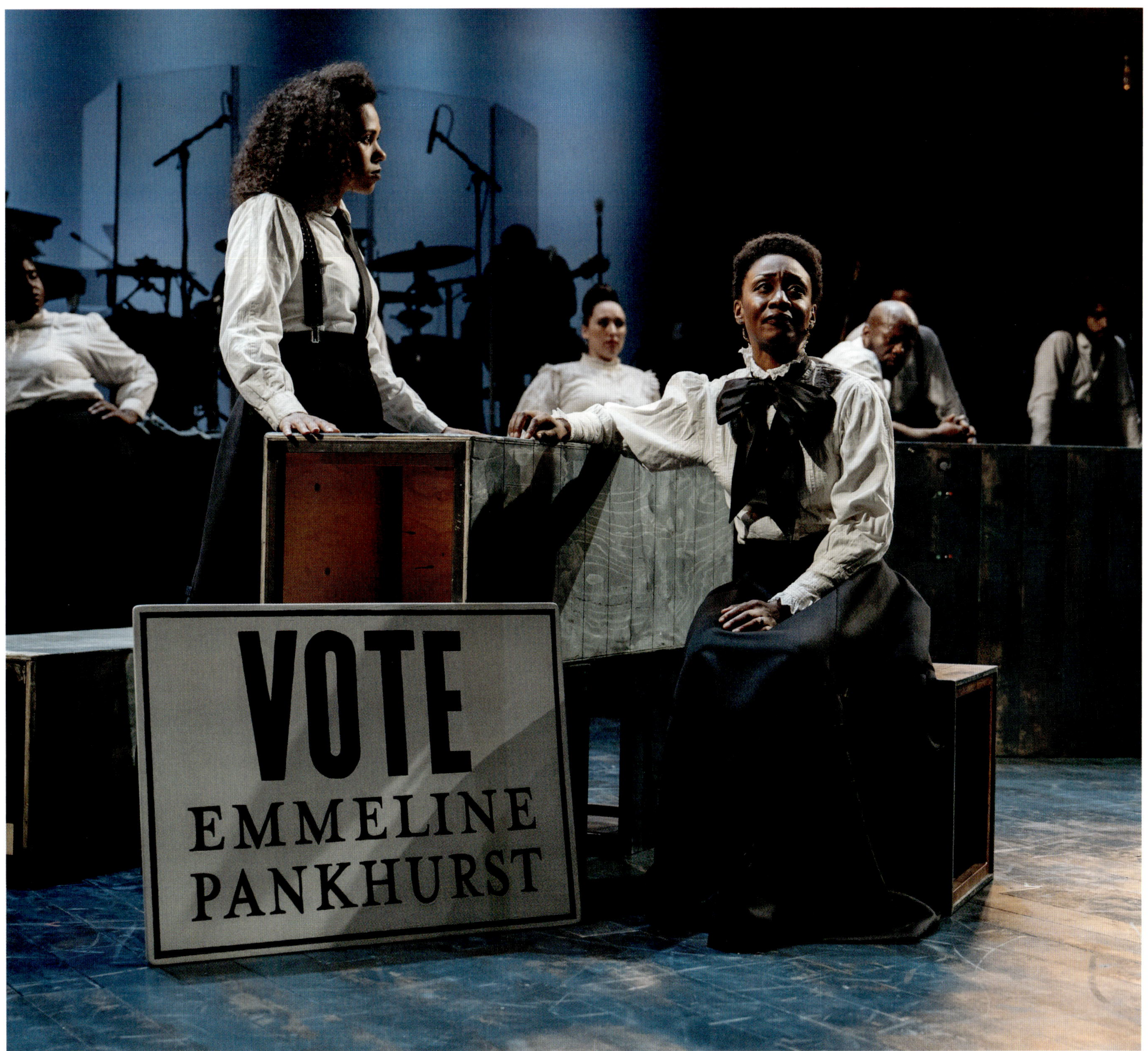
VOTE
EMMELINE
PANKHURST

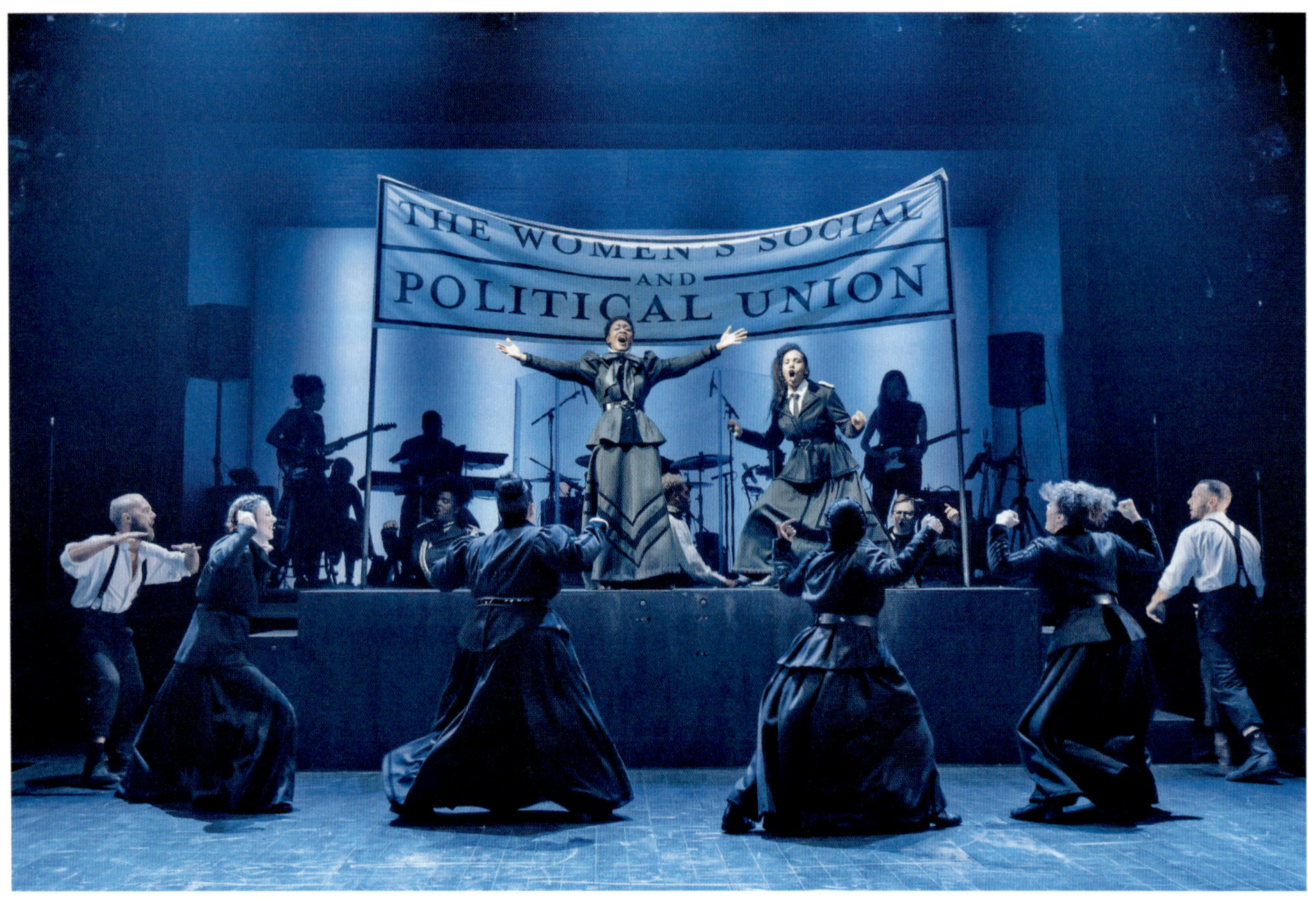

SYLIVIA explored the colourful, unconventional and often turbulent life of Sylvia Pankhurst.

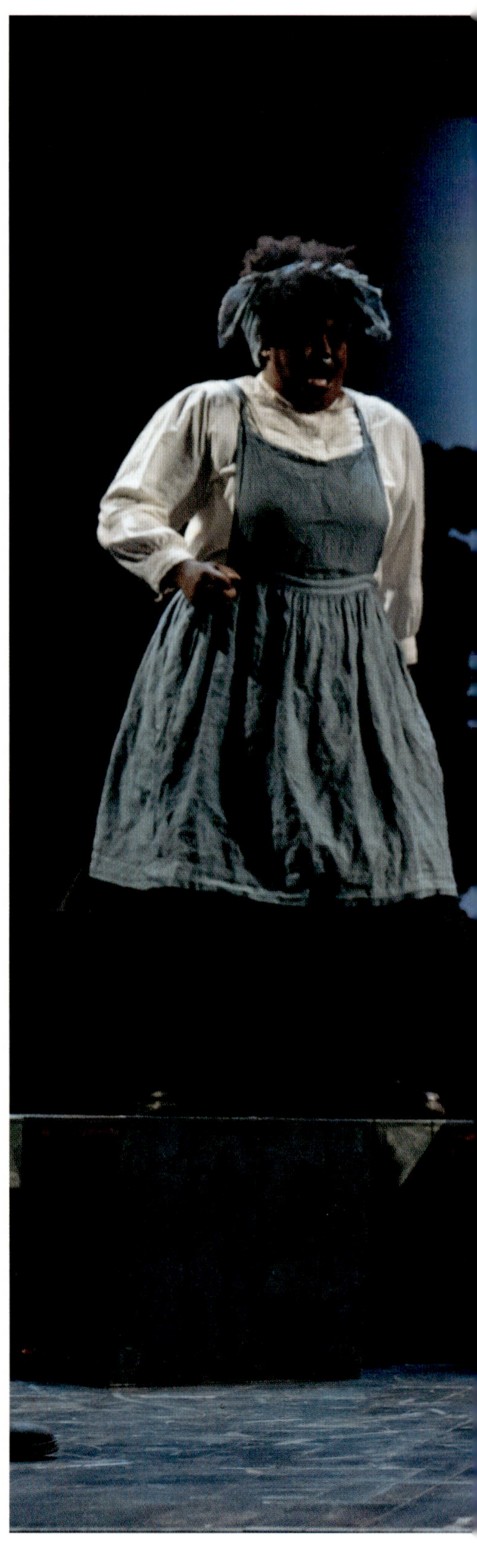

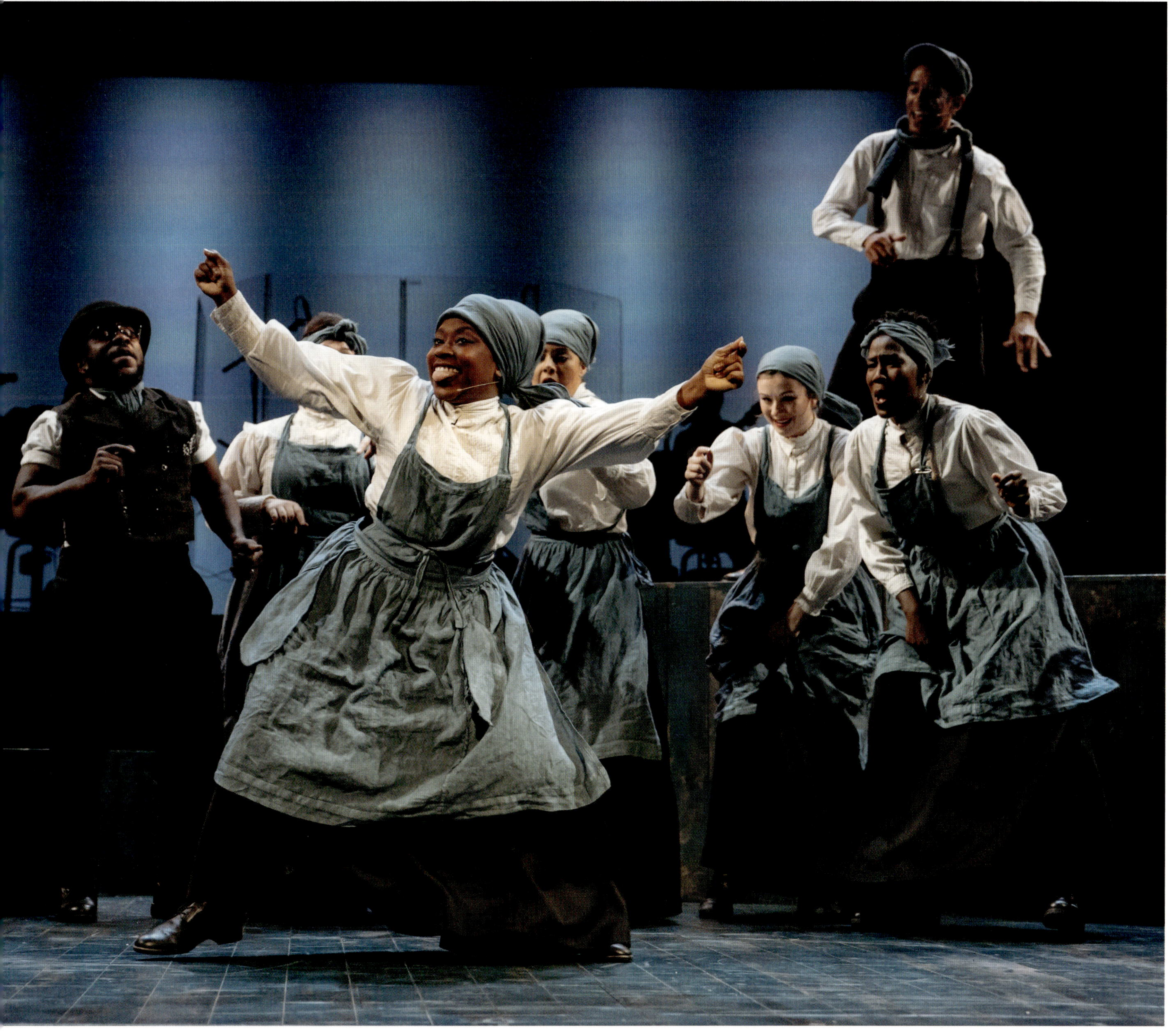

Waters darker

than my own skin

deep enough

UNWRITTEN
POEMS

Jay Bernard
Malika Booker
Kat Francois
Ishion Hutchinson
Jay T. John
Antony Joseph
Charnell Lucien
Vladimir Lucien
Rachel Manley
Karen McCarthy Woolf
Tanya Shirley

hallow enough

Charnell Lucien

Unwritten Poems invited ten contemporary poets from the Caribbean and the international Caribbean diaspora to respond to the history of the Caribbean men who fought alongside the British Army in the First World War.

Although 15,600 men joined the British West Indian Regiment's 11 battalions during the war, these soldiers' stories remain largely unheard, and while the wealth of First World War poetry has had a profound impact on our perceptions of the conflict, very little of it addresses or is drawn from the war's impact on the Caribbean men who served, their families and communities, and the relationship between the Caribbean and the UK in the decades that followed. The poets considered what it meant to be cast into and then omitted from a story or events, left voiceless in a cultural landscape that treasures self-expression.

As part of the BBC's Contains Strong Language festival, the *Unwritten Poems* performances were recorded for a special edition of *The Verb*, presented by Ian McMillan on BBC Radio 3. The poems were also performed on National Poetry Day at the Birmingham Literature Festival, and published in an anthology by Nine Arches Press (*Unwritten: Caribbean Poems After the First World War*) in October 2018.

Hull, 28 — 30 September 2018 / BBC Radio 3 / Royal Birmingham Conservatoire, 4 October 2018

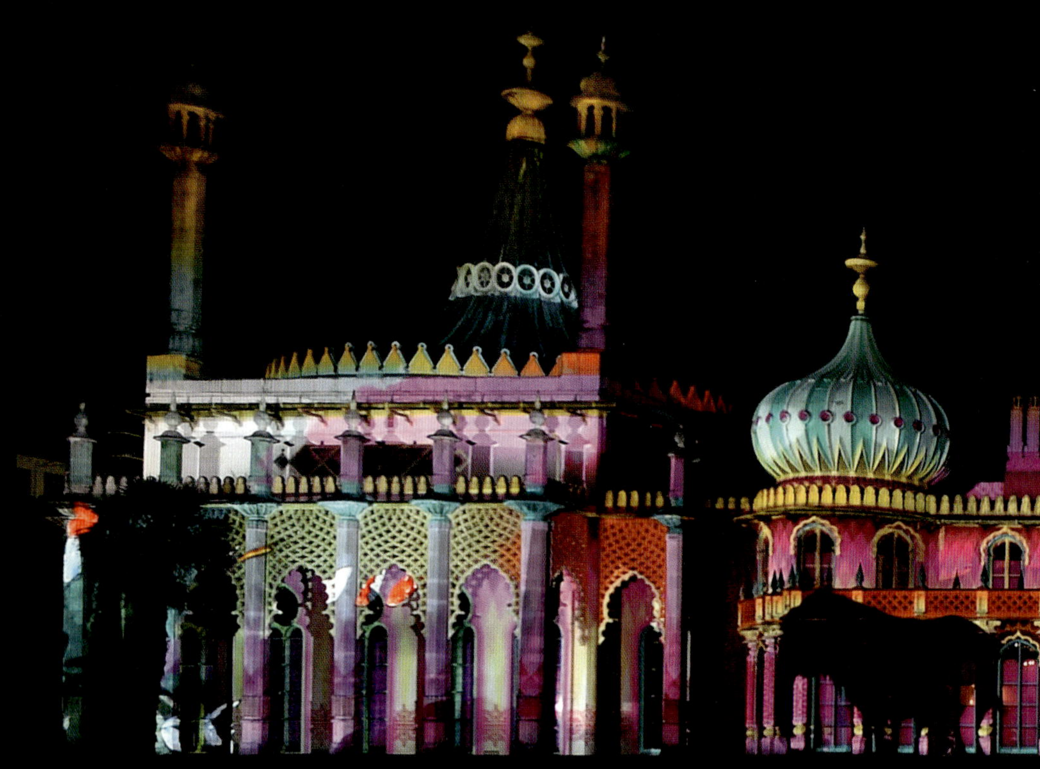

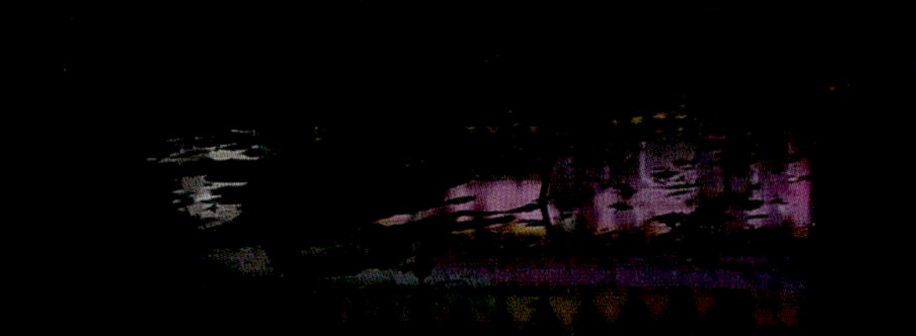

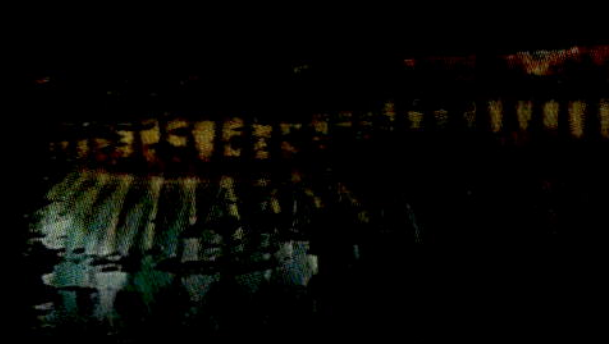

DR BLIGHTY

Nutkhut

More than a million men travelled from India to
fight for the Allies during the First World War, and the
experiences of these volunteer forces constitute one
of the great untold stories in military history. *Dr Blighty*
was a project staged by Nutkhut during the 50th
Brighton Festival to commemorate different aspects
of this history. Between 1914 and 1916, Brighton's Royal
Pavilion was used as a hospital for over 2,300 Indian
servicemen who had been wounded on the Western
Front. The event brought to life the experiences of
these soldiers, and the locals who came to know and
care for them.

   Dr Blighty consisted of a week of activities at the
pavilion. A set of 2,300 traditional clay *diya* lamps were
made — one to represent each soldier — and lamp-
making workshops were held. A spectacular after-dark
video projection created by QED Productions and
NOVAK transformed the pavilion building itself, drawing
huge crowds and telling the story of the Hindu, Sikh
and Muslim soldiers who travelled to Europe to fight
in the war.

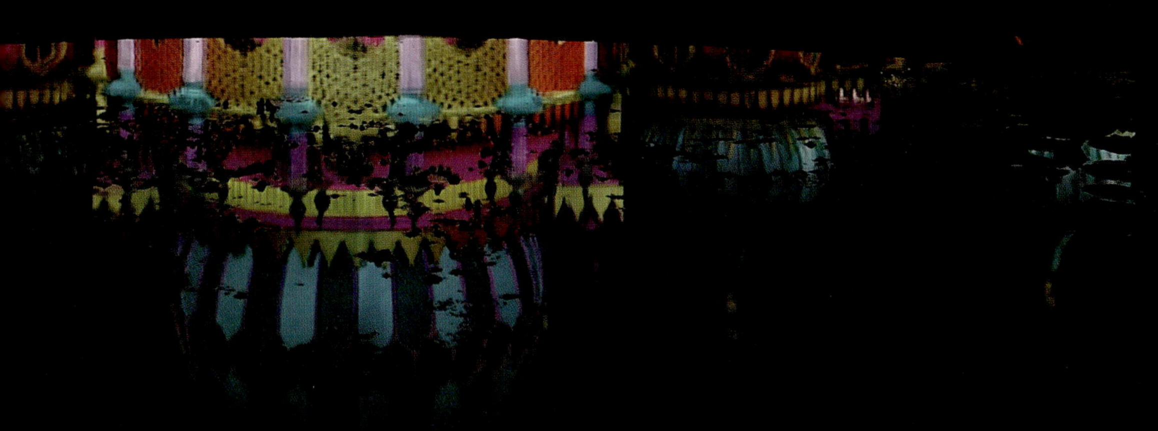

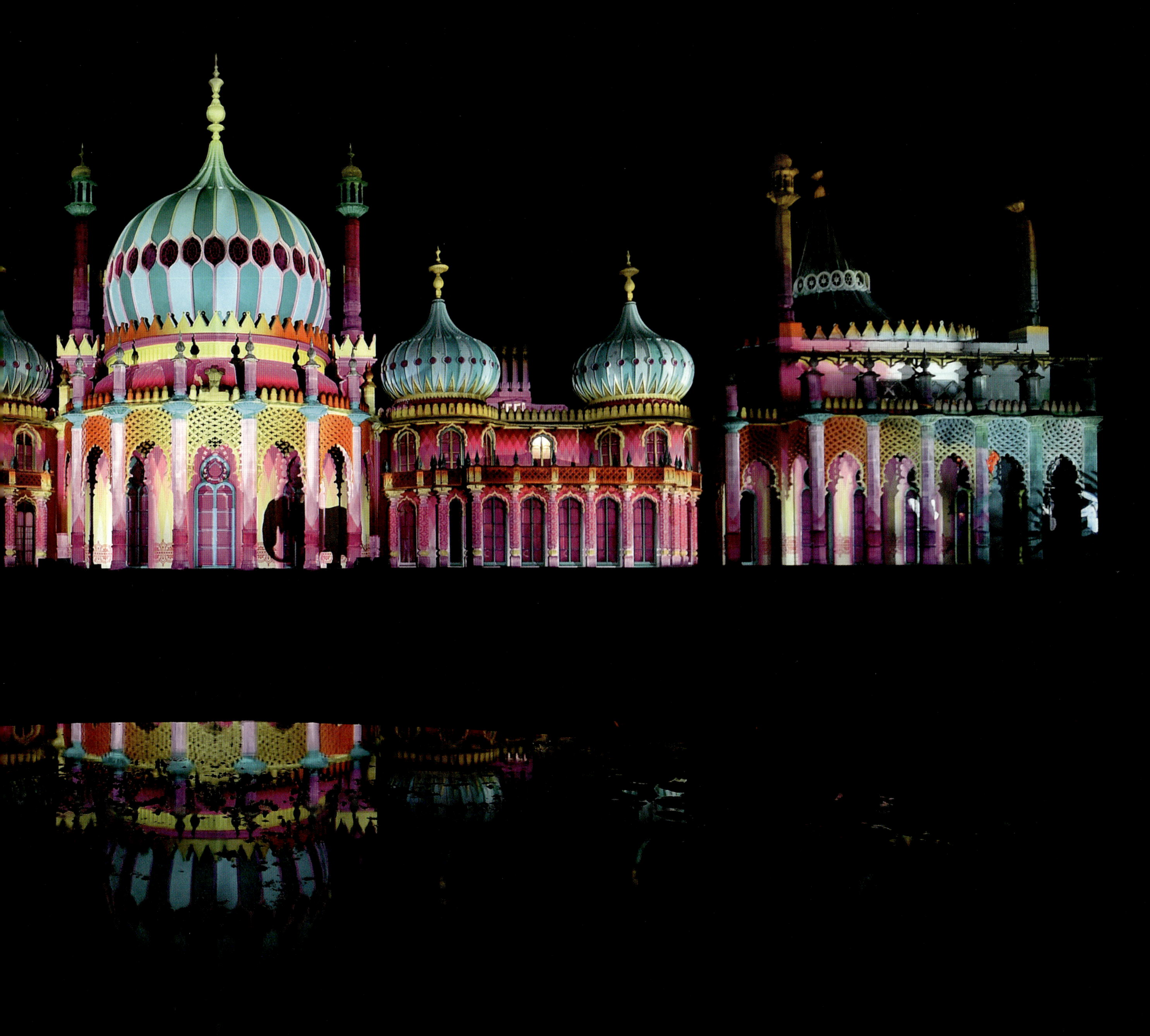

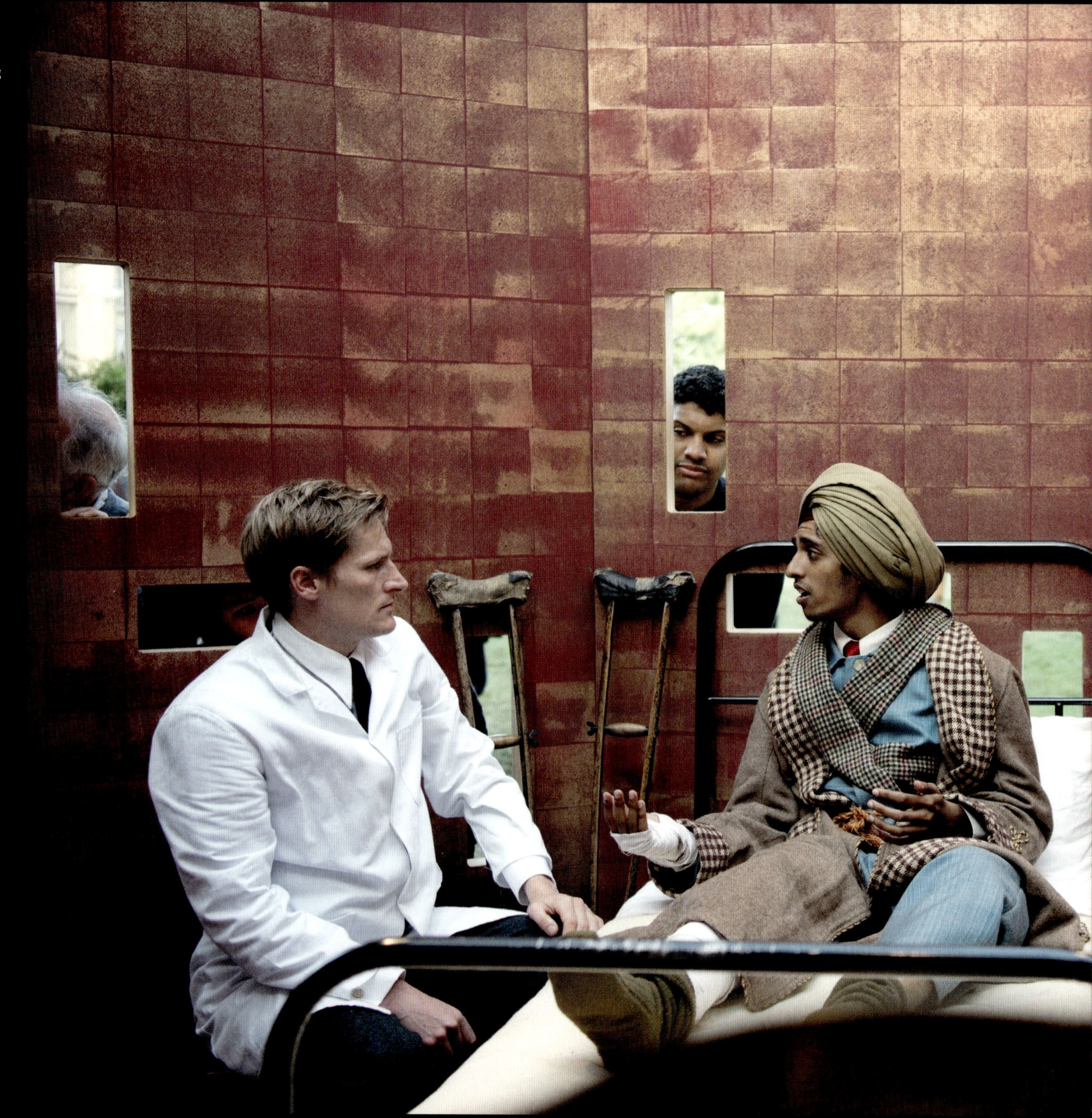

Right. Actors recreated scenes of the pavilion during wartime, when thousands of Indian servicemen woke to find themselves recuperating in a Regency palace.

Opposite. The public were able to engage and reflect on the work by writing their own imaginary letters to those who had stayed in the hospital.

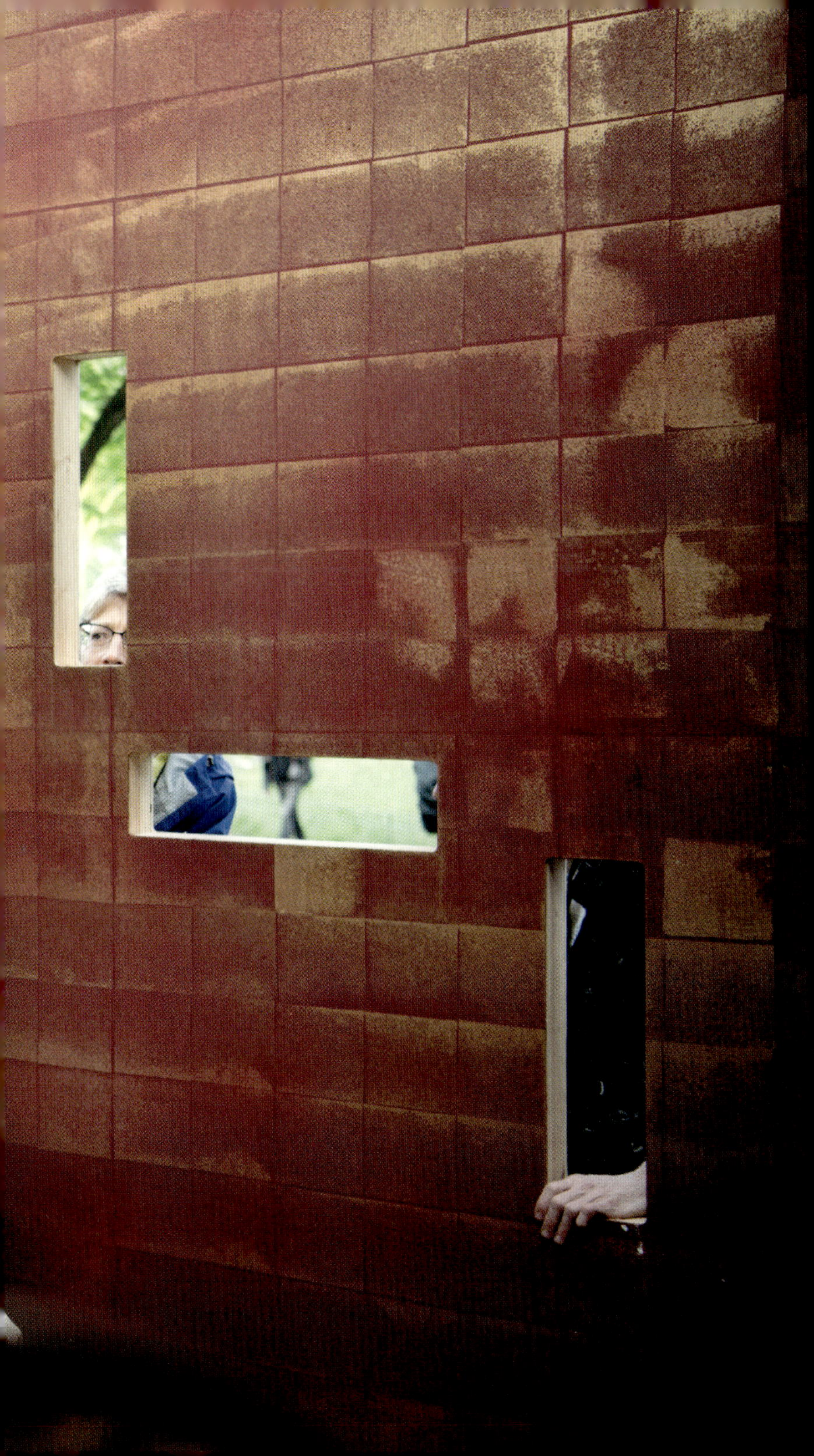

During the day, an immersive walk-through installation in the gardens captured the essence of the hospital, peopled by actors and enhanced by a specially created soundtrack.

As part of the event, two concerts were held at the nearby Brighton Dome, fusing Western and Eastern classical music traditions. The first featured the Philharmonia Orchestra together with a traditional Indian score by musician Kala Ramnath. Alongside the music were readings by Art Malik from the letters and diaries of the Indian servicemen who had recuperated at the pavilion. Later that night, a second performance had Debashish Bhattacharya playing a traditional raga concert alongside tabla player Gurdain Rayatt.

Over 50,000 people experienced *Dr Blighty* in person, while the popularity of the projections meant that the images were spread far and wide on social media, increasing the audience to more than a million online.

Royal Pavilion Gardens and Brighton Festival,
24 — 29 May 2016

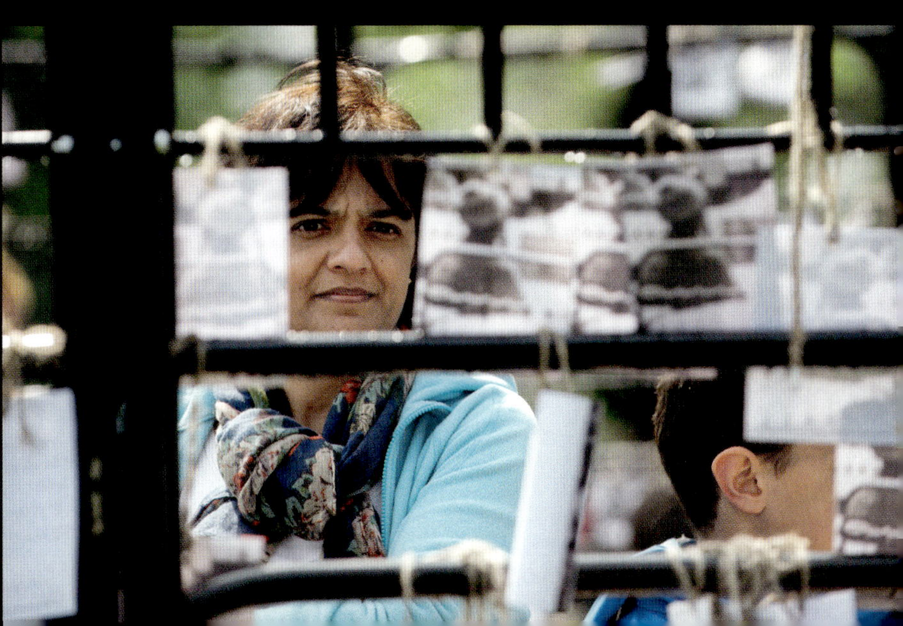

'An otherworldly requiem that makes a fitting tribute to the contribution of black South Africans to the First World War.'

The Stage

SS MENDI: DANCING THE DEATH DRILL

Isango Ensemble
Fred Khumalo

In early 1917, the SS *Mendi* set sail from Cape Town, taking hundreds of black South African volunteers to support the Allied forces fighting in France. The volunteers were part of the South African Native Labour Corps, which supplied manual workers to aid the war effort on the Western Front by building roads, railways and trenches. But early in the morning of 21 February 1917, the *Mendi* collided with a cargo ship amid thick fog in the English Channel south of the Isle of Wight and sank, killing 616 South Africans and 33 of the *Mendi*'s crew. Controversially, the story of the *Mendi* was not included in school curriculums during the apartheid years in South Africa, and only survived as a result of being passed down orally from generation to generation.

SS Mendi: Dancing the Death Drill was a theatre production based on Fred Khumalo's historical novel *Dancing the Death Drill*. It focused on one of the ship's passengers, Pitso Motaung, who sailed aboard the *Mendi* and was among the few who lived to tell the tale. Khumalo took the title of his book from the report of a pastor onboard the *Mendi* who led those around him in a dance, or 'death drill', as the ship went down, urging them to die like warriors. Performed by 14 members of the South African theatre company Isango Ensemble, *SS Mendi: Dancing the Death Drill* drew new attention to these many forgotten lost lives, and told the story of how this maritime disaster gave rise to a life of hope, courage and resilience.

Nuffield Southampton Theatres, 29 June — 14 July 2018 / Linbury Studio, Royal Opera House, London, 18 April — 4 May 2019

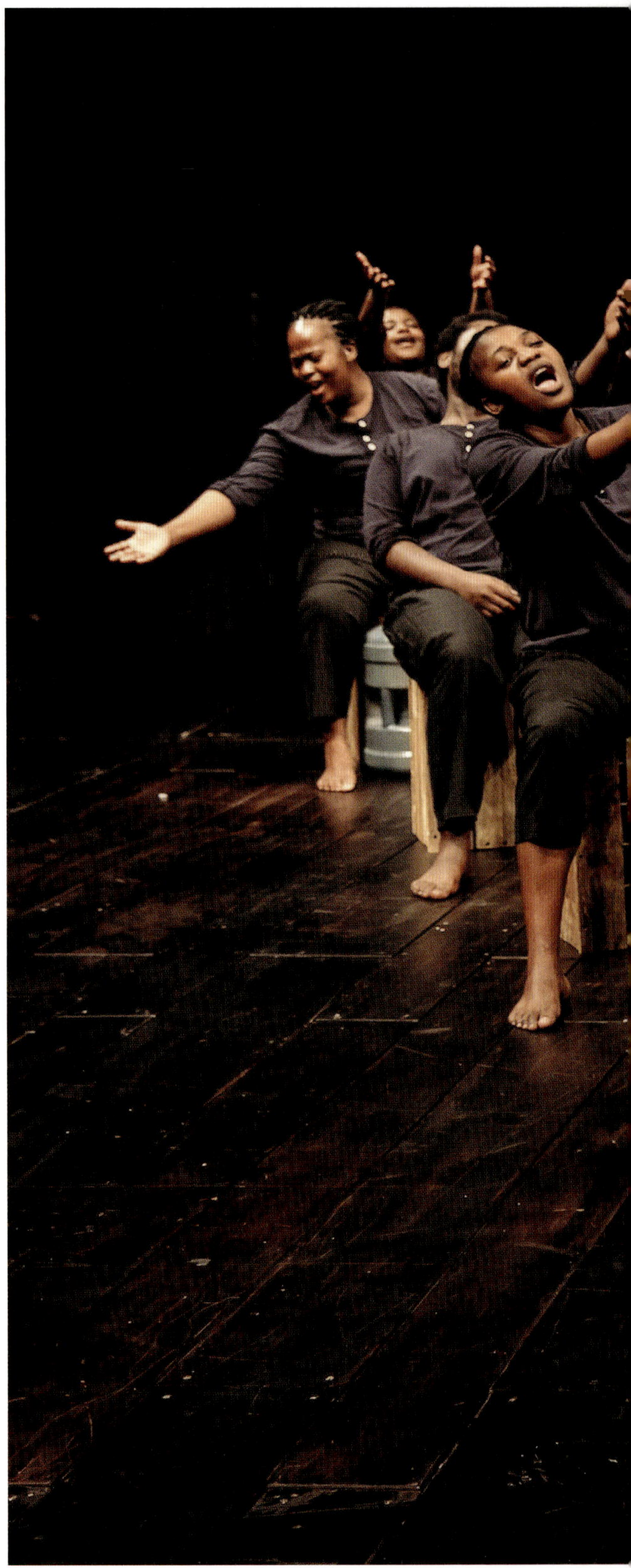

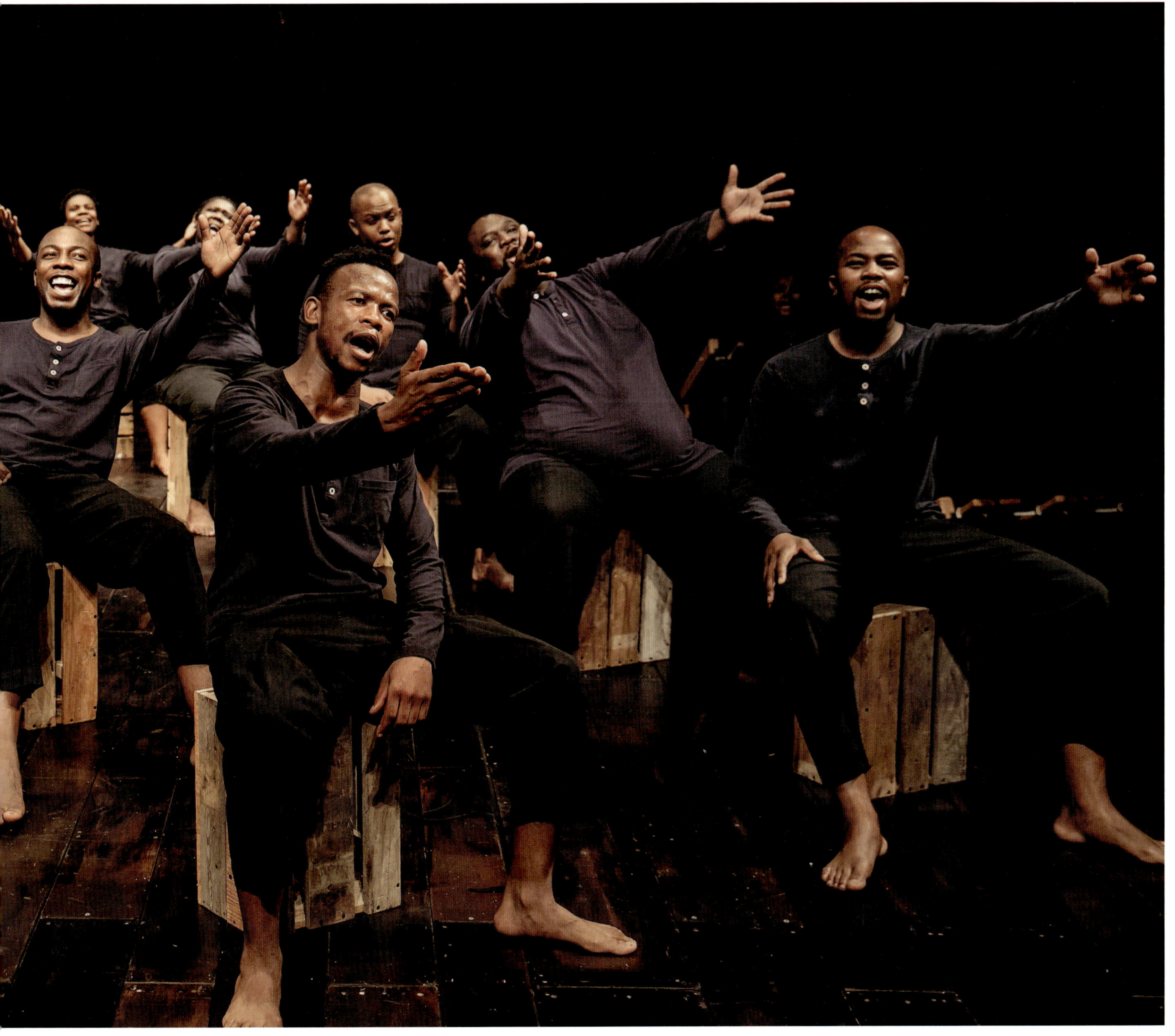

A FOREIGN FIELD

Torsten Rasch

A Foreign Field is a 40-minute cantata for choir, soloists and orchestra, written by the celebrated German composer Torsten Rasch, setting writings of the First World War to music. It was commissioned jointly by Germany's Chemnitz Opera (where it was also performed) and the historic Three Choirs Festival, which takes place every July, rotating among the cathedrals of Hereford, Gloucester and Worcester.

Rasch's powerful libretto was inspired by poets on opposite sides of the conflict — the Dymock Poets (the group that included Edward Thomas, Rupert Brooke and Robert Frost, who wrote, read and walked together in the Gloucestershire countryside before the war intervened) and their Austro-German contemporaries Georg Trakl and Rainer Marie Rilke. At the heart of the work are extracts from the writings of Edward Thomas to his wife, Helen. Thomas was killed on the Western Front in 1917. The composition's title was taken from Brooke's poem 'The Soldier'. Brought together in music, the words of these writers form an impassioned, moving memorial to the suffering endured on both sides.

The work received its premiere at Worcester Cathedral as part of the 2014 festival, and was later broadcast on BBC Radio 3. Baldur Brönnimann conducted the Philharmonia Orchestra, accompanied by the Three Choirs Chorus and choristers from all three English cathedrals, alongside their Chemnitz counterparts. A German premiere then took place in Chemnitz on 4 March 2015.

Worcester Cathedral, 31 July 2014 / BBC Radio 3 broadcast, 19 September 2014

The writings of early 20th-century poets on both sides of the divide inspired Rasch's composition, which was premiered at Worcester Cathedral.

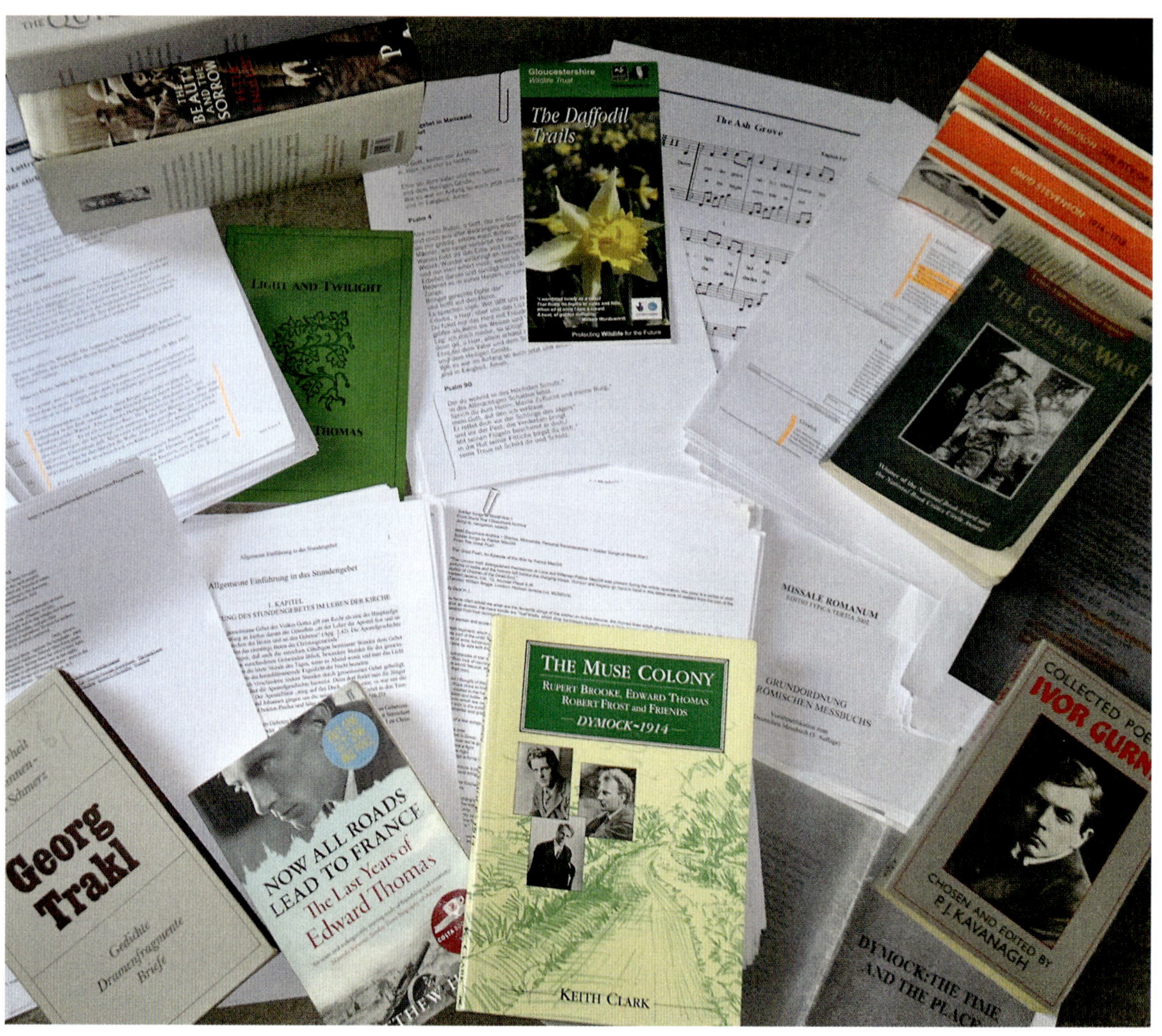

IF IT WASN'T FOR THEIR WELLIES

John Maxwell Geddes

Drawing on the heritage of communities such as those associated with the North British Rubber Company, which supplied the British Army with vital supplies of rubber boots and fire hoses, *If It Wasn't for Their Wellies* united Edinburgh's older residents with exceptional young musicians performing the work of composer John Maxwell Geddes to commemorate the First World War.

This project came under the banner of Live Music Now Scotland's *Composing with Care* scheme, which arranges for musicians to visit care homes in order to hear the stories of elderly residents. These stories then provide the inspiration for new pieces of music by professional composers. For *If It Wasn't for Their Wellies*, hours of source material in the form of memories, stories and songs were gathered from care-home residents and lunch-club users by the soprano

Emma Versteeg and accompanist Maryam Sherhan, as well as baritone Phil Gault and accompanist Geoffrey Tanit. This then provided the basis for a cycle of songs by Geddes entitled *A Castle Mills Suite*.

The new composition was performed in the care homes and centres that had inspired its composition, and then taken on tour, celebrating the wartime memories of Edinburgh's families through music. It was also recorded as part of Live Music Now Scotland's 30th anniversary.

Edinburgh, August 2014

The Glaswegian composer John Maxwell Geddes (1941–2017) worked with the BBC Scottish Symphony Orchestra for over 50 years and composed three symphonies, numerous chamberworks, arrangements of folk songs and film music.

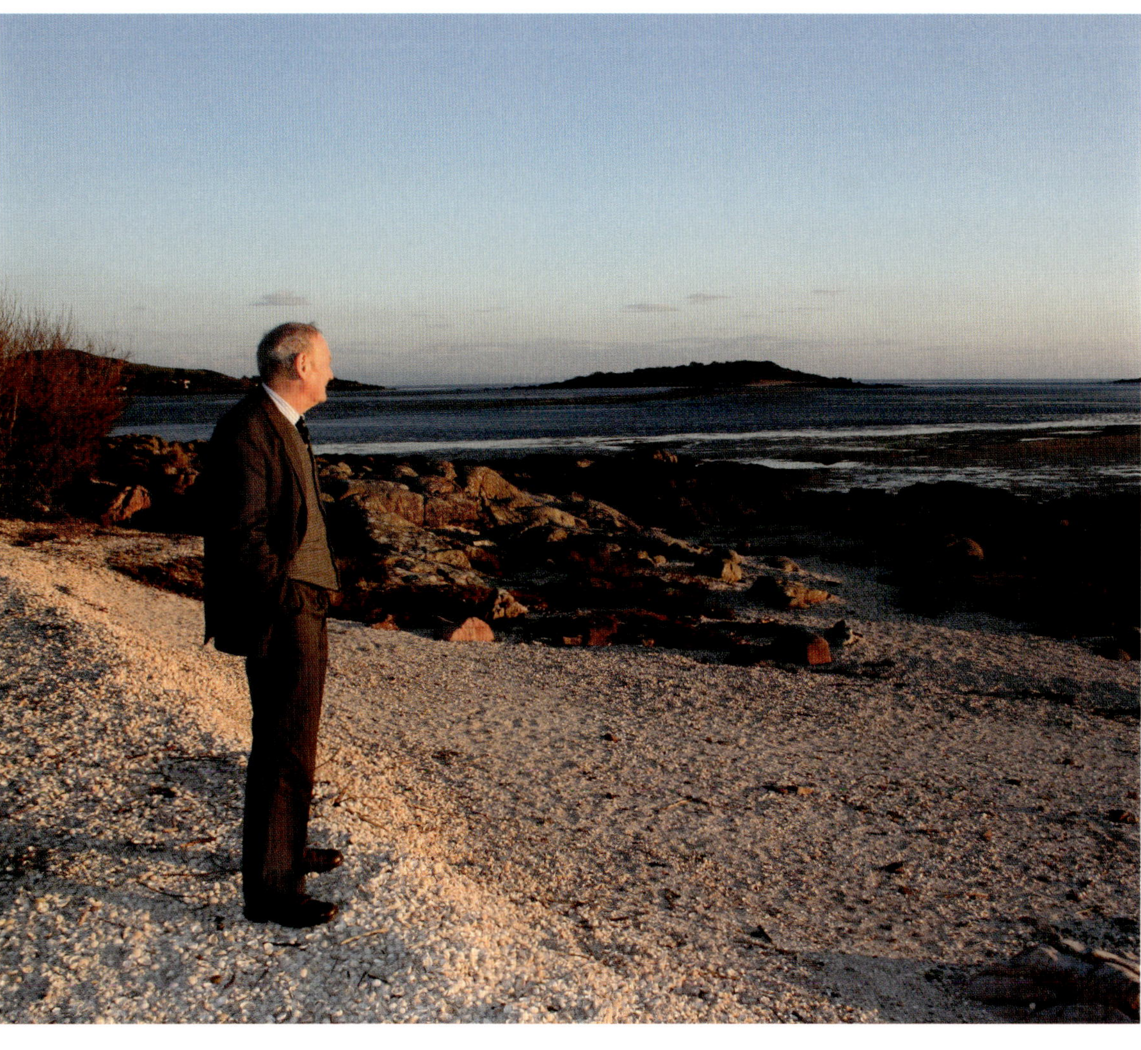

1914 DAY BY DAY

Steve Bell
Peter Brookes
Steven Camley
Kate Charlesworth
Alan Cowsill and
   Lalit Kumar Sharma
Achim Greser and
   Heribert Lenz
Ferg Handley and
   John McCrea
Jon McNaught
Woodrow Phoenix
Zoom Rockman
Posy Simmonds
Ralph Steadman

In the weeks prior to August 2014, a series entitled *1914 Day by Day* was featured on BBC Radio 4, in which Professor Margaret MacMillan (author of *The War that Ended Peace*) chronicled the weeks leading up to Britain's entry into the First World War. To complement the series, 15 celebrated cartoonists and graphic artists then responded as if in real time to these events of a century ago, as relations between the great powers deteriorated into war, with two cartoonists producing a piece of art each week. Their illustrated commentary on the issues and incidents of that fraught period, as seen through modern eyes, was published online and distributed via social media, bringing home to a new audience the frightening speed with which global war can descend.

The artists were Steve Bell (*The Guardian*), Peter Brookes (*The Times*), Steven Camley (*Glasgow Herald*), Kate Charlesworth (*The Cartoon History of Time*), Alan Cowsill and Lalit Kumar Sharma (*The Strange Case of Dr Jekyll and Mr Hyde,* Marvel), Achim Greser and Heribert Lenz (*Frankfurter Allegemeine*), Ferg Handley and John McCrea (Marvel/Lucasfilm & Marvel/Commando), Jon McNaught (*Dockwood*), Woodrow Phoenix (*Rumble Strip*), Zoom Rockman (*The Zoom!*), Posy Simmonds (*Tamara Drewe*) and Ralph Steadman (*New Statesman*).

The original artworks were exhibited at London's Cartoon Museum alongside the exhibition 'Never Again — The First World War in Cartoon and Comic Art'.

The Cartoon Museum, London, 11 June — 14 October 2014

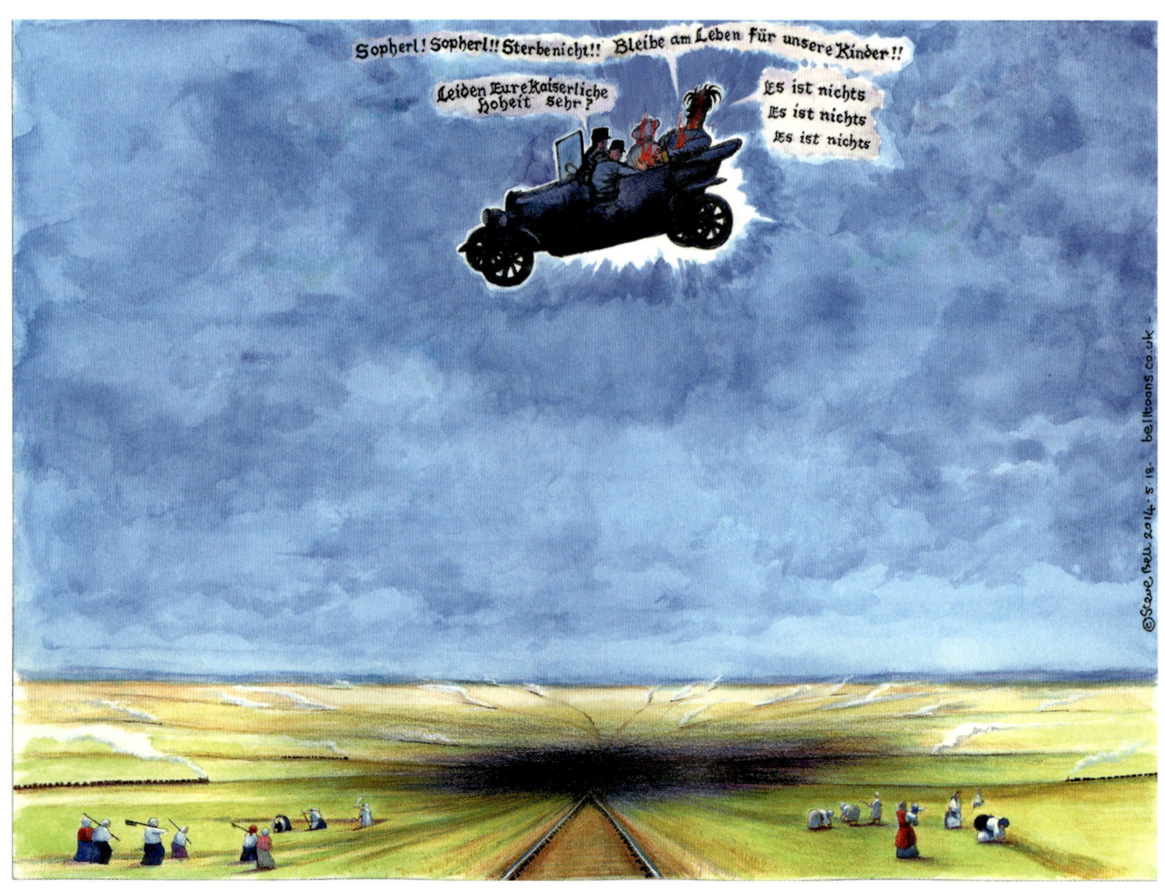

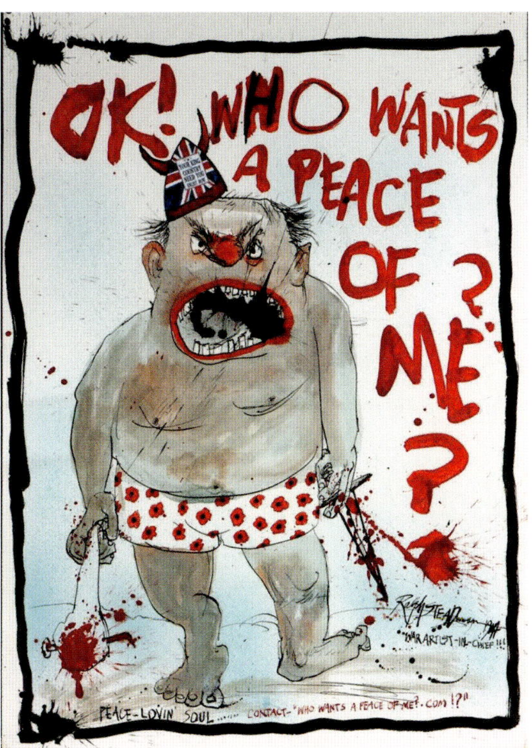

Opposite. Steve Bell's cartoon depicted the archduke and his wife in the open-top car that left them wide open to attack on the streets of Sarajevo.

Below. The ugly side of war, as depicted by Ralph Steadman, whose father fought in the First World War.

Left. *A Blank Cheque for War*, by Peter Brookes. This was inspired by the German kaiser's promise to back the Austro-Hungarian Empire if Vienna's proposed attack on Serbia resulted in war.

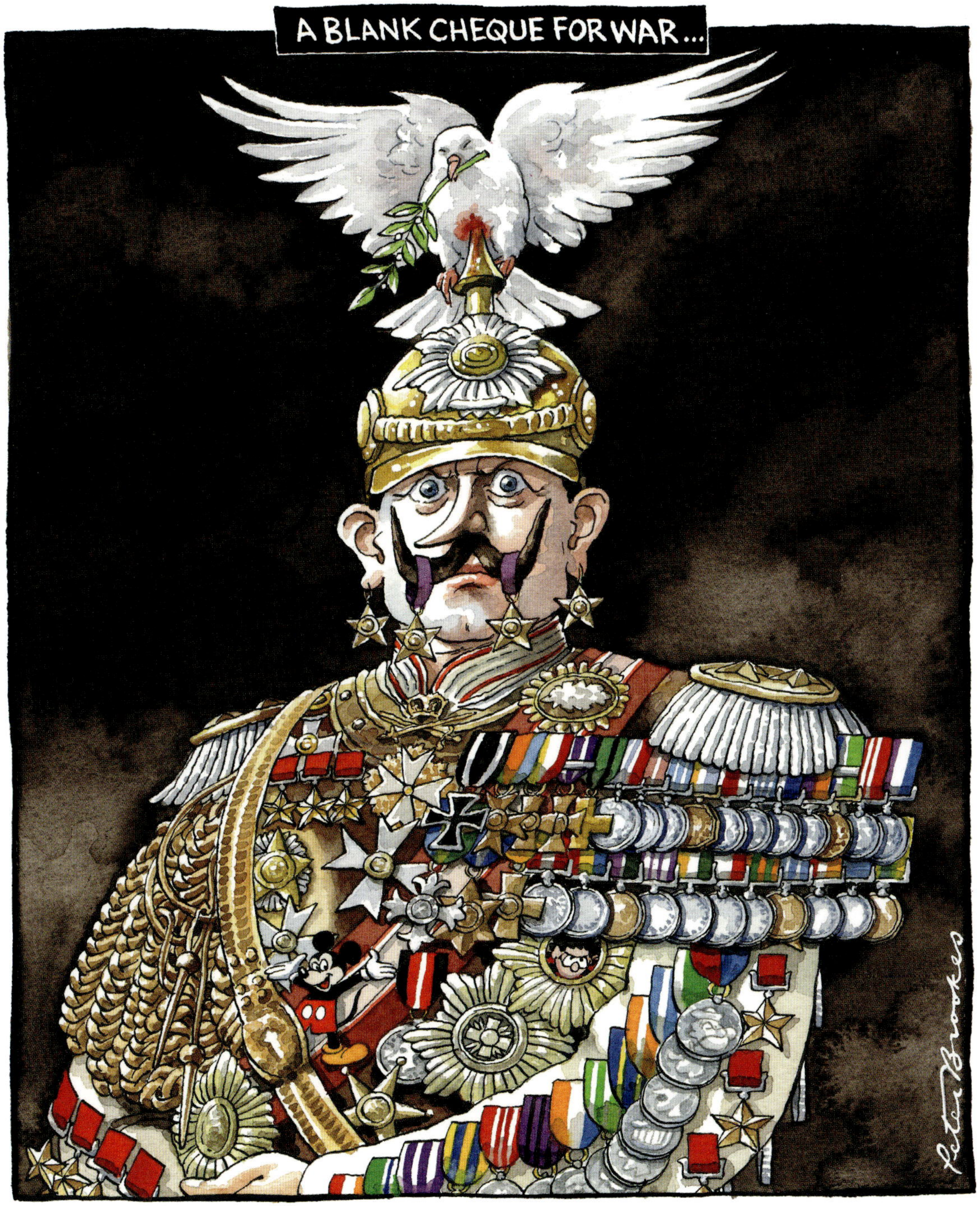

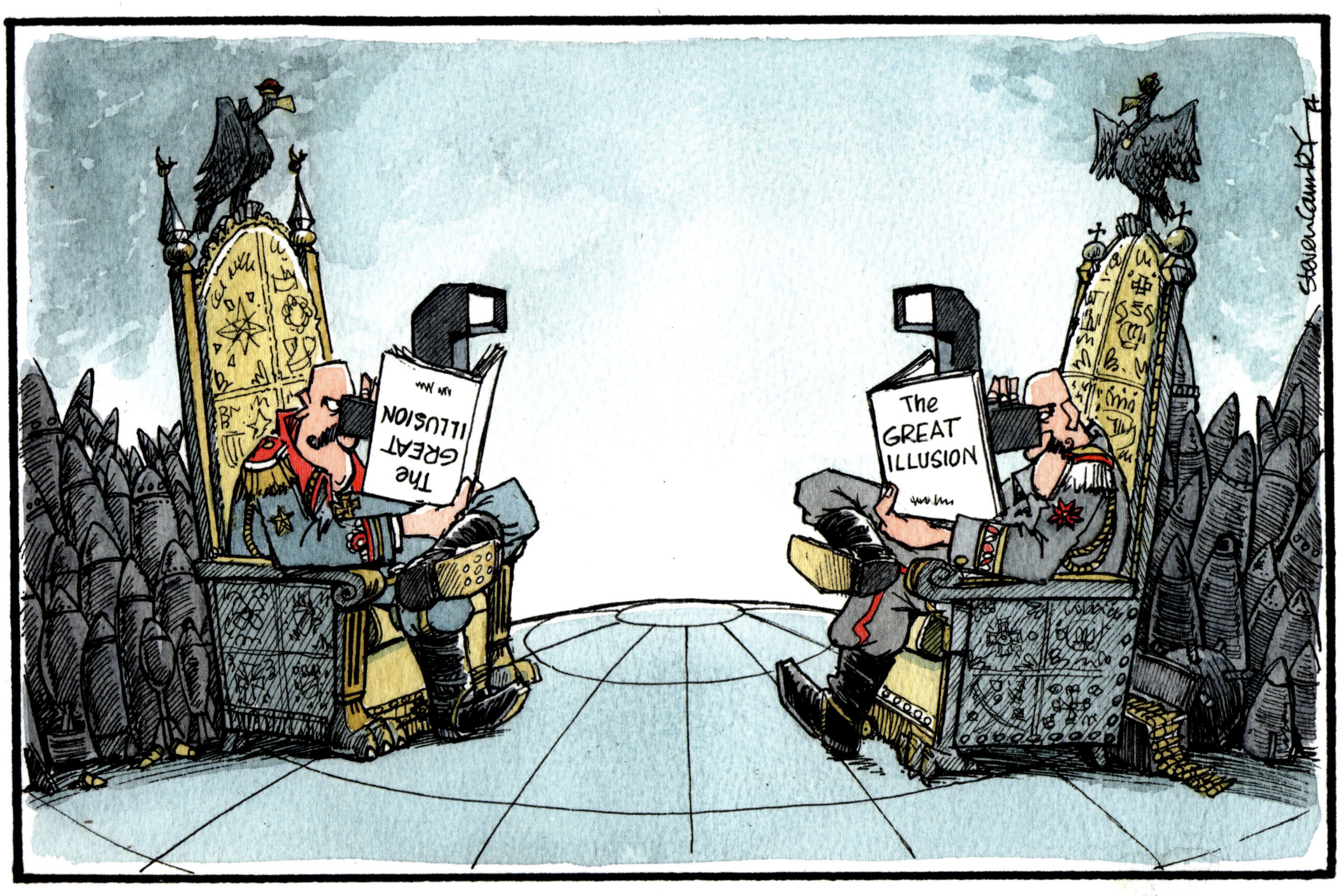

The GREAT ILLUSION
The GREAT ILLUSION

Opposite. *The Great Illusion*, by Steven Camley — a tribute to the author Norman Angell and his book of that name, which argued against the idea that war and conquest would bring economic advantages.

Right. *Shadow Play*, by Posy Simmonds, depicting figures representing Austria–Hungary, Russia, France and England. All are geared up for war, and waiting to declare their intentions.

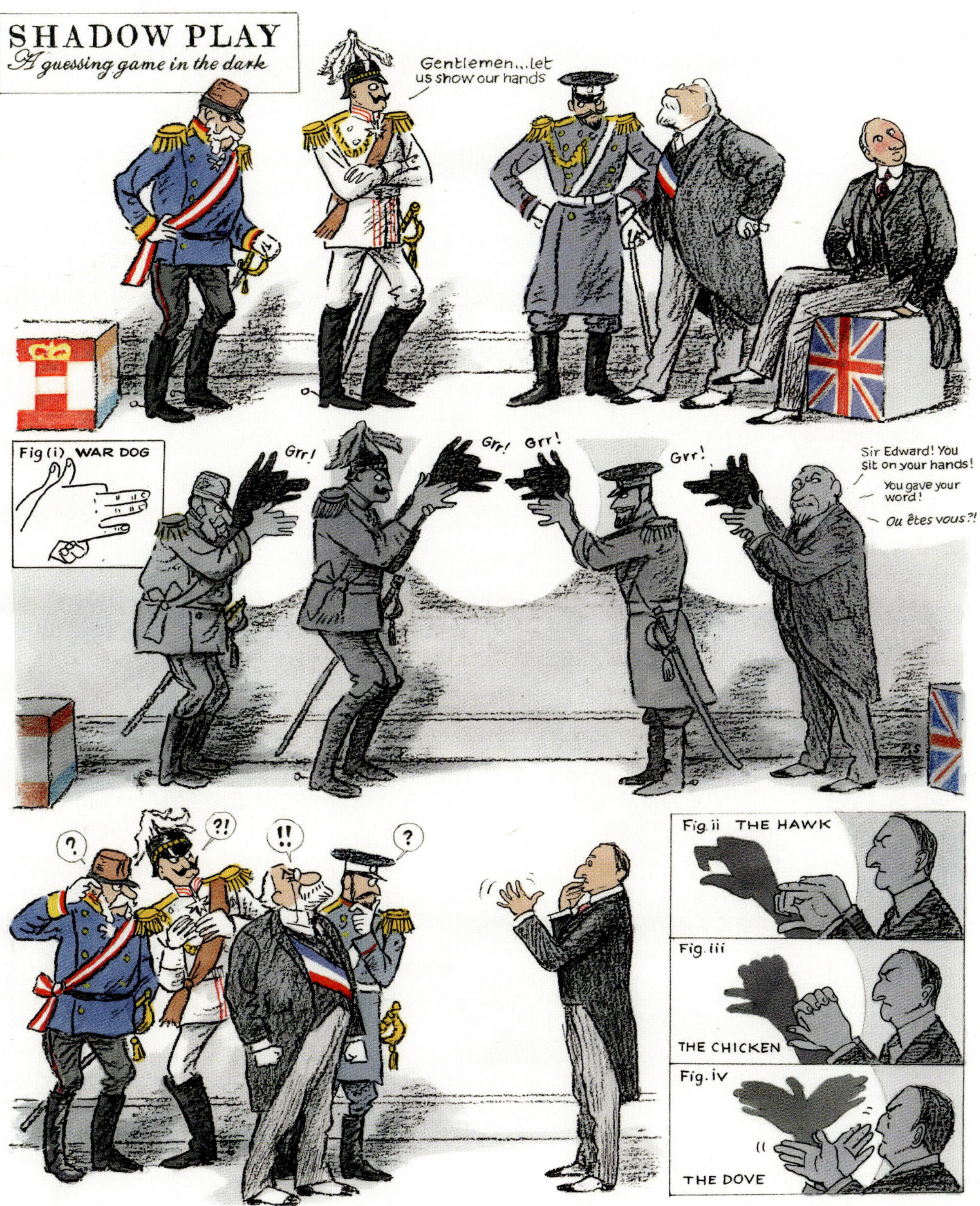

CEREMONY

Phil Collins

The Russian Revolution took place in 1917, in a country exhausted by the First World War. The event shaped the political landscape of the 20th century. But it was in Manchester, not Imperial Russia, that the idea of communism was born. Friedrich Engels, co-founder of communist theory with his friend Karl Marx, lived in Manchester for 20 years. His philosophy was shaped by what he observed in the world's first industrial city.

At the initiative of award-winning artist Phil Collins, a decommissioned statue of Engels travelled in 2017 from a Ukrainian village across Europe to be permanently installed outside HOME, Manchester's centre for international contemporary art, theatre and film, in the city centre. Over the course of a year, Collins collaborated with local organisations, activists and communities to explore Engels' legacy and the lives of workers today. He described *Ceremony* as 'the search for a statue of Engels and its journey back home, the everyday stories of people from Manchester, and a homecoming party to inaugurate the statue, with Russia's 1917 revolution as a pivotal moment in the process'.

The second part of *Ceremony* was a film that used footage produced in 2017 to weave these three strands together. Initially it was broadcast on the BBC and then presented as a gallery installation at several locations, as part of the final 14-18 NOW season.

Baltic Centre for Contemporary Art, Gateshead, 22 June — 30 September 2018 / HOME, Manchester, 7 July — 19 August 2018 / MAC, Belfast, 10 August — 28 October 2018 / Cooper Gallery, Dundee, 18 January — 16 February 2019

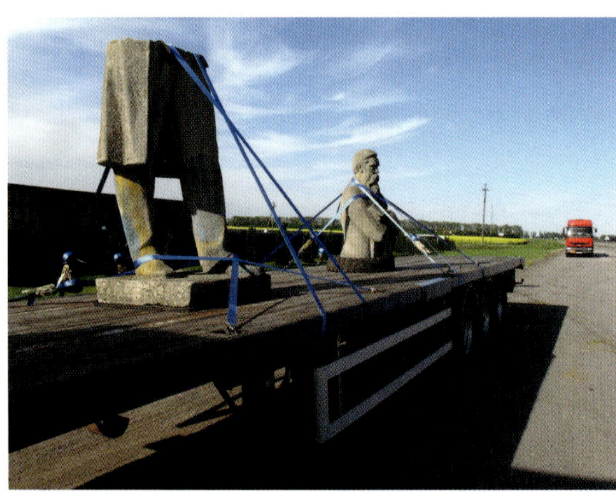

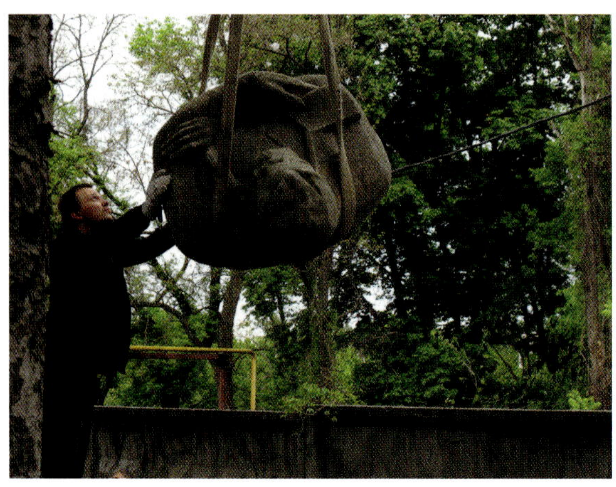

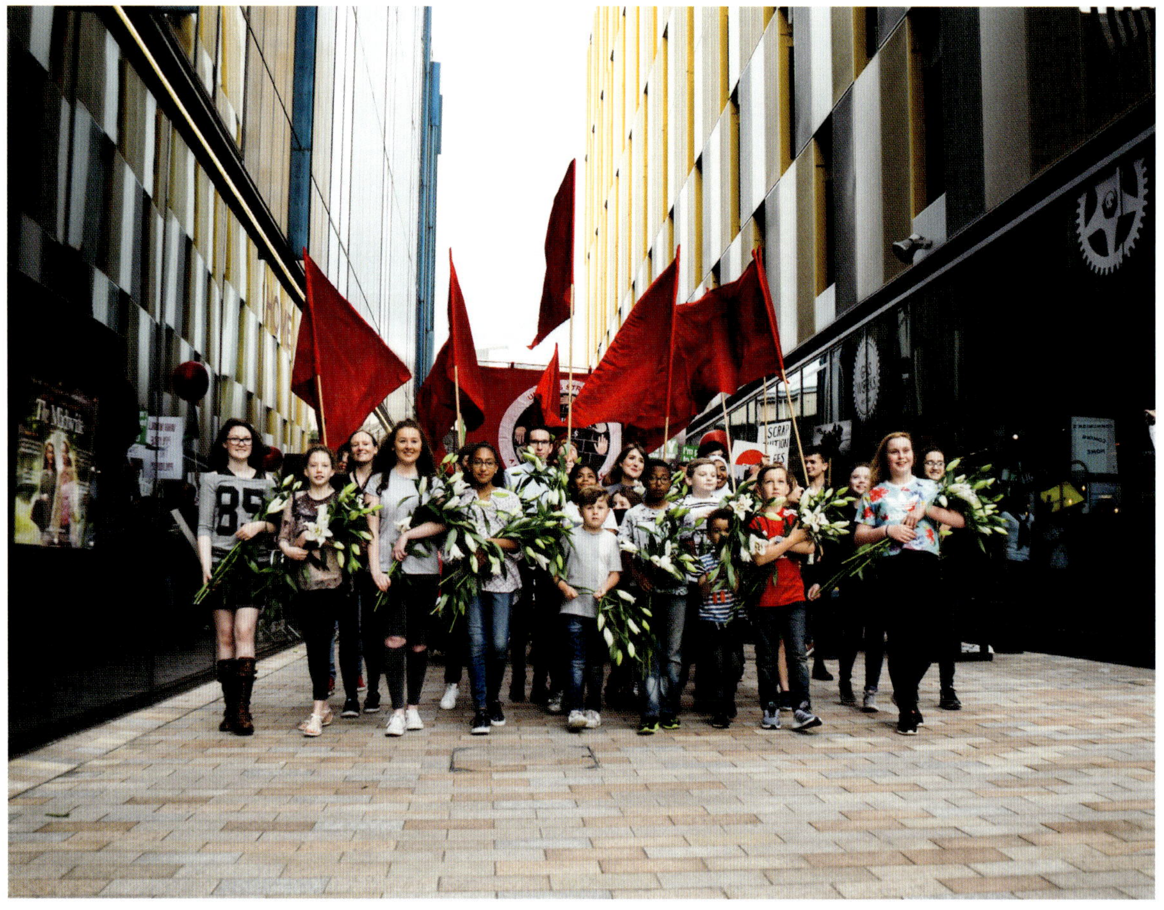

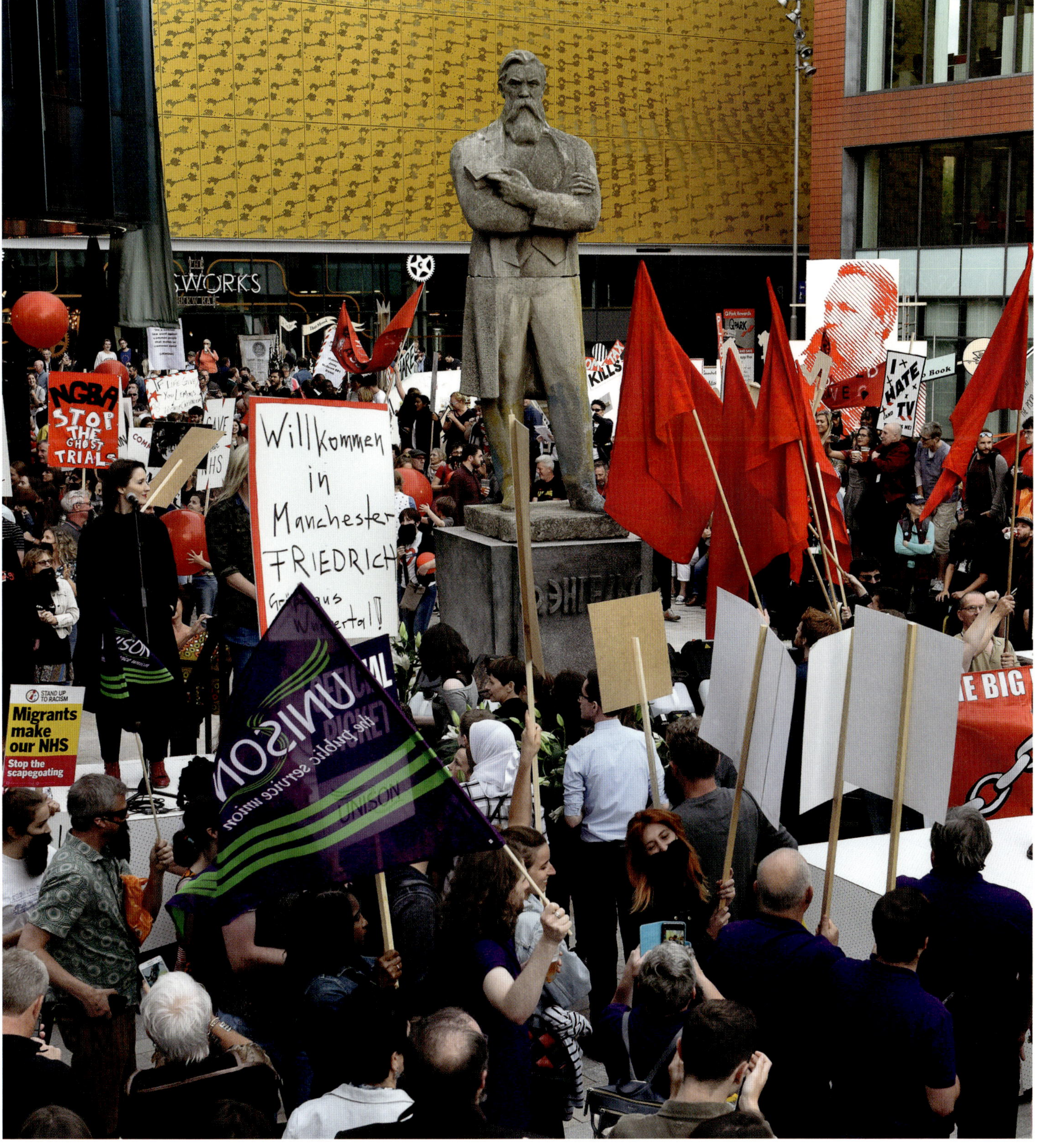

After extensive research
trips, Collins located the
concrete statue (in two
halves) in eastern Ukraine.
When it had completed its
journey, crowds gathered
for the live inauguration
in 2017, in Manchester's
Tony Wilson Place.

MAKE ME UP

Rachel Maclean

Make Me Up, by the multimedia artist Rachel Maclean, is a darkly comic film that takes a satirical look at the contradictory pressures faced by woman today. It examines how, although television and social media can be fun and expressive spaces to explore identity, they are simultaneously a gilded prison that encourages women to conform to strict beauty ideals.

In the film, the character of Siri wakes to find herself trapped inside a candy-coloured dreamhouse. Despite the cutesy décor, the place is far from benign, and she and her inmates are encouraged to compete for survival while being watched over by surveillance cameras, 24/7. Presiding over the group is an authoritarian diva who speaks entirely with the voice of Kenneth Clark from the 1960s BBC series *Civilisation*. As she forces the women to go head to head in a series of demeaning tasks, Siri, with the help of fellow inmate Alexa, starts subverting the rules and soon reveals the sinister truth that underpins their world.

Make Me Up was (together with *Sortition* and *Poet in da Corner*; see following pages) one of three works that formed *Represent* — a 2018 series inspired both by the centenary of Votes for Women and the remaining inequalities in society. The series invited three radical young female artists to explore their experiences of democracy, equality and inclusion in contemporary Britain.

BFI London Film Festival, 12 October 2018 / BBC Four broadcast, 4 November 2018 / UK-wide cinema screening, October — November 2018

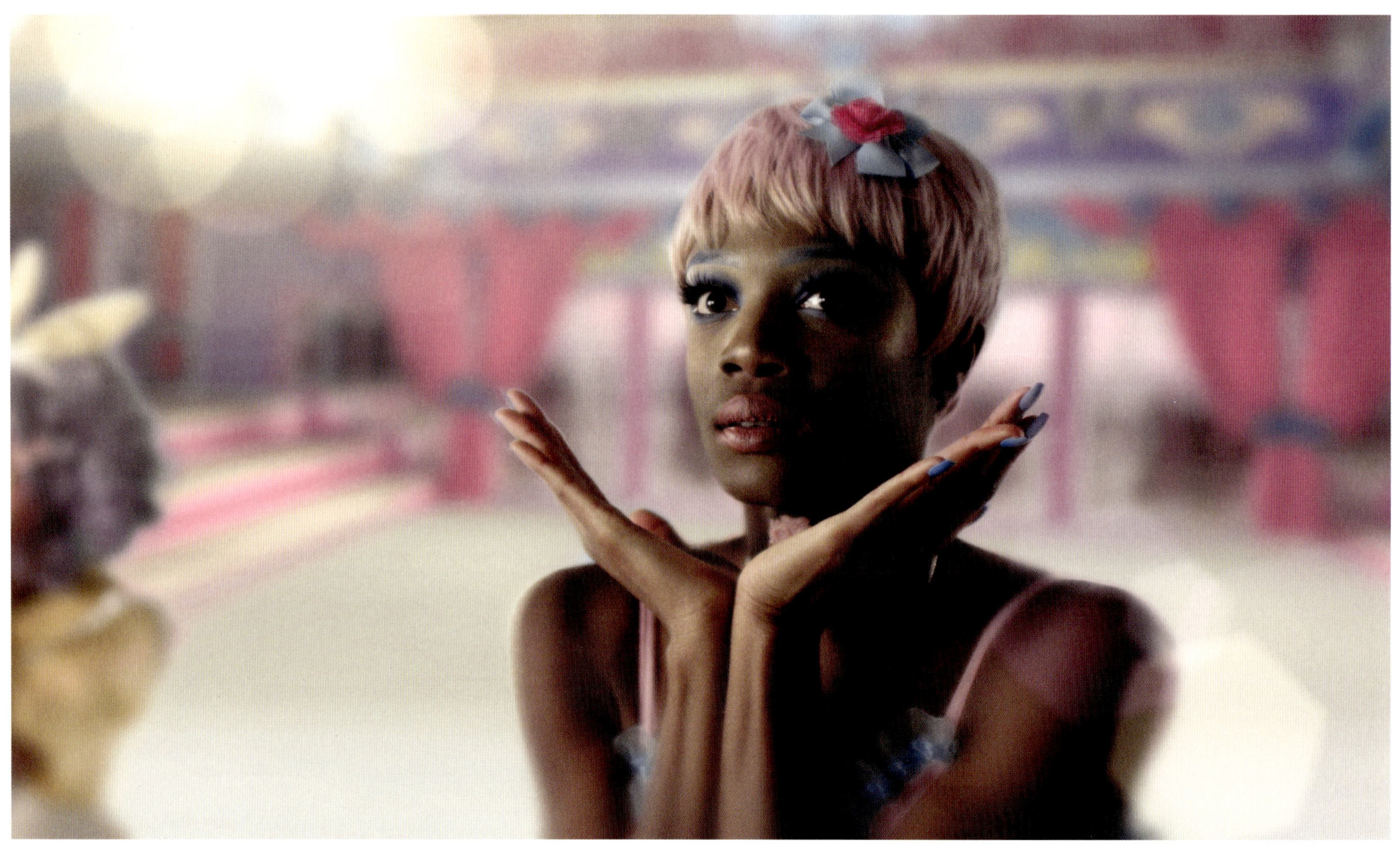

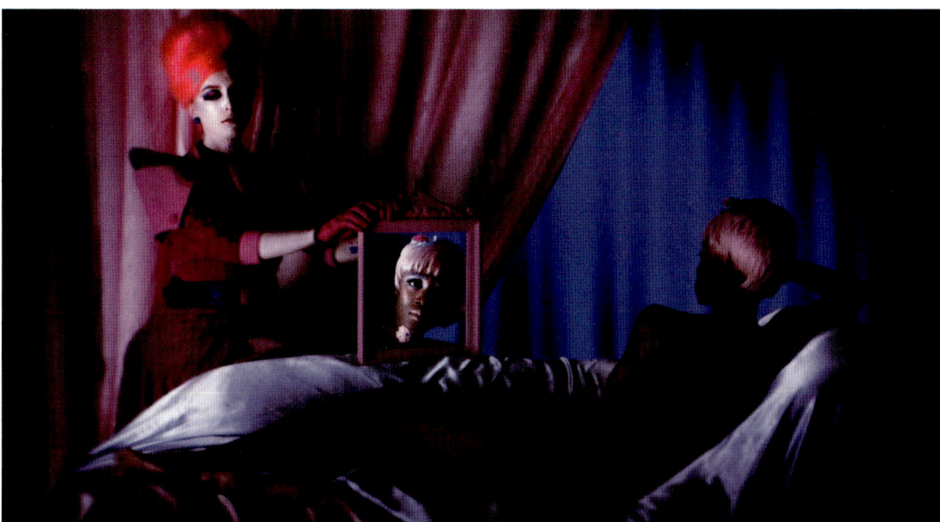

The characters of Siri
(below) and fellow inmate
Alexa (opposite and left)
are encouraged to aim for
feminine perfection by the
all-powerful Figurehead.

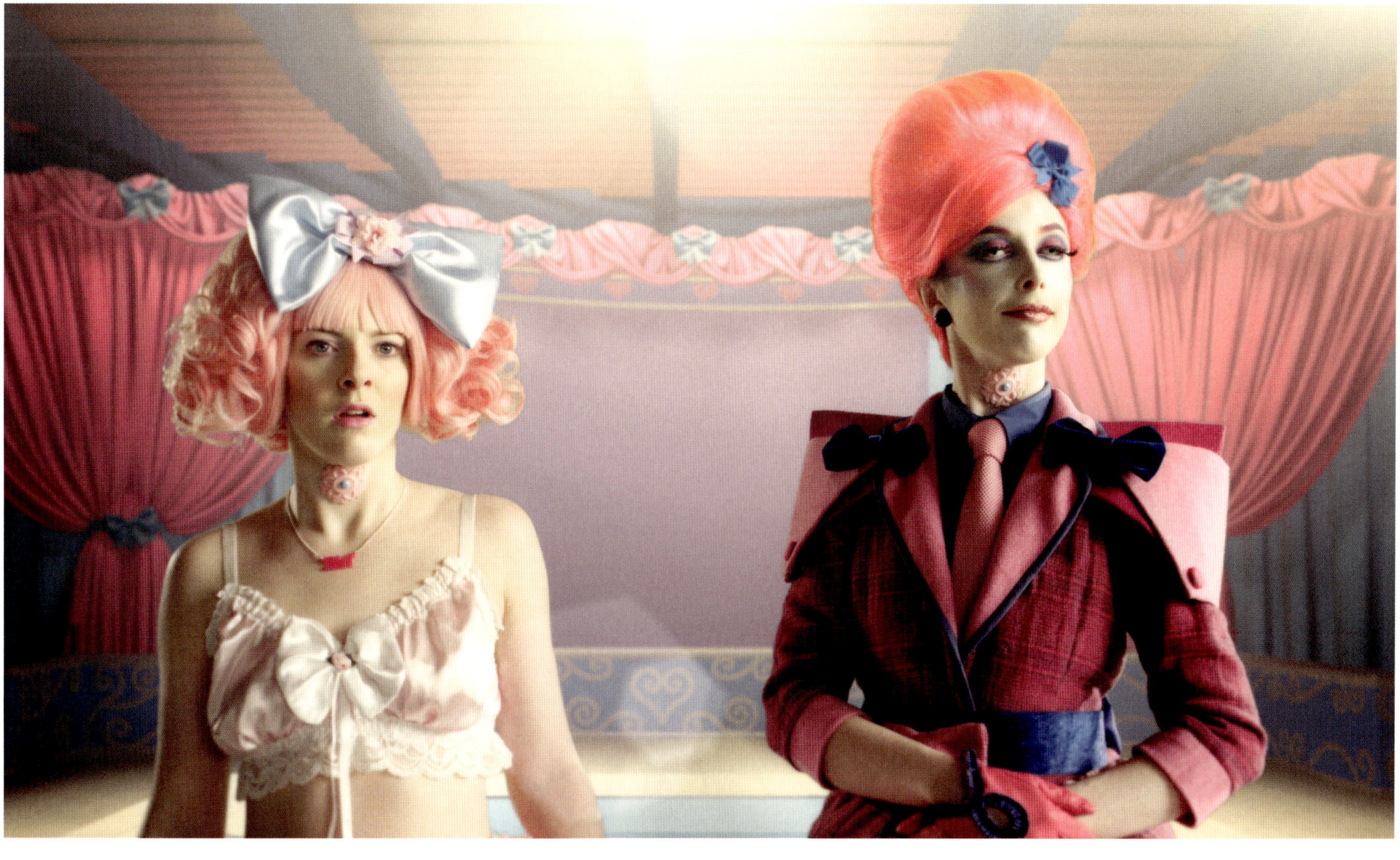

POET IN DA CORNER

Debris Stevenson

Poet in da Corner was a bold new theatre show written by and featuring Debris Stevenson — a coming-of-age story inspired by Dizzee Rascal's seminal grime album *Boy in da Corner*. In a strict Mormon household somewhere in the seam between East London and Essex, a girl is given the album by her best friend — 57 minutes and 21 seconds later, her life begins to change, from feeling muted by dyslexia, to spitting the power of her words; from being conflicted about her sexuality, to finding the freedom to explore; from feeling alone, to being given the greatest gift by her closest friend.

In this semi-autobiographical piece, audiences stepped into a technicolour world where music, dance and spoken word collided. Debris Stevenson is a young poet, lyricist and dancer who has performed her unique work everywhere from BBC Radio 3's *The Verb* to London's Roundhouse; *Poet in da Corner* was the story of how grime allowed her to redefine herself as a person and as an artist.

Poet in da Corner was also part of *Represent*, a 2018 series inspired both by the centenary of Votes for Women and by the remaining inequalities in society.

Royal Court Theatre, London, 12 September 2018 — 6 October 2018

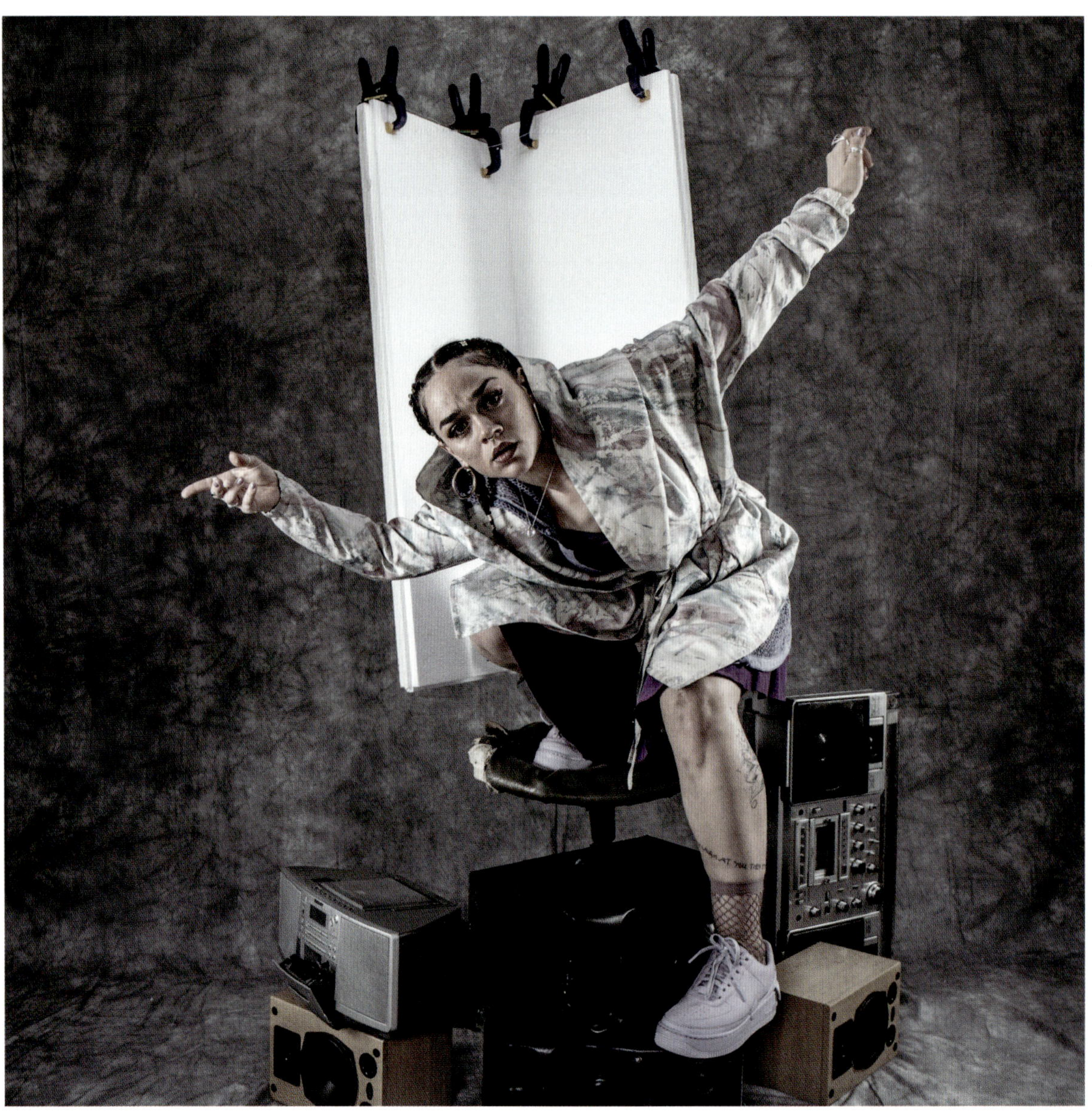

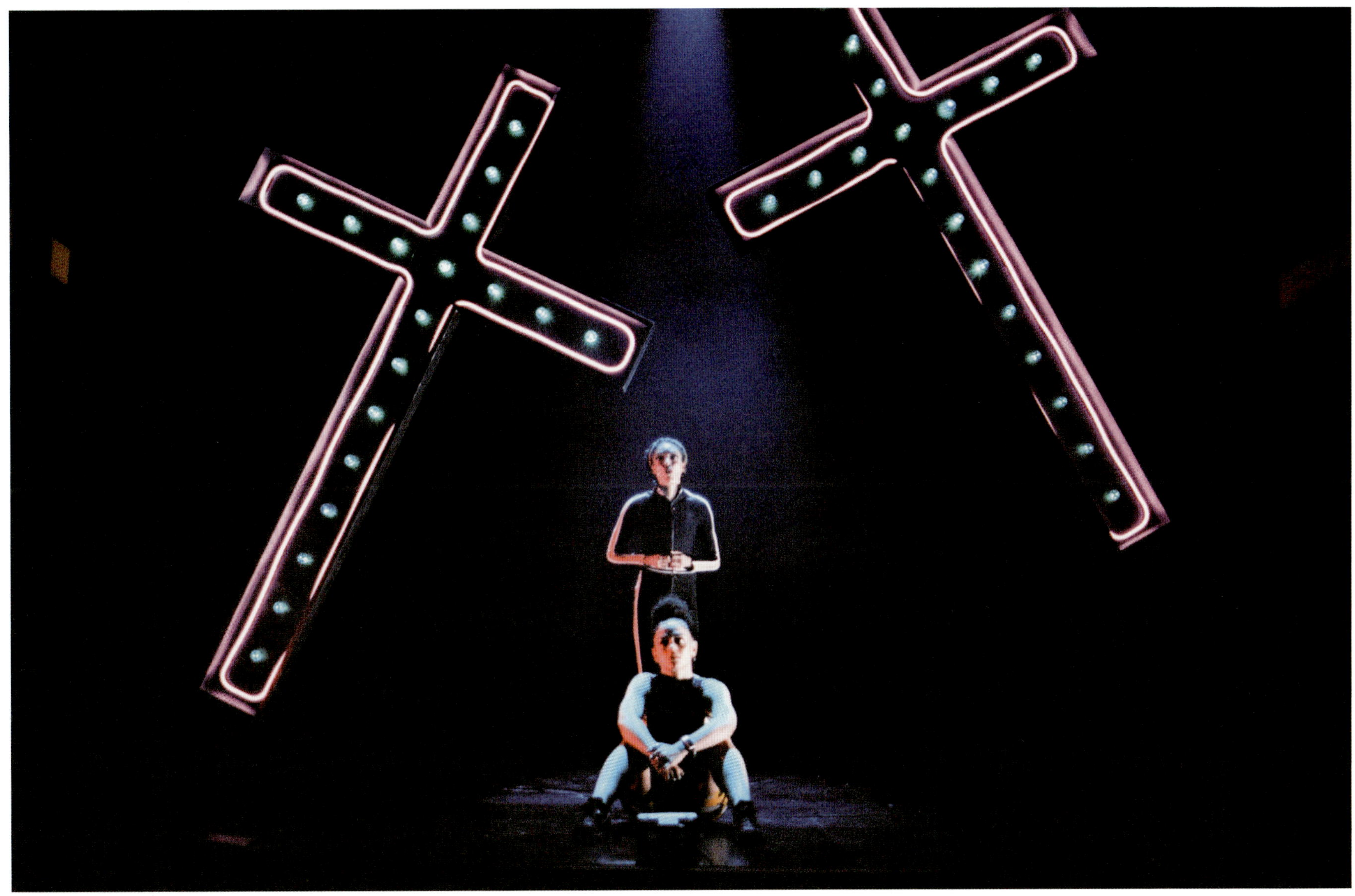

Debris Stevenson's coming-of-age story was told through a blend of dance, songs and spoken word — an ode to the transformative powers of grime.

SORTITION

Selina Thompson

Developed a century after the first women won the right to vote in the UK, performance artist Selina Thompson's provocative new work *Sortition* turned this moment of democratic history on its head.

Created with and by a set of non-voters from across the UK, along with a team of political provocateurs, experts and troublemakers, *Sortition* imagined what the country would look like with representatives selected not by election but by lottery — at random. Thompson considered the distinction between using your own voice and electing someone to speak for you in a work exploring how young people make themselves heard in Britain today.

The development of *Sortition* culminated in 2018, with Selina sharing the creative journey in dialogue with critical thinker Maddy Costa. *Sortition* then continued to grow into 2019, as the relevance and place of our notion of democracy in society continued to be challenged.

Sortition was also part of *Represent*, a 2018 series inspired both by the centenary of Votes for Women and by the remaining inequalities in society.

Developed on residency at Arnolfini, Bristol, July — November 2018

Artist and performer Selina Thompson created a participatory work that encouraged young people to question the way we govern ourselves, 100 years after the first women won the right to vote.

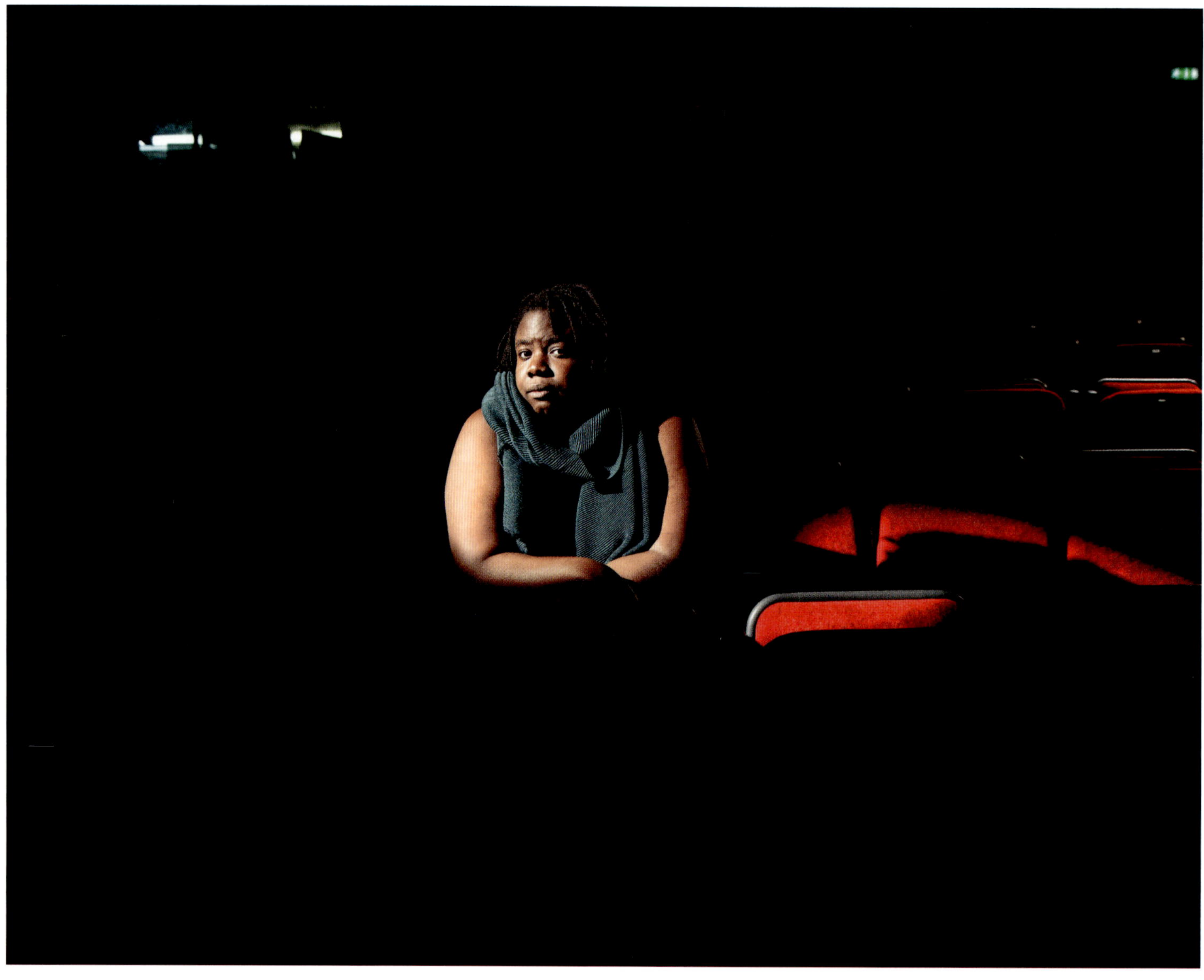

ONE WORLD

Mark Wallinger

Inspired by the Christmas truce matches of 1914, when soldiers from both sides emerged from trenches and met to exchange gifts and play football, artist Mark Wallinger took the football itself as his canvas for this work, co-commissioned by Liverpool Biennial and 14-18 NOW.

Transforming the football into a globe, Wallinger took inspiration from the image of Earth that was taken during the Apollo 8 lunar orbit on 24 December 1968. Captured at the moment of earthrise, it's an image of enduring beauty, depicting a peaceful planet floating in the vastness of space.

A limited edition of 2,000 *One World* footballs was released to community football projects across the UK, and recipients were then encouraged to upload their own #OneWorld videos.

From 2 November 2018

As Wallinger explained, 'It is 100 years since the Armistice was agreed in 1918, and 50 years since the iconic *Earthrise* photograph; an image of a fragile world without borders. Let's celebrate how football can unite us.'

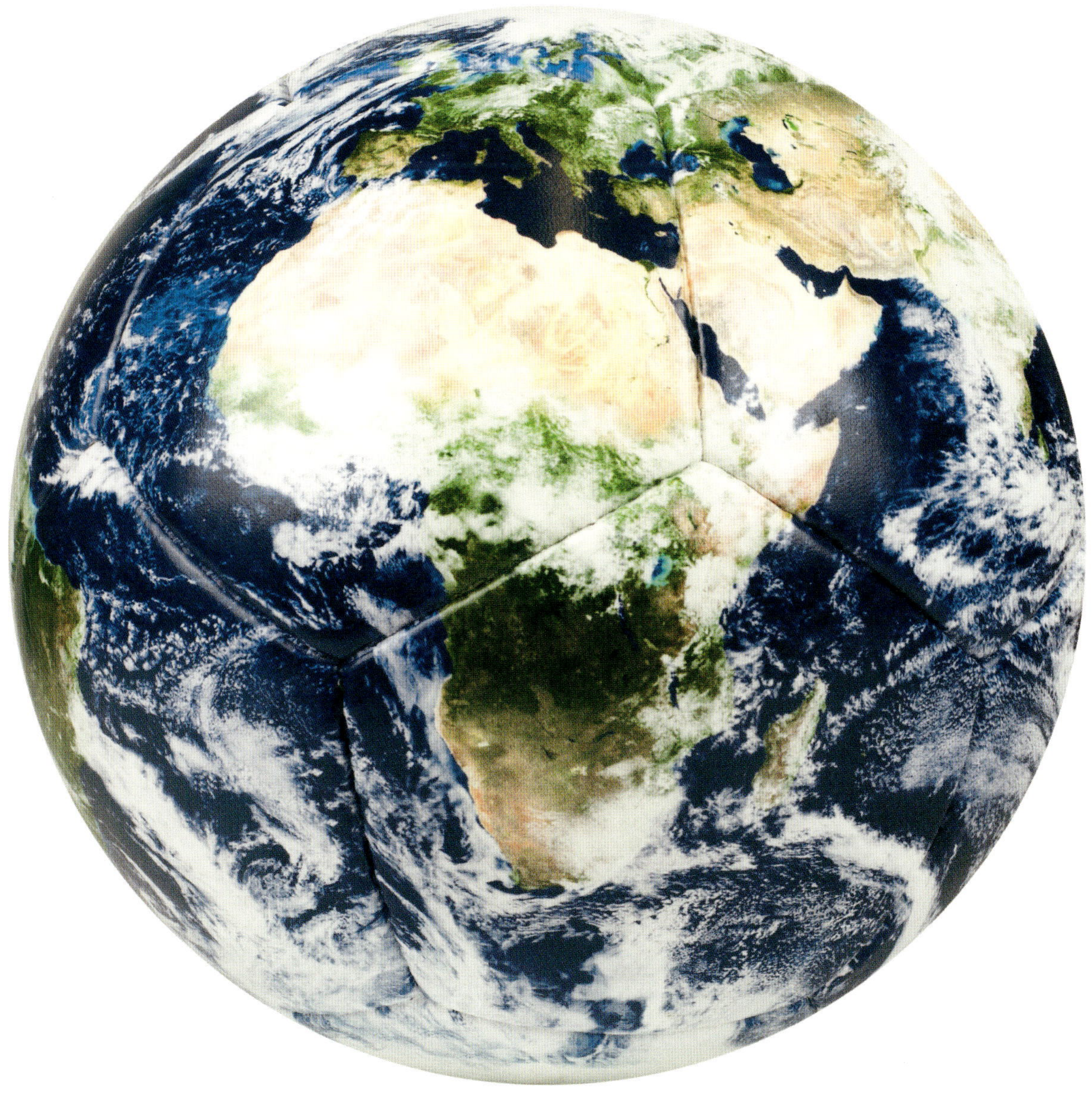

Dame Millicent Garrett Fawcett was a writer, activist and campaigner for women's suffrage. As president of the National Union of Women's Suffrage Societies (NUWSS) from 1890 to 1919, she was instrumental in gaining the vote for women. The suffrage campaign had been largely suspended during the First World War to focus on the war effort, but by the war's conclusion a groundswell of support for the cause had built up — prompted in no small part by the active roles played by women during wartime. This led to the Representation of the People Act 1918, issuing women the right to vote for the very first time. Although restricted to those over 30, this accounted for around 8.5 million individuals.

To commemorate the centenary of the Act, a statue of Fawcett by the artist Gillian Wearing was unveiled in London's Parliament Square. This was the culmination of an online petition to erect the first statue of a woman in the square, and it was also the first to be created by a woman. Its unveiling on 24 April 2018 was a major event in the Mayor of London's #BehindEveryGreatCity campaign, celebrating the role of women in the capital. The statue is a contemporary depiction of Fawcett at 50, when she became president of the NUWSS. Representing both her individual courage and the broader collective struggle, the names and portraits of 59 men and women who campaigned for women's suffrage are inscribed on the plinth.

Parliament Square, London, from 24 April 2018

MILLICENT FAWCETT

Gillian Wearing CBE

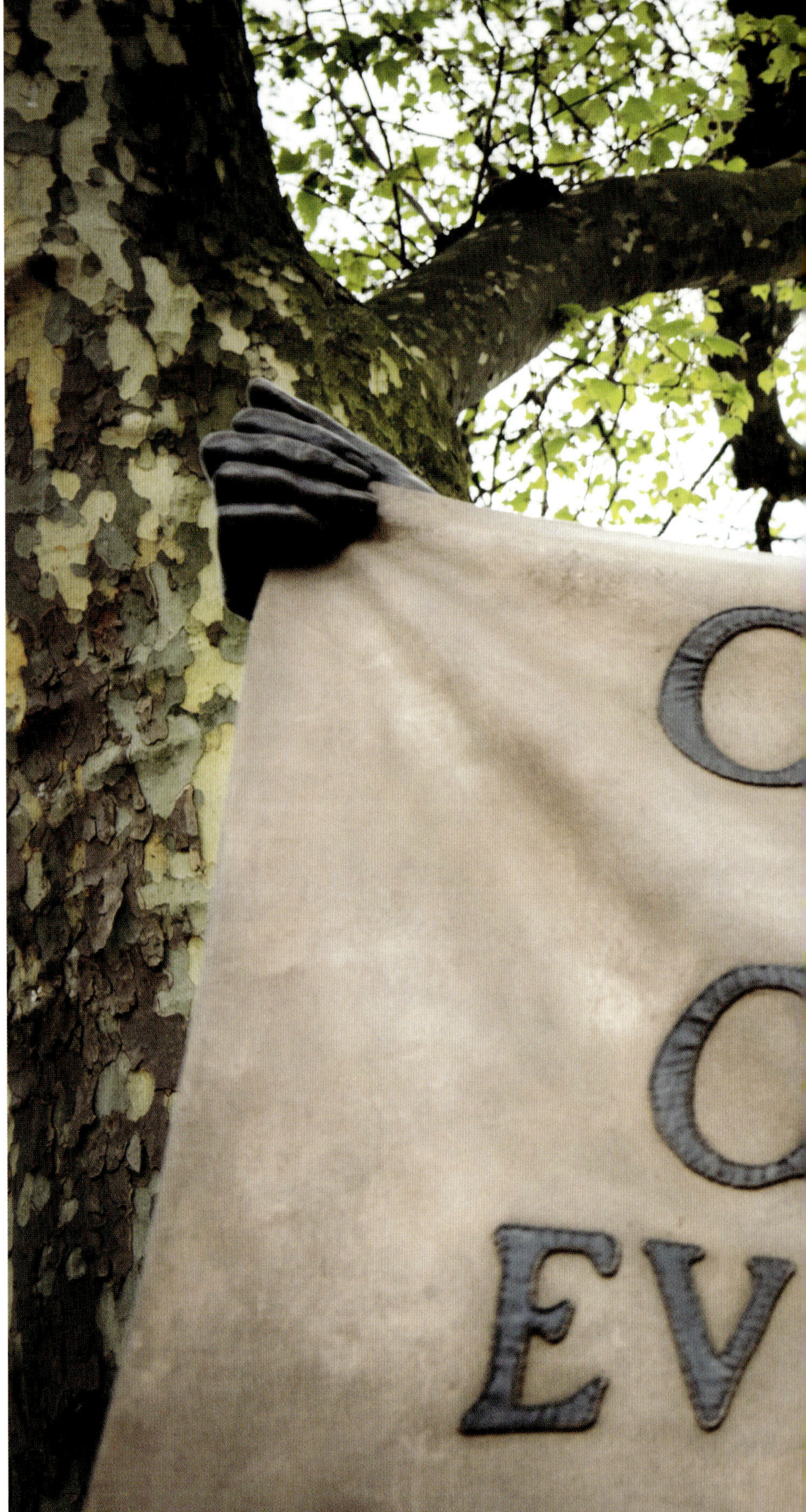

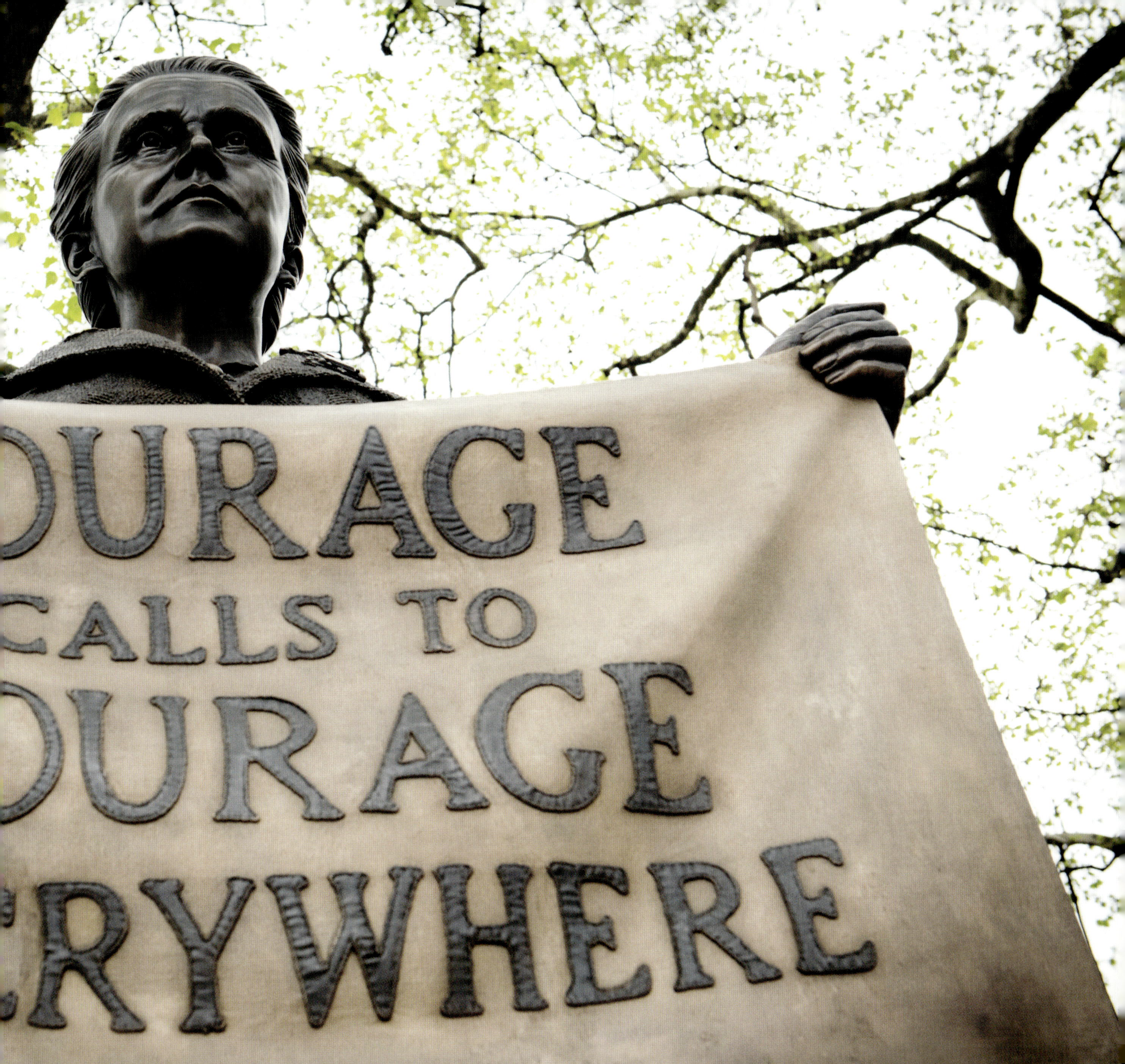
COURAGE
CALLS TO
COURAGE
EVERYWHERE

This page. The components
of the statue and banner were
created at the AB Fine Art
Foundry in East London.

Previous page and opposite.
The finished bronze statue
on its plinth in Parliament
Square, with etched tiles
featuring the portraits of
other key players in the fight
for suffrage.

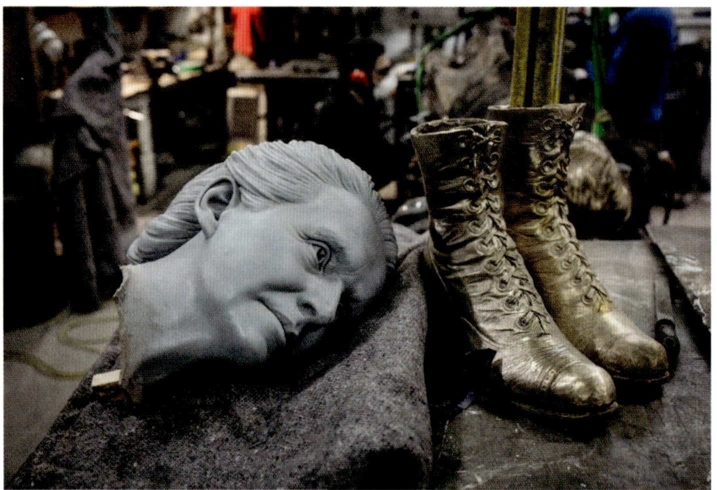

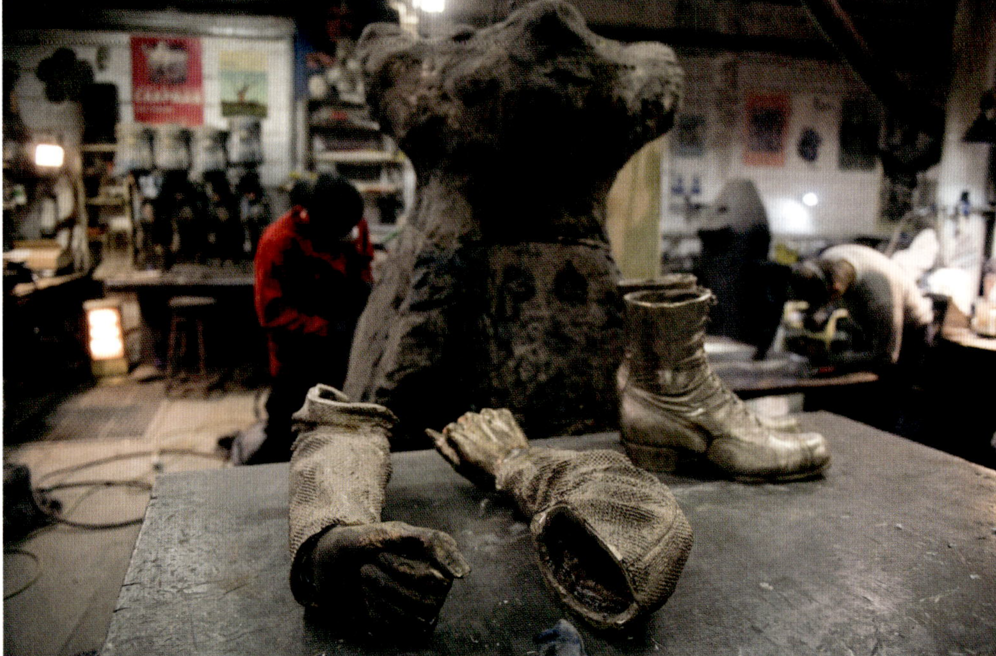

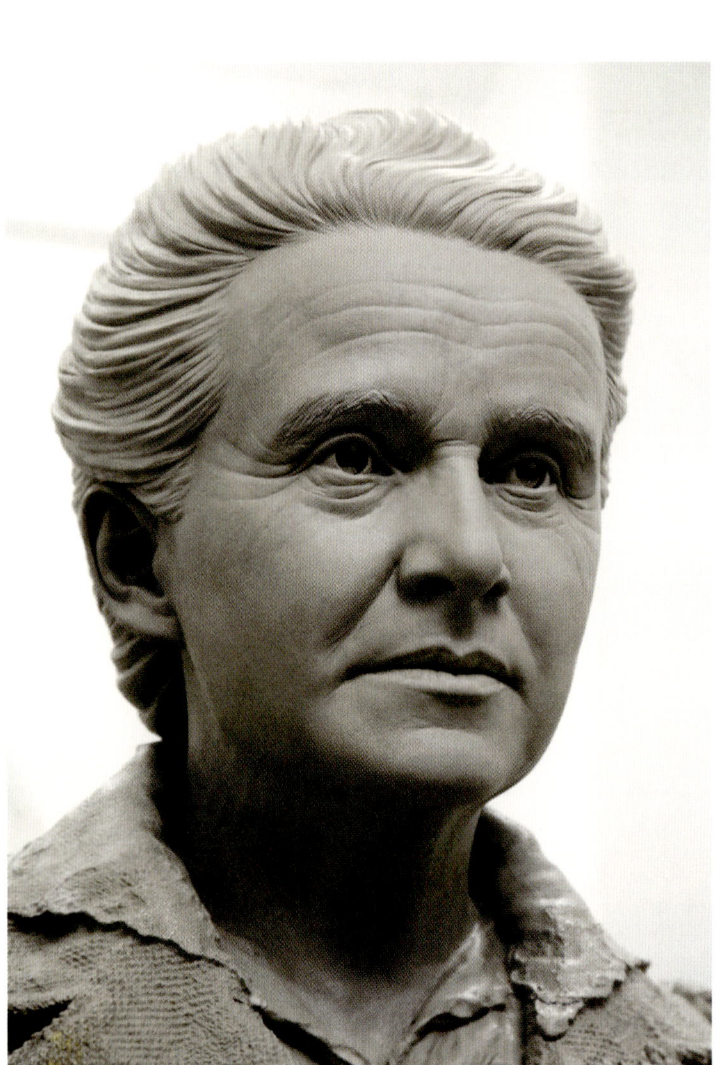

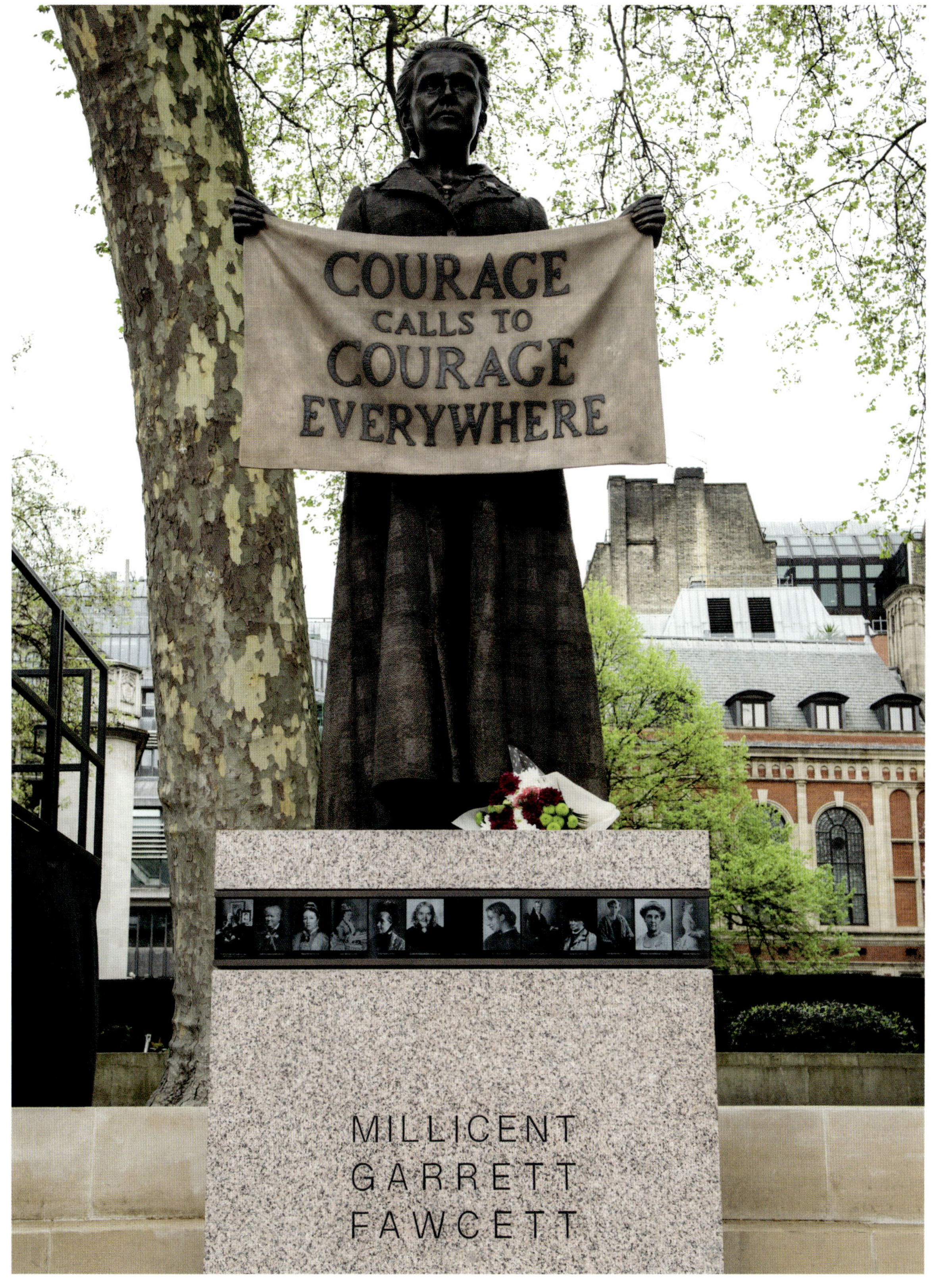

'*Women, your country needs you … Let us show ourselves worthy of citizenship, whether our claim to it be recognised or not.*'

Millicent Fawcett, *The Common Cause*,
14 August 1914

*The ambition of PROCESSIONS was
to create a single unifying moment of
celebration and commemoration, when
communities could take to the streets
creating a glorious portrait of women*
and girls in the 21st century ...
The voices that had sounded so loudly
in that first joyful victory in 1918 rang
out again as the continuing campaign
for women's equality resounded
through the streets 100 years later.*

WOMEN MAKING HISTORY

Helen Marriage

'Let us go then, and make banners … and let them all be beautiful!' The words of artist and women's suffrage campaigner Mary Lowndes echo across the years since the first campaigning women from Britain and Ireland took to the streets to fight for equality and their right to vote. *PROCESSIONS* was inspired by the actions of these ancestors — women in long skirts and hats who stare out from the pages of history books, glaring defiantly at their opponents, but also glaring at us — daring their descendants to emulate their courage as we struggle for the causes we hold dear today.

Creative director Darrell Vydelingum suggested the idea of recreating one of the huge processions organised by the early women's movement at the turn of the century. In 1908, over 350,000 people from across the country turned out to march from Hyde Park to Kensington in the gathering campaign for universal suffrage. We imagined a single day of mass action across the four political capitals — Belfast, Cardiff, Edinburgh and London. For maximum impact this was to be preceded by months of painstaking work by groups in cities, towns and villages nationwide, coming together to create hand-stitched artworks expressing the hopes, fears, aspirations and arguments of the many diverse communities taking part.

A visit to the Women's Library, currently housed at the London School of Economics, to see the collection of suffragist and suffragette banners from that time, cemented our idea that a nationwide initiative to revive the old skills of banner-making amongst women* and girls would lie at the heart of our project. Text and textiles have often been central to women's protest — a way of saying on the outside what is felt on the inside by those with no real voice in society. Even today, women's voices are rarely heard in the boardroom or the corridors of power, while those in marginalised communities are even less audible.

Each of our 100 commissioned groups worked with a woman artist, engaged specifically to help the group realise their wildest ambitions. As each group stitched and sewed, they talked and learnt. For many it was the first opportunity to think about their own voice in the political process; for others it was a chance to learn about the courage of those women who had fought for their right to vote. For most, it was the first time they had signed up to be part of a major contemporary artwork. Individually and collectively they created an extraordinary series of banners that led the processions in each city, held high by women fired up by their own creative imagination and the realisation that their voices would be heard.

The ambition of *PROCESSIONS* was to create a single unifying moment of celebration and commemoration, when communities could take to the streets creating a glorious portrait of women* and girls in the 21st century. Wearing scarves of green, white and violet, tens of thousands gathered on 10 June 2018 in the four political capitals in huge streaming processions representing a vast unfurling of the suffragette flag. The voices that had sounded so loudly in that first joyful victory in 1918 rang out again as the continuing campaign for women's equality resounded through the streets 100 years later.

Those who came together to honour the sacrifices and achievements of the past showed that these moments of commemoration also offer an occasion to reflect on our present situation, and an opportunity to imagine the kind of world we'd like to build for those who follow on behind us.

Those identifying as women and non-binary

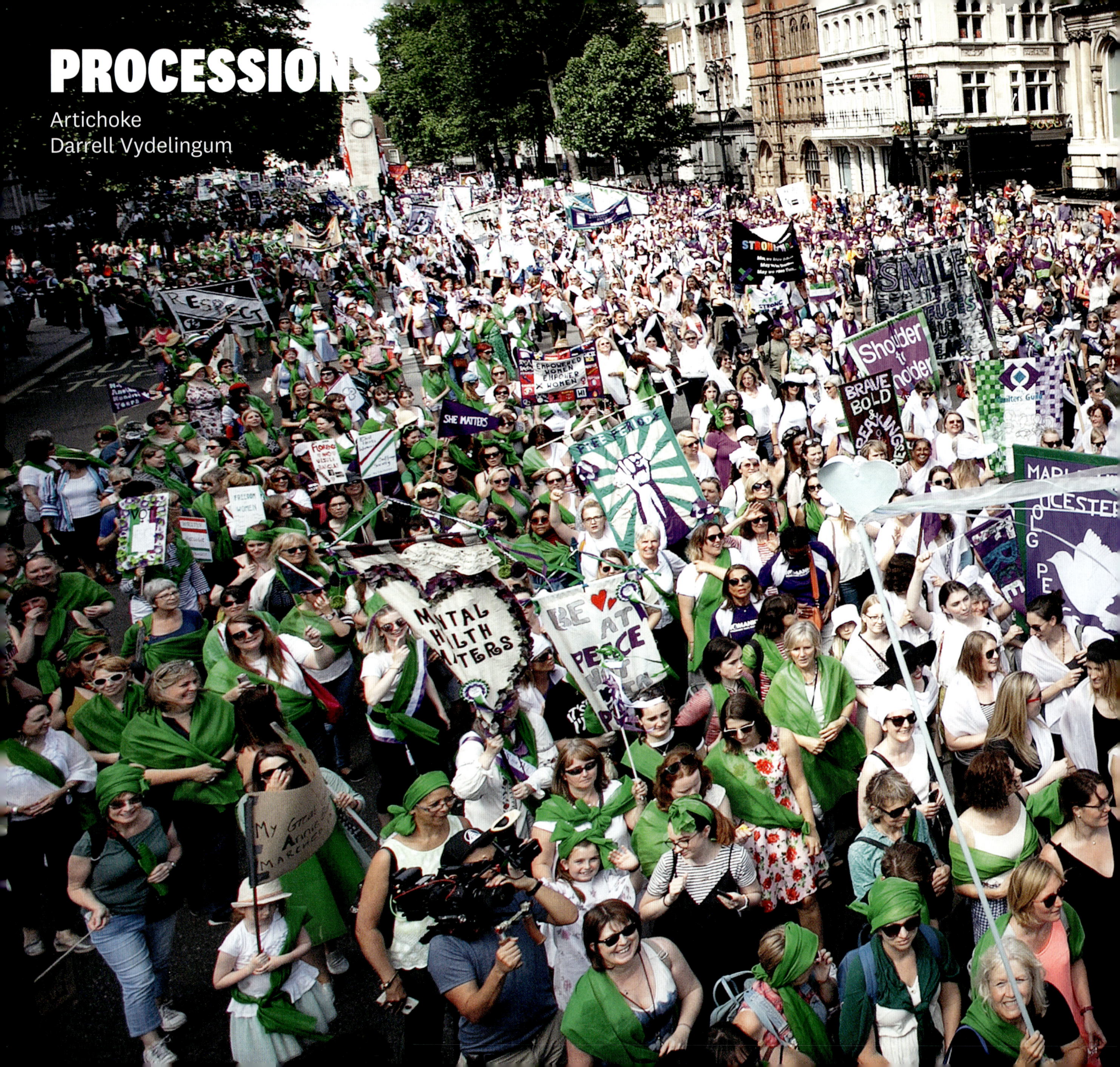

PROCESSIONS
Artichoke
Darrell Vydelingum

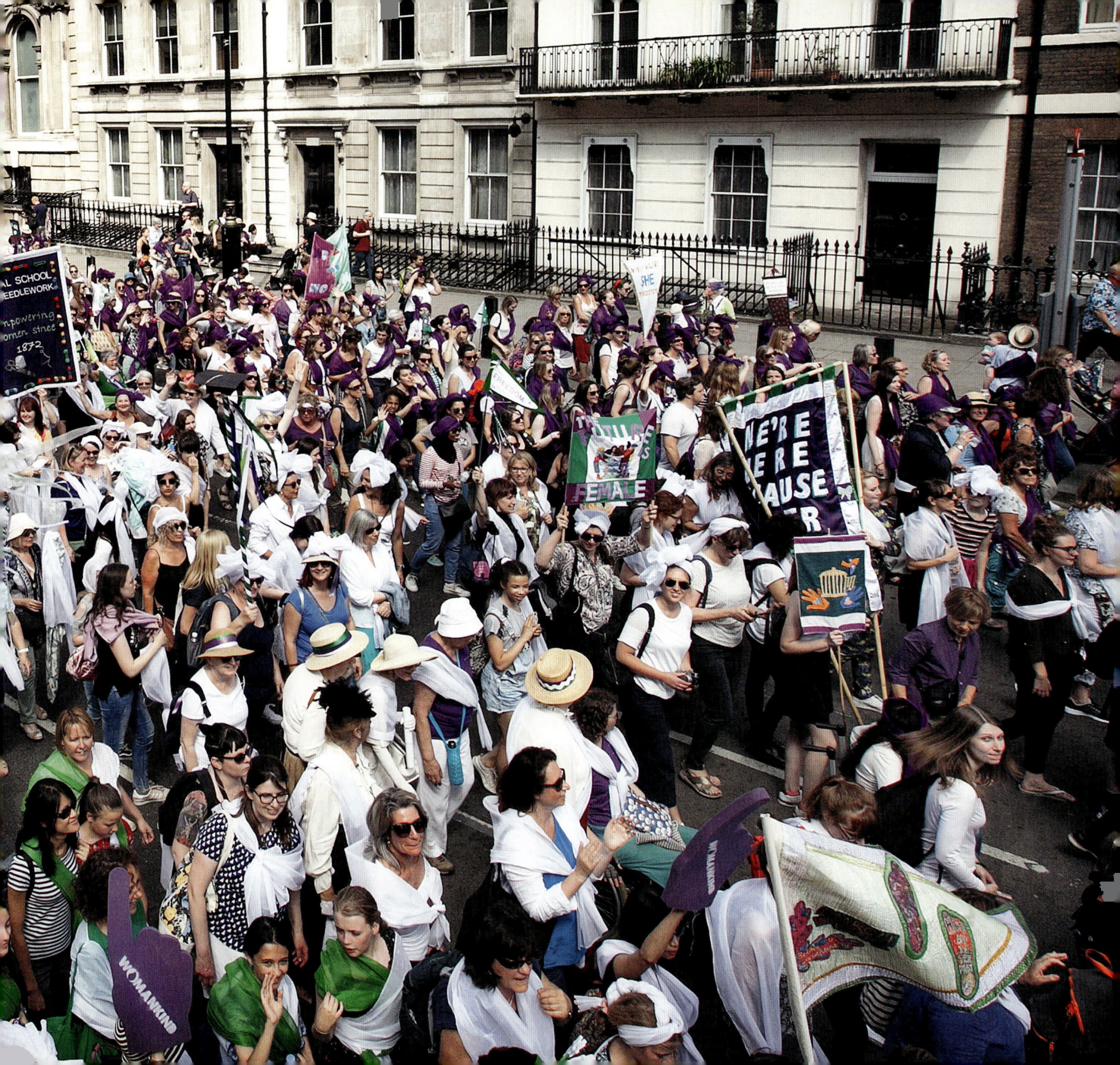

AL SCHOOL
EEDLEWORK
npowering
omen since
1872
FEMALE
WE'RE
ERE
AUSE
WOMANKIND

On Sunday 10 June 2018, to mark the 100th anniversary
of women's suffrage in the UK, the streets of its four
political capitals — Belfast, Cardiff, Edinburgh and
London — were filled with colour as tens of thousands
of women and girls took part in *PROCESSIONS*, an
extraordinary mass-participation artwork, based on
an original idea by creative director Darrell Vydelingum,
produced by public art specialists Artichoke and
commissioned by 14-18 NOW.

Participants were given scarves to wear in one
of the three iconic suffragette colours — green, white
and violet — and were choreographed to walk together
through the streets, creating the effect of a vast,
living suffragette flag unfurling across the four cities.
The routes concluded with each procession walking
underneath an arch that read 'My Vote Really Makes
a Difference'.

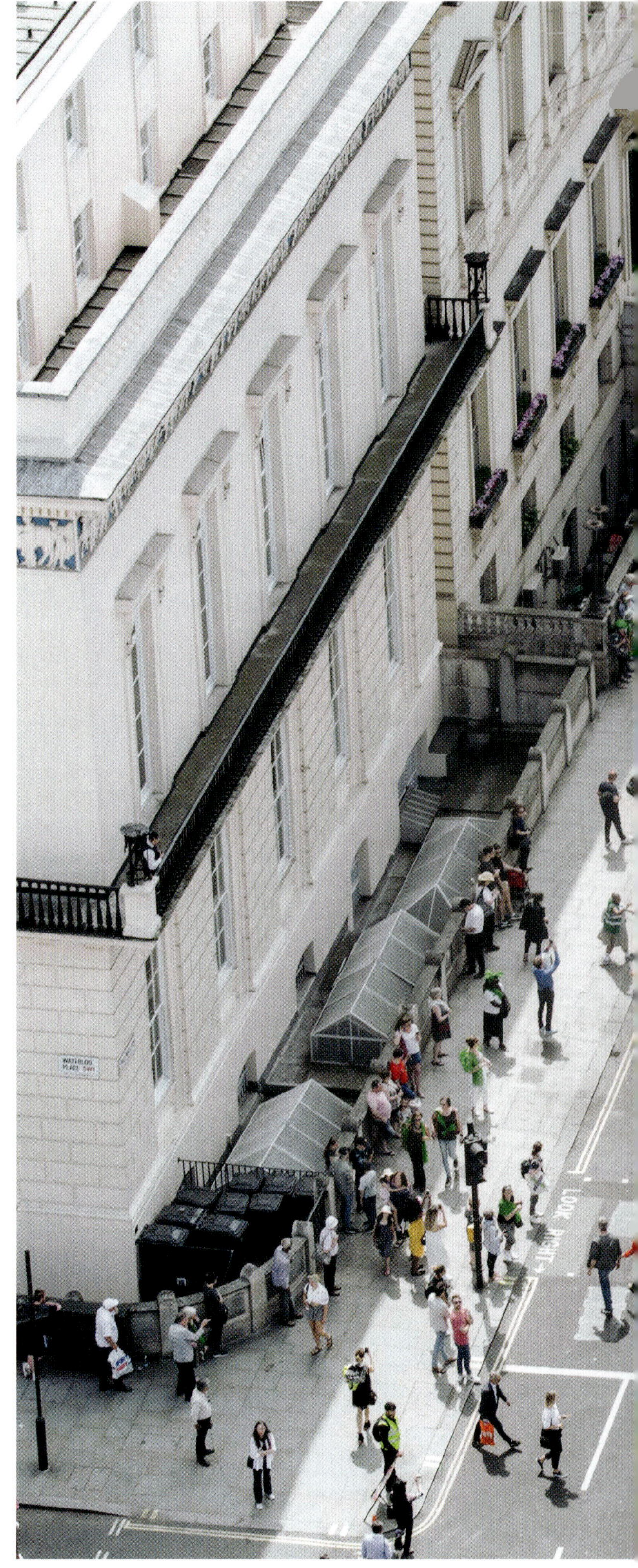

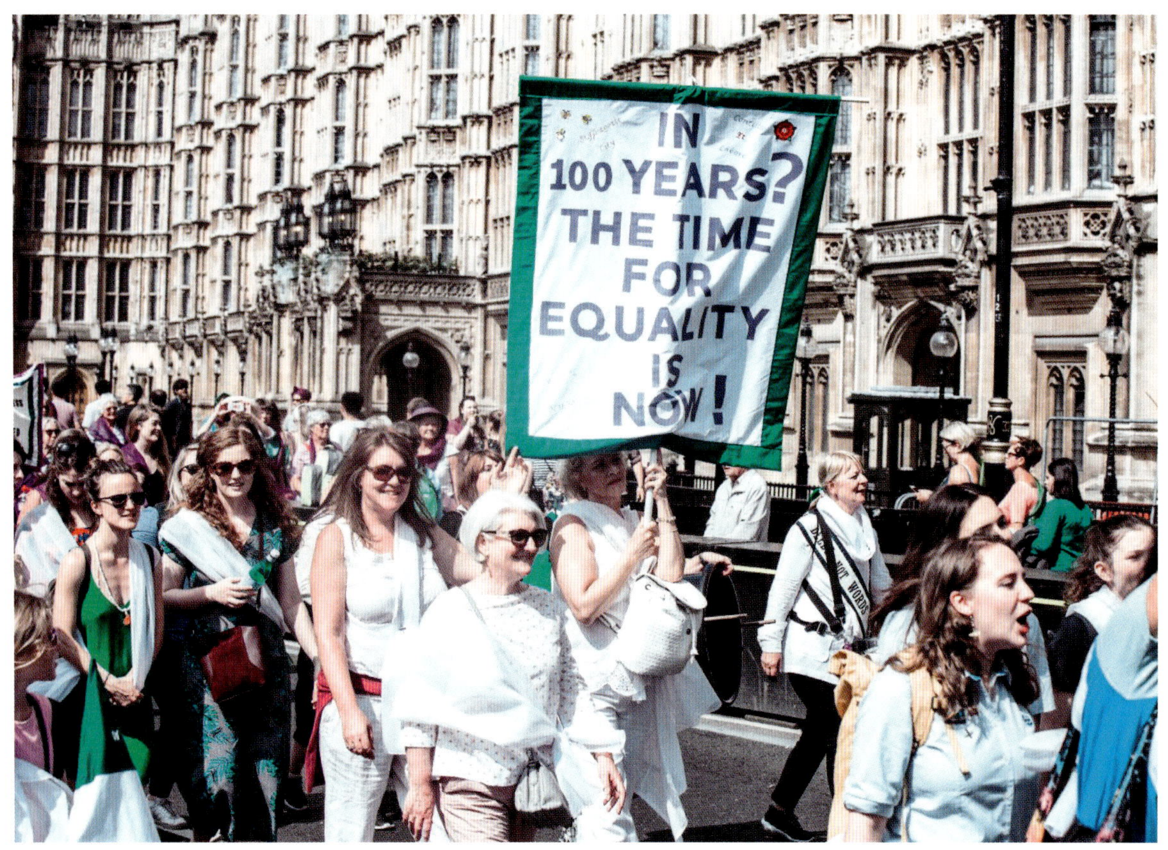

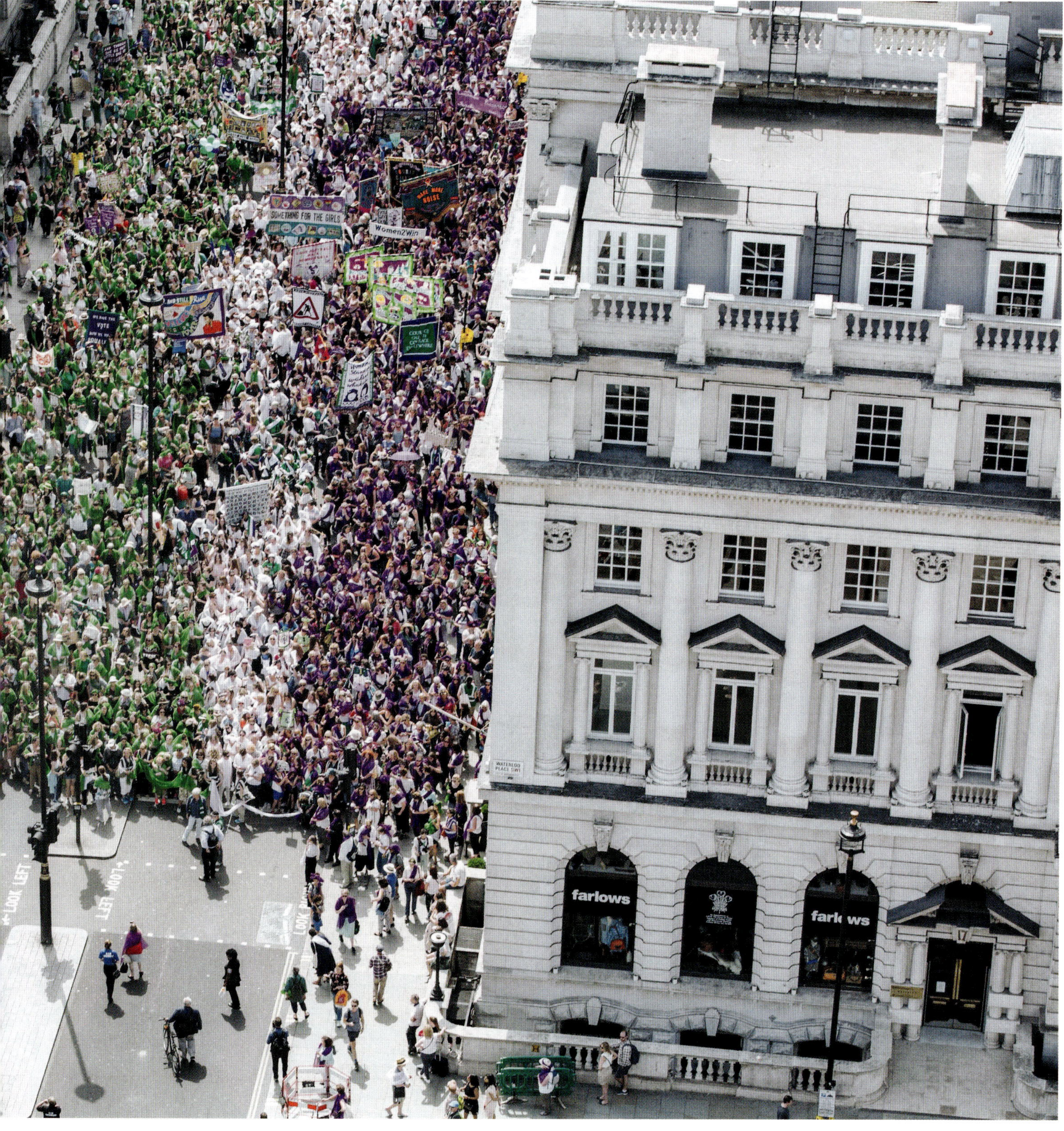

PROCESSIONS took to the streets to celebrate the profound changes achieved by and for women 100 years ago, and to highlight the continued need for equality.

The organisers worked with Clare Hunter, community textile artist, banner-maker and writer, who developed a toolkit based on an original 1909 guide to banner-making written by Mary Lowndes, founding member of the Artists' Suffrage League. Hunter's toolkit provided inspiration, guidance and practical instructions for individuals and groups involved in the parades to create their own banners. One hundred women artists were also commissioned to work with communities across the UK to create 100 centenary banners for *PROCESSIONS*, including one made by a group of inmates at Holloway prison, where many of the original suffragettes served time.

PROCESSIONS was a lively, positive and emotional celebration of an important centenary for human rights in the UK. Participants from all walks of life sang and danced along the routes. For those who took part and those who saw it, it was a reminder of the ways in which women came together on the streets a century ago to make themselves and their message visible with handmade flags, banners, pins and rosettes. The 2018 banners represented and celebrated the diverse voices of the women and girls who took part. They also carried messages of commemoration for the women of 1918 and for the work still to be done for the future of female empowerment.

The event was broadcast live on BBC One and shared across the globe on social media.

Belfast, Cardiff, Edinburgh and London,
10 June 2018 / BBC One

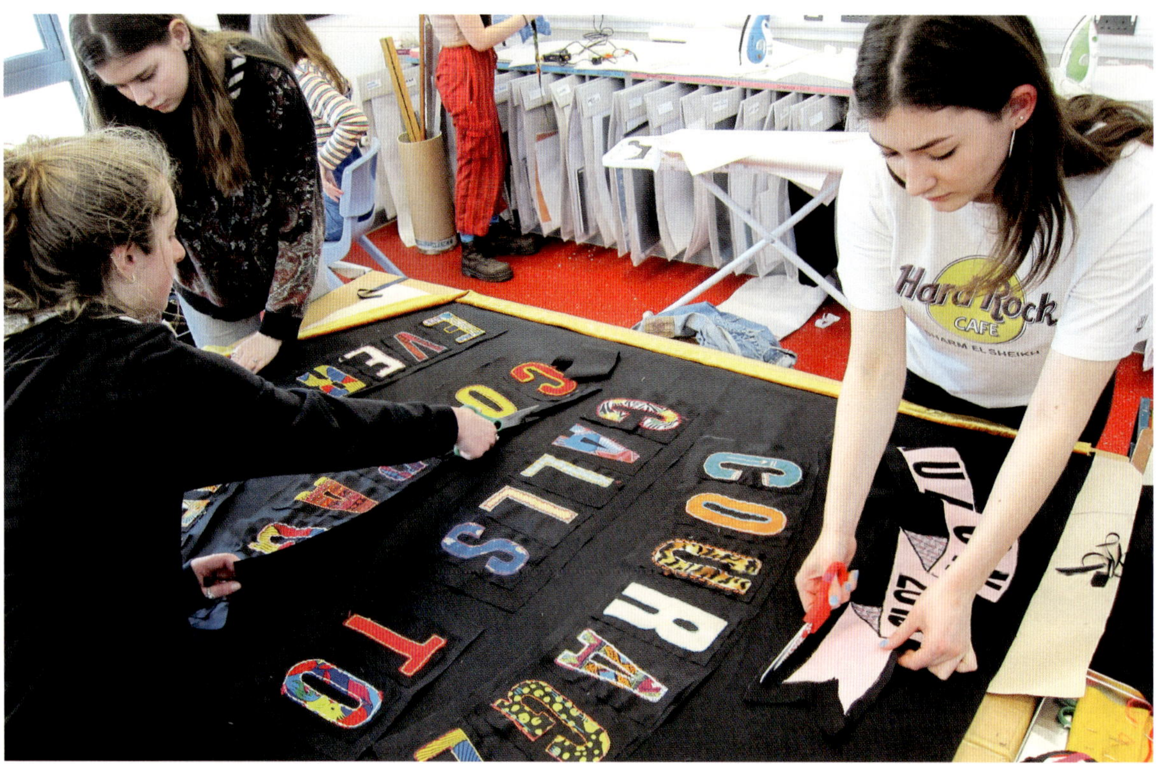

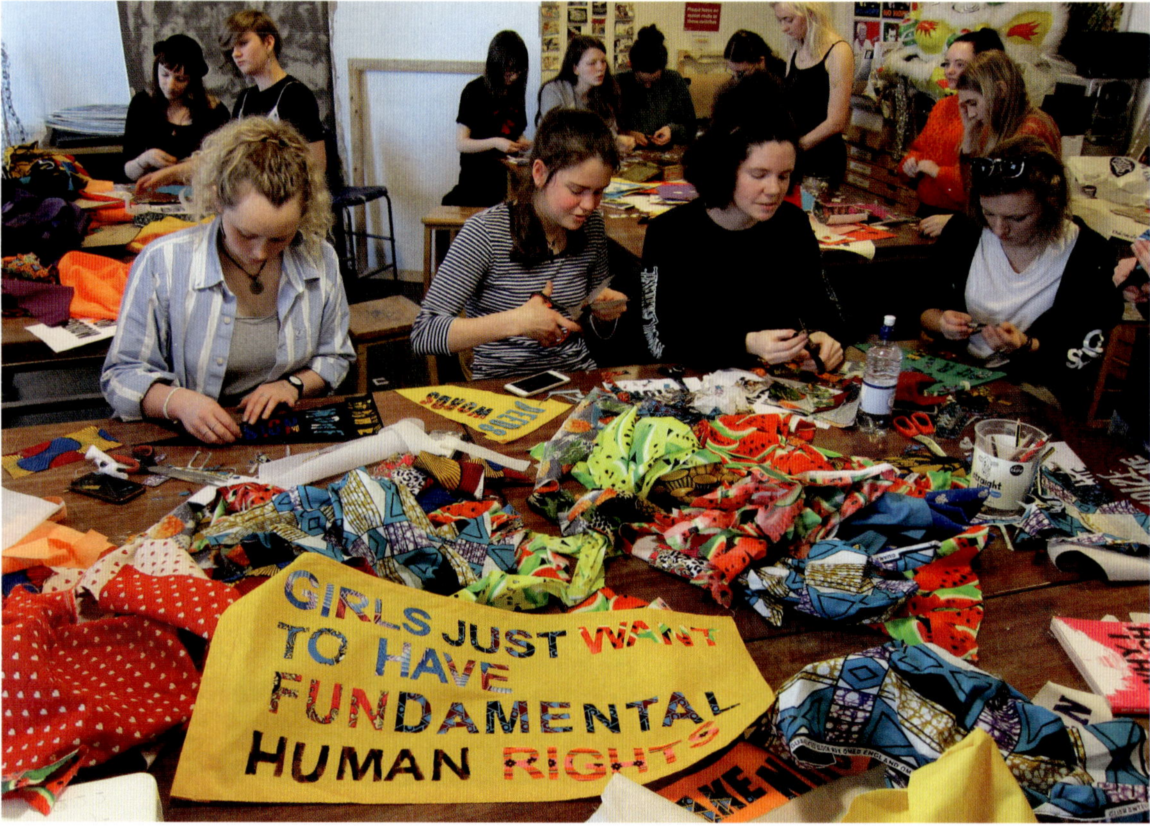

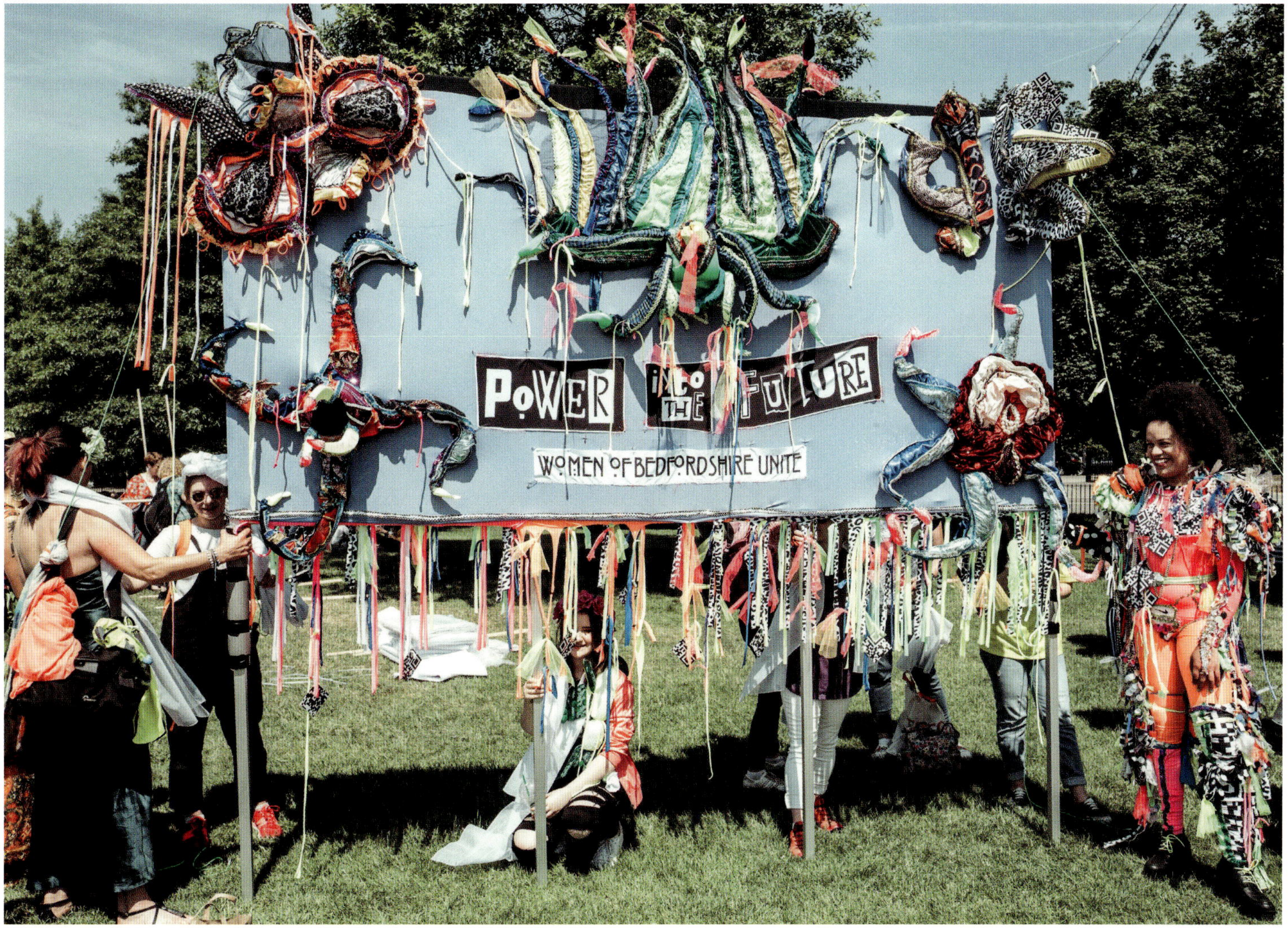

Cloth banners embroidered and appliqued with tributes, images and decorations were a reminder of the handmade banners made by the first generation of women's suffrage campaigners as well as an expression of the hopes and concerns of women today.

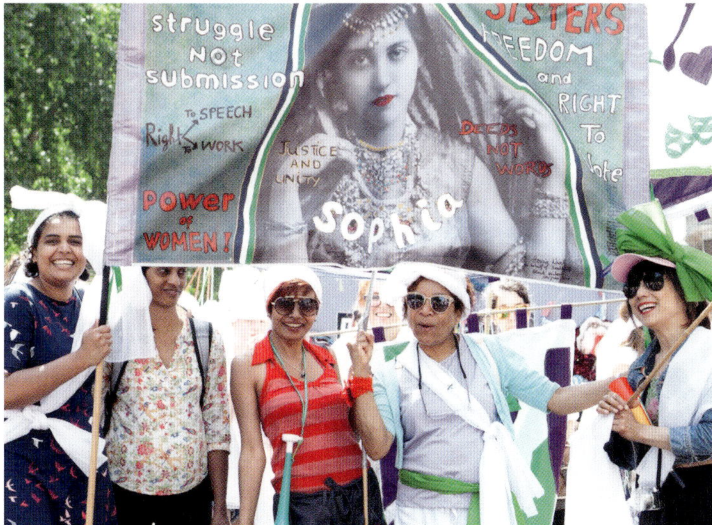

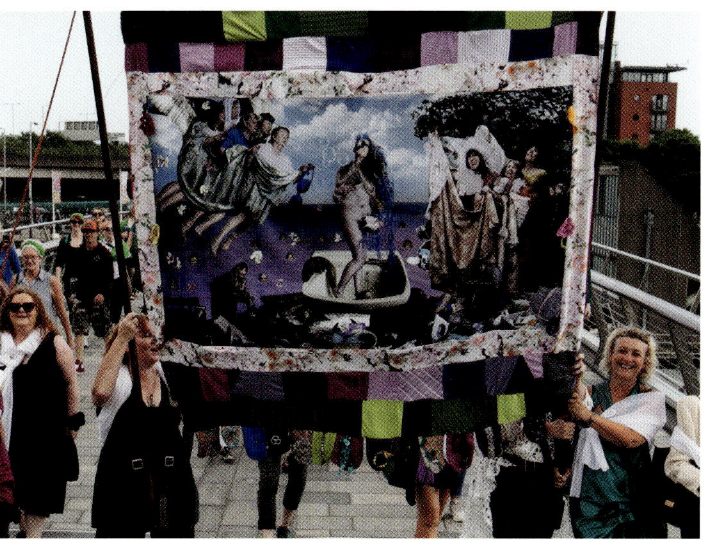

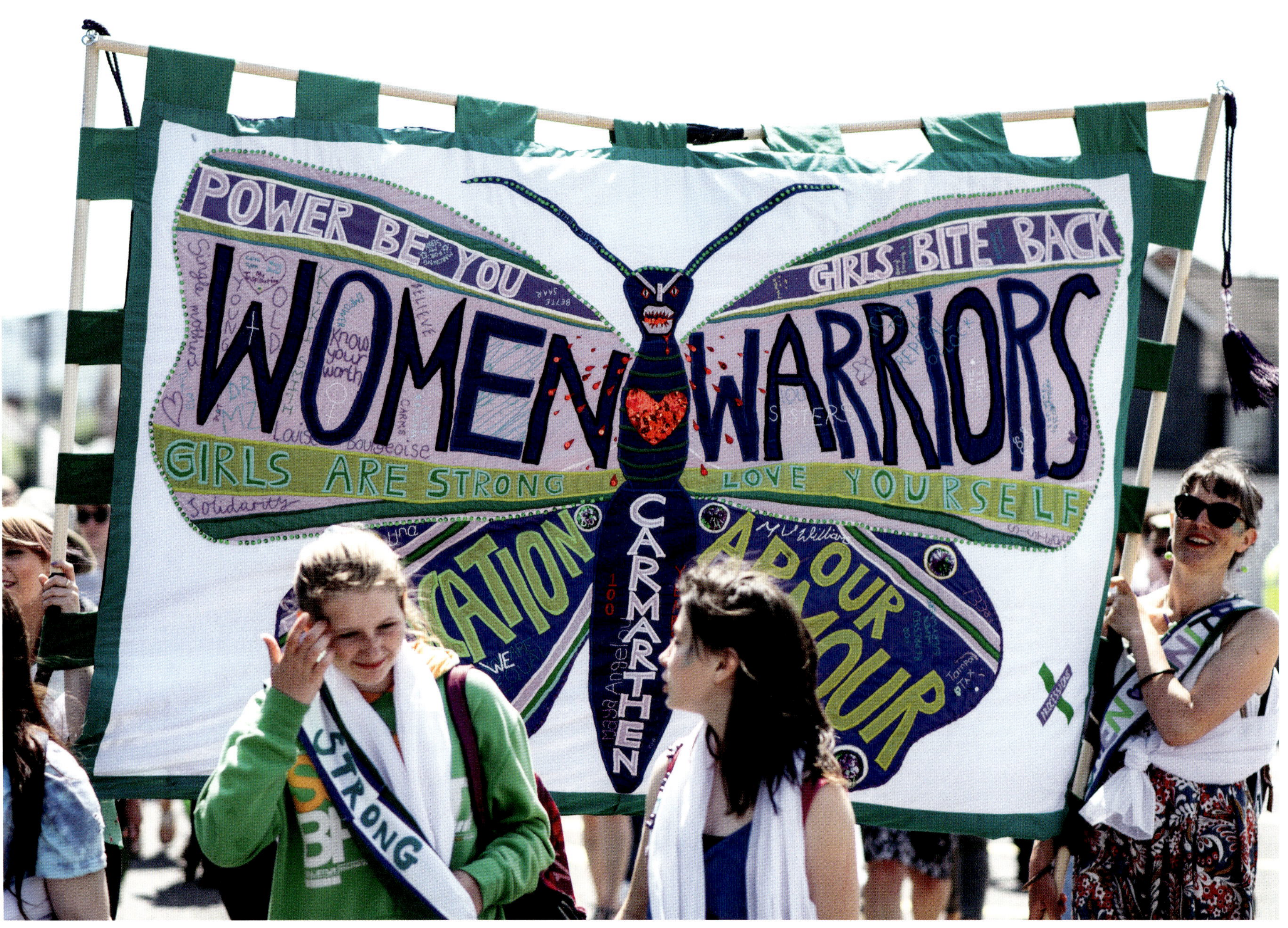
POWER BE YOU
GIRLS BITE BACK
WOMEN WARRIORS
GIRLS ARE STRONG
LOVE YOURSELF
know your worth
Solidarity
CARMARTHEN
STRONG

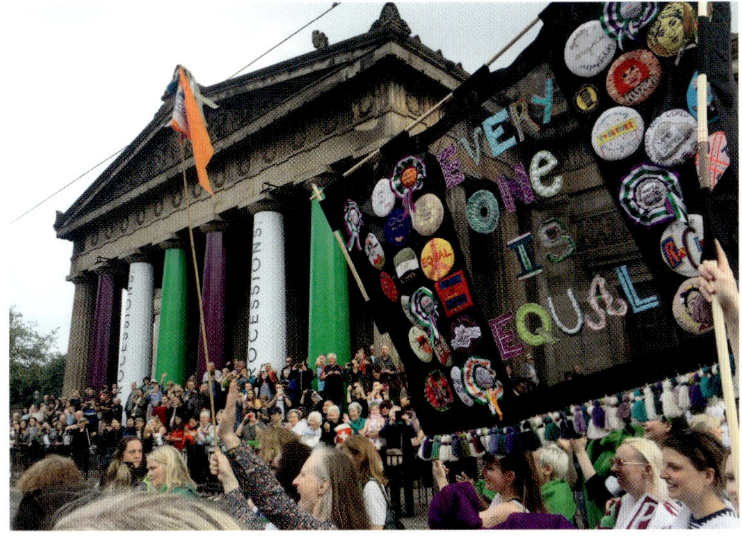

Banners were produced in support of a huge range of different groups and interests across the United Kingdom, yet all participants came together as a 'moving flag' that united diverse communities and age groups in a common cause.

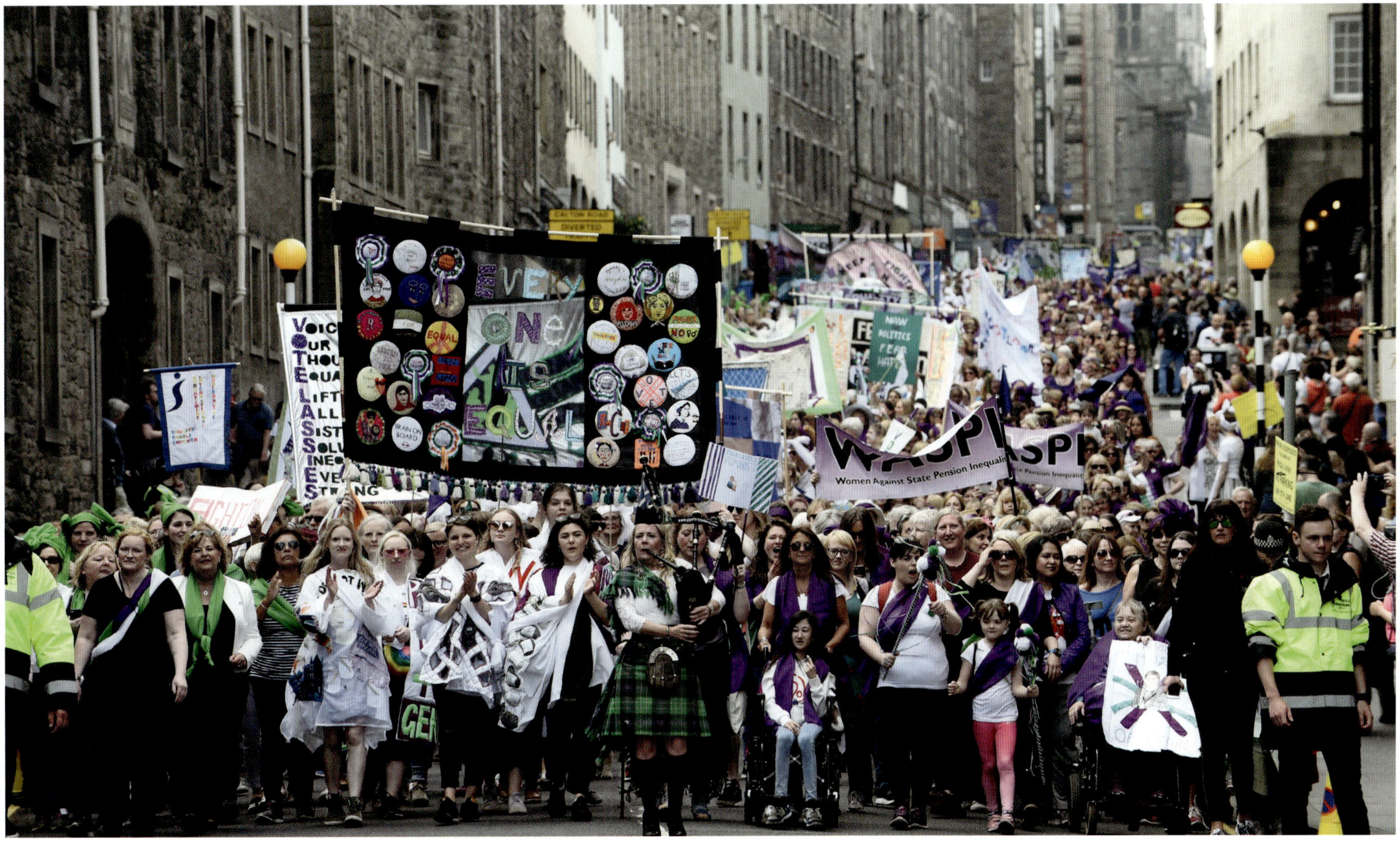

HARLEM HELLFIGHTERS: JAMES REESE EUROPE AND THE ABSENCE OF RUIN

John Akomfrah
Jason Moran
Bradford Young

On New Year's Day 1918, James Reese Europe — an iconic figure in the evolution of African-American music — landed in Brest with the US 369th Infantry Regiment, known as the 'Harlem Hellfighters'. As well as their achievements in combat, Europe's crack military music ensemble popularised the new spirit of jazz to a war-torn French nation fascinated with black culture. And this is but the beginning of a story that continues to fascinate and intrigue.

A century later, composer, pianist and visual artist Jason Moran — himself a major and innovative force in today's jazz world — celebrated the legacy of a hero of black music, in a multi-dimensional reflection on the impact of the African-American presence in Europe in the closing years of the First World War, and its resonance both in Europe and in the United States, with contributions from John Akomfrah, and visual materials from cinematographer Bradford Young. The Harlem Hellfighters story provided the genesis of the extraordinary impact of African-American music on Europe and the Americas, and a century of profound cultural and political change that is still evolving.

Barbican, London, 30 October 2018 / Cardiff Royal Welsh College of Music & Drama, 31 October 2018 / Berliner Festspiele, Germany, 3 November 2018 / Paisley Arts Centre, Scotland, 4 November 2018 / Kennedy Center for the Performing Arts, Washington, D.C., 8 December 2018

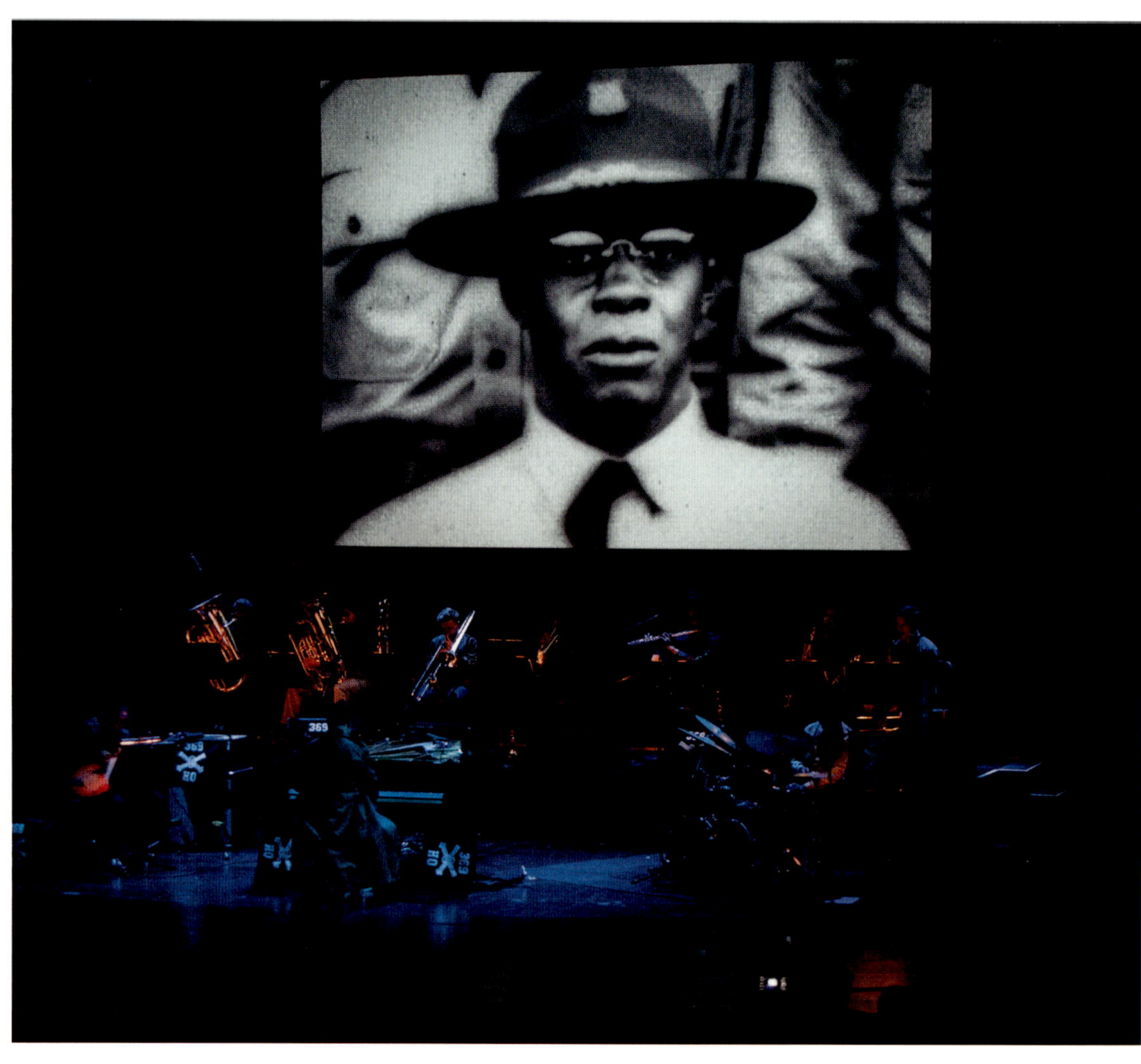

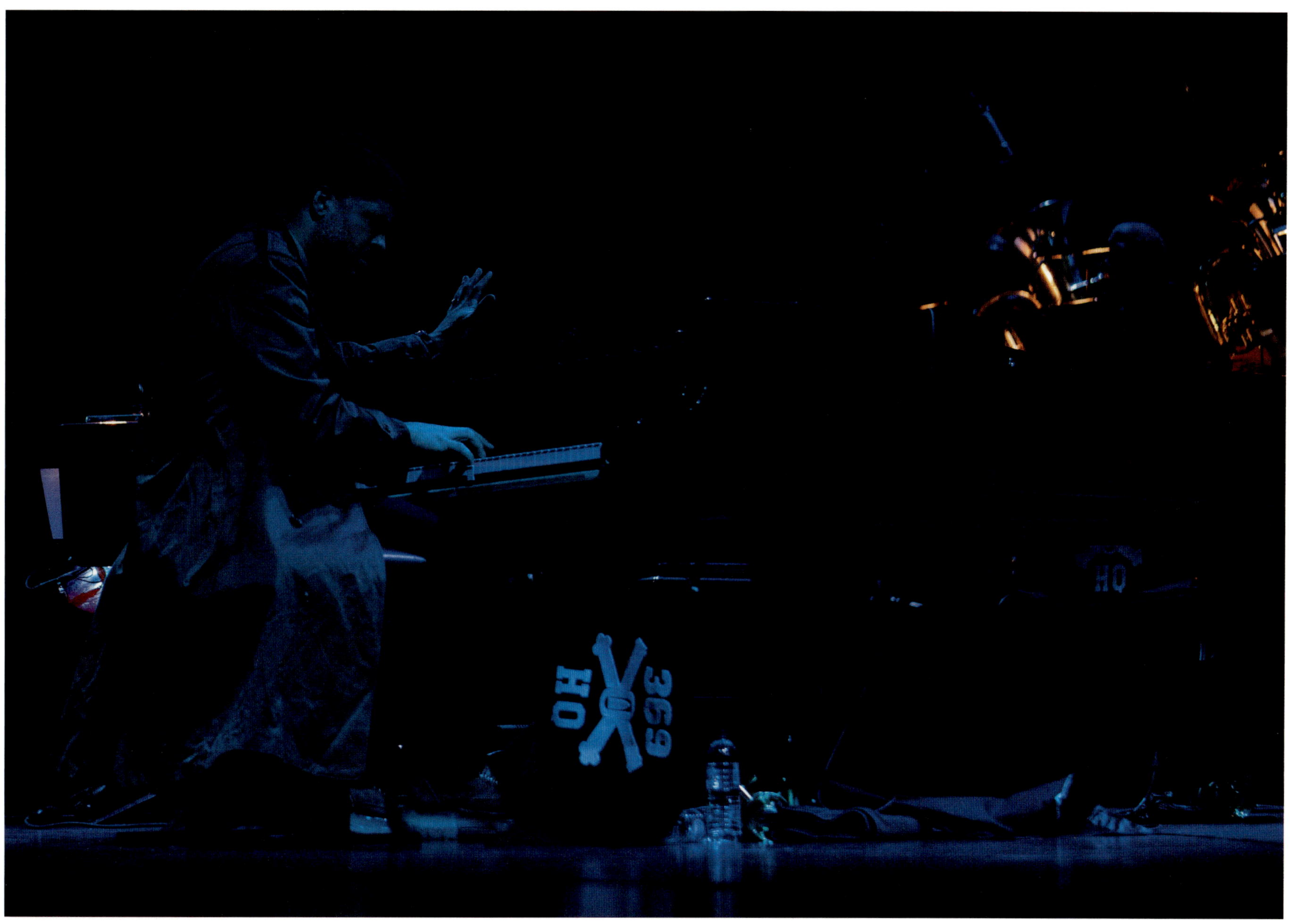

Jason Moran leading his trio The Bandwagon (bassist Tarus Mateen and drummer Nasheet Waits), along with seven other musicians, with the image of James Reese Europe projected behind them.

CLARION CALL

Hannah Fox
Byron J. Scullin
Tom Supple

Over the 11 days of Ipswich's SPILL Festival of Performance, a large-scale outdoor sonic artwork rang out from the waterfront into the town's public spaces. This sonic intervention called out to the setting sun in daily incantations, its voices reflecting contemporary Britain while exploring the local history of the First World War.

Devised by Melbourne-based artists Byron J. Scullin, Hannah Fox and Tom Supple, and produced by Pacitti Company, *Clarion Call* used audio technology originally employed in war and emergencies to create a soundscape of immense scale. The voices and songs of women and girls from across the community, including local schools and a military wives' choir, were projected from 500 speakers alongside the voices of Elizabeth Frazier (Cocteau Twins) and Beth Gibbons (Portishead).

The song at the heart of *Clarion Call* was Shirley Collins' interpretation of 'Our Captain Cried All Hands', a piece that relates to women's experiences and the maritime aspects of war, particularly fitting for the Ipswich Waterfront setting.

Ipswich Waterfront, 25 October — 4 November 2018

Audiences gathered at Ipswich waterfront every sunset over the 11 days of SPILL, to hear the sonic artwork of over 100 female voices.

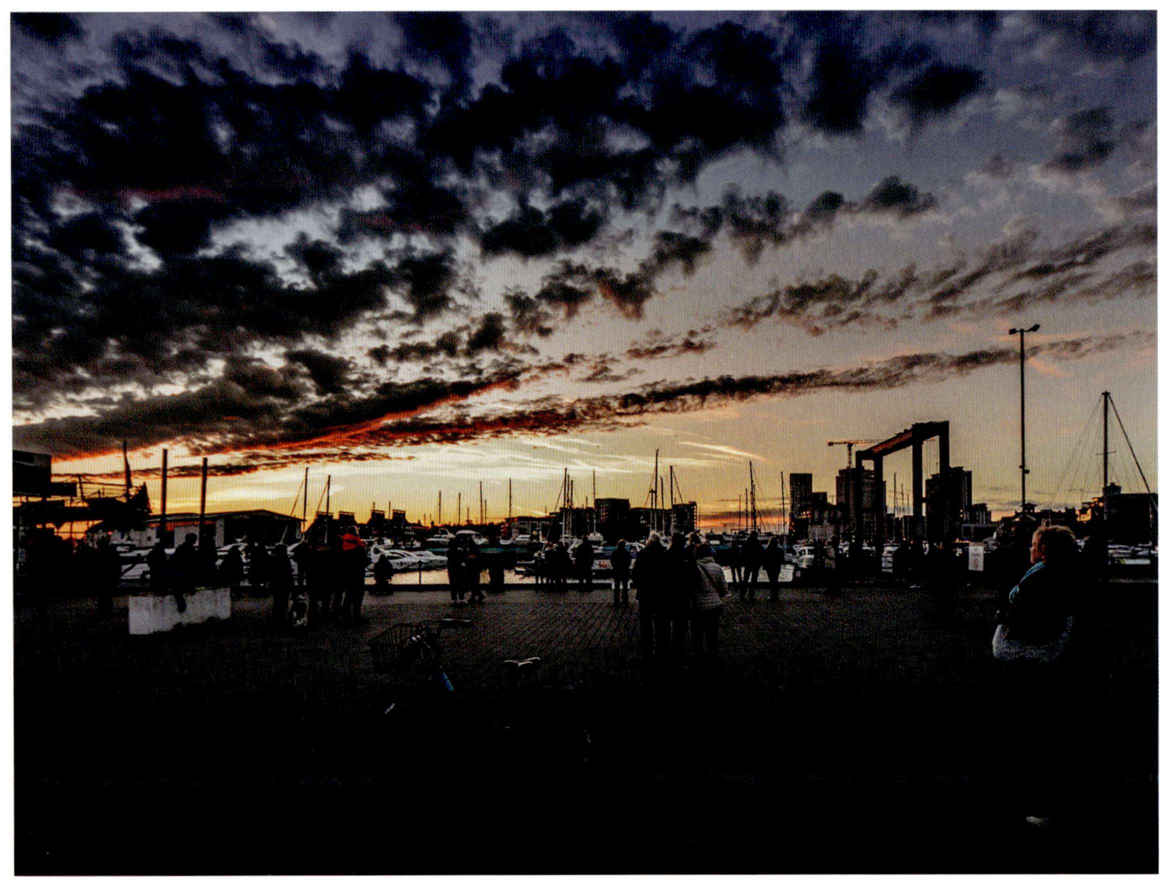

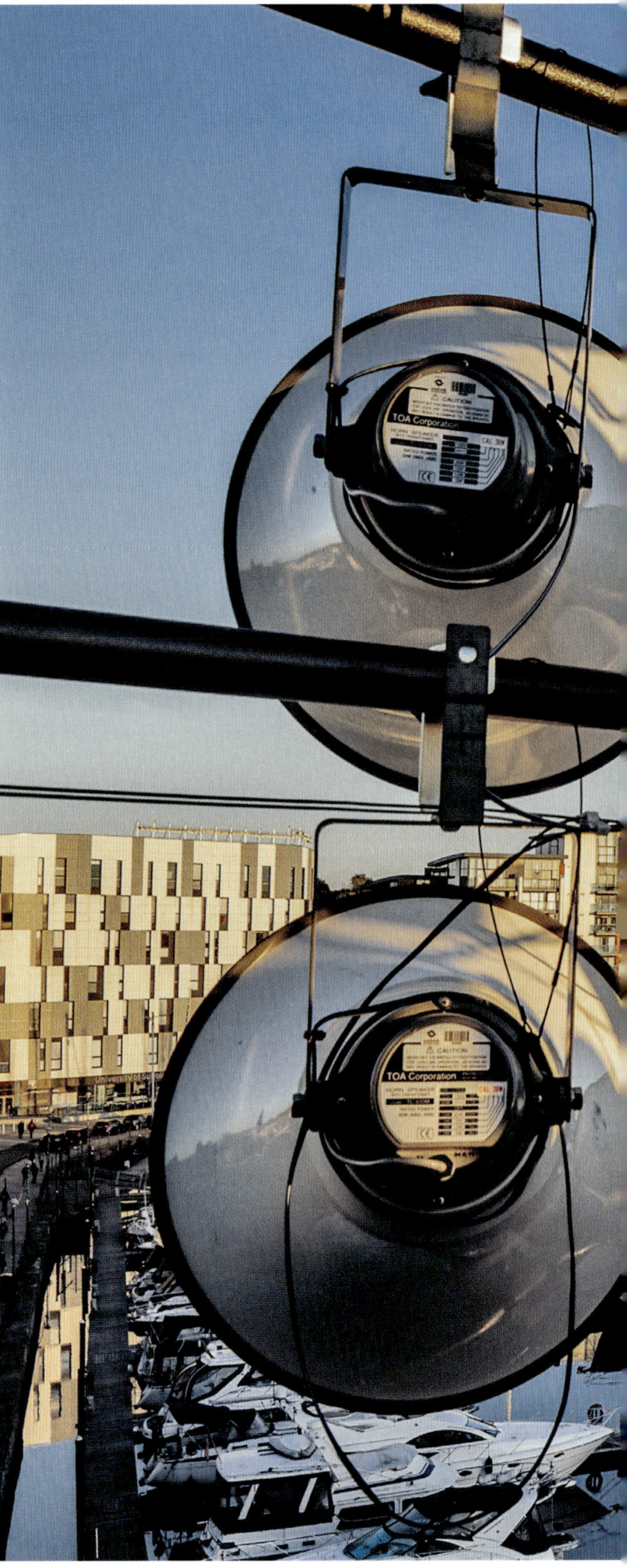

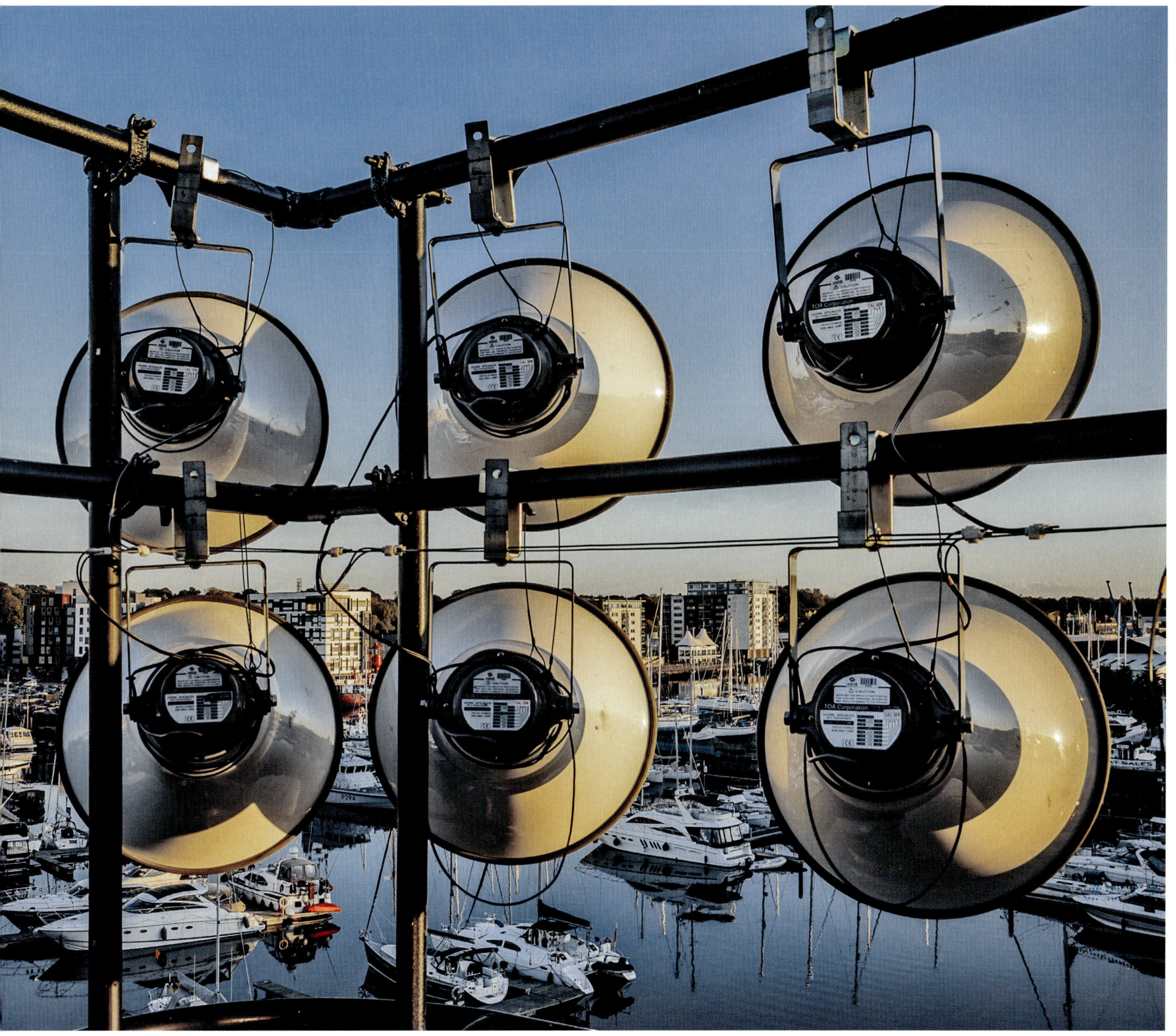

CAUSE AND EFFECT

Akala
Awate
Gaika
Nabihah Iqbal
Lowkey
Hollie McNish
Bridget Minamore
Amy True

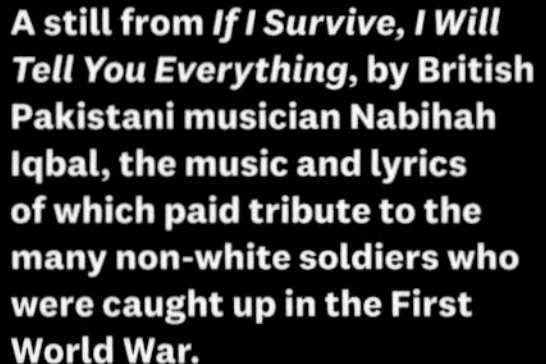

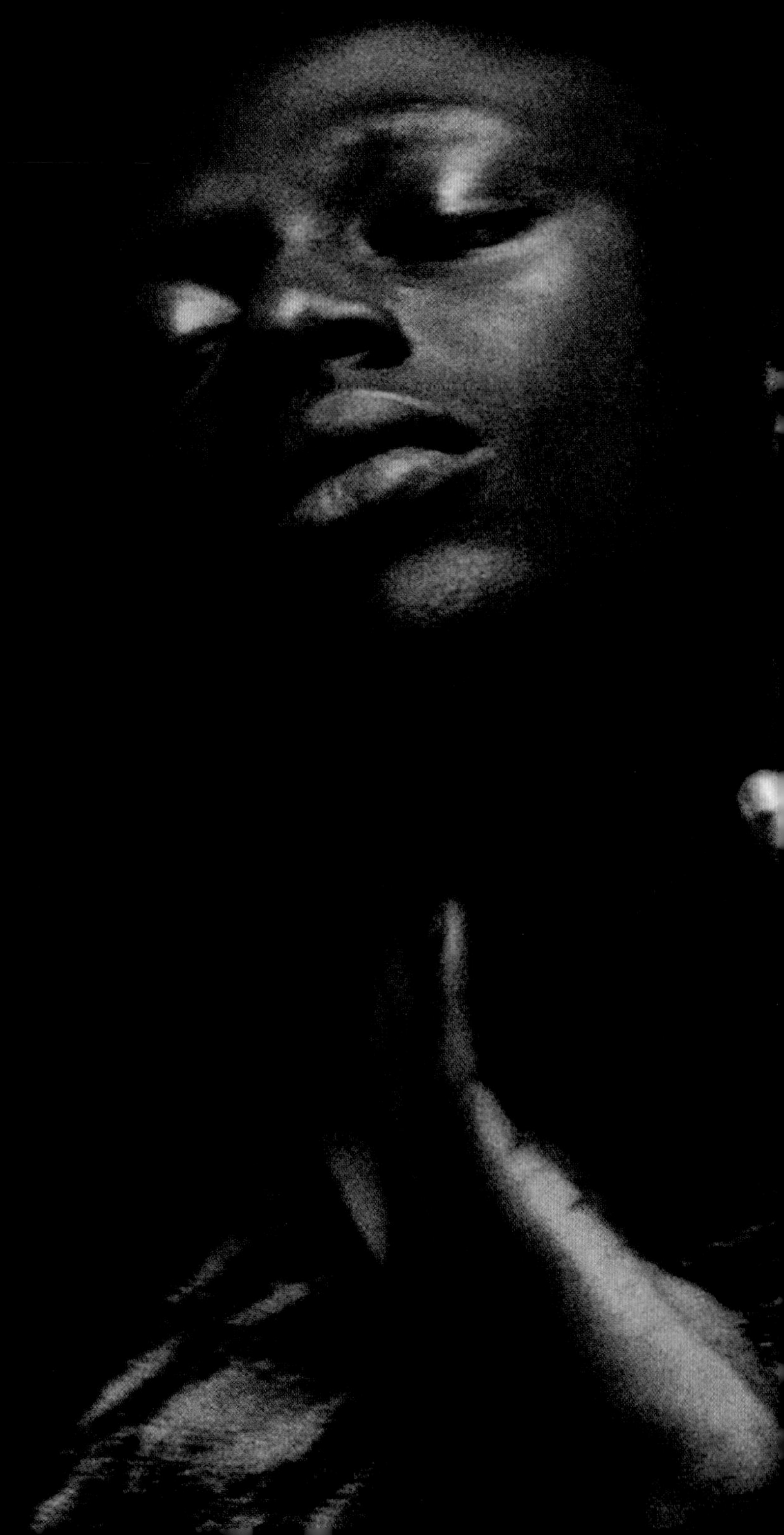

A still from *If I Survive, I Will Tell You Everything*, by British Pakistani musician Nabihah Iqbal, the music and lyrics of which paid tribute to the many non-white soldiers who were caught up in the First World War.

A digital project bringing together some of the UK's most exciting new and emerging music and spoken-word artists, *Cause and Effect* investigated the complex, fractured relationship between the First World War and young people in Britain today.

One hundred years after its final salvos, the First World War can sometimes feel like ancient history — a distant, grainy event with little relevance to our contemporary world. And yet there are countless connections to be drawn between then and now: between the post-war growth in women's rights and today's continuing fight for gender equality; between the rise of the labour movement in the 1920s and the struggle for workers' rights in the 21st-century gig economy; and even between the post-war carve-up of North Africa and the ongoing conflicts in the Middle East.

Eight leading music and spoken-word artists explored these subjects and others through a series of dynamic new digital works. Using music, spoken word and film to engage with contemporary themes that connect us with the conflict, *Cause and Effect* retraced the narrative thread that runs from 1914–18 to now.

From 25 October 2018

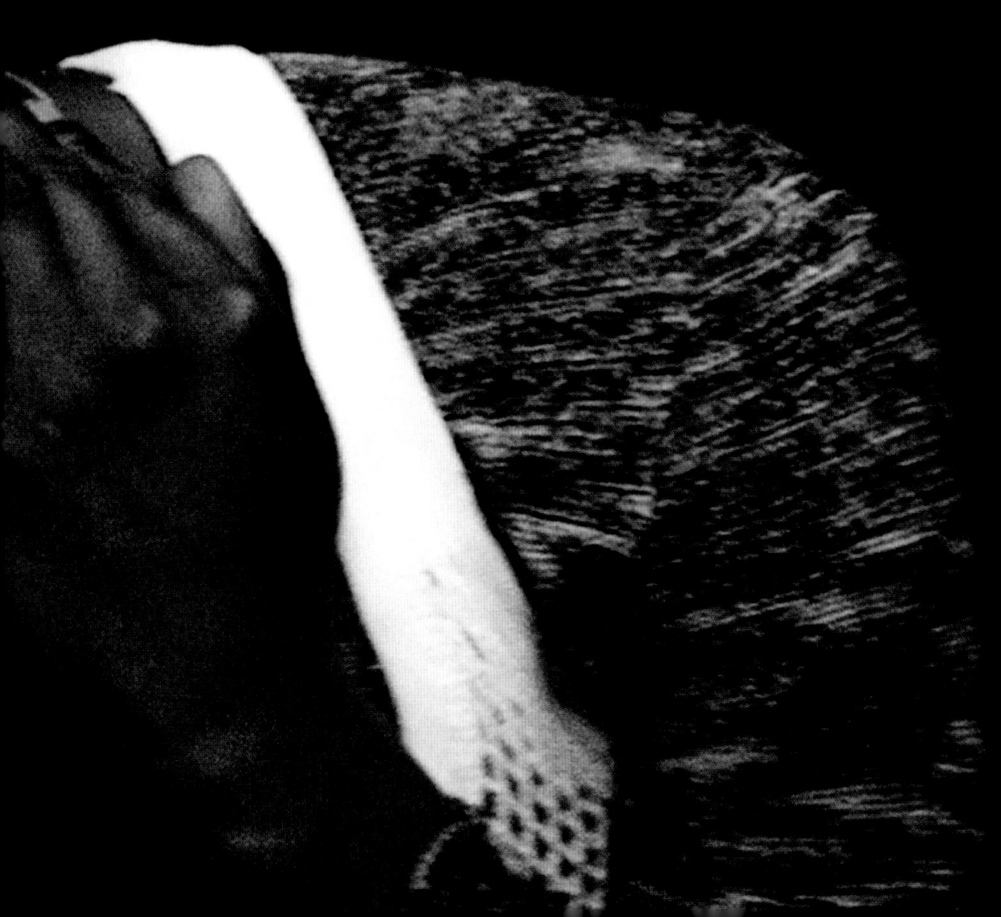

RICHARD THOMPSON

Richard Thompson has been hailed by *Rolling Stone* magazine as 'a perennial dark-horse contender for the title of greatest living rock guitarist'. He is also one of this country's greatest songwriters, capable of breathtaking drama and sublime delicacy.

For the 2014 centenary, Thompson was commissioned to write four songs reflecting the experience of the First World War. His response was to seek inspiration from wartime correspondence — letters between soldiers at the front, and their families, friends and lovers back home. The new songs were then planted as 'seeds of inspiration', scattered among his concert appearances that summer at venues throughout the country, including WOMAD and the Cambridge Folk Festival.

UK-wide tour, 2014

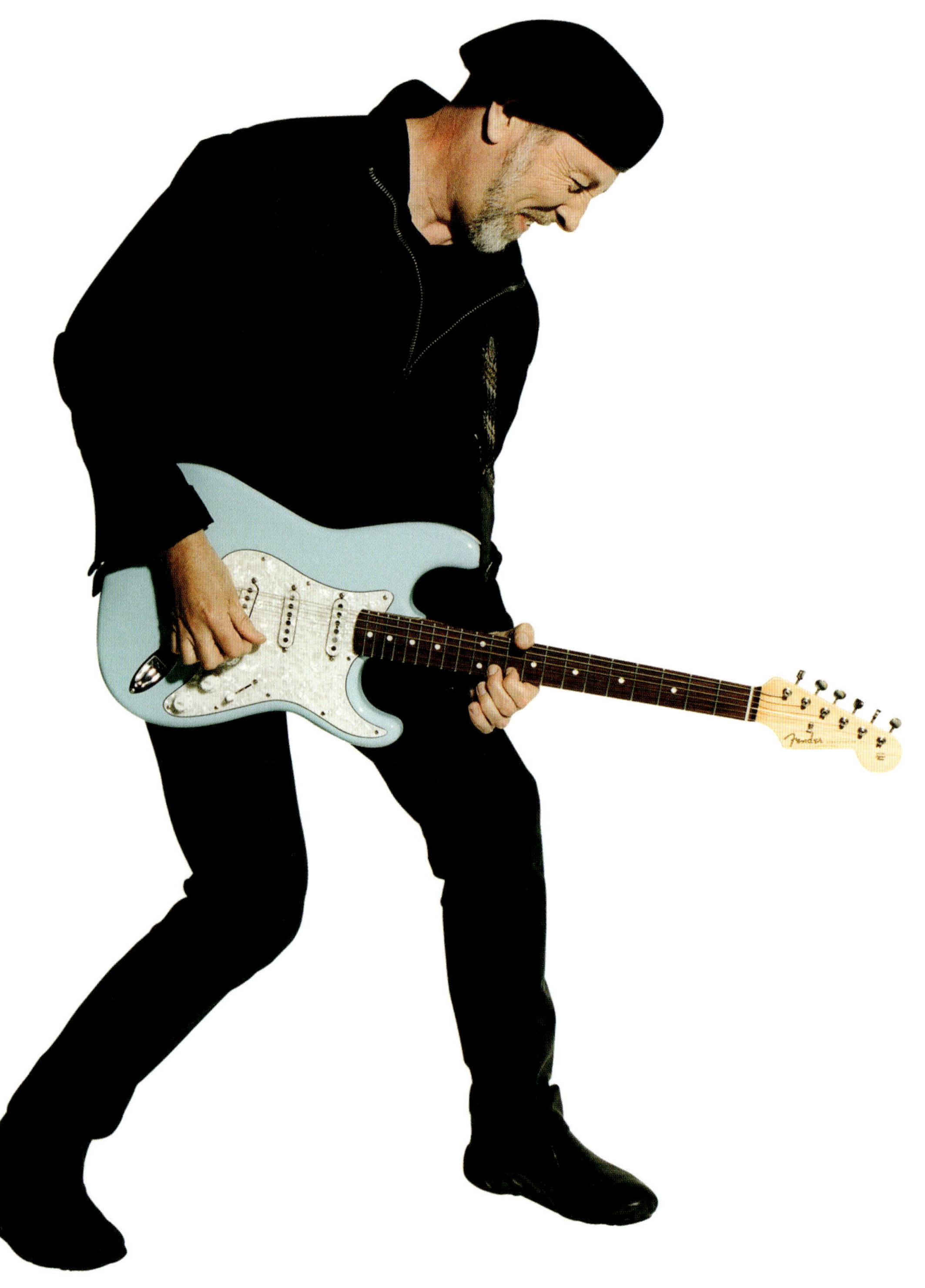

The legendary British songwriter Richard Thompson wrote a suite of songs inspired by letters written to and from the front.

BLOOD

Lemn Sissay

Someone has bricked up The Foyle.
The hands of dawn crawl across it
I'm drawn through the window
Into the air under a bruised sky.
It's still a river. It's a still river.

From *At All*
Lemn Sissay

Through a collaboration with the Verbal Arts — an organisation that strives to enable often divided, marginalised and disconnected communities in Northern Ireland to share their stories with one another — the writer and artist Lemn Sissay worked intensively with young people from Derry/Londonderry to consider the lasting impact in Ireland of the years 1914 to 1918, and to write new poetry.

Sissay worked primarily with young men aged between 16 and 24 who had a history of mental health issues, substance use or behaviour problems. Many participants, like the poet himself, had experienced the fostering and social care system.

Sissay's own contribution was a poem entitled *At All*, a surreal rumination on the imagined effects of the city's River Foyle being bricked up overnight, and the reactions of the people of the town. It was inspired by a conversation with two apprentice bricklayers. The poem was then interpreted by the young people in a temporary public installation of banners positioned across the city. The impact of the whole project on many of its participants was profound.

Verbal Arts, Derry/Londonderry,
January — December 2014

THE 306: DAWN, DAY AND DUSK

Oliver Emanuel
Gareth Williams
National Theatre of Scotland
Perth Theatre

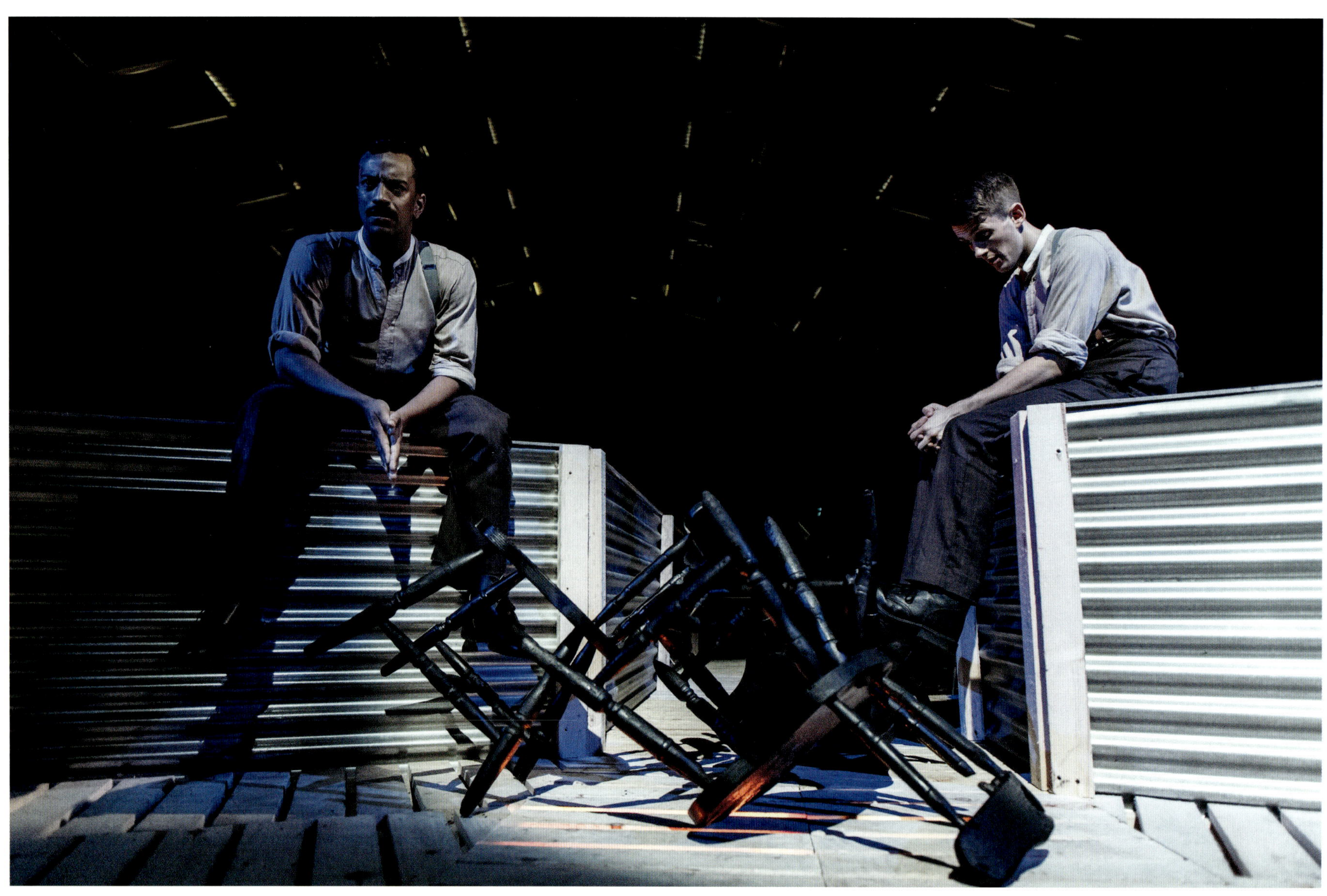

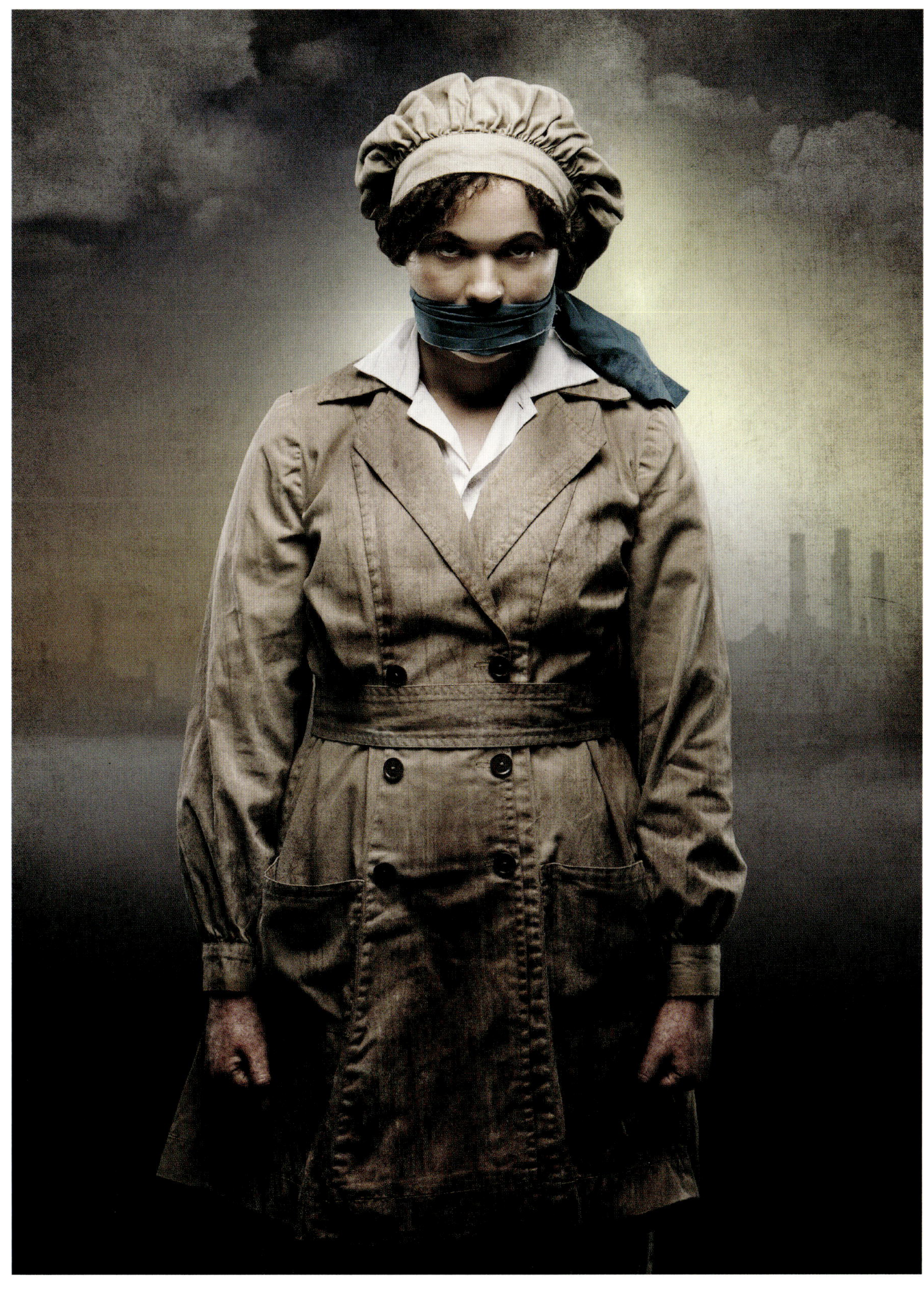

Between 1914 and 1918, many British soldiers were convicted of military offences — including cowardice, mutiny and desertion — and were executed. In 2006, 306 of them received posthumous pardons. *The 306* was a compelling musical theatre trilogy created by playwright Oliver Emanuel and composer Gareth Williams, intended to bring these lives back into sharp focus, challenging our notions of patriotism, heroism and glory.

The first part, *The 306: Dawn*, premiered in 2016 and was directed by Laurie Sansom. It was set around the events of the Battle of the Somme, marking the centenary of the Somme Offensive, and following the story of three of the condemned soldiers — 17-year-old Joseph Byers from Glasgow, 25-year-old Londoner Harry Farr, and 24-year-old Joseph Willie Stones, from Durham.

The 306: Day, the second production in 2017, was directed by Jemima Levick. This charted the struggles of the women and families left behind on the home front, as well as their fight to be heard over the clamour of conflict. Mirroring *Dawn*, this part followed the lives of three ordinary women.

The concluding chapter, *The 306: Dusk*, brought the trilogy into the modern day. Directed by Wils Wilson and set on a single day (11 November 2018), it explored the depth of feeling around the First World War, a century on from its conclusion, and the way in which the spectre of trauma continues to haunt soldiers in the modern day.

Dawn: Dalcrue Farm, Perth, 24 May — 11 June 2016
Day: Scottish tour, 5 — 13 May 2017
Dusk: Perth Theatre, Scotland, 12 — 27 October 2018

'In 2012, Gareth Williams and
I were looking at all the planned
memorials for the First World
War. It felt like all the stories were
about bravery and sacrifice and
heroism — but what about those
who failed to live up to this ideal?
This story challenges what we
think about the war and how we
memorialise the dead.'

Oliver Emanuel

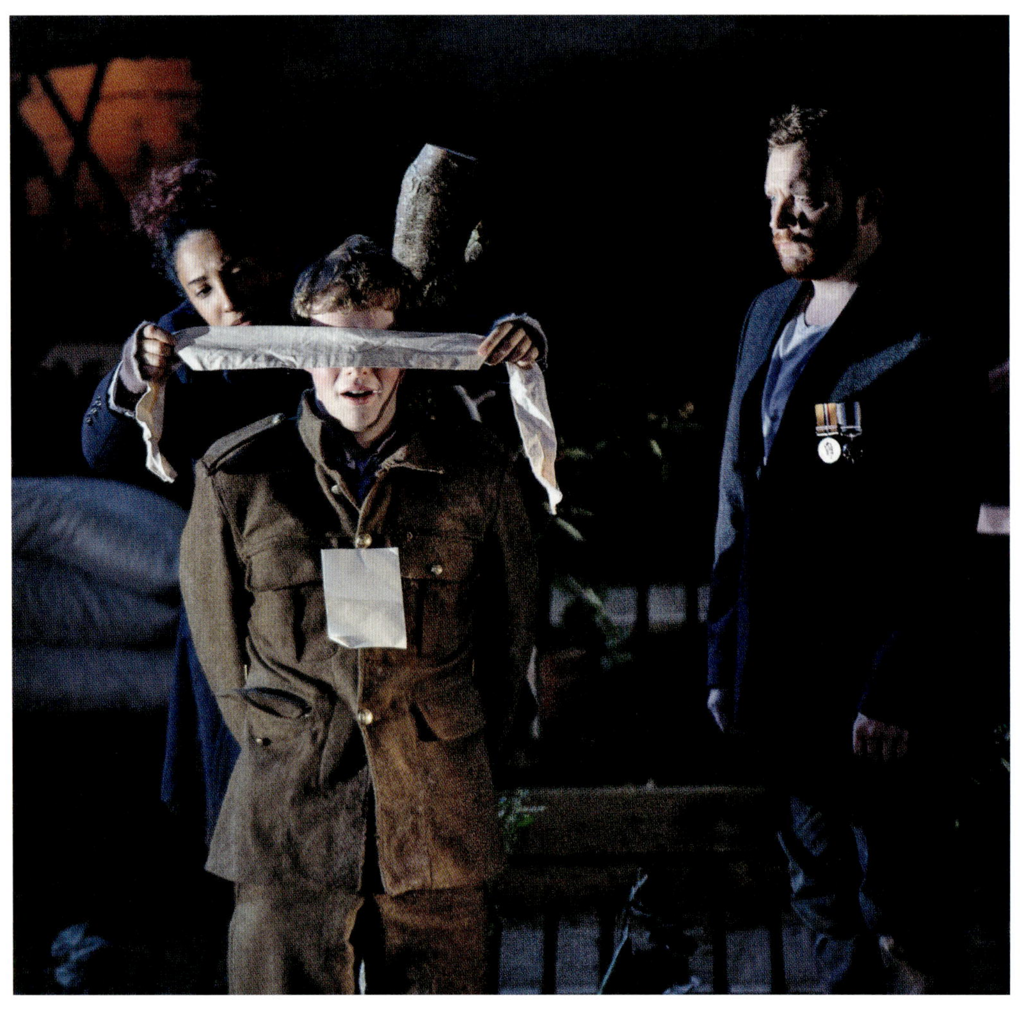

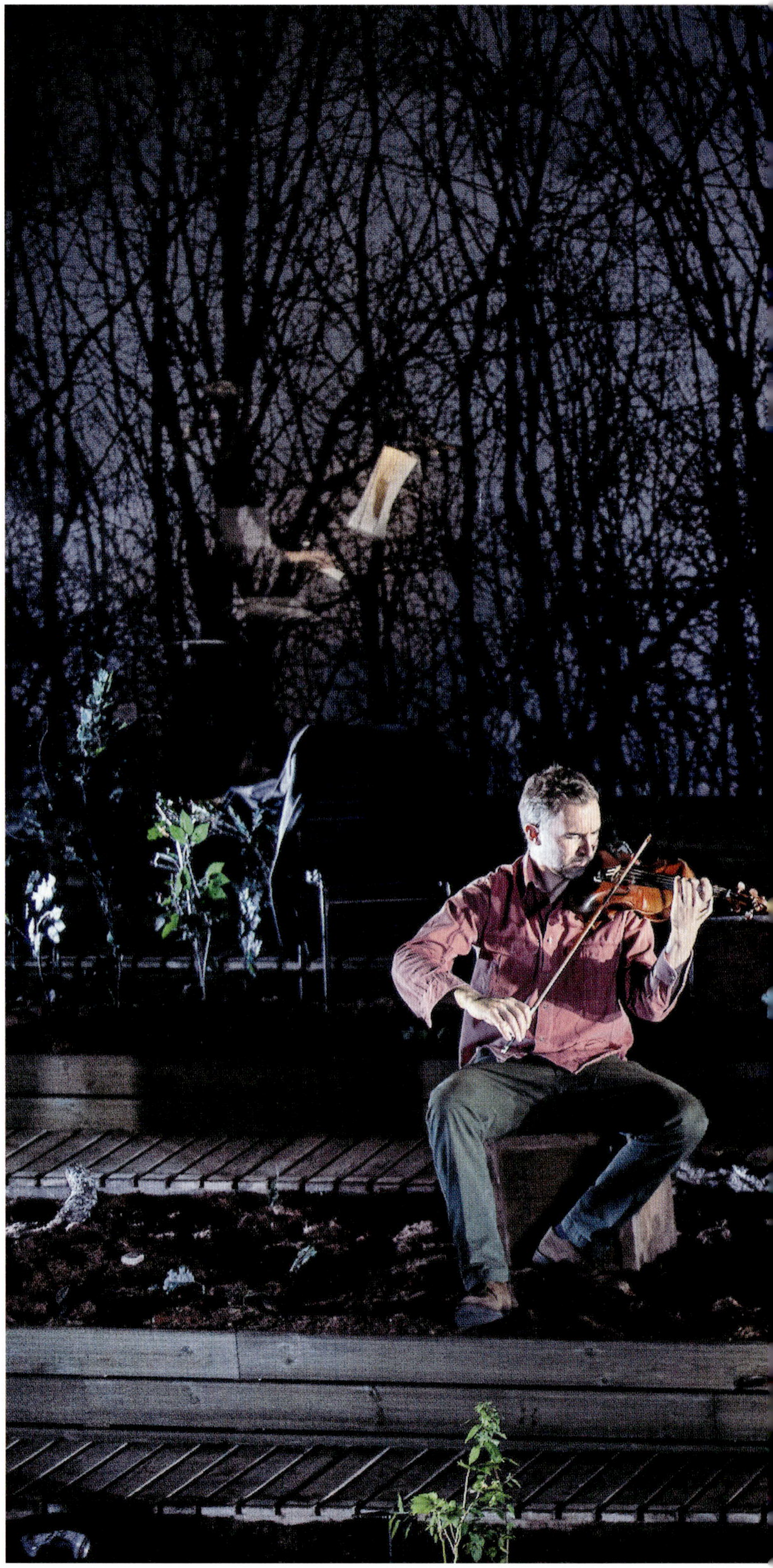

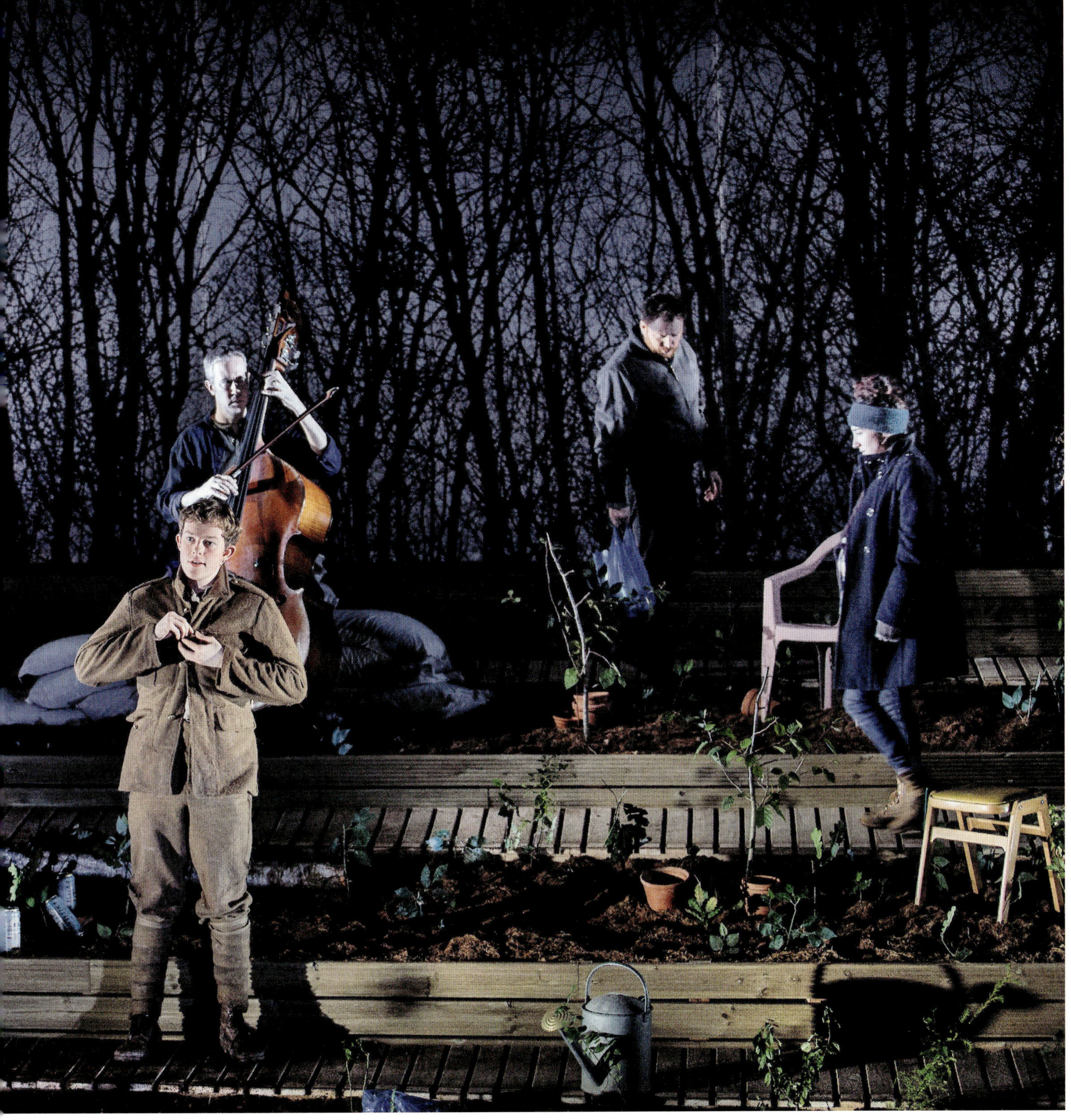

The concluding part of the trilogy was set in 2018 on the centenary of Armistice Day, exploring the lives of three disparate characters.

WAR DAMAGED MUSICAL INSTRUMENTS

Susan Philipsz

War has always been accompanied by music. Drums, bugles, fifes and trumpets have marched generations of men and women into battle, and brought them together at its end. For this commission, sound artist Susan Philipsz brought to life a selection of instruments disfigured by conflict: caught in explosions, shot through by gunfire, crushed under rubble.

Philipsz developed the installation over a number of years. Each wounded instrument played a single note from 'The Last Post', the bugle call sounded to mark the completion of an officer's evening checks of sentry posts to secure a camp, which also serves as a memorial to those lost in conflict. The damage inflicted upon the instruments by war created a moving symphony of injured sound played through speakers hung in the cavernous Duveen Galleries at Tate Britain, parts of which operated as the Queen Alexandra Military Hospital during the war. Walking through the central section, visitors heard a group of instruments used during the First World War: a tuba from the German trenches and a cavalry trumpet retrieved from a ship torpedoed by a submarine in 1918.

Described by *The Guardian* as creating music that was 'as uplifting as it is painful', these ravaged notes were coaxed from their instruments by musicians from Britain and Germany, using the power of sound to connect us to the physical suffering of war.

Tate Britain, London / 21 November 2015 — 3 April 2016

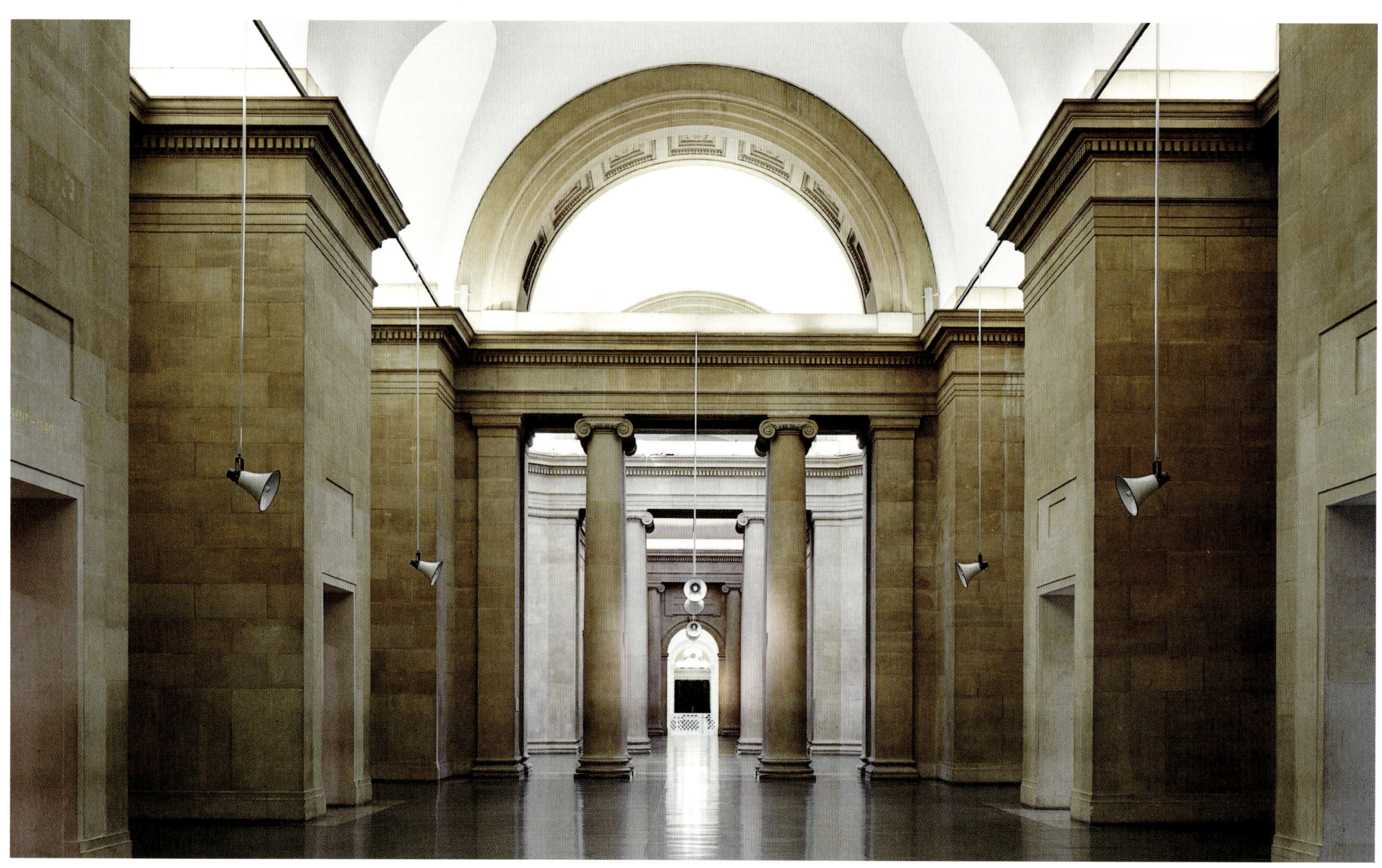

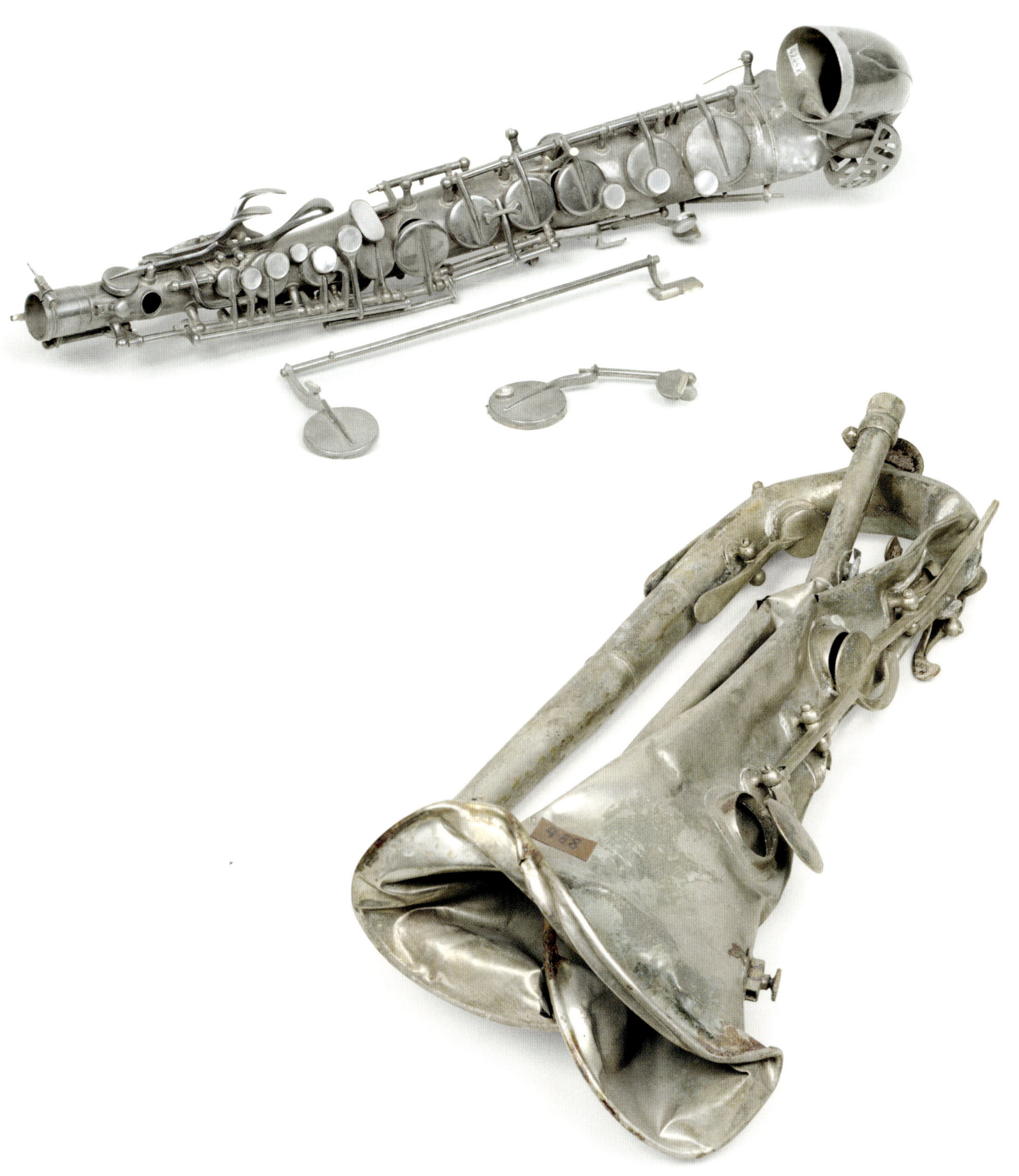

Opposite. The speakers in
place in the Duveen Galleries.

Left. A crushed bugle and
alto saxophone were among
the damaged instruments used
in this deeply affecting record
of loss and destruction.

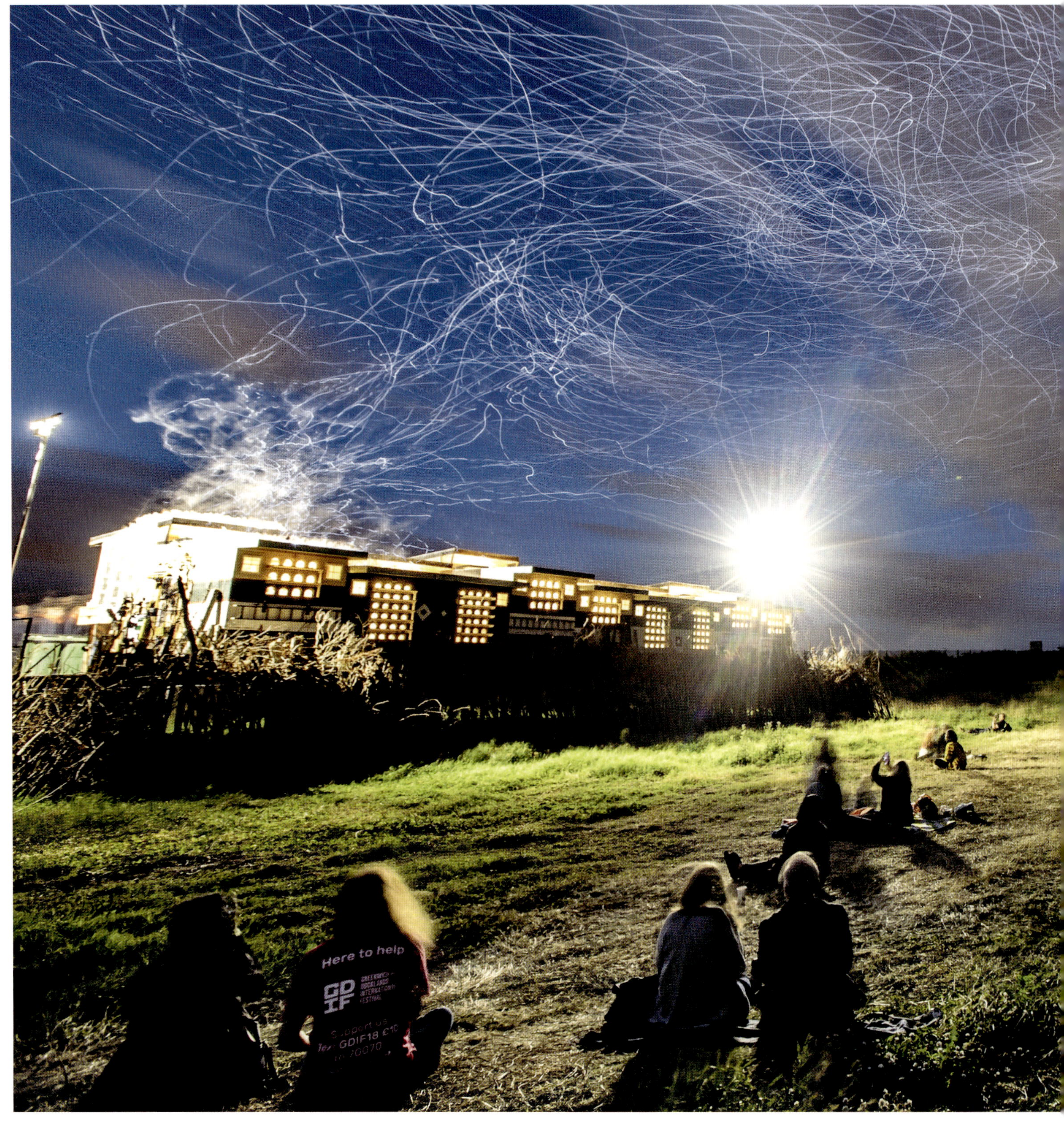

Riley's flock of trained birds were summoned from their coops at dusk, in tribute to the First World War pigeons that made their flights at night, to avoid attacks by hawks.

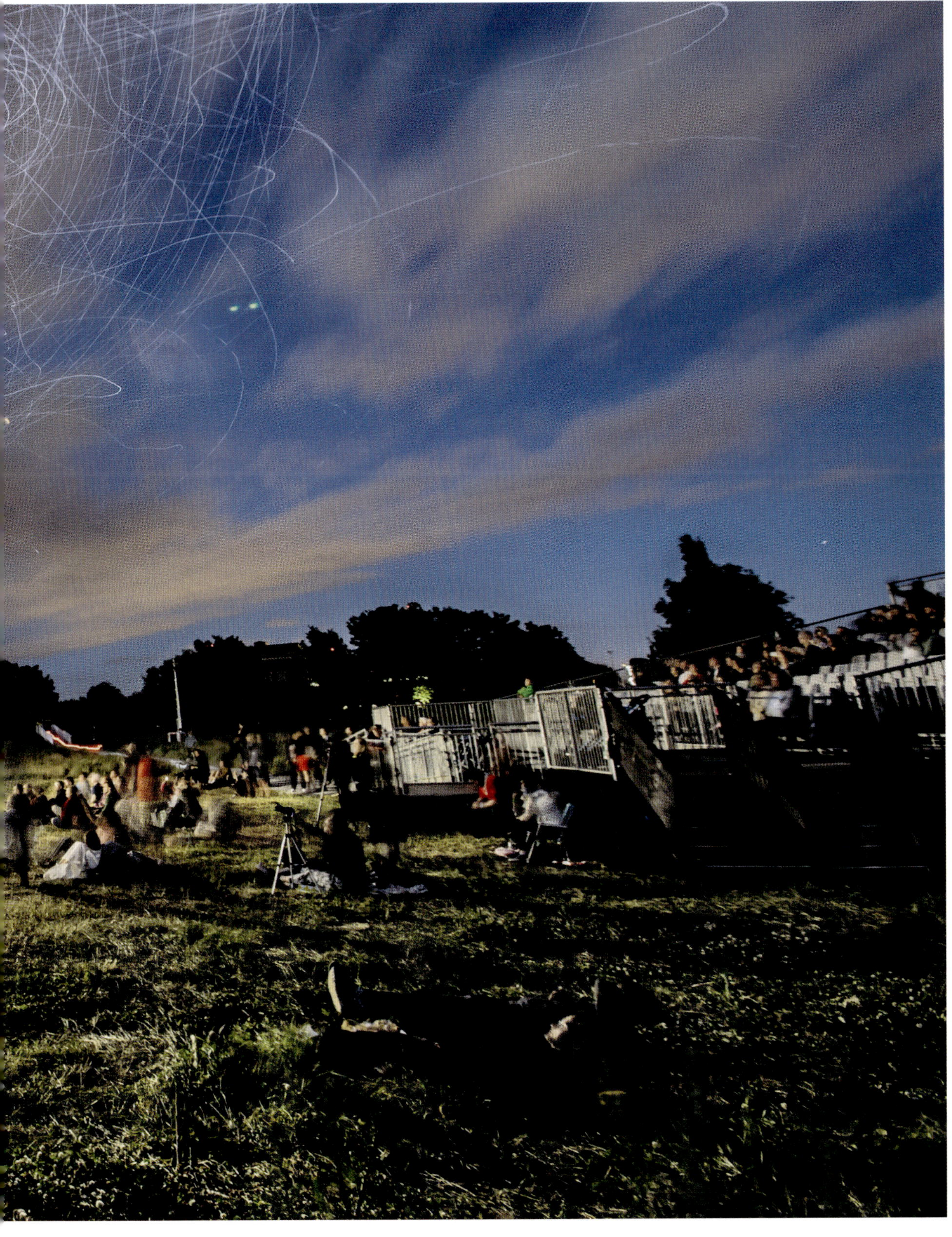

FLY BY NIGHT

Duke Riley

Taking place at dusk above the River Thames, in London's Thamesmead, *Fly by Night* paid beautiful homage to some of the First World War's overlooked heroes: the military pigeons that played crucial roles delivering messages between distant personnel. More than 100,000 pigeons contributed to the British war effort, carrying messages from ship to shore, from battlefield to command post, and from pilots to forces on the ground. An incredible 95 per cent of these messages arrived safely, changing the course of battles and saving many lives.

Fly by Night was first presented by Duke Riley and Creative Time in New York City in 2016. For the London rendition of this epic spectacle, over 1,500 pigeons soared into the skies to create a glorious airborne installation. The location chosen this time was one of military significance — the site of the old Royal Arsenal munitions factory — and the creative team were supported throughout the project by local volunteers.

Purpose-built coops, based on those used during the First World War, had provided the pigeons' home for 11 weeks before *Fly By Night*. Then, for each performance, upon a signal from Riley and his team, the birds flew out of their coops and up into the sky. In the fading light, small LED lights attached to bands on their legs — where once a message would have been attached — illuminated the sky with swirling patterns of light. Then the birds returned home to their coop, just as their ancestors did 100 years before.

East Thamesmead, 21 — 23 June 2018

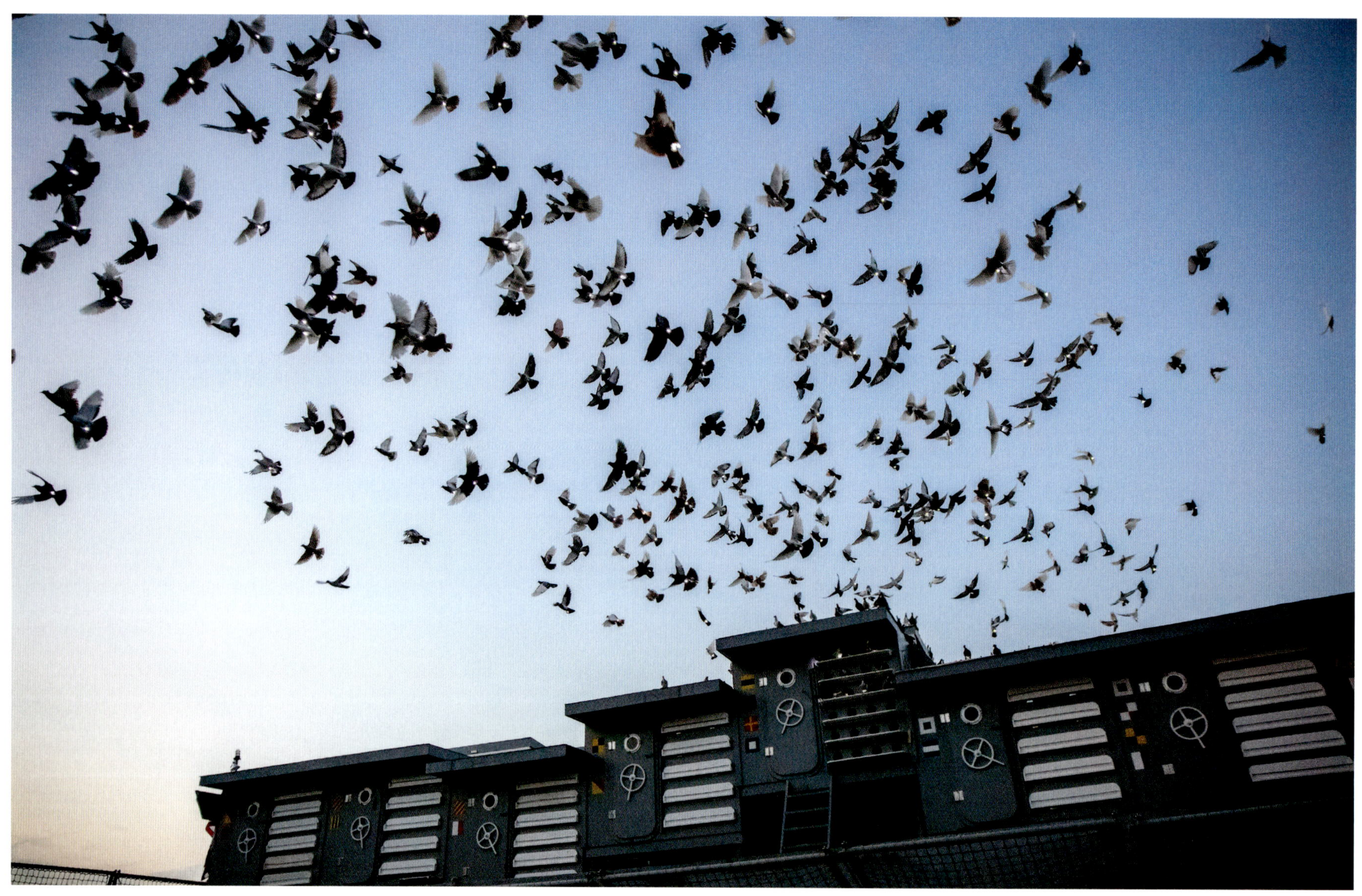

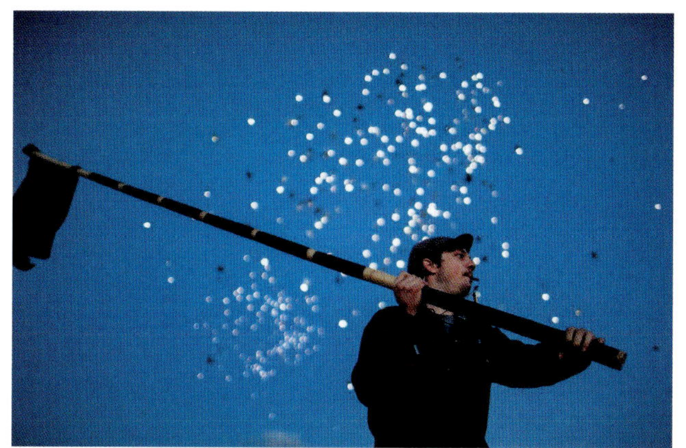

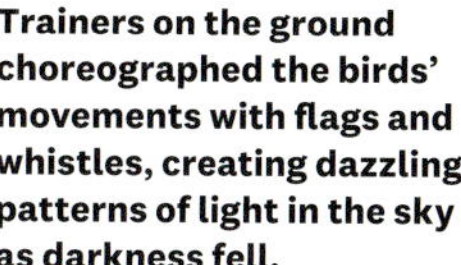

Trainers on the ground choreographed the birds' movements with flags and whistles, creating dazzling patterns of light in the sky as darkness fell.

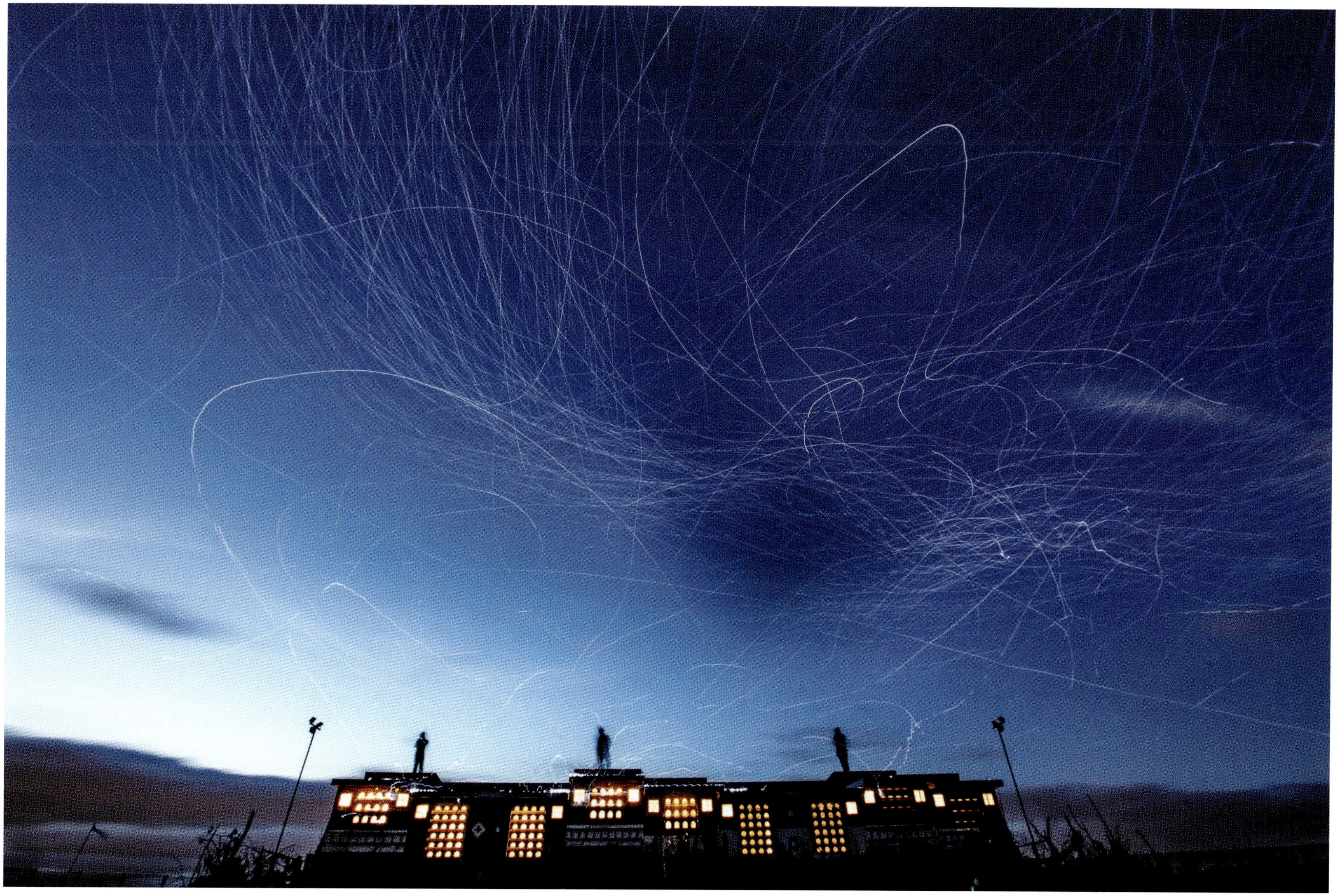

On the seventh day of the Battle of the Somme, the 38th (Welsh) Division was given the order to capture Mametz Wood, an objective that generals calculated would take several hours. The struggle that ensued lasted for five days and, with 4,000 of the 38th Division killed or wounded in the process, was one of the First World War's bloodiest conflicts.

Mametz was a large-scale, site-specific production, written by Owen Sheers, directed by Matthew Dunster and designed by Jon Bausor for National Theatre Wales. It was performed in the ancient Great Llancayo Upper Wood, near Usk in Monmouthshire, providing audiences with an immersive experience that gave them a uniquely evocative glimpse into life and death in the trenches and on the battlefields of the Somme.

Among the soldiers who took part in the battle were the writers David Jones and Llewelyn Wyn Griffith. Both men wrote accounts of the battle, and passages from Jones's 'In Parenthesis' and Wyn Griffith's 'Up To Mametz' are interwoven throughout the script of this living monument to the experiences, fears and hopes of the 38th at Mametz. The script of the play was published in a dual-language Welsh–English edition by Faber & Faber and is a set text for A-level drama in Wales.

Great Llancayo Upper Wood, Monmouthshire, 24 June — 5 July 2014

MAMETZ

Owen Sheers
National Theatre Wales

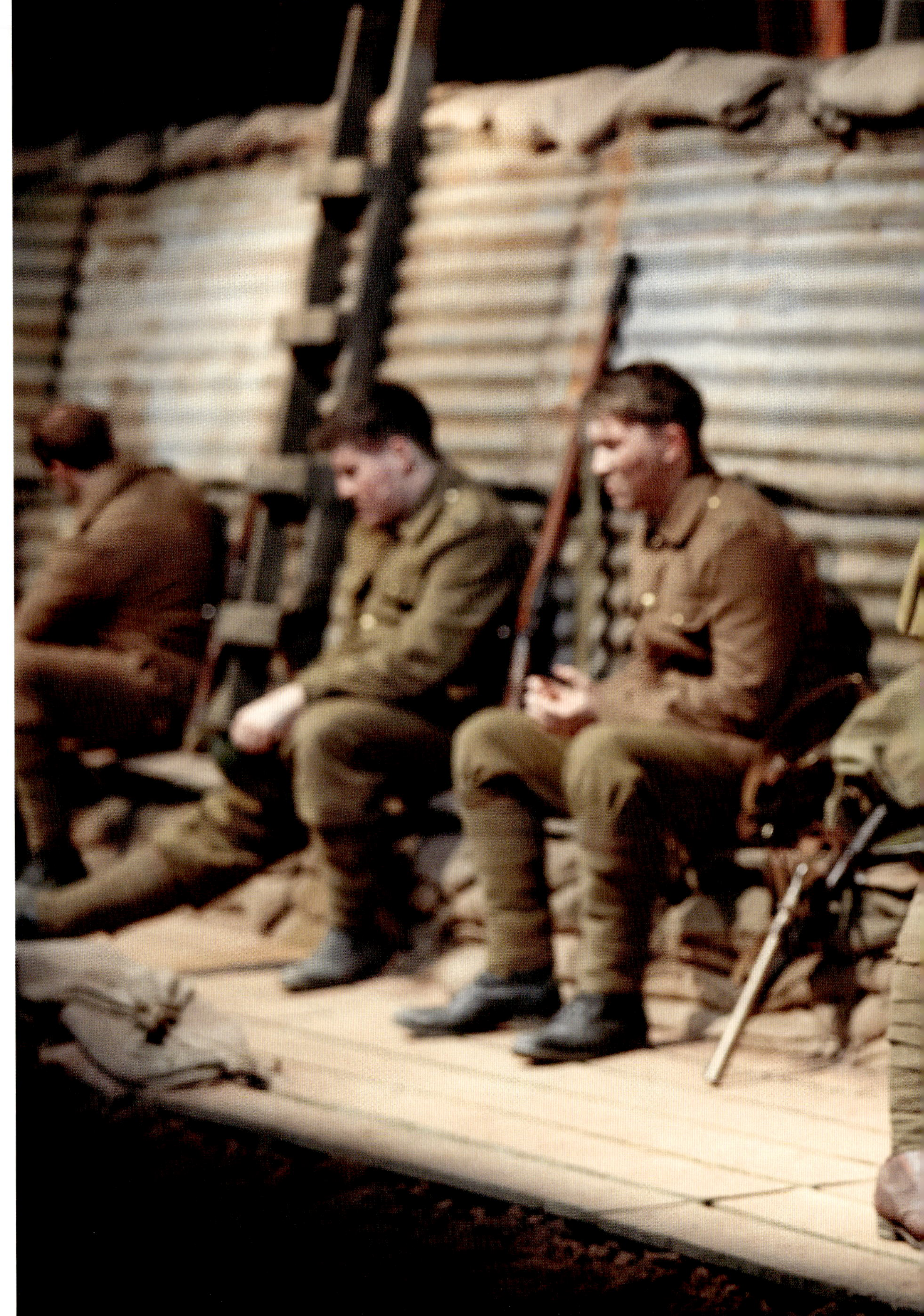

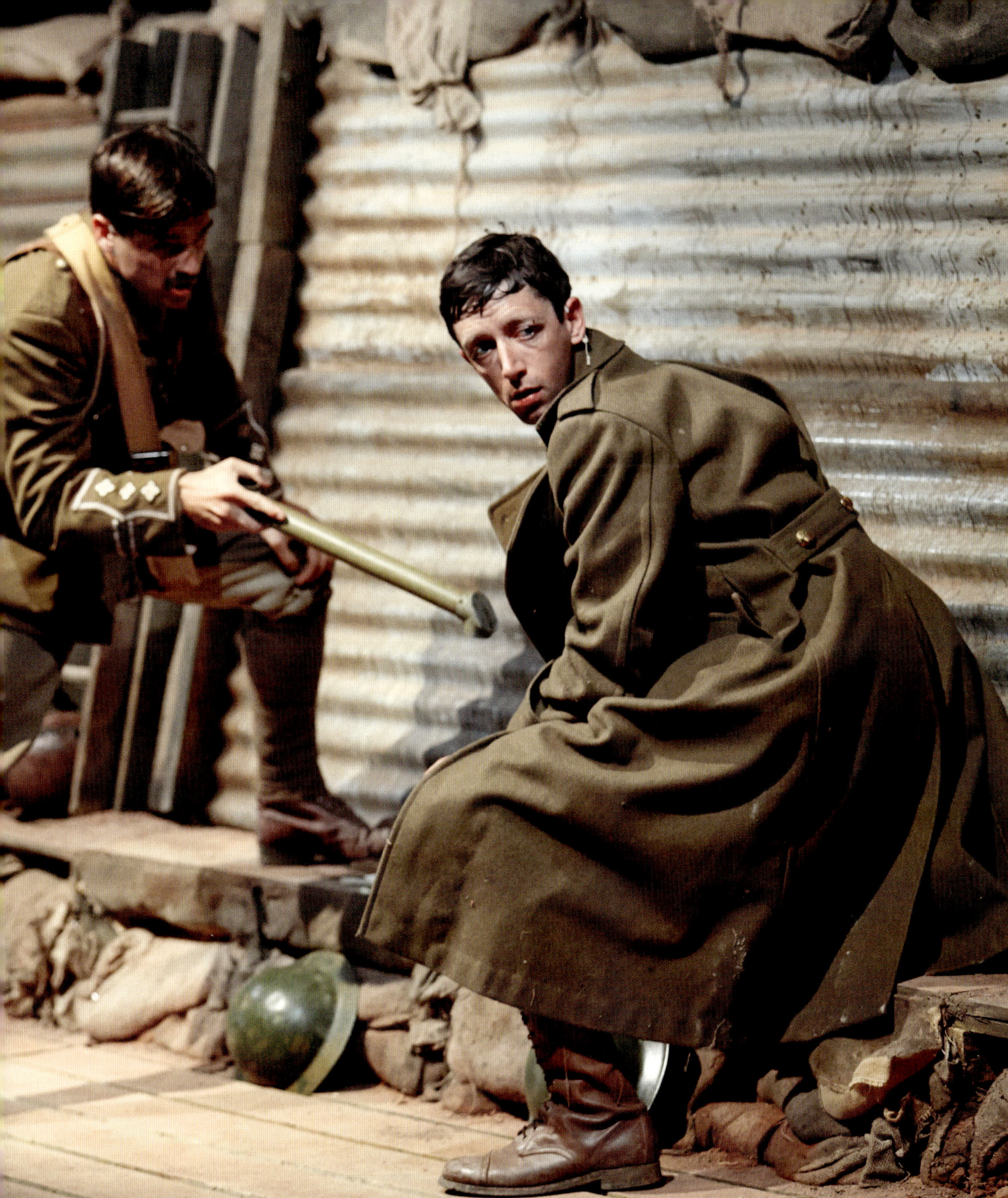

Members of the cast captured both the tedium and tension of trench life.

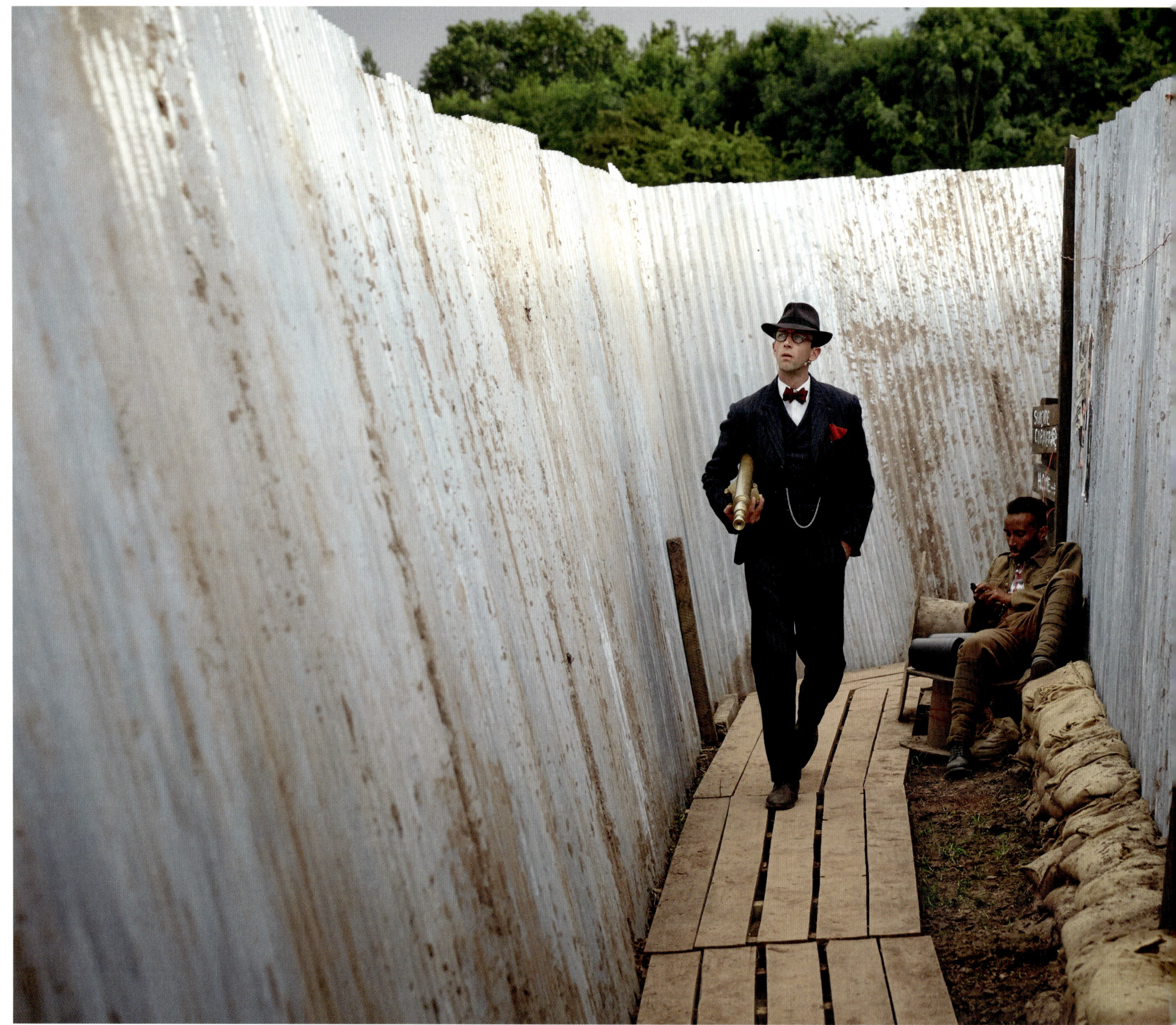

Left. At times, the audience was addressed directly by a character based on the real-life Dutch physicist Willem de Sitter, relating contemporary developments in the theory of time and relativity to the events unfolding on stage.

Below. The production took audiences into the trenches and onto the battlefield, evoking the experiences of those who were there.

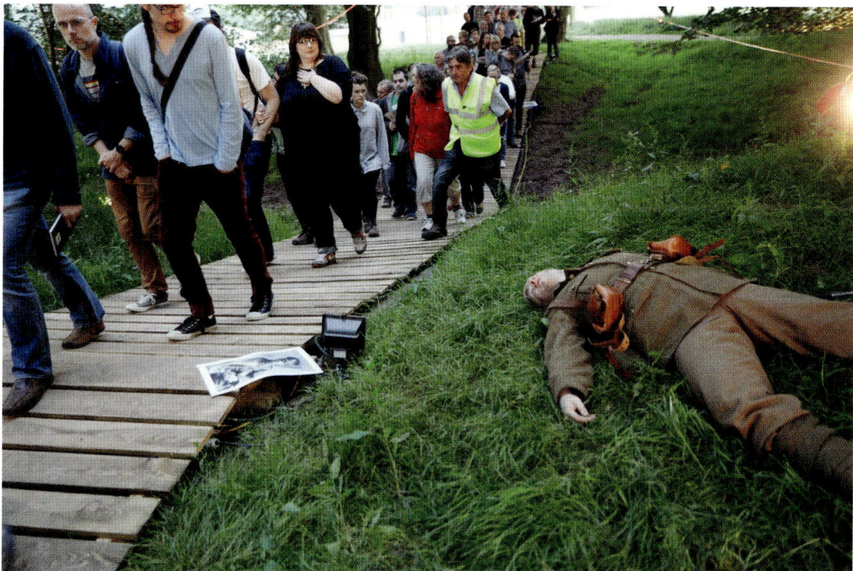

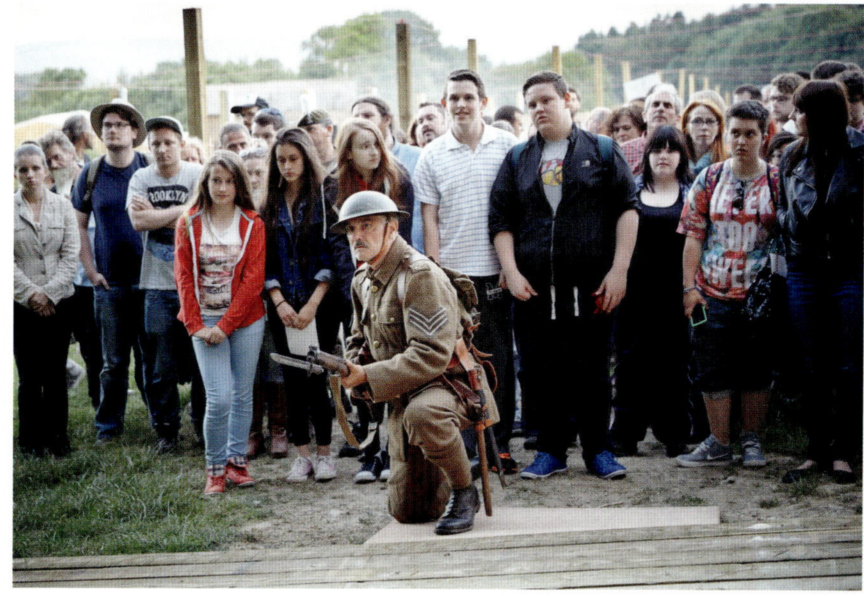

INCREDIBLE JOURNEYS

The Story Museum

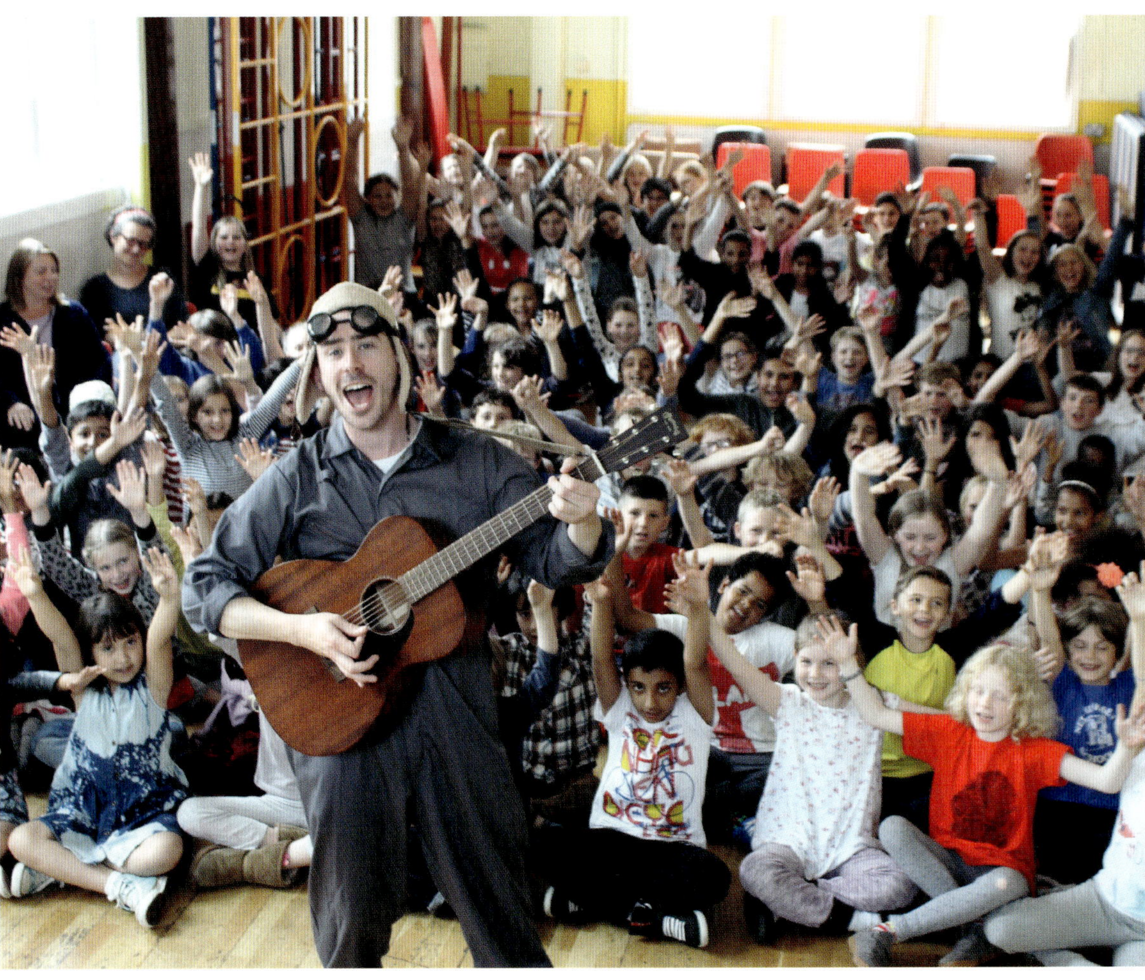

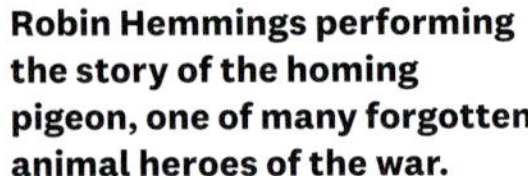

Robin Hemmings performing the story of the homing pigeon, one of many forgotten animal heroes of the war.

In 2016 The Story Museum in Oxford and 14-18 NOW co-commissioned six leading storytellers to create a modern fable that would give children and their families an imaginative introduction to the First World War. Each tale took the point of view of an animal — real or imagined — and live performances then presented a selection of these stories, threaded together with humour, song and audience participation.

'El Shimla — the War Camel', 'The Tale of Ali Pasha — the Tortoise Who Travelled Far', 'The Spider's War', 'Lizzie the Elephant', 'Koala in Gallipoli' and 'The Pigeon Who Had Three Names' told stories of endurance, friendship or battlefield heroism from around the world through the eyes of such characters as the bear that inspired Winnie-the-Pooh, the camels that fought alongside T. E. Lawrence in the Arab Revolt of 1916–18, and a modest homing pigeon.

The Story Museum, Oxford, 18 — 19 June 2016 / Lincoln Castle, 16 — 17 July 2016

'*We embraced this opportunity to ask some of our finest storytellers to give voice to the countries, creatures and cultures whose roles in the far-flung "theatres" of the First World War fall beyond the spotlight.*'

Tish Francis, co-director, The Story Museum

SOMME 100

A creative, collective act

As the country prepared for war, Heaton Park in Manchester served as a training camp for a number of the Manchester Regiment battalion. Many of these soldiers had been recruited to serve alongside their friends, relatives and colleagues — hence the battalions' nickname, the 'Pals' (see page 36). After their training, the Manchester Pals were dispatched to France, where they fought in the Battle of the Somme alongside regiments from across the UK and around the world.

On 1 July 2016, as part of the National Commemoration of the Centenary of the Battle of the Somme, Heaton Park was the venue for a multimedia collective event. Under the artistic direction of Alan Lane, and creative production of Sara Robinson, *Somme 100* included a performance by a national children's choir, newly commissioned short films, dance performed by volunteers alongside professionals, and a concert by the Hallé Orchestra. The event concluded with the reading of a newly commissioned poem by Lemn Sissay (see page 253).

Also on display was the newly created *Path of the Remembered*. Prior to the event, the public had been invited to contribute 'memory squares' — designs inspired by individuals whose lives were affected by the Battle of the Somme — which were uploaded to an online gallery. These were then printed onto 5,000 individual tiles and laid out in an 80-metre-long path. Part of this path was made into a permanent memorial in Heaton Park.

Heaton Park, Manchester / 1 July 2016

The choreography was specially created to enable a cast of 300 volunteers to perform alongside professional dancers.

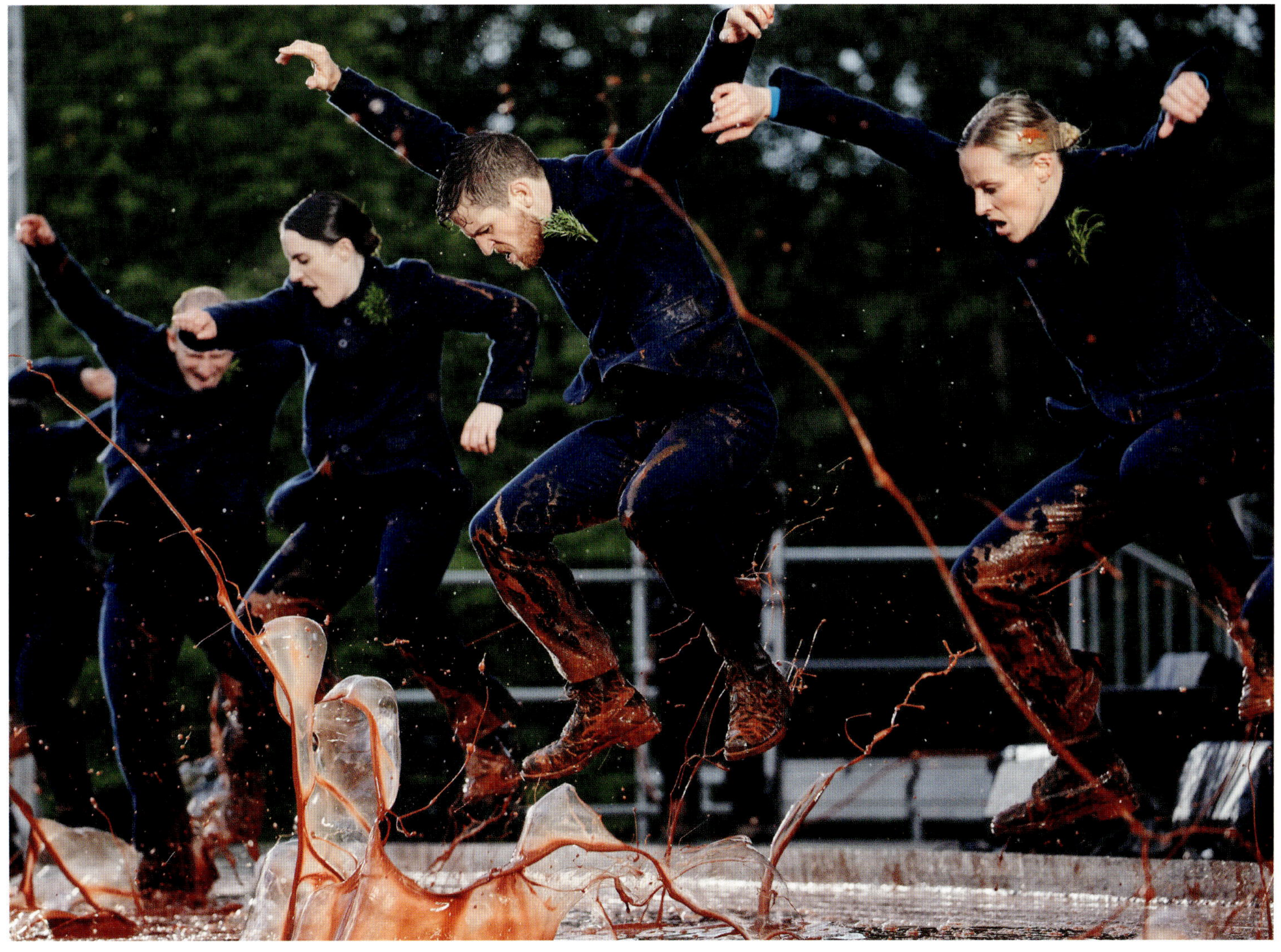

In 1918 and 1919, Glasgow Museums purchased a collection of boxes containing charms and amulets 'worn by the fighting men in the Great War'. The handwritten title of one of the charms (a soapstone monkey) is 'I Say Nothing'. These, along with three mule hooves, a moss-filled pillow and a book of French grammar riddled with shrapnel holes, were among the objects to which Christine Borland found herself drawn during her year of research at Glasgow Museums Resource Centre.

Of particular interest to the artist was a modest white ceramic invalid feeder cup in one of the handling kits of the Open Museum, the community outreach team for Glasgow Museums. The teapot-like object, examples of which were used both to nurse the sick during the war and force-feed hunger-striking suffragettes in the years leading up to 1914, speaks of the duality of institutional care and brutality.

Through an expanded focus on this object, Borland explored the potential for a simple object to embody something much more than the reality of its humble form or material. While the stasis of storage — or, indeed, the passing of time — can render historical objects mute, *I Say Nothing* aimed to give them a voice.

Kelvingrove Art Gallery, Glasgow,
from 12 October 2018

I SAY NOTHING

Christine Borland

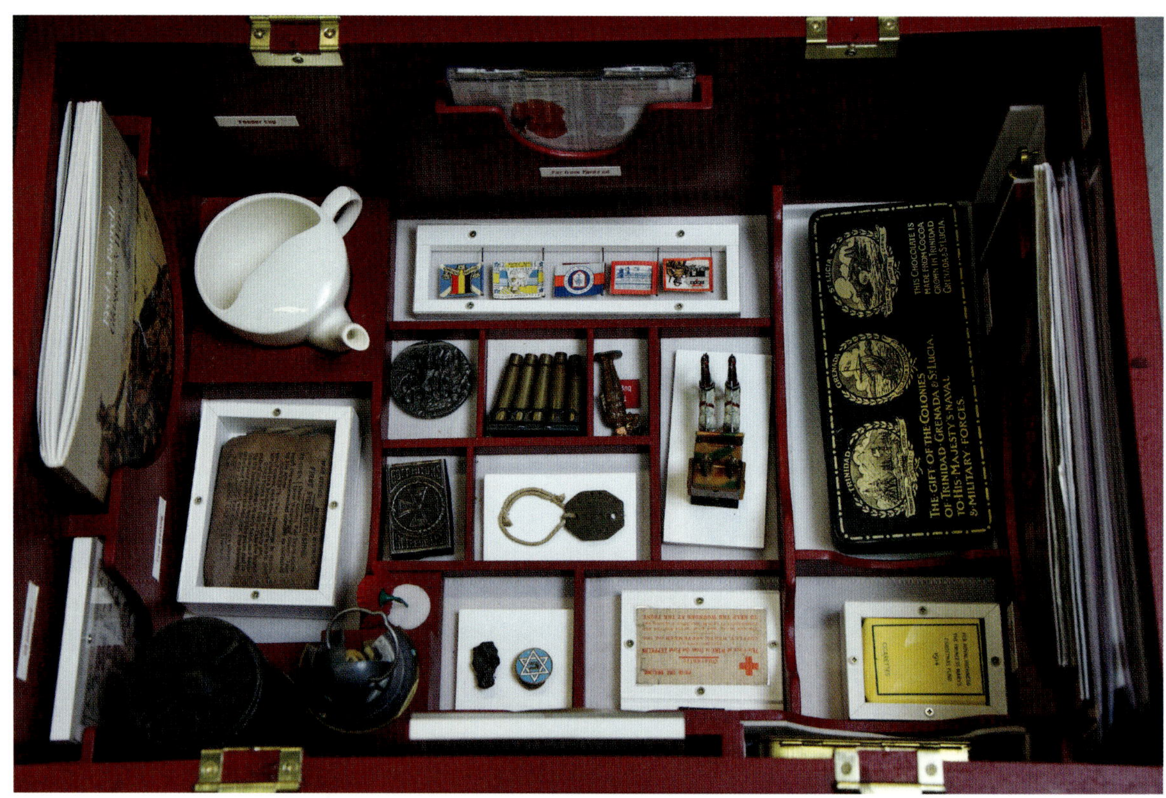

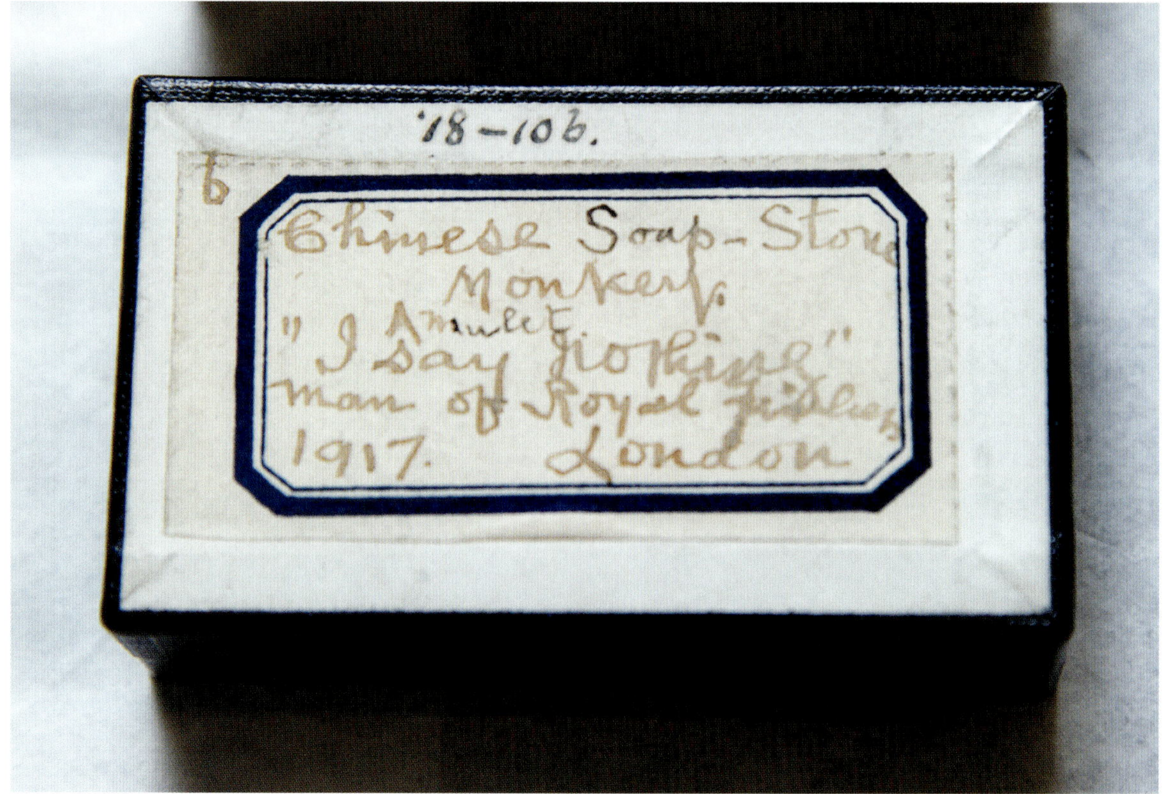

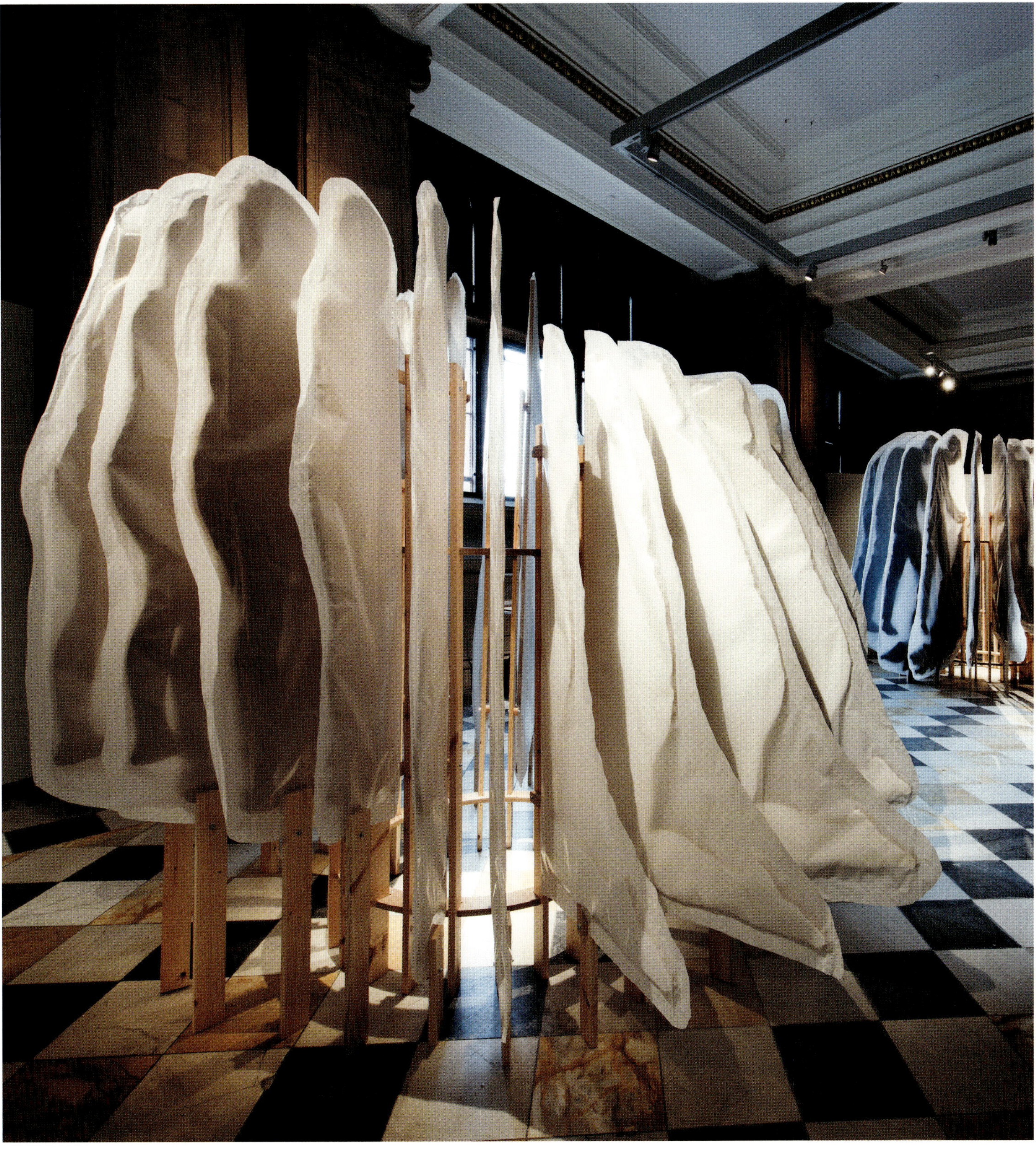

Left. Christine Borland
used the 19th-century
technique of photosculpture
to produce MDF silhouettes
showing imagined scenarios
using the invalid feeder cup.
Arranged in two circular
groupings, these silhouettes
were wrapped in glassine,
a material historically
used to protect objects
in museum stores.

Opposite. Boxes once
containing amulets that had
belonged to soldiers who
fought in the war, including
the box that provided the
title for Borland's work.

AT TIMES LIKE THESE MEN WERE WISHING THEY WERE ALL KINDS OF INSECTS

Graham Gingles

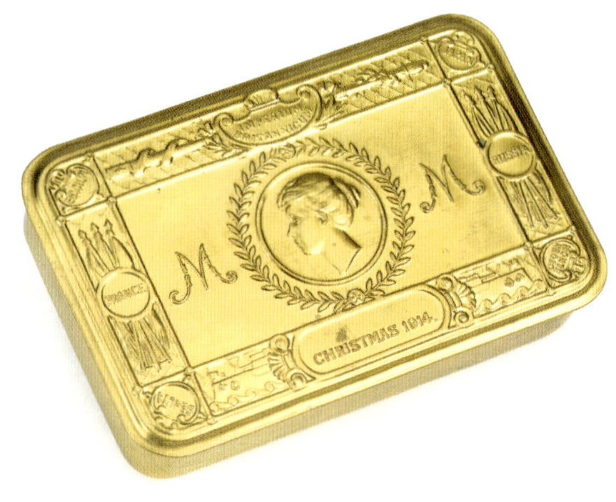

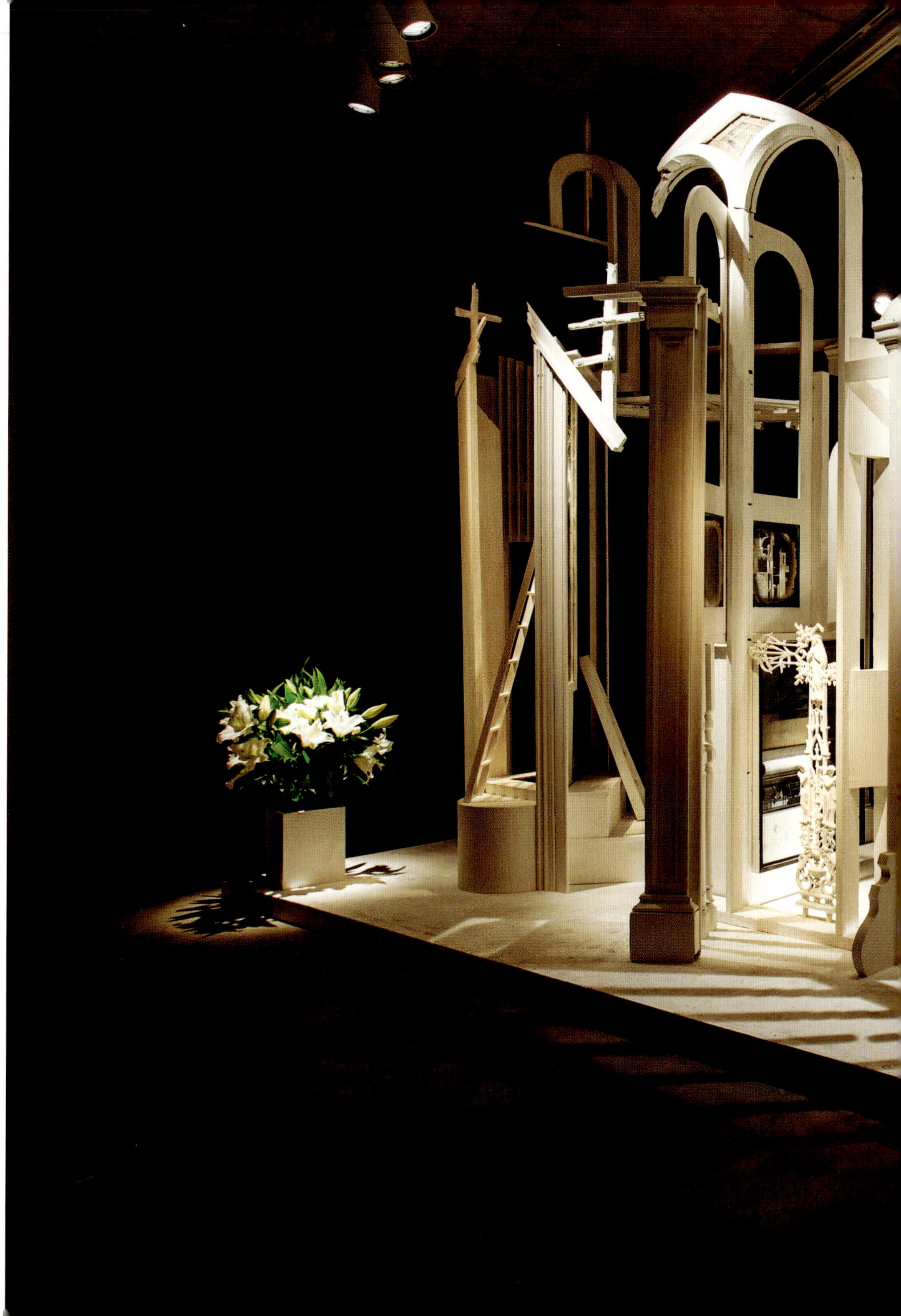

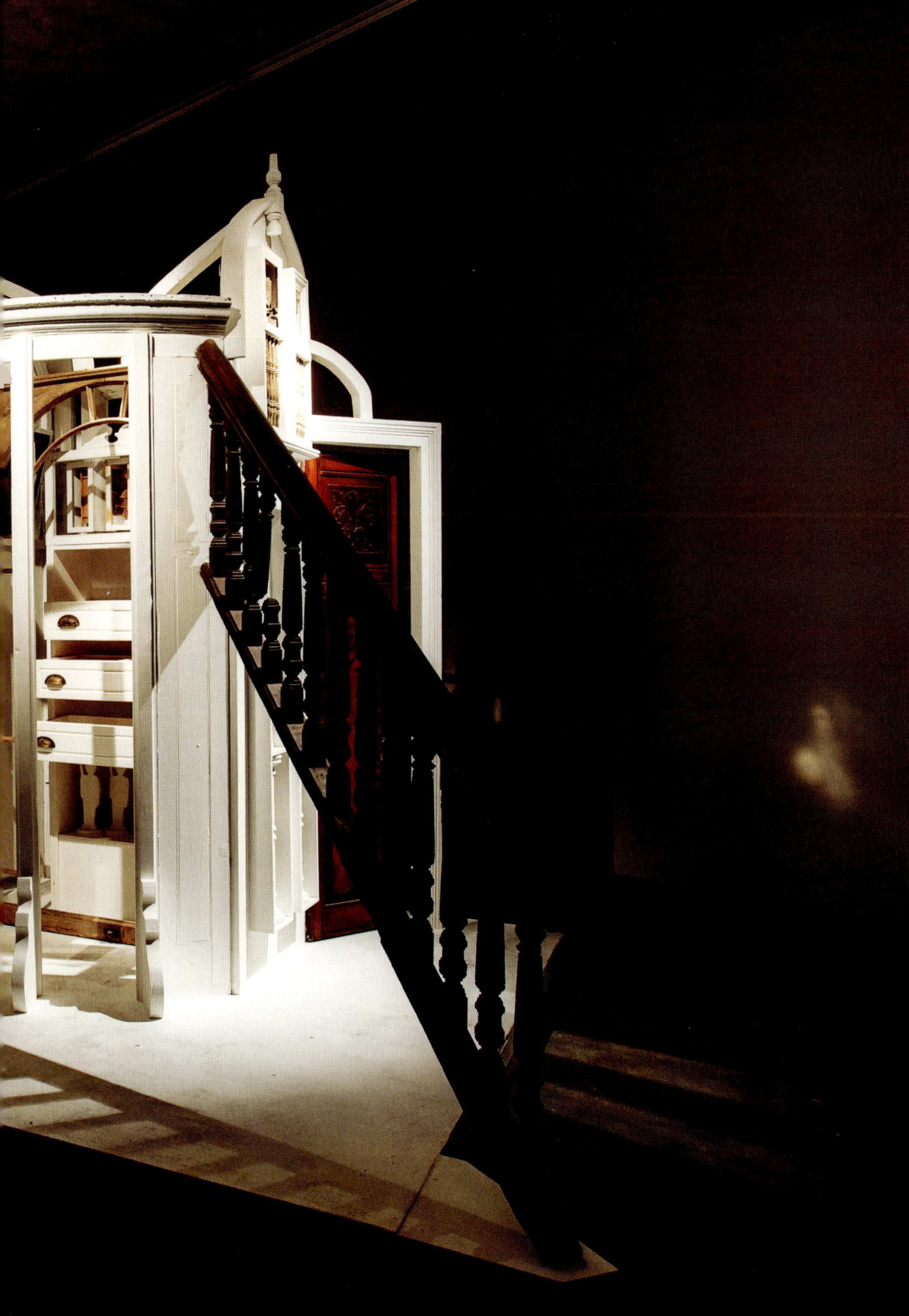

The 17-year-old Princess Mary captured the public imagination when she launched a fundraising campaign to ensure that on Christmas Day 1914 every uniformed man and woman, whether overseas or at home, would receive a 'gift from the nation'. Packed with presents ranging from lighters and cigarettes to chocolate and spices, these embossed brass boxes would become one of the most enduring keepsakes of the First World War — symbols of compassion in times of danger and hardship.

This project began when the MAC Belfast gave an original Princess Mary box to Northern Irish artist Graham Gingles, inspiring him to explore the experiences of men at the front and, in particular, the wartime diaries of Robert McGookin, a soldier from Gingles' hometown of Larne, in County Antrim.

Gingles is best known for intimate mixed-media boxed constructions that combine drawings, sculptures and photographs. For this installation, however, he scaled up his approach dramatically — to room size. This theatrical, maze-like structure occupied the entirety of the Sunken Gallery at the MAC, which itself became a box into which the visitor entered in order to peer into the structure's nooks and crannies. The title of this compelling treatment of memory and loss, referring to the horror of the trenches, came from McGookin himself.

The MAC, Belfast, 3 July — 17 August 2014

MAKE ART NOT WAR

Bob and Roberta Smith

Coinciding with the end of the centenary, artist Bob and Roberta Smith OBE RA invited students aged 16 to 18 to take part in *Make Art Not War*, responding to the bold provocation 'What does peace mean to you?' Young people across the UK were asked to respond creatively in any media, from writing, art and design to photography, theatre and film. To provide inspiration, a series of short films was made by artists from the 14-18 NOW programme, including Jeremy Deller, Rachel Whiteread and Yinka Shonibare CBE, who all contributed commissions inspired by the First World War. The films gave insight into each artist's creative process as well as their own reflection on the provocation.

Make Art Not War was about fuelling young people across the country to find confidence in their own creativity, to develop original thinking, and to express their ideas and opinions relating to the Armistice and the possibility of peace. Creative learning in the UK charts its beginnings back to 1918 and the start of the Child Art Movement. This legacy programme was centred on providing excellent resources and developing the essential creative skills that are vital for young people entering today's workforce.

The programme was devised by 14-18 NOW and Bob and Roberta Smith, with leading academics Professor Bill Lucas and Pauline Tambling CBE. Resources can be accessed at www.1418now.org.uk/commissions/make-art-not-war/

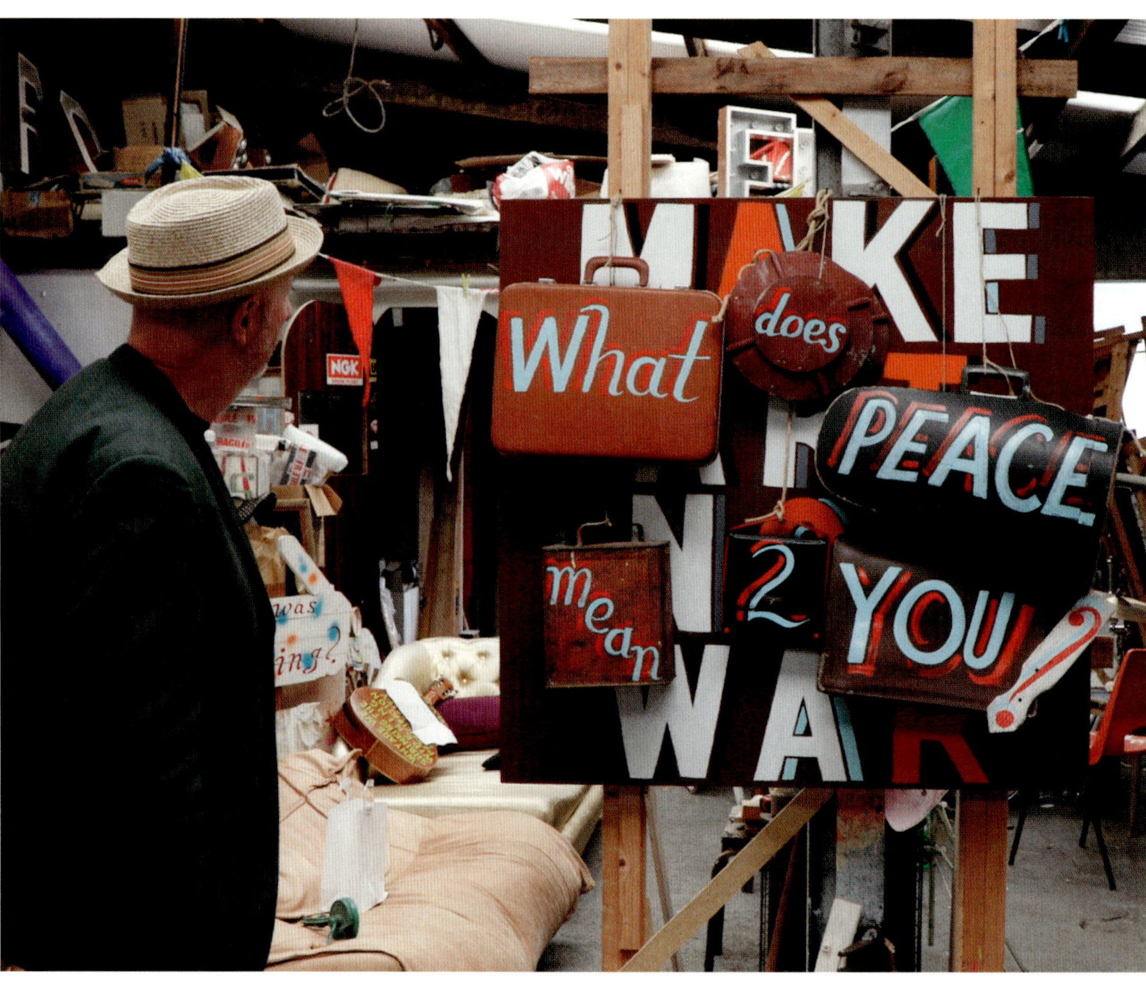

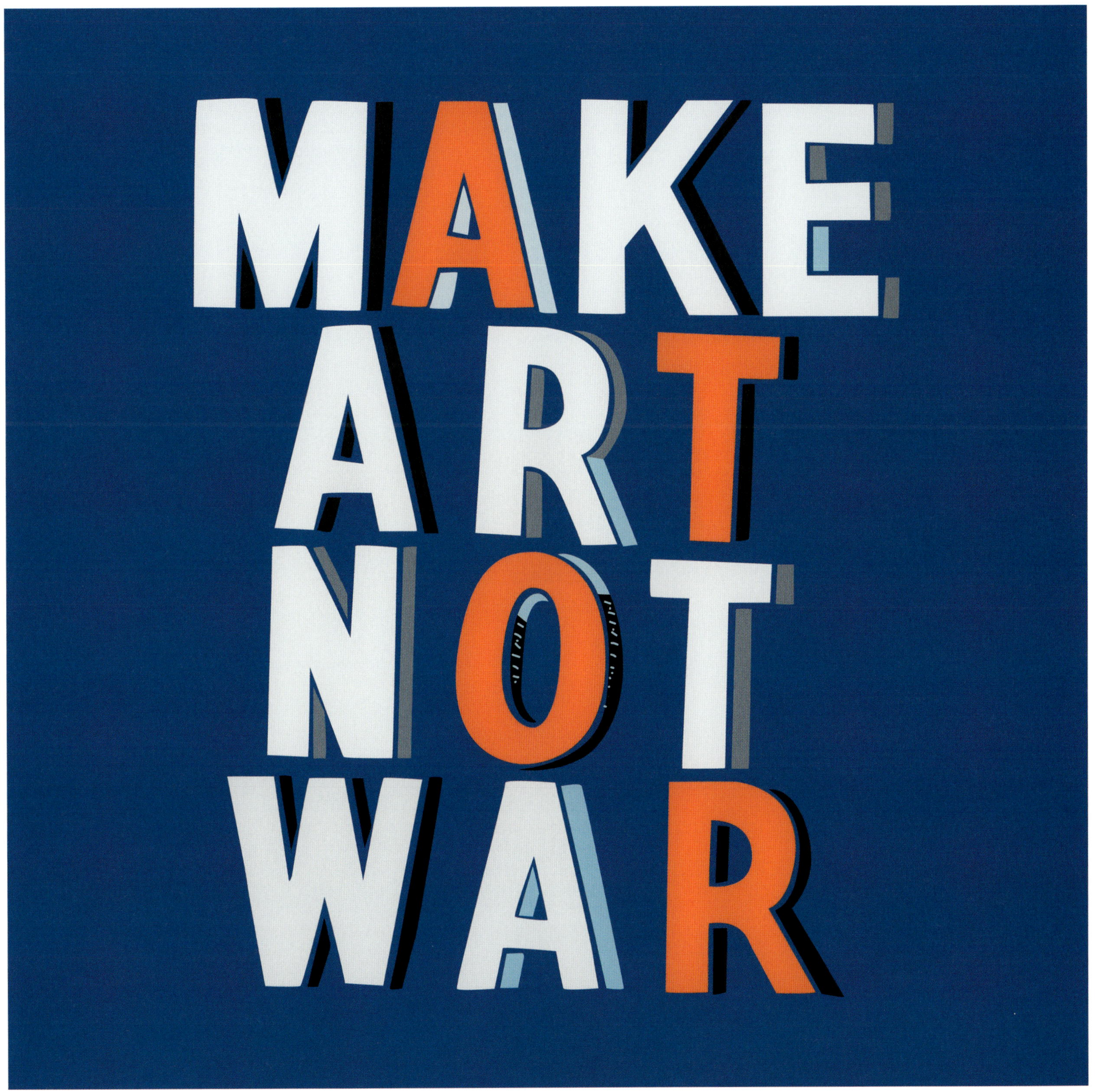

MAKE
ART
NOT
WAR

10 million military deaths alone
240 an hour, every hour for 4 years
4 deaths a minute night & day

11/11

Danny Boyle

On 11 November, 1918, the great tide of blood that had swept Western Europe and many other parts of the world since 1914 was at last stemmed by the Armistice. It is a day we have marked every year since. The 100th year had to feel different.

14-18 NOW, the organisation that did so much — by bringing the past into the present — to make us freshly aware of the sacrifices of that terrible war, wanted to suggest a way in which we could all acknowledge those sacrifices together. This was not intended to replace the formal ceremonies that would take place at the Cenotaph and war memorials all over the country, but something that could underline the significance of a century and be celebrated alongside them.

'Have you news of my boy Jack? / Not this tide.'

Rudyard Kipling's poem 'My Boy Jack' was written in 1917 in response to the losses in the Battle of Jutland. It also reflects his deeply personal feelings about the disappearance of his son John at the Battle of Loos in 1915. The poem has come to represent, for many of us, our own feelings about the millions of unknown soldiers lost to history.

Kipling's tide, and the thought of those men and women who left these shores to serve, made me think of the beaches that surround these islands as a possible space where people could come together and commemorate the century since their fight ended: to say goodbye.

The shoreline belongs to everyone, it is a democratic space, where only the sea rules; at once a personal and public landscape. And these same beaches are where so many soldiers and service people left from. I liked the idea of people coming together in their own way, or with their local community, to celebrate and commemorate, sure, but without too much formal ceremony.

We wanted to create portraits of some of those who were lost, drawn in the sand between low and high tide. The portraits were created as the tide went out in the morning, and were gently erased by the sea as the tide returned. I could think of no more fitting site, for instance, than Folkestone beach, the port through which ten million men and women passed on their way to and from France.

Some of them, like the poet Wilfred Owen, did not come back. He swam from Folkestone beach the day before he left for the front for the last time in 1918. So we drew his portrait there. He, and the other poets, brought the war home in a way that the newspapers and newsreels could not, so — in honour of them — we asked the poet laureate, Carol Ann Duffy, to write a new poem to mark the event. I have brought my daughters up on Duffy's work and she remains, for me, one of the blazing talents of English poetry. I like to think Wilfred Owen would have been pleased with the simplicity and beauty of what she wrote.

The closing line of her poem — 'Your faces drowning in the pages of the sea' — gave us the title for this project: *Pages of the Sea*. So, no speeches, but a simple poem that could be read silently or aloud, singly or in chorus, on any beach, anywhere. It was up to participants to choose how to do that, joining at their local beach to fill the shorelines around the UK, and standing together as they watched the faces of the dead disappear.

Our beaches are spaces where time is relevant only in relation to the tide; where it's possible perhaps to imagine standing beside those young expectant folk who could not imagine what awaited them, and to say a final goodbye and an endless thank you.

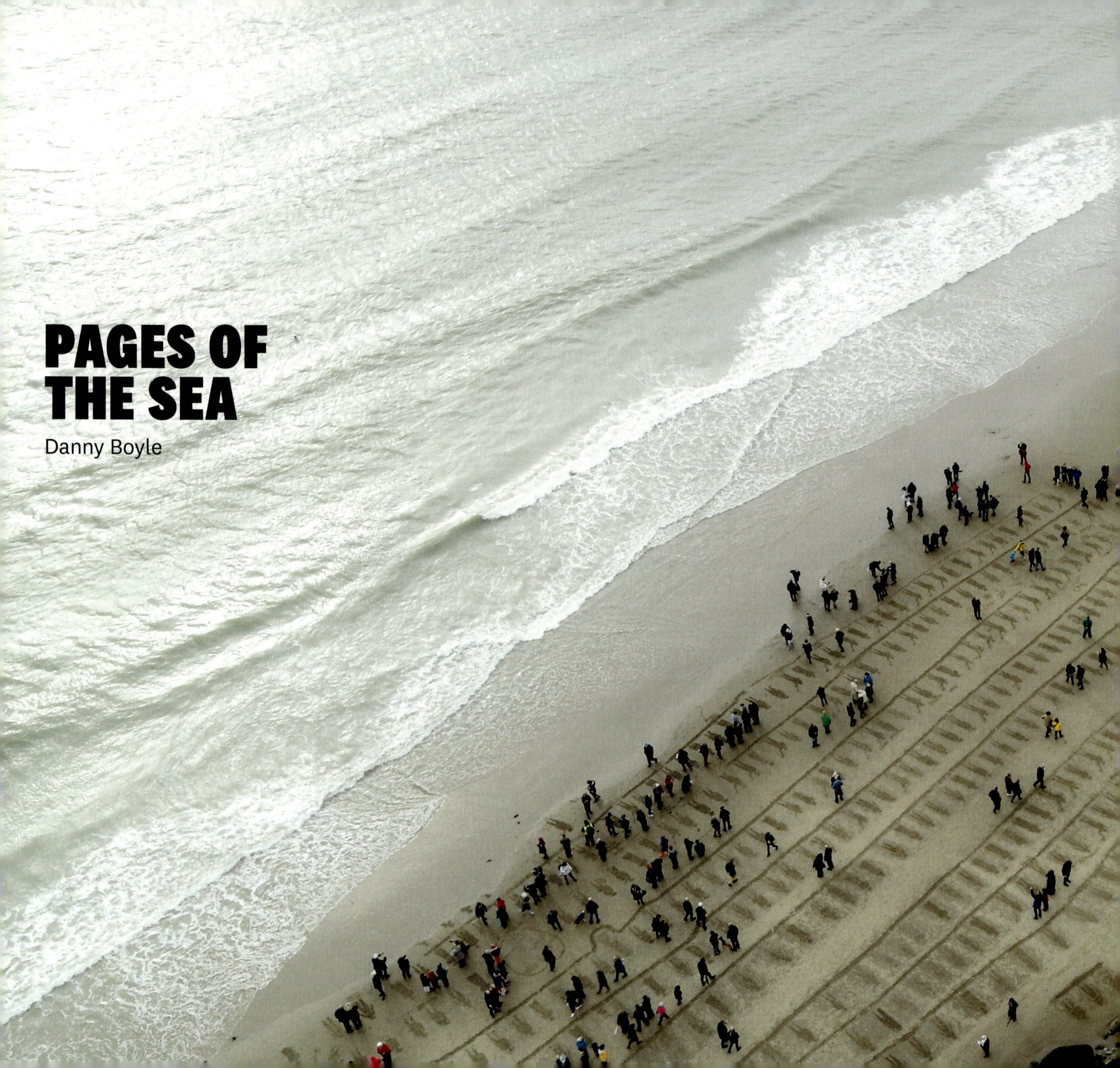
PAGES OF
THE SEA
Danny Boyle

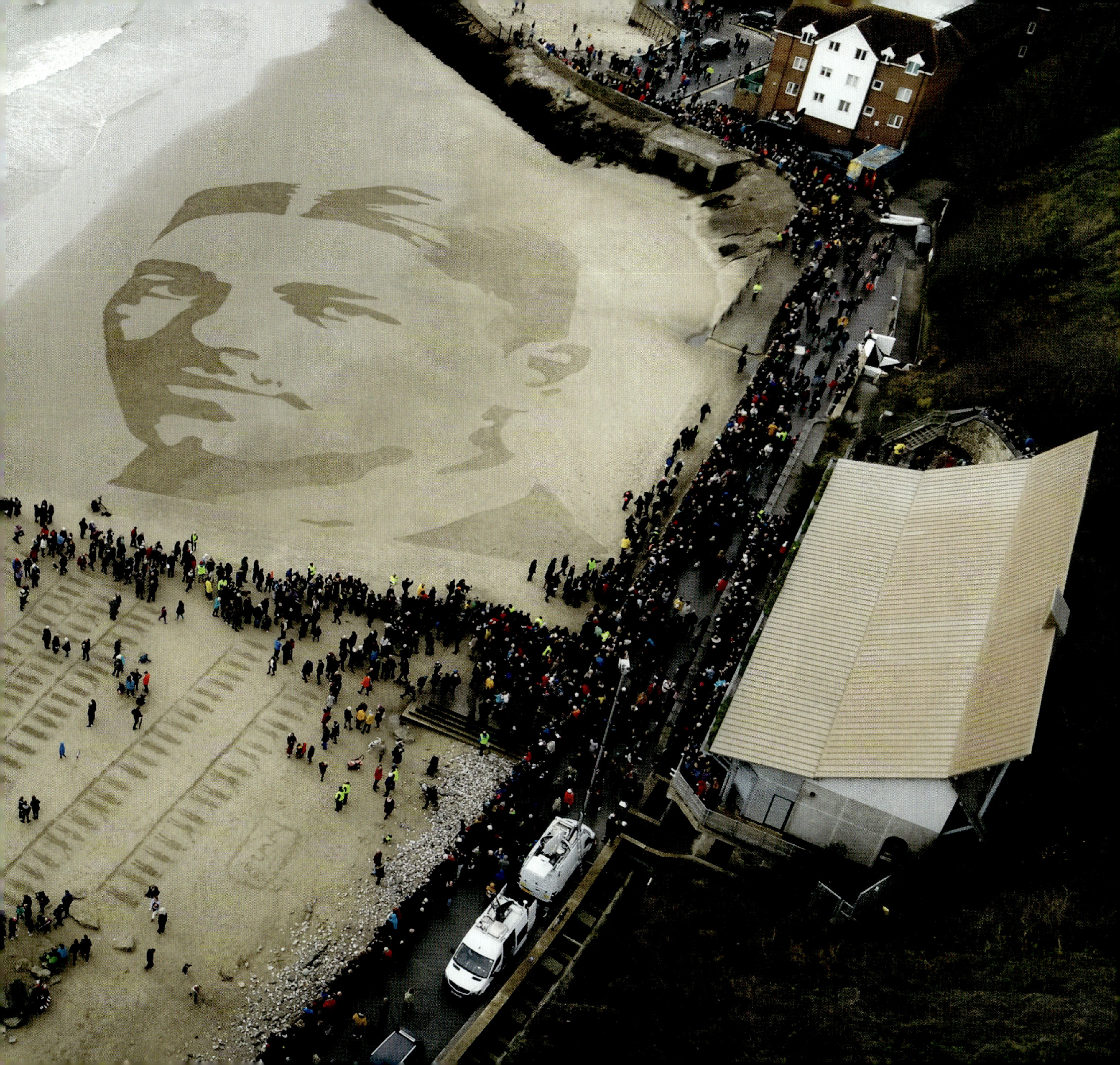

On the centenary of the Armistice, tens of thousands of people took part in a commission created by film-maker Danny Boyle which invited people to gather on 32 beaches around the UK for a UK-wide gesture of remembrance for the men and women who left their home shores during the First World War.

Large-scale portraits of casualties, designed by sand artists Sand In Your Eye, were drawn into the sand on each beach and washed away as the tide came in — representing a small selection of the millions who gave their lives to the war. The portraits were chosen by Boyle to represent a range of stories — ordinary people who gave their lives to the war effort, from doctors and poets to munition workers, privates and officers.

Visitors to each beach were asked to join in by creating silhouettes of people in the sand, remembering the millions of lives lost or changed forever by the conflict. The community near each beach personalised their own event, tailored to reflect the sacrifices of their local community. In Swansea, white kites were decorated and flown as the waves washed away the face of Dorothy Watson, a munitions worker who was killed in an explosion aged 19. In Ayr, Walter Tull was remembered to the sound of pipers — the first black officer to serve in the British Army. Perranporth in Cornwall saw horses, flags and dancing by young people, with lanterns along the shore as the night closed in. Many people also took part in community projects in the preceding weeks near each beach, discovering their local history.

Poet Carol Ann Duffy was invited by Danny Boyle to write a poem to mark the centenary. Her sonnet, ‘The Wound in Time’, was read by individuals, choirs, families and communities as they gathered on the beaches. The poem was also printed on cards featuring over 14,000 different images of casualties from the First World War.

Aerial photographs of the sand portraits went on to became one of the outstanding symbols of the Armistice centenary, as the pictures were circulated around the world via the press and social media. In this way, over 25 million people in the UK were made aware of the event and touched by its impact, with many confirming that it had made the First World War more relevant to their lives.

UK-wide, 11 November 2018

Previous page: Crowds paid tribute to poet and soldier Wilfred Owen, etched into the sand at Folkestone Beach.

Right. Volunteers arrived early in the morning at Murlough Beach, Northern Ireland, to create a tribute to fallen soldier John McCance (see also page 283).

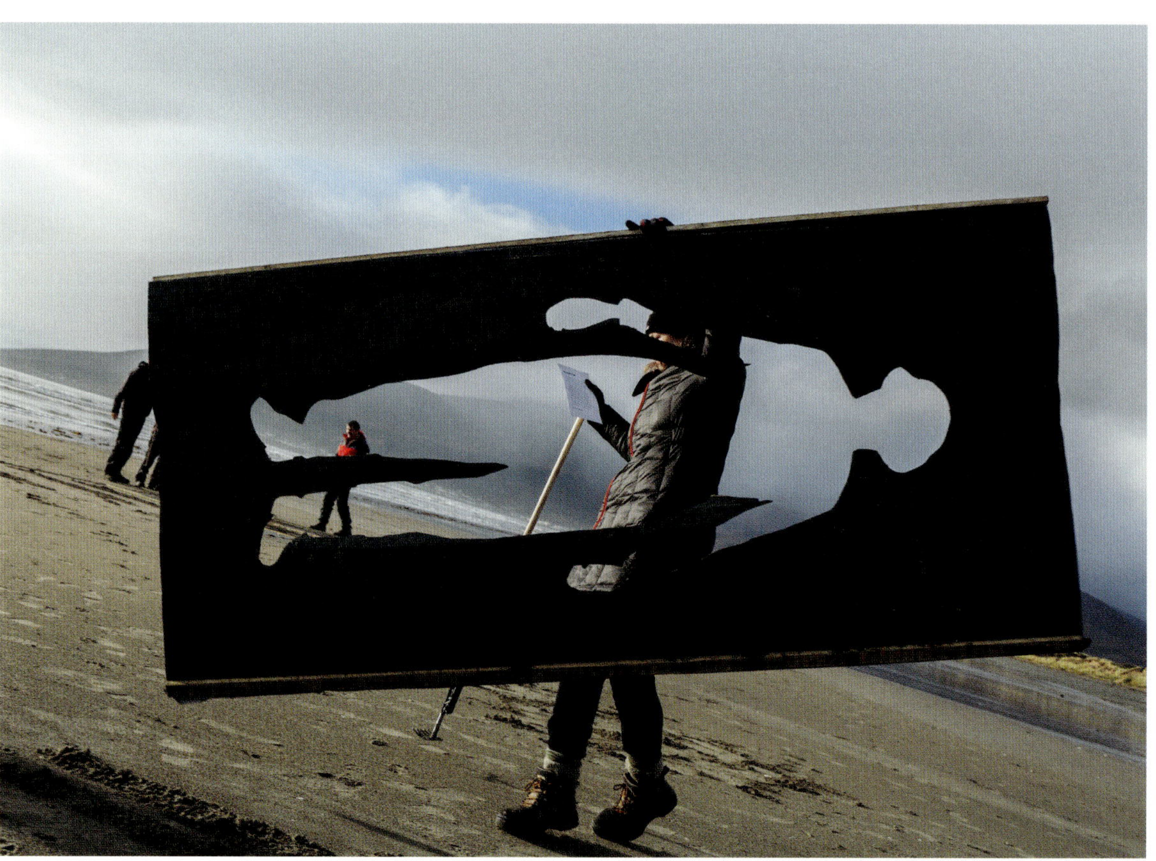

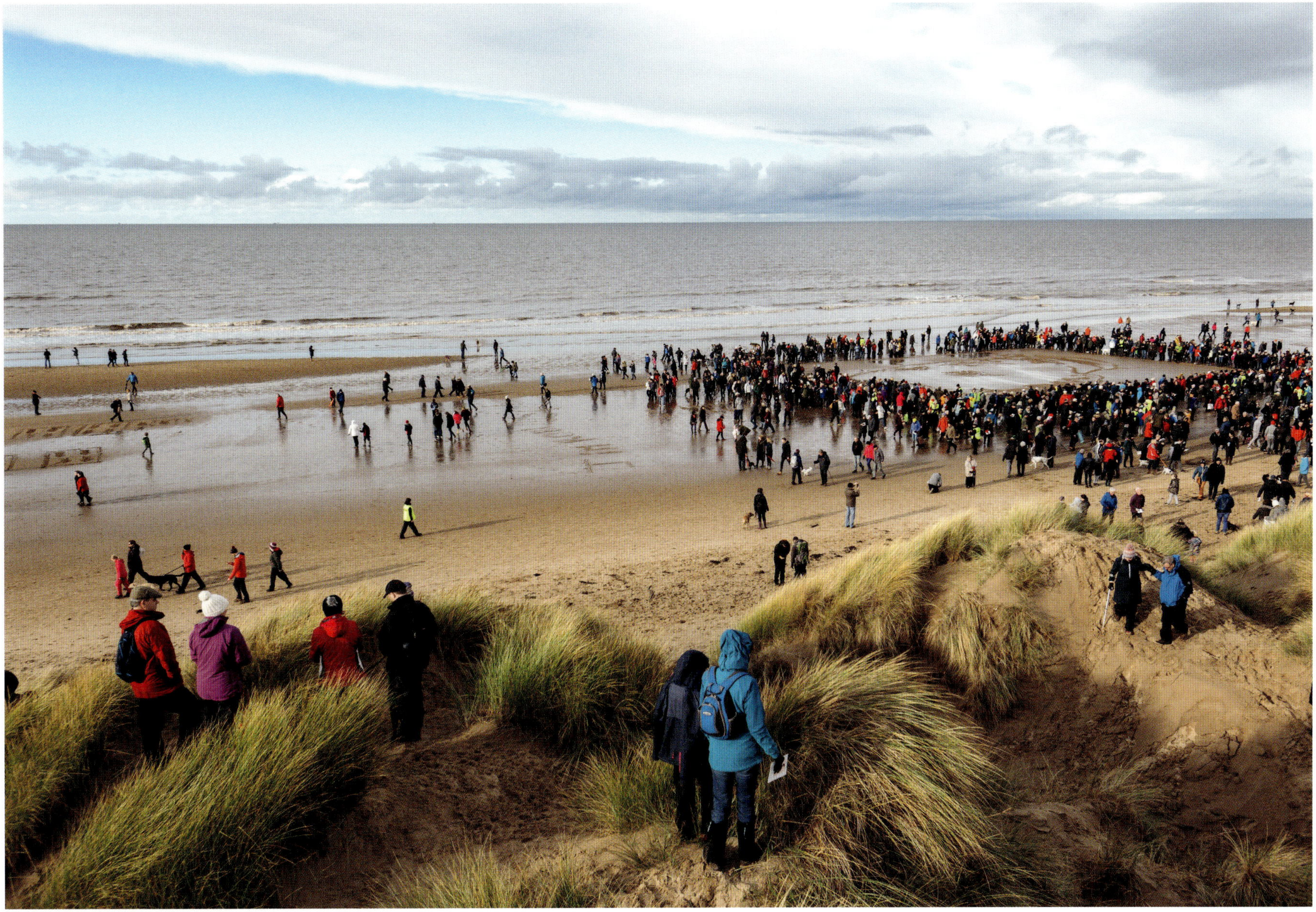

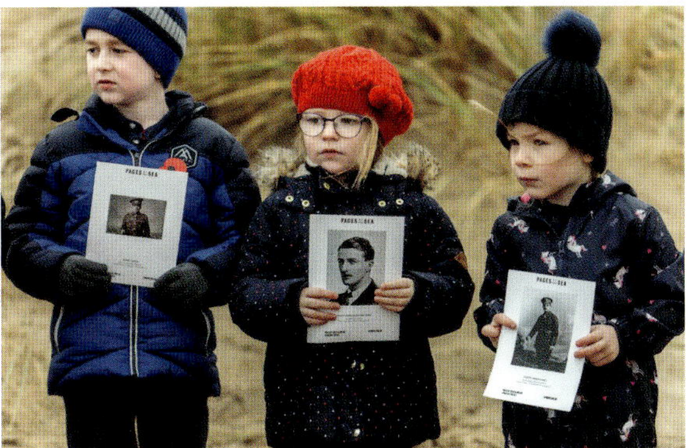

Young and old gathered on
Formby Beach, Merseyside,
to create a silhouette of
Captain John Basil Armitage,
who fought in the Battle of
the Somme.

THE WOUND IN TIME

It is the wound in Time. The century's tides,

chanting their bitter psalms, cannot heal it.

Not the war to end all wars; death's birthing place;

the earth nursing its ticking metal eggs, hatching

new carnage. But how could you know, brave

as belief as you boarded the boats, singing?

The end of God in the poisonous, shrapneled air.

Poetry gargling its own blood. We sense it was love

you gave your world for; the town squares silent,

awaiting their cenotaphs. What happened next?

War. And after that? War. And now? War. War.

History might as well be water, chastising this shore;

for we learn nothing from your endless sacrifice.

Your faces drowning in the pages of the sea.

Carol Ann Duffy, 2018

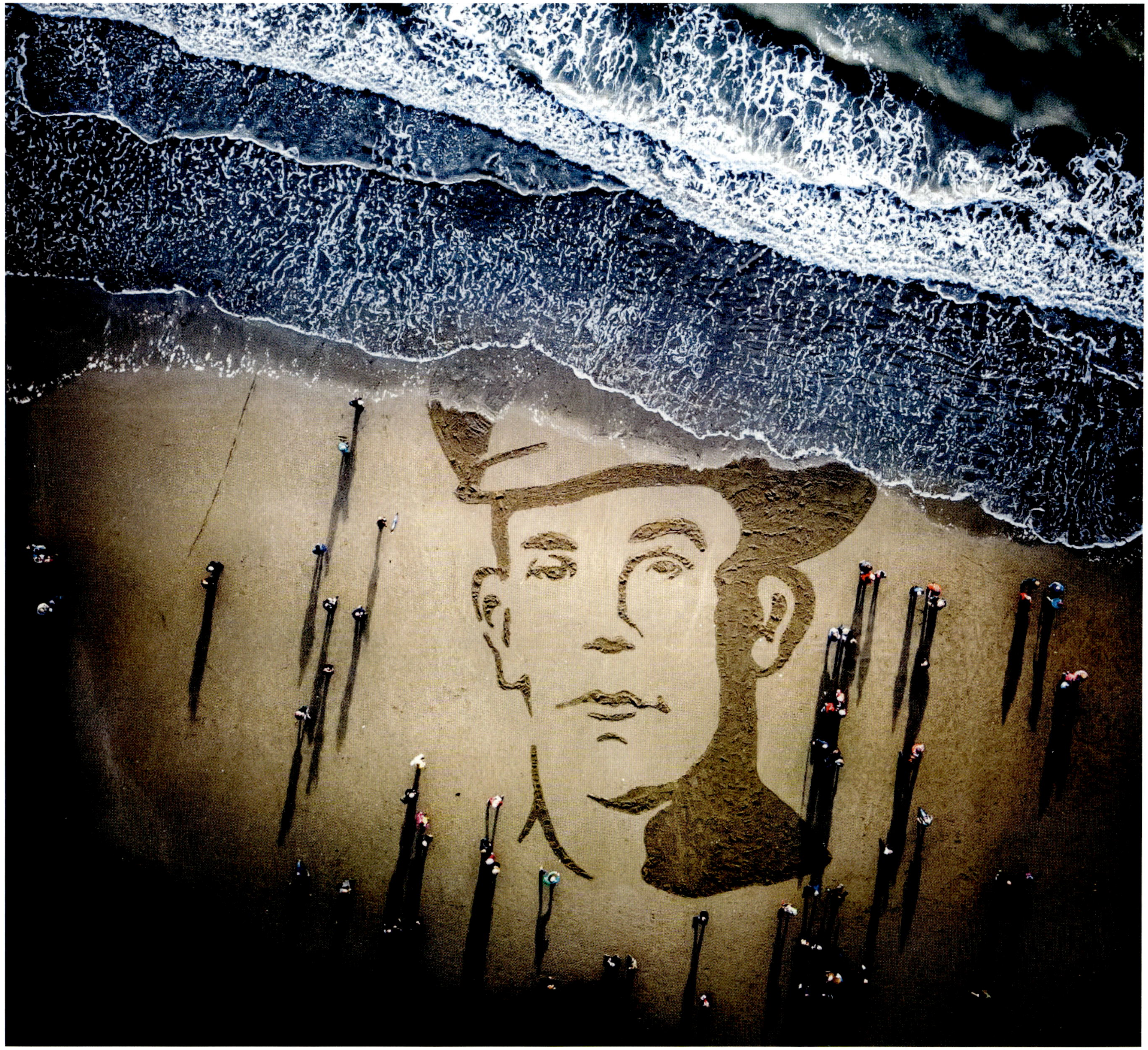

Below. Ellis Humphrey Evans,
Welsh poet and member of the
Royal Welsh Fusiliers, depicted
at Colwyn Bay.

Opposite. Sand portrait of
Rachel Ferguson on Downhill
Beach, Derry.

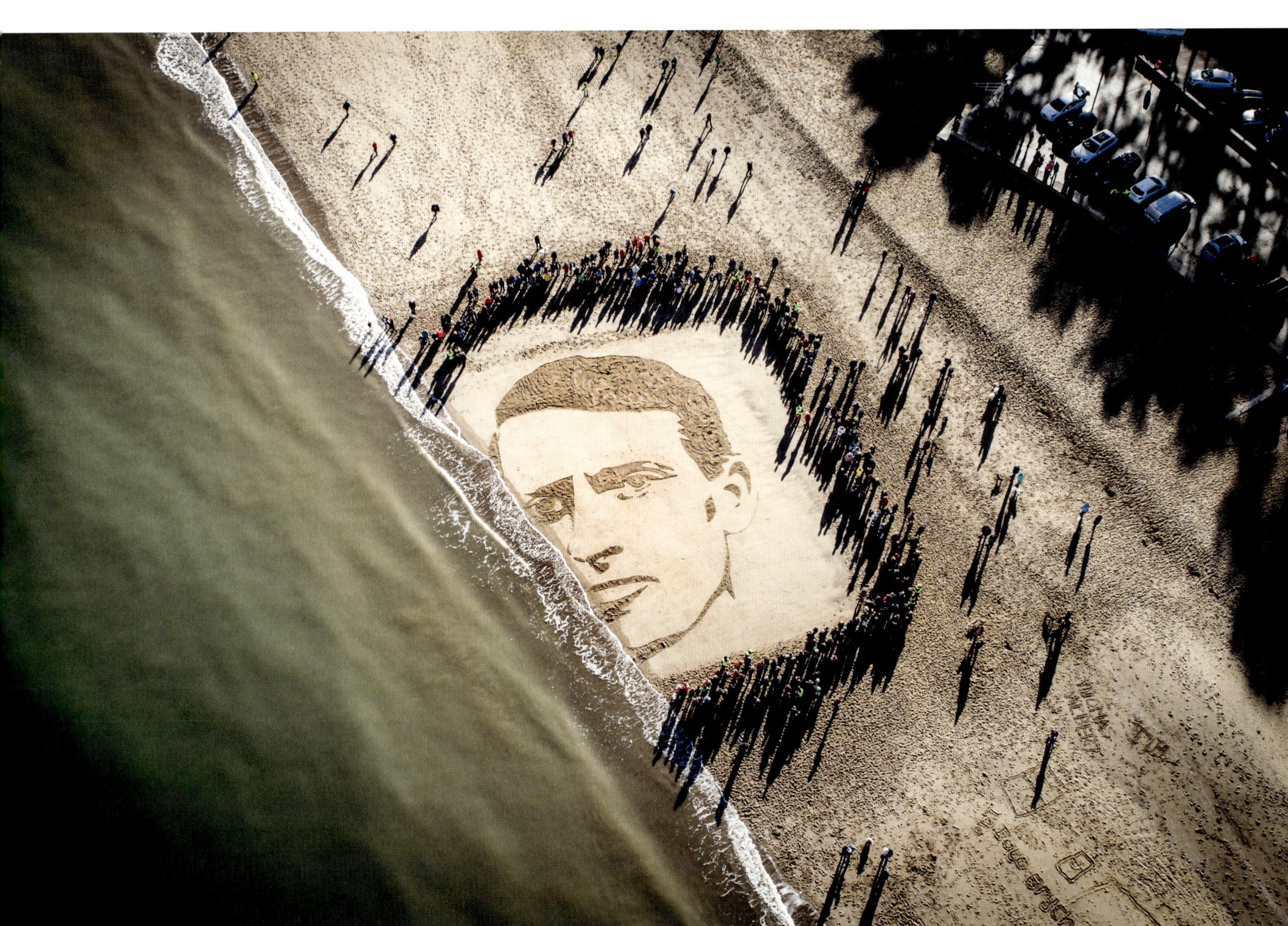

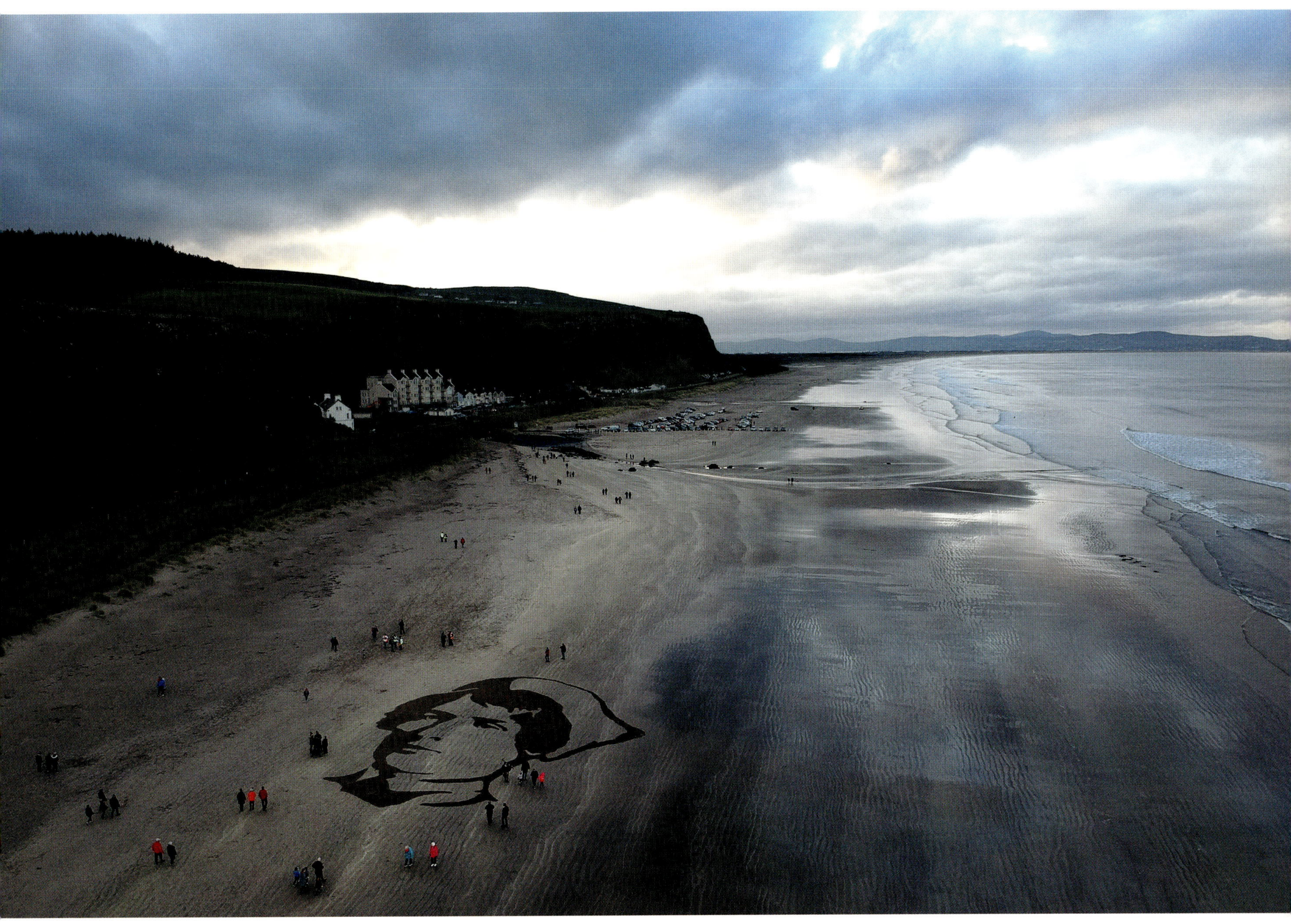

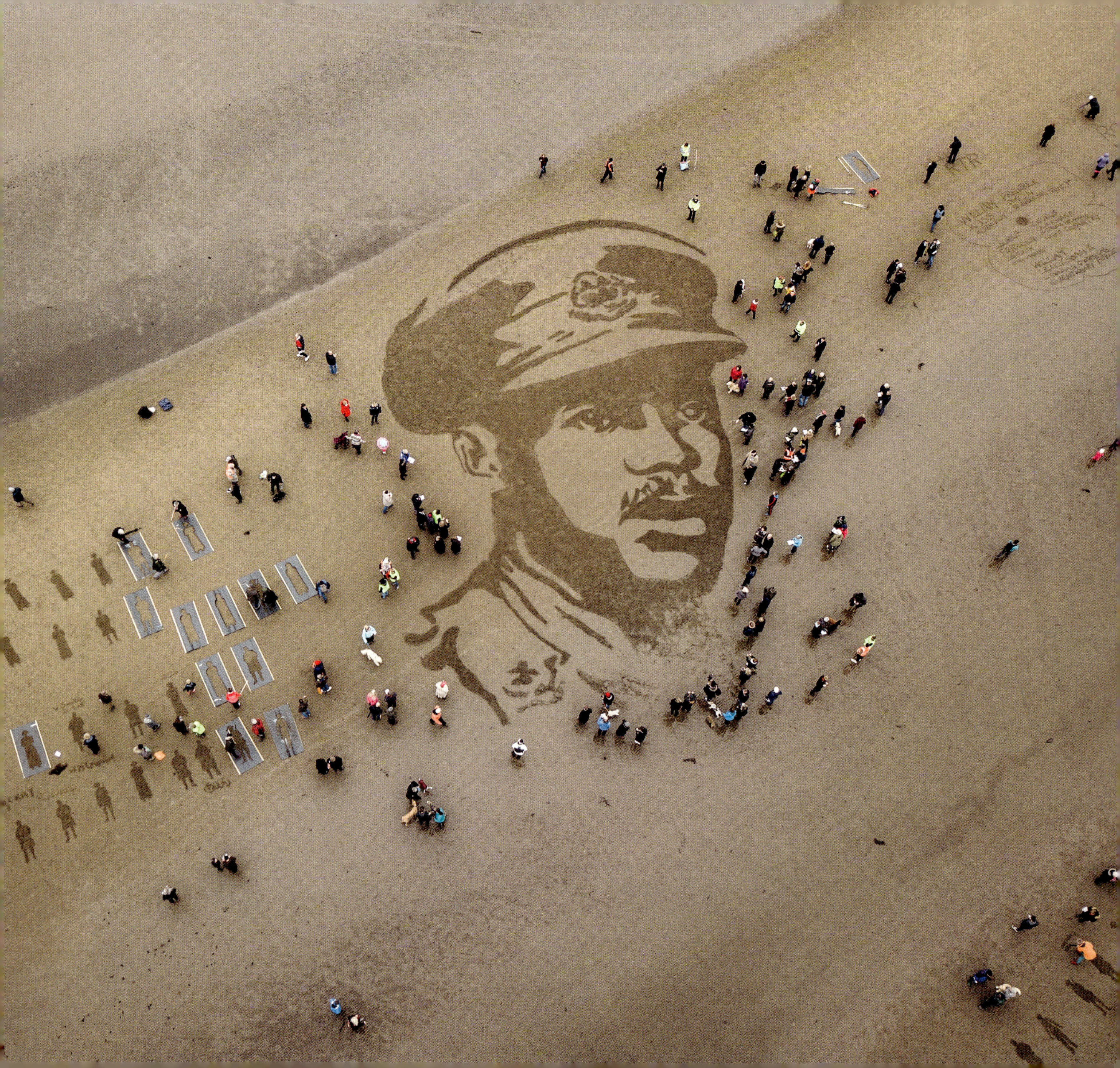

COMMISSIONING CREDITS

The 306: Dawn (p.254)
A National Theatre of Scotland, 14-18 NOW and Perth Theatre co-production, in association with Red Note Ensemble. Written by Oliver Emanuel, composed by Gareth Williams, directed by Laurie Sansom. Image credit: Manual Harlan.

The 306: Day (p.254)
Presented by National Theatre of Scotland, Perth Theatre, and Stellar Quines. In association with Red Note Ensemble. Written by Oliver Emanuel, composed by Gareth Williams, directed by Jemima Levick. Image credit: Christopher Bowen Photography.

The 306: Dusk (p.254)
A National Theatre of Scotland and Perth Theatre production, co-commissioned by 14-18 NOW. Written by Oliver Emanuel, composed by Gareth Williams, directed by Wils Wilson. Image credit: Drew Farrell.

100: The Day Our World Changed — Wildworks (p.60)
Co-commissioned by 14-18 NOW and The Lost Gardens of Heligan. Image credit: Steve Tanner and Ian Kingsnorth.

100: UnEarth — Wildworks (p.64)
Co-commissioned by 14-18 NOW and The Lost Gardens of Heligan. Image credit: Steve Tanner and Ian Kingsnorth.

1914 Day by Day (p.220)
Co-commissioned by 14-18 NOW and The Cartoon Museum in association with BBC Radio 4.

24-Decade History of Popular Music — Taylor Mac (p.122)
Co-commissioned by 14-18 NOW and Belfast International Arts Festival. Image credits: p.122 Johnny Fraser, courtesy Belfast International Arts Festival; p.123 Ves Pitts.

Across and In-Between — Suzanne Lacy (p.40)
Co-commissioned by 14-18 NOW and Belfast International Arts Festival. Supported by the Irish Government. Image credit: Helen Sloan and Ross Mulhall.

After a War (p.170)
Co-commissioned by 14-18 NOW and LIFT. Image credits: p.170 courtesy Tim Etchells; p.171 Joost van den Broek; p.172 (top) Ellie Kurttz, courtesy LIFT and (bottom) JC Caceres, courtesy Lola Arias; p.173 Rene Huemer.

Aldeburgh Festival (p.47)
Co-commissioned by 14-18 NOW and Aldeburgh Festival. Image credit: Matt Jolly.

All the Hills and Vales Along — James MacMillan (p.106)
Co-commissioned by 14-18 NOW and the London Symphony Orchestra. Image credit: Robin Mitchell.

Anya Gallaccio (p.114)
Co-commissioned by 14-18 NOW and Aldeburgh Music's SNAP visual arts programme, with the support of the National Trust. Image credit: Anya Gallaccio — Untitled Landscape 2014. Installation at Orford, Ness, SNAP, Art at the Aldeburgh Festival 2014. Image credit: Owain Thomas, courtesy Snape Maltings and the National Trust.

The Art of Border Living (p.152)
Co-commissioned by 14-18 NOW, the Verbal Arts Centre and The Foghorn Company. Supported by the Irish Government. Image credit: Joseph Molloy.

Asunder — Bob Stanley (p.168)
Co-commissioned by 14-18 NOW and Sunderland Cultural Partnership. Image credits: p.168 North News & Pictures; p.169 courtesy Tyne & Wear Archives & Museums.

At Times Like These Men Were Wishing They Were All Kinds of Insects — Graham Gingles (p.272)
Co-commissioned by 14-18 NOW and The MAC. Image credits: p.272 Princess Mary Gift box, courtesy IWM (EPH 2041); p.273 Simon Mills.

BBC Late Proms — John Tavener (p.68)
Co-commissioned by the BBC for the BBC Proms, as part of 14-18 NOW. Image credit: Chris Christodoulou.

Beware of Pity — Complicité and Schaubühne Berlin (p.142)
Presented by the Barbican and 14-18 NOW. Co-produced by Complicité and the Schaubühne. Live stream and post-show talk presented in partnership with Goethe-Institut London. Image credit: Gianmarco Bredasola.

Black Dog — Dave McKean (p.98)
Co-commissioned by 14-18 NOW, The Lakes International Comic Art Festival and On a Marché sur la Bulle. Image credit: Dave McKean.

Blood — Lemn Sissay (p.253)
Co-commissioned by 14-18 NOW and Verbal Arts.

Bloodyminded (p.54)
Co-commissioned by 14-18 NOW and Attenborough Centre for the Creative Arts. Media Partner Pathfinder International. Image credit: Christa Holka.

The Casement Project — Fearghus Ó Conchúir (p.35)
Co-commissioned by 14-18 NOW. Produced by Fearghus Ó Conchúir in association with Project Arts Centre. An ART:2016 National Project supported by the Arts Council/An Chomhairle Ealaíon and supported by Culture Ireland, as part of the Ireland 2016 Centenary Programme. Image credit: Matthew Thompson.

Walter Daniel John Tull — the first ever black officer to command white troops — was depicted in the sand at Ayr in Ayrshire.

Cause and Effect (p.250)
Commissioned by 14-18 NOW and produced by Roundhouse.

Ceremony — Phil Collins (p.224)
Co-commissioned by 14-18 NOW, HOME, Manchester and Manchester International Festival. Produced by HOME, Manchester, Manchester International Festival, Shady Lane Productions and Tigerlily Productions.

Supported by Arts Council England's Ambition for Excellence, the BBC, the Henry Moore Foundation and My Festival Circle.

Image credits: p.224 (top left and bottom left) Shady Lane Productions and (right) Tarnish Vision, p.225 Joel Fildes. All images courtesy of Shady Lane Productions, Berlin.

Charlie Ward — Sound&Fury (p.174)
Co-commissioned by 14-18 NOW and Fuel. Image credit: Carolyn Hill.

Clarion Call — Hannah Fox, Byron J. Scullin and Tom Supple (p.248)
Co-commissioned by 14-18 NOW and Pacitti Company for the SPILL Festival of Performance. Developed with the support of Dark Mofo Festival, Tasmania. Image credit: Guido Mencari.

**The Coffin Jump —
Katrina Palmer** (p.32)
Co-commissioned by 14-18 NOW and Yorkshire Sculpture Park, made possible with Art Fund support. Special thanks to Sir David Verey, The Henry Moore Foundation and The Clothworkers' Company. With additional support from Melanie Gee, Larissa Joy and thanks to Midge & Simon Palley, Nicholas & Jane Ferguson and Tony McCallum. Image credits: p.32 Danny Lawson, courtesy PA; p.33 Jonty Wilde, courtesy Yorkshire Sculpture Park.

**Contagion —
Shobana Jeyasingh** (p.194)
Co-commisioned by 14-18 NOW and Shobana Jeyasingh Dance, supported by Wellcome, Oak Foundation and the Deborah Loeb Brice Donor Advised Fund at CAF America. Image credits: p.194 (top) Jane Hobson and (bottom) Chris Nash; p.195 Jane Hobson.

Dazzle Ships Series (p.14)
Co-commissioned by Liverpool Biennial. Supported by Bloomberg Philanthropies.

Archive image credits: p.18 courtesy IWM: (top) SP 1650 and (bottom) Art.IWM ART 991; p.19 courtesy IWM: (top to bottom) Art.IWM DAZ 0004 2, Art.IWM DAZ 0004 1, Art.IWM DAZ 0029 2, Art.IWM DAZ 0034 1, Art.IWM DAZ 0034 2, Art.IWM DAZ 0035 1 and Art. IWM DAZ 0008 2.

**Carlos Cruz-Díez, *Induction Chromatique à Double Fréquence pour* L'Edmund Gardner *Ship*, 2014
Edmund Gardner, Liverpool**
Co-commissioned by 14-18 NOW, Liverpool Biennial and Tate Liverpool in partnership with National Museums Liverpool (Merseyside Maritime Museum). With support from Ernest Cook Trust, Cammell Laird, International Paint, Weightmans. Image credits: (top) courtesy of The Cruz-Díez Art Foundation and (bottom) Helen Hunt.

Tobias Rehberger, *Dazzle Ship London*, 2014 HMS *President* (1918), London
Co-commissioned by 14-18 NOW and Liverpool Biennial in association with the University of the Arts London Chelsea College of Arts, HMS *President* (1918) and Tate Liverpool, in partnership with National Museums Liverpool (Merseyside Maritime Museum. Supported by Bloomberg Philanthropies, Goethe-Institut London and Schroder Charity Trust. Image credit: p.23 Chris Wainwright, courtesy Lydiat/ Wainwright Studios.

**Sir Peter Blake, *Everybody Razzle Dazzle*, 2015
Snowdrop, Mersey ferry, Liverpool**
Snowdrop, Mersey ferry, Liverpool. Commissioned by Liverpool Biennial, 14-18 NOW and Tate Liverpool in partnership with Merseytravel and National Museums Liverpool (Merseyside Maritime Museum). Image credit: Mark McNulty.

**Ciara Phillips, *Every Woman*, 2016
MV Fingal, Edinburgh**
Co-commissioned by 14-18 NOW and Edinburgh Art Festival with support from Scottish Government, Creative Scotland, City of Edinburgh Council, The Royal Yacht Britannia Trust, Forth Ports, Sherwin-Williams. Dazzle Ship series co-commissioned with Liverpool Biennial. Supported by Bloomberg Philanthropies. Image credit: Ross Attenburgh, courtesy Ultra Photography.

Tauba Auerbach, *Flow Separation*, 2018 — 2019, New York
Commissioned by Public Art Fund and 14-18 NOW. Supported by Bloomberg Philanthropies. Courtesy Paula Cooper Gallery. Image credit: Nicholas Knight, courtesy Public Art Fund, NY.

Does It Matter? (p.144)
Co-commissioned by 14-18 NOW and Channel 4. Produced by Artsadmin and Xenoki. Part of the Unlimited programme. Image credits: p.144 film still from *Ghosts*, courtesy Simon Mckeown; p.145 film still from *Resemblance*, courtesy Claire Cunningham.

Dr Blighty — Nutkhut (p.212)
Co-commissioned by 14-18 NOW, Brighton Festival and Royal Pavilion & Museums, Brighton & Hove. Image credits: pp.212–213 Tabitha Fireman, courtesy of Getty Images; pp.214–215 Linda Nylind.

The Empire Café (p.180)
Part of the Glasgow 2014 Cultural Programme. Supported by the British Council. Image credit: Graham Fagen.

**End of Empire —
Yinka Shonibare CBE** (p.56)
Co-commissioned by 14-18 NOW and Turner Contemporary. Image credit: Stephen White.

Everything that happened and would happen — Heiner Goebbels (p.70)
Co-commissioned by 14-18 NOW, Artangel, Park Avenue Armory and Ruhrtriennale. World premiere co-presented by Artangel and Manchester International Festival as a pre-Factory event. Contextual programme supported by the Embassy of the Federal Republic of Germany London, with thanks to Goethe-Institut London. Image credit: Thanasis Deligiannis.

Fashion & Freedom (p.28)
Co-commissioned by 14-18 NOW and Manchester Art Gallery, supported by the British Fashion Council. Image credit: Jez Tozer.

Fierce Light (p.192)
Co-commissioned by 14-18 NOW, Norfolk & Norwich Festival and Writers' Centre Norwich.

Five Telegrams — Anna Meredith and 59 Productions (p.86)
Co-commissioned by 14-18 NOW, BBC Proms and Edinburgh International Festival. Image credit: Justin Sutcliffe, courtesy of 59 Productions Ltd.

Flight — Geraldine Pilgrim (p.176)
Co-commissioned by 14-18 NOW and Lake District National Park, part of Lakes Alive Festival. Supported by South Lakeland District Council and Cumbria County Council. Image credit: Matthew Lloyd, courtesy Getty Images.

Fly by Night — Duke Riley (p.260)
Co-commissioned by 14-18 NOW,
LIFT, Peabody, Greenwich + Docklands
International Festival and the
London Borough of Bexley. Originally
commissioned by Creative Time.
Image credits: pp.260–261 Victor
Frankowski, courtesy LIFT; p.262 Tod
Seelie, courtesy Creative Time; p.263
Victor Frankowski, courtesy LIFT.

**The Forbidden Zone —
Duncan Macmillan, Katie Mitchell
and Schaubühne Berlin** (p.154)
Co-produced by Prospero (Théâtre
National de Bretagne — Rennes,
Théâtre de Liège, Emilia Romagna
Teatro Fondazione, Schaubühne am
Lehniner Platz, Göteborgs Stadsteater,
World Theatre Festival Zagreb and
Festival of Athens and Epidaurus).
Image credits: pp.154–155 Stephen
Cummiskey; p.156 Gianmarco Bresdola;
p.157 Stephen Cummiskey.

**A Foreign Field —
Torsten Rasch** (p.218)
Commissioned by public subscription
for the Three Choirs Festival 2014
and StädtischeTheater Chemnitz,
Erich-Schellhorn-Stiftung as part
of 14-18 NOW. Performance kindly
supported by the Elmley Foundation
and Anwen Walker. Choristers
supported by Lee Bolton Monier-
Williams. Image credit: Torsten Rasch.

Furious Folly — Mark Anderson (p.102)
Co-commissioned by 14-18 NOW and
the Town of Poperinge. Image credits:
p.102 Hide the Shark; pp.103–105
Michaël Depestele.

**Garden within a Garden —
Imran Qureshi** (p.108)
Commissioned by 14-18 NOW, Bradford
Museums and Galleries, City of Bradford
MD Council and Yorkshire Festival.
Image credit: Kippa Matthews.

**Goodbye to All That —
Lavinia Greenlaw** (p.88)
Commissioned by 14-18 NOW.

**Great & Tiny War —
Bobby Baker** (p.166)
Commissioned by 14-18 NOW with
Daily Life Ltd and Wunderbar. Image
credit: Andrew Whittuck.

**The Head & the Load —
William Kentridge, Philip Miller,
Thuthuka Sibisi and
Gregory Maqoma** (p.82)
Co-commissioned by 14-18 NOW, Park
Avenue Armory, Ruhrtriennale and
MASS MoCA with additional support
from Holland Festival. *The Head & the
Load* acknowledges the kind assistance
of Marian Goodman Gallery, Goodman
Gallery and Lia Rumma Gallery. Image
credit: Stella Olivier.

**I Say Nothing —
Christine Borland** (p.270)
Co-commissioned by 14-18 NOW and
Glasgow Museums, made possible by
Art Fund support. Image credits: p.270
(top) invalid feeder cup in Glasgow
Museums' Open Museum World War I
handling kit and (bottom) box for World
War I soapstone monkey charm, 'I Say
Nothing', now empty, inscribed by the
collector Edward Lovett about 1917;
p.271 installation view. All courtesy
CSG CIC Glasgow Museums Collection.

**If It Wasn't for Their Wellies —
John Maxwell Geddes** (p.219)
Co-commissioned by 14-18 NOW and
Live Music Now Scotland, part of Live
Music Now Scotland's Composing with
Care initiative.

**In Parenthesis — Iain Bell and
Welsh National Opera** (p.182)
Commissioned by the Nicholas John
Trust, with 14-18 NOW, and supported
by WNO Commissions Group. Image
credit: Bill Cooper.

Incredible Journeys (p.268)
Co-commissioned by 14-18 NOW and
The Story Museum. Image credit:
The Story Museum 2016.

Iolaire (p.58)
Co-commissioned by 14-18 NOW and
An Lanntair. Image credits: p.58
Christian Cooksey, courtesy Braeside
Photography; p.59 film still — track 12:
Sálm II (Reprise) by Dalziel + Scullion
and Christian Cooksey.

**Harlem Hellfighters: James Reese
Europe and the Absence of Ruin —
John Akomfrah, Jason Moran and
Bradford Young** (p.246)
Co-commissioned by 14-18 NOW,
Berliner Festspiele / Jazzfest Berlin,
Serious and the John F. Kennedy
Center for Performing Arts, with
support from the Federal Agency
for Civic Education, Germany. Image
credit: Camille Blake and Jazzfest
Berlin 2018, Berliner Festspiele.

**Letter to an Unknown Soldier —
Neil Bartlett and Kate Pullinger** (p.48)
Commissioned by 14-18 NOW,
produced in association with Free
Word. Image credits: pp.48–50 Dom
Agius; p.51 Gideon Mendel.

LIGHTS OUT — Bedwyr Williams (p.90)
Co-commissioned by 14-18 NOW
and Artes Mundi. Image credit: p.97
Artes Mundi.

**LIGHTS OUT —
Bob and Roberta Smith** (p.90)
Commissioned by 14-18 NOW.
With thanks to Belfast City Council.
Produced by Factotum. Image credit:
p.96 Brian Morrison.

LIGHTS OUT — Jeremy Deller (p.90)
Co-commissioned by 14-18 NOW and
The Space. Produced by Somethin' Else.
Image credit: p.93 stills from *LIGHTS
OUT* film, courtesy Jeremy Deller.

LIGHTS OUT — Nalini Malani (p.90)
Co-commissioned by 14-18 NOW
and Edinburgh Art Festival. With the
generous support of the National
Galleries of Scotland. Produced by
Edinburgh Art Festival. Image credit:
pp.94–95 Stuart Armitt.

LIGHTS OUT — Ryoji Ikeda (p.90)
Co-commissioned by 14-18 NOW and
the Mayor of London. Produced by
Artangel. With thanks to The Royal
Parks. Originally commissioned by
Dream Amsterdam Foundation and
Forma, 2008. With thanks to the
Daiwa Anglo-Japanese Foundation,
The Great Britain Sasakawa Foundation
and Gallery Koyanagi (Tokyo). Image
credits: pp.92–93 Jonathan Perugia;
p.94 (left, top and top right) Will
Eckersley and (bottom) Ewa Hertzog.

**London Sinfonietta —
George Benjamin** (p.34)
Co-commissioned by 14-18 NOW and
London Sinfonietta, supported by the
Embassy of the Federal Republic of
Germany, London. First presented as
part of BBC Proms 2018. Image credit:
Chris Christodoulou.

**Make Art Not War —
Bob and Roberta Smith** (p.274)
Produced by ArtsMediaPeople
with contemporary artist, Bob and
Roberta Smith, leading academic
Professor Bill Lucas, Director of the
Centre for Real World Learning at
the University of Winchester and the
former CEO of Creative & Cultural
Skills, Pauline Tambling CBE. Image
credits: p.274 Proudfoot; p.275
Bob and Roberta Smith.

Make Me Up — Rachel Maclean (p.226)
Produced by Hopscotch Films with
NVA. Commissioned for the BBC,
Creative Scotland and 14-18 NOW,
supported by Jerwood Arts.
Image credit: stills courtesy of
Rachel Maclean.

**Mametz — Owen Sheers and National
Theatres Wales** (p.264)
Co-commissioned by 14-18 NOW
and National Theatre Wales. With
funding from Arts Council of Wales
and the Welsh Government. Image
credit: Mark Douet.

**Man and the dark —
Rebecca Warren** (p.190)
Co-commissioned by 14-18 NOW
and the Henry Moore Institute. Image
credit: Rebecca Warren, courtesy
Maureen Paley, London.

**Memorial — Alice Oswald and
Jocelyn Pook** (p.146)
Co-commissioned by 14-18 NOW and
the Barbican, with assistance from the
Australia Council for the Arts and the
Australian Government's Major Festivals
Initiative. Image credit: Shane Reid.

Memorial Ground — David Lang (p.153)
Co-commissioned by 14-18 NOW and
the East Neuk Festival with the support
of Creative Scotland and in partnership
with the Big Big Sing. Image credit:
Colin Hattersley.

**Memories of August 1914 —
Royal de Luxe** (p.36)
Co-commissioned by 14-18 NOW and
Liverpool City Council. Image credit:
Ant Clausen.

**Millicent Fawcett —
Gillian Wearing** (p.232)
Commissioned by the Mayor of London
with 14-18 NOW, Firstsite and Iniva.
Image credits: p.233 Caroline Teo; p.234
(top) Caroline Teo, (bottom left) Jo
Baxendale and (bottom right) Caroline
Teo; p.235 Caroline Teo. All courtesy
of GLA.

**Mimesis: African Soldier —
John Akomfrah** (p.24)
Co-commissioned by 14-18 NOW,
New Art Exchange, Nottingham and
Smoking Dogs Films.

Supported by Arts Council England,
with additional support from Sharjah
Art Foundation. Image credits: p.24
courtesy John Akomfrah; p.25 (top)
courtesy IWM / Film courtesy Smoking
Dogs Film and (bottom) courtesy
John Akomfrah.

Nissen Hut — Rachel Whiteread (p.150)
Co-commissioned by 14-18 NOW and
the Forestry Commission. Image credit:
Courtesy Forestry Commission.

**Not Yet at Ease —
Raqs Media Collective** (p.196)
Co-commissioned by 14-18 NOW and
Firstsite, Colchester. Image credit:
Installation view, Raqs Media Collective,
Not Yet At Ease, 2018. Photo by Douglas
Atfield, courtesy Firstsite.

**Now the Hero \ Nawr yr Arwr —
Marc Rees** (p.76)
Commissioned by 14-18 NOW.
Produced by Taliesin Arts Centre/
Swansea University in partnership
with the City & County of Swansea and
Swansea International Festival and with
the generous support of Arts Council of
Wales, the Welsh Government, the City
& County of Swansea, the Colwinston
Charitable Trust, Swansea University
and Heritage Lottery Fund — Awards for
All. Image credits: p.76 Warren Orchard;
p.77 David Brangwyn; p.78 Warren
Orchard; p.79 (top) Warren Orchard and
(bottom) Johan Butenschøn Skre.

One World — Mark Wallinger (p.231)
Co-commissioned by 14-18 NOW and
Liverpool Biennial. Image credit:
Football uses photo courtesy NASA,
photo by Mike Smith.

The Opening Act (p.181)
Co-commissioned by 14-18 NOW, Bragg
Central and The Space. Image credit:
Gideon Mendel.

Orchestra of Syrian Musicians (p.112)
Co-commissioned by 14-18 NOW and
Holland Festival. Presented by Africa
Express and Southbank Centre.
Image credit: Ayman Oghanna.

Pages of the Sea — Danny Boyle (p.278)
Commissioned by 14-18 NOW and
delivered with: National Trust; Activate
Performing Arts; Creative Foundation;
Eden Project; National Theatre Scotland;
Nerve Centre; Sunderland Culture;
Taliesin. With Aberystwyth Arts Centre;
The Grand Theatre of Lemmings; Magna
Vitae; MOSTYN; SeaChange Arts;
Swansea Council; Swansea University;
Theatre Orchard; and Visit Blackpool.

The community activation and
engagement programme supported by
The National Lottery Community Fund.
With additional support from Backstage
Trust, Bloomberg Philanthropies,
Calouste Gulbenkian Foundation (UK
Branch) and National Rail.

Image credits: p.280 Murlough
Beach, photo by Oskar Proctor, courtesy
National Trust; p.281 Formby Beach,
photo by Paul Harris, courtesy National
Trust; p.283 Murlough Beach, photo by
Kevin Scott, courtesy Belfast Telegraph;
p.284 Colwyn Bay, photo by Andy
Sayle; p.285 Downhill Beach, photo
by Charles McQuillan, courtesy Getty
Images; p.286 Ayr Beach, photo by
Katielee Arrowsmith, courtesy SWNS;
p.292 Culla Bay Beach, photo by Cara
Forbes; p.295 Redcar Beach, photo by
Darran Moore.

**Poet in da Corner —
Debris Stevenson** (p.228)
Co-commissioned by 14-18 NOW and
the Royal Court Theatre, supported
by Jerwood Arts. Image credits: p.228
Benji Reid; p.229 Vicky Grout.

**Poppies: Wave and Weeping Window —
Artist Paul Cummins & Designer
Tom Piper** (p.158)
Wave and *Weeping Window* are from
the installation *Blood Swept Lands
and Seas of Red* — poppies and original
concept by artist Paul Cummins and
installation designed by Tom Piper —
by Paul Cummins Ceramics Limited in
conjunction with Historic Royal Palaces,
originally at HM Tower of London 2014.
Supported by the Backstage Trust,
Clore Duffield Foundation and DAF:

A PACCAR Company. Learning and
Engagement supported by The Foyle
Foundation. With thanks to MTEC.

Image credits: pp.158–159 Ian Gavan,
courtesy Getty Images; p.160 (top)
Matt Keeble, courtesy Getty Images
and (bottom) Ellie Kurttz; p.161 Andrew
Tryner, courtesy Lincolnshire County
Counci; p.162 Jamie Howden; p.163
Michael Bowles, courtesy Getty Images;
p.164 Nigel Roddis, courtesy Getty
Images; p.165 Colin Davison.

**PROCESSIONS — Artichoke and
Darrell Vydelingum** (p.238)
Commissioned by 14-18 NOW and
produced by Artichoke. R&D supported
by Calouste Gulbenkian Foundation
(UK Branch). Proud partner NatWest.

Image credits: pp.238–239
PROCESSIONS 2018 London, photo
by Sheila Burnett; pp.240–241
PROCESSIONS 2018 London, photo
by Amelia Allen; p.242 Somerset Art
Works workshop images taken at Strode
and Richard Huish Colleges, photo by
Lead Artist Dorcas Casey; p.243 (top)
PROCESSIONS 2018 London, photo
by Amelia Allen; p.243 (bottom left)
PROCESSIONS 2018 London, photo
by Anita Corbin; p.243 (bottom right)
PROCESSIONS Belfast, photo by Brian
Morrison; p.244 PROCESSIONS 2018
Cardiff, photo by Two Cats In The Yard
Photography; p.245 PROCESSIONS
2018 Edinburgh, photo by (top) Claire
Eva and (bottom) Lesley Martin.

Radio Relay (p.69)
Co-commissioned by 14-18 NOW and
Golden Thread Gallery. Image credit:
Graham Fagen.

Richard Thompson (p.252)
Co-commissioned by 14-18 NOW and
produced by Serious. Image credit:
Pamela Littky, courtesy Serious.

Shelter — Anne Tallentire (p.44)
Co-commissioned by 14-18 NOW and
Nerve Centre. Image credits: p.44
Paola Bernardelli; p.45 video
still courtesy Anne Tallentire.

**Shot at Dawn —
Chloe Dewe Mathews** (p.72)
Co-commissioned by 14-18 NOW
and the Ruskin School of Art at the
University of Oxford. Image credit:
Chloe Dewe Mathews.

Somme 100 (p.269)
Co-commissioned by 14-18 NOW.
Produced by Manchester City Council
on behalf of HM Government. Image
credit: Mark Waugh, courtesy
Huckleberry Films.

Sortition — Selina Thompson (p.230)
Co-commissioned by 14-18 NOW and
Arnolfini, supported by Jerwood Arts.
Image credit: Jana Rumley.

**SS Mendi: Dancing the Death Drill —
Isango Ensemble and
Fred Khumalo** (p.216)
Co-commissioned by 14-18 NOW,
Repons Foundation and Nuffield
Southampton Theatres. Image credit:
The Other Richard.

Still — Simon Armitage (p.26)
Co-commissioned by 14-18 NOW,
Norfolk & Norwich Festival and Writers'
Centre Norwich. Image credits: p.26
extract from *Still* by Simon Armitage.
Image courtesy IWM (Q 63948) and
publication by Enitharmon Press; p.27
extract from *Still* by Simon Armitage.
Image courtesy IWM (Q 53) and
publication by Enitharmon Press.

**SYLVIA — ZooNation: The Kate
Prince Company** (p.206)
Co-commissioned by 14-18 NOW.
An Old Vic, Sadler's Wells and
ZooNation: The Kate Prince Company
production. Image credit: artwork
by Hugo Glendinning, production
photography by Manuel Harlan.

**These Rooms — ANU and CoisCéim
Dance Theatre** (p.124)
Co-commissioned by 14-18 NOW,
LIFT and Shoreditch Town Hall.
Supported by Culture Ireland as
part of GB18: Promoting Irish Arts in
Britain. *These Rooms* began as an Arts
Council of Ireland Open Call National
Project in ART2016. Image credits:
p.124 Pat Renmond; pp.125–127
Hugo Glendinning.

**They Shall Not Grow Old —
Peter Jackson** (p.200)
Co-commissioned by 14-18 NOW and
Imperial War Museums in association
with the BBC. Produced by WingNut
Films Production and Executive
Produced by House Productions.
Special thanks to Matthew & Sian
Westerman with additional support
from The Taylor Family Foundation,
The Moondance Foundation, the
British Council, Jacqueline & Richard
Worswick, and one anonymous donor.
Image credit: pp.200–205 Colourised
footage artistic rendition 2018 — *They
Shall Not Grow Old* by WingNut Films
with Peter Jackson. Original black-
and-white film, courtesy IWM.

**This Is Not for You —
Graeae Theatre** (p.42)
Co-commissioned by 14-18 NOW
and Blesma, The Limbless Veterans,
supported by Calouste Gulbenkian
Foundation (UK Branch), The Drive
Project and National Centre for Circus
Arts. Image credit: Alison Baskerville,
courtesy Graeae Theatre Company.

Traces of the Great War (p.138)
Co-commissioned by 14-18 NOW,
La Mission du Centenaire de la Première
Guerre mondiale, On a Marché sur la
Bulle and Lakes International Comic
Art Festival. Image credits: p.138 Robbie
Morrison and Charlie Adlard; p.139
Edmond Baudoin; p.140 Ken Niimura
and Joe Kelly; p.141 Mary Talbot and
Bryan Talbot. All courtesy On a Marché
sur la Bulle / LICAF.

**Triumph to Exist —
Magnus Lindberg** (p.46)
Co-commissioned by 14-18 NOW,
London Philharmonic Orchestra,
Orchestre National de Lille and
Gulbenkian Orchestra. Image credit:
Vetta, courtesy Getty Images.

**Unwritten Poems —
Karen McCarthy Woolf** (p.210)
Co-commissioned by 14-18 NOW and
BBC Contains Strong Language.

**War Damaged Musical Instruments —
Susan Philipsz** (p.258)
Commissioned by 14-18 NOW and
Curated by Tate Britain. Image credits:
p.258 installation view in the Duveen
Galleries, Tate Britain. Photo by Julian
Abrams; p.259 courtesy Collection
Musikinstrumenten-Museum Berlin.

**We're here because we're here —
Jeremy Deller and Rufus Norris** (p.130)
Commissioned by 14-18 NOW.
Conceived and created by Jeremy
Deller with Rufus Norris. Produced
by Birmingham Repertory Theatre and
the National Theatre with Lyric Theatre
Belfast, Manchester Royal Exchange,
National Theatre of Scotland, National
Theatre Wales, Northern Stage,
Playhouse Derry/Londonderry, Salisbury
Playhouse, Sheffield Theatres and
Theatre Royal Plymouth. Supported by:
Aberystwyth Arts Centre, The Belgrade
Theatre, Birmingham Metropolitan
Academy of Performing Arts, Bolton
Octagon, Bristol Old Vic, Storyhouse,
Left Coast, Leicester Curve, Nuffield
Theatre, Oldham Coliseum, Pontio,
Shetland Arts, The Garrick Lichfield
and Volcano. Media partner: BBC.

We're here because we're here was
made possible by an Ambition for
Excellence Award from Arts Council
England and the Heritage Lottery
Fund, with additional support from
Paul Hamlyn Foundation, Creative
Scotland and Art Fund. Image credits:
pp.130–131 Adrian Harris; p.132 Andrew
Fox; p.133 Eoin Carey; p.136 (top) Mark
Douet and (bottom) Keith Morris; p.137
Andrew Fox.

**When You Look You May Not See;
If History Could Be Folded, Where
Would You Put The Crease? —
Richard Wentworth** (p.120)
Co-commissioned by 14-18 NOW
and Art on the Underground. Image
credits: p.120 Thierry Bal; p.121
Alastair Fyfe.

WOMAD — Siyaya (p.107)
Co-commissioned by 14-18 NOW and
WOMAD. Image credit: Gideon Mendel.

XENOS — Akram Khan (p.186)
Commissioned by 14-18 NOW and
sponsored by COLAS. Image credits:
p.186 Nicol Vizioli; pp.187–189
Jean-Louis Fernandez.

Young Men — BalletBoyz (p.116)
Co-commissioned by BalletBoyz,
14-18 NOW, BBC and Sadler's Wells.
Image credit: stills from Young Men
by BalletBoyz and Manilla
ProductionPage.

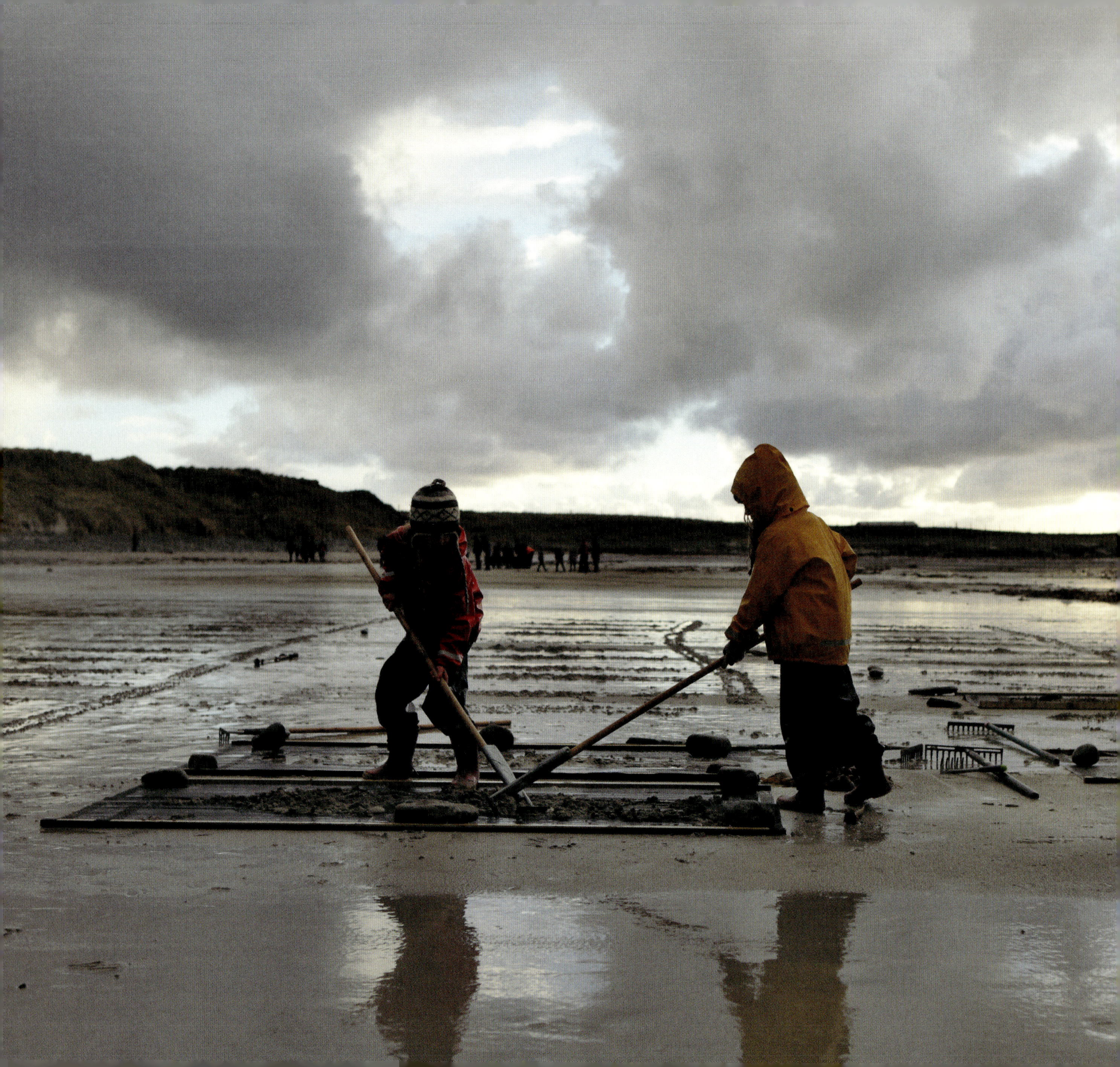

14-18 NOW TEAM AND BOARD

Team
Jenny Waldman, CBE
Nigel Hinds
Sud Basu
Linda Bernhardt
Alice Boff
Gemma Brown
Tamsin Dillon
Francesca Duncan
Emma Dunton
Claire Eva
Sarah Goodfellow
Angela McSherry
Chloë Morley
Ellie Pridgeon
Morag Small
Isabelle Taylor
Nadia Vistisen
Judy Vaknin
Pak Ling Wan

ArtsMediaPeople
Bolton & Quinn
The Cogency
Effect Digital
MHM
The Unloved
Stacey Wright PR

Special thanks to:
Anthony Blackstock, Jon Card, Anna Christoforou, Rachel Clarke, Vicky Corley-Smith, Jen Crook, Katie Cross, Lindsey Dear, Charlotte Egan, Phoebe Greenwood, More Partnership, Will Fulford-Jones, Majeeda Goodall, Amy Grant, Sarah Jenkins, Caroline Jones, Megan Klarenbach, Kate Ottway, Gary Townsend Vila, Emily Wallis, Jane Wentworth Associates, Phil Wilce, Jasmine Wilson, Will Saunders

President
Lady Susie Sainsbury of Turville, CBE

Board
Vikki Heywood, CBE Chairman
Ade Adepitan, MBE
Alex Beard, CBE
Lord Hall of Birkenhead
David Isaac, CBE
Diane Lees, CBE
Rhoda Macdonald
Tim Marlow
John Mathers
Clare PIllman
MT Rainey, OBE
Sir Anthony Seldon
Jenny Waldman, CBE

Special thanks to: Bonnie Greer, OBE, Tabitha Jackson, Jonathan Watkins

Artistic Advisors
Lavinia Greenlaw
Nigel Hinds
Ruth Mackenzie, CBE
Michael Morris
Tessa Ross, CBE
Cian Smyth

Development Advisory Group
David Isaac, CBE, Co-Chair
MT Rainey, OBE, Co-Chair
Jeremy Bennett
Patrick Handley
Clive Jones, CBE
Lady Emma Kitchener, OBE
Rhoda Macdonald
David Potter
Christophe Rust
General Sir Richard Shirreff, KCB, CBE
Jean-Michel Steg
Sir Richard Trainor, KBE

Artist Ambassadors
Yasmin Alibhai-Brown, MBE
Malorie Blackman
Kate Charlesworth
Lee Child
Paul Cummins, MBE
Jeremy Deller
Chloe Dewe Mathews
Sebastian Faulks, CBE
Bonnie Greer, OBE
Margaret MacMillan, OC
Rufus Norris
Tom Piper, MBE
Kamila Shamsie
Owen Sheers
Posy Simmonds
Richard Wentworth

Children create silhouettes on Culla Bay Beach, part of *Pages of the Sea*.

14-18 NOW FUNDERS AND SUPPORTERS

Thank you to our funders and supporters who have enabled the 14-18 NOW programme.

We are grateful to Imperial War Museums, which has been our host and partner throughout the centenary, and to our primary media partner, the BBC.

Principal Funders
Arts Council England
Department for Digital, Culture,
    Media and Sport
Heritage Lottery Fund

Programme Supporters
Backstage Trust
Big Lottery Fund
Bloomberg Philanthropies
Clore Duffield Foundation
DAF: A PACCAR Company
Jerwood Arts
NatWest
Matthew & Sian Westerman
Mayor of London

Mtec
Scottish Government
The Taylor Family Foundation
TH_NK

Art Fund
British Council
Tim and Sarah Bunting
Calouste Gulbenkian Foundation
    (UK Branch)
The Clothworkers' Company
Embassy of the Federal Republic
    of Germany
The Foyle Foundation
Government of Ireland
Goethe Institut London
Henry Moore Foundation
Institut Français
The Moondance Foundation
Paul Hamlyn Foundation
Pinsent Masons
Rail Delivery Group
Schroder Charity Trust
The Space
U.S. Embassy in London
Welsh Government
And an anonymous donor

Honorary Commissioning Circle
Dame Vivien Duffield, DBE
Mark Pigott, KBE
Lady Susie Sainsbury of Turville, CBE

Commissioning Circle
David & Jenny Altschuler
Heidi & Carlo Baravelle
Peter & Ali Bennett Jones
Melanie Gee
Debra Hauer & Denis Raeburn
Vikki Heywood, CBE & Clive Jones, CBE
Nigel Hinds & Judith Ackrill
David Isaac, CBE
Larissa Joy
Gailen Krug
Kate Nelson Best
MT Rainey, OBE
Christophe Rust & Hillevi Gillanders
Sir Anthony & Lady Joanna Seldon
Lea Simpson
Jean-Michel & Diane Steg
Sir David Verey, CBE
KT Wong Foundation
Jacqueline & Richard Worswick
And an anonymous donor

Individual Supporters
Michel & Christine Boël
Adam & Noreen Cleal
Nicholas & Jane Ferguson
Andrew Hochhauser, QC & Graham
    Marchant
Jonathan Levy
Rupert & Elizabeth Nabarro
Tony & Tiger McCallum
Midge & Simon Palley
Nicholas & Margo Snowman
Jenny Waldman & Richard Bull
Anna Yang

Crowds gather on Redcar Beach to read Carol Ann Duffy's poem next to the sand portrait of Theophilius Jones, part of *Pages of the Sea*.

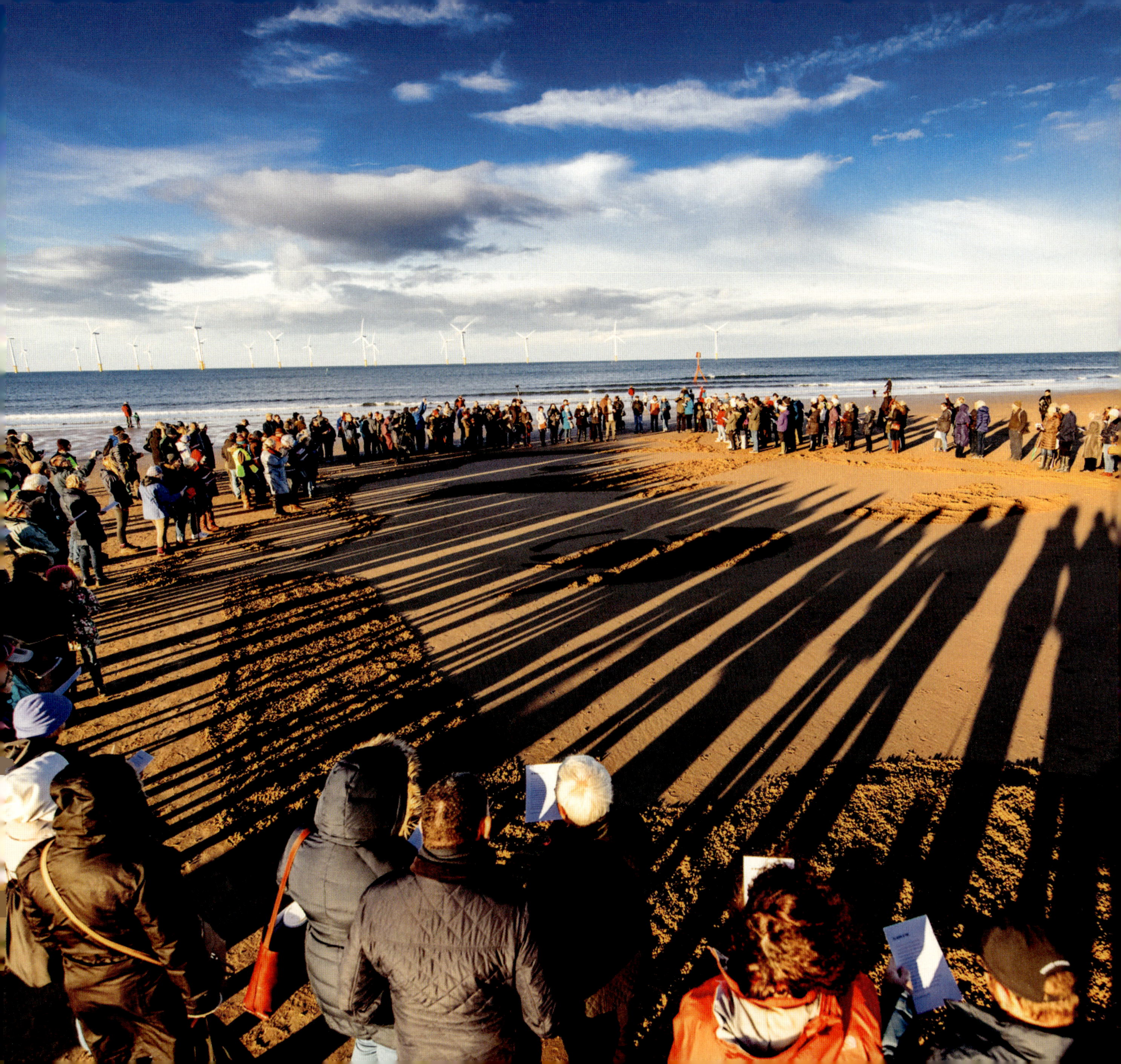

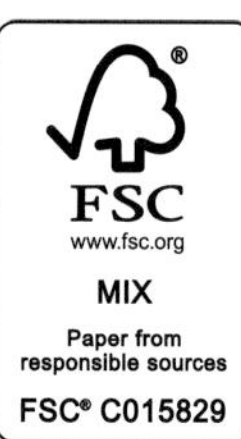

FSC
www.fsc.org
MIX
Paper from
responsible sources
FSC® C015829